THE HISTORY OF HUMAN MARRIAGE

MACMILLAN AND CO., Limited
LONDON . BOMBAY . CALCUTTA . MADRAS
MELBOURNE

THE MACMILLAN COMPANY
NEW YORK . BOSTON . CHICAGO
DALLAS . SAN FRANCISCO

THE MACMILLAN CO. OF CANADA, Ltd.
TORONTO

THE HISTORY OF
HUMAN MARRIAGE

BY

EDWARD WESTERMARCK

PH.D.; HON. LL.D., ABERDEEN
MARTIN WHITE PROFESSOR OF SOCIOLOGY IN THE UNIVERSITY OF LONDON
PROFESSOR OF PHILOSOPHY AT THE ACADEMY OF ÅBO (FINLAND)
AUTHOR OF "THE ORIGIN AND DEVELOPMENT OF THE MORAL IDEAS," "MARRIAGE
CEREMONIES IN MOROCCO," ETC.

IN THREE VOLUMES

VOL. III

FIFTH EDITION REWRITTEN

MACMILLAN AND CO., LIMITED,
ST. MARTIN'S STREET, LONDON
1925

COPYRIGHT

First Edition, 1891
Second Edition, 1894
Third Edition, 1901
Fourth Edition, 1911
Fifth Edition, 1921
Reprinted, 1925

PRINTED IN GREAT BRITAIN

CONTENTS

CHAPTER XXVII

MONOGAMY AND POLYGYNY

CHAPTER XXVIII

MONOGAMY AND POLYGYNY

(*Concluded*)

CHAPTER XXIX

POLYANDRY

CHAPTER XXX

POLYANDRY

(*Concluded*)

CHAPTER XXXIII

THE DURATION OF MARRIAGE AND THE RIGHT TO DISSOLVE IT

(Concluded)

CHAPTER XXXI

GROUP-MARRIAGE AND OTHER GROUP-RELATIONS

CHAPTER XXXII

THE DURATION OF MARRIAGE AND THE RIGHT TO DISSOLVE IT

THE HISTORY OF HUMAN MARRIAGE

CHAPTER XXVII

MONOGAMY AND POLYGYNY

AMONG the lower animals certain species are by instinct monogamous and other species polygynous. In mankind, on the other hand, we find marriages of one man with one woman (monogamy), of one man with several women (polygyny), of several men with one woman (polyandry), and of several men with several women (group-marriage). In the present chapter I shall deal with monogamy and polygyny, which are by far the most frequent forms of human marriage.

Among the South American Indians there are certain tribes which are said to be monogamous,[1] and a few others

[1] Guaycurûs (Lozano, *Descripcion chorographica del terreno, &c. de las Provincias del Gran Chaco*, p. 70 ; v. Martius, *Beiträge zur Ethnographie Amerika's*, i. 104), Canelas (Ignace, 'Les Capiekrans,' in *Anthropos*, v. 477) and Shambioa belonging to the Gês (Castelnau, *Expédition dans les parties centrales de l'Amérique du Sud*, i. 446), Paressí (von den Steinen, *Unter den Naturvölkern Zentral-Brasiliens*, p. 434), Chavantes (v. Martius, *op. cit.* i. 274), Curetús, Purupurús (Wallace, *Travels on the Amazon*, pp. 509, 515), Mundrucûs (*ibid.* p. 516 *sq.* ; v. Martius, *op. cit.* i. 104 ; Tocantins, 'Estudos sobre a tribu "Mundurucu",' in *Revista trimensal do Instituto Historico Geographico e Ethnographico do Brasil*, vol. xl. pt. ii. 113), Otomacos (Gumilla, *El Orinoco ilustrado*, i. 197), Ackawoi (Brett, *Indian Tribes of Guiana*, p. 275). Sir E. F. Im Thurn says (*Among the Indians of Guiana*, p. 223) that the Macusis and Ackawoi are not polygynous except perhaps in the cases of individuals who choose to break through the customs of their tribe.

in which the chiefs alone are allowed to have more than one wife.[1] In the large majority of tribes polygyny is undoubtedly allowed, but in most of these it is reported to be infrequent or exceptional.[2] From my own collection of facts, as well as from the tables given by Messrs. Hobhouse,

---

[1] Guarani (Charlevoix, *History of Paraguay*, i. 202 ; *cf.* Hernandez, *Organización social de las doctrinas Guaraníes de la Compañia de Jesús*, i. 84), Chiriguanos (v. Martius, *op. cit.* i. 217 ; see also Cardús, *Las Misiones Franciscanas entre los infieles de Bolivia*, p. 247), Jabaána, Paravilhana (v. Martius, *op. cit.* i. 627, 632), Karayá (Krause, *In den Wildnissen Brasiliens*, pp. 322, 325 ; *Idem*, ' Bericht über seine ethnographische Forschungsreise in Zentralbrasilien,' in *Zeitschr. f. Ethnol.* xli. 499. According to Ehrenreich [*Beiträge zur Völkerkunde Brasiliens*, p. 27], however, it not infrequently happens among them that a married man is compelled to take a second wife when the first one becomes too old), Maynas in Eastern Ecuador and North-Eastern Peru (Chantre y Herrera, *Historia de las Misiones de la Compañia de Jesús en el Marañón español*, p. 73). Among the Huitoto Indians of the Putumayo region it is only in extremely rare cases that even a chief has more than one wife (Hardenburg, *Putumayo*, p. 154). Mr. Whiffen, in his book *The North-West Amazons* (p. 159), says that the conviction was forced on him that monogamy, not polygamy, is the rule among the Indians of that neighbourhood, with the exception of the chiefs north of the Japura, who have, so far as he could make out, more than one wife. Among the tribes on the Tikie a chief may have four wives, but this is not the case south of that river, where chiefs, like ordinary members of the tribe, have only one.

[2] Yahgans (according to private communication from Mr. Thomas Bridges) and some of the Onas (Gallardo, *Tierra del Fuego—Los Onas*, p. 227 ; among those of the north hardly anybody has more than one wife) of Tierra del Fuego, West Patagonians between the Magellan Straits and the Gulf of Peñas (Skottsberg, *Wilds of Patagonia*, p. 97 ; *Idem*, ' Observations on the Natives of the Patagonian Channel Region,' in *American Anthropologist*, N.S. xv. 596), Tehuelches (Musters, *At Home with the Patagonians*, p. 187 ; Prichard, *Through the Heart of Patagonia*, p. 93), Abipones (Dobrizhoffer, *Account of the Abipones*, ii. 138), Minuanes, Pampas, Guanas (Azara, *Voyages dans l'Amérique méridionale*, ii. 33, 44, 95), Mocobis (Kohler, *Pater Florian Baucke, ein Jesuit in Paraguay* 1748–1766, p. 313), Matacos on the Bermejo and the right bank of the Pilcomayo (Cardús, *op. cit.* p. 254), Tobas (*ibid.* p. 264), Lengua Indians of the Paraguayan Chaco (Grubb, *An Unknown People*, p. 214 *sq.*), Coroados (Hensel, ' Die Coroados der brasilianischen Provinz Rio Grande do Sul,'

Wheeler, and Ginsberg,[1] I gather that the number of South
American tribes in which polygyny is fairly common does
not amount to a third of the number of tribes in which it is
practised only occasionally or not at all. To the former
belonged the Araucanians, some of whose chiefs had as many
as twenty wives,[2] whereas the poor had to content themselves with one or two at most.[3] Among the Guatós,
according to Castelnau, " chaque homme a de deux à
quatre femmes, mais quelques uns en ont dix et même
douze " ; [4] and Father Gumilla states that of the peoples
on the Orinoco the Otomacos were the only one to whom
polygyny was unknown, whilst among others there was not
a man who had less than two or three wives.[5] In the Lesser
Antilles polygyny was very prevalent, nearly every man,
according to Du Tertre, having several wives and some as
many as six or seven ;[6] but the aborigines of Hispaniola
seemed to Columbus to live in monogamy, with the exception of the king or chief.[7]

Among the North American tribes polygyny is evidently
more frequent than among the Indians of the southern part
of the continent, although the cases in which it is said to be

in *Zeitschr. f. Ethnol.* i. 130), Tupinambase (*Captivity of Hans Stade
of Hesse, in A.D. 1547–1555, among the Wild Tribes of Eastern
Brazil*, p. 142), Botocudos (v. Tschudi, *Reisen durch Südamerika*,
ii. 283), Uaupés (v. Martius, *op. cit.* i. 600 ; Wallace, *op. cit.* p. 497 ;
Coudreau, *La France équinoxiale*, ii. 176), Passés (v. Martius, *op. cit.*
i. 511), various Guiana Indians (Schomburgk, ' On the Natives of
Guiana,' in *Jour. Ethnol. Soc. London*, i. 270 ; Bernau, *Missionary
Labours in British Guiana*, p. 60 ; Rodway, *Guiana : British, Dutch,
and French*, p. 219 ; Pelleprat, *Relation des missions des PP. de la
Compagnie de Jesus dans les Isles, & dans la terre ferme de l'Amerique
Meridionale*, ii. 61).

¹ Hobhouse, Wheeler, and Ginsberg, *Material Culture and Social
Institutions of the Simpler Peoples*, pp. 180, 186, 188, 190, 194, 206.

² Guevara, *Historia de la Civilizacion de Araucanía*, i. 208.

³ Molina, *Geographical, Natural, and Civil History of Chili*, ii. 116.

⁴ Castelnau, *op. cit.* ii. 374.

⁵ Gumilla, *op. cit.* i. 197.

⁶ Du Tertre, *Histoire générale des Antilles*, ii. 378.

⁷ Ling Roth, ' Aborigines of Hispaniola,' in *Jour. Anthr. Inst.*
xvi. 272.

more or less unusual[1] or absent are at least twice as numerous
as those in which it is said to be general.[2] Hennepin states
that in many tribes there are savages to be met with who
have even ten or twelve wives ;[3] and Catlin says that " it is
no uncommon thing to find a chief with six, eight, or ten,
and some with twelve or fourteen wives in his lodge."[4]
Among the Navaho " probably about a third of the male
adults are polygamists " ;[5] and of the Plains Indians we
are told that " of the lovers which any Indian maiden may
have, it is safe to say that at least half have already one,

[1] As among the Pima of Arizona (Russell, ' Pima Indians,' in
Ann. Rep. Bur. Ethnol. xxvi. 184), Illinois, Alibamu (Bossu, *Travels
through Louisiana*, i. 128, 231), Pawnee (Dunbar, ' Pawnee Indians,'
in *Magazine of American History*, iv. 266), Mandan (Catlin, *Illustrations of the Manners, &c. of the North American Indians*, i. 119),
Iroquois (Hennepin, *New Discovery of a Vast Country in America
between New France and New Mexico*, ii. 480 ; Loskiel, *History of
the Mission of the United Brethren among the Indians in North America*,
i. 58), Hurons (Parkman, *Jesuits in North America*, p. xxxiv.),
Delaware (Harrington, ' Preliminary Sketch of Lenápe Culture,'
in *American Anthropologist*, N.S. xv. 215), Luiseño (Sparkman,
' Culture of the Luiseño Indians,' in *University of California Publications in American Archæology and Ethnology*, viii. 214) and Chimariko
(Dixon, *Chimariko Indians*, p. 301) of California, Indians of Washington Territory (Swan, *Northwest Coast*, p. 170), Nootka (Sproat,
Scenes and Studies of Savage Life, p. 98 ; Mayne, *British Columbia
and Vancouver Island*, p. 276), Chipewyan (Richardson, *Arctic
Searching Expedition*, ii. 23), Takulli, Chinook (Bancroft, *Native
Races of the Pacific States of North America*, i. 123, 241), Tlingit
(*ibid.* i. 110 ; v. Langsdorf, *Voyages and Travels in various Parts
of the World*, ii. 133), Ingalik (Dall, *Alaska*, p. 196). See also Heriot,
Travels through the Canadas, pp. 326, 551 *sq.* ; Harmon, *Journal of
Voyages and Travels in the Interior of North America*, pp. 292, 339 ;
Buchanan, *Sketches of the History, &c. of the North American Indians*,
p. 338. Hodge says (*Handbook of North American Indians*, i. 809)
that monogamy is " found to be the prevalent form of marriage
throughout the continent."
[2] The cases of occasional polygyny and regular monogamy
tabled by Hobhouse, Wheeler, and Ginsberg (*op. cit.* pp. 180, 182,
184, 186, 190, 196, 206, 208) are twice as numerous as those of
general polygyny, and my own collection of facts shows a still
larger proportion.
[3] Hennepin, *op. cit.* ii. 482.   [4] Catlin, *op. cit.* i. 118.
[5] Stephen, ' Navajo,' in *American Anthropologist*, vi. 356.

two, or more wives."[1] On the other hand, polygyny is
said not to occur among certain tribes inhabiting the
Isthmus of Tehuantepec,[2] the Moqui of New Mexico,[3]
and the Coco-Maricopa and some other tribes on the
banks of the Gila and the Colorado.[4] Among the Aztecs
of Pueblo Viejo the principle of monogamy is strictly
enforced, and if a woman deviates from it she has to be
cured by the shaman, or some accident will befall her—a
jaguar or a snake will bite her, or a scorpion sting her,
or lightning strike her.[5] Certain Californian Indians allow
a plurality of wives to chiefs only;[6] but among the
monogamous Karok the chief possesses no such privilege,
and though a man may own as many women for slaves as
he can purchase, he brings obloquy upon himself if he
cohabits with more than one.[7] Nor is polygyny found
among the Yurok of California.[8] According to Morgan,
polygyny was not permitted nor practised by the Iroquois;[9]
but this statement does not agree with the accounts of earlier
writers.[10] Of the Hurons[11] and Apache,[12] on the other hand,
we are told that the men formerly were satisfied with one
wife each, or that " only one woman was deemed the proper
share of one man," although polygyny subsequently was
introduced among them. Among the Eskimo there are
tribes of which it is said that " at least half of their married
men have two wives,"[13] but these are rare exceptions, mono-

---

[1] Dodge, *Our Wild Indians*, p. 201.

[2] Bancroft, *op. cit.* i. 661.

[3] Schoolcraft, *Archives of Aboriginal Knowledge*, iv. 87.

[4] Domenech, *Seven Years' Residence in the Deserts of North
America*, ii. 305.

[5] Lumholtz, *Unknown Mexico*, i. 481.

[6] Waitz, *Anthropologie der Naturvölker*, iv. 243. Mason, *Eth-
nology of the Salinan Indians*, p. 163 (Chumash and Costanoan).
The same is said of the Calidonian Indians (Gisborne, *Isthmus of
Darien*, p. 155).

[7] Powers, *Tribes of California*, p. 22.   [8] *Ibid.* p. 56.

[9] Morgan, *League of the Iroquois*, p. 324.

[10] Hennepin, *op. cit.* ii. 480.   Loskiel, *op. cit.* i. 58.

[11] Charlevoix, *Voyage to North-America*, ii. 36.

[12] Cremony, *Life among the Apaches*, p. 249.

[13] Gilder, *Schwatka's Search*, p. 246 (Iwillik and Kinipetu).

gamy being the prevailing form of marriage among most of them.[1] Dalager wrote in the eighteenth century that on the west coast of Greenland hardly one man in twenty had two wives, and that it was still more uncommon for a man to have three or four.[2] Cranz says that a Greenlander who took a third or fourth wife was blamed by his countrymen.[3] Concerning the natives of the east coast of Greenland, Holm asserts that there is no instance of a man having more than two wives,[4] and similar statements are made as regards other Eskimo.[5] Murdoch writes of those living in the neighbourhood of Point Barrow:—" As is the case with most Eskimo, most of the men content themselves with one wife, though a few of the wealthy men have two each. I do not recollect over half a dozen men in the two villages who had more than one wife each, and one of these dismissed his younger wife during our stay. We never heard of a case of more than two wives."[6]

Of the Asiatic Eskimo, the Chukchee, Dr. Bogoras says that the majority of them are monogamists, and that only a very small number of men have more than two wives ; among the Maritime Chukchee even bigamists are extremely rare, whereas in some localities inhabited by Reindeer

[1] Cranz, *History of Greenland*, i. 147. Kumlien, *Contributions to the Natural History of Arctic America*, p. 16 *sq.* (Eskimo of Cumberland Sound). Turner, ' Ethnology of the Ungava District, Hudson Bay Territory,' in *Ann. Rep. Bur. Ethnol.* xi. 188 (Koksoagmiut of Labrador). Boas, ' Central Eskimo,' *ibid.* vi. 579. Gilder, *op. cit.* p. 246 *sq.* (Netchillik). Lyon, *Private Journal during the Voyage of Discovery under Captain Parry*, p. 352 (Eskimo of Iglulik and Winter Island). Franklin, *Narrative of a Journey to the Shores of the Polar Sea*, p. 263. Hodge, *op. cit.* i. 435 (Eskimo in general).

[2] Dalager, quoted by Nansen, *First Crossing of Greenland*, ii. 321 n. 1.

[3] Cranz, *op. cit.* i. 147.

[4] Holm, ' Konebaads - Expeditionen til Grønlands Østkyst 1883–85,' in *Geografisk Tidskrift, udgivet af Bestyrelsen for det kongelige danske geografiske Selskab.* viii. 91.

[5] Gilder, *op. cit.* p. 246 (Eskimo round Repulse Bay). Parry, *Journal of a Second Voyage for the Discovery of a North-West Passage from the Atlantic to the Pacific*, p. 528 (Eskimo of Melville Peninsula).

[6] Murdoch, ' Ethnological Results of the Point Barrow Expedition,' in *Ann. Rep. Bur. Ethnol.* ix. 411.

Chukchee one-third and more of all the marriages are polygynous.[1] Among the Koryak, on the other hand, polygyny seems to be more frequently practised by the Maritime than by the Reindeer people. Out of 95 married men among the former, who were questioned by Dr. Jochelson, 13, that is 13·6 per cent., had two wives each and not a single one more than two ; whereas among the Reindeer Koryak out of 65 married men three had two wives and one three, the percentage of men having more than one wife thus being only 6 per cent. The majority of marriages recorded in the myths of the Koryak are likewise monogamous.[2] So also, to all appearances, the institution of polygyny must have existed to a very limited extent among the Yukaghir ;[3] and the same is the case among the Gilyak.[4] Of the Ainu of Yesso v. Siebold states that only the chief of the village and, in some places, the wealthier men are allowed to have more than one wife ;[5] and Miss Bird was told that among the tribes of Volcano Bay polygyny is not practised even by the chiefs.[6] It seems, indeed, that among the large majority of the peoples of Northern and Central Asia and, generally, among the uncivilised or semi-civilised tribes belonging to the former Russian empire polygyny is, or before the introduction of Christianity was, not much in vogue although perfectly legitimate.[7] Among the Yakut it was " fully

[1] Bogoras, *Chukchee*, pp. 598, 599, 611. See also Nordenskiöld, *Vegas färd kring Asien och Europa*, ii. 142 ; Iden-Zeller, ' Ethnographische Beobachtungen bei den Tschuktschen,' in *Zeitschr. f. Ethnol.* xliii. 850.

[2] Jochelson, *Koryak*, p. 752. See also Dittmar, ' Ueber die Koräken,' in *Mélanges russes tirés du bulletin historico-philologique de l'Académie impériale des sciences de St.-Pétersbourg*, iii. 25.

[3] Jochelson, *Yukaghir*, p. 110 *sq.*

[4] Sternberg, reviewed in *L'Anthropologie*, v. 343.

[5] v. Siebold, *Ethnologische Studien über die Aino auf der Insel Yesso*, p. 31.

[6] Isabella Bird, *Unbeaten Tracks in Japan*, ii. 100.

[7] Kamchadal (Georgi, *Beschreibung aller Nationen des russischen Reichs*, p. 341), Tartars (*ibid.* pp. 103, 116, 118), Tungus (*ibid.* p. 324 ; Miss Czaplicka, *Aboriginal Siberia*, p. 106), Gold inhabiting the middle portion of the Amoor (Laufer, ' Preliminary Notes on Explorations among the Amoor Tribes,' in *American Anthropologist*, N.S. ii. 320), Turkomans (Yavorsky, reviewed in *L'Anthropologie*,

developed " when the Cossacks first came among them, but
nowadays it is not so frequent.[1] Rockhill observes that
" the preponderance of testimony tends to prove that
monogamy is the rule, and polygamy the exception, among
the Koko-nor Tibetans " ; and he believes that this is the
case among all nomadic Tibetans.[2]

The same is undoubtedly true of the uncivilised tribes of
India and Indo-China. Among most of those who have
polygyny at all it is expressly said to be exceptional or
infrequent,[3] and among several of them polygyny is practised or permitted only when the first wife is barren or does

viii. 356), Buryat (Melnikow, ' Die Burjäten des Irkutskischen Gouvernements,' in *Verhandl. Berliner Gesellsch. Anthrop.* 1899, p. 442),
Kirghiz (Finsch, *Reise nach West-Sibirien*, p. 167), Kalmucks (Pallas,
Merkwürdigkeiten der Morduanen, Kasaken, Kalmücken, &c., p. 263
sq.), Samoyed (Arnesen, ' Från Gyda-viken till Obdorsk,' in *Ymer*,
iii. 144), Mordvin and Cheremiss (*Åbo Tidningar*, 1794, no. 51),
Ossetes (v. Haxthausen, *Transcaucasia*, p. 402), &c.

[1] Miss Czaplicka, *op. cit.* p. 112.
[2] Rockhill, *Land of the Lamas*, p. 80.
[3] Gonds and Korkús (Forsyth, *Highlands of Central India*,
p. 148), hill tribes of the Central Provinces (Hislop, *Papers relating
to the Aboriginal Tribes of the Central Provinces*, p. 3), Bhuiyas
(Macmillan, ' Bhuiyas,' in *Calcutta Review*, ciii. 178), Kols, Abors
(Rowney, *Wild Tribes of India*, pp. 68, 158), Tipperahs (Dalton,
Descriptive Ethnology of Bengal, p. 110), Chittagong Hill tribes in
general (Hutchinson, *Account of the Chittagong Hill Tracts*, p. 23),
Kaupuis (Watt, ' Aboriginal Tribes of Manipur,' in *Jour. Anthr.
Inst.* xvi. 355), Lushais, Old Kukis (Shakespear, *Lushei Kuki Clans*,
pp. 50, 155), Kacháris (Endle, *Kacháris*, p. 30), Nagas (Hodson,
Nāga Tribes of Manipur, p. 94), Mikirs (Stack, *Mikirs*, p. 19 *sq.*),
Karens (Low, ' Karean Tribes or Aborigines of Martaban and
Tavai,' in *Jour. Indian Archipelago*, iv. 418 *sq.*), Palaungs inhabiting
the uplands of the Shan States and a portion of the north-east of
Upper Burma, as also other peoples of Burma and the Shan States
(Lowis, *Note on the Palaungs of Hsipaw and Tawnpeng*, p. 10;
Fytche, *Burma Past and Present*, ii. 74 ; Shway Yoe, *The Burman*,
p. 59 ; Colquhoun, *Amongst the Shans*, p. 292), Muhsös (Jamieson,
Description of Habits and Customs of the Muhsös, p. 2), Stiêns
(Mouhot, *Travels in the Central Parts of Indo-China, &c.*, i. 253),
Laosians (Bock, *Temples and Elephants*, p. 186 ; Taupain, reviewed
in *L'Anthropologie*, ii. 488). In the Punjab, according to Mr. Crooke
(*Tribes and Castes in the North-Western Provinces and Oudh*, i.
p. cxcviii.), " the proportion of husbands who have more than
one wife is probably under 1 per cent."

not give birth to male offspring.[1] Among the Santals,
according to Skrefsrud, it is out of the question for a man to
have more than one wife, unless he be a younger brother
who has inherited his elder brother's widow ; and if he has
ten brothers older than himself who die, he marries the widows
of all of them.[2] Most of the Kukis, on the other hand, are
said by Mr. Soppitt to be so strictly monogamous that a man
marries the widow of a deceased elder brother only in case
he is not already married, but then he is bound to marry
her ; " even if he be a mere child, he will, on becoming of
age, marry the woman, however old she may be."[3] But,
according to an older account, although the Kukis have
only one wife, they may keep as many concubines as they
please.[4] Among the Old Kukis,[5] or some of them,[6] and the

---

[1] Kârakat Vellâlans on the Palni mountains in the Madura
country (Nelson, *Madura Country*, ii. 33), Kotas (Breeks, *Account
of the Primitive Tribes of the Nīlagiris*, p. 46 ; Grigg, *Manual of the
Nīlagiri District in the Madras Presidency*, p. 206 ; Ward says
[*ibid.* Appendix, p. lxxvii.] that the man is at liberty to take
a second wife if the first has no male issue after three successive
female births), Oráons (Dehon, ' Religion and Customs of the Uraons,'
in *Memoirs Asiatic Soc. Bengal*, i. 164), Kacháris (Endle, *op. cit.*
p. 30 ; Kachári custom sanctions the taking of a second wife mainly
with a view to handing down the father's name to posterity), Rábhás,
Hajongs, Deoris and Baráhis (*ibid.* pp. 85, 86, 94), Mútsa in Indo-
China (Colquhoun, *Amongst the Shans*, p. 71). The Nepalese seldom
take a second wife in case they have children (Waddell, *Among the
Himalayas*, p. 311). Among the Coorgs polygyny chiefly occurs
in cases where the first marriage is not blessed with male issue,
and it also happens that a young widow is taken to wife by another
member of the same house (Richter, *Manual of Coorg*, p. 140).
[2] Hertel, *Indisk Hjemmemission blandt Santalerne ved H. P.
Børresen og L. O. Skrefsrud*, p. 74. Mr. Man says (*Sonthalia and the
Sonthals*, p. 15) that polygamy, although not exactly 'prohibited,
is not very popular with them. According to Risley (*Tribes and
Castes of Bengal. Ethnographic Glossary*, ii. 229), ' a wife will admit
her younger sister to intimate relations with her husband, and if
pregnancy occurs scandal is avoided by his marrying the girl as a
second wife."
[3] Soppitt, *Short Account of the Kuki-Lushai Tribes on the North-
East Frontier*, p. 15.
[4] Macrae, ' Account of the Kookies,' in *Asiatick Researches*, vii. 192.
[5] Stewart, ' Notes on the Northern Cachar,' in *Jour. Asiatic Soc.
Bengal*, xxiv. 621.   [6] Shakespear, *op. cit.* p. 155.

Koch [1] polygyny and concubinage are said to be forbidden ;
whilst among the Pádam,[2] Mikirs,[3] and Munda Kols [4] a
man, although not expressly forbidden to have many wives,
is blamed if he has more than one. The cases of polygyny
found among the Mikirs have been attributed to Assamese
influence and the weakening of tribal sanctions.[5] The
Nagas of Upper Assam,[6] Khasis,[7] Kisáns,[8] and Meches [9]
confine themselves to one consort at a time, and the same is,
according to Lewin, the case with the Toungtha and Mrús ;[10]
but Superintendent Hutchinson states that although polygyny in the Chittagong Hill tracts " is reserved entirely for
the wealthy," the Bunjogees and Pankhos are the only tribes
there that do not allow it.[11] The Nayādis, living in the
rural and jungle tracts of South Malabar, and the Kavaras,
a Tulu caste found in the Chittur Taluk of the Cochin State,
are strictly monogamous ;[12] and among the Kadams and
Ka-káu of Indo-China polygyny is said not to exist or to
be forbidden.[13]

Among the wild tribes of the Malay Peninsula polygyny
is either rare or unknown. The Semang, so far as we know,
are habitually monogamists ; married people among them
seem to be in the highest degree faithful to each other, and
adultery is punished with great severity.[14] Among the
Sakai polygyny is said to be permitted but seldom prac-

---

[1] Dalton, *op. cit.* p. 91.   [2] *Ibid.* p. 28.

[3] *Ibid.* p. 54.   Butler, *Travels and Adventures in the Province of
Assam*, p. 138.

[4] Jellinghaus, ' Sagen, Sitten und Gebräuche der Munda-Kolhs
in Chota Nagpore,' in *Zeitschr. f. Ethnol.* iii. 370.

[5] Butler, *op. cit.* p. 138.   Stack, *op. cit.* p. 20.

[6] Dalton, *op. cit.* p. 41.   [7] Gurdon, *Khasis*, p. 77.

[8] Dalton, *op. cit.* p. 132.   [9] Rowney, *op. cit.* p. 145.

[10] Lewin, *Wild Races of South-Eastern India*, pp. 193, 194, 235.

[11] Hutchinson, *op. cit.* pp. 23, 161.

[12] Anantha Krishna Iyer, *Cochin Tribes and Castes*, i. 51 ; ii. 385.
Of the Panans in the Cochin State it is said (*ibid.* i. 173) that polygyny
does not prevail among them.

[13] Colquhoun, *Amongst the Shans*, pp. 72, 80.

[14] Skeat and Blagden, *Pagan Races of the Malay Peninsula*,
ii. 55, 56, 59.   Martin, *Die Inlandstämme der Malayischen Halbinsel*,
p. 864.   Stevens, *Materialien zur Kenntniss der Wilden Stämme auf
der Halbinsel Malâka*, ii. 132.   The Semang of Ijoh " have, as a rule,

tised,[1] and of those of Selangor we are even told that a man could not have more than one wife ;[2] but the Sakai of Perak are, on the other hand, represented as polygynists.[3] Most of the Benua, according to Logan, have one wife only,[4] whilst other authorities inform us that polygyny is not permitted among them ;[5] Favre met one who had two wives, but " he was censured and despised by the whole tribe."[6] Polygyny is said to be forbidden among the Mantra,[7] and unknown among the Biduanda Kallang in Johor [8] and the Orang Muka Kuning.[9] The two latter belong to the Orang Laut, who were generally monogamists, except that a man might marry his brother's widow as a second rank wife.[10] The Jakun or Malayan tribes, including the Blandas and Besisi of Selangor, " are as a rule fairly strict

one wife, but if all parties consent may have two, never three " (Swettenham, ' Comparative Vocabulary of the Dialects of some of the Wild Tribes inhabiting the Malayan Peninsula,' in *Jour. Straits Branch Roy. Asiatic Soc.* no. 5, p. 156).

[1] [Maxwell, in] *Jour. Straits Branch Roy. Asiatic Soc.* no. 1, p. 112. Low, in *Jour. Indian Archipelago,* iv. 430. Miklucho Maclay, ' Ethnological Excursions in the Malay Peninsula,' in *Jour. Straits Branch Roy. Asiatic Soc.* no. 2, p. 215. *Cf.* Skeat and Blagden, *op. cit.* ii. 56.

[2] Campbell, quoted by Skeat and Blagden, *op. cit.* ii. 68.

[3] de la Croix, ' Étude sur les Sakaies de Perak,' in *Revue d'ethnographie,* i. 339. de Morgan, ' Négritos de la presqu'île Malaise,' in *L'homme,* ii. 558. Of the Sakai of Kuala Kernam in Perak, however, Knocker says (' Notes on the Wild Tribes of the Ulu Plus, Perak,' in *Jour. Roy. Anthr. Inst.* xxxix. 147) that " a man had one wife at a time."

[4] Logan, ' Orang Binua of Johore,' in *Jour. Indian Archipelago,* i. 270.

[5] Favre, ' Account of the Wild Tribes inhabiting the Malayan Peninsula,' in *Jour. Indian Archipelago,* ii. 264. Newbold, *Account of the British Settlements in the Straits of Malacca,* ii. 408.

[6] Favre, *loc. cit.* p. 264.

[7] Bourien, ' Wild Tribes of the Interior of the Malay Peninsula,' in *Trans. Ethn. Soc. London,* N.S. iii. 80.

[8] Logan, ' Biduanda Kallang of the River Pulai in Johore,' in *Jour. Indian Archipelago,* i. 300.

[9] *Idem,* ' Orang Muka Kuning,' in *Jour. Indian Archipelago,* i. 339.*

[10] Stevens, ' Mittheilungen aus dem Frauenleben der Ôrang Bĕlendas, der Ôrang Djâkun und der Ôrang Lâut,' in *Zeitschr. f. Ethnol.* xxviii. 88.

monogamists " ;[1] Favre states that the Jakun are only
allowed to keep one wife,[2] and Mr. Skeat does not remember
a single case in which a Besisi man had more than one.[3]
Concerning the aboriginal tribes of the Malay Peninsula in
general Dr. Martin assumes that they were all essentially
monogamous, and that the polygyny which is found among
some of them is due to Malay influence ; among the pure
tribes, he observes, adultery is commonly punished with
death.[4] Messrs. Annandale and Robinson state that polygamy, in the sense of having more than one wife at a time, is
extremely rare among the Malayo-Siamese peasantry of the
Patani States.[5]

In some parts of the Nicobar Islands polygyny is now
and again found to occur among chiefs and wealthier men,[6]
but in other parts the people are strict monogamists.[7]
Among the Andamanese polygyny is said to be unknown,[8]
and " though there is a freedom of intercourse between the
sexes before marriage, after it the husband keeps faithful
to his wife, as a rule, and she to him."[9] All our authorities
agree that the Veddas of Ceylon never have more than one
wife, and even adultery seems to be unknown among them;[10]

[1] Skeat and Blagden, op. cit. ii. 56.
[2] Favre, Account of the Wild Tribes inhabiting the Malayan
Peninsula, p. 67.   [3] Skeat and Blagden, op. cit. ii. 76.
[4] Martin, op. cit. pp. 865, 874.
[5] Annandale and Robinson, Fasciculi Malayenses, ii. 72.
[6] Kloss, In the Andamans and Nicobars, p. 238.
[7] Ibid. p. 220. Chopard, 'A few Particulars respecting the
Nicobar Islands,' in Jour. Indian Archipelago, iii. 273. Distant,
'Inhabitants of Car Nicobar,' in Jour. Anthr. Inst. iii. 4.
[8] Man, 'Aboriginal Inhabitants of the Andaman Islands,' in
Jour. Anthr. Inst. xii. 135. Portman, History of Our Relations
with the Andamanese, i. 39, 285 ; ii. 826. Kloss, op. cit. p. 188.
According to Lowis (Census of India, 1911, vol. ii. [Andaman and
Nicobar Islands] pp. 67, 100) polygyny is "almost unknown " at
Port Blair in the Andaman Islands and very rare in the Nicobar
Islands.   [9] Portman, op. cit. i. 39.
[10] Bailey, 'Account of the Wild Tribes of the Veddahs of Ceylon,'
in Trans. Ethn. Soc. N.S. ii. 291 sq. Hartshorne, 'Weddas,' in
Indian Antiquary, viii. 320. Nevill, 'Vaeddas of Ceylon,' in Tapro-
banian, i. 178. Deschamps, Carnet d'un voyageur, pp. 313, 381. Sarasin,
Ergebnisse naturwissenschaftlicher Forschungen auf Ceylon, iii. 458 sq.

" nothing short of murder would content the injured party."[1]

In the Malay Archipelago, says Crawfurd, polygyny and concubinage exist only among a few of the higher ranks, and may be looked upon as a kind of luxury of the great ; for it would be absurd to regard either one or the other as an institution affecting the whole mass of society.[2] That polygyny, where it occurs at all, is rare or exceptional is also affirmed by other writers with reference to various peoples inhabiting those islands ;[3] indeed I have not come across a single case in which it is said to be general,[4] whereas there are many peoples among whom it is reported to be unknown or prohibited.   In Sumatra a man married by *semando*, that is, a regular treaty between the parties on the footing of equality, cannot take a second wife without repudiating the first one.[5] Among the Kubus monogamy is the rule, although polygyny is allowed ;[6] but other wild tribes of Sumatra, such as the Orang Mamaq,[7] Orang Akit,

---

[1] Nevill, *loc. cit.* p. 178.

[2] Crawfurd, *History of the Indian Archipelago*, i. 76 *sq.*

[3] Raffles, *History of Java*, i. 81.   Marsden, *History of Sumatra*, p. 270.   Junghuhn, *Die Battaländer auf Sumatra*, ii. 133 ; v. Brenner, *Besuch bei den Kannibalen Sumatras*, p. 249 ; Wilken, *Over de verwantschap en het huwelijks- en erfrecht bij de volken van het maleische ras*, p. 40 n. 1 (Battas).   Low, *Sarawak*, p. 147 ; Boyle, *Adventures among the Dyaks of Borneo*, p. 25 *sq.* (Malays of Sarawak).   Crocker, ' Notes on Saràwak and Northern Borneo,' in *Proceed. Roy. Geograph. Soc.* N.S. iii. 199 (Milanows).

[4] According to Hobhouse, Wheeler, and Ginsberg (*op. cit.* p. 212), polygyny is " general " among the Niase ; but I fail to find any authority confirming this statement. Modigliani (*Un Viaggio a Nías*, p. 546) rejects Horner's assertion that they are monogamists, but maintains that those who have more than one wife are few in number. According to Hollander-van Eck (*Handleiding bij de beoefening der land- en volkenkunde van Nederlandsch Oost-Indië*, i. 601), most men have to content themselves with a single wife on account of the bride price ; and Rosenberg (*Der malayische Archipel*, p. 155) says nothing more than that a Niase may marry as many women as he is able to buy.

[5] Marsden, *op. cit.* pp. 263, 270.

[6] Hagen, *Die Orang Kubu auf Sumatra*, p. 133. Volz, ' Zur Kenntniss der Kubus in Südsumatra,' in *Archiv f. Anthrop.* N.S. vii. 98, 104.   [7] Hagen, *op. cit.* p. 164.

and Sakai,[1] are represented as strict monogamists. In
Borneo there are many tribes where polygyny does not
occur.[2] Thus the Hill Dyaks marry but one wife, and a chief
who once broke through this custom lost all his influence ;
even adultery is said to be entirely unknown among them.[3]
So also the traditional law of the Sea Dyaks allows a man to
have only one wife ; "polygamy is considered very dis-
pleasing to the gods, and if a man does take to himself two
wives, the other people of the village compel him to give
one up, and sacrifices are offered to the gods and spirits to
avert any evil effects upon the community for the crime."[4]
Among the nomadic Punans in the central highlands of
Borneo each man has usually one wife ; polyandry occurs
among them—generally in cases where a woman married
to an elderly man has no children by him,—but Mr. Hose
knows of no instances of polygyny, although there are cases
in which a Punan woman has become the second wife of a
man of some other tribe.[5] The Toála of South Celebes live
in monogamy ;[6] and the same was formerly the case with the
Alfoors of Minahassa, whose occasional polygyny in later
times, according to Dr. Hickson, is a degeneration from the
old customs brought about perhaps by Muhammadan
influence.[7] Strict monogamy prevails among the natives
of many of the smaller islands, such as the Galela of Hal-
mahera,[8] and the Watubela,[9] Leti,[10] Mentawi,[11] and Poggy

[1] Moszkowski, *Auf neuen Wegen durch Sumatra*, pp. 40, 105.

[2] Rejang tribe of the Milanows (Low, *op. cit.* p. 342), Kayans of
Baram (St. John, *Life in the Forests of the Far East*, i. 113), Dusuns
(Burbridge, *Gardens of the Sun*, p. 255), Sibuyaus (Keppel, *Expedition
to Borneo of H.M.S. Dido*, i. 56).

[3] Low, *op. cit.* p. 300.   Haughton, quoted by Ling Roth, *Natives
of Sarawak*, i. 126.

[4] Gomes, *Seventeen Years among the Sea Dyaks of Borneo*, pp. 70,
127 *sq.*   See also Low, *op. cit.* p. 195 ; Ling Roth, *op. cit.* i. 126.

[5] Hose and McDougall, *Pagan Tribes of Borneo*, ii. 183.

[6] Sarasin, 'Ueber die Toála von Süd-Celebes,' in *Globus*, lxxxiii.
280.   [7] Hickson, *A Naturalist in North Celebes*, p. 277.

[8] Riedel, 'Galela und Tobeloresen,' in *Zeitschr. f. Ethnol.* xvii. 77.

[9] *Idem, De sluik- en kroesharige rassen tusschen Selebes en Papua*,
p. 206.   [10] Bickmore, *Travels in the East Indian Archipelago*, p. 125.

[11] Rosenberg, *op. cit.* p. 199.   Hollander-van Eck, *op cit.* i. 615.

Islanders.[1] The early discoverers of the Philippine
Islands found there legal monogamy combined with concubinage.[2] Among the Bagobo and some other tribes of
Southern Mindanao a man " may not take a second mate
until a child has been born to the first union, or the wife
has been proved beyond doubt to be barren."[3] Among the
Subanu, a mountain folk in the same island, a plurality of
wives is permissible but not common.[4]   The Igorot of
Luzon are strictly monogamous, and in case of adultery the
guilty party can be compelled to leave the hut and the family
for ever.[5] Of the Italons, Malayan head-hunters of Luzon,
Father Arzaga wrote that they make a contract of marriage
with one wife only, which lasts till death, and do not allow
concubinage.[6] So also the Tinguianes, a sub-Malayan
people of Luzon, are monogamists.[7] Among the Negritos
of Zambales, in the same island, well-to-do people have
more than one wife,[8] but generally the Negritos of the
Philippines are strictly monogamous.[9] The wild Tag-

---

[1] Crisp, 'Account of the Inhabitants of the Poggy, or, Nassau
Islands,' in *Asiatick Researches*, vi. 87. Rosenberg, *op. cit.* p. 199.
Hollander-van Eck, *op. cit.* i. 615. Adultery is punished with
death.

[2] [de Mas,] *Informe sobre el estado de las Islas Filipinas en* 1842,
i. 'Estado de los Filipinos a la llegada de los españoles,' p. 20. de
Morga, *Philippine Islands at the close of the Sixteenth Century*, p. 300.
Mallat, *Les Philippines*, i. 57.

[3] Cole, 'Wild Tribes of Davao District, Mindanao,' in *Field
Museum of Natural History, Anthropological Series*, xii. 103, 133, 192.

[4] Finley and Churchill, *Subanu*, p. 40.

[5] Meyer, 'Die Igorrotes von Luzon,' in *Verhandl. Berliner
Gesellsch. Anthrop.* 1883, p. 385. Mas, *op. cit.* ii. 'Poblacion,' p. 18.
Reyes Lala, however, says (*Philippine Islands*, p. 98) that polygyny
sometimes occurs among the Igorot, although adultery is almost
unknown.

[6] Arzaga, quoted by Mozo, *Noticia de los gloriosos triumphos por
los religiosos del orden de N. P. S. Agustin en las Islas Philipinas*,
p. 19. See also Blumentritt, *Versuch einer Ethnographie der Philippinen*, p. 33.

[7] Foreman, *Philippine Islands*, p. 216.

[8] Reed, *Negritos of Zambales*, p. 60.

[9] Schadenberg, 'Ueber die Negritos der Philippinen,' in *Zeitschr.
f. Ethnol.* xii. 135. Piehler, 'Die Ajitas (Aëtas) der Philippinen,'

banuas of Palawan do not allow polygyny.[1] The savages of Formosa are also generally rigorous monogamists.[2]

In Guam, one of the Ladrone Islands, a husband contented himself with one wife and a wife with one husband at a time, though divorces were frequent.[3] In the Pelew Islands polygyny is found only among the well-to-do people ;[4] and in the Caroline Islands, or some of them, it is likewise said to be more or less exceptional[5]—indeed, Don Luis de Torres heard of no man there having two wives.[6] The Papuans of the Maclay Coast of New Guinea are monogamists ;[7] and of those of Dorey we are told that not only is polygyny forbidden but concubinage and adultery are unknown.[8] Among the natives of Mailu, in British New Guinea, polygyny is very infrequent ; Dr. Malinowski has only one polygynous marriage to record amongst the total number of marriages in the pedigrees of Mailu village.[9] The 76 Koita marriages

in *Globus*, xcvi. 201. Garcia, quoted by Bille, *Beretning om Corvetten Galathea's Reise omkring Jorden*, ii. 181. Mallat, *op. cit.* ii. 121. Bowring, *Visit to the Philippine Islands*, p. 173. Proust de la Girondière, *Twenty Years in the Philippines*, p. 271.

[1] Worcester, *Philippine Islands*, p. 108.

[2] Davidson, *Island of Formosa*, p. 583. Müller, ' Ueber die Wildenstämme der Insel Formosa,' in *Zeitschr. f. Ethnol.* xlii. 230. Shinji Ishii, ' Life of the Mountain People in Formosa,' in *Folk-Lore*, xxviii. 127 (Taiyal tribe).

[3] Safford, ' Guam and its People,' in *American Anthropologist*, N.S. iv. 716.

[4] Kubary, ' Die Palau-Inseln in der Südsee,' in *Jour. Museum Godeffroy*, iv. 56.

[5] ' Die Carolinen,' in *Deutsche Rundschau für Geographie und Statistik*, viii. 65. Christian, *Caroline Islands*, p. 73 *sq.* (Ponapéans). Born, ' Einige Beobachtungen ethnographischer Natur über die Oleaï-Inseln,' in *Mittheil. Deutsch. Schutzgeb.* xvii. 189 (natives of the Oleaï Islands, politically belonging to the Western Carolines).

[6] Arago, *Narrative of a Voyage round the World*, ii. 17.

[7] Miklucho-Maclay, ' Anthropologische Bemerkungen über die Papuas der Maclay-Küste in Neu-Guinea,' in *Natuurkundig Tijdschrift voor Nederlandsch Indie*, xxxiii. 245. *Idem*, ' Ethnologische Bemerkungen über die Papuas der Maclay-Küste in Neu-Guinea,' *ibid.* xxxv. 89.

[8] Finsch, *Neu-Guinea*, p. 101. Earl, *Papuans*, p. 81.

[9] Malinowski, ' Natives of Mailu,' in *Trans. Roy. Soc. South Australia*, xxxix. 572.

recorded by Dr. Seligman include only four instances of polygyny.[1] At Wagawaga, in the Southern Massim area, " it is denied that any man has more than one wife at the present day, and it is stated that even in the old days very few men had two " ;[2] and throughout the domain of the Northern Massim polygyny is a privilege theoretically restricted to the families of chiefs, although this rule is not always strictly kept.[3] From various writers on New Guinea savages we learn that polygyny is not much practised,[4] though there are also a few statements to the contrary.[5] Thus among the Mafulu mountain people a man will often have two or three, sometimes even four, wives, and a chief or rich man may have six.[6] In many of the islands in the Pacific Ocean polygyny was indulged in by the chiefs,[7] who often had a large number of wives. Parkinson knew chiefs in Bougainville, of the Solomons, who had as many as fifty.[8] Guppy speaks of a Shortland chief who had between eighty

[1] Seligman, *Melanesians of British New Guinea*, p. 83.
[2] *Ibid.* p. 509.   [3] *Ibid.* p. 712.
[4] Lawes, in *Proceed. Roy. Geograph. Soc.* N.S. ii. 614. Thomson, *British New Guinea*, p. 193. Pitcairn, *Two Years among the Savages of New Guinea*, p. 61. Stone, *A few Months in New Guinea*, p. 93. Finsch, *Neu-Guinea*, p. 82. Bink, in *Bull. Soc. d'Anthr. Paris*, ser. iii. vol. xi. 396. Neuhauss, *Deutsch Neu-Guinea*, i. 161. Hagen, *Unter den Papua's*, p. 225 (Bogadjim). Vetter, ' Bericht über papuanische Rechtsverhältnisse bei den Jabim,' in *Nachrichten über Kaiser Wilhelms-Land*, 1897, p. 88. Kohler, ' Ueber das Recht der Papuas auf Neu-Guinea,' in *Zeitschr f. .vergl. Rechtswiss.* vii. 370. Chalmers, ' Toaripi and Koiari Tribes,' in *Report of the Second Meeting of the Australasian Association for the Advancement of Science, held at Melbourne, in* 1890, p. 314.
[5] Beardmore, ' Natives of Mowat, Daudai, New Guinea,' in *Jour. Anthr. Inst.* xix. 460. Neuhauss, *op. cit.* i. 152 (the natives of the village Sialum, at Cape Wilhelm). Among the Inland Papuans of Dutch New Guinea polygyny is frequent but not the rule (Moszkowski, ' Die Völkerstämme am Mamberamo in Holländisch-Neuguinea,' in *Zeitschr. f. Ethnol.* xliii. 339).
[6] Williamson, *Mafulu Mountain People of British New Guinea*, p. 169.
[7] Robertson, *Erromanga*, p. 397. de Rochas, *La Nouvelle Calédonie*, p. 228 ; Lambert, *Mœurs et superstitions des Néo-Calédoniens*, p. 95. Stair, *Old Samoa*, p. 175 ; &c.
[8] Parkinson, *Dreissig Jahre in der Südsee*. p. 481

and a hundred.[1] In Fiji there were, according to John
Williams, chiefs who had a hundred;[2] but according to
another account the highest chiefs only had harems of from
ten to fifty women, counting concubines, those of the inland
tribes five or six wives, and those of tributary tribes
seldom more than two.[3] In various places—such as Buin[4]
and other parts of the Solomons,[5] Futuna,[6] the Sandwich
Islands,[7] and New Zealand[8]—polygyny seems in fact to have
been restricted to the chiefs or a privilege connected with
chieftainship or high rank.   In Lepers' Island a man who
has a young wife generally takes an elderly woman, a widow,
for a second, to look after the first;[9] and the majority of the
Treasury men are said to have two wives, who are usually
widely separated by age.[10] But the general rule in the
South Sea Islands was undoubtedly that the bulk of the
people were monogamists.[11] From the Duke of York group

---

[1] Guppy, *Solomon Islands*, p. 44 *sq.*

[2] Williams, *Missionary Enterprises in the South Sea Islands*, p. 557.

[3] Thomson, *Fijians*, p. 172.

[4] Thurnwald, *Forschungen auf den Salomo-Inseln und dem Bismarck-Archipel*, iii. 81.

[5] Elton, ' Notes on Natives of the Solomon Islands,' in *Jour. Anthr. Inst.* xvii. 95 (the islands east of Guadalcanar).

[6] Mangeret, *Mgr Bataillon et les missions de l'Océanie*, i. 243.

[7] Ellis, *Tour through Hawaii*, p. 414. *Cf.* Jarves, *History of the Hawaiian Islands*, p. 42.

[8] Best, ' Maori Marriage Customs,' in *Trans. and Proceed. New Zealand Institute*, xxxvi. 29. Tregear, *The Maori Race*, p. 296.

[9] Codrington, *Melanesians*, p. 245.   [10] Guppy, *op. cit.* p. 45.

[11] Stephan and Graebner, *Neu-Mecklenburg (Bismarck-Archipel)*, p. 110. Strauch, in *Zeitschr. f. Ethnol.* ix. 62 (New Hanover). Schnee, *Bilder aus der Südsee*, pp. 38 (Bismarck Archipelago), 96 (Gazelle Peninsula of New Britain).   Burger, *Die Küsten- und Bergvölker der Gazellehalbinsel*, p. 55 (mountain district). Parkinson, *op. cit.* p. 66 (north-eastern part of the Gazelle Peninsula). Turner, *Samoa*, p. 317 (Tanna of the New Hebrides). Cook, *Voyage to the Pacific Ocean*, i. 401 (Tonga); ii. 157 (Tahiti).—In the tables given by Hobhouse, Wheeler, and Ginsberg (*op. cit.* pp. 198, 200, 202) polygyny is represented as general among the Koita and at Bogadjim in New Guinea, in Florida, New Caledonia, and Fiji, and among the Maori. But these statements are contrary to the information at my disposal. Among the Koita, as we have seen, Dr. Seligman found only four polygynous marriages among the 76 marriages

we have some statistical data : out of 663 married men 600 had one wife each, 57 two wives, 5 three wives, and 1 four wives—that is, 10·5 per cent. were polygamists.[1] In a few of the smaller islands there seems to have been strict monogamy.[2]

As regards the former Tasmanians we have very conflicting information. Lloyd states that a plurality of wives was the universal law amongst them, and that amongst the Oyster Bay tribe in 1821 he scarcely ever knew an instance of a native having but one wife, two or three being the usual allowance.[3] But according to other writers polygyny,

recorded by him. At Bogadjim, according to Hagen (*Unter den Papua's*, p. 225), polygyny is permitted but little practised : one man had three wives, a few men had two, but the large majority only one. In Florida, according to Dr. Codrington (*op. cit.* p. 245), " one wife is commonly enough for a . . . man, who says that he can neither manage nor afford more than one." The New Caledonians, says Rochas (*op. cit.* p. 228), " have generally only one wife " ; and concerning those of the Belep Islands we are told by Père Lambert (*op. cit.* p. 95) that, whilst the chiefs usually are polygamists, only a very small number of their subjects have two wives. In Fiji, according to Thomson (*op. cit.* p. 172 ; see also Zimmermann, *Die Inseln des indischen und stillen Meeres*, i. 400), " the bulk of the people were monogamists." As regards the Maori, Dieffenbach states (*Travels in New Zealand*, ii. 37) that polygyny was " very uncommon " among them, and Best (*loc. cit.* p. 29), who is probably the greatest authority on their marriage customs, that " the bulk of the people married but one wife."

[1] Schnee, *op. cit.* p. 96. ' Statistik der Eingeborenen-Bevölkerung der Neu-Lauenburg-Gruppe,' in *Mittheil. Deutsch. Schutzgeb.* xiv. 128.

[2] Ninigo and Kaniet, to the west of the Admiralty Islands (Parkinson, *op. cit.* p. 442), Santa Christina or Tauata in the Marquesas Group (Waitz-Gerland, *Anthropologie der Naturvölker*, vi. 128), Easter Island (Geiseler, *Die Oster-Insel*, p. 29 ; Cooke, ' Te Pito Te Henua,' in *Smithsonian Report*, 1897, pt. i. 716). In Laur and Kandass of New Ireland every man had one wife only, except the chief of Watpi, who had three (Stephan and Graebner, *op. cit.* p. 110).

[3] Lloyd, *Thirty-three Years in Tasmania and Victoria*, p. 44 *sq* Dove (' Moral and Social Characteristics of the Aborigines of Tasmania,' in *Tasmanian Journal of Natural Science*, i. 252) says that polygamy prevailed " among the Tasmanians, and West (*History of Tasmania*, ii. 78) that it " was tolerated."

C 2

if not unknown, was quite exceptional ;[1] and Nixon says that they " never kept more than one wife at one time."[2] In most Australian tribes monogamy is evidently the rule, polygyny being practised chiefly by the old men and chiefs.[3] But there seem to be exceptions to the rule : Father Bischofs says that among the Niol-Niol in North-Western Australia the grown-up men, from twenty-five to thirty years of age, had for the most part two or three wives each and not infrequently four.[4] On the other hand, there are also a few tribes in which polygyny is said not to occur at all[5] or to be forbidden.[6]

It is in Africa that we find polygyny at its height, both in point of frequency and so far as the number of wives is concerned. In Unyoro, according to Emin Pasha, it would be absolutely improper for even a small chief to have fewer than ten or fifteen wives, and poor men have three or four each.[7] Among the Nandi rich men have had as many as forty ;[8] and Serpa Pinto tells us of a minister in the Barotse-

[1] Calder, 'Native Tribes of Tasmania,' in *Jour. Anthr. Inst.* iii. 22. Bonwick, *Daily Life and Origin of the Tasmanians*, p. 71. Brough Smyth, *Aborigines of Victoria*, ii. 386.

[2] Nixon, *Cruise of the Beacon*, p. 29. Milligan (quoted *ibid.* p. 29) states that " they were monogamous."

[3] Howitt, *Native Tribes of South-East Australia*, pp. 206, 245, 256. Strehlow, *Die Aranda- und Loritja-Stämme in Zentral-Australien*, vol. iv. pt. i. 98, 102. Henderson, *Excursions and Adventures in New South Wales*, ii. 110. Cameron, ' Notes on some Tribes of New South Wales,' in *Jour. Anthr. Inst.* xiv. 352. Bonney, ' Some Customs of the Aborigines of the River Darling,' *ibid.* xiii. 135. Bonwick, *ibid.* xvi. 205. Mrs. Langloh Parker, *Euahlayi Tribe*, p. 55. Hodgson, *Reminiscences of Australia*, p. 213. Freycinet, *Voyage autour du monde*, ii. 766. Curr, *The Australian Race*, ii. 196, 361; iii. 36. Waitz-Gerland, *op. cit.* vi. 771. Malinowski, *The Family among the Australian Aborigines*, p. 307. It is said that in the Larrakia tribe, Port Darwin, about ten per cent. of those who are married have two wives (Curr, *op. cit.* i. 252).

[4] Bischofs, ' Die Niol-Niol,' in *Anthropos*, iii. 35.

[5] Curr, *op. cit.* i. 402 (Eucla tribe).

[6] *Ibid.* ii. 371 (Karawalla and Tunberri tribes on the lower Diamantina), 378 (Birria tribe : " the possession of more than one wife is absolutely forbidden, or was so before the coming of the whites ").

[7] *Emin Pasha in Central Africa*, p. 85.   [8] Hollis, *Nandi*, p. 64.

land who at the time of his visit to that country had more than seventy.[1] Among the Matabele, says Decle, " polygamy is the rule, the average number of a man's wives ranging from two up to several hundreds."[2] The number of wives possessed by the King of Benin has been estimated by different writers at 600, 1,000, over 3,000,[3] and 4,000 ; but he gave some away to men who had rendered him some service.[4] In Ashanti the law limited the king to 3,333 wives, but whether it required him to reach this number is not known.[5] King Mtēssa of Uganda is said to have had 7,000 wives,[6] and the same is the case with the king of Loango.[7] This is, to my knowledge, the high-water mark of polygyny anywhere.

As to the frequency of polygyny I may refer to some figures based on the tables published by Messrs. Hobhouse, Wheeler, and Ginsberg. Out of 110 cases relating to the prevalence of polygyny and monogamy among African peoples there are 89, that is 81 per cent., in which polygyny is represented as general,[8] whilst it is so only in 30 per cent. of the cases relating to the same forms of marriage among simple peoples in other parts of the world.[9] The difference is sufficiently great to be of significance, although the value of the figures must be largely relative. It cannot be supposed that the term " general " implies that polygyny is practised by the majority of the married men. Yet there are peoples among whom this is expressly said to be the case. In Ondonga, for instance, according to Schinz, most men have two wives each, many have only one, and a few more than two.[10] Among the Warega in the Belgian Congo "presque

[1] Serpa Pinto, *How I crossed Africa*, ii. 33.
[2] Decle, *Three Years in Savage Africa*, ii. 160.
[3] Landolphe, *Mémoirs contenant l'histoire de ses voyages*, i. 335 n. 2.
[4] Ling Roth, *Great Benin*, p. 40.
[5] Wilson, *Western Africa*, p. 180.
[6] Stuhlmann, *Mit Emin Pascha ins Herz von Afrika*, p. 184.
[7] Reade, *Savage Africa*, p. 44.
[8] Hobhouse, Wheeler, and Ginsberg, *op. cit.* pp. 180, 192, 194, 196, 198, 206, 208, 210, 212.
[9] This statement is based on the figures given *ibid.* p. 159.
[10] Schinz, *Deutsch-Süd-West-Afrika*, p. 311.

tous les ménages sont polygames ; toutefois il est rare qu'un mari ait plus de dix femmes."[1] Of the Banjange in Kamerun [2] and the Mossi in the Western Sudan [3] we are told that the majority of the men have from two to four wives each. And an old Dutch writer states that in Benin " there is no man so poor but that he has ten or twelve wives at the least."[4] But, on the other hand, we also hear that among many African peoples monogamy is the predominant[5] and among a few even the exclusive form of marriage.

The Central African Pygmies seem to be mostly mono-gamous,[6] in spite of Sir Harry Johnston's statement that polygamy among them " depends on the extent of their barter goods."[7] According to Hutereau, most Batua of Tanganyika do not practise polygamy,[8] and the Wambutti

---

[1] Delhaise, *Les Warega*, p. 175.

[2] Schuster, ' Die sozialen Verhältnisse des Banjange-Stammes,' in *Anthropos*, ix. 951.

[3] Mangin, ' Les Mossi,' in *Anthropos*, ix. 479.

[4] Quoted by Ling Roth, *Great Benin*, p. 37.

[5] Betsileo (Shaw, ' Betsileo,' in *Antananarivo Annual*, no. iv. 8) and Sakalava (Walen, ' Sakalava,' *ibid.* no. viii. 54) of Madagascar, some tribes in Northern Rhodesia (Gouldsbury and Sheane, *Great Plateau of Northern Rhodesia*, p. 168), Bechuanas (Holub, *Seven Years in South Africa*, i. 392), Herero (v. François, *Nama und Damara Deutsch-Süd-West-Afrika*, p. 195 ; Hahn, ' Die Ovaherero,' in *Zeitschr. Gesellsch. Erdkunde Berlin*, iv. 489), Wamuera and Wamakua (Adams, quoted by Fülleborn, *Das Deutsche Njassa- und Ruwuma-Gebiet*, p. 61), lower classes of the Wadshagga (Volkens, *Der Kilimandscharo*, p. 252), Wapokomo (Gregory, *Great Rift Valley*, p. 343), peasantry of the Baganda (Roscoe, *Baganda*, p. 95), Madi (Felkin, ' Notes on the Madi or Moru Tribe of Central Africa,' in *Proceed. Roy. Soc. Edinburgh*, xii. 322 *sq.*), Wandorobbo belonging to the Masai (Merker, *op. cit.* p. 231), Tedâ (Nachtigal, *Sahara und Sudan*, i. 447), Bambara (Delafosse, ' Le peuple Siéna ou Sénoufo,' in *Revue des études ethnographiques et sociologiques*, i. 457, 483), Ewhe tribes in Togoland (Spieth, *Die Ewe-Stämme*. p. 62*), Pangwe (Tessmann, *Die Pangwe*, ii. 262).

[6] Schmidt, *Die Stellung der Pygmäenvölker in der Entwicklungs-geschichte des Menschen*, p. 187.

[7] Johnston, *Uganda Protectorate*, p. 539.

[8] Hutereau, ' Notes sur la Vie familiale et juridique de quelques populations du Congo Belge,' in *Annales du Musée du Congo Belge*, p. 3.

of Ituri emphatically deny that any man has more than one wife in his hut.[1] Among the South African Bushmen polygyny occurred more frequently. Kicherer, who visited them in 1799, says that the men had several wives ;[2] and Campbell found in the earlier part of the nineteenth century that they had frequently four or five wives.[3] Stow observes that although it is certain that among the greater portion of them a plurality of wives was allowed, the men of some of the tribes never took more than one.[4] In modern days, says Theal with reference to the same people, " the instances of a man living with more than one woman at a time have been exceedingly rare. Miss Lloyd, after long inquiry, could learn of but one such case, and other investigators could hear of none whatever."[5] The Auin of Gam, however, are said to have on an average two and not infrequently five wives each, whereas those of Rietfontein[6] and the Namib Bushmen[7] are strict monogamists. Among the Hottentots polygyny was allowed but evidently not much practised ;[8] in many of their kraals not a single case of it was found.[9]

[1] David, ' Notizen über die Pygmäen des Ituriwaldes,' in *Globus*, lxxxvi. 196. See also *ibid.* p. 197.

[2] Kicherer, *Extract from the Narrative of his Mission in South Africa*, p. 6.

[3] Campbell, *Narrative of a Second Journey in the Interior of South Africa*, 1. 30.

[4] Stow, *Native Races of South Africa*, p. 95.

[5] Theal, *History of the Boers in South Africa*, p. 19. See also *Idem, Yellow and Dark-skinned People of Africa south of the Zambesi*, p. 47.

[6] Kaufmann, ' Die Auin,' in *Mittheil. Deutsch. Schutzgeb.* xxiii. 157.

[7] Trenk, ' Die Buschleute der Namib,' in *Mittheil. Deutsch. Schutzgeb.* xxiii. 168. The Tati Bushmen " are mostly mono- gamists " (Dornan, ' Tati Bushmen [Masarwas] and their Language,' in *Jour. Roy. Anthr. Inst.* xlvii. 47).

[8] Thunberg, ' Account of the Cape of Good Hope,' in Pinkerton, *Collection of Voyages and Travels*, xvi. 141. Le Vaillant, *Travels from the Cape of Good-Hope, into the Interior Parts of Africa*, ii. 72. Campbell, *op. cit.* ii. 347. Kretzschmar, *Südafrikanische Skizzen*, p. 209. Wandrer, in Steinmetz, *Rechtsverhältnisse von eingeborenen Völkern in Afrika und Ozeanien*, p. 317. *Cf.* Schinz, *op. cit.* p. 96.

[9] Theal, *History of the Boers*, p. 48. *Idem, Yellow and Dark- skinned People*, p. 85.

Of certain Kafir tribes we are told that " the average number of wives to each married man amongst the common
people is about three " ; [1] but in other tribes monogamy
predominated, [2] and at present the great majority of men
have only one wife. [3] The Quissama of Angola, so far as
Mr. Hamilton was able to ascertain, practised monogamy. [4]
The Mongwandi of the Upper Mongala region, according to
Grenfell, tend towards monogamy, great chiefs alone pos-
sessing several wives, and the Banza of the region between
the Mongala River and the east bank of the Lower Mubangi
" are monogamous in principle." [5] In a sociological study
on the Lower Congo Mr. Phillips remarks, " It is a mistaken
opinion that in a polygamous society most men have more
than one wife : the relative numbers of the sexes forbid
the arrangement being extended to the whole population ;
really only the wealthier can indulge in a plurality of wives,
the poorer having to be content with one or often with none." [6]
Proyart says the same of the people of Loango, adding that
the rich who can use the privilege of having many wives
are far from being numerous. [7] In his report on the Edo-
speaking peoples of Nigeria Mr. Thomas states that while
in the greater part of the country inhabited by them
" monogamy is rare except in the case of poor men, and
two husbands out of five on an average will be found to
have two wives," it seems to be exceedingly rare in the Sobo
country to find a husband with more than one. [8] Among
the Bali tribes in the northern *Hinterland* of Kamerun the
legal form of marriage is monogamy, and from the point of

[1] Maclean, *Compendium of Kafir Laws and Customs*, p. 44.

[2] Barrow, *Account of Travels into the Interior of Southern Africa*,
i. 206. Lichtenstein, *Travels in Southern Africa*, i. 261 *sq.*

[3] Kidd, *The Essential Kafir*, p. 227 *sq.*

[4] Price, 'Description of the Quissama Tribe,' in *Jour. Anthr
Inst.* i. 189.

[5] Johnston, *George Grenfell and the Congo*, p. 676 *sq.*

[6] Phillips, ' Lower Congo,' in *Jour. Anthr. Inst.* xvii. 225. See
also Chavanne, *Reisen und Forschungen im Kongostaate*, p. 398 *sq.*
(Bafióte).

[7] Proyart, ' History of Loango,' in Pinkerton, *op. cit.* xvi. 568 *sq.*

[8] Thomas, *Anthropological Report on the Edo-speaking Peoples of
Nigeria*, i. 58.

view of family rights and rights of inheritance this form is
strictly honoured ; yet "in practice is a man allowed
polygamy, though only with women of the slave class and
only with unmarried ones," and these have no rights whatever.[1] Baumann observes that the Wambugwe, as an
exception to an almost universal rule in Central Africa, are
so strictly monogamous that not even their chiefs have
more than one wife.[2] Among the Bogos polygyny is a
luxury found only among the noble and wealthy ; in the
whole of their country, says Munzinger, there are hardly
fifty men who have two wives and hardly five who have
three.[3] So, also, polygyny is confined to a few men only
among other peoples in North-Eastern Africa—the Marea,
the Beni Amer, &c.[4] Lane says that in Egypt not more
than one husband in twenty has two wives.[5] In Algeria[6]
and Morocco the great bulk of the people are likewise
monogamous ; in the latter country there are villages even
of a considerable size where no man has more than one wife,
unless it be perhaps some well-to-do person who has a second
wife in another village where he owns property. Among
the Moorish tribes in the Western Sahara Vincent did not
meet a single man who had a plurality of wives.[7] The
Beni Mzab[8] and the Touareg[9] are monogamists. So also the
Guanches of the Canary Islands lived in monogamy, except
the inhabitants of Lancerote.[10]

[1] Hutter, *Wanderungen und Forschungen in Nord-Hinterland
von Kamerun*, p. 377.

[2] Baumann, *Durch Massailand zur Nilquelle*, p. 186.

[3] Munzinger, *Ueber die Sitten und das Recht der Bogos*, p. 64 sq.

[4] *Idem, Ostafrikanische Studien*, pp. 209 (Takue), 248 (Marea),
326 (Beni Amer), 524 (Bazes).

[5] Lane, *Manners and Customs of the Modern Egyptians*, i. 252.

[6] Hanoteau and Letourneux, *La Kabylie*, ii. 167. Bel, ' La
population musulmane de Tlemcen,' in *Revue des études ethnographiques et sociologiques*, i. 443.

[7] Chavanne, *Die Sahara*, p. 454.   [8] *Ibid.* p. 315.

[9] *Ibid.* pp. 181, 182, 315. Duveyrier, *Exploration du Sahara*,
p. 429. Hourst, *Sur le Niger et au pays des Touaregs*, p. 209.

[10] Abreu de Galindo, *History of the Discovery and Conquest of the
Canary Islands*, p. 68. Bontier and Le Verrier, *The Canarian*,
Major's Introduction, p. xxxix.

From the geographical distribution of polygyny and monogamy among the lower races we shall now turn our attention to their prevalence at different grades of economic culture. To judge by my collection of facts, polygyny has not been practised on a larger scale by any of the lower hunters and food-collectors, except some Australian and Bushman tribes, nor by any incipient agriculturists, at least among those of the lower type. On the other hand, a considerable number of these low hunting and slightly agricultural tribes are strictly monogamous. To this class belong some of the South American Indians referred to above, the aboriginal tribes of the Malay Peninsula, the Andaman Islanders, the Veddas of Ceylon, certain tribes in the Malay Archipelago as the Orang Mamaq and Orang Akit,[1] the monogamous Negritos of the Philippine Islands, a few Australian tribes (which, however, I regard as doubtful cases), and some at least of the Central African Pygmies. Among the higher hunters, most of whom are found in North America, polygyny is more frequent, although in the majority of their tribes it is practised only occasionally ; and exclusive monogamy is very rare, though not unknown, if the Californian Karok and Yurok and the Guaycurûs are to be reckoned among them.[2] Among pastoral peoples I have found none which can be regarded as strictly monogamous ;[3] and both among them and the higher agriculturists polygyny is undoubtedly more frequent than among the hunters and incipient agriculturists, although cases of regular monogamy

---

[1] The Punans in the interior of Borneo, who cultivate no crops and have no domestic animals but live entirely upon the wild produce of the jungle, vegetable and animal, would have to be included in this list but for the occurrence, however occasional, of polyandry among them.

[2] Although the Guaycurûs are themselves pure hunters, they hold the Guanas as tributaries and tillers of the soil (v. Martius, *op. cit.* i. 226 *sq.* ; Hobhouse, Wheeler, and Ginsberg, *op. cit.* p. 24).

[3] Hobhouse, Wheeler, and Ginsberg (*op. cit.* p. 194) represent the Tobas as regular monogamists, but this is not in agreement with a statement made by Cardús, *op. cit.* p. 264. Besides, such pastoral life as they have has been an importation from the whites (Hobhouse, Wheeler, and Ginsberg, *op. cit.* p. 161).

are more frequent among the higher agriculturists than among the higher hunters. This has also been pointed out by Messrs. Hobhouse, Wheeler, and Ginsberg, who say that " the *extent* of polygamy as distinct from the recognition of it as good custom, increases almost continuously, only being more marked among the pastoral peoples."[1] According to their tables polygyny is more frequent among the cattle-keeping agriculturists than among the pure agriculturists and more frequent among the higher pastoral tribes (who have taken to agriculture as a secondary employment) than among the lower ones.[2] It should, however, be noticed that the cases in which polygyny is represented as " general " are comparatively much more numerous among African than among non-African pastoral peoples and higher (that is, pure and cattle-keeping) agriculturists, amounting among the former to 84 per cent. of all African cases relating to the prevalence of polygyny and monogamy and among the latter only to 32 per cent. of the non-African cases. The difference between African and non-African peoples is greater among the higher agriculturists than among the pastoral peoples, the cases of " general " polygyny being among the higher agriculturists 86 per cent. in Africa and 30 per cent. outside Africa and among the pastoral peoples respectively 76 and 57 per cent. At the same time the cases in which monogamy is represented as " regular " are comparatively much more numerous among the non-African than among the African higher agriculturists, amounting

---

[1] Hobhouse, Wheeler, and Ginsberg, *op. cit.* p. 161.

[2] *Ibid.* p. 160. According to these writers, the cases of " general " polygyny are among the higher hunters 32 per cent. of the total cases recorded, those of " occasional " polygyny 61 per cent., and those of " regular " monogamy 6 per cent.; among the incipient agriculturists they are respectively 18, 59, and 23 per cent.; among the lower pastoral peoples respectively 53, 40, and 7 per cent.; among the pure agriculturists respectively 43, 39, and 17 per cent.; among the higher pastoral peoples respectively 74, 26, and 0 per cent.; and among the cattle-keeping agriculturists respectively 64, 25, and 11 per cent. Among the lower hunters they are respectively 29, 57, and 14 per cent.; but as about a third of the cases recorded refer to Australian tribes, the figures are more or less arbitrary (*ibid.* 160)

among the former to 21 per cent. of all non-African cases
recorded and among the latter only to 4 per cent. of the
African cases recorded. Among the non-African higher
hunters—and they are all non-African—the percentage of
cases in which polygyny is " general " slightly exceeds the
percentage of such cases among the non-African higher
agriculturists, the former being 33 per cent. and the latter
30 per cent. ; whilst the cases in which monogamy is
" regular " are considerably fewer among the higher hunters
than among the non-African higher agriculturists, being
respectively 6 and 21 per cent. If, on the other hand, we
compare non-African higher agriculturists with non-African
incipient agriculturists—and, like the higher hunters, the
incipient agriculturists also are all non-African—we find that
among the former the cases of " general " polygyny amount
to 30 per cent. and among the latter to 20 per cent., whilst
the cases of " regular " monogamy are about equal, respectively 21 and 22 per cent.[1] These figures tend to show that
even among non-African peoples the higher agriculturists
are more addicted to polygyny than the incipient agriculturists, although the difference is very much smaller than
between the higher agriculturists of Africa and the incipient
agriculturists. And the higher agriculturists outside Africa
are also undoubtedly more addicted to polygyny than the
lower hunters, at least if the Australian tribes are excluded.
I have gone into these details because the fact that polygyny
is much more prevalent among the higher agriculturists of
Africa than among those elsewhere should serve as a warning
not to assume that the frequency of polygyny at the higher
grades of economic culture among the simpler peoples is
merely due to economic causes.

Where polygyny occurs it may be modified in a monogamous direction both from the social and the sexual point
of view. Among some of the simpler peoples all the wives
of a polygynous marriage are said to have equal rights,[2]

---

[1] All these figures are based on cases recorded *ibid.* p. 180 *sqq.*

[2] Onas (Gallardo, *op. cit.* p. 222), Karayá (Krause, *In den Wildnissen Brasiliens*, pp. 322, 325), people of Dardistan (Biddulph,
Tribes of the Hindoo Koosh, p. 76), Jabim (Vetter, in *Nachrichten
über Kaiser Wilhelms-Land*, 1897, p. 89), Pygmies of Central Africa

and a similar equality may, of course, prevail among others, of whom nothing is said on the subject. But the general rule is undoubtedly that one of the wives holds a higher social position than the rest or is regarded as the principal wife ;[1] and in the large majority of these cases it is the first married wife to whom such a distinction is assigned,[2]

(Hutereau, *op. cit.* p. 4), Bambala, Bayaka (Torday, *Camp and Tramp in African Wilds*, pp. 95, 135), Bangongo (Torday and Joyce, *Les Bushongo*, p. 115), Boloki (Weeks, *Among Congo Cannibals*, p. 125), Tubori of Fianga (Lamouroux, 'La région du Toubouri,' in *L'Anthropologie*, xxiv. 682).

[1] Guarani (Hernandez, *op. cit.* i. 85), Central Eskimo (Boas, in *Ann. Rep. Bur. Ethnol.* vi. 579), natives of the Gazelle Peninsula of New Britain (Hahl, ' Ueber die Rechtsanschauungen der Eingeborenen eines Theiles der Blanchebucht und des Innern der Gazelle Halbinsel,' in *Nachrichten über Kaiser Wilhelms-Land*, 1897, p. 80), Marquesas Islanders (Tautain, ' Étude sur le mariage chez les Polynésiens des îles Marquises,' in *L'Anthropologie*, vi. 645), Awemba (Gouldsbury and Sheane, *Great Plateau of Northern Rhodesia*, p. 165), Wafipa (Fromm, ' Ufipa,' in *Mittheil. Deutsch. Schutzgeb.* xxv. 98), Baluba (v. Wissmann, Wolf, v. François, and Mueller, *Im Innern Afrikas*, p. 159 *sq.*), Bassari (Klose, *Togo unter deutscher Flagge*, p. 508 *sq.*), Cross River natives (Partridge, *Cross River Natives*, p. 255).

[2] Araucanians (Molina, *op. cit.* ii. 116), Mocobis (Kohler, *Pater Florian Baucke*, p. 313), the tribes of the North-West Amazons north of the Japura (Whiffen, *op. cit.* p. 160), Tupinambase (*Captivity of Hans Stade*, p. 143), Jurís, Passés, Uainumá, Miranhas (v. Martius, *op. cit.* i. 105), Mundrucûs (*ibid.* i. 392), Uaupés (Wallace, *Travels on the Amazon*, p. 497), Guaraunos (Chaffanjon, *L'Orénoque et le Caura*, p. 11), Tamanacs (v. Humboldt, *Personal Narrative of Travels to the Equinoctial Regions of the New Continent*, v. 548), Indians of Guiana (Schomburgk, in Ralegh, *Discovery of the Empire of Guiana*, p. 110 note), Roucouyennes of French Guiana (Coudreau, *Chez nos Indiens*, p. 132), Mosquito Indians (Bancroft, *op. cit.* i. 729), Pima Indians of Arizona (Russell, ' Pima Indians,' in *Ann. Rep. Bur. Ethnol.* xxvi. 184), Apache (Cremony, *op. cit.* p. 249), Pawnee (Dunbar, in *Magazine of American History*, iv. 266), Omaha (Dorsey, in *Ann. Rep. Bur. Ethnol.* iii. 261), Chippewa (Kohl, *Kitchi-Gami*, p. 111), Achomawi and Atsugewi Indians of Northern California (Dixon, in *American Anthropologist*, N.S. x. 217), Cree (Franklin, *Narrative of a Journey to the Shores of the Polar Sea*, p. 70), Tlingit, Kaniagmiut (Holmberg, ' Ethnographische Skizzen über die Völker des russischen Amerika,' in *Acta Soc. Scientiarum Fennicae* iv. 313, 399), Aleut (Erman, ' Ethnographische Wahrnehmungen an

presumably because monogamy is, or formerly was, the rule among the people and polygyny either a novelty or an excep-

den Küsten des Berings-Meeres,' in *Zeitschr. f. Ethnol.* iii. 162), Chinook (Waitz, *op. cit.* iii. 338), Eskimo of Melville Peninsula (Parry, *op. cit.* p. 528), Eskimo of the Ungava District of Labrador (Turner, in *Ann. Rep. Bur. Ethn.* xi. 190).—Chukchee (Bogoras, *op. cit.* p. 600), Koryak (Jochelson, *Koryak*, p. 754), Yukaghir (*Idem, Yukaghir,* p. 110), Tungus, Yakut (Saucr, *Expedition to the Northern Parts of Russia performed by Billings,* pp. 49, 129), Samoyed (Castrén, in *Helsingfors Morgonblad,* 1843, no. 54), Central Asiatic Turks (Vámbéry, *Das Türkenvolk,* p. 248), Ossetes (Kovalewsky, *Coutume contemporaine et loi ancienne,* p. 155), Kádars in the Cochin State (Anantha Krishna Iyer, *op. cit.* i. 9), Muduvars (Thurston, *Castes and Tribes of Southern India,* v. 92), Saorias (Bainbridge, ' Saorias of the Rajmahal Hills,' in *Memoirs Asiatic Soc. Bengal,* ii. 57), Khamtis, Santals (Dalton, *op. cit.* pp. 8, 216), Tangkhuls (Hodson, *Nāga Tribes of Manipur,* p. 94), Meitheis (*Idem. Meitheis,* p. 77), some of the Old Kukis (Shakespear, *op. cit.* p. 155), Kachins of Burma (Gilhodes, in *Anthropos,* viii. 374), Battas of Sumatra (Junghuhn, *op. cit.* ii. 133), natives of Waëpote in Buru (Martin, *Reisen in den Molukken,* p. 290), Bagobo (Schadenberg, in *Zeitschr. f. Ethnol.* xvii. 12), Bila-an, and Kulaman of Mindanao (Cole, in *Field Museum of Natural History, Anthropological Series,* xii. 103, 144, 157).—Ladrone Islanders (Waitz-Gerland, *op. cit.* vol. v. pt. ii. 107), Pelew Islanders (Kubary, *Die socialen Einrichtungen der Pelauer,* p. 62), Ponapéans (Finsch, ' Ueber die Bewohner von Ponapé (östl. Carolinen),' in *Zeitschr. f. Ethnol.* xii. 317), Western Islanders of Torres Straits (Haddon, in *Reports of the Cambridge Anthropological Expedition to Torres Straits,* v. 230), natives of Erromanga of the New Hebrides (Robertson, *Erromanga,* p. 397), Tongans (Cook, *Voyage to the Pacific Ocean,* i. 401), Tahitians (Ellis, *Polynesian Researches,* i. 273 *sq.*), Maori (Taylor, *Te Ika a Maui,* p. 338 ; Best, in *Trans. and Proceed. New Zealand Institute,* xxxvi. 29), tribes of Western Victoria (Dawson, *Australian Aborigines,* p. 33), Narrinyeri (Taplin, *Folklore, &c. of the South Australian Aborigines,* p. 35).—Betsileo of Madagascar (Shaw, in *Antananarivo Annual,* no. iv. 8 *sq.*), Auin belonging to the Kalahari Bushmen (Kaufmann, in *Mittheil. Deutsch. Schutzgeb.* xxiii. 157), Hottentots (Hahn, *Tsuni-Goam,* p. 18 ; Kohler, Das Recht der Hottentotten,' in *Zeitschr. vergl. Rechtswiss.* xv. 342), Kafirs (Alberti, *De Kaffers aan de Zuidkust van Afrika,* p. 139 ; Kropf, *Das Volk der Xosa Kaffern,* p. 152 *sq.* ; Fritsch, *Die Eingeborenen Süd-Afrika's,* p. 92 ; not always), Angoni belonging to the Zulu race (Wiese, ' Beiträge zur Geschichte der Zulu im Norden des Zambesi,' in *Zeitschr f. Ethnol.* xxxii. 192 ; not always), Kimbunda (Magyar, *Reisen in Süd-Afrika,* p. 283 ; usually), Bechuanas (Livingstone, *Missionary*

tion.[1] In exceptional cases only we hear that the higher position of one of the wives depends not on priority of marriage but on superiority of rank,[2] or that the principal

Travels and Researches in South Africa, p. 185), Basuto (Casalis, *Basutos*, p. 186 *sq.*), Herero (Dannert, *Zum Rechte der Herero*, p. 38 ; Brincker, ' Charakter, Sitten und Gebräuche speciell der Bantu Deutsch-Südwestafrikas,' in *Mittheil. d. Seminars f. oriental. Sprachen Berlin*, vol. iii. pt. iii. 83), Mountain Damara (François, *op. cit.* p. 251), Thonga (Junod, *Life of a South African Tribe*, pp. i. 125, 186, 272 *sq.*), Warega of the Belgian Congo (Delhaise, *op. cit.* p. 175), Konde people (Fülleborn, *op. cit.* p. 344), people of Bukoba (Richter, ' Der Bezirk Bukoba,' in *Mittheil. Deutsch. Schutzgeb.* xii. 85), Makua (v. Behr, ' Die Völker zwischen Rufiyi und Rovuma,' *ibid.* vi. 82), Washambaa in Usambara (Storch, ' Sitten, &c. bei den Bewohnern Usambaras und Pares,' *ibid.* viii. 312 ; usually), Wabende (Avon, ' Vie sociale des Wabende au Tanganika,' in *Anthropos*, x.–xi. 99), Wanyamwezi (Decle, *op. cit.* p. 348), Baganda (Roscoe, *Baganda*, p. 83), Akikúyu (Routledge, *op. cit.* p. 134), Nandi (Hollis, *Nandi*, p. 64), Masai (Merker, *op. cit.* p. 27 *sq.* ; Hinde, *The Last of the Masai*, p. 76), Banjange (Schuster, ' Die sozialen Verhältnisse des Banjange-Stammes [Kamerun],' in *Anthropos*, ix. 955), natives of British Nigeria (Mockler-Ferryman, *British Nigeria*, p. 233), Yoruba (Ellis, *Yoruba-speaking Peoples*, p. 182 *sq.*), Ewhe (*Idem, Ewe-speaking Peoples*, p. 204 ; see also Spieth, *op. cit.* p. 63* *sq.*), Baoulé (Clozel and Villamur, *Les coutumes indigènes de la Côte d'Ivoire*, p. 100), Siéna (Delafosse, in *Revue des études ethnographiques et sociologiques*, i. 483), Mossi of the Western Sudan (Mangin, in *Anthropos*, ix. 487), Baya (Poupon, ' Étude ethnographique des Baya de la circonscription du M'Bimou,' in *L'Anthropologie*, xxvi. 125), Bavili (Dennett, *At the Back of the Black Man's Mind*, p. 37).

[1] There is no reason to regard the higher position granted to the first married wife as indicating a transition from polygynous to monogamous habits, as has been suggested, *e.g.*, by Post (*Die Ge schlechtsgenossenschaft der Urzeit*, p. 27) and Spencer (*Principles of Sociology*, i. 664 *sq.*).

[2] Wadshagga (Volkens, *Der Kilimandscharo*, p. 252), Angoni (Wiese, ' Beiträge zur Geschichte der Zulu im Norden des Zambesi,' in *Zeitschr. f. Ethnol.* xxxii. 192 ; sometimes), Marshall Islanders (Erdland, ' Die Stellung der Frauen in den Häuptlingsfamilien der Marshallinseln,' in *Anthropos*, iv. 107 ; apparently). Among the Maori the principal wife of a man of noble birth or position was generally a high-born woman (Tregear, *op. cit.* p. 296 ; *cf.* Best, in *Trans. and Proceed. New Zealand Institute*, xxxvi. 29). Among the Fo negroes in Togoland the first free (not slave) wife is the chief wife (Wolf, ' Beitrag zur Ethnographie der Fō-Neger in Togo,' in *Anthropos*, vii. 297).

wife is the mother of the first-born.[1]   Often she is distinguished from the other wives by a special designation.
The Garos, according to Major Playfair, call her *jik-mamung*
or *jik-mongma* (the latter meaning " elephant-wife ") and
the others *jik-gité*, which is equivalent to " concubine."[2]
In Erromanga the oldest wife of a chief was his *retepon*,
or " wife," whereas the others were merely his *ovasiven*,
" women," or *nocte*, " property."[3]   Among the Yoruba
the first married wife is styled *iyale*, " mistress of the house,"
whilst the junior wives are termed *iyawo*, " trade-wives,"
or " wives of commerce," probably because they sell in the
markets.[4]   The Thonga call the first wife the " great one,"
nsati lwe' nkulu, and those who are taken in marriage afterwards the " little wives "; and when Junod asked an old
native why such a difference is made between the wives, he
was told that " the first one is the true one and the others
are but thieves."[5]   Even where the head wife has no other
privileges she is more or less the mistress of the house ; she
is entrusted with keeping the others in order, and her
authority over them may even be so great that they are
practically her handmaids.   She is often consulted by the
husband when he wishes to take a second wife,[6] and her
veto may be decisive.[7]   Sometimes we hear that she inhabits

---

[1] Among the Guaraunos the first wife or the wife who has first
given birth to a child is the most respected one and rules over the
other wives when the husband is away (Chaffanjon, *L'Orénoque
et le Caura*, p. 11).   Thomson says (*Story of New Zealand*, i. 179)
that among the Maori " the mother of the first-born was the head
wife, and the others were little better than slaves."

[2] Playfair, *Garos*, p. 69.   According to Chunder Dey (' Account
of the Garos,' in *Calcutta Review*, cxxviii. 161) the chief wife is
called *jik phongma*, or " the eternal wife."

[3] Robertson, *Erromanga*, p. 397.

[4] Ellis, *Yoruba-speaking Peoples*, p. 182 *sq.*

[5] Junod, *Life of a South African Tribe*, i. 186, 273.

[6] Jochelson, *Koryak*, p. 754.   Clozel and Villamur, *Les coutumes
indigènes de la Côte d'Ivoire*, p. 100 (Baoulé).   Delafosse, in *Revue
des études ethnographiques et sociologiques*, i. 483 (Siéna).   Poupon,
in *L'Anthropologie*, xxvi. 124 (Baya).

[7] Dorsey, in *Ann. Rep. Bur. Ethnol.* iii. 261 (Omaha).   Chunder
Dey, in *Calcutta Review*, cxxviii. 161 (Garos ; according to Playfair
[*op. cit.* p. 69] the first wife is entitled to compensation if the husband
takes a second without her permission).

the principal hut,[1] or is the only wife who has a separate
sleeping-tent,[2] or that she " takes her station next the
principal fire, which comes entirely under her management,"[3]
or that " her place in the lodge is usually by her husband's
side."[4] Among the Mocobis of the Gran Chaco the other
wives do not even live in the husband's hut, but remain with
their parents.[5] Among the Yukaghir the man shared his bed
with the first wife, whereas the others, who slept elsewhere,
were visited by him only at night, in a somewhat clandestine
fashion.[6] Among the Saorias a husband who has intercourse with a younger wife without the consent of the elder
one is liable, on complaint, to a fine according to circumstances.[7] Among the Meitheis of Assam " in polygamous
households the husband's attentions to the several wives
are strictly regulated according to precedence, the eldest
getting twice the nominal share of the wife next below her " ;
but although this is the rule, it seems that the rule is often
broken.[8] Among some of the Old Kukis the first wife is
entitled to the company of her husband for five nights, the
second for four, and the third for three.[9] Sometimes we
are told that the first wife is better kept[10] or receives more
food and presents[11] than the others, and she may have to
work less ;[12] but, on the other hand, she may also be in the
first place responsible for the husband's well-being.[13] Among
the Baganda she had charge of all his fetishes.[14] Among
some peoples she is never deposed[15] or can be divorced only

[1] Junod, *Les Ba-Ronga*, p. 40.   [2] Jochelson, *Koryak*, p. 756.
[3] Parry, *op. cit.* p. 528 (Eskimo of Melville Peninsula).
[4] Kohl, *Kitchi-Gami*, p. 111 (Chippewa).
[5] Kohler, *Pater Florian Baucke*, p. 313.
[6] Jochelson, *Yukaghir*, p. 110.
[7] Bainbridge, in *Memoirs Asiatic Soc. Bengal*, ii. 57.
[8] Hodson, *Meitheis*, p. 77.   [9] Shakespear, *op. cit.* p. 155.
[10] Merker, *Die Masai*, p. 27.
[11] Schuster, in *Anthropos*, ix. 955 (Banjange of Kamerun).
[12] Coudreau, *Chez nos Indiens*, p. 132 (Roucouyennes of French
Guiana).
[13] Martin, *Reisen in den Molukken*, p. 290 (natives of Waëpote in
Buru).
[14] Roscoe, *Baganda*, p. 83.
[15] Dorsey, in *Ann. Rep. Bur. Ethnol.* iii. 261 (Omaha).

if she has been unfaithful to her husband.[1] Among some natives of Mindanao, on the death of the husband she acts as administrator of his property,[2] or one-half of it goes to her and the other half to his children, whereas the second and succeeding wives inherit nothing;[3] but in either case the children of the latter share equally with those of the first. Of some other peoples, also, we are told that no difference in the right of inheritance or in rights generally exists between the children of different wives;[4] but very frequently the opposite is the case, the children[5] or sons[6] or the eldest son[7] of the first wife taking precedence over those of the later wives in inheritance or succession or otherwise. The chief of the Basuto, when asked by foreigners how many children he has, alludes in his answer only to those of his first wife; and if he says that he is a widower it means that he has lost his real wife and has not raised any of the others to the rank she occupied.[8] Among the Maori the first or head

[1] Waitz, *op. cit.* ii. 110 (negroes). Vergette, *Certain Marriage Customs of some of the Tribes in the Protectorate of Sierra Leone,* p. 22.

[2] Cole, in *Field Museum of Natural History, Anthropological Series,* xii. 144 (Bila-an).

[3] *Ibid.* p. 157 (Kulaman).

[4] v. Martius, *op. cit.* i. 126 (Brazilian aborigines). Richter, in *Mittheil. Deutsch. Schutzgeb.* xii. 85 (people of Bukoba). Heese, ' Sitte und Brauch der Sango,' in *Archiv f. Anthrop.* N.S. xii. 137. Best, in *Trans. and Proceed. New Zealand Institute,* xxxvi. 30 (Maori).

[5] Sproat, *op. cit.* p. 100 (Nootka). Prejevalsky, *Mongolia,* i. 69 (Mongols); ii. 121 (Tangutans). de Morga, *op. cit.* p. 300; Mallat, *op. cit.* i. 57 (natives of the Philippines at the time of their discovery). Storch, in *Mittheil. Deutsch. Schutzgeb.* viii. 312 (Washambaa in Usambara). Kohler, in *Zeitschr. vergl. Rechtswiss.* xv. 342 (Hottentots).

[6] Turner, in *Ann. Rep. Bur. Ethnol.* xi. 190 (Eskimo of the Ungava district, Labrador). Bainbridge, in *Memoirs Asiatic Soc. Bengal,* ii. 57 (Saorias).

[7] Kropf, *op. cit.* p. 153 (Xosa Kafirs). Wiese, in *Zeitschr. f. Ethnol.* xxxii. 192 (Angoni). Dannert, *op. cit.* p. 42 *sq.* (Herero). Decle, *op. cit.* p. 348 (Wanyamwezi). Volkens, *op. cit.* p. 253 (Wadshagga). Burrows, *Land of the Pigmies,* p. 86 (Mangbettu). Hollis, *Nandi,* p. 64. Routledge, *op. cit.* p. 134 (Akikúyu).

[8] Casalis, *op. cit.* p. 187. *Cf.* Livingstone, *op. cit.* p. 185 (Makololo).

wife of a chief was of his own people and probably his equal in rank, whereas the second wife might be a slave.[1] The Ewhe in the interior of Togoland believe that a man's first wife also was his wife—and indeed his only one—during his previous state of existence. Among those who live on the coast, again, it is the custom for a man to be provided with the first wife by his maternal uncle, whereas he procures any subsequent wife himself.[2] Casalis writes of the Basuto:— " A very marked distinction exists between the first wife and those who succeed her. The choice of the *great* wife (as she is always called) is generally made by the father, and is an event in which all the relations are interested. The others, who are designated by the name of *serete* (heels), because they must on all occasions hold an inferior position to the mistress of the house, are articles of luxury, to which the parents are not obliged to contribute."[3] Among several peoples, as we have seen, it is for the first wife alone that a man has to serve with her father.[4]

The difference between the position of the first wife and that of subsequent ones is not infrequently so great that our authorities represent the former as the only real or legitimate wife and the others as concubines, and speak of monogamy combined with concubinage. In many or most of these cases we are probably justified in regarding the marriage as polygynous and the concubines as inferior wives. If " concubinage " is used as a term not for a mere *liaison* of some duration but for a relation recognised by custom or law, I think it anyhow should be restricted to relations that only imply sexual licence, whereas marriage is something more than a regulated sexual relation between man and woman. But to apply this distinction in practice is often impossible on account of our ignorance of the actual status of the so-called concubine. If she lives under the roof and protection of the man who keeps her and it is considered his duty to support her and their common offspring, she has a claim to be treated as a wife by the soci-

---

[1] Best, in *Trans. and Proceed. New Zealand Institute*, xxxvi. 29 (Maori).   [2] Spieth, *op. cit.* p. 63* *sq.*
[3] Casalis, *op. cit.* p. 186 *sq.*   [4] *Supra*, ii. 364.

ologist, however humble her position may be in the family. So, also, when we hear that a man has concubines besides having several wives, this may really mean that not one but several of his wives occupy a higher position than others, who are then called concubines. There may be a distinction not only between the first wife and the subsequent ones, but also between different wives belonging to the latter class. Among the Ewhe-speaking peoples of the Slave Coast, for instance, the first wife, who is termed the " head-wife," supervises the internal arrangements of the entire household and is consulted by her husband ; the second wife acts as the assistant of the first, and those married later are classed together. But besides the " wives " there are concubines, usually slave-girls, whose condition is but little inferior to that of the third, fourth, and later wives.[1]

In a few cases mentioned above the higher position of the first wife implies certain sexual privileges. More often we are told that it is the custom for the husband to cohabit with his wives in turn.[2] Among the Caribs he lived a month with each wife in her separate hut.[3] Among the wild Indians of Chili, according to Darwin, the cazique lives a week in turn with each of his wives.[4] Among the Bavuma, " if a man has more than one wife, he resides with each four days at a time. If his attentions were prolonged beyond that period, he would be publicly denounced by the other wives as guilty of a gross breach of etiquette."[5]

---

[1] Ellis, *Ewe-speaking Peoples,* p. 204 *sq.*

[2] Grandidier, *Ethnographie de Madagascar,* ii. 194 *sq.* Stannus, ' Notes on some Tribes of British Central Africa,' in *Jour. Roy. Anthr. Inst.* xl. 309. Gottschling, ' Bawenda,' *ibid.* xxxv. 374. Magyar, *op. cit.* p. 283 (Kimbunda). Kaufmann, in *Mittheil. Deutsch. Schutzgeb.* xxiii. 136 (Auin). Torday and Joyce, *Les Bushongo,* p. 115 *sq.* (Bangongo). Bufe, ' Die Bakundu,' in *Archiv f. Anthropologie,* N.S. xii. 235. Felkin, in *Proceed. Roy. Soc. Edinburgh,* xii. 323 (Madi of Central Africa). Krasheninnikoff, *History of Kamschatka,* p. 215.

[3] Du Tertre, *op. cit.* ii. 378.

[4] Darwin, *Journal of Researches,* p. 366.

[5] Cunningham, *Uganda,* p. 141. Among the Banyoro the husband likewise lives with each of his wives for four days in turn (*ibid.* p. 37).

The Kafirs, again, have an old traditional law requiring a
husband who has many wives to devote three succeeding
days and nights to each of them ;[1] and a similar rule prevails
among the Swahili.[2] It is prescribed in the Koran that a
husband shall be impartial to his several wives.[3] Another
matter is how far theory and practice coincide. We have
reason to suspect that in polygynous marriages one of the
wives is for the time being the favourite.

Among the Banjange of Kamerun, says Schuster, there
are two wives in polygynous marriages who are particularly
prominent, namely, the first wife, who rules over the others
and enjoys certain other privileges, and the favourite wife,
with whom the husband generally lives and sleeps.[4] Among
the Baganda only the head wives have definite privileges,
but " in large establishments the favourite for the day
wears some distinguishing ornament ; in some cases it is
a small bell hung round the neck."[5] In Bokhara a rich
man generally has two, three, or four wives, but one of them,
as a rule, holds precedence in the husband's love.[6] If a
Koryak has several wives, one of them is likewise in most
cases the favourite, whilst the others chiefly work for him.[7]
Of the Omaha Indians we are told that on the general
hunting expeditions, when they separate into distinct bands,
a married man takes with him his favourite wife.[8] Among
the Apache the chiefs " can have any number of wives they
choose, but one only is the favourite."[9] Sometimes the
wife who has proved most fruitful and given birth to the
healthiest children is most favoured by the husband ;[10]

---

[1] v. Weber, *Vier Jahre in Afrika*, i. 329.

[2] Velten, *Sitten und Gebräuche der Suaheli*, p. 140.

[3] *Koran*, iv. 3.   [4] Schuster, in *Anthropos*, ix. 955.

[5] Felkin, ' Notes on the Waganda Tribe of Central Africa,' in
Proceed. Roy. Soc. Edinburgh, xiii. 757.

[6] Georgi, *op. cit.* p. 153.   [7] Dittmar, *loc. cit.* p. 25.

[8] James, *Account of an Expedition from Pittsburgh to the Rocky
Mountains*, i. 232.

[9] Schoolcraft, *Archives of Aboriginal Knowledge*, v. 210.   *Cf. ibid.*
i. 236 (Comanche).

[10] Lane, *Manners and Customs of the Modern Egyptians*, i. 253.
Polak, *Persien*, i. 226 *sq.*

and among the Indians of Western Washington and North-Western Oregon, according to Gibbs, the man usually lives with his first wife at least after his interest in subsequent wives has cooled down.[1] But temporary precedence is no doubt given to the wife who for the moment offers the greatest sexual attraction. Speaking of the modern Egyptians, Lane remarks that " in general, the most beautiful of a man's wives or slaves is, of course, for a time his greatest favourite," although in many, if not most, cases the lasting favourite is not the most handsome.[2] An Arab sheikh said to Sir Samuel Baker :—" I have four wives ; as one has become old, I have replaced her with a young one ; here they all are (he now marked four strokes upon the sand with his stick). This one carries water ; that grinds the corn ; this makes the bread ; the last does not do much, as she is the youngest, and my favourite."[3] Frequently, as will be seen, a fresh wife is taken when the first one grows old ; and in such cases the sexual relations inside the polygynous marriage are likely to be monogamous, although the old wife remains the mistress of the house.

Polygyny, or a sort of concubinage hardly distinguishable from genuine polygyny, is found among most peoples of archaic civilisation. It was permitted among the ancient Mexicans,[4] Mayas,[5] Chibchas,[6] and Peruvians,[7] although it was probably practised chiefly by the rich.[8] The first wife took precedence of the subsequent wives, or they had only one " true and lawful wife," though as many less legitimate

---

[1] Gibbs, loc. cit. p. 198 sq.   [2] Lane, op. cit. i. 253 sq. n. 5.
[3] Baker, Nile Tributaries of Abyssinia, p. 265. Cf. ibid. p. 263 sq.
[4] Clavigero, History of Mexico, i. 322. Bancroft, op. cit. ii. 265.
Waitz, op. cit. iv. 130.
[5] Bancroft, op. cit. ii. 671.
[6] Waitz, op. cit. iv. 360, 366. Spencer, Descriptive Sociology, Ancient Mexicans, &c., p. 4.
[7] Garcilasso de la Vega, First Part of the Royal Commentaries of the Incas, i. 310. Acosta, Natural and Moral History of the Indies, ii. 424.
[8] Prescott, History of the Conquest of Mexico, p. 72. Idem, History of the Conquest of Peru, p. 54.

wives or concubines as they liked. In Mexico, at least, neither the wives of " second rank " nor their children could inherit property.[1] In the counsels of a Mexican father to his son we even find the remarkable declaration that, for the multiplication of the species, God ordained one man only for one woman.[2] In Nicaragua bigamy, in the strict judicial sense of the term, was punished with exile and confiscation of property.[3]

In China there are, besides the legal principal wife, so-called wives " by courtesy " or lawful concubines ; whereas the law forbids the taking of a wife, in the full sense of the term, during the lifetime of the first.[4] The wife is invested with a certain amount of power over the concubines, who may not even sit in her presence without special permission.[5] She addresses her partner with a term corresponding to our " husband," whilst the concubines call him " master."[6] These are generally women with large feet and of low origin, not infrequently slaves or prostitutes ; whereas the wife is almost invariably, except, of course, in the case of Tartar ladies, a woman with small feet.[7] A wife cannot be degraded to the position of a concubine, nor can a concubine be raised to the position of a wife so long as the wife is alive, under a penalty in the one case of a hundred and in the other of ninety blows.[8] But the question upon which the legitimacy of the offspring depends is not whether the woman is wife

---

[1] Bancroft, *op. cit.* ii. 265.

[2] Sahagun, *Historia general de las cosas de Nueva España*, vi. 21, vol. ii. 143.

[3] Squier, ' Observations on the Archæology and Ethnology of Nicaragua,' in *Trans. American Ethn. Soc.* vol. iii. pt. i. 127.

[4] Medhurst, ' Marriage, Affinity, and Inheritance in China,' in *Trans. Roy. Asiatic Soc. China Branch*, iv. 21. Parker, ' Comparative Chinese Family Law,' in *China Review*, viii. 78. Jamieson, ' Translations from the General Code of Laws of the Chinese Empire ; vii.—Marriage Laws,' *ibid.* x. 80. Ball, *Chinese at Home*, p. 48.

[5] Gray, *China*, i. 212.

[6] Medhurst, *loc. cit.* p. 15. When dying, concubines who have not had children are removed from the dwelling-house to a humbler abode, not being entitled to die in the dwelling-house of their master Gray, *op. cit.* i. 213).   [7] Gray, *op. cit.* i. 212 *sqq.*

[8] Jamieson, *loc. cit.* p. 80. Medhurst, *loc. cit.* pp. 15, 21.

or concubine, but whether she has been received into the house of the man or not.[1] It is difficult even to guess at the extent of concubinage in China, as there are no statistics on the subject. Among the labouring classes it is no doubt rare to find more than one woman to one man ; but tradesmen, official persons, landholders, and those in easy circumstances frequently take one or more concubines—Wells Williams thinks that perhaps two-fifths of such persons have them.[2] The best feelings of the nation are evidently at heart against the practice.[3] In Corea the mandarins are even bound by custom, besides having several wives, to retain several concubines in their " yamen."[4] In Japan concubinage of the Chinese type existed as a legal institution until it was abolished with the promulgation of the Criminal Code of 1880 ;[5] and " the long-established custom still lingers to some extent."[6] The old Taihō Code of 701 gave concubines, as well as wives, the position of relatives in the second degree ;[7] and children of a concubine had the same legal rights as those of a wife.[8]

In ancient Egypt polygyny seems to have been permitted but to have been unusual.[9] Royal double marriages, however, frequently occurred ; Rameses II., for example, had two great " royal consorts," and when he concluded his treaty with the Cheta king, he brought the daughter of that monarch also home to Egypt as his wife.[10] The Pharaohs

[1] Parker, loc. cit. p. 79.   [2] Williams, Middle Kingdom, i. 792.
[3] Ball, op. cit. p. 47.   [4] Ross, History of Corea, p. 315.
[5] Hozumi, Ancestor-Worship and Japanese Law, p. 142.
[6] Nakajima, ' Marriage (Japanese and Korean),' in Hastings, Encyclopædia of Religion and Ethics, viii. 459.
[7] Hozumi, op. cit. p. 142. Idem, Lectures on the New Japanese Civil Code, p. 101.
[8] Rein, Japan, p. 423. Küchler, ' Marriage in Japan,' in Trans. Asiatic Soc. Japan, xiii. 129.
[9] Gardiner, ' Ethics and Morality (Egyptian),' in Hastings, op. cit. v. 481. Erman, Life in Ancient Egypt, p. 151 sq. Nietzold, Die Ehe in Ägypten zur ptolemäisch-römischen Zeit, p. 15. Herodotus said (ii. 92) that among the Egyptians, as among the Greeks, each man took to himself a single wife.
[10] Erman, op. cit. p. 152. Müller, Die Liebespoesie der alten Ägypter, p. 5. Griffith, ' Marriage (Egyptian),' in Hastings, op. cit. viii. 444.

had large *harīms*, and it is improbable that concubinage
on a considerable scale was confined to the royal house,
although we are ill-instructed on this point.[1] Dr. Alan
Gardiner points out to me that evidence of non-royal
polygyny in Egypt is very hard to find. A certain noble
speaks about " his fathers, his mothers, his wives, and his
children " ;[2] and a passage of the unpublished Papyrus
Mayer (11 c, 7 *sq.*), from the twentieth Dynasty, shows that
a certain " guardian " Puro had two wives simultaneously,
who were called as witnesses in a law-suit.[3]

The Babylonian Code of Ḥammurabi assumes that
marriage shall be monogamous. Yet " if a man has married
a wife and a sickness has seized her," he may take a second
wife ;[4] and, according to Johns' translation, " if a man has
espoused a votary (that is, a woman who has served as a
sacred servant in the temple), and she has not granted him
children and he has set his face to take a concubine, that
man shall take a concubine," although he shall not put her
on an equality with the wife.[5] But according to Winckler's
translation the latter paragraph refers to any wife who
remains childless, not only to one who has previously been
a votary.[6] Slave-concubinage was frequently practised in
the days of Ḥammurabi, and a female slave who had borne
her master children could not be sold.[7] Among the Hebrews,
on the other hand, a man could in any circumstances take
a plurality of wives, and there was no difference in the legal
status of different wives, although a distinction was made
between a wife and a slave-concubine.[8] In the case of the
levirate marriage the Pentateuch actually ordains a second
marriage, a man being compelled to marry his childless

---

[1] Gardiner, *loc. cit.* p. 482. Erman, *op. cit.* p. 153.
[2] Griffith, *Inscriptions of Siût and Dêr Rîfeh*, xiv. 77.
[3] Dr. Alan Gardiner.
[4] *Code of Laws promulgated by Ḥammurabi*, trans. by Johns,
§ 148, p. 29. *Die Gesetze Hammurabis*, trans. by Winckler, § 148,
p. 43.
[5] Johns' translation, § 145, p. 28 *sq.*
[6] Winckler's translation, § 145, p. 41.
[7] Johns' translation, § 146, p. 29. Winckler's translation, § 146,
p. 43.
[8] Benzinger, *Hebräische Archäologie*, p. 104.

brother's widow whether he be married before or not.[1] From certain passages in Genesis[2] and the Proverbs,[3] and from the general tendency of the Song of Songs,[4] it has been argued that monogamy was the Biblical ideal.[5] But Deuteronomy[6] certainly presupposes that a man will often have two wives, and the law of Exodus[7] takes it for granted that female slaves will become the concubines either of their owner or of his sons.[8] The provisions of the Talmudic law frequently refer to cases where one man contracts marriage with more than one wife.[9] It is probable, however, that among the ancient Israelites, as among most other peoples practising polygyny, the bulk of the population lived in monogamy, and that in post-exilic times polygyny was a rare exception.[10] There was no limit to the number of wives a man might have. We read of Solomon, who had " seven hundred wives, princesses, and three hundred concubines ";[11] and of Rehoboam, who " took eighteen wives, and three-score concubines."[12] But in the Talmud it is said that " the wise men have given good advice, that a man should not marry more than four wives."[13] Among European Jews polygyny was still practised during the Middle Ages, and among Jews living in Muhammadan countries it occurs even to this day.[14] An express prohibition of it was not pronounced until the convening of the Rabbinical Synod at Worms, in the beginning of the eleventh century. This

[1] *Deuteronomy*, xxv. 5 *sqq.*
[2] *Genesis*, ii. 24 ; iv. 19.   [3] *Proverbs*, xxxi. 10 *sqq.*
[4] See Harper, *Song of Solomon*, p. xxxiv. *sq.*
[5] Abrahams, ' Marriage (Jewish),' in Hastings, *op. cit.* viii. 461. Greenstone, ' Polygamy,' in *Jewish Encyclopedia*, x. 120.
[6] *Deuteronomy*, xxi. 15.
[7] *Exodus*, xxi. 7 *sqq. Cf. Deuteronomy*, xxi. 10 *sqq.*
[8] See Barton, ' Marriage (Semitic),' in Hastings, *op. cit.* viii. 469.
[9] Mielziner, *Jewish Law of Marriage and Divorce*, p. 30.
[10] *Ibid.* p. 29. Andree, *Zur Volkskunde der Juden*, p. 146 *sq.* Krauss, *Talmudische Archäologie*, ii. 27 *sq.* Greenstone, *loc. cit.* p. 120.
[11] 1 *Kings*, xi. 3.   [12] 2 *Chronicles*, xi. 21.
[13] Hughes, *Dictionary of Islam*, p. 462.
[14] Andree, *Zur Volkskunde der Juden*, p. 147 *sqq.* Polak, *Persien*, i. 209. Löbel, *Hochzeitsbräuche in der Türkei*, p. 270. Greenstone, *loc. cit.* p. 121.

prohibition was originally made for the Jews living in Germany and Northern France, but it was successively adopted in all European countries. Nevertheless, the Jewish Marriage Code retained many provisions which originated at a time when polygyny was still legally in existence.[1]

In Arabia Muhammad set a limit to the number of wives a man might possess, by ordaining that his legal wives should be not more than four ; but he might enjoy as concubines any number of slaves he was able to possess.[2] The Prophet himself, however, was allowed as many wives as he wished.[3] Where two or more wives belong to one man, the first married generally enjoys the highest rank and is called " the great lady." But no distinction in inheritance is made between the children of different wives, nor even between the child of a wife and that borne by a slave to her master, if the master acknowledge the child to be his own.[4] As a matter of fact, the large majority of men in Muhammadan countries live in monogamy ; this is the case in Asia[5] as well as in Africa.[6] In Persia, according to Colonel Macgregor, only two per cent. have a plurality of wives.[7] Among the Muhammadans of India there are 1,021 wives to every 1,000 husbands, so that, even if no husbands have more than two wives, all but 21 per thousand must be monogamous.[8] Ameer Ali states that " among many of the educated classes versed in the history of their ancestors and able to compare it with the records of other nations, the practice of polygamy is regarded with disapprobation amounting almost to disgust."[9] A growing section of Islamists, particularly among the Mutazalas, even consider

---

[1] Mielziner, *op. cit.* p. 30.   [2] *Koran*, iv. 3.   [3] *Ibid.* xxxiii. 49.

[4] Lane, *Manners and Customs of the Modern Egyptians*, i. 252.

[5] Burckhardt, *Notes on the Bedouins and Wahábys*, pp. 61, 158. Van-Lennep, *Bible Lands*, p. 558 (Palestine). Elphinstone, *Account of the Kingdom of Caubul*, i. 241 ; Pennell, *Among the Wild Tribes of the Afghan Frontier*, p. 195. Pischon, *Der Einfluss des Islâm auf das häusliche, sociale und politische Leben seiner Bekenner*, p. 13 (Turks).   [6] *Supra*, iii. 25.

[7] Ameer Ali, *Mahommedan Law*, ii. 25. See also Polak, *op. cit.* i. 209.

[8] *Imperial Gazetteer of India*, i. 482.   [9] Ameer Ali, *op. cit.* ii. 24 *sq.*

it positively unlawful ; indeed, so early as the third century of the era of Hegira, during the reign of al-Māmūn, the first Mutazalite doctors taught that the developed Koranic laws inculcated monogamy. Much emphasis is laid on the fact that the clause in the Koran which contains the permission to contract four contemporaneous marriages is immediately followed by the sentence, " And if ye fear that ye cannot be equitable, then [marry] only one." It is argued that, as it is impossible for all ordinary men who have a plurality of wives to be quite impartial to each wife, monogamy must be considered the law for them.[1]

Polygyny has been permitted among most of the so-called Aryan peoples. Herodotus wrote of the ancient Persians, " Each of them has several wives, and a still larger number of concubines."[2] This, however, can hardly have been true of the common people ;[3] and it also seems that in polygynous households one of the wives was the principal wife.[4] In the Avesta there is no positive testimony either concerning monogamy or concerning polygyny. From this Geiger draws the conclusion that polygyny was not prohibited to the Avesta nation ; for if it had been so, contrary to the custom which we know to have prevailed elsewhere in the country of Iran, there would certainly have been no lack of passages opposing it.[5] The Parsees of India nowadays prohibit bigamy, but it was frequently practised among them till half a century ago.[6]

---

[1] *Ibid.* ii. 24. Pennell, *op. cit.* p. 195. [2] Herodotus, i. 135.

[3] Rapp, ' Die Religion und Sitte der Perser und übrigen Iranier nach den griechischen und römischen Quellen,' in *Zeitschr. Deutsch. Morgenl. Gesellsch.* xx. 109 *sq.* Spiegel, *Eránische Alterthumskunde,* iii. 677.

[4] Rapp, *loc. cit.* p. 109. Spiegel, *op. cit.* iii. 680. Rawlinson, *Five Great Monarchies of the Ancient Eastern World,* iii. 216.

[5] Geiger, *Civilization of the Eastern Iránians,* i. 68 *sq.* A different opinion has been expressed by C. de Harlez and Darab Peshotan Sanjana (*Position of Zoroastrian Women in Remote Antiquity,* p. 42 *sqq.*), but, as it seems to me, without good reason. The former says (in the Introduction to his translation of the Avesta, p. clxxi.), " La polygamie ne semble pas y avoir été admise ; cependant elle paraît autorisée lorsqu'une première union était restée sans fruit."

[6] Framjee A. Ráná, *Parsi Law,* p. 50 *sq.*

That polygyny was practised among the Vedic Indians
is clearly proved by many passages in the Rig-Veda and
other texts ; but it was probably as a rule confined to kings
and wealthy lords, monogamy being recognised as the
ordinary and natural form of marriage.[1] In a Vedic hymn,
which dwells upon the duality of the two Aświns, the pairs
of deities are compared with pairs of almost everything that
runs in couples, including a husband and wife and two lips
uttering sweet sounds.[2] Zimmer is of opinion that polygyny
is dying out in the Rig-Veda period, monogamy being
developed from polygyny ;[3] but there is nothing to prove
that it had previously been more frequent.[4] In the case of
the king four wives are regularly mentioned—namely, the
mahiṣī, the anointed, *i.e.*, the first wedded ; the *parivṛktī*,
or sonless and therefore discarded ;[5] the *vāvātā*, or favourite ;
and the *pālāgalī*, who has been explained[6] as the daughter
of the last of the eight special court officials. But the
mahiṣī seems to have been the wife proper, though the others
were evidently not mere concubines.[7] None of the Hindu
law-books restricts the number of wives whom a man is
permitted to marry ; yet some preference is often shown
for monogamy.[8] Āpastamba says that if a householder has
a wife who is willing and able to perform her share of the
religious duties and who bears sons, he shall not take a
second;[9] and in the 'Laws of Manu' we read that the maxim,

---

[1] Zimmer, *Altindisches Leben*, p. 324 *sq.* Delbrück, ' Die indogermanischen Verwandtschaftsnamen,' in *Abhandl. Königl. Sächsischen
Gesellsch. Wissensch.* xxv. 540 *sq.* Kaegi, *Rigveda*, p. 15. Roth,
' On the Morality of the Veda,' in *Jour. American Oriental Soc.*
iii. 339. Mandlik, *Vyavahára Mayúkha*, p. 398 *sq.* Macdonell and
Keith, *Vedic Index of Names and Subjects*, i. 478. Keith, ' Marriage
(Hindu),' in Hastings, *op. cit.* viii. 452.
[2] *Rig-Veda*, ii. 39.   [3] Zimmer, *op. cit.* p. 323 *sqq.*
[4] *Cf.* Weber, ' Vedische Hochzeitssprüche,' in *Indische Studien*,
v. 222 n.**
[5] Thus translated by Weber, ' Collectanea über die Kastenverhältnisse in den Brâhmaṇa und Sûtra,' in *Indische Studien*, x. 6.
[6] By Weber, *ibid.* x. 6 n. 2.
[7] Delbrück, *loc. cit.* p. 540.   Jolly, *Recht und Sitte*, p. 64.
[8] *Laws of Manu*, v. 168; ix. 101 *sq.*   Jolly, *op. cit.* p. 65.   Keith,
loc. cit. p. 453.   [9] *Āpastamba*, ii. 5. 11. 12.

" Let mutual fidelity continue until death," may be considered as the summary of the highest law for husband and
wife.[1] A peculiar sanctity seems always to have been
attributed to the first marriage, as being that which was
contracted from a sense of duty and not merely for personal
gratification.[2] The first married wife should be of the same
caste as her husband.[3] She had precedence over the others,
and her first-born over his half-brothers.[4] She sat by her
husband at religious ceremonies. She was entitled to adopt
a son if she had no sons at the time of her husband's death.[5]
At the present day, although the Hindu law places no
restriction upon polygyny, most castes object to their
members having more than one wife, except for special
reasons, such as the failure of the first wife to bear a son,
or her affliction with some incurable disease or infirmity ;
and in such cases the consent of the caste *panchayat* must
generally be obtained before a man marries again. Much
the same rules prevail among the Buddhists.[6] According
to the Imperial Gazetteer of India, there are among the
Hindu and Buddhists only 1,008 and 1,007 wives respectively
to every 1,000 husbands.[7] It should be added that the
keeping of concubines by wealthy Hindus is a recognised
usage. The Smritis allowed a man to have, in addition to
wives proper, concubines (*dāsī, bhujiṣyā*), who were distin-

---

[1] *Laws of Manu*, ix. 101.

[2] Mayne, *Treatise on Hindu Law and Usage*, p. 112.   v. Schroeder,
Indiens Literatur und Cultur, p. 430.

[3] *Laws of Manu*, iii. 12.   Jolly, *op. cit.* p. 64.

[4] *Laws of Manu*, ix. 122 *sqq.*

[5] Steele, *Law and Custom of Hindoo Castes*, p. 31.   In Siam
" the wife who has been the object of the marriage ceremony,
called Khan mak, takes precedence of all the rest and is really the
sole legitimate spouse ; and she and her descendants are the only
legal heirs to the husband's possessions " (Bowring, *Kingdom and
People of Siam*, i. 119). According to a later account (Young,
Kingdom of the Yellow Robe, p. 99), the children of a subordinate
wife are legally entitled to a share of their father's property upon
his death, although they do not share on equal terms with the
children of the first wife.

[6] Gait, *Census of India*, 1911, vol. i. (India) Report, p. 246.

[7] *Imperial Gazetteer of India*, i. 483.

guished by not being married in due form, and who could
not in any case become their husband's heirs. They were,
however, entitled to maintenance by his brothers on his
death,[1] and intercourse with one of them was regarded as
adultery.[2]

Polygyny occurred among the ancient Slavs,[3] but generally, it seems, only chiefs and nobles were addicted to it.[4]
Concerning the pagan Russians Ewers says that of the wives
of a prince one probably had precedence.[5] As late as
1249 the Prussians formally promised thenceforth not to
take two or three wives, but to content themselves with a
single one.[6] Among some Southern Slavs bigamy is even
now allowed in case the wife is unfruitful or becomes insane.
In Bulgaria, where bigamy in such circumstances is
said to be fairly frequent, the second wife is called " the
substitute " (namiestnica).[7]

In ancient Scandinavia the kings indulged in polygynous
practices, and not they alone ; a man could not only have
as many concubines as he chose, but also more than one
legitimate wife.[8] Among the West Germans, according
to Tacitus, only a few persons of noble birth had a plurality
of wives.[9] There is no direct evidence of polygyny among
the Anglo-Saxons, but it cannot have been entirely unknown to them, as it is prohibited in some of their law-

---

[1] *Nârada*, xiii. 26.

[2] *Ibid.* xii. 79. Jolly, *op. cit.* p. 64 *sq.* Keith, *loc. cit.* p. 453.

[3] Ewers, *Das älteste Recht der Russen*, p. 105 *sqq.* Volkov, ' Rites
et usages nuptiaux en Ukraïne,' in *L'Anthropologie*, ii. 171.

[4] Krek, *Einleitung in die slavische Literaturgeschichte*, p. 361 *sq.*
Macieiowski, *Slavische Rechtsgeschichte*, ii. 191 *sqq.*

[5] Ewers, *op. cit.* p. 108.

[6] Hartknoch, *Alt- und Neues Preussen*, p. 176.

[7] Krauss, *Sitte und Brauch der Südslaven*, pp. 229, 233. See also
Macieiowski, *op. cit.* iv. 376 (Montenegro).

[8] *Heimskringla*, trans. by Laing, ed. by Anderson, i. 127 *sq.* Geijer,
Samlade skrifter, v. 88. Weinhold, *Altnordisches Leben*, p. 248.
Vigfusson and Powell, *Corpus Poeticum Boreale*, ii. 474. v. Amira,
' Recht,' in Paul, *Grundriss der germanischen Philologie*, iii. 161.
Gudmundsson and Kålund, ' Skandinavische Verhältnisse,' *ibid.*
iii. 422 *sq.* Hoops, *Reallexikon der Germanischen Altertumskunde*,
iii. 426.   [9] Tacitus, *Germania*, ch. 18.

books.[1] The general custom among the ancient Irish was to have one wife, but we sometimes find a king or chief with two.[2] It has been assumed that polygyny or concubinage occurred in ancient Gaul ;[3] but this assumption is based on a probable misinterpretation of the word *uxores* in a statement made by Caesar,[4] where this plural seems to be simply due to the plural *viri*.[5] The laws of ancient Wales did not permit polygyny.[6]

In the Homeric poems genuine polygyny appears to be ascribed to Priamus alone,[7] but he was a Trojan. From the historic age we hear of the Spartan king Anaxandridas who, at the suggestion of the Ephors, took a second wife because the first one had no children and he refused to divorce her. But this was " quite against all Spartan custom " ;[8] indeed, no such thing was ever allowed to any other Spartan.[9] It is true that King Ariston is said to have had two wives and even to have married a third,[10] but he is not said to have had the wives at one and the same time. There can be little doubt that monogamy was the only recognised form of marriage in Greece. Hruza points out that polygyny was not definitely prohibited by law at Athens and that cases of it actually occurred there ;[11] but neither of these facts justifies the conclusion that an Athenian could simultaneously have more than one lawful wife. On the contrary, there is every reason to believe that the validity of a second marriage

---

[1] *Laws of Ethelred*, vi. 12. *Laws of Cnut*, i. 7. *Law of the Northumbrian Priests*, 61. *Cf.* Roeder, *Die Familie bei den Angelsachsen*, p. 79.

[2] Joyce, *Social History of Ancient Ireland*, ii. 7.

[3] d'Arbois de Jubainville, *Cours de littérature celtique*, vi. 291. Schrader, *Reallexikon der indogermanischen Altertumskunde*, p. 635.

[4] Caesar, *De bello Gallico*, vi. 19. 3.

[5] *Cf.* Jullian, *Histoire de la Gaule*, ii. 408.

[6] Rhys and Brynmor-Jones, *The Welsh People*, p. 210.

[7] *Ilias*, xxi. 88 ; xxii. 48, 51.

[8] Herodotus, v. 39 *sq.*

[9] Pausanias, *Descriptio Graeciae*, iii. 3. 9.

[10] Herodotus, vi. 61 *sqq.*

[11] Hruza, *Beiträge zur Geschichte des griechischen und römischen Familienrechtes*, ii. 31 *sqq.*

presupposed the dissolution of the first,[1] or at all events that
the taking of a second wife was regarded as an offence against
the first, probably giving her the right of dissolving her
marriage.[2] Owing to exceptional circumstances, however,
bigamy may have been legal at Athens for a few years,
between 411 and 403 B.C. O. Müller maintains that after
the Sicilian expedition a law was passed there allowing a
married man to take a secondary wife, with a view to increasing the citizen body, which had been so much reduced
that marriageable girls could not find husbands ; but this
institution was abolished on the restitution of the democracy.[3] Concubinage existed at Athens at all times, and was
hardly censured by public opinion.[4] But it was well
distinguished from marriage : it conferred no rights on the
παλλακή, and the children were νόθοι, bastards.[5] The law
hardly took any notice of it at all, except that it authorised
a man to slay with impunity an offender caught *flagrante
delicto* whom he found either with his wife or with his
concubine.[6]

Roman marriage was strictly monogamous. A second
marriage concluded by a married person was invalid,
although it was not subject to punishment during the Republic and the early Empire ; Diocletian was the first who
punished bigamy.[7] Liaisons between married men and
mistresses were not uncommon by the close of the Republic ;[8] but such a relation was not considered lawful concubinage in after times. According to Paulus, a man who
had an *uxor* could not have a *concubina* at the same time.[9]

[1] See Beauchet, *Histoire du droit privé de la République Athénienne*,
i. 41 *sqq.*

[2] v. Wilamowitz-Moellendorff and Niese, *Staat und Gesellschaft
der Griechen und Römer*, p. 34.

[3] Müller, ' Untersuchungen zur Geschichte des attischen Bürger-
und Eherechts,' in *Jahrbücher f. classische Philologie*, xxv. Supple-
mentband, p. 796 *sq.*

[4] *Cf. Oratio in Neaeram*, in Demosthenes, p. 1386.

[5] Beauchet, *op. cit.* i. 82 *sqq.* Hruza, *op. cit.* ii. 66, 70 *sqq.*

[6] Demosthenes, *Oratio contra Aristocratem*, § 55, p. 637. Lysias,
Pro caede Eratosthenis apologia, § 31.

[7] Mommsen, *Römisches Strafrecht*, p. 701.

[8] Cicero, *De oratore*, i. 40, § 183.   [9] *Digesta*, i. 16. 144.

Marital faithfulness, however, was not required. The Romans defined adultery as sexual intercourse with another man's wife ; the intercourse of a married man with an unmarried woman was not regarded as adultery.[1]

Considering that monogamy prevailed as the only legitimate form of marriage in Greece and Rome, it cannot be said that Christianity introduced obligatory monogamy into the Western world. Indeed, although the New Testament assumes monogamy as the normal or ideal form of marriage, it does not expressly prohibit polygyny, except in the case of a bishop and a deacon.[2] It has been argued that it was not necessary for the first Christian teachers to condemn polygyny because monogamy was the universal rule among the peoples in whose midst it was preached ; but this is certainly not true of the Jews, who still both permitted and practised polygyny at the beginning of the Christian era. Some of the Fathers accused the Jewish Rabbis of sensuality ;[3] but no Council of the Church in the earliest centuries opposed polygyny, and no obstacle was put in the way of its practice by kings in countries where it had occurred in the times of paganism. In the middle of the sixth century Diarmait, king of Ireland, had two queens and two concubines.[4] Polygyny was frequently practised by the Merovingian kings. Charles the Great had two wives and many concubines ; and one of his laws seems to imply that polygyny was not unknown even among priests.[5] In later times Philip of Hesse and Frederick William II. of Prussia contracted bigamous marriages with the sanction of the Lutheran clergy.[6] Luther himself approved of the bigamy of the former, and so did Melanch-

---

[1] Vinnius, *In quatuor libros institutionum imperialium commentarius*, iv. 18. 4, p. 993.   *Cf. Digesta*, i. 16. 101. 1 ; Mommsen, *op. cit.* p. 688 *sq.*

[2] 1 *Timothy*, iii. 2, 12.   [3] Krauss, *Talmudische Archäologie*, ii. 28.

[4] d'Arbois de Jubainville, *op. cit.* vi. 292.

[5] Thierry, *Narratives of the Merovingian Era*, p. 17 *sqq.* v. Hellwald, *Die menschliche Familie*, p. 558 n. 1.   Hallam, *Europe during the Middle Ages*, i. 420 n. 2.

[6] Friedberg, *Lehrbuch des katholischen und evangelischen Kirchenrechts*, i. 436, note to § 143.

thon.[1] On various occasions Luther speaks of polygyny
with considerable toleration. It had not been forbidden by
God; even Abraham, who was a "perfect Christian," had two
wives. It is true that God had allowed such marriages to
certain men of the Old Testament only in particular
circumstances, and if a Christian wanted to follow their
example he had to show that the circumstances were similar
in his case ; [2] but polygamy was undoubtedly preferable to
divorce.[3] In 1650, soon after the Peace of Westphalia,
when the population had been greatly reduced by the
Thirty Years' War, the Frankish *Kreistag* at Nuremberg
passed the resolution that thenceforth every man should be
allowed to marry two women.[4] Certain Christian sects
have even advocated polygyny with much fervour. In 1531
the Anabaptists openly preached at Munster that he who
wants to be a true Christian must have several wives.[5] And
the Mormons, as all the world knows, regard polygyny as a
divine institution. Sir Richard Burton observes that
among them, as among polygamists generally, the first
wife is *the* wife and assumes the husband's name and title.[6]

[1] Köstlin, *Martin Luther*, ii. 475 *sqq.*   [2] *Ibid.* i. 693 *sq.*
[3] *Ibid.* i. 347 ; ii. 257.   [4] v. Hellwald, *op. cit.* p. 559 note.
[5] *Ibid.* p. 558 n 1.   [6] Burton, *City of the Saints*, p. 518.

CHAPTER XXVIII

MONOGAMY AND POLYGYNY

(Concluded)

FROM the survey of facts we now come to the question how to explain them. Why are some peoples polygynous and others strictly monogamous; and why is polygyny more frequent, or the number of wives in polygynous marriages larger, among some polygynous peoples than among others ? These questions cannot be answered in every detail; but it is easy to show that there are certain circumstances that have a tendency to produce polygyny and others that make for monogamy. One factor which has undoubtedly exercised much influence upon the form of marriage is the numerical proportion between the sexes.

It has been asserted that monogamy is the natural form of human marriage, because there is an almost equal number of men and women. But this is a fallacious argument. The proportion of the sexes varies, and in some cases varies greatly, among different peoples. Sometimes they are about equal in number, sometimes there are more men than women, sometimes there are more women than men. Now there can be no doubt that a frequent cause of polygyny is an excess of marriageable women and a frequent cause of monogamy a comparative scarcity of them.

We know little about the proportion of the sexes among the South American Indians, who as a rule are not much addicted to polygyny. With reference to the Yahgans, Mr. Bridges wrote to me from Tierra del Fuego, where, as he says, polygyny is practised " in some districts very

rarely, in others more frequently, but in no part generally":—
" On several occasions when some hundreds of natives
have been gathered together, I have taken censuses of them,
and have always found the sexes equal or nearly so. . . .
War was unknown, though fightings were frequent, but
women took part in them as energetically as the men, and
suffered equally with them—if anything more." Among
the Pampas the women are a minority, in consequence of
the terrible wars made on them by the gauchos of Rosas.[1]
Azara states that among the Guanas the men are much more
numerous than the women, whereas among the Guarani
there are fourteen women to thirteen men.[2] Among the
Brazilian Indians, according to v. Martius, the number
varied in some villages in favour of the male sex, in others
in favour of the female.[3]   In some cases we hear of an excess
of females and polygyny connected with it.   In his description of the Lengua Indians of the Paraguayan Chaco Mr.
Grubb writes :—" Polygamy is not the natural instinct of
the Indian.   It is only found to exist among tribes where,
owing to devastating wars, the men have been so reduced
in number that the women largely outnumber them, . . .
but it gradually ceases as the balance of the sexes is restored.
. . . The tribes practising polygamy lie on the south-west
frontier, and are strong and powerful, with warlike in-
stincts."[4] Speaking of the polygyny of rich Araucanians,
who have a considerable number of wives, Molina observes
that there does not " arise any inconvenience from the
scarcity of women, as the number of females is much greater
than the males, which is always the case in those countries
where polygamy is permitted."[5]   Concerning the Guaraunos
M. Chaffanjon writes, " Le nombre des femmes dépassant
celui des hommes, la polygamie s'ensuit."[6]

Among the Indian tribes of North America, who, generally
speaking, practised polygyny more extensively than the

[1] Guinnard, *Three Years' Slavery among the Patagonians*, p. 134.
[2] Azara, *op. cit.* ii. 93, 59 *sq.*
[3] v. Martius, *op. cit.* i. 304 *sq.* note **.
[4] Grubb, *An Unknown People*, p. 215 *sq.*
[5] Molina, *op. cit.* ii. 116.   *Cf.* Guinnard, *op. cit.* p. 134.
[6] Chaffanjon, *op. cit.* p. 11.

South American tribes, there were often more women than men.[1] The census of the Creeks taken in 1832 showed 6,555 men and 7,142 women ; that of the Indian population around Lakes Superior, Huron, Michigan, the Upper Mississippi, &c., in the same year, 3,144 men and 3,571 women, excluding children ; that of the Nez Percés in Oregon, taken in 1851 by Dr. Dart, 698 men and 1,182 women.[2] The last-mentioned Indians were much addicted to polygyny.[3] In some other tribes the excess of women was greater still.[4] "As all nations of Indians in their natural condition," says Catlin, "are unceasingly at war with the tribes that are about them, . . . their warriors are killed off to that extent, that in many instances two, or sometimes three women to a man are found in a tribe."[5] An old Apache warrior, wise in the traditions of his people, told Cremony that there was a time when it was considered proper for a man to have one wife only, but that the losses by war and other causes "had so reduced the number of the males that it was judged politic to make a change in this custom."[6] Of the Seri Indians we are told that "the tribal population is preponderantly feminine, so that polygyny naturally prevails."[7] On the other hand, among the Upper Californians[8] and the Loucheux Indians[9] the females are said to be fewer than the males.

[1] Lumholtz, *Unknown Mexico*, i. 264 (Tarahumare). Powers, *Tribes of California*, p. 243 (Shastika). Lisiansky, *Voyage round the World*, p. 237 (natives of the Sitka Islands). Meares, *Voyages to the North-West Coast of America*, p. 268.

[2] Schoolcraft, *Archives of Aboriginal Knowledge* (*Indian Tribes of the United States*), iv. 577; iii. 601 *sq.*; v. 707. For other tribes see *ibid.* iii. 615, 632; iv. 590.

[3] Hobhouse, Wheeler, and Ginsberg, *op cit.* p. 184.

[4] Morgan, *Systems of Consanguinity and Affinity of the Human Family*, p. 477. Catlin, *Illustrations of the Manners, &c. of the North American Indians*, i. 212. *Cf.* Schoolcraft, *op. cit.* iii. 562 *sq.*

[5] Catlin, *op. cit.* i. 119.   [6] Cremony, *op. cit.* p. 249.

[7] McGee, ' Seri Indians,' in *Ann. Rep. Bur. Ethn.* vol. xvii. pt. i. 279.

[8] Coulter, ' Notes on Upper California,' in *Jour. Roy. Geograph. Soc.* v. 67.

[9] Hardisty, ' Loucheux Indians,' in *Smithsonian Report*, 1866, p. 312. Kirby, ' Journey to the Youcan,' *ibid.* 1864, p. 418.

Among some of the Eskimo tribes there is a preponderance of women, owing to the higher mortality among the men. Dr. Sutherland found that the average age of 109 Eskimo was nearly 22 years—that of the females 24·5 and that of the males 19·3 years.[1] The men pass most of their time at sea, in snow and rain, heat and cold, and many of them are drowned ; and the result of this manner of living is that few of them attain the age of fifty, whereas many women reach the age of seventy or even eighty. Such circumstances naturally lead to polygyny.[2] Among the Iwillik and Kinipetu, where at least half of the married men had two wives, there was a surplus of women.[3] On the other hand, there was no such surplus among the Netchillik, where the number of unmarried young men was comparatively large and but a few men had two wives ; among their children there were plenty of boys and only few girls—as their neighbours said, because they killed many of their female babes as soon as they were born.[4] Nor was there any excess of women among the Ita Eskimo of Western Greenland, who, destitute of boats and with fewer sources of livelihood at their disposal, were, as a compensation, less exposed to the perils of the sea ; and the consequence of this was monogamy.[5] Among the Eskimo of Cumberland Sound the males outnumber the females ; and " the scarcity of women at present in proportion to the men makes polygamy a luxury only to be indulged in by the wealthy."[6] Among the Chukchee, according to the data in the census of 1897 as collected by Gondatti and Bogoras, the number of women as compared to that of men forms in the Maritime portion of the tribe 108 per cent. and among the Reindeer Chukchee 101 per cent., and the total for the whole tribe is 102 per cent. The difference between the Maritime and Reindeer Chukchee depends on the far greater danger and

[1] Sutherland, ' On the Esquimaux,' in *Jour. Ethnol. Soc. London,* iv. 213.

[2] King, in *Jour. Ethnol. Soc. London,* i. 152. Reclus, *Primitive Folk,* p. 31. Armstrong, *Personal Narrative of the Discovery of the North-West Passage,* p. 195.

[3] Gilder, *op. cit.* p. 246.   [4] *Ibid.* p. 246 *sq.*

[5] Reclus, *op. cit.* p. 31 *sq.*   [6] Kumlien, *op. cit.* p. 16 *sq.*

risk of life which the Maritime hunters incur.[1] That polygyny, as we have seen, is rare among the former is not surprising considering how small the surplus of females is, but the general proportion of the sexes among the Reindeer Chukchee does not account for the fact that in some of their localities one-third or more of all the marriages are poly-gynous. The decline of polygyny among the Yakut is attributed partly to their decreasing prosperity and the rather large bride price, but partly also to the fact that girls die more frequently in infancy than boys, being less carefully tended.[2]

There is a considerable shortage of women at Port Blair in the Andaman Islands, where polygyny is on that account said to be almost unknown,[3] and among the inhabitants of the Nicobars.[4] The males are said to outnumber the females among the monogamous Veddas of Ceylon,[5] Orang Laut of Malacca,[6] and Orang Akit of Sumatra,[7] as also among the Kubus,[8] who as a rule live in monogamy. Elsewhere in Sumatra men and women are about equal in number,[9] whilst in Sarawak the women are less numerous than the men;[10] and in neither of these places, as we have seen, is polygyny much practised. The exceptional prevalence of polygyny at Sialum in Kaiser Wilhelm Land is due to the great pre-ponderance of women,[11] whereas among the Jabim most of the men are said to have to content themselves with one wife because the excess of women is very slight.[12] The predominance of monogamy in New Caledonia is attributed to a similar cause;[13] indeed, according to M. Moncelon,

---

[1] Bogoras, *op. cit.* p. 550 *sq.*

[2] Miss Czaplicka, *Aboriginal Siberia*, p. 112.

[3] Lowis, *op. cit.* p. 66 *sq.*   [4] *Ibid.* p. 99.

[5] Sarasin, *Ergebnisse naturwissenschaftlicher Forschungen auf Ceylon*, iii. 462 *sq.*

[6] Stevens, in *Zeitschr. f. Ethnol.* xxviii. 88.

[7] Moszkowski, *Auf neuen Wegen durch Sumatra*, p. 40. *Idem*, 'Ueber zwei nicht-malayische Stämme von Ost-Sumatra,' in *Zeitschr. f. Ethnol.* xl. 229.

[8] Hagen, *Die Orang Kubu auf Sumatra*, p. 133.

[9] Marsden, *op. cit.* p. 272.   [10] Low, *Sarawak*, p. 146.

[11] Neuhauss, *op. cit.* i. 152.   [12] Vetter, *loc. cit.* p. 88.

[13] de Rochas, *op. cit.* p. 228.   Lambert, *op. cit.* p. 95.

the men even outnumber the women.[1]   From various islands
in the Pacific Ocean we have records of a striking excess of
males over females.[2]   Mr. Inglis states that on the side
of the island of Aneiteum (New Hebrides) where he had
his mission, there were, in 1876, 446 males, out of whom
277 were unmarried, and only 267 females, out of whom
98 were unmarried ; the whole population was professedly
Christian.[3]   At Port Olry, in the same group, Dr. Speiser
found that the number of women amounted to about one-
fourth of that of the men.   He says that one reason for
this disproportion is the custom of killing all the widows
of a chief, which was all the more pernicious because the
chiefs, as a rule, owned most of the young females ; but
this custom is now dying out.[4]   On some of the Solomons,
according to Mr. Elton, "especially on Ugi and San
Christoval, there are more men than women " ;[5] and the
same is, according to Dr. Thurnwald, the case in Buin.[6]
A census taken in 1912 among the coast people of the
Gazelle Peninsula of New Britain showed 1,510 males
and 1,266 females.[7] About the middle of the last century
Thomson wrote that in every New Zealand village there
was an excess of males ; infanticide was then rare,[8] but it
was said that children often perished from want of suitable
care, and that girls, being less valuable than boys, suffered
most from this cause.[9]   The Maori census of 1881 gave

[1] Moncelon, in *Bull. Soc. d'Anthr. Paris*, ser. iii. vol. ix. 367.

[2] Mallicolo (Eckardt, ' Der Archipel der Neu-Hebriden,' in
*Verhandlungen des Vereins für naturwissenschaftliche Unterhaltung
zu Hamburg*, iv. 21 n.*), Luf to the west of the Admiralty Islands
(Parkinson, *op. cit.* p. 442), Sandwich Islands (Ellis, *Tour through
Hawaii*, p. 414 ; Marcuse, *Die Hawaiischen Inseln*, p. 109), Maupiti
(Montgomery, *Journal of Voyages and Travels by Tyerman and
Bennet*, ii. 12).   Melville (*Typee*, p. 281) says of the Typees of
Nukahiva :—" The males considerably outnumber the females.
This holds true of many of the islands of Polynesia."

[3] Inglis, *In the New Hebrides*, p. 339 *sq.*

[4] Speiser, *Two Years with the Natives in the Western Pacific*, p. 118.

[5] Elton, in *Jour. Anthr. Inst.* xvii. 94.

[6] Thurnwald, *op. cit.* iii. 81.   [7] Burger, *op. cit.* p. 29 n. 1.

[8] *Cf.* Tregear, *Maori Race*, p. 50.

[9] Thomson, *Story of New Zealand*, ii. 287.

1,235 males, and the census of 1886 1,169 males, to 1,000 females ; the Registrar-General came to the conclusion that there was a much higher death-rate among the adult Maori females than among the adult males.[1] On the other hand, we are told by Colenso that polygamy did not cause a disproportion of marriageable women among the Maori, as many males were being continually killed in their frequent battles.[2] The missionary Ellis thought that in Tahiti, at the time of his arrival, there were probably four or five men to one woman ;[3] here,[4] as in some of the other islands,[5] female infanticide reduced the number of women. In Easter Island, according to the estimates of Cook and La Pérouse, the males were twice as numerous as the females.[6] In 1868, when H.M.S. " Topaze " visited the island, there were about 900 natives left, and of these more than two-thirds were males.[7] In 1872 La Flore's expedition found 275 inhabitants, of whom only 55 were females.[8] Ten years later Geiseler counted 67 men, 39 women, and 44 children.[9] Infanticide is said to have been very rare, but the island has been visited again and again by raiders who carried off large numbers of inhabitants, and others have been removed by Chilian and Tahitian Jesuits.[10] In 1911, when the population amounted to 228 individuals, there were as many women as men.[11] The larger number of males in many of the Pacific islands was undoubtedly a cause of the predominance of monogamous practices noticed

[1] Gisborne, *Colony of New Zealand*, ii. 283, 325.
[2] Colenso, *Maori Races of New Zealand*, p. 26. *Cf.* Tregear, *op. cit.* p. 297.
[3] Ellis, *Polynesian Researches*, i. 258.   [4] *Ibid.* i. 257 *sq.*
[5] Sandwich Islands (Ellis, *Tour through Hawaii*, p. 414 ; Marcuse, *op. cit.* p. 109), Maupiti (Montgomery, *op. cit.* ii. 12).
[6] Tregear, ' Easter Island,' in *Jour. Polynesian Soc.* i. 101. La Pérouse, *Voyage round the World*, ii. 28. *Cf.* v. Kotzebue, *Voyage of Discovery into the South Sea*, iii. 226.
[7] Cooke, in *Smithsonian Report*, 1897, pt. i. 712.
[8] Stolpe, ' Påskön,' in *Ymer*, iii. 167.
[9] Geiseler, *op. cit.* p. 19.
[10] *Ibid.* p. 30. Tregear, in *Jour. Polynesian Soc.* i. 101.
[11] Knoche, ' Einige Beobachtungen über Geschlechtsleben und Niederkunft auf der Osterinsel,' in *Zeitschr. f. Ethnol.* xliv. 661.

above. In Easter Island it led to obligatory monogamy, so strictly enforced that even the head men had to content themselves with a single wife.[1]

From Africa we extremely seldom hear of any people among whom the males outnumber the females. This, however, is stated to be the case in the Quissama tribe of Angola[2]—one of the few African tribes who are said to be monogamous. Among the Wapokomo of British East Africa the inhabitants of some of the smaller villages seem to be monogamous, owing to the paucity of women caused by raids made on them by Somal and Swahili.[3] Among a large number of African peoples, on the other hand, there are more women than men ; and this fact goes a long way to explain the great prevalence of polygyny in Africa. According to Ellis, it was supposed by the missionaries in Madagascar that in consequence of the destructive ravages of war there were, among the free portion of the inhabitants, in some of the provinces five, and in others three, women to one man.[4] Among the Auin, belonging to the Kalahari Bushmen, some of whom are much addicted to polygyny, there are more women than men ;[5] and as regards the Bushmen in general, Theal expresses the opinion that the proportion between the sexes made them first polygamists and then monogamists.[6] Among the Kafirs polygyny was largely the result of their constant feuds and wars, which caused the number of women to be much greater than that of men ; but nowadays it is unusual to find men with more than one wife or two wives, since no longer a sufficient number of men are being killed off in war.[7] Among the Thonga polygyny was very much fostered by the Gungunyane wars, which greatly diminished the number of men.[8] Of the

---

[1] Geiseler, *op. cit.* p. 29.   [2] Price, in *Jour. Anthr. Inst.* i. 189.
[3] Gregory, *op. cit.* p. 343.
[4] Ellis, *History of Madagascar,* i. 152.
[5] Kaufmann, in *Mittheil. Deutsch. Schutzgeb.* xxiii. 136.
[6] Theal, *Yellow and Dark-skinned People of Africa south of the Zambesi,* p. 47.
[7] Lichtenstein, *Travels in Southern Africa,* i. 244.   Theal, *op. cit.* p. 235.   Kidd, *The Essential Kafir,* p. 227.
[8] Junod, *Life of a South African Tribe,* i. 272.

Awemba in Northern Rhodesia we are told that there is still a superfluity of women, with polygyny as the result, owing to the practice of sparing them in warfare.[1] Speaking of the Central Africans, more particularly those of Congo, Mr. Ward observes that the number of women is generally greatly in excess of the male population because men are so frequently killed in their incessant intertribal battles.[2] There are said to be, or to have been, more women than men among the Edeeyahs of Fernando Po,[3] the Kru of the Grain Coast,[4] the Negroes of the Gold Coast,[5] the Latuka,[6] the Waguha of West Tanganyika,[7] and the Wateïta.[8] A census taken in Lagos in 1872 showed among the population of African origin 27,774 men and 32,353 women.[9] In Ma Bung, in the Timannee country, Major Laing counted three women to one man.[10] Among the Bantu Kavirondo, according to Mr. Hobley, " the women outnumber the men probably three or four to one."[11] Dr. Felkin states that among the Baganda the proportion of females to males was about $3\frac{1}{2}$ to one ;[12] and Mr. Roscoe says that some of their old people told him that there were fully three women to one man.[13]

As appears from statements quoted above, the preponderance of women depends among many peoples, partly at least, on the higher mortality of the men, whether this mortality be due to the dangerous life the men have to

[1] Gouldsbury and Sheane, *op. cit.* pp. 165, 168.
[2] Ward, *A Voice from the Congo*, p. 251.
[3] Allen and Thomson, *Narrative of the Expedition sent to the River Niger, in* 1841, ii. 204.
[4] *Ibid.* i. 117.   [5] Bosman, *loc. cit.* p. 424.
[6] *Emin Pasha in Central Africa*, p. 225.
[7] Mr. A. J. Swann, in a letter.
[8] Thomson, *Through Masai Land*, p. 51.
[9] Vogt, ' Die Bewohner von Lagos,' in *Globus*, xli. 253.
[10] Laing, *Travels in the Timannee, Kooranko, and Soolima Countries*, p. 59.
[11] Hobley, *Eastern Uganda*, p. 18. *Cf.* Johnston, *Uganda Protectorate*, pp. 746, 748.
[12] Felkin, in *Proceed. Roy. Soc. Edinburgh*, xiii. 744. See also Wilson and Felkin, *Uganda and the Egyptian Soudan*, i. 150.
[13] Roscoe, *Baganda*, p. 97.

lead in order to gain their subsistence or, as is often the case, to the destructive influence of war.[1] Another cause is the importation of women from other peoples. Leighton Wilson remarks that " to supply the demand for women in Ashanti the surrounding country must be greatly drained of its female population, while none born in the kingdom are ever taken to these neighbouring districts to supply their losses." And so also in Southern Guinea there is a larger female than male population in the maritime districts only, where the men multiply their wives by drawing upon the bush tribes for them.[2] Dr. Felkin says that the large excess of females over males among the Baganda is due to three causes :—there is a constant influx of women into the country as prisoners of war ; a great number of males are killed in war ; and more females are born than males. To the last-mentioned cause Dr. Felkin attaches much importance ; but it appears that it is largely a consequence of the importation of foreign women. For it was found that the excess of female births occurs chiefly in cases where the mother is an imported woman, whereas the excess in births from pure Baganda women is only slight.[3] These interesting facts will be more fully stated and discussed in another connection.[4] With reference to the same people Mr. Roscoe quotes the statement made by some old natives, that " more girls than boys were born " ;[5] and concerning another Bantu people, the Banyoro, to the north-west of Uganda, he writes :—" The birth rate of girls appears to be in excess of that of boys. Twenty-seven mothers who were questioned by Miss Attlee gave the total of children born to them as 101. Of these, 60 were girls and 41 were boys."[6] It is a pity that the investigation was

---

[1] War is also said to be a cause of the disproportion between the sexes among the Californian Shastika (Powers, *op. cit.* p. 243), the people of Baghirmi (Nachtigal, *op. cit.* ii. 616), and the Waguha (Mr. Swann, in a letter).

[2] Wilson, *Western Africa*, pp. 181, 266.

[3] Felkin, in *Proceed. Roy. Soc. Edinburgh*, xiii. 744 *sq. Idem,* ' Contribution to the Determination of Sex,' in *Edinburgh Medical Journal*, vol. xxxii. pt. i. 233 *sqq.*   [4] *Infra*, p. 176 *sq.*

[5] Roscoe, *Baganda*, p. 97.   [6] *Idem, Northern Bantu*, p. 48 *sq.*

not made on a larger scale. In the Mangbettu country, according to Emin Pasha, " far more female children are born than males."[1] Among the Konde people in "German East Africa," according to Zache, there is a conspicuous disproportion between boys and girls, the former being in the minority ; and Fülleborn adds that infanticide is not customary among them.[2] Magyar states that among the Kimbunda " the number of girls exceeds by far that of boys."[3] Mr. McCall Theal doubts whether among the Southern Bantu the sexes are equal in number at birth, and points out that the census of the Cape Colony in 1904, when war had long ceased to have any effect upon the Bantu inhabitants, showed the number of males to be 692,728 and of females 732,059, that is, nearly 106 women and girls to 100 men and boys.[4] Speaking of the Thonga, on the eastern coast of South Africa, M. Junod, on the other hand, remarks that " in ordinary circumstances, women are not more numerous than men in Bantu tribes."[5] And concerning the Akikúyu, in British East Africa, Mr. and Mrs. Routledge write that " such investigations as it has been possible to make confirm the natural anticipation that the births in each sex are fairly equal " ; but they add that it is difficult to arrive at figures, even approximately correct, with regard to the size of the families.[6] When Bruce travelled to discover the source of the Nile, he was in the habit of asking the people with whom he came into contact in towns and in the country " how many children they had, or their fathers, their next neighbours, or acquaintance," and arrived at the conclusion that " through the Holy Land, the country called Horan, in the Isthmus of Suez, and the parts of the Delta, unfrequented by strangers " the proportion of the sexes was something less than three women to one man, and " from Suez to the Straits of Babel-

[1] Emin Pasha in Central Africa, p. 209.
[2] Zache, quoted by Fülleborn, op. cit. p. 345.
[3] Magyar, Reisen in Süd-Afrika, p. 284.
[4] Theal, Yellow and Dark-skinned People, p. 235.
[5] Junod, Life of a South African Tribe, i. 271.
[6] Routledge, op. cit. p. 135.

mandeb, which contains the three Arabias," fully four women
to one man.[1] This statement, though contradicted, has
hardly been proved to be entirely groundless ; and the
same may be said of Montesquieu's well-known assertion
that in the hot regions of the Old World more girls are
born than boys,[2] which was opposed by Süssmilch[3] and
Chervin.[4] However exaggerated it be on account of its
generality, it nevertheless seems to be true of certain African
peoples. It is interesting to note that in the United States,
contrary to what is the case among the white population,
" it would seem that an excess of male births does not
characterise the negro race, but rather the contrary."[5]

It has been suggested that polygyny leads to the birth of
a greater proportion of female infants.[6] In support of this
suggestion Burton quotes M. Remy and Mr. Hyde, according
to whom the censuses of the Mormons showed a great excess
of female births ;[7] but Mr. Newcomb found among them
" the usual preponderance of male births."[8] Dr. Campbell,
who attended to this subject in the harems of Siam, concluded
that the proportion of male to female births is the same as
from monogamous unions ;[9] and Mr. Sanderson found that
among the Kafirs resident in Natal and the adjoining countries there was no surplus of female births in their polygynous families.[10] The facts collected by the latter, however,
are too few to warrant any positive deductions of a general
character ; and the like must be said of the information on

[1] Bruce, *Travels to Discover the Source of the Nile*, i. 284 *sq.*
[2] Montesquieu, *De l'esprit des loix*, book xvi. ch. 4.
[3] Süssmilch, *Die göttliche Ordnung in den Veränderungen des
menschlichen Geschlechts*, ii. 258, 259, &c.
[4] Chervin, *Recherches medico-philosophiques sur les causes physiques
de la polygamie dans les pays chauds*, pp. 38, &c.
[5] Newcomb, *Statistical Inquiry into the Probability of Causes of
the Production of Sex in Human Offspring*, p. 8.
[6] Burton, *City of the Saints*, p. 521.   *Idem, Abeokuta*, i. 212 note.
[7] *Idem, City of the Saints*, p. 521.
[8] Newcomb, *op. cit.* p. 27.
[9] Summary of Campbell's paper ' On Polygamy ' in *Anthropological Review*, vol. viii. p. cviii.
[10] Sanderson, ' Polygamous Marriage among the Kafirs of Natal,'
in *Jour. Anthr. Inst.* viii. 254 *sqq.*

the subject which Mr. Cousins and Mr. Eyles have sent me from the same part of South Africa. Anyhow it is impossible to believe that polygynous intercourse *per se* could cause such an excess. As Darwin remarks, hardly any animal has been rendered so highly polygynous as English race-horses, and nevertheless their male and female offspring are almost exactly equal in number.[1]

Although our knowledge of the proportion between the sexes among the lower races is very defective, I think we may safely say that whenever there is a marked and more or less permanent majority of women in a savage tribe polygyny is allowed. I have found no reliable statement to the contrary, and cannot believe that savage custom would make monogamy obligatory if any considerable number of women were thereby doomed to celibacy. On the other hand, there may very well be polygyny where the sexes are equal in number or the males form the majority ; we find polygyny, for instance, among Australian tribes and the natives of Buin in spite of their surplus of men. In such cases some men have to live unmarried at least for part of their life, and unmarried men are found even where there are more females than males. But although an excess of females leads to polygyny, it is never the sole or complete cause of polygyny, indeed it is only an indirect cause of it. Whilst the existence of available women facilitates polygyny or makes it possible, the direct cause of it is generally the men's desire to have more than one wife. There are various reasons for this desire.

First, monogamy requires of a man periodical continence. He has to live apart from his wife for a certain time every month. At the lower stages of civilisation a menstruous woman is an object of superstitious fear ; ignorance of the nature of female periodicity often leads to the idea that the flow of blood comes from a wound caused by the bite of a supernatural animal or by congress with such an animal or with an evil spirit.[2] And being looked upon as a danger to those around her the menstruous woman is subject to

[1] Darwin, *Descent of Man*, i. 378 *sq.*
[2] Crawley, *Mystic Rose*, p. 191 *sqq.*

taboos of various kinds : she must not touch or prepare
food which is to be eaten by somebody else, she must not
eat with her husband, she may be secluded altogether.[1]
Among the natives of the Kimberley district in West
Australia, for instance, during the period of menstruation
the females isolate themselves for a week, carefully avoiding
even the most casual meeting with men.[2] Ridley tells us
of an Australian native who, finding that his wife had lain
on his blanket during menstruation, killed her, and died
of terror in a fortnight.[3] Sexual intercourse with a
menstruous woman is naturally looked upon as particularly
dangerous ; the Araucanians [4] and the tribes near Fort
Johnston in British Central Africa,[5] for example, believe
that such intercourse exposes the man to some disease which
may easily prove fatal.   No wonder, then, that married life
among so many peoples has to be interrupted during the
monthly periods of the wife.[6] Yet the prohibition is not
universal.   The Akamba in East Africa have, in fact, the
very opposite custom : " when a married woman menstruates,
the husband cohabits with her that night, the idea being
that she will probably conceive."[7]

[1] *Ibid.* p. 165 *sq.*
[2] Hardman, ' Notes on some Habits and Customs of the Natives
of the Kimberley District,' in *Proceed. Roy. Irish Academy,* ser.
iii. vol. i. 73.
[3] Ridley, ' Report on Australian Languages and Traditions,' in
Jour. Anthr. Inst. ii. 268.
[4] Guevara, ' Folklore Araucano,' in *Anales de la Universidad de
Chile,* cxxvii. 625.   [5] Stannus, in *Jour. Roy. Anthr. Inst.* xl. 305.
[6] Schoolcraft, *op. cit.* v. 183 (Blackfeet).   Jones, ' Kutchin
Tribes,' in *Smithsonian Report,* 1866, p. 326.   Dall, *Alaska,* p. 403
(Kaniagmiut).   Steller, *Beschreibung von dem Lande Kamtschatka,*
p. 347 *sq.*   Riedel, *De sluik- en kroesharige rassen tusschen Selebes en
Papua,* p. 263 (Aru Islanders).   Alberti, *De Kaffers aan de Zuidkus
van Afrika,* p. 136 *sq.*   Junod, *Life of a South African Tribe,* i. 187
(Thonga).   Hutter, *op. cit.* p. 379 (Bali).   Martrou, ' Les " Eki "
des Fang ' (in Kamerun), in *Anthropos* i. 755.   Landolphe, *op. cit.*
ii. 51 (people of Benin).   Ellis, *Ewe-speaking Peoples,* p. 206 ;
Spieth, *op. cit.* p. 62* (Ewhe).   Bosman, *loc. cit.* pp. 423, 527 (West
African negroes).   Waitz, *op. cit.* ii. 121 (negroes).   Andree,
Zur Volkskunde der Juden, p. 142.   Ploss-Bartels, *Das Weib,*
i. 458 *sqq.*   [7] Hobley, *Ethnology of A-Kamba,* p. 65.

Among many peoples the husband must also abstain from his wife during her pregnancy,[1] or at least during the latter stage of it.[2] A pregnant woman is often regarded as unclean : she may be forbidden to wait upon her husband, or to eat with him, or to eat of game caught by hounds, as it is believed that otherwise these would never again be able to hunt.[3] Sexual intercourse with her may injure or kill the child.[4] Among the Warega in the Belgian Congo the husband may cohabit with his pregnant wife until her delivery draws near, but if he has connection with any other woman it is supposed that the child will die.[5] So also among the Bahuana men do not abstain from their

---

[1] Whiffen, *North-West Amazons*, p. 146 (Witoto and Boro). de Poincy, *Histoire naturelle et morale des Isles Antilles*, p. 548. Bancroft, *op. cit.* ii. 267 (Azteks). Ashe, *op. cit.* p. 249 (Shawnee). Lahontan, *New Voyages to North-America*, p. 458 ; Charlevoix, *Voyage to North-America*, ii. 41 (Algonkin). Zimmermann, *op. cit.* i. 27 (Malays). Riedel, *op. cit.* p. 263 (Aru Islanders). Keate, *Account of the Pelew Islands*, p. 321. Seligman, *Melanesians of British New Guinea*, p. 582 (Southern Massim). Johnston, *George Grenfell and the Congo*, ii. 671. Weeks, *Among the Primitive Bakongo*, p. 148. *Idem, Among Congo Cannibals*, p. 137 (Boloki). Torday and Joyce, ' Notes on the Ethnography of the Ba-Mbala,' in *Jour. Anthr. Inst.* xxxv. 420. *Iidem*, ' Notes on the Ethnography of the Ba-Yaka,' *ibid.* xxxvi. 51. Landolphe, *op. cit.* ii. 51 (people of Benin). Ellis, *Ewe-speaking Peoples*, p. 206. Reade, *Savage Africa*, pp. 45, 243 ; Waitz, *op. cit.* ii. 120 *sq.* (various negro tribes). Mangin, in *Anthropos*, ix. 488 (Mossi of the Western Sudan). Merker, *Die Masai*, p. 50. Hollis, *Nandi*, p. 66. Felkin, in *Proceed. Roy. Soc. Edinburgh*, xiii. 745 (Baganda). v. Behr, in *Mittheil. Deutsch. Schutzgeb.* vi. 83 (Makua). Fülleborn, *op. cit.* p. 61 (tribes in the Ruwuma district). Johnston, *British Central Africa*, p. 411. Beauregard, ' En Asie ; Kachmir et Tibet,' in *Bull. Soc. d'Anthr. Paris*, ser. iii. vol. v. p. 264 n. 6 (Massagetae). Gray, *China*, i. 185.

[2] Laufer, in *American Anthropologist*, N.S. ii. 320 (Gold on the Amoor). Kaufmann, in *Mittheil. Deutsch. Schutzgeb.* xxiii. 157 (Auin). Alberti, *op. cit.* p. 136 *sq.* (Kafirs ; *cf.* Kropf, *op. cit.* p. 153). Hutter, *op. cit.* p. 379 (Bali). Martrou, in *Anthropos*, i. 755 (Fang of Kamerun). [3] Crawley, *op. cit.* p. 167.

[4] Weeks, *Bakongo*, p. 148. *Idem, Among Congo Cannibals*, p. 137 (Boloki). Fülleborn, *op. cit.* p. 61 (tribes in the Ruwuma district). Merker, *Masai*, p. 51. Mangin, in *Anthropos*, ix. 488 (Mossi of the Western Sudan). Gray, *China*, i. 185.

[5] Delhaise, *op. cit.* p. 147.

wives during the early stages of pregnancy, and it may even be said " that the only time during which a woman contents herself with her husband is during pregnancy, since it is believed that adultery at this period would prove fatal to the child."[1] Sometimes intercourse between married people is not only allowed but is considered favourable or even necessary to the growth of the fetus.[2] But ideas of this kind, which certainly do not encourage polygyny, are no doubt quite exceptional.

In a still higher degree than the obligatory abstinence from conjugal intercourse during pregnancy does the necessity to refrain from such intercourse after child-birth lead to polygynous practices. Sometimes the period of abstinence lasts for a certain number of months, in other cases it lasts for years. Of a great number of simple peoples we are told that the husband must not cohabit with his wife until the child is weaned ;[3] and this prohibition is severe enough, as the suckling-time lasts sometimes for about a year or a little longer,[4] but more often for two or

---

[1] Torday and Joyce, in *Jour. Anthr. Inst.* xxxvi. 288.   In Sierra Leone it is also believed that if a married woman during pregnancy is guilty of adultery, she will have a miscarriage or the child will be stillborn (Vergette, *op. cit.* p. 8).

[2] Junod, *Life of a South African Tribe*, i. 188 (Thonga).   Johnston, *George Grenfell and the Congo*, ii. 676 (Niam-Niam).

[3] Whiffen, *op. cit.* p. 146 (Witoto and Boro of the North-West Amazons).   Riedel, *op. cit.* p. 263 (Aru Islanders).   v. Kotzebue, *op. cit.* iii. 210 (Caroline Islanders).   Haddon, in *Reports of the Cambridge Anthropological Expedition to Torres Straits*, v. 229 (Western Islanders).   Kaufmann, in *Mittheil. Deutsch. Schutzgeb.* xxiii. 136 (Auin).   Alberti, *op. cit.* p. 137 (Kafirs).   Johnston, *British Central Africa*, p. 411 (the more polygamous tribes).   *Idem*, *George Grenfell and the Congo*, ii. 672.   Torday and Joyce, in *Jour. Anthr. Inst.* xxxvi. 292 (Bahuana).   Weeks, *Among Congo Cannibals*, p. 137 (Boloki).   Landolphe, *op. cit.* ii. 51 (people of Benin).   Reade, *Savage Africa*, p. 45 (Ashanti).   *Emin Pasha in Central Africa*, p. 84 (Banyoro).   v. Behr, in *Mittheil. Deutsch. Schutzgeb.* vi. 83 (Makua).   Gray, *China*, i. 185.

[4] Torday and Joyce, in *Jour. Anthr. Inst.* xxxv. 410 (Bambala). *Iidem*, *ibid.* xxxvi. 51 (Bayaka).   Hutter, *op. cit.* p. 379 (Bali). Martrou, in *Anthropos*, i. 755 (Fang of Kamerun).   Merker, *op. cit.* p. 50 (Masai).

three[1] or even four, five, or six[2] years. This long suckling-time is due chiefly to want of soft food and animal milk.[3] But though milk can be obtained,[4] and even when the people have domesticated animals able to supply them with it,[5] this kind of food is often avoided ; the Dravidian aborigines of Central India, for example, regard it as an excrement,[6] and to the Chinese milk is insupportably odious.[7] It is feared that intercourse during the period of suckling would

[1] Felkin, in *Proceed. Roy. Soc. Edinburgh*, xiii. 745 (Baganda ; two years, but in the lowest class of society only a few months' separation is usual). Le Jeune, ' Relation de ce qvi s'est passé en la Novvelle France, en l'année 1635,' in *Jesuit Relations*, viii. 127 (Hurons). Charlevoix, *Voyage to North-America*, ii. 41 (Algonkin). Thomson, *Fijians*, p. 175 *sq.* (Seemann says [*Viti*, p. 191] that in Fiji " the relatives of a woman take it as a public insult if any child should be born before the customary three or four years have elapsed "). Kropf, *op. cit.* p. 153 (some Kafirs). Fülleborn, *op. cit.* p. 61 (tribes in the Ruwuma district). Poupon, in *L'Anthropologie*, xxvi. 125 (Baya of West Africa). Ellis, *Ewe-speaking Peoples*, p. 206. *Idem, Yoruba-speaking Peoples*, p. 185.

[2] Grubb, *Among the Indians of the Paraguayan Chaco*, p. 63. Dunbar, in *Magazine of American History*, iv. 267 (Pawnee). Weeks, *Bakongo*, p. 148. Klose, *Togo unter deutscher Flagge*, pp. 254 (Ewhe) 508 (Bassari).

[3] *Cf.* Brett, *Indian Tribes of Guiana*, p. 102 ; Egede, *Description of Greenland*, p. 146 ; Thomson, *Fijians*, pp. 177, 180 ; Brough Smyth, *Aborigines of Victoria*, i. 48 n.* Bonwick, ' Australian Natives,' in *Jour. Anthr. Inst.* xvi. 205. *Idem, Daily Life and Origin of the Tasmanians*, p. 78. Lippert remarks (*Die Geschichte der Familie*, p. 22), " Thierische Milch ist so wenig die allgemeine Nahrung der Menschheit auf einer sehr frühen Kulturstufe gewesen, dass vielmehr sämmtliche Völker der neuen Welt aus eigner Entwicklung gar nie diese Stufe erklommen haben."

[4] Grubb, *Indians of the Paraguayan Chaco*, p. 63. Carver, *Travels through the Interior Parts of North America*, p. 262. Powers, *Tribes of California*, p. 271.

[5] Dalton, *Descriptive Ethnology of Bengal*, p. 38 (Akas). Lewin, *Wild Races of South-Eastern India*, p. 261 (Kukis). Oldham, ' Communications respecting the Cassia Tribe,' in *Jour. Ethn. Soc. London*, iii. 240 (Khasis). Harkness, *Description of a Singular Aboriginal Race inhabiting the Neilgherry Hills*, p. 78 (Kotas).

[6] Crooke, *Things Indian*, p. 92.

[7] Huc, *Travels in Tartary*, i. 281. Wilson, *Abode of Snow*, p. 179. For further instances see Westermarck, *Origin and Development of the Moral Ideas*, ii. 326.

harm the child,[1] that it would make it rachitic,[2] or, by
affecting the milk or drying up the supply of it, cause the
death of the suckling.[3] Speaking of the Fijian belief
that cohabitation during this period would impoverish the
mother's milk, Sir Basil Thomson observes that behind
the superstition there is an important truth, namely,
that a second conception taking place during the suckling-
time must cause the child to be prematurely weaned, which
would be followed by serious consequences as " there is
nothing between the mother's milk and solid vegetable
food."[4] Among the Thonga, though conjugal intercourse
is absolutely prohibited before " the tying of the cotton
string "—a rite which takes place when the child is one
year old—it is afterwards allowed, but the mother must not
conceive another child before she has weaned the one she
is nursing, nay, she must not conceive before her milk has
entirely passed away, after the weaning ceremony ; if she
became pregnant before then it is believed that the weaned
child " would become thin, paralysed, with big holes below
the shoulders."[5] The Bambala, again, have the idea that
if the man does not abstain from his wife for about a year,
during which time the child is suckled, it would prove fatal
to the woman ; and " in the event of her death soon after
childbirth, the husband is accused of being the cause and
heavily fined, or, more often, compelled to submit to the
poison ordeal."[6] But intercourse with a woman in child-
bed may also be shunned by the man because she is regarded
as unclean—a very widespread notion.[7] Among the

---

[1] Fülleborn, op. cit. p. 61. Thomson, ' Notes on the Basin of the
River Rovuma,' in Proceed. Roy. Geograph. Soc. N.S. iv. 75 (Wama-
konde and other tribes in the Ruwuma district).   Gray, China, i.
185.

[2] Velten, op. cit. p. 12 (Swahili).

[3] Kropf, op. cit. p. 153 (some Kafirs). Poupon, in L'Anthropologie, xxvi. 125 (Baya of West Africa). Weeks, Bakongo, p. 148.
See also Idem, Among Congo Cannibals, p. 137 (Boloki), where it is
said that intercourse during the suckling-time is supposed to cause
the child to die.

[4] Thomson, Fijians, p. 177.   [5] Junod, op. cit. i. 55, 57, 59.

[6] Torday and Joyce, in Jour. Anthr. Inst. xxxv. 410.

[7] Ploss-Bartels, op. cit. ii. 413 sqq.

Northern Indians, for instance, a mother has to remain in a small tent placed at a little distance from the others during a month or five weeks;[1] and similar customs are found among many other peoples.[2] According to early Aryan traditions, as von Zmigrodzki remarks, a witch and a woman in child-bed are persons so intimately connected that it is impossible to distinguish between them.[3]

One of the chief causes of polygyny is the attraction which female youth and beauty exercise upon the men. A fresh wife is often taken when the first grows old. A few instances will suffice to illustrate this widespread practice. Speaking of the Channel Indians distributed from the Magellan Straits to the Gulf of Peñas, who as a rule have one wife only, Dr. Skottsberg observes that a man with an old and ugly wife occasionally secures a younger one in addition.[4] In Guiana " an Indian is never seen with two young wives ; the only case in which he takes a second is when the first has become old."[5] Among the Karayá, who like many other South American Indians have the custom of young men marrying old women, a man is not infrequently compelled to take a second wife when the first one gets advanced in years.[6] Among the Bushmen, according to Stow, the young men frequently contented themselves with one wife, whereas few of middle age had less than two, a young and an old one.[7] Of the Batwa in North-Eastern Rhodesia we are told that when the first wife has given birth to a few children and is becoming aged and worn out, the husband procures another who is young, and when she too is *passée*

---

[1] Hearne, *Journey from Prince of Wales's Fort to the Northern Ocean*, p. 93.

[2] Wallawalla, a Shahaptian tribe (Wilkes, *op. cit.* iv. 400 *sq.*), Tlingit, Mosquito Indians, Maori (Waitz, *op. cit.* iii. 328; iv. 291; vi. 131), Tongans (West, *Ten Years in South-Central Polynesia*, p. 254), &c.

[3] v. Zmigrodzki, *Die Mutter bei den Völkern des arischen Stammes*, p. 177.

[4] Skottsberg, *Wilds of Patagonia*, p. 97.

[5] Schomburgk, in Ralegh, *Discovery of Guiana*, p. 110 note.

[6] Ehrenreich, *Beiträge zur Völkerkunde Brasiliens*, p. 27.

[7] Stow, *op. cit.* p. 95.

he takes a third.[1]   Among the Akikúyu " the first wife
is usually about the same age as her husband ; the man's
later wives are considerably younger than he is, and the
older he grows the more difference there is in age between
himself and his latest acquisition."[2]   Among the Kunnuvans,
a hill tribe of the Palnis in South India, it often happens
that a little boy is married to his paternal aunt's grown-up
daughter, who may then consort with any man she pleases,
while the boy-husband is considered as the father of the
children.   When he in his turn reaches the years of manhood,
he finds his wife too old, and therefore often takes another
wife of his own age.   This custom, says Father Dahmen,
accounts in great part for the polygamy prevalent among
the Kunnuvans and indulged in by nearly all those who
have the means of supporting more than one wife.[3]   So
also in China and Corea, where the first wife is generally
a woman from three to eight years older than her husband,[4]
the difference in age leads to polygyny or concubinage.
But even when a man soon after he has attained manhood
marries a woman of his own age, he may still be in the prime
of life when the youthful beauty of his wife has passed
away for ever.   This is especially the case at the lower
stages of civilisation, where women seem to get old much
sooner than among ourselves.

Thus Patagonian women are said to lose their youth at
a very early age, " from exposure and hard work."[5]   Of
the Indians of the Paraguayan Chaco Mr. Grubb writes,
" Having to move so constantly from place to place, it is
no wonder that the poor women age quickly, more especially
as the children are often not weaned till they are five or
six years old."[6]   Among the Indians of British Guiana at
the age of twenty-five the women have lost all the appearance
of youth, whereas men of forty years do not look older than

[1] v. Rosen, *Träskfolket*, p. 276.   [2] Routledge, *op. cit.* p. 134.
[3] Dahmen, ' Kunnuvans or Mannadis,' in *Anthropos*, v. 326.
[4] Ross, *History of Corea*, p. 311.
[5] Musters, ' On the Races of Patagonia,' in *Jour. Anthr. Inst.*
i 196.   See also Skottsberg, *op. cit.* p. 97.
[6] Grubb, *Among the Indians of the Paraguayan Chaco*, p. 63.

Europeans of the same age ; [1] of the Warraus Schomburgk
even says that " when the woman has reached her twentieth
year, the flower of her life is gone."[2]   Among the Mandan
the beauty of the women vanishes soon after marriage.[3]
The native women of California, according to Powers, are
rather handsome in their free and untoiling youth, but
after twenty-five or thirty they break down under their
heavy burdens and become ugly.[4]   Among the Loucheux
Indians women get "coarse and ugly as they grow old,
owing to hard labour and bad treatment."[5]

Koryak women soon grow old ;[6] and the same is true of
the Ainu women in Yesso, partly, it is said, because of the
exposed life they lead as children, partly because of the
early age at which they marry and become mothers, and
partly because of the hard life they continue to lead afterwards.[7]   Among the Manipuris and Garos the women,
pretty when young, soon become " hags."[8]   At two and
twenty Dyak beauty " has already begun to fade, and the
subsequent decay is rapid."[9]   The Papuan women in the
Mimika district of Dutch New Guinea become mothers as
soon as they are capable of bearing children, and then wither
up and shrivel away under the toil and strain of their
laborious existence.[10]   In New Zealand, Tahiti, Hawai,
and other islands of the South Sea, the beauty of the native
women soon decays—" the result," we are told, " of hard
labour in some cases, and in others of early intercourse with
the opposite sex, combined with their mode of living, which
rapidly destroys their youthful appearance."[11]   Among
the aborigines of New South Wales the women age early and

---

[1] Bernau, op. cit. p. 59.
[2] Schomburgk, Reisen in Britisch-Guiana, i. 122.
[3] Catlin, op. cit. i. 121.   [4] Powers, op. cit. pp. 20, 44.
[5] Hardisty, in Smithsonian Report, 1866, p. 312.
[6] Jochelson, Koryak, p. 413.
[7] St. John, ' Ainos,' in Jour. Anthr. Inst. ii. 249.
[8] Dalton, op. cit. pp. 50, 66.   [9] Boyle, op. cit. p. 199 note.
[10] Rawling, Land of the New Guinea Pygmies, p. 133.
[11] Angas, Savage Life and Scenes in Australia and New Zealand,
i. 311.   Waitz-Gerland, op. cit. vi. 15, 22.

" become meagre skeletons, more like baboons than human beings."[1]

In Africa, also, female beauty fades quickly. The Egyptian women, from the age of about fourteen to that of eighteen or twenty, are generally models of loveliness in body and limbs, but when they reach maturity their attractions do not long survive.[2] In Eastern Africa, according to Burton, the beauty of women is less perishable than in India and Arabia ; but even there charms are on the wane at thirty, and when old age comes on the women are no exceptions to " the hideous decrepitude of the East."[3] Arab girls in the Sahara preserve only till about their sixteenth year that youthful freshness which the women of the north still possess in the late spring of their life.[4] In Kordofan " a woman in her twenty-fourth year is considered *passée*."[5] Among the Bakwileh women have no trace of beauty left after twenty-five.[6] Speaking of the Wolofs in Senegambia, Winwood Reade remarks that the girls are very pretty with their soft and glossy black skin, but " when the first jet of youth is passed, the skin turns to a dirty yellow and creases like old leather ; their eyes sink into the skull, and the breasts hang down like the udder of a cow, or shrivel up like a bladder that has burst."[7] Zöller maintains that the incredibly short duration of female youthfulness among the negroes is only in a small degree due to a tendency in the race, and attributes it chiefly to their habits of life, especially the extremely early marriages of the women and the hard work which they have to perform.[8]

[1] Henderson, *Excursions and Adventures in New South Wales*, ii. 120.
[2] Lane, *Manners and Customs of the Modern Egyptians*, i. 50. On the Arabs of Upper Egypt see Baker, *Nile Tributaries of Abyssinia*, pp. 124, 265.
[3] Burton, *First Footsteps in East Africa*, p. 119.
[4] Chavanne, *Die Sahara*, p. 397. *Cf. ibid.* p. 81.
[5] Pallme, *Travels in Kordofan*, p. 63.
[6] Valdau, ' Om Ba-kwileh-folket,' in *Ymer*, v. 163.
[7] Reade, *Savage Africa*, p. 447.
[8] Zöller, *Forschungsreisen in der deutschen Colonie Kamerun*, ii. 72 *sq.*

According to Magyar, early marriages likewise account for the fact that among the Kimbunda the women already at the age between twenty-five and thirty are so utterly unattractive that men who can afford to have younger wives " non solent amplius cum illis coire."[1] So also among the Herero,[2] Ovambo,[3] and Kafirs,[4] women begin to wither soon after maturity, as we are told on account of hard labour ; and the Bushmen women, it is said, soon become sterile from the same cause.[5] In Unyoro Emin Pasha never saw a woman above twenty-five with babies.[6] Even from a physiological point of view hard labour seems to shorten female youth ; statistics show that among the poorer women of Berlin menstruation ceases at a rather earlier age than among the well-to-do classes.[7] It has been said that in hot countries women lose their youthfulness much sooner than in colder regions, whereas men are not affected in the same way by climate ; but, so far as I know, we are in want of exact information on this point.

A further cause of polygyny is man's taste for variety. The sexual instinct is dulled by long familiarity and stimulated by novelty. A shereef from Morocco was once in my presence asked by some English ladies why the Moors did not content themselves with a single wife like the Europeans. His answer was, " Why, one cannot always eat fish."[8] In Egypt, according to Lane, " fickle passion is the most evident and common motive both to polygamy and repeated divorces."[9]

It is not, however, from sexual motives alone that a man

[1] Magyar, *op. cit.* p. 283.   [2] Chapman, *op. cit.* i. 342.
[3] Andersson, *Lake Ngami*, pp. 50, 196.
[4] v. Weber, *Vier Jahre in Afrika*, ii. 199, 200, 216.
[5] Thulié, ' Instructions sur les Bochimans,' in *Bull. Soc. d'Anthr. Paris*, ser. iii. vol. iv. 421.
[6] *Emin Pasha in Central Africa*, p. 85.
[7] Krieger, *Die Menstruation*, p. 174.
[8] Mr. Wilson (*Persian Life and Customs*, p. 263) records a similar answer given by a Mussulman who was asked what he thought of polygamy. " It is like eating," he said ; " you do not confine yourself to one kind of food, but set several kinds on the table."
[9] Lane, *op. cit.* i. 252. *Cf. supra*, ii. 198.

may wish to have more than one wife.   He may do so also because he is desirous of offspring, wealth, and authority.

The barrenness of a wife, or the birth of female offspring only, is a very common reason for the choice of another partner in addition to the former one.   Among the Greenlanders, for instance, who considered it a great disgrace for a man to have no children, particularly no sons, a husband generally took a second wife if the first could not satisfy his desire for offspring.[1]   Among the Chukchee the absence of children is considered so great a misfortune that a good woman, if childless, herself insists that her husband shall take another wife.[2]   So also among the Munda Kols of Chota Nagpur[3] and the Hindus of Southern India[4] a barren wife sometimes advises her husband to take a fresh partner, as Rachel gave Jacob Bilhah.[5]   The desire for offspring is one of the principal causes of polygyny in the East.[6]   Professor Hozumi says that the legal recognition of concubinage in Japan found its justification in the paramount importance of having an issue to perpetuate the ancestral cult.   He thinks, however, that this institution took its rise in the licentiousness of chiefs and warriors, and that the dreaded misfortune of the extinction of the cult was rather a pretext ; for it was usual for the nobles to keep concubines notwithstanding that they had children by their wives, and the prevalence of the custom of adopting a son to succeed to the family worship made the recourse to concubinage practically unnecessary.[7]   The polygyny of the ancient Hindus seems to have been due chiefly to the dread of dying childless ; and the same motive persists among their modern

---

[1] Cranz, *op. cit.* i. 147.   [2] Bogoras, *op. cit.* p. 600.
[3] Jellinghaus, in *Zeitschr. f. Ethnol.* iii. 370.
[4] Padfield, *The Hindu at Home*, p. 96.   [5] *Genesis*, xxx. 1 *sqq.*
[6] Gray, *China*, i. 184.   Ball, *Chinese at Home*, p. 48 *sq.*   Ward, *Land of the Blue Poppy*, p. 57 (Tibetans).   Benzinger, *Hebräische Archäologie*, p. 105.   Blunt, *Bedouin Tribes of the Euphrates*, i. 227.   Wallin, *Reseanteckningar från Orienten*, iii. 267.   Le Bon, *La civilisation des Arabes*, p. 424.
[7] Hozumi, *Ancestor Worship and Japanese Law*, p. 139 *sqq.*   Cf. Crasselt, in *Anthropos*, iii. 552 ; Nakajima, in Hastings, *op. cit.* viii. 459.

descendants. The Nambuthiris, or Brahmans of Malabar, Cochin, and Travancore, are said to indulge in polygyny partly to gratify " their desire to have a son to perform funeral and other ceremonies for the spirits of the departed, and partly to dispose of the superfluous number of girls."[1] Sleeman thinks that not one Hindu in ten of those who can afford to maintain more than one wife will venture " upon a sea of troubles " in taking a second, if he has a child by the first.[2] Many Persians take a fresh wife only when the first one is childless ;[3] and in Egypt, according to Lane, " a man having a wife who has the misfortune to be barren, and being too much attached to her to divorce her, is sometimes induced to take a second wife, merely in the hope of obtaining offspring."[4] It was for such a reason that Anaxandridas, king of Sparta,[5] and Diarmait, king of Ireland,[6] contracted a second marriage. Among various peoples mentioned above polygyny is practised or permitted only when the first wife is barren or does not give birth to male offspring.

Polygyny, however, is practised as a means not only of obtaining offspring but of obtaining a *large* progeny. We have previously discussed the reasons why men like to have children ;[7] but there are also reasons why they may like to have many children. Man in a savage or barbarous state of society is proud of a large family, and he who has most kinsfolk is most honoured and most feared.[8] Among the Chippewa, says Keating, "the pride and honour of parents depend upon the extent of their family."[9] Concerning certain Indians of North America, among whom the

---

[1] Anantha Krishna Iyer, *op. cit.* ii. 210.

[2] Sleeman, *Rambles and Recollections of an Indian Official*, i. 51.

[3] Wilson, *Persian Life and Customs*, p. 264.

[4] Lane, *op. cit.* i. 252.   [5] *Supra*, iii. 48.

[6] d'Arbois de Jubainville, *op. cit.* vi. 292 *sq.*

[7] *Supra*, vol. i. ch. x.

[8] *Cf.* v. Martius, *Beiträge zur Ethnographie Amerika's zumal Brasiliens*, i. 353 note ; Waitz, *op. cit.* iii. 115 ; Livingstone, *Missionary Travels and Researches in South Africa*, p. 15 ; d'Escayrac de Lauture, *Die afrikanische Wüste*, p. 132.

[9] Keating, *op. cit.* ii. 156.

dignity of a chief was elective, Heriot remarks that "the choice usually fell upon him who had the most numerous offspring, and who was therefore considered as the person most deeply interested in the welfare of the tribe."[1] Speaking of African polygyny, Burton observes that the " culture of the marriage tie is necessary among savages and barbarians, where, unlike Europe, a man's relations and connections are his only friends ; besides which, a multitude of wives ministers to his pride and influence, state and pleasure." [2] I was told that in some Berber tribes in Morocco polygyny is much practised owing to the prevalence of the blood-feud, which makes it highly desirable for a man to have many sons. Bosman speaks of a viceroy tributary to the negro king of Fida who, assisted only by his sons and grandsons with their slaves, repulsed a powerful enemy who came against him ; this viceroy, with his sons and grandsons, could make out the number of two thousand descendants, not reckoning daughters or any that were dead.[3] " There is nothing," says Leighton Wilson, " which an untutored African covets more than a numerous progeny. Children as they grow up to maturity enrich him, give him prominence and respectability in society, and when he is dead they perpetuate his name among men. For the generality of his wives, if he has a considerable number, he cares very little, except so far as they enrich him with children."[4] In a state of nature, next to a man's wife the real servant, the only one to be counted upon, is the child ; Casalis observes that in the language of the Bechuanas the word *motlanka*, like the Greek παῖς and the Latin *puer*, signifies at the same time boy and servant.[5] Sons work for their parents until they marry, daughters are a source of income through the bride price paid for them.[6]

---

[1] Heriot, *op. cit.* p. 551.

[2] Burton, in *Trans. Ethn. Soc.* N.S. i. 320 *sq.* *Cf. Idem, First Footsteps in East Africa*, p. 121.   [3] Bosman, *loc. cit.* p. 481.

[4] Wilson, *Western Africa*, p. 269.   [5] Casalis, *op. cit.* p. 188 note.

[6] Poupon, in *L'Anthropologie*, xxvi. 125 (Baya).   Klose, *op. cit.* p. 256 (Ewhe).   Schuster, in *Anthropos*, ix. 952 (Banjange of Kamerun).   Weeks, *Bakongo*, p. 147.   Junod, *Life of a South African Tribe*, i. 126 (Thonga).

The desire for children must be a particularly potent cause of polygyny in countries where families are small. Dr. Hewit observed long ago that women are naturally less prolific among rude than among polished nations ;[1] and this assertion, although not true universally,[2] may be true in the main. " It is a very rare occurrence for an Indian woman," says Catlin, " to be ' blessed ' with more than four or five children during her life ; and, generally speaking, they seem contented with two or three."[3] Similar statements are made by many other writers with reference to uncivilised peoples both in America [4] and elsewhere.[5] The small number of children is to some extent due to

[1] Schoolcraft, *Archives of Aboriginal Knowledge*, vi. 180 *sq.*
[2] Among the Yahgans (Bove, *op. cit.* p. 133), Guiana Indians (Brett, *op. cit.* p. 413 n. 2), Kamchadal (Georgi, *op. cit.* p. 342), Santals (Man, *Sonthalia*, p. 15), Punans (Hose and McDougall, *op. cit.* ii. 183), Marea (Munzinger, *Ostafrikanische Studien*, p. 248), Somal (Burton, *First Footsteps in East Africa*, p. 119), Matabele (Decle, *op. cit.* p. 160), Fors, and Baganda (Felkin, in *Proceed. Roy. Soc. Edinburgh*, xiii. 207, 745) the women are stated to be more or less prolific.   [3] Catlin, *op. cit.* ii. 228.
[4] Azara, *op. cit.* ii. 59 (Guarani). Bovallius, *Resa i Central-Amerika*, i. 249 (Talamanca Indians). Baegert, ' Inhabitants of the Californian Peninsula,' in *Smithsonian Report*, 1863, p. 368. Dunbar, in *Magazine of American History*, iv. 267 (Pawnee). Schoolcraft, *op. cit.* v. 684 (Comanche). Gibbs, *loc. cit.* p. 209 (Indians of Western Washington and North-Western Oregon). Bancroft, *op. cit.* i. 169, 218, 242 (Haida, Columbians about Puget Sound, Chinook). Hearne, *op. cit.* p. 313 (Northern Indians). Mackenzie, *Voyages from Montreal to the Frozen and Pacific Oceans*, p. 147 (Beaver Indians). Ross, ' Eastern Tinneh,' in *Smithsonian Report*, 1886, p. 305. Dall, *Alaska*, p. 194 (Ingalik). Armstrong, *op. cit.* p. 195 (Eskimo). Cranz, *op. cit.* i. 149 (Greenlanders).
[5] Ahlqvist, ' Unter Wogulen und Ostjaken,' in *Acta Soc. Scientiarum Fennicae*, xiv. 290 (Ostyak). Lewin, *Wild Races of South-Eastern India*, p. 255 (Kukis). Wallace, *Malay Archipelago*, i. 142 (Dyaks). Marsden, *History of Sumatra*, p. 257. Waitz-Gerland, *op. cit.* vi. 780 ; Sturt, *Narrative of an Expedition into Central Australia*, ii. 137 ; Angas, *op. cit.* i. 81 *sq.* ; Eylmann, *Die Eingeborenen der Kolonie Südaustralien*, p. 120 (Australian aborigines). Velten, *op. cit.* p. 28 (Swahili on the coast). Mungo Park, *Travels in the Interior of Africa*, p. 219 (Mandingo). Nachtigal, *op. cit.* i. 448 (Tedâ). Spieth, *op. cit.* p. 217 *sq.* (Ewhe in Ho). Burton, *Abeokuta and the Camaroons Mountains*, i. 207 (Egbas).

abortion, which is frequent in the savage world ;[1] partly
to the long period of suckling, not only because a woman
less easily becomes pregnant during the time of lactation,
but on account of the continence in which she often has
to live during that period ; and partly, it would seem, to
inability to produce more children. Mr. Heape considers
it highly probable that the reproductive power of man has
increased with civilisation, precisely as it may be increased
in the lower animals by domestication—" that the effect
of a regular supply of good food, together with all the other
stimulating factors available and exercised in modern
civilised communities, has resulted in such great activity
of the generative organs, and so great an increase in the
supply of the reproductive elements, that conception in
the healthy human female may be said to be possible almost
at any time during the reproductive period."[2] Polygyny
also tends to reduce the number of children born by each
married woman. Dr. Felkin observes that among the
Baganda, although in the poorer families the women are
prolific, it being common enough to meet with mothers of
six or even seven children, yet on account of polygamy
most of the women have only one or two ;[3] and Grenfell
says that in the Congo region there are only few children in
each polygamous household owing to the provocation of
miscarriages.[4] But it is impossible to doubt that polygyny,
generally speaking, has a tendency to increase the number
of children born to the same man, though there may be
exceptions to the rule.[5] Moreover, whilst in many savage
tribes the birth-rate is low, the mortality of children is very
great.[6] The records of the Baptist Mission on the Congo,

---

[1] Ploss-Bartels, *Das Weib*, i. 913 *sqq.*

[2] Heape, *Sex Antagonism*, p. 39.

[3] Felkin, in *Proceed. Roy. Soc. Edinburgh*, xiii. 745.

[4] Johnston, *George Grenfell*, ii. 672.

[5] *Cf.* Weeks, *Bakongo*, p. 150; Munzinger, *Ueber die Sitten und das Recht der Bogos*, p. 65 ; Thurnwald, *op. cit.* iii. 83 (natives of Buin).

[6] Bove, *op. cit.* p. 133 (Yahgans). Whiffen, *op. cit.* p. 146 (Indians of the North-West Amazons). Brett, *op. cit.* p. 413 n. 2 (Indians of Guiana). Powers, *Tribes of California*, p. 231 (Wintun). Schoolcraft, *Indian Tribes of the United States*, iii. 238 (Dakota). Shaw, ' Betsileo,' in *Antananarivo Annual and Madagascar Magazine*, no.iv.9.

which extend over more than twenty years, show that a
large percentage of the children die; this is said to be
chiefly due to unsuitable, indigestible, or insufficient food.[1]
Among the Matabele the mortality of children is stated to
be enormous, chiefly owing to the lack of care. " More
than seventy per cent.," says Decle, " die before they reach
the age of five months; and for that reason, if polygamy
ceases to exist, the native races will disappear from Africa."[2]
Speaking of Equatorial Africans, Winwood Reade observes,
" Propagation is a perfect struggle; polygamy becomes a
law of nature; and even with the aid of this institution,
so favourable to reproduction, there are fewer children
than wives."[3] Among African races in particular the
desire for large families seems to be an important cause of
polygyny. They are not generally addicted to infanticide,
contrary to many other savage peoples, especially in Australia and the South Sea Islands, where infanticide was
practised to such an extent that the prospect of having a
large progeny could not possibly have been an inducement
to taking a plurality of wives.[4]

Polygyny contributes to a man's material comfort or
increases his wealth through the labour of his wives. " If
I have but one wife, who will cook for me when she is ill ? "
is a question often asked by the wife-loving Zulu when argu-
ing in support of his darling custom.[5] Among the Yahgans
of Tierra del Fuego[6] and the Eskimo on the east coast of
Greenland [7] one reason why a man desires to have two wives
is to obtain rowers for his boat, and another motive for
bigamy among the latter is to have women to dress the
skins of the animals killed by the hunter. " The object
of the Kutchin," says Kirby, " is to have a greater number
of poor creatures whom he can use as beasts of burden for

[1] Johnston, George Grenfell, ii. 672.
[2] Decle, op. cit. p. 160.   [3] Reade, Savage Africa, p. 242.
[4] See Westermarck, Origin and Development of the Moral Ideas,
i. 396 sqq.
[5] Tyler, Forty Years among the Zulus, p. 117.   Cf. Wilson, Western
Africa, p. 115 (Kru people of the Grain Coast).
[6] Bove, op. cit. p. 131.
[7] Holm, in Geografisk Tidskrift, viii. 91.

hauling his wood, carrying his meat, and performing the drudgery of his camp."[1] A Californian Modok defends his having several wives on the plea that he requires one to keep house, another to hunt, another to dig roots.[2] Speaking of the Hurons, Charlevoix says that "some nations have wives in all the places where they stay any considerable time for hunting."[3] The Reindeer Chukchee generally ascribe polygyny to economic considerations. "If I possess one herd," they say, "I need but one house and one wife to look after it ; if, however, I own two herds, I must have two separate households and a woman for each of them."[4] Among the Central Australian Arunta many a chief has from three to ten wives, who as a rule live in different places and are obliged to accompany him when he wants them and to supply him with vegetable food.[5] A Shortland chief declared that the main objection he had against missionaries settling on his islands was that they would insist on his giving up nearly all his wives, thereby depriving him of those by whose labour his plantations were cultivated and his household supplied with food.[6] The more wives an Eastern Central African has the richer he is :—"It is his wives that maintain him. They do all his ploughing, milling, cooking, &c. They may be viewed as superior servants who combine all the capacities of male servants and female servants in Britain—who do all his work and ask no wages."[7] Mr. Weeks observes that "a woman on the Congo is the best gilt-edged security in which a man can invest his surplus wealth." He rarely if ever loses the money he has invested in a wife ; should she die he demands from her maternal uncle's family another wife in the place of the deceased, and if the family has not another woman free for this purpose then the marriage money must be returned in full.[8] Among the Tartars, again, according

---

[1] Kirby, in *Smithsonian Report*, 1864, p. 419.
[2] Powers, *op. cit.* p. 259.
[3] Charlevoix, *Voyage to North-America*, ii. 36.
[4] Bogoras, *op. cit.* p. 598.   [5] Strehlow, *op. cit.* vol. iv. pt. i. 98.
[6] Guppy, *op. cit.* p. 44 *sq.*   *Cf.* Thurnwald, *op. cit.* iii. 81.
[7] Macdonald, *Africana*, i. 141 *sq.*   Fülleborn, *op. cit.* p. 229.
[8] Weeks, *Bakongo*, p. 147.

to Marco Polo, wives were of use to their husbands as traders.[1]

The usefulness of wives as labourers accounts no doubt in part for the increasing practice of polygyny at the higher grades of economic culture, which has been noticed above. But it is certainly not the only cause, nor even the only economic cause, of this increase. Economic progress leads to a more unequal distribution of wealth, and this, combined with the necessity of paying a bride price the amount of which is more or less influenced by the economic conditions, makes it possible for certain men to acquire several wives while others can acquire none at all. Speaking of the Iroquois, Colden long ago remarked that "in any nation where all are on a par as to riches and power, plurality of wives cannot well be introduced ";[2] and Morgan observed that "in its highest and regulated form it presupposes a considerable advance of society, together with the development of superior and inferior classes, and of some kinds of wealth."[3]

A multitude of wives, however, may increase not only a man's wealth but also his social importance, reputation, and authority, apart from the influence of the number of his children. The following are some of the advantages that a Thonga is said to derive from it. " In the evening, each of his wives will bring him the pot which she has cooked for him. He will become large and stout himself, and the stouter he gets the more he will be respected. He treats his children and visitors and strangers and poor people, and his magnificence and hospitality are extolled. He will become famous, perhaps even more esteemed than the chief himself. Conclusion : the greatness of an African is before all a matter of pots and the matter of pots is closely connected with polygamy."[4] We often hear that a multitude of wives makes a man able to be liberal and keep open

[1] Marco Polo, *Kingdoms and Marvels of the East*, i. 252.
[2] Colden, quoted by Schoolcraft, *Indian Tribes of the United States*, iii. 191.
[3] Morgan, *Systems of Consanguinity and Affinity*, p. 477.
[4] Junod. *Life of a South African Tribe*, i. 127 *sq.*

doors for foreigners and guests[1]—occasionally even that
it enables him to give friends or followers a share in some of
the wives.[2] It increases his influence by connecting him
with other families.[3] It is a sign of valour, skill, or wealth.
Among the Tupis the more wives a man has the more valiant
he is esteemed.[4] Among the Aleut the best hunters had
the greatest number.[5] The Apache " who can support or
keep, or attract by his power to keep, the greatest number of
women, is the man who is deemed entitled to the greatest
amount of honour and respect."[6] The Konde people
consider it the same thing to be rich and to have many
wives.[7] Statements such as " polygamy is held to be the
test of a man's wealth and consequence," or " a man's
greatness is ever proportionate to the number of his wives,"
are frequently met with in books cf travels. When a
Congo native " wants to impress you with the greatness of
his chief or the importance of the head of his family, he
tells you the number of his wives, and he does not mind adding a dozen to the sum total."[8] Polygyny, as associated with
greatness, is thus regarded as honourable or praiseworthy,
whereas monogamy, as associated with poverty, is thought

[1] Chantre y Herrera, *op. cit.* p. 73 (Maynas in Eastern Ecuador
and North Eastern Peru). Rodway, *op. cit.* p. 219 (Guiana Indians).
Catlin, *op. cit.* i. 118 (Mandan and other North American Indians).
Tregear, *Maori Race,* p. 296. Livingstone, *Missionary Travels
and Researches in South Africa,* p. 196 (Makololo). Weeks, *Congo
Cannibals,* p. 137 (Boloki). Wilson, *Western Africa,* p. 115 (Kru
people of the Grain Coast).

[2] Tessmann, *op. cit.* ii. 262 *sq.* (Pangwe). Rolland, quoted by
Theal, *History of the Boers,* p. 19 (Basuto).

[3] Roth, *North Queensland Ethnography : Bulletin No. 8. Notes
on Government, &c.,* p. 5. Büttner, ' Sozialpolitisches aus dem
Leben der Herero,' in *Das Ausland,* lv. 854. Zöller, *Kamerun,* ii.
59 (Dualla).

[4] ' Extracts out of the Historie of John Lerius,' in Purchas,
His Pilgrimes, xvi. 562. *Cf.* de Poïncy, *op. cit.* p. 547 (Caribs).

[5] Dall, *op. cit.* p. 388. Coxe, *Account of the Russian Discoveries
between Asia and America,* p. 183.

[6] Bancroft, *op. cit.* i. 512 n. 120.

[7] Merensky, quoted by Fülleborn, *op. cit.* p. 344.

[8] Weeks, *Among Congo Cannibals,* p. 137.

mean.[1] The former has tended to become a more or less definite class distinction, and among certain peoples, as we have seen, it is not even permitted to others but chiefs or nobles. Of the Sakalava in Madagascar we are told that a chief is allowed to have four wives, whereas the king can have as many as he likes. " Were a Sakalava chief to take to himself more than four wives, or six at most, he would be considered as attempting to rival the king."[2]

Among polygynous peoples, as elsewhere, social influence or authority is frequently associated with wealth. But even when it is not so, it may be a cause of polygyny. This is the case in the Australian tribes, where the old men possess exceptional power, and in consequence can indulge in polygyny while many of the younger men have to live unmarried. In the other tribes at the lowest stages of civilisation, whether they be lower hunters or incipient agriculturists, there is no class of people invested with much authority ; and among nearly all of them, as we have seen, polygyny is either unknown or very rare.

Among the causes of polygyny we have still to notice the levirate, or the custom of a man marrying his deceased brother's widow. Sometimes a man never takes another wife unless he thus inherits her.[3] The levirate may, in fact, make it necessary for a married man to become a polygynist. In India, for example, as Mr. Gait observes, there is a certain amount of compulsory polygamy owing to the practice whereby certain castes expect a man to marry his elder brother's widow. The Garos expect him in certain cases to marry his widowed mother-in-law.[4]

From circumstances that lead to polygyny we shall now turn our attention to such as make for monogamy. Where the sexes are about equal in number, or there is an excess of men, and a woman consequently has a fair chance

[1] Shaw, ' Betsileo,' in *Antananarivo Annual*, no. iv. 8. Scott Robertson, *Káfirs of the Hindu-Kush*, p. 534. Spencer, *Principles of Sociology*, i. 657.

[2] Walen, ' Sakalava,' in *Antananarivo Annual*, no. viii. 54. *Cf.* Grandidier, *op. cit.* ii. 190 (Merină of Madagascar).

[3] *Supra*, iii. 9, 11   [4] Gait, *op. cit.* p. 246.

of getting a husband for herself, she will hardly care to become the second wife of a man who is already married, or her parents will hardly compel her to marry such a man, unless some particular advantages, economic or social, are gained by it. Hence the absence of disparity in wealth or rank in a society tends to make monogamy general. Again, where there is inequality of wealth or otherwise considerable social differentiation, the poor or low class people may have to be satisfied with one wife even though there be an excess of females. We often hear that a man must live in monogamy owing to the price he has to pay for a bride or the expenses connected with a wedding. A few instances may serve as an illustration. Mr. Eyles wrote to me that among the Zulus many men have but one wife because women must be bought with cattle. Among the Gonds and Korkús of Central India, according to Forsyth, " polygamy is not forbidden, but, women being costly chattels, it is rarely practised."[1] An ordinary Batta can hardly ever afford to buy more than a single wife.[2] Among the Subanu of Mindanao a plurality of wives is not common, " mostly for want of sufficient means for the marriage portion and to pay for the ceremony and the usual feast provided for relatives and friends."[3] In the Chittagong Hill tracts polygyny " is reserved entirely for the wealthy, as they alone can afford the luxury of paying for and supporting a plurality of wives, to say nothing of meeting the heavy expenses of providing the necessary feasts for the community."[4] So also among the Hindus one important deterrent to polygyny seems to be the very great expense connected with an orthodox marriage.[5] The difficulty of maintaining several wives is frequently said to be a cause of monogamy. Such a difficulty easily arises where life is supported by hunting and the amount of female labour is limited, or where the produce of agriculture is insufficient to feed a larger family owing to the poverty of the soil, the primitive methods of cultivation, or the small size of the landed property.

---

[1] Forsyth, *op. cit.* p. 148.   [2] Junghuhn, *op. cit.* ii. 133.
[3] Finley and Churchill, *op. cit.* p. 40.
[4] Hutchinson, *op. cit.* p. 23.   [5] Padfield, *op. cit.* p. 97.

Among the Eskimo, says Mr. Hodge, " monogamy is prevalent, as the support of several wives is possible only for the expert hunter."[1] Among the Maritime Chukchee, who live by fishing and sea-hunting, even bigamy is extremely rare, because a man cannot afford to maintain an extra family ; " in fact, he is barely able to provide for one woman and her children."[2] In New Ireland "most men have only one wife, probably because the land is too poor to feed a larger family."[3] Among various peoples polygyny is more or less checked by the man's obligation to serve for his wife for a certain number of years,[4] or by his having to settle down with his father-in-law for the whole of his life. Dr. Boas says of the Central Eskimo :—" Should the newly married couple join the wife's family this would serve as a check to polygamy, which, however, is quite allowable. It is only when the new family settles on its own account that a man is at full liberty to take additional wives."[5]

The expenses of having several wives are very frequently increased by the necessity of providing each of them with a separate dwelling. In my collection of facts the cases where each wife is said to live in a house by herself are nearly six times as many as those in which the wives are said to live together, although I have taken equal care to record both classes of facts ; but the figures are not large (41 and 7 respectively) owing to the limitation of my notes on this point. The custom of giving a separate house to each wife is intended to prevent quarrels and fights ; and thus we may say that even when this aim is achieved— which is not always the case—female jealousy is an obstacle to the practice of polygyny.

We often hear that no jealousy or rivalry disturbs the peace in polygynous families.[6] In many cases we are told

---

[1] Hodge, *op. cit.* i. 809.   [2] Bogoras, *op. cit.* p. 611.
[3] Stephan and Graebner, *op. cit.* p. 110.
[4] See, *e.g.,* Dittmar, *loc. cit.* p. 25 (Koryak).
[5] Boas, in *Ann. Rep. Bur. Ethnol.* vi. 579.
[6] *Captivity of Hans Stade,* p. 143 (Tupinambase). 'Extracts of the Historie of John Lerius,' in Purchas, *op. cit.* xvi. 562 (Tupis). v. Koenigswald, ' Die Cayuás,' in *Globus,* xciii. 381. de Poincy. *op. cit.* p. 544 ; Du Tertre, *op. cit.* ii. 378 (Caribs). Perrin du Lac.

that the women do not object to polygyny ;[1] or that they rejoice at the arrival of a new wife ;[2] or that the first wife herself brings her husband a fresh wife or a concubine, or advises him to take one when she becomes old herself or if she proves barren or has a suckling child or in order to be relieved of some of her work or for some other reason.[3] Among the Onas of Tierra del Fuego the first wife often wishes that the husband shall take another one so as to get assistance in transporting his shelters.[4] Among the Apache " the women are by no means averse to sharing the affections of their lords with other wives, as the increased number lessens the work for each individual."[5] Among the Californian Modok the women are said to be opposed to any change in the polygynous habits of the men.[6] Speaking of

Voyage dans les deux Louisianes et chez les nations sauvages du Missouri, p. 80. Parry, *op. cit.* p. 528 (Eskimo of Melville Peninsula). Iden-Zeller, in *Zeitschr. f. Ethnol.* xliii. 850 (Chukchee). Thurston, *Castes and Tribes of Southern India*, v. 92 (Muduvars ; not always). Petrie, *Reminiscences of Early Queensland*, p. 61. Hill and Thornton, *Notes on the Aborigines of New South Wales*, p. 7. Colenso, *op. cit.* p. 26 ; Tregear, *op. cit.* p. 296 (Maori). Alberti, *op. cit.* p. 138 (Kafirs). Magyar, *op. cit.* p. 283 (Kimbunda). v. Wissmann, Wolf, v. François, and Mueller, *op. cit.* p. 160 (Baluba). Burrows, *op. cit.* p. 86 (Mangbettu). Felkin, in *Proceed. Roy. Soc. Edinburgh*, xii. 323 (Madi). Heese, in *Archiv f. Anthropologie*, N.S. xii. 137 (Sango).

[1] Taplin, *Folklore, &c. of the South Australian Aborigines*, p. 35 (Narrinyeri). Cole, in *Field Museum of Natural History, Anthropological Series*, xii. 103 (Bagobo of Mindanao). Roscoe, *Northern Bantu*, p. 174 (Bagesu). Tyler, *op. cit.* p. 119 (Zulus).

[2] Schadenberg, in *Zeitschr. f. Ethnol.* xvii. 12. (Bagobo). Pfeil, *op. cit.* p. 32 *sq.* (natives of the Bismarck Archipelago).

[3] v. Martius, *op. cit.* i. 106 (Brazilian aborigines). Cranz, *op. cit.* i. 147 (Greenlanders). Bogoras, *op. cit.* p. 600 (Chukchee). Jochelson, *Koryak*, p. 754. v. Siebold, *op. cit.* p. 31 *sq.* (Ainu). Landtman, *Nya Guinea fården*, p. 81 (Kiwai Papuans). Colenso, *op. cit.* p. 26 (Maori). Kropf, *op. cit.* p. 152 *sq.* ; v. Weber, *op. cit.* ii. 158 ; Waitz, *op. cit.* ii. 389 (Kafirs). Mockler-Ferryman, *British Nigeria*, p. 233. Partridge, *Cross River Natives*, p. 255. Dennett, *At the Back of the Black Man's Mind*, p. 37 (Bavili). Le Bon, *La civilisation des Arabes*, p. 424 ; Rein, *Japan*, p. 425.

[4] Cojazzi, *Los indios del Archipiélago Fueguino*, p. 16.

[5] Cremony, *op. cit.* p. 249.

[6] Meacham, quoted by Powers, *op. cit.* p. 259.

the Plains Indians, Colonel Dodge remarks, "Jealousy would seem to have no place in the composition of an Indian woman, and many prefer to be, even for a time, the favourite of a man who already has a wife or wives, and who is known to be a good husband and provider, rather than tempt the precarious chances of an untried man."[1] Among the Kru people of the Grain Coast the women are quite as much interested in the continuance of polygyny as the men :—" A woman would infinitely prefer to be one of a dozen wives of a respectable man, than to be the sole representative of a man who had not force of character to raise himself above the one-woman level. . . . She would greatly prefer the wider margin of licentious indulgence that she would enjoy as one of a dozen wives, than the closer inspection to which she would be subjected as the only wife of her household."[2] Among the Warega of the Belgian Congo " les femmes ne demandent pas mieux que d'être très nombreuses ; c'est une preuve de richesse et cela diminue leurs travaux."[3] Among the Mossi of the Western Sudan the first wife eagerly wishes her husband to take many wives because it increases her own authority.[4] The leading wife of a Kikúyu chief asked Mrs. Routledge to tell the English ladies that in her country the women like their husbands to have as many wives as possible.[5] Speaking of the Makololo women, Livingstone observes :—" On hearing that a man in England could marry but one wife, several ladies exclaimed that they would not like to live in such a country : they could not imagine how English ladies could relish our custom, for, in their way of thinking, every man of respectability should have a number of wives, as a proof of his wealth. Similar ideas prevail all down the Zambesi."[6] According to the missionary Moffat, a Bechuana woman " would be perfectly amazed at one's ignorance, were she to be told that she would be much happier in a

[1] Dodge, op. cit. p. 201.   [2] Wilson, Western Africa, p. 112 sq.
[3] Delhaise, op. cit. p. 176.
[4] Mangin, in Anthropos, ix. 487 sq.
[5] Routledge, op. cit. p. 124.   See also ibid. p. 133 sq.
[6] Livingstone, Narrative of an Expedition to the Zambesi, p. 284 sq.

single state, than being the mere concubine and drudge of a haughty husband."[1] But although we thus often hear that the women put up with or approve of polygyny[2]— because it implies a division of labour, or because it increases the reputation of the family or the authority of the first wife, or because it gives greater liberty to the married women—we are more frequently told that it is a cause of quarrels and domestic misery. For jealousy is not exclusively a masculine passion, although it is generally more violent in the male than in the female sex. It is not unknown among the lower animals: a female rabbit bites another female of her own species that wants to pair in her presence.[3]

To take some instances.[4] When a Yahgan has as many as four women, his hut is every day transformed into a field of battle, and many a young and pretty wife must even atone with her life for the precedence given her by the

---

[1] Moffat, *Missionary Labours and Scenes in Southern Africa*, p. 251.

[2] See also Kropf, *op. cit.* p. 153 (Xosa Kafirs) ; Reade, *Savage Africa*, p. 259 *sq.* (Equatorial Africans) ; Baker, *Nile Tributaries*, p. 125 *sqq.* (Arabs of Upper Egypt).

[3] Burdach, *Die Physiologie als Erfahrungswissenschaft*, i. 372. Professor Lester Ward (*Dynamic Sociology*, i. 623 n. *) witnessed a scene which he interprets as evidence of female jealousy :—" There were three hens with a cock ; between the cock and one of the hens a successful courtship took place, immediately after which the successful hen was attacked first by one and then by the other of the two unsuccessful ones and driven away to some distance."

[4] For other instances of female jealousy in mankind see Molina, *op. cit.* ii. 116 (Araucanians) ; v. Martius, *op. cit.* i. 392 (Mundrucûs) ; Matthews, *Ethnography and Philology of the Hidatsa Indians*, p. 53 ; James, *Account of an Expedition from Pittsburgh to the Rocky Mountains*, i. 231 *sqq.* (Omaha) ; Charlevoix, *Voyage to North-America*, ii. 37 *sq.* (Algonkin) ; Hearne, *op. cit.* p. 310 (Northern Indians) ; Franklin, *Narrative of a Journey to the Shores of the Polar Sea*, p. 70 (Cree) ; *Idem, Narrative of a Second Expedition to the Shores of the Polar Sea*, p. 301 ; Kirby, in *Smithsonian Report*, 1864, p. 419 (Kutchin) ; Turner, in *Ann. Rep. Bur. Ethnol.* xi. 270 (Indians of the Ungava district of Labrador), 189 (Eskimo of the same district) ; Kumlien, *op. cit.* p. 16 *sq.* (Eskimo of Cumberland Sound) ; Lyon, *op. cit.* p. 355 (Eskimo of Iglulik and Winter Island) ; Bogoras, *op. cit.* p. 601 *sq.* (Chukchee) ; Steller, *op. cit.* p. 288 (Kamchadal) ; Kearns, *Tribes of South India*, p. 72 (Reddies) ; Rowney, *op. cit.* p. 38 (Bhils) ; Cooper, *Mishmee Hills*, p. 102 (Assamese) ; St. John,

common husband.[1] Among the Charruas it often happens that a woman abandons her husband if he has a plurality of wives, as soon as she is able to find another man who will take her as his only wife.[2] If a Toba takes a second wife the first one does not leave the newcomer in peace until she is either conqueror or conquered.[3] The natives of Guiana are said to live in comfort as long as the man is content with one wife, but when he takes another, " the natural feelings of woman rebel at such cruel treatment, and jealousy and unhappiness have, in repeated instances, led to suicide."[4] Among the Tamanacs, according to v. Humboldt, " the husband calls the second and third wife the ' companions ' of the first ; and the first treats these ' companions ' as rivals and ' enemies ' ('ipucjatoje ')."[5] A Delaware or Iroquois Indian had seldom two and hardly ever more wives, because his love of ease renders domestic peace a most valuable treasure.[6] Of the Dakota it is said that "polygamy is the cause of a great deal of their miseries and troubles. The women, most of them, abhor the practice, but are overruled by the men. Some of the women commit suicide on this account."[7] The Greenlanders have a saying that "whales, musk oxen, and reindeer deserted the country because the women were jealous at the conduct of their husbands."[8]

[1] *Life in the Forests of the Far East*, i. 56 (Sea Dyaks) ; Riedel, *op. cit.* pp. 335, 448 (natives of Babber and Wetter) ; Kubary, *Die socialen Einrichtungen der Pelauer*, p. 61 (Pelew Islanders) ; Landtman, *op. cit.* p. 81 (Kiwai Papuans of British New Guinea) ; Neuhauss, *op. cit.* i. 161 (natives of Kaiser Wilhelm Land) ; Parkinson, *op. cit.* p. 394 (Moánus of the Admiralty Islands) ; Lambert, *op. cit.* p. 96 (New Caledonians) ; Turner, *Samoa*, p. 97 ; Stair, *op. cit.* p. 178 (Samoans) ; Ellis, *Polynesian Researches*, i. 269 (Tahitians) ; Thomson, *Story of New Zealand*, i. 179 ; Yate, *Account of New Zealand*, p. 97 (Maori).   [1] Bove, *op. cit.* p. 131.

[2] Azara, *op. cit.* ii. 22 *sq.*   [3] Cardús, *op. cit.* p. 264.

[4] Brett, *op. cit.* p. 351 *sq.* Cf. Schomburgk, in *Jour. Ethn. Soc. London*, i. 270.

[5] v. Humboldt, *op. cit.* v. 548 *sq.*   [6] Loskiel, *op. cit.* i. 58.

[7] Prescott, in Schoolcraft, *Indian Tribes of the United States*, iii. 234 *sq.* Cf. *ibid.* iii. 236.

[8] Nansen, *First Crossing of Greenland*, ii. 329. Cf. *ibid.* ii. 321, 329 *sq.*

Among the Ainu Mr. Batchelor always found that "though a man's wives live in separate houses, they are often not on speaking terms with one another."[1] Experience has taught the Lushais that two wives in one house is not conducive to peace, and consequently polygamy is almost entirely confined to the chiefs, since few others can afford to keep up two establishments.[2] Among the Malayo-Siamese peasantry of the Patani States polygyny is extremely rare "partly for economic reasons and partly because it is recognised that double unions lead to friction in the family."[3] At Wagawaga, in British New Guinea, where at the present day no man seems to have more than one wife, it is stated "that even in the old days very few men had two, as it was found that the old and new wife quarrelled so persistently as to cause discomfort to their common husband."[4] In Buin of the Solomons monogamy is the rule not only for economic reasons but because the first wife often knows how to prevent the husband from taking a fresh one.[5] When the missionary Williams asked a woman in Fiji how it was that she and so many other women there were without a nose, the answer was, "It is due to a plurality of wives; jealousy causes hatred, and then the stronger tries to cut or bite off the nose of the one she hates."[6] In Tikopia many a wife who believed another woman to be preferred by the husband committed suicide.[7] In the Australian tribes jealousy is common among the women.[8] Among some of them "a new woman would always be beaten by the other wife, and a good deal would depend on the fighting powers of the former whether she kept her position or not."[9]

---

[1] Batchelor, *op. cit.* p. 231.   [2] Shakespear, *op. cit.* p. 50 *sq.*

[3] Annandale and Robinson, *op. cit.* ii. 72.

[4] Seligman, *op. cit.* p. 509.   [5] Thurnwald, *op. cit.* iii. 81 *sq.*

[6] Williams and Calvert, *op. cit.* p. 152 *sq.*

[7] Waitz-Gerland, *op. cit.* vol. v. pt. ii. 191 *sq.*

[8] *Ibid.* vi. 758, 781. Freycinet, *op. cit.* ii 766. Westgarth, *Australia Felix*, p. 68. Taplin, 'Narrinyeri,' in Woods, *Native Tribes of South Australia*, p. 11. Eylmann, *Die Eingeborenen der Kolonie Südaustralien*, p. 130. Lumholtz, *Among Cannibals*, p. 213.

[9] Palmer, in *Jour. Anthr. Inst.* xiii. 282.

In Africa also jealousies and quarrels frequently arise between the wives of the same man,[1] even where the women are said to argue in favour of polygyny. The Malagasy word for polygyny, *fampirafesană*, means "that which engenders enmity," being derived from or related to the word *răfy*, " enemy " or "adversary."[2] " So invariably," says Mr. Sibree, " has the taking of more wives than one shown itself to be a fruitful cause of enmity and strife in a household. . . . The different wives are always trying to get an advantage over each other, and to wheedle their husband out of his property ; constant quarrels and jealousy are the result, and polygamy becomes inevitably the causing of strife, ' the making an adversary.' "[3]   In the Thonga language there is a special term, *bukwele*, that " indicates the peculiar jealousy of a wife towards her co-wives."[4] Messrs. Gouldsbury and Sheane observe that " though there was, and still is, a superfluity of women among the Awemba, owing to the practice of sparing them in warfare, while destroying the males, yet it cannot be said that our Central African woman favours polygamy, as is asserted of her South African sister. For the Wemba woman polygamy may be truly described as serving as the battlefield of her status."[5]   Speaking of the Ngoni in British Central Africa, Mr. Elmslie remarks that " nowhere do quarrels and witchcraft practices foment more surely than in a polygamous household."[6]   Among the Wamuera in the Ruwuma district polygyny proper is said to be rare on

[1] Passarge, ' Die Bushmänner der Kalahari,' in *Mittheil. Deutsch. Schutzgeb.* xviii. 265. Maclean, *op. cit.* p. 44 ; v. Weber, *op. cit.* i. 329 *sq.* ; Shooter, *op. cit.* p. 78 (Kafirs). Tyler, *op. cit.* p. 119 ; Fritsch, *Die Eingeborenen Süd-Afrika's,* p. 142 (Zulus). Casalis, *op. cit.* p. 189 (Basuto). Velten, *op. cit.* p. 139 *sq.* (Swahili). Macdonald, *Africana,* i. 134 (Eastern Central Africans). Dennett, *Notes on the Folklore of the Fjort (French Congo),* p. 21. *Idem, At the Back of the Black Man's Mind,* p. 37 (Bavili). Wilson, *Western Africa,* p. 115 (Kru people of the Grain Coast). Felkin, in *Proceed. Roy. Soc. Edinburgh,* xiii. 756 (Baganda).
[2] Grandidier, *op. cit.* ii. 191.   [3] Sibree, *op. cit.* p. 161.
[4] Junod, *Life of a South African Tribe,* i. 274.
[5] Gouldsbury and Sheane, *op. cit.* p. 165. See also *ibid.* p. 168.
[6] Elmslie, *Among the Wild Ngoni,* p. 58.

account of the jealousy of the free married women.[1] Mr.
Weeks thinks that on the Lower Congo there are in polygamous marriages ninety-nine unhappy unions for one
really happy one.[2] Concerning the Bogos and neighbouring
peoples—in Abyssinia and on its northern frontier—
Munzinger states that he has come to the conclusion that
a man who has a single wife is ten times happier than one
who has several, in consequence of the jealousy which the
wives of the same man feel towards each other even though
they live in different houses ; one of their most serious
curses runs, " Keep two wives."[3] In Egypt quarrels
between the various women belonging to one man are very
frequent, and often the wife will not even allow her female
slave or slaves to appear unveiled in the presence of her
husband.[4] In other Muhammadan countries polygyny
is likewise the cause of strife or unhappiness.[5] In Persia,
says Dr. Polak, a married woman cannot feel a greater pain
than if her husband takes a fresh wife whom he prefers to
her ; then she is quite disconsolate.[6] In India, both among
Muhammadans and Hindus, there is much intriguing and
disquiet in polygynous families ;[7] and the same seems to
have been the case in ancient times—in the Rig-Veda
there are hymns in which wives curse their fellow-wives.[8]
In Hebrew the popular term for the second wife was haṣ-
ṣârâh, meaning " female enemy."[9] In China many women
dislike altogether the idea of getting married because they
fear the misery which is in store for them if their husbands
take other wives ; hence some become Buddhist or Taouist

[1] Adams, quoted by Fülleborn, op. cit. p. 61.

[2] Weeks, Bakongo, p. 149.

[3] Munzinger, Ueber die Sitten und das Recht der Bogos, p. 65.

[4] Lane, Modern Egyptians, i. 253 sq.

[5] d'Escayrac de Lauture, op. cit. p. 250 sq. Pischon, Der Einfluss
des Islâm auf das häusliche, sociale und politische Leben seiner
Bekenner, p. 14.

[6] Polak, Persien, i. 226. See also Wilson, Persian Life and Customs,
p. 265 sq.

[7] Balfour, Cyclopædia of India, iii. 251.

[8] Dutt, ' Social Life of the Hindus in the Rig-Veda Period,' in
Calcutta Review, lxxxv. 79.

[9] Benzinger, op. cit. p. 145.

nuns, and others prefer death by suicide to marriage.[1] Statements of this kind cannot but shake our confidence in the optimistic assertions of Dr. Le Bon and other defenders of polygyny.

Domestic troubles may be more easily averted if the wives are chosen from one family, as they not infrequently are. The practice of marrying women who are sisters is particularly widespread among American Indians,[2] but is also found among various other peoples in different parts of the world.[3] In many cases the man has even a claim to the

[1] Gray, *op. cit.* i. 185.

[2] Chiriguanos of the Gran Chaco (Church, *op. cit.* p. 238), Caribs (Du Tertre, *op. cit.* ii. 378), Minnetarees (a Hidatsa division) and Mandan (Lewis and Clarke, *Travels to the Source of the Missouri River*, p. 307), Dakota (Carver, *op. cit.* p. 367), Indians of the Californian Peninsula (Baegert, in *Smithsonian Report*, 1863, p. 368), Luiseño Indians on the coast of California (Sparkman, in *University of California Publications in American Archæology and Ethnology*, viii. 214), British Columbia Indians (Teit, ' Thompson Indians of British Columbia,' in *Publications of the Jesup North Pacific Expedition*, i. 326 ; *Idem*, ' Indian Tribes of the Interior,' in *Canada and its Provinces, vol. XXI. The Pacific Province*, pt. i. 309), Northern Indians (Hearne, *op. cit.* p. 129 *sq.*), Cree (Mackenzie, *op. cit.* p. xcvi. *sq.*), Eastern Tinne (Ross, in *Smithsonian Report*, 1866, p. 310), Kaviak of Alaska (Dall, *op. cit.* p. 138). See *supra*, ii. 392. For other facts see Frazer, *Totemism and Exogamy*, iv. 141 *sqq.*, and particularly the same writer's *Folk-Lore in the Old Testament*, ii. 266 *sqq.*, which was published after the present chapter was written.

[3] Hindus (Gait, *op. cit.* i. 246), Negritos of Zambales (Reed, *op. cit.* p. 61), natives of Nauru in the Marshall Islands (Jung, ' Die Rechtsanschauungen der Eingeborenen von Nauru,' in *Mittheil. Deutsch. Schutzgeb.* x. 66), natives of Kaiser Wilhelm Land (Neuhauss, *op. cit.* i. 150, according to tales), Western Islanders of Torres Straits (Rivers, in *Reports of the Cambridge Anthropological Expedition to Torres Straits*, v. 244), Banks Islanders (*Idem, History of Melanesian Society*, i. 49 ; formerly), natives of East Mallicolo in the New Hebrides (Serbelov, in *American Anthropologist*, xv. 279), Maori (Best, in *Trans. and Proceed. New Zealand Institute*, xxxvi. 29, 63 ; Tregear, *op. cit.* p. 298 ; formerly), Kalahari Bushmen (Passarge, in *Mittheil. Deutsch. Schutzgeb.* xviii. 265), Basoga (Roscoe, *Northern Bantu*, p. 210). Among the Nilotic Kavirondo '' a wife who is proved to be sterile is not divorced, but her parents send her sister to become the man's wife, and he is expected to pay another

sisters, or at least the younger sisters, of his wife, as they
grow up.[1] Perrot says that among the Algonkin wives
who are sisters "always live together without any strife,
all that is furnished by their husband being for the common
use of their family, who cultivate the land together ";[2]
and we often hear that a man who wishes to have several
wives by preference chooses sisters for the very purpose of
securing more domestic peace.[3] But there are also said to be
other motives for the practice. The Ostyak " believe that
a man's marrying with a wife's sister brings good luck, and

sum as a marriage-fee for her " (ibid. p. 282). See also supra, ii.
392 ; infra, p. 263 sq.; Frazer, Totemism and Exogamy, iv. 145 sqq. ;
Idem, Folk-Lore in the Old Testament, ii. 275 sqq.
  [1] Cheyenne and Arapaho (Algonkin) and other southern Plains
tribes of North American Indians (Dodge, op. cit. p. 201 sq.),
Pawnee (Grinnell, Story of the Indian, p. 46 ; Dunbar, in Magazine
of American History, iv. 266), Hidatsa (Matthews, op. cit. p. 53),
Omaha (Fletcher and La Flesche, in Ann. Rep. Bur. Ethnol. xxvii.
313 ; James, Expedition from Pittsburgh to the Rocky Mountains,
i. 230), Indians of Oregon (Schoolcraft, Archives of Aboriginal
Knowledge, v. 654 ; Bancroft, op. cit. i. 277), Mortlock Islanders
(Kubary, in Mittheil. Geograph. Gesellsch. Hamburg, 1878–79,
p. 260), Line Islanders (Tutuila, in Jour. Polynesian Soc. i. 267),
Malagasy (Waitz, op. cit. ii. 438), Thonga (Junod, Life of a South
African Tribe, i. 251 sq.), Bantu Kavirondo (Hobley, Eastern Uganda,
p. 17). Other instances are given by Frazer in the works referred to.
  [2] Perrot, in Blair, Indian Tribes of the Upper Mississippi Valley,
i. 72. See also Boller, Among the Indians, p. 195 ; Schinz, Deutsch-
Süd-West-Afrika, p. 172 sq. (Herero).
  [3] Onas of Tierra del Fuego (Cojazzi, op. cit. p. 16), Indians of
French Guiana (Pelleprat, op. cit. ii. 61), Illinois (' Account of Monsieur de la Salle's Last Expedition in North America,' in Collections
of the New-York Historical Society, for the Year 1814, ii. 238 ; Bossu,
op. cit. i. 128), Pawnee (Dunbar, in Magazine of American History,
iv. 266), Sauk and Foxes (Marston, in Blair, op. cit. ii. 167 ; Forsyth,
ibid. ii. 214), and other Indian tribes in North America (Hennepin,
New Discovery of a Vast Country in America between New France
and New Mexico, p. 482 : " They frequently marry three sisters,
and give this reason for so doing, that they agree better together
than with strangers " ; Domenech, Seven Years' Residence in the
Great Deserts of North America, ii. 306), Malayo-Siamese population
of the Patani States (Annandale and Robinson, op. cit. ii. 73).
See also Frazer, Folk-Lore in the Old Testament, ii. 268 (Apache),
269 (Ojibway), 275 (Caribs), 299 (some natives of Ceram).

by doing this they pay the father only half the price, or *kalym* first-paid."[1] When a Samoan was seen to be resolved upon taking a fresh wife, the principal one often endeavoured to get her own sister or sisters " added to the family roll of wives, so that she might have some control over them. This plan was frequently adopted to avoid strangers being brought into the family."[2] The Omaha custom of marrying sisters was explained as serving the purpose of " holding the family intact, for should the children be bereft of their own mother they would come under the care of her close kindred and not fall into the hands of a stranger." Our informants add that " this interpretation seems borne out by the approval still expressed when a woman weds the brother of her late husband or a man marries the sister of his dead wife or the widow of his brother ; even when there is a marked disparity in the ages of the parties, it is said, ' The marriage does not make a break in the family and it shows respect for the dead.' "[3] The practice of marrying a deceased wife's sister is widespread.[4] So far as the Koryak are concerned, Dr. Jochelson also explains it as a method of maintaining the family union ; they do not seem to marry a living wife's sister, but to strengthen the union between the two families the brother of a married

---

[1] Miss Czaplicka, *Aboriginal Siberia*, p. 126. Among the Cheyenne, Arapaho, and other southern Plains tribes of North American Indians the husband of the eldest daughter of a family has a right to take her full sisters as wives, as they arrive at a marriageable age, without paying anything for them (Dodge, *op. cit.* p. 202).

[2] Stair, *op. cit.* p. 175.

[3] Fletcher and La Flesche, in *Ann. Rep. Bur. Ethnol.* xxvii. 313.

[4] Roucouyennes (Coudreau, *Chez nos Indiens*, p. 128), Pima of Arizona (Russell, in *Ann. Rep. Bur. Ethnol.* xxvi. 184), Luiseño (Sparkman, *loc. cit.* p. 214), Iroquois (Loskiel, *op. cit.* i. 65), Algonkin (Lahontan, *op. cit.* p. 462), Thompson Indians of British Columbia (Teit, in *Publications of the Jesup North Pacific Expedition*, i. 325), Shuswap in the interior of British Columbia (*Idem, ibid.* ii. 591), Kamchadal (Steller, *op. cit.* p. 347), Koryak (Jochelson, *Koryak*, pp. 748, 750), Banks Islanders (Rivers, *History of Melanesian Society*, i. 48 *sq.*), Maori (Best, in *Trans. and Proceed. New Zealand Institute*, xxxvi. 29, 63), Namib Bushmen (Trenk, in *Mittheil. Deutsch. Schutzgeb.* xxiii. 168). Other instances are given by Frazer in the works referred to.

woman will court her husband's sister if she has any.[1] In various cases, as we have seen, a man marries a sister of his wife if the latter dies soon or before bearing a child.[2]

Among some peoples there are, side by side with marriages between a man and two or several sisters, marriages with two women who are mother and daughter[3] or aunt and niece.[4] M. Junod thinks that among the Thonga " the preference accorded to a wife's sisters, or nieces, might very well owe its origin to the following cause : when a group has ascertained that its women are well treated in another group, it welcomes near alliances with that group, thinking that, in this dreadful lottery of marriage, one must not despise the guarantee given by a previous happy union."[5]

Female jealousy may be an obstacle to polygyny either because the husband for his own sake dreads its consequences or because his wife simply prevents him from taking another wife or because he has too much regard for her feelings to do so. Even in the savage world a married woman often occupies a respected and influential position, and the relations between man and wife may be of a very tender character. This is said to be the case among many monogamous or almost monogamous savages. Among the tribes of the North-West Amazons the women are generally well treated and consulted by their husbands, and their influence is very great ; " the tribal reputation of a man rests largely in the hands of his wife."[6] Among the Karayá the position of a wife is said to be very good : she gives her opinion in

---

[1] Jochelson, *Koryak*, p. 750. Among the Maori two sisters would also sometimes marry two brothers (Best, *loc. cit.* p. 29).

[2] *Supra*, ii. 392. See also Frazer, *Folk-Lore in the Old Testament*, ii. 278 (Matabele), 279 (Baganda), 280 (Banyoro), 281 (Awemba), 298 (Battas), 300 (natives of the Louisiade Archipelago).

[3] Onas (Cojazzi, *op. cit.* p. 16), Chiriguanos (Church, *op. cit.* p. 238), Caribs (Du Tertre, *op. cit.* ii. 378), Negritos of Zambales (Reed, *op. cit.* p. 61), Maori (Best, *loc. cit.* p. 29).

[4] Omaha (Fletcher, *loc. cit.* p. 313 ; James, *op. cit.* i. 252), Thonga (Junod, *op. cit.* i. 252).

[5] Junod, *op. cit.* i. 253.   [6] Whiffen, *op. cit.* p. 68 *sq.*

all matters of importance, she has no hard work to perform, she generally lives on very peaceful terms with her husband,[1] and adultery on his part would be avenged by her nearest relatives.[2] Among the Huitoto Indians serious disagreements very rarely arise between husband and wife.[3] The Guaycurûs generally treat their wives well.[4] Among the Zapotecs and other nations inhabiting the Isthmus of Tehuantepec, who do not permit polygyny, "gentleness, affection, and frugality characterise the marital relations."[5] The Santal " treats the female members of his family with respect " ;[6] his wife is not only the ruler of the house, but her influence extends to social and political matters.[7] Among the Kukis women are generally held in consideration ; " their advice is taken, and they have much influence."[8] The Pádam wives, according to Colonel Dalton, are treated by their husbands with a regard that seems singular in so rude a race ; " but," he adds, " I have seen other races as rude who in this respect are an example to more civilised people. It is because with these rude people the inclination of the persons most interested in the marriage is consulted, and polygamy is not practised."[9] The Munda Kols of Chota Nagpur call a wife " the mistress of the house," and she takes up a position similar to that of a married woman in Europe.[10] Dr. Martin states that among the " pure " aboriginal tribes of the Malay Peninsula a wife is uniformly treated well by her husband, and that they look upon each other as companions.[11] Among the

---

[1] Krause, *In den Wildnissen Brasiliens*, p. 325. *Idem*, in *Zeitschr. f. Ethnol.* xli. 499.
[2] Ehrenreich, *Beiträge zur Völkerkunde Brasiliens*, p. 27.
[3] Hardenburg, *op. cit.* p. 154.
[4] Sánchez Labrador, *op. cit.* ii. 26. Waitz, *op. cit.* iii. 472.
[5] Bancroft, *op. cit.* i. 661.
[6] Hunter, *Annals of Rural Bengal*, i. 217. See also Man, *Sonthalia*, p. 15. [7] Hertel, *op. cit.* p. 84.
[8] Lewin, *Wild Races of South-Eastern India*, p. 254.
[9] Dalton, *op cit.* p. 28.
[10] Jellinghaus, in *Zeitschr. f. Ethnol.* iii. 369.
[11] Martin, *Die Inlandstämme der Malayischen Halbinsel*, p. 872.

Nicobarese " the position of women is, and always has been, in no way inferior to that of the other sex. They take their full share in the formation of public opinion, discuss publicly with the men matters of general interest to the village, and their opinions receive due attention before a decision is arrived at. In fact, they are consulted on every matter, and the henpecked husband is of no extraordinary rarity in the Nicobars."[1]   Among the Andamanese, according to Mr. Portman, husbands are affectionate to their wives ; the latter, it is true, have to perform all the drudgery, but " have a good deal of influence and are under no restrictions," and the old women are much respected.[2]   Mr. Man says of the same people that " the consideration and respect with which women are treated might with advantage be emulated by certain classes in our own land."[3]   The Dyak women do not hold an inferior and humiliating position ; they do no more than a fair share of the work, and when people meet to discuss any matter of general importance the women are allowed to take part in the discussion. A great deal of conjugal affection exists, and " the men very often love their wives and think a great deal of their opinion."[4]   Among the Alfoors of Minahassa " the woman is, and probably has been for many generations, on a footing of equality with her husband."[5]   Among the savages of Formosa man and wife are said to have equal rights.[6]   Among the monogamous natives of Guam, of the Ladrone Islands, if a woman discovered her husband to be unfaithful she called together the other women of her village, who armed themselves with spears, went to the offender's house, destroyed any growing crops he might own, and menaced him with the spears until he was forced to

[1] Kloss, *op. cit.* p. 242.   See also *ibid.* p. 220.

[2] Portman, *op. cit.* i. 34.

[3] Man, in *Jour. Anthr. Inst.* xii. 327.

[4] Gomes, *op. cit.* pp. 86, 129.   Bock, *Head-Hunters of Borneo,* p. 210 *sq.*   Selenka, *Sonnige Welten,* p. 33.

[5] Hickson, *op. cit.* p. 282.

[6] Müller, in *Zeitschr. f. Ethnol.* xlii. 230.   Davidson, *op. cit.* p. 566 (Atayals).

flee from the house.[1] Among the natives of Mailu, in British New Guinea, " in the matter of marital authority there seems to be a great independence on the part of both partners " ; Dr. Malinowski never saw any of the women as much as rebuked or spoken to unkindly by her husband, but there were present all the signs of friendly and unconstrained relations between them.[2] Concerning the monogamous Easter Islanders, it is said that, owing to the preponderance of the male over the female portion of the community, " the women are a source of great solicitude ; much consideration is shown them ; they are fairly well taken care of, and are treated, generally, with kindness, not to say affection."[3] Among the Central African Pygmies there is " much attachment between husband and wife."[4] " Among the Bushmen," says Fritsch, " the female sex makes life-companions, among the A-bantu beasts of burden."[5] Of the Auin we are told that the position of a wife is hardly inferior to that of her husband, who is often enough henpecked by her ; [6] and among the Namib Bushmen the widow takes in the matter of inheritance precedence over the eldest son.[7] Grenfell says of the Mongwandi of the Upper Mongala region that their tendency towards monogamy " arises partly from the high value—morally and commercially—placed on women," and of the Banza, who " are monogamous in principle," that in their tribe, as an exception, men attend to agriculture and women enjoy generally much consideration.[8] Among the monogamous Moors of the Western Sahara the women exercise a considerable influence over the men, who take great pains

[1] Safford, in *American Anthropologist*, N.S. iv. 716. Concerning the Ladrone Islanders in general Arago says (*op. cit.* ii. 5) that " the women have at all times exercised the greatest influence," and that " the men were in a species of subjection to them." See also Meinicke, *op. cit.* ii. 408.

[2] Malinowski, in *Trans. Roy. Soc. South Australia*, xxxix. 571.
[3] Cooke, in *Smithsonian Report*, 1897, p. 716. See also Geiseler, *op. cit.* p. 41. [4] Johnston, *Uganda Protectorate*, p. 539.
[5] Fritsch, *op. cit.* p. 444.
[6] Kaufmann, in *Mittheil. Deutsch. Schutzgeb.* xxiii. 157.
[7] Trenk, *ibid.* xxiii. 169.
[8] Johnston, *George Grenfell and the Congo*, ii. 676 *sq.*

to pay them homage.[1] Among the Touareg " la femme est l'égale de l'homme, si même, par certains côtés, elle n'est dans une condition meilleure."[2] The Guanches of the Canary Islands treated their women with much respect.[3]

As for other uncivilised peoples who are strictly or almost exclusively monogamous, I can at least say that I am not aware of a single case in which any such people is reported to treat its women badly. It is true that the position of women may be comparatively good also among peoples who are addicted, and even much addicted, to polygyny ; of the highly polygamous Warega, for example, we are told that " les femmes mariées jouissent d'une considération presqu' égale à celle de l'homme."[4] But the case is different with many other peoples who practise polygyny on a large scale. Hence I think we may assume that consideration for the woman's feelings is one cause of monogamy among the lower races, although this consideration itself may be due to circumstances which also in other respects make for mono- gamy, such as scarcity of women or economic conditions unfavourable to polygyny. And there can be no doubt that the same cause has been operating among civilised nations among whom polygyny is forbidden.

Apart from the general regard for the feelings of women, there are in sexual love itself certain elements that tend to make men inclined to restrict themselves to one wife, at least for some time. " The sociable interest," says Bain, " is by its nature diffused : even the maternal feeling admits of plurality of objects ; revenge does not desire to have but one victim ; the love of domination needs many subjects ; but the greatest intensity of love limits the regards to one " The beloved person acquires, in the imagination of the lover, an immeasurable superiority over all others. " The be- ginnings of a special affection," the same psychologist continues, " turn upon a small difference of liking ; but

---

[1] Chavanne, *Die Sahara*, p. 454.

[2] Duveyrier, *Exploration du Sahara*, p. 339. *Cf.* Chavanne, *op. cit.* p. 181 ; Hourst, *Sur le Niger et au pays des Touaregs*, p. 209.

[3] Bory de St. Vincent, *Essais sur les Isles Fortunées*, p. 105. Mantegazza, *Rio de la Plata e Tenerife*, p. 630.

[4] Delhaise, *op. cit.* p. 193. *Cf. ibid.* p. 169.

such differences are easily exaggerated ; the feeling and the estimate acting and re-acting, till the distinction becomes altogether transcendent."[1] This absorbing passion for one is not confined to the human race. Hermann Müller,[2] Brehm,[3] and other good observers have shown that it is experienced by birds ; and Darwin found it among certain domesticated mammals.[4] The love-bird rarely survives the death of its companion, even if supplied with a fresh and suitable mate.[5] M. Houzeau states, on the authority of Frédéric Cuvier :—" Lorsque l'un des ouistitis (*Harpale jacchus*) du Jardin des Plantes de Paris vint à mourir, l'époux survivant fut inconsolable. Il caressa longtemps le cadavre de sa compagne ; et quand à la fin il fut convaincu de la triste réalité, il se mit les mains sur les yeux, et resta sans bouger et sans prendre de nourriture, jusqu'à ce qu'il eût lui-même succombé."[6] In mankind the absorbing passion for one is found not only among civilised but also among savage men and women. Among the Indians of Western Washington and North-Western Oregon " instances are not rare of young women destroying themselves on the death of a lover."[7] Suicide from unsuccessful or disappointed love is by no means infrequent in the savage world, and although apparently more common among women it also occurs in the case of men.[8] In Tahiti unsuccessful suitors

---

[1] Bain, *Emotions and the Will*, p. 136 *sq.*
[2] Müller, *Am Neste*, p. 102.   [3] Brehm, *Bird-Life*, pt. iv. ch. ii.
[4] Darwin, *Descent of Man*, ii. 293 *sqq.*   [5] Brehm, *op. cit.* p. 288 *sq.*
[6] Houzeau, *Études sur les facultés mentales des animaux*, ii. 117.
[7] Gibbs, *loc. cit.* p. 198.
[8] Lasch, ' Der Selbstmord aus erotischen Motiven bei den primitiven Völkern,' in *Zeitschrift für Socialwissenschaft*, ii. 579 *sqq.* Westermarck, *Origin and Development of the Moral Ideas*, ii. 232. See the authorities quoted there, and besides, Kroeber, ' A Mission Record of the California Indians,' in *University of California Publications in American Archæology and Ethnology*, viii. 6 ; Russell, in *Ann. Rep. Bur. Ethnol.* xxvi. 184 (Pima) ; James, *op. cit.* i. 244 (Omaha) ; Waitz, *op. cit.* iii. 102 (North American Indians) ; Moncelon, in *Bull. Soc. d'Anthr. Paris*, ser. iii. vol. ix. 366 (New Caledonians). Ancient love poems of the Tamil allude to the custom of a disappointed lover proclaiming his love in the streets and committing suicide (Kanakasabhai [Pillai], *Tamils Eighteen hundred Years ago*, p. 123).

have been known to take their own lives in despair.[1] In Pentecost, of the New Hebrides, unrequited love has led to suicide or to rapid pining away and death.[2] In Fiji Sir Basil Thomson has " met with several cases of what is called *ndongai*, which corresponds with what is called ' broken heart ' in Europeans. Two young people who have come together once or twice, and who have been suddenly separated, sicken and pine away, and unless their intrigue can be resumed, they do not recover."[3] On the Gold Coast, according to Cruickshank, love " is frequently distinguished by an order and a constancy full of distracting fears and doubts, and seeks its gratification, regardless of the greatest sacrifices. The African rushes into battle, shouting the name of his lady-love to inspire him to deeds of daring ; the canoeman gives additional vigour to the stroke of his paddle at the mention of her name ; the weary hammock-bearer plucks up a new spirit through the same all-powerful spell, and the solitary wayfarer beguiles the tediousness of his journey by a song in her praise." And the obstacles thrown in the way of the union of the lovers occasionally lead to very disastrous consequences, such as suicide.[4] Davis tells us of a negro who after vain attempts to redeem his sweetheart from slavery became a slave himself rather than be separated from her.[5] Dalton represents the Pahária lads and lasses as forming very romantic attachments : " if separated only for an hour," he says, " they are miserable."[6] Curr speaks in his recollections of squatting in Victoria of a native youth who had lost his heart to a girl, and says that this set him thinking " of how little real difference there is in the feelings of men."[7] And the rude Australian girl sings in a strain of romantic affliction, " I never shall see my darling again."[8] But although the absorbing character

---

[1] Wilkes, *op. cit.* iv. 45. Seemann, *Viti*, p. 192. Ellis, *Polynesian Researches*, i. 267.

[2] Speiser, *op. cit.* p. 235.   [3] Thomson, *Fijians*, p. 241.

[4] Cruickshank, *Eighteen Years on the Gold Coast of Africa*, ii. 207 sqq.

[5] Waitz, *op. cit.* ii. 117.   [6] Dalton, *op. cit.* p. 273.

[7] Curr, *Recollections of Squatting in Victoria*, p. 145.

[8] Waitz-Gerland, *op. cit.* vi. 756.

of his love prevents a man for some time from taking
another wife, it does not necessarily prevent his doing so
for long. Sensual love is fickle ; it is dominated by the
desire for change. On the other hand, when love implies
sympathy and affection arising from mental qualities there
is a tie between husband and wife which lasts long after youth
and beauty are gone. This leads to a monogamy that is
enduring.

Monogamy is the only form of marriage that is permitted
among every people. Wherever we find polygyny, polyandry, or group-marriage, we find monogamy side by side
with it. On the other hand, it is also in many cases the
only form of marriage which is permitted by custom or law.
This may be due to the mere force of habit ; or, possibly,
to the notion that some men must not appropriate a plurality
of wives when others in consequence can get none at all ;
or to the feeling that polygyny is an offence against the
female sex ; or to the condemnation of lust. As regards
the obligatory monogamy of Christian nations, we have to
remember not only that monogamy was the exclusive form
of marriage recognised in the societies on which Christianity
was first engrafted, but that polygyny was hardly compatible
with the spirit of a religion which regarded every gratification of the sexual impulse with suspicion and incontinence
as the gravest sin. In its early days the Church showed little
respect for women, but its horror of sensuality was immense.

Our examination into the causes of monogamy and
polygyny makes it possible for us to explain why progress
in civilisation up to a certain point has proved favourable
to polygyny, whilst in its highest forms it leads to monogamy.
The first tendency is, as we have seen, largely due to economic
and social circumstances—the accumulation and unequal
distribution of wealth and increasing social differentiation ;
but it should also be noticed that the considerable surplus
of females which among many of the higher savages is caused
by their wars is not found at the lowest stages of civilisation, where war does not seriously disturb the proportion
of the sexes. The retrograde tendency towards monogamy
in the highest grades of culture, again, may be traced to a

variety of causes. No superstitious beliefs keep civilised men apart from their wives during pregnancy and for a long time after child-birth. The desire for offspring has become less intense. A large family, instead of being a help in the struggle for existence, is often considered an insufferable burden. A man's kinsfolk are no longer his only friends, and his wealth and influence do not depend upon the number of his wives and children. A wife ceases to be a mere labourer, and manual labour is to a large extent replaced by the work of domesticated animals and the use of implements and machines.[1] The sentiment of love has become more refined and, in consequence, more enduring. To a cultivated mind youth and beauty are by no means the only attractions of a woman, and besides, civilisation has given female beauty a new lease of life. The feelings of the weaker sex are held in higher regard, and the causes which may make polygyny desired by the women themselves no longer exist. The better education bestowed on them, and other factors in modern civilisation, enable them to live comfortably without the support of a husband.

Will monogamy be the only recognised form of marriage in the future ? This question has been answered in different ways. According to Spencer, " the monogamic form of the sexual relation is manifestly the ultimate form ; and any changes to be anticipated must be in the direction of completion and extension of it."[2] Dr. Le Bon, on the other hand, thinks that European laws will in the future legalise polygyny ;[3] and M. Letourneau remarks that although we may now look upon monogamy as superior to any other form of marriage yet known, " we need not consider it the Ultima Thule in the evolution of connubial ceremonies."[4]

[1] Among the Bechuanas, says Mr. Conder (' Present Condition of the Native Tribes in Bechuanaland,' in *Jour. Anthr. Inst.* xvi. 86), a man became in former days richer the more wives he had because they used to hoe his mealies ; " now, however, ploughs have been introduced, and the men take pride in driving a team of eight oxen in a plough."

[2] Spencer, *Principles of Sociology*, i. 752.

[3] Le Bon, *La civilisation des Arabes*, p. 424.

[4] Letourneau, *Sociology*, p. 378.

Professor v. Ehrenfels even regards the adoption of polygyny as necessary for the preservation of the Aryan race.[1]   Yet I think we may without hesitation assert that if mankind will advance in the same direction as hitherto, if consequently the causes to which monogamy in the most progressive societies owes its origin will continue to operate with constantly growing force, if especially the regard for the feelings of women, and the women's influence on legislation, will increase, the laws of monogamy are not likely to be changed.   It is certainly difficult to imagine a time when Western civilisation would legalise the marriage of one man with several women simultaneously.

[1] v. Ehrenfels, ' Die konstitutive Verderblichkeit der Monogamie und die Unententbehrlichkeit einer Sexualreform,' in *Archiv f. Rassen- und Gesellschafts-Biologie*, iv. 615–651, 803 *sqq. Idem*, ' Erwiderung auf Dr. A. Ploetz' Bemerkungen zu meiner Abhandlung über die konstitutive Verderblichkeit der Monogamie,' *ibid.* v. 97 *sqq.*

CHAPTER XXIX

POLYANDRY

POLYANDRY is a much rarer form of marriage than polygyny.

Cases of it have been noticed in America. Among the Avanoes and Maypures, along the Orinoco, v. Humboldt found that brothers often had but one wife.[1] The same is the case among the Maquiritarés, the eldest brother, who is called " chief," being strictly obeyed by the others.[2] A Warrau of British Guiana, on being asked why a man should have two wives and a woman not be allowed two husbands, " directly said that his tribe did not consider either practice to be bad ; and that he knew a Warau woman who had three."[3] Among the Roucouyennes in French Guiana, according to M. Coudreau, " la polyandrie demi-avouée est fréquente, la polyandrie ouvertement affichée n'est pas rare."[4] Mr. Simson mentions the occurrence of polyandry among the Záparo Indians of Ecuador ; two men, whom he selected to be his travelling companions, had five wives—two each and one in common.[5] The Cañaris Indians of Quito traced their descent from a mythical bird with the face of a woman, who had commerce with two men who were brothers, and gave in consequence birth to six sons and daughters, the ancestors of the tribe.[6] Mr. Grubb observes that on the

---

[1] v. Humboldt, *Personal Narrative of Travels*, v. 549.
[2] Chaffanjon, *L'Orénoque et le Caura*, p. 283 *sq.*
[3] Brett, *Indian Tribes of Guiana*, p. 178.
[4] Coudreau, *Chez nos Indiens*, p. 132.
[5] Simson, *Travels in the Wilds of Ecuador*, pp. 173, 178.
[6] *Narratives of the Rites and Laws of the Yncas*, p. 8 *sq.*

frontiers of the Paraguayan Chaco polyandry is sometimes met with. Among the Lengua Indians he found one instance of it, namely, in the case of a woman exceedingly capable and intelligent, but of an exceptionally wayward disposition, who had two husbands living in different parts of the country. Her conduct, however, was strongly condemned, especially by the women of her tribe, and she was eventually forced to content herself with the senior husband.[1]

Father Lafitau wrote, " Par une suite de la Ginécocratie, la Polygamie, qui n'est pas permise aux hommes, l'est pourtant aux femmes chez les Iroquois Tsonnontouans (that is, the Seneca tribe of the Iroquois), où il en est, lesquelles ont deux maris, qu'on regarde comme légitimes."[2] Among the Cree it often happened that when a man was in love with the wife of a friend, he told the husband about it, with the result that the latter, if he was fond of him, proposed that they should become " brothers in love," which implied that the other man had access to his wife.[3] Polyandry has been found among some of the Eskimo. Nils Egede mentions the case of a Greenland woman who had two husbands, but both she and they were *angekoks ;*[4] and Cranz, in his description of the Greenlanders, speaks of " women who cohabit with several husbands," though he says that such women are subjected to universal censure.[5] A Netchilirmiut informed Ross that he and his half-brother had but one wife between them ; and unions of this kind seem to have been held quite justifiable among his people, although they were not very common.[6] Of the Western Eskimo Seemann states that " two men sometimes marry the same woman."[7] Veniaminoff tells us that in ancient

[1] Grubb, *An Unknown People in an Unknown Land,* p. 215 *sq.*
[2] Lafitau, *Mœurs des sauvages amériquains,* i. 555. See also Charlevoix, *Voyage to North-America,* ii. 36.
[3] Leden, ' Unter den Indianern Canadas,' in *Zeitschr. f. Ethnol.* xliv. 824.   [4] Nansen, *Eskimo Life,* p. 145. *Cf. infra,* p. 194 *sq.*
[5] Cranz, *History of Greenland,* i. 147.
[6] Ross, *Second Voyage in search of a North-West Passage,* p. 356. See also *ibid.* p. 373, and *infra,* p. 195.
[7] Seemann, *Voyage of Herald,* ii. 66.

times a Tlingit woman, besides her real husband, could
have a legal paramour, who usually was the brother of the
husband.[1] Erman speaks of "lawful polyandry" among
the Aleut,[2] as also of the right of certain married women
to have intercourse for a time with another man besides
their real husband. These secondary unions were originally
formed with hunters or traders of their own tribe who visited
their island, but were subsequently extended to Russians
living in the same place, who in return had to contribute
to the maintenance of the family ; and since then such
a paramour was called by the Russian name *polovinshchik*,
meaning "half-partner."[3] Langsdorf states that in Una-
laska, one of the Aleutian Islands, a woman sometimes
"lives with two husbands, who agree among themselves
upon the conditions on which they are to share her."[4]
Among the Kaniagmiut two or even three men sometimes
lived with one wife, "without suspicion or jealousy ";[5] but
the second husband (and presumably the third also) was
only a deputy who acted as husband and master of the
house during the absence of the true lord, and on the latter's
return not only yielded to him his place but became in the
meantime his servant.[6]

Among the Chukchee, who occupy the north-eastern
extremity of Asia, there are group-relations, of which I
shall speak in a subsequent chapter, but sometimes also
unions of a polyandrous character. Married men among
them are generally reluctant to make bachelors their
"companions in wives," since the bachelor only gains from
entering the union and gives nothing in return ; but if a

---

[1] Holmberg, 'Ethnographische Skizzen über die Völker des
russischen Amerika,' in *Acta Soc. Scien. Fennicae*, iv. 315 *sq.* Dall,
Alaska, p. 416.

[2] Erman, *Travels in Siberia*, p. 531 note.

[3] *Idem*, 'Ethnographische Wahrnehmungen und Erfahrungen
an den Küsten des Berings-Meeres,' in *Zeitschr. f. Ethnol.* iii. 163.

[4] v. Langsdorf, *Voyages and Travels*, ii. 47. Christianity, however, has extirpated this custom among the Aleut (v. Hellwald, ' Das
Volk der Aleuten,' in *Das Ausland*, liv. 792).

[5] Coxe, *Russian Discoveries between Asia and America*, p. 300.

[6] Erman, in *Zeitschr. f. Ethnol.* iii. 163. Holmberg, *loc. cit.*
p. 399.

married man has no children and desires to have some, he may for that reason be anxious to make a union with a strong single man, who thus becomes, not a husband in the proper sense of the word, but a " companion."[1] Sternberg tells us that among the Gilyak custom permits the younger brother to have intercourse with the elder brother's wife during her husband's absence, although it, nowadays at least, forbids the converse ; if the husband finds his younger brother with his wife, only the expression of his face reveals that he is not indifferent, as he cannot take action.[2] Maksimoff, however, questions whether the younger brother really has a right to cohabit with his sister-in-law, though intercourse between them is considered less blameworthy than adultery with a stranger.[3] But we hear from another source that polyandry prevails among the Smerenkur Gilyak ;[4] and among the Ainu occasional cases of it occur in districts bordering on Gilyak territory, though it is unknown among them elsewhere.[5]

In earlier editions of Strabo's 'Geography' polyandry is said to have existed among the mountaineers of Media.[6] This statement has been altered by certain editors so as to imply polygyny instead of polyandry,[7] but, as it seems, for no good reason.   A Chinese writer of the thirteenth century, Ma-touan-lin, states that among the Getae and the Massagetae of Turkestan it was the custom for brothers to have one wife between them.   Of the latter it is said that the children born of these unions belonged to the eldest brother ; and that if a man had no brothers, he associated with other

---

[1] Bogoras, *Chukchee*, p. 603 *sq.*

[2] Sternberg, quoted by Miss Czaplicka, *Aboriginal Siberia*, p. 99 *sq.* *Idem*, reviewed in *L'Anthropologie*, v. 342.   Bogoras, *op. cit.* p. 608.

[3] Miss Czaplicka, *op. cit.* p. 100 n. 2.

[4] Ravenstein, *Russians on the Amur*, p. 391.

[5] Miss Czaplicka, *op. cit.* p. 104.

[6] Strabo, *Geographica*, xi. 13. 11.

[7] Strabo's *Geographica* edited by C. Müller and F. Dübner, pp. 451, 1018.   The same work edited by Meineke, ii. 740.   See also the German translation by Groskurd, ii. 428 n. 1, and the French translation by Tardieu, ii. 456.   The former defends the alteration by the curious argument that polyandry is unheard of in the East.

men, since elsewise he was compelled to live singly through-out his life.[1] The Arabic traveller Alberuni wrote in the eleventh century that the people inhabiting the mountains stretching from the region of Panchîr into the neighbourhood of Kashmir lived under the rule that several brothers had one wife in common.[2] Dr. Sachau observes that the author meant the alpine countries of the Hindu-Kush between Kashmir and a line from Faizabad to Kabul, *i.e.*, the Hazâra country, Svât, Citrâl, and Kafiristan.[3]

In Tibet polyandry has prevailed from time immemorial ; and it is still very common there, although it is said to have been even more common in former days than it is now.[4] According to Ahmad Shah, " polyandry in Tibet is much more nearly universal than polygamy in any Mohammadan land," and, though all the forms of marriage co-exist, " the right thing there is polyandry."[5] It is obviously more frequent in certain parts of the country than in others.[6] According to Rockhill, it exists only in agricultural districts, being unknown among the nomads ;[7] whereas Baber asserts that polygyny obtains in the valley farms and polyandry among the shepherds of the uplands.[8] The former was frequently told by Tibetans that polyandry did not exist to any great extent among the better classes of society ;[9] and many learned and worthy lamas assured him " that it is a sinful practice, solely attributable to the very lax morality of the people, and by no means a recog-

[1] Rémusat, *Nouveaux mélanges asiatiques*, i. 240, 241, 245.
[2] *Alberuni's India*, i. 108.   [3] *Ibid.* ii. 295.
[4] Puini, *Il Tibet secondo la relazione del viaggio del P. Ippolito Desideri* (1715–1721), p. 148.
[5] Ahmad Shah, *Four Years in Tibet*, p. 52.
[6] See Sarat Chandra Das, *Journey to Lhasa and Central Tibet*, p. 327 ; Puini, *op. cit.* p. 147.
[7] Rockhill, *Land of the Lamas*, p. 211 *sq.*
[8] Baber, ' Travels and Researches in the Interior of China,' in *Roy. Geo. Soc. Supplementary Papers*, i. 97. See also Talboys Wheeler, *History of India*, i. 116 ; Waddell, *Among the Himalayas*, p. 197. According to Mr. Kingdon Ward (*Land of the Blue Poppy*, p. 57), polygyny is common in Eastern Tibet.
[9] Rockhill, ' Tibet,' in *Jour. Roy. Asiatic Soc.* N.S. xxiii. 230 n. 2. See also Grenard, *Tibet*, p. 257.

nised institution "—an opinion which was also held by the
early Christian missionaries in the country.[1] Orazio Penna,
who was in Lhasa about 1740, states that noble and well-
to-do men generally have one wife each, and a few of them
even more than one ;[2] at present polygyny is confined to
the wealthier class, principally the chiefs,[3] and men whose
first wife has proved barren.[4] That polyandry mainly
prevails among the poorer people is also suggested by statements like these, that " if his means admit of such a luxury,
a man takes a wife to himself,"[5] and that " any casual
influx of wealth, as from trade or other sources, immediately
leads to the formation of separate establishments by the
several members of a house."[6] But, on the other hand,
we hear from Turner, who visited Tibet in the latter part of
the eighteenth century, that polyandry was also found
frequently in the most opulent families,[7] and from Mr.
Andrew Wilson that it prevailed among all classes, being
superseded by polygyny only where the people were a good
deal in contact with either Hindus or Muhammadans.[8]

In Tibet the husbands are as a rule brothers. The
choice of the wife is the right of the elder brother, and the
contract he makes is understood to involve a marital contract with all the other brothers as well, if they choose to

---

[1] Rockhill, *Land of the Lamas*, p. 213 n. 3. See also Grenard, *op.
cit.* p. 257. Orazio Penna di Billi (*Breve notizia del regno del Thibet,*
p. 71) says, " Circa li maritaggi tra le persone non molto comode
vi è un pessimo abuso, non però ordinato dalla legge, ma introdotto
dall' abuso, che quanti fratelli sono in una casa pigliano una sol
moglie per tutti."

[2] Penna di Billi, *op. cit.* p. 71.   So also Antonio Georgi says, in
his *Alphabetum Tibetanum* (quoted by Puini, *op. cit.* p. 139), " Ab hoc
turpitudinis genere alieni sunt viri nobiles, et cives honesti."

[3] Rockhill, *Land of the Lamas*, p. 212 *sqq.   Idem,* in Sarat Chandra
Das, *op. cit.* p. 216 n. 1.   *Cf.* Desgodins, *Le Thibet d'après la correspondance des missionaires,* p. 244 ; Bonvalot, *Across Thibet,* ii. 126.

[4] Ahmad Shah, *op. cit.* p. 54.

[5] Bonvalot, *op. cit.* ii. 126. See also Desideri, in Puini, *op. cit.*
p. 132.

[6] Cunningham, *History of the Sikhs,* p. 18.

[7] Turner, *Embassy to the Court of the Teshoo Lama,* p. 349.

[8] Wilson, *Abode of Snow,* p. 209.

avail themselves of it.[1]   Yet in Eastern Tibet and Sikkim, according to Mr. Earle, it does not necessarily follow that the wife will cohabit with all the younger brothers ; " she exercises much liberty in this respect, and it will depend upon her pleasure as to whether she will cohabit with any particular younger brother." The same authority adds that " if the eldest brother of a group of brothers does not marry, but the second or third brother does so, then the wife will be the common wife of such second or third brother and his younger brothers only.   Elder brothers, in such cases, will separate and leave the family, having no claim on the wives of the younger brothers."[2]   In many parts of the country, however, the husbands are not necessarily brothers.   Thus Mr. Earle informs us that in Eastern Tibet, as well as in Sikkim, cousins, both on the father's and mother's side, and half-brothers may be admitted as members of the group, though only if the husband agrees and has no brothers of his own.[3]   The Abbé Desgodins speaks of *proches parents*, or near relatives in general, as well as brothers, being co-husbands in the east part of the country.[4] According to Sarat Chandra Das, who visited Lhasa and Central Tibet, " it is not unusual for a father or uncle to live with his son's or nephew's wife, and even in high life a father makes himself a partner in the marital rights over his son's wife."[5]   Mr. Sherring mentions a viceroy of Gartok, the capital of Western Tibet, who on the loss of his own wife became a joint husband of his son's ; and he adds that it is apparently an orthodox custom in Tibet for father and sons to share the same wife, the only condition being that she shall not be the son's mother.[6]   Du Halde wrote that husbands were " d'ordinaire de la même

---

[1] Desideri, in Puini, *op. cit.* p. 131.   Wilson, *op. cit.* p. 214. Ahmad Shah, *op. cit.* p. 52.   Grenard, *op. cit.* p. 253.

[2] Earle, quoted by Risley, *People of India*, p. 211.

[3] *Ibid.* p. 211.   [4] Desgodins, *op. cit.* p. 244.

[5] Sarat Chandra Das, *op. cit.* p. 327.   With reference to this statement Rockhill remarks (*ibid.* p. 327 n. 2) that he hardly imagines that the author intends to convey the idea that such an arrangement is a custom of the Tibetans.

[6] Sherring, *Western Tibet and the British Borderland*, p. 305.

famille,"[1] which seems to imply that they were not always so. Sarat Chandra Das had a guide whose wife was also married to another man not at all related to him ; but he called him by a term meaning " joint brother."[2] Grenard states that a Tibetan who is unable to have a child by his wife or wives sometimes introduces a stranger into his house and charges him to perpetuate his line in his place and stead ; " in reality, this stranger becomes a conventional brother, having the same rights as a brother born."[3] According to Bonvalot's description of polyandry at Seresumdo, any young men who are desirous of sharing the first husband's happiness may present themselves, and " if terms can be arranged, take their place, too, around the family hearth, thus becoming members of the household and co-husbands."[4]

The number of husbands depends, of course, in the first place on the number of brothers. In the neighbourhood of Teshoo Loomboo a family residence was pointed out to Turner in which five brothers were living together very happily with one woman.[5] Wilson once met a family where the number of brother-husbands was six, though the youngest of them was only a boy. Instances of three and five husbands were not uncommon ; " but," he says, " without having gone rigidly into the matter, I should say that the most instances of polyandry were those of two husbands, and that, not because there was any objection to five or six, but simply because no greater number of brothers was usually to be found in a family."[6]

All the husbands live together with their common wife as members of the same household. Indeed, according

---

[1] Du Halde, *Description de l'Empire de la Chine*, iv. 572.
[2] Sarat Chandra Das, *op. cit.* p. 285 *sq.*   See also *ibid.* p. 311.
[3] Grenard, *op. cit.* p. 260.
[4] Bonvalot, *op. cit.* ii. 124 *sq.*   Ahmad Shah (*op. cit.* p. 52 *sq.*) even tells us that a woman cannot have more than three husbands from the same family, though if she wants to have a fourth husband—which rarely happens—she may solicit him from outside the family circle ; but this statement probably refers to Ladakh (see *infra,* p. 121).
[5] Turner, *op. cit.* p. 349   [6] Wilson. *op. cit.* p. 210.

to Sarat Chandra Das, " the wife is claimed by the younger
brothers as their wife only so long as they continue to live
with the eldest one. When they separate from their eldest
brother, they cannot ask him to pay compensation for their
share in the wife, and she remains the lawful wife of the
eldest brother."[1] But according to M. Grenard, a brother
who leaves the paternal roof and settles down apart to
live on his own industry still retains his rights over the
wife of his brothers as over the paternal inheritance,
although *they* have no rights over the wife whom he
introduces into his new home ; she belongs to him alone,
because she does not live on the property of the family.[2]
Yet even when members of the same household, the brothers
are not generally at home together,[3] and in any case some
arrangement seems to be made to secure to every one his
proper share. In Eastern Tibet, according to Mr. Kingdon
Ward, each husband lives with the wife for a month or more
at a time, and signalises the fact that he is in possession of
her by hanging his boots up outside the door.[4]

As regards the sons born of these marriages Desideri
states that they are called the sons of the eldest brother-
husband and the nephews of the other ones.[5] Other
authorities inform us that the children call the eldest husband " father " and the others " younger " or " little
fathers."[6] According to Du Halde, " on partage les enfans,
en donnant à l'aîné le premier qui vient au monde, et aux
cadets ceux qui naissent dans la suite."[7] Orazio Penna
says that when a child is born it is attributed to him
by whom the mother asserts that she has conceived it.[8]

[1] Sarat Chandra Das, *op. cit.* p. 327.   [2] Grenard, *op. cit.* p. 256.
[3] See *infra*, p. 192.   [4] Kingdon Ward, *op. cit.* p. 57.
[5] Desideri, in Puini, *op. cit.* p. 131.   In a Chinese work it is said
that " when a child has grown up, he is taken by one of the brothers,
the other brothers being considered its uncles " (Rockhill, in *Jour.
Roy. Asiatic Soc.* N.S. xxiii. 231 n. 1).
[6] Ahmad Shah, *op. cit.* p. 53.   Sherring, *op. cit.* p. 305 *sq.*
[7] Du Halde, *op. cit.* iv. 572.   The same statement is made by
Grosier, *General Description of China*, i. 322.   According to a Chinese
work, the children are divided by choice among the husbands
(Wilson, *op. cit.* p. 211 n. †; Rockhill, in *Jour. Roy. Asiatic Soc.*
N.S. xxiii. 230).   [8] Penna di Billi, *op. cit.* p. 71.

According to Rockhill, the offspring " treat as father whomever their mother teaches them to recognise by that name," and call the other husbands uncles.[1] Wilson tells us that " there is no noticeable difference in the relationship of a child to his different fathers."[2]

With reference to Eastern Tibet and Sikkim Mr. Earle writes :—" If the eldest brother (i.e., the real husband) dies, the wife passes to one of the younger brothers according to her own selection. Should her choice fall on the next brother, she will still be the common wife of the younger brothers. Should, however, she select any of the younger brothers, she will be the common wife only of those younger than him, and, if he be the youngest, she will be his wife only."[3]

Fraternal polyandry is more or less common in vast districts of the Himalayan region from Assam to the dependencies of Kashmir, chiefly among people of Tibetan affinities. It is found among the Hill Miris,[4] Daflas,[5] and Sissee Abors[6] on the northern frontier of Assam. The Khasis of Assam have also been charged with the practice of polyandry, but according to Captain Fisher it is disclaimed by the upper classes among them, and with the poorer sort too " it would often seem to mean rather facility of divorce than the simultaneous admission of a plurality of husbands."[7] Major Gurdon says that they at the present day are monandrists, and that there is no evidence to show that polyandry ever existed amongst them.[8] In Bhutan, in the Eastern Himalayas, fraternal polyandry prevails chiefly in the northern and central parts of the country, which are nearest to Tibet ;[9] and polygyny is found only

---

[1] Rockhill, *Land of the Lamas*, p. 212 *sq.*

[2] Wilson, *op. cit.* p. 212.

[3] Earle, quoted by Risley, *op. cit.* p. 211.

[4] Dalton, *Descriptive Ethnology of Bengal*, p. 33.

[5] *Ibid.* p. 36.   [6] Rowney, *Wild Tribes of India*, p. 158.

[7] Fisher, ' Memoir of Sylhet,' in *Jour. Asiatic Soc. Bengal*, vol. ix. pt. ii. 834.

[8] Gurdon, *Khasis*, p. 77.

[9] Pemberton, *Report on Bootan*, p. 116. See also Dalton, *op. cit.* p. 98 ; White, *Sikhim and Bhutan*, p. 320.

amongst the rich.[1] According to Mr. Wilson polyandry does not exist in Sikkim,[2] but from accounts given by Mr. Claude White, late Political Agent in Sikkim,[3] and Mr. Earle, late Deputy-Commissioner of Darjeeling,[4] I gather that it is frequently practised there. Among the Lepchas, a Mongolian tribe of Sikkim, Western Bhutan, Eastern Nepal, and Darjeeling, polyandry, though comparatively rare, is not entirely unknown, the younger brothers sharing the favours of the eldest brother's wife.[5] Vigne observes that among some of the natives of alpine Bengal one woman is married to a whole family of brothers ;[6] but in the Darjeeling district, according to Mr. Earle, there are instances of a number of men, not brothers or near relations, taking a wife between them, although this appears to be a novel practice introduced for purposes of economy.[7]

Polyandry of the fraternal type is practised in various parts of the Punjab, such as Sirmur,[8] the Jounsar and Bawar hill districts east of Sirmur,[9] the Kanawar subdivision of Bashahr State,[10] Kotgarh in Simla District,[11] and the Kulu subdivision of Kangra District,[12] especially Lahul.[13]

---

[1] Risley and Gait, Census of India, 1901, vol. i. (India) Report, p. 448.
[2] Wilson, op. cit. p. 207.   [3] White, op. cit. p. 320.
[4] Earle, quoted by Risley, People of India, p. 211.
[5] Risley, Tribes and Castes of Bengal. Ethnographic Glossary, ii. 9.
[6] Vigne, Travels in Kashmir, i. 37.
[7] Earle, quoted by Risley, People of India, p. 211.
[8] Fraser, Tour through Part of the Snowy Range of the Himālā Mountains, p. 207 sqq.   Balfour, Cyclopædia of India, iii. 246.
[9] Dunlop, Hunting in the Himalaya, p. 180 sq.
[10] Rebsch, quoted by Stulpnagel, ' Polyandry in the Himâlayas,' in Indian Antiquary, vii. 134. Miss Gordon Cumming, In the Himalayas, p. 406. Pandit Harikishan Kaul, Census of India, 1911, vol. xiv. (Punjab) Report, p. 289.
[11] Stulpnagel, loc. cit. pp. 133, 135.
[12] Harcourt, Himalayan Districts of Kooloo, Lahoul, and Spiti, p. 241. Ujfalvy, Aus dem westlichen Himalaja, p. 35 sqq. Calvert, Vazeeri Rupi, p. 32. Pandit Harikishan Kaul, op. cit. pp. 287, 289.
[13] Harcourt, op. cit. pp. 242, 304. Ujfalvy, op. cit. p. 36. In his report on Spiti, Captain Hay says that polyandry was in full force in that canton. Harcourt (op. cit. p. 242) denies the accuracy of this statement, whilst Ujfalvy (op. cit. p. 36) thinks that its existence

According to Mr. Pandit Harikishan Kaul, " the custom is common among the Kanets of the higher hills, but the lower castes also practise it, and the Rajputs and other castes residing in the tracts where this custom is prevalent also appear to have been influenced by it."[1] Masson wrote in 1842 that it was no unusual arrangement among the Sikhs for the brothers of a family to have a wife in common ; he knew soldiers requesting permission to visit their homes, alleging that their brothers had gone on a journey and their wives were alone, and the plea was considered a good one.[2] The Jâts in some of the eastern Punjab districts are stated to have followed the same custom, though without full recognition ; but inquiries show that it has completely died out among them.[3] The Khokhars of the Punjab practised polyandry before they embraced Islam.[4] Dr. Stulpnagel says that most of the cases of polyandry in the villages of the Kotgarh district, and in Bussahir and Kulu, are found among the well-to-do people, whereas the poor prefer polygyny, on account of the value of the women as household drudges ;[5] but this is certainly not true of those parts of Lahul where brothers prefer to have separate wives, since there " nearly all the men in the higher class are polygamists." [6]

In polyandrous families in the Punjab all the brothers have usually one joint wife, and as a general rule the husbands must be full brothers.[7] Yet sometimes step-brothers and cousins who are on as intimate terms as full brothers are allowed to share the common wife ; and in rare cases even persons belonging to different families marry a joint wife in Spiti is probable, though not proved. But Mr. Pandit Harikishan Kaul (*op. cit.* p. 289) affirms that it occurs there ; and Mr. Hose mentions a case within his own experience, where two Spiti men not related took a common wife, made their land joint, and " became brothers " (Risley and Gait, *op. cit.* p. 448 n. *).

[1] Pandit Harikishan Kaul, *op. cit.* p. 287.
[2] Masson, *Narrative of Journeys in Balochistan*, i. 435.
[3] Pandit Harikishan Kaul, *op. cit.* p. 289.
[4] Elliot, *History of India*, viii. 202. See *infra*, p. 119 n. 4.
[5] Stulpnagel, *loc. cit.* p. 135.   [6] Harcourt, *op. cit.* p. 242.
[7] Durga Singh, ' Report on the Panjab Hill Tribes,' in *Indian Antiquary*, xxxvi. 277.

by agreement, and merge their separate properties into a
joint holding.[1] The rule about access to the wife differs
in different places in the Punjab. " The elder brother usually
has the preference, and it is only in his absence that the
younger brother can enjoy her company. But where the
younger brothers go out for trade or on other business and
one of them comes back periodically, the eldest brother
allows him the exclusive use of the wife during his short
visit. Where, however, all the brothers stay at home,
the wife not unfrequently bestows her favours on all of them
equally, by turn, one evening being reserved for each. The
house usually has two rooms, one for the wife and the other
for the husbands."[2] In Kulu, according to Ujfalvy, when
parents sell a daughter to several brothers, she belongs
during the first month to the eldest brother, during the second
to the next eldest, and so on.[3] We are often told that when
one brother goes into the wife's room, he leaves his shoes
or hat at the door, which is equivalent to the notice " engaged "; and if another brother wishes to visit the wife,
he has, on seeing the signal, to return to the men's apart-
ment.[4] " All the sons of the wife by whichsoever husband
begotten, are generally called the sons of the eldest brother,
but the son calls all the husbands of his mother, as his
fathers. Indeed, the larger the number of fathers, the
prouder the son feels."[5] In Kulu the children speak of

---

[1] Pandit Harikishan Kaul, *op. cit.* p. 287. Risley and Gait,
op. cit. p. 448 n. *   [2] Pandit Harikishan Kaul, *op. cit.* p. 287.

[3] Ujfalvy, in *Bull. Soc. d'Anthr. Paris*, ser. iii. vol. v. 227.

[4] Pandit Harikishan Kaul, *op. cit.* p. 287. Ujfalvy, *Aus dem
westlichen Himalaja*, p. 36 (Kulu). Kirkpatrick, ' Polyandry in the
Panjâb,' in *Indian Antiquary*, vii. 86 (Jâts). Ghula'm Ba'sit also
tells us of the Khokhars of the Punjab that " when one husband
went into the house of the woman, he left something at the door
as a signal " (Elliot, *op. cit.* viii. 202 ; see also the description of
polyandry in Ferishta's *History of the Rise of the Mahomedan
Power in India*, i. 184, which seems to refer to the Khokhars and
not to the Gakkars, who settled in the Punjab at a later date [Rose,
' The Khokhars and the Gakkars in Panjab History,' in *Indian
Antiquary*, xxxvi. 1]).

[5] Pandit Harikishan Kaul, *op. cit.* p. 287. See also Dunlop,
op. cit. p. 181 (Jounsar).

an " elder " and a " younger " father.[1]   In Sirmur " the
first born child is the property of the elder brother, and the
next in succession are supplied in turn."[2]   Sometimes the
wife is permitted to name the father of each boy, and if she is
not particularly scrupulous, she names each time the richest
of the brothers as the father.[3]

An interesting form of polyandry prevails in Ladakh,
now politically a division of the Kashmir State, with a
population of the Tibetan stock.   Mr. Knight gives the
following account of it.   As soon as the eldest son of a family
marries, he enters into possession of the family estate, a
small portion only being retained by his parents for the
support of themselves and their unmarried daughters.
The eldest son is then obliged to support the two sons next
to himself in age ; and these two are not allowed to contract
independent marriages, but share the wife of their eldest
brother, becoming the minor husbands of the lady.   If
there are more brothers than two, the others do not share
the family wife, but have to leave the estate and seek their
fortune outside, becoming lamas, or earning their living by
working as coolies, or, if they be fortunate, as *magpas*—
a term which will be soon explained.   The two younger
brothers, though minor husbands to the wife, are always
in an inferior position, and are often little better than
servants to the eldest brother, who is looked upon as the
sole owner of the property by the Kashmir State.   According
to Moorcroft and Trebeck, the younger brothers can even be
turned out of doors at his pleasure, without its being incumbent upon him to provide for them.[4]   The children of
this polyandrous marriage recognise all three husbands as
fathers, but pay most respect to the eldest, as the head of
the family ; according to Drew, they speak of their elder
and their younger fathers,[5] according to Bellew, they take

[1] Ujfalvy, *Aus dem westlichen Himalaja*, p. 36.

[2] Fraser, *op. cit.* p. 209.   See also Pandit Harikishan Kaul, *op. cit.*
p. 287.

[3] Pandit Harikishan Kaul, *op. cit.* p. 287.

[4] Moorcroft and Trebeck, *Travels in the Himalayan Provinces of
Hindustan and the Panjab*, i. 322.

[5] Drew *Jummoo and Kashmir Territories*, p. 251.

the name of the eldest husband.[1] If the eldest brother dies,
the wife, provided she has no children, can rid herself of
his brothers, who are her minor husbands, by a simple
ceremony. One of her fingers is attached with a thread to
a finger of her dead husband. The thread is then broken,
and by this action she is divorced from the corpse, and
consequently from the two surviving brothers at the same
time.

But besides being married to the three brothers, a wife
can in Ladakh, if she prefers it—and she generally does
prefer it,—enter into another marriage contract, with a
man from a different family. She selects some well-formed
young man, who has at least three elder brothers and therefore has no interest in the lands of his family or share in his
eldest brother's wife, and makes this person her *magpa*,
as this sort of husband is called. The *magpa* husband of an
heiress must behave himself if he wishes to retain his position.
He is the property of his wife, and cannot leave her, except
in the case of gross misconduct on her part. But if she is
displeased with him, she can turn him out of doors, and be
rid of him without any excuse or form of divorce. She
generally gives him a sheep or a few rupees when thus dis-
charging him ; and she is then quite free to take unto herself
another *magpa*.[2] Drew also speaks of the wife's right of
choosing an additional husband from a different family,
and mentions instances in which women who were married
to two or perhaps three brothers availed themselves of the
privilege ; but he has also known cases of four brothers
becoming husbands to the same wife, and believes that there
is no limit to the number of such husbands.[3] According to
Ujfalvy, a woman who is married to four or five brothers
is allowed to choose a fifth or sixth husband after her own
pleasure.[4] Cunningham, on the other hand, states that
polyandry in Ladakh is strictly confined to brothers, and
that the most usual number of husbands is two, although

[1] Bellew, *Kashmir and Kashghar*, p. 118.
[2] Knight, *Where Three Empires meet*, p. 138 *sqq.*
[3] Drew, *op. cit.* p. 250 *sq.*
[4] Ujfalvy, *Aus dem westlichen Himalaja*, p. 36.

three or even four are not uncommon.[1] According to Moor-croft and Trebeck, a younger son is usually made a lama, but " should there be more brothers, and they agree to the arrangement, the juniors become inferior husbands to the wife of the elder " ; and on the death of the eldest brother his property, authority, and widow devolve upon his next brother.[2] Matin-uz-Zaman Khan, again, says in the Census Report of India for 1911 that all the brothers, except such as elect to become lamas or pass over into other families as *khanadamads* (*mukhpa*), live jointly and have but one wife common to them all. The eldest brother alone undergoes the wedding formalities, while the younger ones have only to promise that they will remain united. The brothers share the favours of the wife equally, though on sufferance of the eldest ; and the children are regarded at law to be of the eldest. If a man has no brothers, a stranger is admitted into the family, shares the wife along with the income of the family property, and assists in all agricultural work and other business of the house ; but this rarely happens.[3] It is impossible to say whether some of these statements are inaccurate or whether they refer to different parts of the country. Although polyandry is quite general in Ladakh,[4] monogamy and polygyny also occur there. It happens that a wealthy girl chooses to have one husband only,[5] and rich men " generally have two or three wives, according to their circumstances."[6]

The mountaineers of the Himalayas are not the only people in Northern India that practise fraternal polyandry. It also occurs, though more or less concealed, among various communities of the plains. Râja Lachhman Sinh was assured on the spot that in almost every Gûjar village in the vicinity of the Jumna, in the Bulandshahr district, polyandry was a fact among the poorer people, although it

---

[1] Cunningham, *Ladák*, p. 306.
[2] Moorcroft and Trebeck, *op. cit.* i. 321 *sq.*
[3] Matin-uz-Zaman Khan, *Census of India*, 1911, vol. xx. (Kashmir) Report, p. 136.
[4] Drew, *op. cit.* p. 250.
[5] Ujfalvy, *Aus dem westlichen Himalaja*, p. 36.
[6] Cunningham, *Ladák*, p. 306. See also Drew, *op. cit.* p. 250.

was not an acknowledged or legal custom ; " the wife was
formally married to one of the brothers, usually to the
eldest, if he were not too old, and her children were known as
his children only, though he as well as the other brothers
knew that she was at the disposal of all of them."[1] There
seems reason to believe that fraternal polyandry in some
cases occurs among the Jâts in the western part of the North-
Western Provinces, although the people would never admit
it ;[2] but there can be no doubt about its prevalence among
the Punjab Jâts. Mr. Kirkpatrick writes that when one of
them is well-to-do " he generally procures a wife for each
of his sons, but if he is not rich enough to bear the expenses
of many marriages he gets a wife for the eldest son only,
and she is expected to, and as a rule does, accept her brothers-
in-law as co-husbands." Though Brahmanical influence
prevents open cohabitation with an elder brother's wife,
no great pains are taken to conceal it ; and it is even a
common thing when women quarrel for one to say to the
other, " You are one so careless of your duty as not to
admit your husband's brothers to your embraces."[3] In
the submontane part of Ambala, amongst all classes of
Hindus, a sister-in-law was looked upon as the common
property, not only of uterine brothers, but of all *bhāis*,
including first cousins. It is said that this laxity has now
disappeared.[4] We are told that among the Santals—a
Dravidian tribe, classed on linguistic grounds as Kolarian,
which is found in Western Bengal, Northern Orissa,
Bhágalpur, and the Santal Parganás—a man's unmarried
younger brothers are permitted to share his wife, " so long
as they respect his dignity and feelings and do not indulge
in amorous dalliance in his presence " ;[5] and according to
another account they retain this privilege even after they

---

[1] Crooke, *Tribes and Castes of the North-Western Provinces,* ii.
444 *sq.*   [2] *Ibid.* iii. 36.
[3] Kirkpatrick, *loc. cit.* p. 86. See also Tupper, *Punjab Customary
Law,* ii. 95 ; Gait, *Census of India,* 1911, vol. i. (India) Report,
p. 239, quoting the *Punjab Census Report* for 1881.
[4] Gait, *op. cit.* p. 239 *sq.*
[5] Craven, ' Traces of Fraternal Polyandry amongst the Santāls,'
in *Jour. Asiatic Soc. Bengal,* vol. lxxii. pt. iii. 89.

marry for themselves.[1] Among the Bhuiyas, an important tribe of Chota Nagpur,[2] and the Kandhs, a Dravidian tribe which up to 1905 were included in the Central Provinces but now belong to Bihār and Orissa,[3] the younger brothers are allowed access to the elder brother's wife till the time of their own marriage ; and there are possibly survivals of a similar privilege in the marriage ceremonies of the Korkús,[4] the Oráons (a Dravidian cultivating tribe of Chota Nagpur),[5] and some other tribes in the Central Provinces.[6] Motte, in describing his journey through Balasore in 1766, wrote that when young married men went into Bengal leaving their families behind, their brothers raised up seed to them during their absence.[7]

Besides the Himalayan region, Southern India is a great centre for polyandry. This custom is extensively practised among the Todas of the Nilgiri Hills. When a boy is married to a girl she usually becomes the wife of his brothers at the same time, and any brother born later will similarly be regarded as sharing his older brothers' rights.[8] According to Dr. Shortt, the girl is led by her parents to the homestead

---

[1] Skrefsrud, ' Traces of Fraternal Polyandry amongst the Santāls,' *ibid.* p. 90.

[2] Russell, *Tribes and Castes of the Central Provinces of India,* ii. 317.

[3] *Ibid.* iii. 468. [4] *Ibid.* iii. 558.

[5] At the wedding there is a certain ceremony by which the bridegroom's brother seals a kind of tacit agreement that from that time he will never touch the wife of his brother (Dehon, ' Religion and Customs of the Uraons,' in *Memoirs Asiatic Soc. Bengal,* i. 164).

[6] Gait, *op. cit.* p. 240. [7] Motte, quoted *ibid.* p. 240.

[8] Rivers, *Todas,* p. 515. Ward, in Grigg, *Manual of the Nílagiri District,* Appendix, p. lxxiv. Hough, *Letters on the Neilgherries,* p. 69. Harkness, *Description of a Singular Race inhabiting the Neilgherry Hills,* p. 121. Shortt, ' Account of the Hill Tribes of the Neilgherries,' in *Trans. Ethn. Soc.* N.S. vii. 240. King, *Aboriginal Tribes of the Nilgiri Hills,* p. 24. Baierlein, *Nach und aus Indien,* p. 249. [Madame Janssen,] ' Die Todas,' in *Globus,* xliii. 371. Marshall says (*A Phrenologist amongst the Todas,* p. 213) that " if the husband has brothers or very near relatives, all living together, they may each, if both she and he consent, participate in the right to be considered her husband also, on making up a share of the dowry that has been paid."

of the future husband, before whom she makes a graceful
genuflexion, bowing her head at the same time, and he then
places his foot on the fore part of her head, which is looked
upon by them as a token of respect and submission. If
there are brothers, they all do the same in turn, and " at
one time the bride was taken to the nearest wood accompanied by the bridegroom and his brothers, who in turn
consummated the marriage."[1] Harkness says that in the
case of fraternal polyandry the supreme authority rests with
the eldest brother.[2] But although in the vast majority of
polyandrous marriages at the present time the husbands are
brothers, there are a few cases in which they are not so but
simply belong to the same clan and are of the same generation ; and Dr. Rivers even mentions an instance in which
a woman had at the same time husbands belonging to
different clans.[3] If the husbands are brothers they all
live together in one village,[4] and the same may be the case
if they are merely members of the same clan ; but in the
latter instance they may also live at different villages, and
then it is the usual rule that the wife shall live with each
husband in turn, generally for a month at a time, although
there is very considerable elasticity in the arrangement.[5]
Harkness tells us of a Toda who, having referred to his
betrothal to his wife Pilluvāni and the subsequent betrothal
of the latter to two other men who were not his brothers,
Khakhood and Tūmbŭt, said, " Now, according to our
customs, Pilluvāni was to pass the first month with me, the
second with Khakhood, and the third with Tūmbŭt."[6]
In speaking of the fraternal husbands Lieut.-Colonel
King, who spent three years on the Nilgiri Hills, says that
the wife cohabits with each of them a month at a time ;[7]
and Breeks states that brothers who have one wife in common
generally live in separate houses and take her in turn.[8] In

---

[1] Shortt, *Hill Ranges of Southern India*, i. 11.
[2] Harkness, *op. cit.* p. 121.   [3] Rivers, *op. cit.* p. 515.
[4] Shortt, *Hill Ranges of Southern India*, i. 11. Rivers, *op. cit.*
p. 516.   [5] Rivers, *op. cit.* p. 517.
[6] Harkness, *op. cit.* p. 122 *sq.*   [7] King, *op. cit.* p. 23.
[8] Breeks, *Account of the Primitive Tribes and Monuments of the
Nīlagiris*, p. 10.

the beginning of the seventeenth century Father Fenicio wrote, " Conjux una est omnibus fratribus, noctu paret senioribus, die vero junioribus " ; [1] or, according to another manuscript, [2] " Two brothers marry the same woman ; she lives with the eldest at night and with the youngest by day."

Ward, whose description of the Nilgiri Hills dates from 1821, says that the boys were divided between the brothers according to seniority.[3] Baierlein[4] and Madame Janssen[5] make a similar statement as to the children in general, and the former thinks that this custom might account for the practice of female infanticide, since the husbands naturally preferred boys to girls. According to Dr. Rivers, on the other hand, the brothers are all equally regarded as the fathers of the child, although if any of them leaves the rest and sets up an establishment of his own, it appears that he may lose his right to be regarded as the father of the children. In the case of non-fraternal polyandry, again, the husband who about the seventh month of the wife's pregnancy performs the ceremony of giving her a mimic bow and arrow becomes for all social purposes the father of the child about to be born and of all future children also until another of the husbands in similar circumstances gives her the bow and arrow.[6]

---

[1] Besse, ' Un ancien document inédit sur les Todas,' in Anthropos, ii. 974.

[2] Translated from the Portuguese by Miss A. de Alberti, in Rivers, op. cit. p. 727.

[3] Ward, loc. cit. p. lxxv.   See also Hough, op. cit. p. 69.

[4] Baierlein, op. cit. p. 249.   [5] ' Die Todas,' in Globus, xliii. 371.

[6] Rivers, op. cit. p. 516 sqq.   The ceremony in question is described ibid. p. 319 sqq., and by Thurston, Ethnographic Notes in Southern India, p. 110 sq.   According to Harkness (op. cit. p. 123), the first husband had the option of claiming the three first children, the second husband the second three, and the third husband the third three, after which the option again revolved to the first one.   The first husband went to the father of the wife two or three months prior to the birth of a child ; delivering to him a small piece of wood he claimed the forthcoming infant, whether male or female, and acknowledged before him and his relations that he would protect and nourish it.

In addition to the regular marriage, there is among the Todas another recognised mode of union by which a woman becomes the formal mistress of another man ; a woman may even have more than one of these lovers, and a man may have more than one mistress.[1] According to Ward, the woman is allowed to choose her paramour " independent of her husbands,"[2] whereas according to King[3] and Rivers[4] she can do so only with their permission. Any children born of such a union are regarded as the children of the regular marriage. Otherwise the position of a lover seems to differ little from that of a husband ; he may take his mistress to live with him at his own village just as if she were his real wife.[5] Nay, according to Ward, the husbands must on all occasions give the precedence to the lover : in case the woman should be at the house of one of her husbands and the lover comes in, the husband immediately retires and leaves her to the paramour.[6] It should be added that although polyandry is still quite common among the Todas, all the other forms of marriage occur side by side with it— monogamy, polygyny, and group-marriage.[7]

Fraternal polyandry is reported to occur among the jungle Kurumbas, another people of the Nilgiris ;[8] and among the Badagas, inhabiting the same hills, it is said to be etiquette " that, when a woman's husband is away, she should be accessible to her brothers-in-law."[9] Polyandry and communism of women in one house were by earlier writers ascribed to the Coorgs or Kodagas, the principal tribe of the Coorg country, whose language is a mixture of the Dravidian tongues.[10] But in his *Manual of Coorg*,

---

[1] Rivers, *op. cit.* p. 526. Ward, *loc. cit.* p. lxxiv. Hough, *op. cit.* p. 69. Harkness, *op. cit.* p. 124. King, *op. cit.* p. 23 *sq.*

[2] Ward, *loc. cit.* p. lxxiv. [3] King, *op. cit.* p. 24.

[4] Rivers, *op. cit.* p. 526. [5] *Ibid.* p. 526.

[6] Ward, *loc. cit.* p. lxxiv. See also Hough, *op. cit.* p. 69.

[7] Breeks, *op. cit.* p. 10. Marshall, *op. cit.* p. 213. Rivers, *op. cit.* p. 518 *sqq.* [8] Thurston, *op. cit.* p. 113.

[9] *Ibid.* p. 113. Thurston, *Castes and Tribes of Southern India.* 1. 105 *sq.* See also Gait, *op. cit.* p. 241.

[10] Wilks, *Historical Sketches of the South of India*, ii. 102 (the first edition was published in 1817). Hough, *op. cit.* p. 71 (1829). Moegling, *Coorg Memoirs*, p. 32 (1855).

published in 1870, the Rev. G. Richter says that, upon a careful examination of the matter, he may state as a fact that, "whatever may have been the custom in bygone ages, there is no such thing now practised amongst the Coorgs as a national rite."[1]

The president of the Malabar Marriage Commission stated that "among carpenters and blacksmiths in the Calicut, Walluvanad and Ponnani Taluks several brothers have one wife between them."[2] A similar observation was made by Sheikh Zeen-ud-deen, who visited Malabar about the middle and latter half of the sixteenth century. He wrote, "The carpenters, and ironsmiths, and painters, and others of their description . . . cohabit two or more together with one woman, but not unless they are brothers or in some way related."[3] According to Fra Paolino da S. Bartolomeo, whose account dates from the end of the eighteenth century, it was the custom among the braziers, and perhaps among some other lower castes on the coast of Malabar, for the eldest brother alone to marry, but when he was absent the rest supplied his place with their sister-in-law.[4] Among the Kammālans, or artisans of Malabar, the eldest brother cohabits with the bride on the wedding day, and special days are set apart for each brother ;[5] but poly-andry is said to be "fast dying out among these and other caste-men, owing to the influence of western civilisation."[6] Of the Izhuvans, also known as Tiyyans, in the northern part of the Cochin State and in the Valluvanad Taluk of South Malabar, we are told that "in a family in which there are four or five brothers living together, the eldest of them marries an adult woman, who, by a simple ceremony, becomes the wife of all." The bridegroom, with his sister and others, goes to the house of the bride-elect and pays the

---

[1] Richter, *Manual of Coorg*, p. 139.
[2] Moore, *Malabar Law and Custom*, p. 58.
[3] Zeen-ud-deen, *Tohfut-ul-mujahideen*, p. 65.
[4] Fra Paolino da S. Bartolomeo, *Viaggio alle Indie Orientali*, p. 200.
[5] Thurston, *Ethnographic Notes*, p. 114.
[6] Anantha Krishna Iyer, *Cochin Tribes and Castes*, i. 347.

price for her ; the union is then completed by the bride
and bridegroom being seated on a mat and given some
milk, plantation fruit, and sugar, and a feast is held, after
which the bridegroom returns home with the bride. " At
this stage, the bride is the wife only of the eldest brother.
If she is however intended as the wife of his brothers, the
sweet preparation is served to them and the bride, either in
the hut of the bridegroom by their mother, or in that of the
bride by their mother-in-law. Thenceforward, she becomes
the common wife of all. It is the custom even now for four
or five brothers to marry a young woman."[1] Mr. Thurston
was told that the Tiyyan woman sleeps in a room and her
husbands outside, and that when one of them is engaged
with her a knife is placed on the door-frame as a signal
that entrance into the room is forbidden to the other husbands.[2] A wedding ceremony similar to that just described
is also found among the Kaniyans, or Kaṇiṣans, of the Cochin
State, who practise fraternal polyandry. The husbands
are often away to earn their livelihood by astrology, but if
several of them happen to be at home together for a few
weeks, each in turn associates with the woman in accordance
with the directions given by their mother. Polygyny is
almost unknown among them.[3] Polyandry of the fraternal
type is further practised by the Tolkollans, or leather-
working caste of Malabar, of whom it is stated that in former
times only those in good circumstances indulged in the
luxury of a private wife ;[4] by the barber classes of Malabar,
said to be Nayars who have fallen from their social estate
owing to the degrading nature of their profession ;[5] and by
the Vilkurups in the Cochin State. Of the last-mentioned
we are told that the children are regarded as the children

[1] *Ibid.* i. 294 *sq.*

[2] Thurston, *Ethnographic Notes*, p. 112. The same practice
was said by Duncan (' Historical Remarks on the Coast of Malabar,'
in *Asiatick Researches*, v. 14 n. *) to occur among various polyandrous
low castes in a few of the southern districts of Malabar.

[3] Anantha Krishna Iyer, *op. cit.* i. 209 *sq.* For the polyandry of
the Kaniyans see also Logan, *Malabar*, i. 141 ; Gait, *op. cit.* p. 241.

[4] Gait, *op. cit.* p. 241.

[5] Gopal Panikkar, *Malabar and its Folk*, p. 30.

of all the brothers, who without any distinction are called fathers.[1]

Among the Kallans of the Madura district it constantly happens that a woman is the wife of ten, eight, six, or two husbands, who are all regarded as fathers of her children.[2] Of the Tottiyans settled in the same country we learn that it is customary for their women after marriage to cohabit with their husbands' brothers and near relatives and with their uncles ; it is even said that ill-luck will attend any refusal to do so, and " so far from any disgrace attaching to them in consequence, their priests compel them to keep up the custom if by any chance they are unwilling."[3] Among the Kunnuva Vellālas of the Madura country, " when an estate is likely to descend to a female on default of male issue, she is forbidden to marry an adult, but goes through the ceremony of marriage with some young male child, or in some cases with a portion of her father's dwelling-house, on the understanding that she shall be at liberty to amuse herself with any man of her caste, to whom she may take a fancy : and her issue, so begotten, inherits the property ; which is thus retained in the woman's family."[4] Among the Vellāla caste in the Coimbatore district, again, it is believed to have been the common practice for the father of a family to live in sexual intercourse with his daughter-in-law during the period when his son, the youthful husband, was in nonage, the offspring of such intercourse being affiliated on the latter.[5] Indeed, when grown-up women are married to very young boys—as is often the case where cousin marriage is in vogue—the wife is during her

[1] Anantha Krishna Iyer, op. cit. i. 182. The polyandry among the Mannans of the northern parts of the Cochin State, mentioned ibid. i. 161, is presumably also fraternal.

[2] Thurston, Castes and Tribes, iii. 77. Idem, Ethnographic Notes, p. 108.

[3] Nelson, Madura Country, ii. 82. Thurston, Castes and Tribes, vii. 186.

[4] Nelson, op. cit. ii. 35. See also Dahmen, ' Kunnuvans or Mannadis,' in Anthropos, v. 326.

[5] Shortt, Hill Ranges of Southern India, i. 37. Idem, in Trans. Ethn. Soc. N.S. vii. 264.

husband's minority commonly allowed to cohabit with his father or with her paternal aunt's son, or some other near relative, or even, in some instances, with any member of the caste she may select. This practice prevails among the Reddies in the Tinnevelly district,[1] the Tottiyans,[2] the Badagas,[3] and various other tribes or castes both in Southern India and in Kashmir.[4] But marriages of this kind cannot be called polyandrous, nor be regarded as evidence of polyandry in the past. They occurred, as we have seen, among the Russian peasants, the father being anxious to marry his son at as early an age as possible in order to secure an additional female labourer, and cohabiting with the wife during the son's minority.[5] They are found even to this day in Serbia.[6] Ahlqvist mentions the occurrence of the same practice among the Ostyak,[7] Smirnov among the Cheremiss and Mordvin,[8] and von Haxthausen among the Ossetes of Caucasia.[9]

Until prohibited by the Governor, Sir Henry Ward, about the year 1860, polyandry prevailed throughout the interior of Ceylon,[10] and in spite of governmental interdict it occurred there later still.[11] In the middle of the nineteenth century, at least, it did not exist in the maritime provinces,[12] but it is recorded to have been at one time universal throughout the island, except among the Veddas.[13] According to Sir Emerson Tennent it prevailed chiefly among the wealthier classes,[14] whilst according to Dr. Davy it was more or less

---

[1] *Idem, Hill Ranges,* i. 37 n. * *Idem,* in *Trans. Ethn. Soc.* N.S. vii. 264 *sq.* note. *Cf.* Kearns, *Tribes of South India,* p. 69.

[2] Hemingway, quoted by Thurston, *Castes and Tribes,* vii. 193.

[3] *Ibid.* i. 106.   [4] Gait, *op. cit.* p. 244.

[5] *Supra,* i. 386.   [6] *Supra,* i. 386.

[7] Ahlqvist, ' Unter Wogulen und Ostjaken,' in *Acta Soc. Scient. Fennicae,* xiv. 292 note.

[8] Smirnov, *Les populations finnoises des bassins de la Volga et de la Kama,* pp. 115, 348.

[9] v. Haxthausen, *Transcaucasia,* p. 402. See also Kovalewsky, *Coutume contemporaine,* p. 177 *sq.*

[10] Tennent, *Ceylon,* ii. 428. Balfour, *Cyclopædia of India,* iii. 250.

[11] Haeckel, *Indische Reisebriefe,* p. 240.

[12] Sirr, *Ceylon and the Cingalese,* ii. 163.

[13] Tennent, *op. cit.* ii. 428.   [14] *Ibid.* ii. 428.

general among the high and low, the rich and poor.[1] One woman had in many cases three or four husbands, and in others five or even more ;[2] Sirr saw a Kandyan matron of high caste who was the wife of eight brothers.[3] The husbands were most usually brothers, especially in the highest caste.[4] Joinville wrote :—" A whole family goes in a body to ask a girl in marriage ; the more numerous the family, the greater title it has to the girl. It is the whole family that marries."[5] Yet it does not seem that brothers always had a wife in common, nor were the husbands always brothers. In the Níti-Nighanduva, a compilation of the native customary law made in 1818 by a commission of respected Sinhalese at Kandy,[6] it is said :—" After the parents have given their daughter in marriage to a man, that man, either to obtain assistance or to prevent a division of the estate (lit., on account of the estate being too small for division) when intending to live in associated marriage, cannot do so except with his wife's consent. If a married man consents to make his marriage a communal one with another person who is not his brother, even though the wife be willing, if the parents do not give their consent, the associated marriage cannot be arranged."[7] If the necessary consent was given, the first husband could bring home several husbands unrelated to him, and the children of those unions were looked upon as his children, though they also inherited the property of their real fathers.[8] The offspring of brother-husbands called all of them father,[9] distinguishing however between "great" and " little father,"[10] and they were the recognised

[1] Davy, *Account of the Interior of Ceylon*, p. 286.
[2] Forbes, *Eleven Years in Ceylon*, i. 332.   Davy, *op. cit.* p. 286.
[3] Sirr, *op. cit.* ii. 162.
[4] *Ibid* ii. 162.   Davy, *op. cit.* p. 286.   Chitty, *Ceylon Gazetteer*, p 116.   Forbes, *op. cit.* i. 332.   van Mökern, *Ostindien*, ii. 83. Perera, *Glimpses of Singhalese Social Life*, p. 11.
[5] Joinville, ' Religion and Manners of the People of Ceylon,' in *Asiatick Researches*, vii. 427.
[6] Jolly, *Recht und Sitte*, p. 44.   [7] *Níti-Nighanduva*, p. 22.
[8] Sirr, *op. cit.* ii. 162 *sq.*
[9] *Ibid.* ii. 162.   van Mökern, *op. cit.* ii. 83.
[10] Thurston, *Ethnographic Notes*, p. 112.

heirs of them all;[1] but if litigation arose concerning property, then the children claimed the eldest brother as their
paternal parent, and the Kandyan laws recognised the
claim.[2] That one husband was the chief husband is also
suggested by Baldaeus' statement from 1672 that " when
husbands have occasion to leave their wives for some time,
they recommend the conjugal duty to be performed by their
own brothers."[3] Besides polyandry all other forms of
marriage—monogamy, polygyny, and group-marriage—
were also recognised by Kandyan law ;[4] but whilst monogamy
was common, polygyny seems to have been rare.[5] Sirr
says that during his residence in Ceylon he never met with
a Sinhalese either in the interior or on the coast who had,
or acknowledged having, more than one wife.[6]

Among the polyandrous peoples of India whom we have
hitherto considered the husbands, or at least most of them,
are brothers, either invariably or as a general rule. But
among one people, the Nayars or Nairs of Cochin, Malabar,
and Travancore, we meet with polyandrous unions of a
different, non-fraternal, type, the prevalence of which has
been testified by a large number of travellers from the
beginning of the fifteenth century onwards.[7] In the course

---

[1] Sirr, *op. cit.* ii. 162. Tennent, *op. cit.* ii. 429.

[2] Sirr, *op. cit.* ii. 162.

[3] Baldaeus, ' Description of Malabar and Coromandel ; as also
of Ceylon,' in Churchill's *Collection of Voyages*, iii. 744.

[4] *Niti-Nighanduva*, p. 22.

[5] Davy, *op. cit.* p. 286. Percival, *Account of the Island of Ceylon*,
p. 178. Van Mökern says (*op. cit.* ii. 83) that polygyny was unknown
in Ceylon, but this is certainly an exaggeration. In the *Niti-Nighanduva* (p. 22) it is even said to be frequently the custom for one man to
have at the same time a number of wives.

[6] Sirr, *op. cit.* ii. 163.

[7] Such as Conti, a Venetian nobleman in whose account, so far
as I know, we find the first statements relating to the polyandrous
habits of the Nayars (*Travels of Nicolò Conti, in the East* [in *India
in the Fifteenth Century*, trans. and edited by R. H. Major]) ; Abd-er-
Razzak, a native of Herát (1442 ; *Narrative of the Journey of Abd-er-
Razzak* [*ibid.*]) ; Hieronimo di Santo Stefano, a Genoese merchant
who visited India at the close of the fifteenth century (*Account of
the Journey of Hieronimo di Santo Stefano* [*ibid.*]) ; Alvares Cabral,
a Portuguese whose description dates from 1500–1502 (' Navigation

of the nineteenth century polyandry was dwindling away
among the Nayars, and may now be said to be extinct,
except in some remote localities, where even cases of non-
fraternal polyandry may still be found, or at least occurred

del captino Pedro Alvares,' in Ramusio, *Navigationi et viaggi*, vol. i.) ;
Ludovico de Barthema, a native of Bologna whose book of travels
was published in 1510 (*Itinerario nello Egypto, nella Surria, nella
Arabia deserta & felice, nella Persia, nella India, & nella Ethiopia*) ;
Barbosa, a Portuguese who visited Malabar in the beginning of the
same century (*Description of the Coasts of East Africa and Malabar in
the beginning of the Sixteenth Century*, trans. by H. E. J. Stanley) ;
Lopez de Castanheda, a Portuguese whose account of the Nayars
appeared in his great work *Historia do descobrimento e conqvista
da India pelos Portugueses*, first published in 1552–1554 ; Sheikh
Zeen-ud-deen, who wrote his description about the middle and
latter half of the sixteenth century (*Tohfut-ul-mujahideen*, trans.
by M. J. Rowlandson) ; Federici, a merchant of Venice who travelled
in the East Indies and other countries during eighteen years in
the latter half of the same century (1563–1581 ; *Viaggio nell' India
Orientale, et oltra l'India*) ; van Linschoten, a Dutchman who sailed
for India in 1583 (*Voyage of J. H. van Linschoten to the East Indies*,
trans. edited by A. C. Burnell and P. A. Tiele) ; François Pyrard,
who visited Calicut in the beginning of the seventeenth century
(*Voyage of François Pyrard of Laval to the East Indies, the Maldives,
the Moluccas and Brazil*, trans. and edited by A. Gray) ; Pietro della
Valle, born in Rome, who visited the same country shortly afterwards, in 1623 (*Travels of Pietro della Valle in India*, trans. by
G. Havers) ; Giuseppe di Santa Maria, who was in Malabar on an
apostolic mission in 1657 (*Prima speditione all' Indie Orientali*) ;
Wouter Schouten, who together with other Dutchmen fought
against the Portuguese in 1662 (*Ost-Indische Reyse*) ; Hamilton,
who spent his time in the East Indies between the years 1688 and
1723 (' New Account of the East Indies,' in Pinkerton's *Collection
of Voyages and Travels*, vol. viii.) ; Visscher, whose letters from
Malabar, written in Dutch, date from the beginning of the eighteenth
century (*Letters from Malabar*, trans. by H. Drury) ; Grose (1750–
1764 ; *Voyage to the East-Indies*) ; Sonnerat (1774–1781 ; *Voyage to
the East-Indies and China*) ; Fra Paolino da S. Bartolomeo (1796 ;
Viaggio alle Indie Orientali) ; Buchanan (1800 ; ' Journey from
Madras through Mysore, Canara, and Malabar,' in Pinkerton's
Collection of Voyages and Travels, vol. viii.) ; James Forbes (1813 ;
Oriental Memoirs).   Ibn Batūta, who visited Malabar already in
the former part of the fourteenth century, says (*Travels*, p. 166 *sq.*)
that the king is succeeded by his sister's son, not his own son ;
but he does not mention the existence of polyandrous practices.

a few years ago.[1] Subramhanya Aiyar wrote in 1901 that the practice at heart among all decent sections of the Nayar people is one of strict monogamy.[2]

The polyandry of the Nayars has played an important though rather deceptive part in the history of marriage, and I shall therefore discuss it at some length. First of all it is necessary to form a clear idea of the people who practised it.

The Nayars, who are generally considered to be Dravidians,[3] constitute the third and last of the honoured castes under the name of the pure " Sudras of the Malayala."[4] They were nobles who engaged in no other occupation but that of arms, in which they exercised themselves continually from the time they could wield them, and they always carried arms when out of their houses.[5] At the age of seven the boys were sent to school to learn the use of all kinds of weapons, their masters first pulling and twisting their joints to make them supple, and then teaching them to fence and handle their arms adroitly.[6] Later on they enlisted to live with the king and promised to die for him, and they did likewise with any other lord from whom they received pay. They lived outside the towns, separate from other people, on their estates, which were fenced in, and there they had all that they required.[7] They remained thus a fighting race towards the close of the eighteenth century,[8] but became subsequently engrossed in agriculture, government service, or their own affairs, and won for themselves the name of

[1] Gopal Panikkar, *op. cit.* p. 30 *sq.* Moore, *op. cit.* p. 57 *sq.* Subramhanya Aiyar, *Census of India*, 1901, vol. xxvi. (Travancore) Report, p. 331. Fawcett, ' Nâyars of Malabar,' in the Madras Government Museum's *Bulletin*, iii. 241. Thurston, *Ethnographic Notes*, p. 120. Nayar, ' Matrimonial Customs of the Nayars,' in *Malabar Quarterly Review*, vii. 189. Anantha Krishna Iyer, *op. cit.* ii. 38, 41 *sq.*

[2] Subramhanya Aiyar, *op. cit.* p. 331.

[3] Anantha Krishna Iyer, *op. cit.* ii. 41. Moore, *op. cit.* p. 59. Stuart, quoted by Thurston, *Castes and Tribes*, v. 283.

[4] Anantha Krishna Iyer, *op. cit.* ii. 1.

[5] Lopez de Castanheda, *op. cit.* i. 47. Pyrard, *op. cit.* i. 380.

[6] Lopez de Castanheda, *op. cit.* i. 48. See also Barbosa, *op. cit.* p. 128 ; Baldaeus, *loc. cit.* p. 579. [7] Barbosa, *op. cit.* p. 128 *sq.*

[8] Anantha Krishna Iyer, *op. cit.* ii. 28.

loyal peaceful citizens.[1] The present Nayar caste includes persons who, by hereditary occupation, are traders, artisans, oilmongers, and even barbers and washermen. It seems that successive waves of immigration brought from the Canarese and Tamil countries different castes and tribes, which adopted the customs and manners and assumed the caste names of the more respectable of the community that surrounded them.[2]

According to Nayar usage, every girl, before she attains puberty, goes through a marriage ceremony, the essential incident of which consists in the nominal husband tying a *tāli*, or tiny plate of gold, round her neck. I have previously[3] discussed this rite, and pointed out that in former times the man who performed it might possibly have deflowered the girl whom he thus technically married ; but even then he had no further rights over her. Subsequently the woman was allowed to cohabit with any Brahman or Nayar she chose, but if she did so with a man belonging to a lower caste she was punished with death[4] or at least became an outcast.[5] She was " under no obligation to admit above a single attachment,"[6] but usually she had several lovers,[7] and was not less respected on that account. The numbers of lovers are given differently by different writers. They are reported to have been two or four,[8] three or four,[9] five or six,[10] from five to eight,[11] ten or more.[12] Tīpū Sultān is said to have issued a proclamation to the Nayars on the occasion of his visit to Calicut in 1788, in which he required them to forsake their sinful practices according to which one woman associated with ten men more shamelessly than the beasts of

[1] Nagam Aiya, *Travancore State Manual*, ii. 348. In 1800 Buchanan (*loc. cit.* p. 735) wrote of the Nayars, " All pretend to be born soldiers ; but they are of various ranks and professions."
[2] Stuart, quoted by Thurston, *Castes and Tribes*, v. 283 *sq.*
[3] *Supra*, i. 184 *sqq.*   [4] Barbosa, *op. cit.* p. 124.
[5] Hamilton, *loc. cit.* p. 374.   Buchanan, *loc. cit.* p. 737.
[6] Grose, *op. cit.* i. 243.
[7] Lopez de Castanheda says (*op. cit.* i. 47) that " there are always several men attached to one woman."
[8] Zeen-ud-deen, *op. cit.* p. 64.   [9] Barbosa, *op. cit.* p. 126.
[10] Alvares Cabral, *loc. cit.* p. 137.
[11] Barthema, *op. cit.* fol. liii. a.   [12] Conti, *op. cit.* p. 20.

the field.[1] Barbosa says that the more lovers a woman had the more highly she was esteemed.[2] Some writers, however, speak as if there were a limit to the number of men who were allowed to visit a Nayar lady. Pyrard asserts that " every woman may have as many as three husbands at once if she likes,"[3] and Hieronimo di Santo Stefano that " every lady may take to herself seven or eight husbands, according to her inclination."[4] According to Grose, the number of lovers was not so much limited by any specific law as by a kind of tacit convention, and it scarcely ever happened that it exceeded six or seven ;[5] whilst Hamilton definitely states that no Nayar woman was allowed to have more than twelve husbands at one time.[6]

When a lover received admission into a house he commonly gave his mistress some ornaments and her mother a piece of cloth ; but these presents were never of such value as to give room for supposing that the women bestowed their favours from mercenary motives.[7] All the lovers contributed to maintain the woman,[8] but she lived apart from them. This is expressly said in the earliest account, that of Conti ;[9] and even to this day it frequently happens that the husband only visits the wife in her house in the night and goes home the next morning. Nagam Aiya says that it is the exception in South Malabar and North Travancore for a wife to be taken to her husband's home,[10] and other writers tell us that she remains in her own *tarwad* (the common residence of the children of the same maternal ancestor) if she is a member of a wealthy *tarwad* [11] or if the husband has no independent means.[12] The lovers cohabited with their

---

[1] Wilks, *op. cit.* ii. 120.   [2] Barbosa, *op. cit.* p. 126.

[3] Pyrard, *op. cit.* i. 384.

[4] Hieronimo di Santo Stefano, *op. cit.* p. 5.

[5] Grose, *op. cit.* i. 243.   [6] Hamilton, *loc. cit.* p. 374.

[7] Buchanan, *loc. cit.* p. 737.

[8] Conti, *op. cit.* p. 20. Barbosa, *op. cit.* p. 126. Lopez de Castanheda, *op. cit.* i. 47. Pyrard, *op. cit.* i. 384. Pietro della Valle, *op. cit.* ii. 379. Graul, *Reise nach Ostindien*, iii. 230.

[9] Conti, *op. cit.* p. 20.   [10] Nagam Aiya, *op. cit.* ii. 358.

[11] Jogendra Nath Bhattacharya, *Hindu Castes and Sects*, p. 107.

[12] Sankara Menon, *Census of India*, 1901, vol. xx. (Cochin) Report, p. 160.

mistress by agreement among themselves. In earlier accounts it is said that the hours of the day and of the night were divided between them, each of them for a certain period taking up his abode in the house ;[1] or that each lover dwelt a day in his turn with the joint mistress, counting from noon of one day to the same time of the next, after which he departed and another came for the like time ;[2] or simply that each lover in turn passed the night with her.[3] A somewhat different account is given by Hamilton, who writes :—" They cohabit with her in their turns, according to their priority of marriage, ten days, more or less, according as they can fix a term among themselves, and he that cohabits with her, maintains her in all things, necessary, for his time, so that she is plentifully provided for by a constant circulation. . . . And all the time of cohabitation she serves her husband as purveyor and cook, and keeps his clothes and arms clean."[4] When one of the lovers visited the woman in her house he left his arms or some other signal at the door, and then nobody else dared to enter as long as he remained with her.[5] By such arrangements difficulties and quarrels were avoided, and it is said that jealousy seldom or never disturbed the relations between the lovers.[6]

With reference to the children born of these unions there is disagreement between our authorities. Conti states that they were allotted to the husbands at the will of the wife ;[7] according to Barthema the mother says " it is the child of this husband or of that husband, and thus the children go

---

[1] Abd-er-Razzak, *op. cit.* p. 17.

[2] Barbosa, *op. cit.* p. 126 *sq.*   Lopez de Castanheda, *op. cit.* i. 47. Pyrard (*op. cit.* i. 384) speaks of " a day and a night at a time."

[3] Barthema, *op. cit.* fol. liii. a.   Zeen-ud-deen, *op. cit.* p. 64.

[4] Hamilton, *loc. cit.* p. 375.

[5] Conti, *op. cit.* p. 20.   Federici, *op. cit.* p. 57.   van Linschoten, *op. cit.* i. 280.   Baldaeus, *loc. cit.* p. 579.   Pyrard, *op. cit.* i. 384. Pietro della Valle, *op. cit.* ii. 379.   Giuseppe di Santa Maria, *op. cit.* p. 160.   Hamilton, *loc. cit.* p. 375.   Grose, *op. cit.* i. 243.   Forbes, *op. cit.* i. 385.

[6] Zeen-ud-deen, *op. cit.* p. 65.   Pyrard, *op. cit.* i. 384.   Pietro della Valle, *op. cit.* ii. 379.   Hamilton, *loc. cit.* p. 375.   Grose, *op. cit.* i. 243.   Forbes, *op. cit.* i. 385.   [7] Conti, *op. cit.* p. 20.

according to the word of the woman."[1] Hamilton informs
us that " when she proves with child, she nominates its
father, who takes care of its education, after she has suckled
it, and brought it to walk or speak."[2] According to Forbes,
also, the wife nominates the father of the child, and he is
obliged to provide for it ;[3] whilst Pyrard says that all the
husbands " contribute to support and maintain the wife and
children."[4] But according to Lopez de Castanheda the
Nayars " never look upon any of the children born of their
mistresses as belonging to them, however strong a resem-
blance may subsist " ;[5] and Barbosa says that the children
" remain at the expense of the mother and of the brothers
of the mother, who bring them up," none of the fathers
recognising them as their children or giving anything for
them.[6] The statements of these two writers are certainly
remarkable, considering the general agreement between the
earliest and the latest among our informants. Perhaps
we may assume that in earlier times Nayar custom varied
with reference to the relations between fathers and children,
although later on, from the seventeenth century if not before,
paternal duties became more generally recognised. On the
other hand there is no dissensus of opinion as regards the
rule of succession among the Nayars, all inheritances going
to the sons of their sisters.[7] Even to this day the children
in all cases " succeed to the property and status of their
mother's *tarwad*."[8]

The polyandrous unions of the Nayars were dissolved
as easily as they were entered into. Barbosa[9] and Castanheda[10] say that any one might forsake his mistress at his

[1] Barthema, *op. cit.* fol. liii. a.   [2] Hamilton, *loc. cit.* p. 375.
[3] Forbes, *op. cit.* i. 385.   [4] Pyrard, *op. cit.* i. 384.
[5] Lopez de Castanheda, *op. cit.* i. 48. [6] Barbosa. *op. cit.* p. 127.
[7] Conti, *op. cit.* p. 20. Barbosa, *op. cit.* p. 124. Lopez de Castanheda, *op. cit.* i. 48. Zeen-ud-deen, *op. cit.* p. 62 *sq.* Pyrard, *op. cit.*
i. 385. Pietro della Valle, *op. cit.* ii. 379. Schouten, *op. cit.* p. 168.
Hamilton, *loc. cit.* p. 375. Grose, *op. cit.* i. 243 *sq.* Sonnerat,
op. cit. ii. 24. Buchanan, *loc. cit.* p. 737. [Papi,] *Lettere sull' Indie
Orientali*, i. 236. Graul, *op. cit.* iii. 231.
[8] Jogendra Nath Bhattacharya, *op. cit.* p. 107.
[9] Barbosa, *op. cit.* p. 127 [10] Lopez de Castanheda, *op. cit.* i. 47.

pleasure, and that, in like manner, the mistress might refuse admittance to or dismiss any of her lovers when she pleased. Even now the " second marriage," known as *sambandham* ("association"), is terminable at the will of either party,[1] although as a matter of fact the right to divorce at will is sparingly exercised.[2] As to the legitimacy of polygynous unions among the Nayars the statements vary. Pyrard says that they might have but one wife at the time;[3] whereas according to Giuseppe di Santa Maria they might have as many as five,[4] and according to Hamilton they were not confined to a set number of wives, as the women were to husbands.[5]

In the above account I have spoken rather of lovers and mistresses than of husbands and wives ; for the polyandrous unions of the Nayars can hardly be called marriages. Several of our authorities expressly assert that the Nayars did not marry or were not allowed to marry ; [6] and to this day the male partner in a *sambandham* connection—to which is practically attached the full sanctity of a monogamous union—occupies, as matter of law, no recognised relation involving rights and responsibilities in regard either to his wife or his children.[7] From a non-legal point of view as well, it is doubtful whether the term marriage can be

[1] Risley, *People of India*, p. 210.
[2] Subramhanya Aiyar, *op. cit.* p. 331.
[3] Pyrard, *op. cit.* i. 384 .
[4] Giuseppe di Santa Maria, *op. cit.* p. 160.
[5] Hamilton, *loc. cit.* p. 375.
[6] Barbosa, *op. cit.* p. 124. Lopez de Castanheda, *op. cit.* i. 47. Zeen-ud-deen, *op. cit.* p. 64. van Linschoten, *op. cit.* i. 280. Visscher, *op. cit.* p. 122. Schouten, *op. cit.* p. 168. Mr. K. M. Panikkar, in a recent article (' Some Aspects of Nāyar Life,' in *Jour. Roy. Anthr. Inst.* xlviii. 272), says that all the evidence we have of polyandry among the Nayars in the sixteenth, seventeenth, and eighteenth centuries are from foreign travellers, whereas the extensive Malayalam literature of that period contains no single allusion to polyandry. He maintains that " the loose character of the sexual tie and the licentious habits of the richer Nampudiri landlords, as far as their immediate Nāyar tenants were concerned, were naturally enough interpreted as polyandry by foreign observers " (*ibid.* p. 293).
[7] Logan, *Malabar*, i. 135. Gopal Panikkar, *op. cit.* p. 22. K. M. Panikkar, in *Jour. Roy. Anthr. Inst.* xlviii. 271.

properly applied to the connections of the Nayars, considering that they were of the loosest and most fugitive character,
that the male partners never lived with the woman, and that
according to some accounts the duties of fatherhood were
entirely ignored. In these respects there was a vast difference between the Nayars and the other peoples of India who
have come under our notice in the present chapter. It is
true that among the latter also men who have access to the
woman are not in every case husbands in the full sense of
the term, but she is legally married to some or at least to
one of them. And there is another difference to be noted.
Nothing indicates that the Nayars who regularly had intercourse with the same woman were brothers. We are told
that brothers almost always lived under the same roof,[1]
but, as we have seen, the woman did not live with her lovers.
It is also noteworthy that the Nayars with their cicisbeism
and matrilineal system of descent lived in the midst of
people who practised fraternal polyandry and among whom
children inherited their fathers.[2]

Non-fraternal polyandry has been attributed to a few
other castes or tribes in South India, which are closely
connected with the Nayars ; these cases will be considered
in the following chapter in the discussion of the origin of
the polyandrous practices of the latter.[3] Among the
matrilineal Muduvars of the Travancore plateau both
polygyny and polyandry are permitted, the former being
common, the latter occasional ; but brothers are prohibited
from having a common wife, as also are cousins on the
father's side. " A man may be polygamous in one village,
and be one of a polyandrous lot of men a few miles off."
But " on the Cardamom Hills, and on the western slopes,

---

[1] Buchanan, loc. cit. p. 738. Conner, ' Extract from the General
Memoir of the Survey of Travancore,' in Journal of Literature and
Science Published under the Auspices of the Madras Literary Society,
i. 69. Graul, op. cit. iii. 230.

[2] Duncan, loc. cit. p. 14. Moore, op. cit. p. 58. Logan, op. cit.
i. 141 (Kaniyans). Anantha Krishna Iyer, op. cit. i. 347. As Mr.
Gait observes (op. cit. p. 239), fraternal polyandry is generally
associated with male kinship.

[3] Infra, p. 203 sq.

where the majority of the tribe live, they are monogamous, and express abhorrence of both the polygamous and polyandrous condition."[1] Generally speaking, polyandry in modern India is restricted to non-Aryan—Tibetan or Dravidian—tribes or castes. Yet it is often supposed to have existed among the early Aryans. We read in the Mahabharata of Draupadī who was won at an archery match by the eldest of the five Pāṇḍava princes and then became the wife of all. It is true that Kuntī, the mother of three of the princes, is represented as having at first sanctioned the union only by a mistake, and that supernatural occurrences are introduced to explain and justify the transaction. Moreover, strong objections are put into the mouth of Draupadī's father, who states that although one king may have many wives it is not permissible for one queen to have more than one husband, and pronounces Draupadī's marriage to be contrary to custom and the Veda. But Yudhishṭhira replies that the practice may plead precedent, and instances the case of Jatilā Gautamī, who is said in an old tale to have had seven husbands, and that of Vārkshī, a saint's daughter, who married ten brothers ; and Vyāsa likewise affirms the lawfulness of the marriage as a recognised custom practised from time immemorial.[2] One of the law-books says that " a bride is given to the family (of her husband), and not to the husband alone," but declares it to be forbidden at present ; [3] whilst another law-book speaks of " the delivery of a marriageable damsel to a family " as a custom found in other countries, that is, the South.[4] None of these

---

[1] Thurston, *Castes and Tribes of Southern India*, v. 92, 94.

[2] This story is found in the first book of the Mahabharata. The particulars of it are given by Muir in his article ' On the Lax Observance of Caste Rules, etc.,' in *Indian Antiquary*, vi. 260 *sqq.*, and by Winternitz, ' Notes on the Mahābhārata, with special reference to Dahlmann's " Mahābhārata," ' in *Jour. Roy. Asiatic Soc.* 1897, p. 735 *sqq.*

[3] *Âpastamba*, ii. 10. 27. 3 *sq.*

[4] *Brihaspati*, xxvii. 20. Jolly, ' Beiträge zur indischen Rechtsgeschichte,' in *Zeitschr. d. Deutschen Morgenländ. Gesellsch.* xliv. 340 *sq.*

statements, however, proves that polyandry was a genuinely
Aryan custom.[1] It was not Vedic.[2] Oppert maintains
that the occurrence of the polyandry of the five Pāṇḍavas
and other peculiar customs closely connects them with the
non-Aryan inhabitants of India.[3] It has also been argued
that the Pāṇḍava princes were Kshatriyas, to whom greater
licence was allowed in their dealings with women, and for
whom the lowest forms of marriage were sanctioned ;[4] that,
if polyandrous practices existed among the aborigines whom
they conquered, these would naturally be imitated by them,
just as the English knights who settled beyond the Pale
became *Hibernis Hiberniores ;*[5] and that the conquerors
would the more readily adopt such practices since they
obviously brought with them as few women as possible.[6]
Polyandry was constantly opposed by Brahmanism.[7] The
nearest approach to it which is recognised by the sacred law
is the rule according to which a married woman, on failure

[1] *Cf.* Hopkins, ' The Social and Military Position of the Ruling
Caste in Ancient India,' in *Jour. American Oriental Soc.* xiii. 354 *sq.* ;
Jolly, *Recht und Sitte,* p. 48 ; Mayne, *Treatise on Hindu Law and
Usage,* p. 79 ; Dahlmann, *Das Mahābhārata als Epos und Rechtsbuch,*
p. 93 *sqq.*

[2] Zimmer, *Altindisches Leben,* p. 325 *sq.* Hopkins, *loc. cit.* p. 355.
Mandlik, *Vyavahāra Mayūkha,* p. 397. Delbrück, ' Die indogermanischen Verwandtschaftsnamen,' in *Abhandlungen d. Königl.
Sächsischen Gesellsch. d. Wissensch.* xxv. 541 *sqq.* Schrader, *Reallexikon der indogermanischen Altertumskunde,* p. 633. Jolly, *Recht
und Sitte,* p. 48. Macdonell and Keith, *Vedic Index of Names and
Subjects,* i. 479 :—" There is no passage containing any clear reference
to such a custom. The most that can be said is that in the Rigveda
and the Atharvaveda verses are occasionally found in which husbands
are mentioned in relation to a single wife. It is difficult to be certain
of the correct explanation of each separate instance of this mode
of expression ; but even if Weber's view (' Vedische Hochzeitssprüche,' in *Indische Studien,* v. 191), that the plural is here used
majestatis causa, is not accepted, Delbrück's explanation (*loc. cit.*
p. 543) by mythology is probably right. In other passages the plural
is simply generic."

[3] Oppert, *On the Original Inhabitants of Bharatavarṣa or India,*
p. 617.

[4] *Laws of Manu,* iii. 26. [5] Mayne, *op. cit.* p. 79.

[6] Wheeler, *History of India,* i. 116.

[7] Jolly, *Recht und Sitte,* p. 48.

of issue by her husband, could be authorised by him to obtain offspring by cohabitation with a brother-in-law or some other near relative (*sapindā*) of the husband.[1] But this rule had its root in the great importance attached to having a child, and can certainly not be regarded as a survival of fraternal polyandry in the proper sense of the term. It seems indeed to have been an ancient Aryan custom that an old or impotent married man could engage a substitute for the production of a legitimate heir. This is said to have been permitted or even ordained by Lycurgus at Sparta,[2] and traces of the same custom have been preserved in German tradition and old peasant customals.[3] At Athens an heiress whose husband—always a near relative— was incapable of performing his marital duty was legally entitled to ask for the embraces of another relative.[4] At Sparta actual polyandry existed according to Polybius, who said that several brothers often had one wife and that the children were brought up in common ;[5] whilst Xenophon states that " at Sparta a wife will not object to bear the burden of a double establishment."[6] Fraternal polyandry is mentioned in old Irish legends.[7] In the Scandinavian ' Ynglingasaga ' there is the mythical statement that the goddess Frigg, during the absence of her husband Odin, was married to his brothers Vili and Vé ;[8] but these are

---

[1] *Laws of Manu*, ix. 59. See also Bühler's remark in *Sacred Books of the East*, xxv. 337 *sq.* n. 59.

[2] Xenophon, *Lacedæmoniorum respublica*, i. 7. Plutarch, *Vita Lycurgi*, xv. 9. We are also told that Lycurgus permitted a man who did not desire to live with a wife permanently but yet was anxious to have children of his own to select another man's wife, well born herself and blest with fair offspring, and with the consent of her husband raise up children for himself through her (Xenophon, *op. cit.* i. 8 ; Plutarch, *op. cit.* xv. 10). See also Plutarch, *Lycurgi et Numæ comparatio*, iii. 2 *sq.*

[3] Grimm, *Deutsche Rechtsalterthümer*, p. 443 *sqq.* (i. 613 *sqq.*) Maurer, *Geschichte der Dorfverfassung in Deutschland*, i. 338 *sq.* Gierke, *Der Humor im deutschen Recht*, p. 56.

[4] Meier and Schömann, *Der attische Process*, p. 290 (356).

[5] Polybius, *Historia*, xii. 6 b. 8.   [6] Xenophon, *op. cit.* i. 9.

[7] d'Arbois de Jubainville, *La famille celtique*, p. 50.

[8] Snorri Sturluson, *Ynglingasaga*, ch. 3, p. 10.

supposed to have been originally only other names for Odin.[1]

Cicisbeism has existed in Europe as a recognised custom. We are told that in former days a Florentine girl of good family, by a clause in the nuptial contract, claimed her right to take a lover whenever it should please her to do so.[2] Lady Montagu, who visited the Court of Vienna in 1716, writes that it is there " the established custom for every lady to have two husbands, one that bears the name, and another that performs the duties. And these engagements are so well known, that it would be a downright affront, and publicly resented, if you invited a woman of quality to dinner, without at the same time inviting her two attendants of lover and husband, between whom she always sits in state with great gravity. These sub-marriages generally last twenty years together, and the lady often commands the poor lover's estate even to the utter ruin of his family." A woman, she adds, " looks out for a lover as soon as she's married, as part of her equipage, without which she could not be genteel." And the husbands " look upon their wives' gallants as favourably as men do upon their deputies, that take the troublesome part of their business off of their hands ; though they have not the less to do ; for they are generally deputies in another place themselves."[3]

We shall return to Asia. Campbell states that among the Orang Tanjong in Ulu Langat of Selangor (the Malay Peninsula) the women—who used to seek their own husbands—were allowed to have more than one, and that a certain woman who lived at Bandar Kanching had as many as four.[4] Dr. Martin doubts the accuracy of this statement on account of its uniqueness ;[5] but Messrs. Skeat and Blagden affirm that cases of polyandry have been recorded

---

[1] Hoops, *Reallexikon der Germanischen Altertumskunde*, iii. 426.
[2] Reclus, *Primitive Folk*, p. 66.
[3] Lady Montagu, *Letters and Works*, i. 244 *sq.*
[4] Campbell, quoted by Skeat and Blagden, *Pagan Races of the Malay Peninsula*, ii. 68.
[5] Martin, *Die Inlandstämme der Malayischen Halbinsel*, p. 871.

among the Sakai of Ulu Langat.[1] Among the Punans, a
nomadic people in the central highlands of Borneo living
entirely upon the wild produce of the jungle, polyandry
occurs, although as a rule they are monogamous.[2] Among
the Dyaks of Sidin, in the western division of Borneo,
according to Kater, a woman may have more than one husband, and the women make use of this privilege without
being the less respected on that account or without making
any secret of it ; but in such cases the management of the
children belongs to the first husband alone.[3] Riedel states
that in the Kei Islands " the women formerly lived with
several men, and the children followed the mother."[4]
Among the Subanu, a mountain people of Mindanao in the
Philippines, " polyandry is occasionally resorted to where
men are too poor to provide the *laxa* (dowry) required to
secure a wife, and two of them join in the purchase of one
woman."[5]

In the Marshall Islands polyandry still exists, although
it has much decreased through missionary influence ; among
the heathen, women of rank can take as many husbands as
they like, and in former days they exercised this right to a
great extent. All the husbands are regarded as the fathers
of the children.[6] Polyandry is, or has been, one of the fixed
customs of the natives of the Marquesas. De Roquefeuil, who
visited those islands in the earlier part of the nineteenth
century, says that nearly every woman there had at least
two husbands, and that it was only the most moderate that
contented themselves with two. The supplementary

---

[1] Skeat and Blagden, *op. cit.* ii. 76.

[2] Hose and McDougall, *Pagan Tribes of Borneo,* ii. 183.

[3] Kater, ' De Dajaks van Sidin,' in *Tijdschrift voor indische
taal-, land- en volkenkunde,* xvi. 185.

[4] Riedel, *De sluik- en kroesharige rassen tusschen Selebes en Papua,*
p. 236.

[5] Finley and Churchill, *Subanu,* p. 29.

[6] Senfft, in Steinmetz, *Rechtsverhältnisse von eingeborenen Völkern
in Afrika und Ozeanien,* p. 433. *Idem,* ' Die Insel Nauru,' in *Mittheil. Deutsch. Schutzgeb.* ix. 106. Jung, ' Rechtsanschauungen der
Eingeborenen von Nauru,' *ibid.* x. 66. Kohler, ' Das Recht der
Marschallinsulaner,' in *Zeitschr. f. vergl. Rechtswiss.* xiv. 416.

husband was generally a brother or friend of the principal husband, and the wife slept between them. The children belonged to him who supported the mother or to him whom she designated to be their father. Polygyny, on the other hand, was so rare that in all those islands men who had more than one wife were specially spoken of.[1] Lisiansky, whose description is of a slightly earlier date, writes of the natives of Nukahiva, one of the Marquesas :—" In rich families, every woman has two husbands ; of whom one may be called the assistant husband. This last, when the other is at home, is nothing more than the head servant of the house ; but, in case of absence, exercises all the rights of matrimony, and is also obliged to attend his lady wherever she goes. It happens sometimes, that the subordinate partner is chosen after marriage ; but in general two men present themselves to the same woman, who, if she approves their addresses, appoints one for the real husband, and the other as his auxiliary : the auxiliary is generally poor, but handsome and well-made."[2] According to Dr. Tautain's description of the marriage customs of the Marquesas Islanders, all the brothers of a man became from the moment of his marriage *vahana pekio*, or secondary husbands to his wife, and all her sisters became *vehine pekio*, or secondary wives to him, which, however, did not prevent them from marrying other men if they were not married already. But the husbands of one woman were not always brothers. If a man carried off another man's wife, he became her principal husband, whilst the original husband, if he followed her, now only became her *vahana pekio* and the principal husband's servant ; and the principal wife of a man could also on her own account take a secondary husband, and often did so. A woman's children were regarded as the children of all her husbands, and called each other brothers or sisters.[3] In the valley of Typee, according to Melville, no man has more than one wife, and no wife of mature years has less

[1] de Roquefeuil, *Journal d'un voyage autour du monde*, i. 308 *sq.*
[2] Lisiansky, *Voyage round the World*, p. 83.
[3] Tautain, ' Étude sur le mariage chez les Polynésiens des îles Marquises,' in *L'Anthropologie*, vi. 644, 646, 648.

than two husbands ; " a second suitor presents himself, of graver years, and carries both boy and girl away to his own habitation."[1] Dr. Rivers says that the polyandry of the Marquesas Islanders is peculiar in that the husbands are of different social status, one husband belonging to a more influential section of the community than the other.[2] I do not know on what authority he makes this statement, but it is certainly contradictory to the information given us both by de Roquefeuil and Dr. Tautain, and is not justified even by Lisiansky's report on the Nukahivans.

In the Hawaian Islands there were polyandry and cicisbeism apart from the group-relations of which I shall speak in the next chapter.[3] Thus it was usual in the families of chiefs that a woman had two husbands ; the first child was regarded as the offspring of the first husband and the second child as belonging to the second husband.[4] Among the Tuhoe tribe of the Maori there are a few isolated cases on record " where, a married woman having committed adultery, it was agreed to by her people that she should have the two husbands " ; but Mr. Best knows of no sign of a polyandrous system among the Maori.[5] In a very ancient Maori legend, however, there is one mention of polyandry, namely, when Hinauri became the wife of the two brothers Ihuatamai and Ihuwareware.[6] In New Caledonia, according to M. Moncelon, polyandry does not seem to have been entirely unknown.[7] The Rev. J. H. Hadfield wrote to me from Lifu in 1888 that an old man knew of three cases of polyandrous marriage having occurred in that island, though the husbands were despised by the rest of the natives ; in two of

[1] Melville, *Typee*, p. 282.
[2] Rivers, ' Marriage (Introductory and Primitive),' in Hastings, *Encyclopædia of Religion and Ethics*, viii. 427.
[3] Stewart, *Journal of a Residence in the Sandwich Islands*, p. 129. Marcuse, *Die Hawaiischen Inseln*, p. 108.
[4] Poepoe, quoted by Rivers, *History of Melanesian Society*, i. 380. See also Jarves, *History of the Hawaiian Islands*, p. 43.
[5] Best, ' Maori Marriage Customs,' in *Trans. and Proceed. New Zealand Institute*, xxxvi. 28.
[6] Grey, *Polynesian Mythology*, p. 49. Tregear, *The Maori Race* p. 298.
[7] Moncelon, in *Bull. Soc. d'Anthr. Paris*, ser. iii. vol. ix. 367.

these cases they were brothers, in the third unrelated. In Mallicolo, of the New Hebrides, two men sometimes had one wife between them.[1] In the Banks Islands cases are known in which two widowers live with one widow and she is called wife to both, any child she may have being called the child of both. " Such cohabitation, however," Dr. Codrington observes, " is not so much marriage as a convenient arrangement for people who find themselves alone in later life." There are also cases where a husband connives at his wife's connection with another man ; but the second man is not a husband, and the thing is thought discreditable.[2] In the Arosi district of San Cristoval, in the Solomon Group, it frequently happens that " a man gives money and goes and lives with a married couple. Often, it is said, he has no access to the woman, and lives with them merely to have someone to cook for him and help in the garden work ; but if he wishes to have access to the woman he may do so on payment, and will have children by her. In some villages there are three or even four men living thus with a woman, but never more ; and all the children born are considered to be the children of the first husband."[3] In Luf, to the west of the Admiralty Islands, nowadays inhabited by about eighty persons only, it is the custom for a married man to allow some other man access to his wife, and it is even said that a woman is in a way the common property of all the men.[4]

The sexual communism of certain Melanesians of New Guinea and natives of Australia will be dealt with in the chapter on group-marriage and group-relations. In the present place I only want to point out that their sexual relations also may in some cases assume a merely polyandrous character, as when, among the Dieri in the neighbourhood of Lake Eyre in Central Australia, a widower may be

[1] Eckardt, ' Der Archipel der Neu-Hebriden,' in *Verhandlungen des Vereins für naturwissenschaftliche Unterhaltung zu Hamburg,* iv. 21 n. *

[2] Codrington, *Melanesians,* p. 245 *sq.*

[3] Fox, ' Social Organization in San Cristoval, Solomon Islands,' in *Jour. Roy. Anthr. Inst.* xlix. 118 *sq.*

[4] Parkinson, *Dreissig Jahre in der Südsee,* pp. 436, 442.

allowed access to his brother's wife and an unmarried man to the wife of somebody else.[1] Among the Gippsland blacks, according to Bulmer, " there is reason to believe that custom sanctioned a single man cohabiting occasionally with his brother's wife ; and also a married man with his wife's sister."[2] Sometimes the facts adduced as evidence of group-marriage actually imply nothing else than polyandrous relations. Thus, with reference to the Wakelbura in Queensland it is simply said that a man's unmarried brothers (own or tribal) have access to his wife and are obliged to protect the children borne by her.[3] Sir James G. Frazer's statement that polyandry is not found in Australia[4] may be quite correct if by polyandry is understood marriage in the full sense of the term ; but then he should also avoid speaking of the present existence of group-marriage in Australia.

In Madagascar polyandry has occurred, though only in exceptional cases. Thus among the former inhabitants of the province of Antangenă, who, in consequence of a civil war, had been driven away from their native country and settled down in another province, several brothers had one woman in common, and the children were recognised as the children of them all. Among the Merină, on the same island, the widow of a man became the wife not only of his eldest brother, but, by his consent, of the other brothers as well— she became, as they said, a *vady marolahÿ*, which means " the spouse of many men " ; but at the end of the eighteenth century this custom was put a stop to. Moreover, until recently a Malagasy woman, though actually having only one husband, was during his absence compelled by ancestral law to receive in the conjugal bed his brothers— or, as it seems, his younger brothers,[5]—as also his brothers-in-law and cousins by alliance, to all of whom she was *tokam-balÿ*, or "common spouse." If any of them was

1 Howitt, *Native Tribes of South-East Australia*, pp. 181, 183.
2 Bulmer, in Curr, *The Australian Race*, iii. 546.
3 Howitt, *op. cit.* p. 224.
4 Frazer, *Totemism and Exogamy*, i. 501.
5 Grandidier, *Ethnographie de Madagascar*, ii. 155 n. 2.

caught in flagrant adultery, he was allowed to atone for his fault by proposing to the husband to share with him the family expenses, as well as the woman and her children, a proposal which, it is said, the injured husband was at liberty to accept or refuse.[1] The queens of Madagascar were perfectly free to take several husbands according to their choice ; a traveller who visited the east coast of the island in 1818 found there a queen who had four, and M. Grandidier has seen one who was accompanied by two.[2] Herr Walter says that in Nossi-Bé, off the north-west coast of Madagascar, a woman is not generally allowed to have more than one husband, but that cases of polyandry nevertheless occur both there and on the main island.[3]

In the description given by Bontier and Le Verrier of the conquest and conversion of the Canarians in 1402 by Jean de Bethencourt we read that in the island of Lancerote most of the women have three husbands, " who wait upon them alternately by months ; the husband that is to live with the wife the following month waits upon her and upon her other husband the whole of the month that the latter has her, and so each takes her in turn."[4] Abreu de Galindo states that among the Canarians no woman had more than one husband, " contrary to what some misinformed authors affirm " ;[5] but this was written at a much later date, in 1632.[6] As v. Humboldt justly remarks, it must be regretted that the missionaries who accompanied Jean de Bethencourt have given us no ampler details on the custom in question.[7]

---

[1] According to Mr. Sibree (*The Great African Island*, p. 253), the Hovas of Madagascar have a word to express the leave given to a wife to have intercourse with another man during her husband's prolonged absence from home.

[2] Grandidier, *op. cit.* ii. 189 n. *a.* See also *ibid.* ii. 154 *sq.*

[3] Walter, in Steinmetz, *Rechtsverhältnisse*, p. 370.

[4] Bontier and Le Verrier, *The Canarian*, p. 139.

[5] Abreu de Galindo, *History of the Discovery and Conquest of the Canary Islands*, p. 68.

[6] *Cf.* Viera y Clavijo, *Noticias de la historia general de las islas de Canaria*, i. 171.

[7] v. Humboldt, *op. cit.* i. 84.

On the African continent there are a few peoples among whom polyandry has been found to exist. According to Thunberg, " a Hottentot sometimes takes two wives, and it frequently happens that a woman marries two husbands, although adultery under certain circumstances is punished with death."[1] Mr. McCall Theal observes that there were polyandrous marriages among the Bantu mountaineers of South Africa : " a man who had not the requisite number of cattle to procure a wife, and whose father was too poor to help him, obtained assistance from a wealthy individual on condition of having joint marital rights."[2] Among the Basuto, according to Mr. Rolland, a chief with many wives " secures the services and adherence of many young men who are too poor to purchase wives, by bestowing one of his own concubines upon them either temporarily or permanently. In either case the children belong to the chief, who is considered as the nominal father and owner."[3] Of the Banyankole or Bahima, a pastoral tribe of Ankole, in Central Africa, the Rev. John Roscoe writes :—" It happens at times that a poor man cannot afford to pay the necessary number of cows to obtain a wife and still have sufficient left to supply him and his wife with milk for their daily need. He therefore seeks the aid of one or more brothers to join him and together they pay the marriage fee and the woman becomes the wife of the party. The eldest brother goes through the marriage customs, but it is understood that she is the wife of all the men in the contract. The woman lives with each in turn until she is with child, when she remains with the eldest until the child is born. Any children born of such a marriage are called the children of the eldest brother. An agreement of this kind does not prevent any member of the party from relinquishing his share in this arrangement and marrying another wife himself, if he

---

[1] Thunberg, *Travels in Europe, Africa, and Asia* (1770–1779), ii. 193. *Cf.* Alexander, *Expedition of Discovery into the Interior of Africa*, i. 169 :—" Sometimes two chiefs will have four wives between them : this is, I think, new."

[2] Theal, *Yellow and Dark-skinned People of Africa south of the Zambesi*, p. 224. *Idem, History of the Boers in South Africa*, p. 19.

[3] Rolland, quoted by Theal, *History of the Boers*, p. 19.

wishes to do so when he has obtained the means."[1] A
married woman may also welcome to her bed any of her
husband's friends or relations with impunity, and any children resulting from such intercourse belong to the husband.[2]
Mr. Roscoe says that the only other Bantu people known
to him to be polyandrists are the Baziba to the south of
Uganda ;[3] but he gives us no further details about their
marriages. According to M. Junod the Bapedi, in South-
East Africa, have a kind of polyandry, which, however,
amounts to nothing more than cicisbeism : after marriage
a woman who has had children can have intercourse with
other men than her husband.[4] In various African tribes
a childless man will secretly introduce his brother,[5] or
possibly some other man,[6] to his wife in order that he may
have a child by her. According to Winwood Reade, the
sisters of the king of Ashanti " may negotiate with whom
and with as many as they please for the contribution of
royal heirs ; provided always that the man is strong,
good-looking, and of a decent position in life."[7] In some
tribes of Sierra Leone " a woman who is a Paramount Chief
may have sexual intercourse with as many men as she
pleases." In the same tribes " a man having many wives,
so long as it does not come openly to his knowledge, has
no objection (and in fact it is looked upon as a right) to
his sons having connection with his wives other than the
actual mother of the son, and any other wife who has
helped to wean him. . . . The same semi-right of use also

---

[1] Roscoe, *Northern Bantu*, p. 121.

[2] *Idem*, ' Bahima,' in *Jour. Roy. Anthr. Inst.* xxxvii. 105.

[3] *Ibid.* p. 105 n. 1.

[4] Junod, *Life of a South African Tribe*, i. 99.

[5] Torday and Joyce, ' Ethnography of the Ba-Mbala,' in *Jour.
Anthr. Inst.* xxxv. 410. *Iidem*, ' Ethnography of the Ba-Yaka,'
ibid. xxxvi. 45. *Iidem, Les Bushongo*, p. 272 (Bohindu). Poupon,
' Étude ethnographique des Baya,' in *L'Anthropologie*, xxvi. 126.
Le Herissé, *L'Ancien Royaume du Dahomey*, p. 208.

[6] Bufe, ' Die Bakundu,' in *Archiv f. Anthropologie*, N.S. xii.
235. Le Herissé, *op. cit.* p. 208 (Dahomans). Weeks, ' Notes on
some Customs of the Lower Congo People,' in *Folk-Lore*, xix. 413.

[7] Reade, *Savage Africa*, p. 43.

applies to nephews, the sons of the man's brothers (but not sisters) and to their sons, but does not apply to grandsons."[1] Mr. Northcote W. Thomas informs me that among the Ifòn of Southern Nigeria sons likewise can have connection with their father's wives in his lifetime. Strabo asserts that polyandry prevailed in Arabia Felix. " All the kindred," he says, " have their property in common, the eldest being lord ; all have one wife and it is first come first served, the man who enters to her leaving at the door the stick which it is usual for every one to carry ; but the night she spends with the eldest."[2]   Glaser[3] and Winckler[4] think that they have found confirmation of this statement in Sabaean and Minaean inscriptions. According to Bukhārī it was a custom of the pagan Arabs that several men cohabited with one wife, and that the latter nominated the father of any child to which she gave birth ; [5] and he also mentions another form of marriage, called *nikāḥ al-istibḍā'*, which consisted in a man prostituting his wife to a noble person in order to get noble offspring.[6]   Nöldeke, however, observes that a Muhammadan theologian can hardly be regarded as a reliable witness as to the customs of Arabic paganism, and he sees in the pretended polyandry in Central Arabia merely a kind of prostitution.[7]   According to Robertson Smith, the former prevalence of " the very

---

[1] Vergette, *Certain Marriage Customs of some of the Tribes in the Protectorate of Sierra Leone*, p. 10.

[2] Strabo, *Geographica*, xvi. 4. 25, C. 783. I have availed myself of Robertson Smith's translation of this passage in his *Kinship and Marriage in Early Arabia*, p. 158.

[3] Glaser, quoted by Winckler, ' Polyandrie bei Semiten,' in *Verhandl. Berliner Gesellsch. Anthr.* 1898, p. 29.

[4] *Ibid.* p. 29. Winckler, ' Die Polyandrie bei den Minäern,' in *Altorientalische Forschungen*, ii. 81 *sqq.*

[5] Bukhārī, iii. 206, quoted by Wellhausen, ' Die Ehe bei den Arabern,' in *Nachrichten von der Königl. Gesellsch. d. Wissensch. zu Göttingen*, 1893, p. 460 *sq.* See also *Alberuni's India*, i. 109.

[6] Bukhārī, quoted by Wilken, *Das Matriarchat bei den alten Arabern*, p. 27.

[7] Nöldeke, review of Wilken, *Het Matriarchaat bij de oude Arabieren*, in *Oesterreichische Monatsschrift für den Orient*, x. 303. *Idem*, review of Robertson Smith, *Kinship and Marriage in Early Arabia*, in *Zeitschr. d. Deutsch. Morgenländ. Gesellsch.* xl. 155.

grossest forms of polyandry . . . over all the Semitic area seems to be proved by the fact that absolute licence continued to be a feature of certain religious rites among the Canaanites, the Aramæans, and the heathen Hebrews."[1] But I can see no reason whatever to look upon these rites as survivals of earlier marriage customs.

It appears from this survey of facts that, so far as direct evidence goes, it is only in a few areas that polyandry is, or has been, practised by a considerable number of the population, whilst among various peoples it has been restricted to more or less exceptional cases. In a single instance, that of the Massagetae of Turkestan, it is represented as the only recognised form of marriage, but this statement, made by an old Chinese writer with reference to a foreign people, must be looked upon with some suspicion. Very frequently polyandry, like polygyny, is modified in a monogamous direction : as one, usually the first married, wife in polygynous families is the chief wife, so one, usually the first, husband in polyandrous families is often, or mostly, the chief husband. Any other man with whom he shares his wife is in various cases spoken of as a secondary husband,[2] or as a deputy or assistant who acts as husband and master of the house during the absence of the true lord but on the latter's return becomes his servant,[3] or merely as a recognised paramour,[4] a " half-partner,"[5] a " brother-in-love,"[6] or a connubial " companion."[7] Very frequently the husbands are brothers, although among various peoples whose polyandry is as a rule fraternal the husbands or paramours may also be otherwise related to one another[8] or even unrelated ;[9] nay, sometimes it is only a certain number of brothers who may have a wife in common whilst the wife is allowed to take an additional husband from another

---

[1] Robertson Smith, *op. cit.* p. 206.   [2] Marquesas Islanders.
[3] Kaniagmiut, Nukahivans.   [4] Tlingit.
[5] Aleut.   [6] Cree.   [7] Chukchee.
[8] Tibetans, some polyandrists of the Punjab, Todas, carpenters and some other castes of Malabar, Sinhalese, Wakelbura, Malagasy, ancient Arabs.
[9] Tibetans, natives of Darjeeling, some polyandrists of the Punjab, Todas, Sinhalese, Marquesas Islanders.

family.[1] Where fraternal polyandry prevails the eldest brother is commonly regarded as the principal husband. He chooses the wife, and the contract he makes may implicitly confer matrimonial rights on all the other brothers,[2] although it may also be that each of them has to undergo a special ceremony in order to be recognised as husband.[3] It is said that the younger brothers can claim the wife as theirs only as long as they continue to live with the eldest one ;[4] that if the latter dies she can rid herself of the other brothers by a simple ceremony, at least if she has no children ;[5] that the minor husbands often are little better than servants to the eldest brother and can be turned out of doors at his pleasure.[6] Several statements seem to imply, or even expressly affirm, that the younger brothers are not really regarded as husbands of the eldest brother's wife although they have access to her, especially in his absence.[7] In some cases all the children are regarded as the children of the eldest brother ;[8] he is called " father," the other husbands being called " uncles,"[9] or a distinction is made between " elder " and " younger " or "great" and " little " fathers.[10] In other cases of polyandry—fraternal or non-fraternal— all the husbands are equally regarded as fathers ;[11] or the children are divided between them according to seniority,[12] or belong to those whom the mother designates to be their fathers.[13] Among many polyandrous peoples the various husbands live or cohabit with their common wife in turn ;[14]

[1] Ladakhis.

[2] *E.g.*, Tibetans, Ladakhis, Gûjar, Punjab Jâts, Todas.

[3] Tiyyans, Kaniyans.   [4] Tibetans.   [5] Ladakhis.   [6] Ladakhis.

[7] Tlingit, Gilyak, Lepchas, some polyandrists of the Punjab, Santals, Bhuiyas, Kandhs, casters in metal of Malabar, Tottiyans, Dieri, Gippsland blacks, Wakelbura, Malagasy.

[8] Massagetae of Turkestan, some polyandrists of the Punjab, Ladakhis, Gûjar, Bahima.

[9] Tibetans.   [10] Tibetans, Kulu, Ladakhis, Sinhalese.

[11] Todas, Vilkurups, Kallans, Marshall Islanders, Marquesas Islanders, Malagasy.

[12] Tibetans, natives of Sirmur, Todas, Hawaians.

[13] Tibetans, Nayars, Marquesas Islanders.

[14] Tibetans, polyandrists of the Punjab (*e.g.*, Kulu), Todas, Kammālans, Kaniyans, Nayars, aborigines of Lancerote, Bahima.

if they are brothers, the eldest one is sometimes expressly said to take the lead,[1] or when she is with child she remains with him until the child is born.[2]   In two cases we are told that the eldest husband spends the nights with the wife.[3]

[1] Kulu, Kammālans.   [2] Bahima.
[3] Ancient Arabs, Todas.

CHAPTER XXX

POLYANDRY

(*Concluded*)

From the description of facts given in the last chapter we shall now proceed to a discussion of the causes to which polyandry may be traced. One of these causes is the numerical proportion between the sexes. Among various polyandrous peoples there are said to be more men than women, and their polyandry has in several cases been directly attributed to this fact.

Thus according to von Humboldt the polyandry of the Avanoes and Maypures along the Orinoco is due to a disproportion between the sexes, the men being in the majority.[1] M. Chaffanjon makes a similar statement with reference to the Maquiritarés.[2] Scarcity of women likewise accounts for the cases of polyandry sometimes practised on the frontiers of the Paraguayan Chaco.[3] Speaking of the occasional polyandry of the Western Eskimo, Seemann observes that this custom " seems to have its origin in the paucity of the softer sex."[4] According to the statistics of Patkanov, from 1912, there were among the Gilyak 2,556 men and only 2,093 women, and their polyandry has been accounted for by this unequal proportion.[5] Ma-touan-lin states that

---

[1] v. Humboldt, *Personal Narrative of Travels*, v. 549.
[2] Chaffanjon, *op. cit.* p. 283.
[3] Grubb, *An Unknown People in an Unknown Land*, p. 215.
[4] Seemann, *Voyage of H.M.S. Herald*, ii. 66.
[5] Miss Czaplicka, *Aboriginal Siberia*, p. 100 n. 1.

among the Massagetae of Turkestan the brothers of a family had one wife in common because there were among them many more men than women.[1]

It has been said that Tibetan polyandry is caused by the scarcity of women in a marriageable state, and that this scarcity is due to the Lama nunneries absorbing so many of the girls.[2] But Koeppen clears the religion of Tibet of any responsibility for polyandry, showing that the practice existed in the country before the introduction of Buddhism;[3] and Professor Puini observes that the number of women who devote themselves to a religious life is much smaller than the number of men.[4] Waddell speaks of " the enormous tax of celibate Lamas which the present priestly government extracts from the people, about one out of every two males " ;[5] whereas according to Rockhill there are very few nuns, at least in Eastern Tibet.[6] Among the laity of Lhasa the women considerably outnumber the men, a preponderance which Waddell attributes both to the immense numbers of men who join the Church as celibates and to the prevalence of polyandry, which tends to drive the surplus women from their homes into the town, where they contract promiscuous marriages, as marriage and divorce are easy in Tibet.[7] Other writers speak of superfluous women who become prostitutes or remain single.[8] Yet if the proportion of the sexes in Tibet were fairly equal, as some recent writers are inclined to believe,[9] the number of unmarried women outside the convents ought to be very

[1] Rémusat, op. cit. i. 245.
[2] Beauregard, ' En Asie ; Kachmir et Tibet,' in Bull. Soc. d'Anthr. Paris, ser. iii. vol. v. 265, 267, 271. Cf. Wilson, op. cit. p. 212.
[3] Koeppen, Die Religion des Buddha, i. 476.
[4] Puini, op. cit. p. 146.
[5] Waddell, Lhasa and its Mysteries, p. 469.
[6] Rockhill, Land of the Lamas, p. 212.
[7] Waddell, op. cit. p. 345 sq. According to a census taken in 1854 there were in Lhasa 27,000 Lamas and 15,000 laity, of whom 9,000 were women (Rockhill, in Jour. Roy. Asiatic Soc. N.S. xxiii. 14).
[8] Earle, quoted by Risley, People of India, p. 212. Bonvalot, op. cit. ii. 126. Landon, Lhasa, p. 267. Grenard, op. cit. p. 263.
[9] Rockhill, Land of the Lamas, p. 212. Puini, op. cit. p. 146. Risley, People of India, p. 212.

large indeed, considering that polygyny is not commonly practised. The old statement that there are more men than women in Tibet may perhaps after all be true. According to Desideri, the polyandry of the Tibetans is due in the first place to the barrenness of their country and the scarcity of cultivable land, and in the second place to the small number of women.[1] Du Halde writes that when the Lamas are reproached for allowing such a shameful practice, " they excuse themselves on account of the few women there are in Tibet, just as in Tartary, where, as a matter of fact, one sees in the families many more boys than girls."[2] Mr. Sherring, in a recent book, evidently takes a similar view of the proportion between the sexes in Tibet ; for in discussing the causes of the decrease of the population he refers to the observation made in the hills of India that where polyandry has existed there have been " small families with males preponderating."[3] M. Grenard directly states that girls are less numerous than boys in Tibet, " at the rate of seven to eight, according to the prefect of Nagchu." He maintains, however, that the insufficiency of daughters was not the cause of the institution or the reason for the continuance of polyandry in that country. On the contrary —he argues—there are too many women in Tibet to-day and many of them do not get married for these two reasons, that on the average there are a few more husbands than wives in the families and that a host of men are devoted to religious celibacy.[4] But this argumentation loses its force when we consider that religious celibacy did not exist in pre-Buddhistic times. Among the Mongols, according to Prejevalsky, " the women are far less numerous than the men " ;[5] and among the Turkomans, as we are informed by Yavorski, there are born 100 boys to 76 girls.[6] Grenard thinks it probable that both the Mongols and the Turkomans

---

[1] Puini, *op. cit.* p. 131.
[2] Du Halde, *op. cit.* iv. 572. A similar statement is made by Grosier, *op. cit.* i. 322.
[3] Sherring, *Western Tibet*, p. 88 *sq.*
[4] Grenard, *op. cit.* p. 263.   [5] Prejevalsky, *Mongolia*, i. 71.
[6] Yavorski, reviewed in *L'Anthropologie*, viii. 356.

formerly practised polyandry,[1] although his argument is not conclusive.

Among the Mongoloid population of the Western Himalaya region, as also among many of the Assam tribes, females are said to preponderate.[2] In the Census Report of Kashmir for 1911 we are told that whilst the Aryan races inhabiting the lower regions of Jammu Province seem disposed naturally to a shortage of women, the Mongolians of Ladakh have a superabundance of them.[3] Sir Alexander Cunningham states that the females outnumber the males in the Buddhist country of Ladakh, whereas the reverse is the case in the Mussulman districts along the Indus.[4] The surplus female population is said to find its way into the monasteries or to pass over to the Mussulman families.[5] On the other hand, Drew, in discussing polyandry and its effects in Ladakh, wrote :—" I could get no satisfactory answer to the inquiry I made of many—what becomes of the surplus of women which must, one would think, be caused by the custom ? I did not learn that there were many old maids, and the number of nuns is less than the number of young men that have been drafted off to become monks. It is possible that polyandry alters the proportion of sexes in the children born —lessens the number of females ; but this is hypothetical ; I could not get statistics to throw light on the subject."[6] In a census of the North-West Provinces taken in the year 1866 the proportions of the sexes were found to be 100 men to 86·6 women, and in the Punjab even 100 to 81·8.[7] Speaking of polyandry in the Jounsar district, Mr. Dunlop observes :— " It is remarkable that wherever the practice of polyandry exists, there is a striking discrepance in the proportions of the sexes among young children as well as adults ; thus, in a village where I have found upwards of four hundred boys,

---

[1] Grenard, *op. cit.* p. 256. [2] *Imperial Gazetteer of India*, i. 480.
[3] Matin-uz-Zaman Khan, *op. cit.* p. 131. See also Moorcroft and Trebeck, *op. cit.* i. 322.
[4] Cunningham, *Ladák*, p. 289.
[5] Matin-uz-Zaman Khan, *op. cit.* p. 137.
[6] Drew, *op. cit.* p. 251.
[7] Marshall, *A Phrenologist amongst the Todas*, p. 100. See also *Imperial Gazetteer of India*, i. 479.

there were only one hundred and twenty girls. . . . In the Gurhwal Hills, moreover, where polygamy is prevalent, there is a surplus of female children."[1] We are told that the polyandry of the Kotgarh district was due to a disproportion between the sexes caused partly by female infanticide and partly by the custom of selling females to rich natives of the plains.[2] Ferishta states that among the " Gakkars "— presumably the Khokhars—[3] of the Punjab it was a custom " as soon as a female child was born to carry her to the door of the house, and there proclaim aloud, holding the child in one hand, and a knife in the other, that any person who wanted a wife might now take her, otherwise she was immediately put to death. By this means, they had more men than women, which occasioned the custom of several husbands to one wife."[4] Among the Gûjars polyandry " was mainly due to the scarcity of women in the tribe, and this scarcity was the result of female infanticide, which several sections of the caste practised very largely before the passing of the Infanticide Act of 1870 "; but as this Act put a stop to the murder of infant girls, " the scarcity of women is no longer felt, the custom of polyandry is dying out, and will soon be a thing of the past."[5] Sir Herbert Risley says that there is no reason to believe that the proportion of the sexes in Sikkim is not fairly equal ;[6] but among the Lepchas and other Himalayan tribes on the northern frontier of Bengal females are expressly stated to be in a minority.[7] Pemberton observed that in the northern and central portions of Bhutan, where polyandry is practised far more extensively than in the southern, the attention of the traveller is arrested by the paucity of children and women, whereas in the latter division they appear quite as numerous as in any of the surrounding countries ; and at Dewangiri, on the southern face of the

---

[1] Dunlop, *op. cit.* p. 181 *sq.*
[2] Rebsch, quoted by Stulpnagel, in *Indian Antiquary*, vii. 133.
[3] See *supra*, iii. 119 n. 4 ; Elliot, *History of India*, viii. 202 *sq.*
[4] Ferishta, *op. cit.* i. 183 *sq.*
[5] Râja Lachhman Sinh, quoted by Crooke, *Tribes and Castes of the North-Western Provinces and Oudh*, ii. 444 *sq.*
[6] Risley, *People of India*, p. 212.
[7] *Imperial Gazetteer of India*, i. 480.

mountains overlooking Assam, where the practice is altogether disavowed and considered infamous, the proportion
of young to grown-up persons, and of females to males,
" appears to follow the laws by which it is ordinarily regulated."[1] In the Census Report for 1901 it is said that there
is no very marked dearth of females in Bhutan, and that the
superfluous women usually become nuns or prostitutes.[2]

All the records which we have of the Todas from different
years show an excess of men over women. In 1871 there
were 140·6 men for every 100 women ; in 1881, 130·4 ;
in 1891, 135·9 ; and in the census of 1901, 127·4. Dr.
Rivers' figures from his genealogical record give, for 1902,
132·2 men for every 100 women.[3] There has thus been a
progressive decrease in the excess of males over females. At
the same time it seems that polyandry also has been somewhat decreasing. Dr. Rivers thinks it probable that it has
become less frequent for several brothers to have only one
wife in common, and that, owing to the greater number of
women, it has become more frequent for them to have
several wives between them.[4] This undoubtedly gives
support to the common view that the polyandry of the Todas
always has been connected with their scarcity of women.
Among the Badagas also there has been found a considerable
surplus of males.[5] According to an estimate of the native
population of the Nilgiri Hills in 1856, there were then
altogether 21,844 males and 14,579 females.[6] In Coorg
" the dearth of females is extraordinarily great."[7] In
Ceylon, too, a considerable disparity between the sexes has
been exhibited by the returns. In the middle of the last
century it was found in the greatest degree among the
Sinhalese, among whom the surplus of men averaged twelve

---

[1] Pemberton, *op. cit.* p. 116.
[2] Risley and Gait, *op. cit.* p. 448.
[3] Rivers, *Todas*, p. 477. Marshall (*op. cit.* p. 100) found in 1870
that Toda males of all ages bore the proportion to females of all
ages of 100 to 75.
[4] Rivers, *op. cit.* p. 518 *sq.*
[5] Metz, *Tribes inhabiting the Neilgherry Hills*, p. 131.
[6] Baikie, *Neilgherries*, p. 111.
[7] *Imperial Gazetteer of India*, i. 479.

per cent., but it was also observable in the case of the Malabar population in the northern province, where the surplus of men averaged six per cent.[1] According to the census of 1891 there were among the Sinhalese 108·8 males to 100 females.[2]

Among many Australian tribes the males are said to be in the majority.[3] In the middle of the last century Westgarth wrote, " In reducing to an average the various evidence on the aboriginal population lately furnished to the Committee of the Legislative Council of New South Wales, it appears that there are at present among the adult aborigines inhabiting that colony rather less than two females to three males, and that there is also about the same proportion in the sexes among the children."[4] Among the Bangerang of Victoria, according to Curr, the males exceeded the females in the proportion perhaps of three to two.[5] In the Adelaide tribe Moorhouse found the males to average even seventy per cent. more than the females.[6] In West Australia Sir G. Grey drew up a list of 222 births, and of these 129 were males and 93 females.[7]

The polyandry occasionally practised in Mallicolo was due to lack of women.[8] Parkinson attributes the sexual com-

---

[1] Pridham, *Account of Ceylon*, i. 451. *Cf.* Davy, *op. cit.* p. 107 note ; Sirr, *op. cit.* ii. 339.

[2] Schmidt, *Ceylon*, p. 242.

[3] Fison and Howitt, *Kamilaroi and Kurnai*, p. 148. Lumholtz, *Among Cannibals*, p. 134. Beveridge, *Aborigines of Victoria and Riverina*, p. 15. Brough Smyth, *Aborigines of Victoria*, i. 51. Eylmann, *Die Eingeborenen der Kolonie Südaustralien*, p. 137. Wilhelmi, ' Manners and Customs of the Australian Natives, in particular of the Port Lincoln District,' in *Trans. Roy. Soc. Victoria*, v. 180. Oldfield, ' Aborigines of Australia,' in *Trans. Ethn. Soc. N.S. iii.* 250 (West Australian natives).

[4] Westgarth, *Australia Felix*, p. 63. See also Henderson, *Excursions and Adventures in New South Wales*, ii. 110.

[5] Curr, *Recollections of Squatting in Victoria*, p. 249.

[6] Eyre, *Journals of Expeditions of Discovery into Central Australia*, ii. 375.

[7] Grey, *Journals of Expeditions of Discovery in North-West and Western Australia*, ii. 251.

[8] Eckardt, in *Verhandl. d. Vereins f. naturwiss. Unterhaltung Hamburg*, iv. 21 n. *

munism in Luf to the same cause.[1] In the Hawaian Islands
the men outnumbered the women,[2] and the same was the
case in Nukahiva[3] and, according to M. Moncelon, in New
Caledonia.[4] Dr. Tautain is inclined to believe that the
polyandry of the Marquesas Islanders, and the sexual
laxity of the Polynesians in general, were due to the fact that
the immigrants mostly consisted of men, their great pirogues
even being tabooed to women ; and he quotes one of their
traditions in support of this opinion.[5] Yet it is difficult to
believe that such a more or less temporary disturbance of the
proportion between the sexes could have produced so lasting
effects. The Malagasy of Antangenă, who settled down in
another province, took to fraternal polyandry because only
a small number of their women accompanied them in their
exile ; but the equilibrium between the sexes was soon
re-established and polyandry disappeared.[6] Polyandric
relations have often been noticed among emigrants. The
East Indian coolies introduced into British Guiana often
practise polyandry, three or four men living with one woman,
as there are on an average not more than 35 women to every
100 men among them.[7] The Klings of the Coromandel
Coast who emigrate to Malacca, Singapore, Java, or other
places, take with them so few women that several men have
to content themselves with one woman between them.[8]
The Rev. L. Fison writes, " Polyandry is to be seen under
our eyes here in Fiji among the ' imported labourers.' " [9]
The surplus of males may be due to different causes.
Von Humboldt explains the paucity of women among the
polyandrous Avanoes and Maypures by the hard work they

[1] Parkinson, op. cit. p. 442.
[2] Ellis, Tour through Hawaii, p. 414. Marcuse, op. cit. p. 109.
[3] Melville, op. cit. p. 281.
[4] Moncelon, in Bull. Soc. d'Anthr. Paris, ser. iii. vol. ix. 367.
Cf. however supra, iii. 56.
[5] Tautain, in L'Anthropologie, vi. 640 sq.
[6] Grandidier, op. cit. ii. 189 n. a.
[7] Kirke, Twenty-five Years in British Guiana, p. 216 sq.
[8] ' Racenanlage und verschiedene Begabung zum Arbeiten,'
in Globus, xxv. 379.
[9] Fison, quoted by Codrington, op. cit. p. 246 n. 1.

have to perform,[1] but this is of course a mere conjecture. Similar explanations have been given with reference to some other uncivilised peoples among whom the women are in the minority. Dr. Jochelson points out that among the Reindeer Koryak there are only 90·8 women to 100 men, whereas among the Maritime division of the same people there are 102·6 women to 100 men, and he thinks that this difference may be accounted for by the fact that the life of a Reindeer Koryak woman is much harder than that of her Maritime sister ;[2] but here again we do not know the proportion of the sexes at birth. In various communities of the Orang Kubu in Sumatra, however, Hagen found that among the adult population the men considerably outnumbered the women, although among the children or newborn there was a slight excess of girls ; and he regards the greater mortality of the females as the result of the hardships of life which those savages have to endure and the weaker resisting power of the female organism.[3] Beveridge observes that among the aborigines of Victoria and Riverina the sexes are about equal at birth, but that after the age of puberty the death-rate is far higher among the females than among the males on account of the drudgery their husbands impose upon them, the ill-treatment to which they are subject, their early maternity, and their profligate life.[4] Some other writers on Australian tribes explain their scarcity of women as a result of female infanticide.[5] In India there are only 963 females per 1000 males, the males outnumbering the other sex throughout the western half of the country, especially in the northern portion. One cause which has produced this deficiency of women has been the destruction of female infants. " But,"

[1] v. Humboldt, op. cit. v. 549.
[2] Jochelson, Koryak, p. 445 sq. See also Kirby, ' Journey to Youcan,' in Smithsonian Report, 1864, p. 418 (Kutchin) ; Lewin, Wild Races of South-Eastern India, p. 195 sq. (Toungtha) ; Miklucho-Maclay, ' Papuas der Maclay-Küste in Neu-Guinea,' in Natuurk. Tijdschr. Nederlandsch Indie, xxxiii. 249.
[3] Hagen, Die Orang Kubu auf Sumatra, p. 25 sq.
[4] Beveridge, op. cit. p. 15 sq.
[5] Curr, Recollections of Squatting in Victoria, p. 249. Westgarth, op. cit. p. 63 sq.

it is said, " even where female infanticide is no longer, or perhaps never was, in vogue, there is no doubt that female children receive far less care than those of the other sex. . . . Nor is it only in infancy that female life is exposed to relatively greater risks than in Europe.   There is also the danger of functional derangement due to premature cohabitation and child-bearing, unskilful midwifery, exposure, and hard labour."[1]

Among various peoples the preponderance of males is said to be due to female infanticide.   Some instances of this have been noticed above, where female infanticide has been given as the cause of polyandrous practices, and others may be added.   All accounts of the Todas agree in attributing to them at one time the practice of destroying newborn girls. Our earliest informant, Ward, wrote in 1821, " Our investigation into the cause of this disparity in the sexes has led to a supposition that they have been in the habit of destroying the females hitherto, at least those born on ominous days of the week."[2]   Nowadays, Dr. Rivers says, they are very chary of acknowledging the existence of the practice, denying it absolutely for the present, and being reluctant to speak about it for the past.   He admits that at the present and during recent times there has been no economical motive for infanticide among the Todas, and he is very doubtful whether such a motive has ever existed.   Yet he thinks that there is not the slightest doubt that it was at one time very prevalent, and that it is still practised to some extent, although it has greatly diminished in frequency.[3]   Several earlier writers on the Todas thought that it had become extinct long ago ;[4] according to Hough, the people themselves affirmed that since 1819 not one infant had been destroyed, and, he adds, " having ascertained that there is now an almost equal number of *young* children of each sex, we may

---

[1] *Imperial Gazetteer of India*, i. 479 *sq.*   Gait, *op. cit.* p. 215 *sqq.*
[2] Ward, in Grigg, *op. cit.* Appendix, p. lxxv.
[3] Rivers, *op. cit.* pp. 478, 518, 521.
[4] Shortt, in *Trans. Ethn. Soc.* N.S. vii. 241, 265.   Breeks, *op. cit.* p. 10.   Marshall, *op. cit.* p. 194 *sqq.*   Baierlein admits (*op. cit.* p. 249 *sq.*) that one could not be sure that it had ceased to be practised.

hope that they speak the truth."[1] Yet even though we take for granted that the Todas have been addicted to female infanticide, we cannot be sure that this has been the only cause of the disproportion of the sexes among them. Dr. Rivers observes that the pedigrees record more girls than boys of five years and under, and takes this to be an indication that female infanticide has almost entirely ceased during the last five years.[2] But the figures in question, showing 45 girls and 44 boys, are too small to exclude the possibility that among the Todas, as among so many other peoples, there has been a disproportion of the sexes at birth. Among the children between six and ten years there were 54 males and 33 females, and among those between eleven and fifteen years 41 males and 20 females.[3] In the Hawaian Islands, also, female infanticide reduced the number of women,[4] but could hardly have been the only cause of the preponderance of men. For according to censuses between 1850 and 1890 there was still among the native population a surplus of males, which in fact steadily increased till the year 1884 ; and the excess was particularly great in the population under fifteen years—8·84 per cent. among all races together.[5] Among the Typees of Nukahiva, according to Melville, infanticide was altogether unknown.[6]

With reference to the conspicuous discrepancy in the proportions of the sexes among young children in the Jounsar district, Mr. Dunlop remarks that " the temptations to female infanticide, owing to expensive marriages and extravagant dowers which exist among the Rajpoots of the plains, are not found in the hills where the marriages are comparatively inexpensive, and where the wife, instead of bringing a large dowry, is usually purchased for a considerable sum from her parents " ; and he adds, " I am inclined to give

---

[1] Hough, op. cit. p. 70.   [2] Rivers, op. cit. p. 480.
[3] Ibid. p. 469. Among the Badagas, according to a census taken in 1828, there were slightly more women than men, but 1,151 boys and only 632 girls (Hough, op. cit. p. 93).
[4] Ellis, Tour through Hawaii, p. 414. Marcuse, op. cit. p. 109.
[5] Marques, ' Population of the Hawaiian Islands,' in Jour. Polynesian Soc. ii. 261.   [6] Melville, op. cit. p. 283 sq.

more weight to Nature's adaptability to national habit, than
to the possibility of infanticide being the cause of the discrepance found in Jounsar."[1]   According to a census made by the
collectors of districts in 1814, there were in the population
of the old English possessions in Ceylon 1161 male children
below the age of puberty to 1,000 female children.[2]
Yet, according to Davy—who thinks that the census is not
far from the truth—the Sinhalese held in abhorrence the
crime of exposing children ; and it was never committed
except in some of the wildest parts of the country, when the
parents themselves were on the brink of starvation and had
either to sacrifice a part of the family or die.[3]   And Haeckel
directly assures us that among this people there is a permanent disproportion between male and female births, ten
boys being born, on the average, to eight or nine girls.[4]
As for the Tibetans, it may at all events be said that they have
never been charged with female infanticide,[5] and it is nowadays practised only by Tibetan women married to Chinese.[6]

With regard to the causes which determine the sex of the
offspring many theories have been set forth, but no conclusion commanding general assent has been arrived at.   I shall
say something about one of these theories, Dr. Düsing's, not
only because it seems to me to be founded on a sound
principle, but because it may have an important bearing upon
our subject.   According to Düsing, the characters of animals
and plants which influence the formation of sex are due to
natural selection.   In every species the proportion between
the sexes has a tendency to keep constant, but the organisms
are so well adapted to the conditions of life that, under
anomalous circumstances, they produce more individuals of
that sex of which there is the greatest need.   When nourishment is abundant, strengthened reproduction is an advantage
to the species, whereas the reverse is the case when nourishment is scarce.   Hence—the power of multiplication de-

---

[1] Dunlop, *op. cit.* p. 181 *sq.*   [2] Davy, *op. cit.* p. 107 note.
[3] *Ibid.* p. 289.
[4] Haeckel, *Indische Reisebriefe*, p. 240.
[5] Turner, *op. cit.* p. 352.
[6] Rockhill, *Land of the Lamas*, p. 213 *sq.* n. 3.

pending chiefly upon the number of females—organisms, when unusually well nourished, produce comparatively more female offspring ; in the opposite case, more male. Dr. Düsing and, before him, Dr. Ploss[1] have adduced several facts to prove that such a connection between abundance and the production of females, and between scarcity and the production of males, actually exists. It is, for example, a common opinion among furriers that rich regions give more female furs, poor regions more male.[2] In mankind male births are said to be in greater excess in country districts, the population of which is often badly fed, than in towns, where the conditions of life are more luxurious ;[3] yet different investigations as to the comparative ratio of the sexes at birth in city and country have yielded contradictory results, as in some cases the ratio of males to females has been found to be higher, and in other cases lower, in the country than in cities.[4] We are told that an excess of male births is noticed among poor people as compared with the well-off classes.[5] Moreover, Ploss found that in Saxony there are born comparatively more boys in the highlands than in the lowlands. In the years 1847–1849 the proportion between male and female births was 105·9 to 100 in the region not exceeding 500 Paris feet above the level of the sea ; 107·3 to

[1] Ploss, ' Ueber die das Geschlechtsverhältniss der Kinder bedingenden Ursachen,' in *Monatsschrift für Geburtskunde und Frauenkrankheiten*, xii. 321 *sqq*.   [2] *Ibid*. p. 340.

[3] v. Oettingen, *Die Moralstatistik*, p. 64 *sq.* Düsing, *Die Regulierung des Geschlechtsverhältnisses bei der Vermehrung der Menschen, Tiere und Pflanzen*, p. 159 *sq.*

[4] Nichols, ' Numerical Proportions of the Sexes at Birth,' in *Memoirs American Anthrop. Association*, i. 294 *sq.*

[5] Düsing, *op. cit.* p. 160 *sqq*. It has been pointed out that in France the proportion of male to female births is for the upper classes as 104·5 to 100, and foi the lower classes as 115 to 100 ; and that among Russian peasants there are 114 male births to 100 female births (Morgan, *Experimental Zoölogy*, p. 384 *sq.*). The old statement that among the Swedish nobility, contrary to the general rule in Sweden, the female births outnumber the male (*ibid.* p. 385 ; Bertillon, ' Natalité [démographie],' in *Diction. encycl. des sciences médicales*, ser. ii. vol. xi. 472) has been confirmed and discussed by Professor Fahlbeck (*Sveriges adel*, i. 391 *sqq.*).

100 at a height of between 1,001 and 1,500 feet ; and 107·8 to 100 at a height of between 1,501 and 2,000 feet.[1]

The theory that want and privation are correlated with an increase of male births and prosperity with an increase of female births has received support from a considerable number of writers.[2] Mr. Heape, however, points out that this theory " depends not solely on the amount or quality of nutriment supplied to the mother but on her capacity to assimilate what is supplied and on her power or her disposition at any given time to transmit it to the ovary."[3] Professor Morgan, on the other hand, thinks it probable that if the nutrition in any way affects the proportion of the sexes it does so not by determining either the sex of the embryo or the egg, but only indirectly by eliminating one or the other kind of egg ; and he observes that this conclusion is borne out by the results of some experiments made by Cuénot and by Schultze.[4] Mr. Punnett, again, who has examined some statistics based on the census of London for 1901, is " inclined to believe that in man at any rate the determination of sex is independent of parental nutrition."[5] But this conclusion has been criticised by Heape, who maintains that it is based on wrong premises.[6]

There are certain facts referring to polyandrous peoples which may seem to agree with Dr. Düsing's theory. With reference to the census of Ceylon for 1814 mentioned above, Davy remarks :—" The disproportion appears to be greatest in the poorest parts of the country, where the population

[1] Ploss, in *Monatsschrift für Geburtskunde und Frauenkrankheiten,* xii. 352.

[2] See Heape, ' Proportion of the Sexes produced by Whites and Coloured Peoples in Cuba,' in *Philosophical Transactions Roy. Soc. London,* ser. B. vol. cc. 275, 317 ; Geddes and Thomson, *Evolution of Sex,* pp. 41, 45 *sqq.* ; Doncaster, *Determination of Sex,* p. 76.

[3] Heape, *loc. cit.* p. 276.

[4] Morgan, *Experimental Zoölogy,* p. 385. Schultze, ' Zur Frage von den geschlechtsbildenden Ursachen,' in *Archiv f. Mikroskopische Anatomie und Entwicklungsgeschichte,* lxiii. 233 *sqq.*

[5] Punnett, ' On Nutrition and Sex-determination in Man,' in *Proceedings of the Cambridge Philosophical Society,* xii. 276.

[6] Heape, *loc. cit.* p. 276.

is thinnest, and it is most difficult to support life ; and smallest where there is least want. Indeed, in some of the fishing villages, where there is abundance of food, the number of females rather exceeds that of the males. May it not be a wise provision of provident Nature to promote, by extreme poverty, the generation of males rather than of females ? "[1] Very frequently there is a striking coincidence of polyandry with the poverty of the countries or the classes of people where it prevails, and if polyandry is due to an excess of males it may be supposed that this excess owes its origin to scarce nourishment. But, as we shall see presently, difficult economic conditions may lead to polyandry for entirely different reasons, and one of its effects would seem to be to *prevent* starvation.

For our present purpose I attach more importance to another inference which Dr. Düsing has drawn from his general theory. He argues that incest is less common in proportion as the number of males is great. The more males, he says, the farther off they have to go from their birthplace to find mates. Incest is injurious to the species ; hence incestuous unions have a tendency to produce an excess of male offspring.[2] Thus, according to Dr. Nagel, certain plants, when self-fertilised, produce an excess of male flowers. According to Dr. Goehlert's statistical investigation, in the case of horses, the more the parent animals differ in colour, the more the female foals outnumber the male.[3] Among the Jews, many of whom marry cousins, there is a remarkable excess of male births. In country districts where comparatively more boys arc said to be

---

[1] Davy, *op. cit.* p. 107 note.

[2] Düsing, *op. cit.* p. 237 *sqq.*

[3] 1,150 unions of horses of the same colour gave 91·3 male foals to 100 female ; 878 unions of horses of somewhat different colours, 86·2 to 100 respectively ; 237 unions of horses of still more different colours, 56 to 100 respectively ; 30 unions of horses of the most widely different colours, 30 to 100 respectively (Goehlert, ' Ueber die Vererbung der Haarfarben bci dcn Pferdcn,' in *Zeitschr. f. Ethnol.* xiv. 145 *sqq.*). See also Crampe, ' Untersuchungen über die Vererbung der Farbe bei Pferden,' in *Landwirthschaftliche Jahrbücher,* xiii. 954 *sqq.*

born than in towns, marriage more frequently takes place between kinsfolk. For an opposite reason, according to Düsing, illegitimate unions show a tendency to produce female births.[1]

The evidence given by Düsing for the correctness of his deduction is certainly very scanty—if, indeed, it can be called evidence. Nevertheless, I am inclined to believe that his main conclusion contains a great deal of truth. Independently of his reasoning, I had come to exactly the same result in a purely inductive way. There is some ground for supposing that mixture of race produces an excess of female births. In his work on the ' Tribes of California ' Mr. Powers observes, " It is a curious fact, which has frequently come under my observation, and has been abundantly confirmed by the pioneers, that among half-breed children a decided majority are girls. . . . Often I have seen whole families of half-breed girls, but never one composed entirely of boys, and seldom one wherein they were more numerous."[2] When I mentioned this statement to a gentleman who had spent many years in British Columbia and other parts of North America, he replied that he himself had made exactly the same observation. In the northern parts of the United States, according to Kohl, female children predominate in the families of the cross-breeds arising from the intercourse of Frenchmen with Indian women.[3] Mr. Starkweather has found that, according to the United States' statistical tables of the sex of mulattoes born in the Southern States, there is an excess of from 12 to 15 per cent. of female mulatto children, whilst, taking the whole population together, the male births show an excess of 5 per cent.[4] In Central America, according to Colonel Galindo, " an extraordinary excess is observable in the births of white and Ladino females over those of the males, the former being in proportion to the latter as six, or at least as five, to four :

[1] Düsing, *op. cit.* p. 242 *sqq.*
[2] Powers, *Tribes of California*, pp. 403, 149.
[3] Kohl, ' Bemerkungen über die Bekehrung canadischer Indianer zum Christenthum,' in *Das Ausland*, xxxii. 58 *sq.*
[4] Starkweather, *Law of Sex*, p. 159 *sq.*

among the Indians the births of males and females are about equal."[1] Mr. Stephens asserts that among the Ladinos of Yucatan the proportion is even as two to one.[2] Taken in connection with the fact mentioned by Mr. Squier, that the whites in Central America are as one to eight in comparison with the mixed population,[3] these statements accord well with the following observation of M. Belly as regards Nicaragua :—" Ce qui me paraît être le fait général," he says, " c'est que dans les villes où l'élément blanc domine, il se procrée en effet plus de filles que de garçons. . . . Mais dans les campagnes et partout où la race indienne l'emporte, c'est le contraire qui se produit, et dès lors la prépondérance du sexe masculin se maintient par la prépondérance de l'élément indigène. Le même phénomène avait déjà été observé au Mexique."[4]

Concerning the proportion of the sexes at birth among the mixed races of South America, I have unfortunately no definite statements at my disposal. But Mr. J. S. Roberton informs me, from Chañaral in Chili, that in that country, with its numerous mongrels, more females are born than males. According to the list of the population of the capitaina of São Paulo, in the year 1815, given by v. Spix and v. Martius—a list which includes more than 200,000 persons—the proportion between women and men is, among the mulattoes, 114·65 to 100 ; among the whites, 109·3 to 100 ; among the blacks, 100 to 129.[5] But this last proportion is of no consequence, as we have no account of the number of negro slaves who were imported into the capitaina. Sir Richard Burton found, from the census returns of 1859 for the town of São João d'El Rei, where there is a large intermixture of the white race with the coloured women, an excess of nearly 50 per cent. of women as compared with men.[6] A census of the population in

[1] Galindo, 'On Central America,' in *Jour. Roy. Geo. Soc.* vi. 126.
[2] Peschel, *Races of Man*, p. 221.
[3] Squier, *States of Central America*, p. 58.
[4] Belly, *À travers l'Amérique Centrale*, i. 253 note.
[5] v. Spix and v. Martius, *Travels in Brazil*, ii. 33.
[6] Burton, *Highlands of the Brazil*, i. 115.

the Province of Rio, taken in the year 1844, also shows a
considerable excess of women, not only, however, among the
mixed population, but among the Indian and negro creoles
as well ;[1] and de Castelnau was astonished at the dis-
proportionately large number of females in Goyaz.[2]
In the native population of Ceylon, according to the
census of 1891, the males considerably outnumbered the
females—among the Sinhalese there were 1,063,139 males
and 978,019 females, among the Tamils 396,115 males and
327,738 females, among the Veddas 652 males and 577 females ; whereas among the Eurasians alone there were more
women than men, although the excess was only slight—
10,697 women and 10,534 men.[3] A similar observation
has been made in the Hawaian Islands. Whilst according
to censuses taken between 1850 and 1890 males were more
numerous than females among the natives, as also, though
in a trifling smaller proportion, among the foreigners born
in the islands, the half-castes were the only stable class in
which the sexes were " about equally divided, with even a
regular slight excess in favour of the females."[4] Von
Görtz states that the families of the offspring of Dutchmen
and Malay women in Java (Lipplapps) consist chiefly of
daughters ;[5] and a census taken in the eighteenth century
also showed that among these mongrels there was a great
excess of women over men.[6]

From Stanley Pool, in Congo, Dr. Sims wrote to me,
" It is the subject of general remark here that the half-
caste children are generally girls ; out of ten I can count,
two only are boys." At the same time he pointed out that
among the native Bateke no disproportion between the
sexes was observable. Mr. Torday, who has had ten years'
experience in Congo, informs me that the children of Bel-
gians and negroes whom he can remember were nearly all

[1] de Castelnau, *Expédition dans les parties centrales de l'Amérique du Sud*, Histoire du voyage, i. 137 *sq.* [2] *Ibid.* i. 328.
[3] Schmidt, *op. cit.* p. 242.
[4] Marques, in *Jour. Polynesian Soc.* ii. 261.
[5] v. Görtz, *Reise um die Welt*, iii. 288.
[6] Süssmilch, *Die Göttliche Ordnung in den Veränderungen des menschlichen Geschlechts*, ii. 260 *sq.*

girls ; among thirty half-castes there were perhaps two boys.
Dr. Bérenger-Féraud writes :—" Dès ma première arrivée
au Sénégal, en 1852, j'avais été frappé de la grande disproportion qu'il y avait pour le chiffre entre les hommes et
les femmes métis que je rencontrais. Ces dernières sont,
en effet, incomparablement les plus nombreuses ; et
d'ailleurs quand on songe qu'on les a désignées depuis
plusieurs siècles sous le nom ' Signarres,' alors qu'on a
oublié de créer une appellation masculine particulière pour
leurs frères, on est porté à penser que les hommes n'entrent
dans cette société que pour des chiffres relativement minimes.
. . . Le nombre des filles est plus grand que celui des
garçons."[1]

Dr. Felkin found that, among the foreign women imported
to Uganda, the excess of females in the first births was
enormous, viz., 510 females to 100 males, as compared with
102 females to 100 males in first births from pure Baganda
women ; whilst in subsequent pregnancies of these imported
women the ratio was 137 females to 100 males. As a matter
of fact, in the families of the poorer classes of Uganda, who
" do all in their power to marry pure Baganda women,"
the sexes are as evenly balanced as in Europe, whereas this
is certainly not the case among the children of chiefs and
wealthy men who have large harems supplied mainly with
foreign wives. " I found," says Dr. Felkin, " that of the
women captured by the slave-raiders in Central Africa, and
brought down to the East Coast, either near Zanzibar or
through the Soudan to the Red Sea, those who had been
impregnated on the way usually produced female children.
Hence the Soudan slave-dealers, instead of having only one
slave to sell, have a woman and a female child."[2] Dr.
Felkin suggests, as an explanation of this excess of female
births, that the temporarily superior parent produces the
opposite sex ; but the facts stated seem strongly to cor-
roborate the theory that intermixture of race is in favour

[1] Bérenger-Féraud, ' Note sur la fécondité des mulâtres au
Sénégal,' in Revue d'Anthropologie, ser. ii. vol. ii. 577, 588.
[2] Felkin, ' Contribution to the Determination of Sex,' in Edinburgh Medical Journal, vol. xxxii. pt. i. 233 sqq.

of female births. Very remarkable are two statements in the Talmud, that mixed marriages produce only girls [1] Mr. Jacobs informed me that his collection of Jewish statistics included details of 118 mixed marriages, of these 28 were sterile, and in the remainder there were 145 female children and 122 male—that is, 118·82 to 100 males.

We must not, of course, take for granted that what applies to certain races of men holds good of all of them ; but it should be observed that the cases mentioned refer to mongrels of very different kinds. [2] And it seems the more likely

[1] Jacobs, ' On the Racial Characteristics of Modern Jews,' in *Jour. Anthr. Inst.* xv. 44 *sq.*

[2] It has, on the other hand, been recently suggested that crossbreeding " increases masculinity " (C. J. and J. Norman Lewis, *Natality and Fecundity*, p. 114 *sq.*), or that " when abnormal sex-proportions appear as the result of hybridisation, the excess is of males rather than of females " (Doncaster, *op. cit.* p 87). In the case of moths some crosses produce only or almost exclusively males, whereas the converse cross between the same two species may yield an excess of females, and considerable excess of males is said to have been observed in crosses between species or varieties of rats and mice (*ibid.* p. 86 *sq.*). According to Professor Whitman, the " width of cross " in doves and pigeons is of first importance in determining sex ratios, and the wider the cross the higher is the proportion of males. Family crosses produce in practically all matings only male offspring. Generic crosses produce from their " stronger " germs—those of spring and early summer—nearly all males ; but if " the birds of such a generic cross be made to ' overwork at egg-production ' . . . then the same parents which in the spring threw all or nearly all male offspring may be made to produce all, or nearly all, female offspring in later summer and autumn " (Riddle, ' Sex Control and known Correlations in Pigeons,' in *American Naturalist*, l. 387 ; I am indebted to my friend, Professor Seligman, for this reference). These observations certainly confirm the theory that hybridisation exercises some influence upon the sex of the offspring, but they also show that it may yield quite opposite results in different cases. So far as mankind is concerned, the only evidence which, to my knowledge, has been adduced in favour of the theory that hybridisation tends to increase masculinity comes from Argentina. According to M. Gache's investigations in Buenos Ayres, covering the period from 1884 to 1894 inclusive, the births resulting from unions of Italian, Spanish, and French male immigrants with native-born Argentine females show a higher masculinity than the births produced either by pure Argentine alliances or by

that in these cases it is the crossing that is the cause of the
excess of females, as facts tend to show that unions between
related individuals or, generally, between individuals who
are very like each other, in various cases at least, have a
tendency to produce a comparatively great number of male
offspring.

In all the in-bred stocks of the Bates herd at Kirkleving-
ton, according to Bell, the number of bull calves was constantly very far in excess of the heifers.[1] Of the in-bred
Warlaby branch of shorthorns Mr. Carr says that it " appears
to have a most destructive propensity to breed bulls."[2]
Experiments made by Schultze on white mice, for the purpose of finding out whether incestuous connections exercise
any influence on the sex of the offspring, gave the result
that among the in-bred creatures there was a comparatively
large excess of male births.   But as in some cases many more
females than males were produced, he drew the conclusion

pure alliances of any of those nationalities of Buenos Ayres.   So
also the unions of Argentine males with females of foreign nationality
provide a higher masculinity than is common among Argentines
themselves (Lewis, op. cit. p. 114 sq.).   The excess of male births,
however, is very slight.   The data collected by Pearl from the
Argentine Republic indicate that the mating between an Italian
father and an Argentine mother gives a ratio of 105·7 males to 100
females, whereas the mating between pure Italians gives a ratio of
100·7 to 100 and that between pure Argentines a ratio of 103·2 to
100 ; and among the children of Spanish and Argentine parents the
differences are still less striking (Doncaster, op. cit. p. 87).   These
facts, however, by no means contradict my suggestion that the
crossing of great racial groups in mankind tends to increase the
proportion of female births ; for, as Mr. Arner rightly points out
(Consanguineous Marriages in the American Population, p. 33), all
of the nationalities involved in the investigations are predominantly
Mediterranean in blood.   Speaking of my suggestion, which was
already made in the earlier editions of the present work, Professor
Ripley remarks in his Huxley Memorial Lecture (' The European
Population of the United States,' in Jour. Roy. Anthr. Inst. xxxviii.
236), " Certain it is that an imposing array of evidence can be
marshalled to give colour to the hypothesis."   In the present edition
I have been able to add some important facts corroborating it.

[1] Bell, History of Improved Short-Horn, or Durham Cattle, p. 351.
[2] Carr, History of the Rise and Progress of the Killerby, Studley, and
Warlaby Herds of Shorthorns, p. 98.

that close interbreeding does not in any decided degree
influence the sex of the progeny.[1] It should be remembered,
however, that there may very well be a genuine tendency
of a certain kind, although it does not always show itself.
  With reference to the Jews, among whom cousin marriages
occur perhaps three times as often as among the surrounding populations,[2] I am able to give the following details
based upon Mr. Jacobs' comprehensive manuscript collection of Jewish statistics, which he has kindly allowed me
to examine.[3] The average proportion of male and female
Jewish births registered in various countries is 114·50 males
to 100 females, whilst the average proportion among the
non-Jewish population of the corresponding countries is
105·25 males to 100 females. But Mr. Jacobs thinks that
the accuracy of these statistics may be called in question,
as the abnormal figures for Austria (128 to 100, in the years
1861–1870) and Russia (129 to 100, in the years 1867–1870),
when compared with those for Posen (108 to 100, in the years
1819–1873) and Prussia (108 to 100, in the years 1875–1881),
render it likely that some uniform error occurs in the
registration of Jewish female children in Eastern Europe.
Fishberg is quite confident that less care is taken in the
registration of females among poor Jews.[4] Moreover, still-
born children are not included in the rates of births, and this
certainly affects the figures as to sex, because, parturition
being more difficult in the case of males than in that of
females, there are not so many still-born females as still-

[1] Schultze, *loc. cit.* p. 208 *sqq.*
[2] Jacobs, in *Jour. Anthr. Inst.* xv. 26. Mr. Jacobs thinks that
English Jews marry their first cousins to the extent of 7·5 per cent.
of all marriages, against a proportion of about 2 per cent. for England
generally, as calculated by Professor G. H. Darwin. Stieda, in his
Eheschliessungen in Elsass-Lothringen (1872–1876), gives the proportion of consanguineous marriages among Jews as 23·02 per
thousand, against 1·86 for Protestants, and 9·97 for Catholics
(Jacobs, *Studies in Jewish Statistics*, p. 53).
[3] Afterwards published by Mr. Jacobs in his *Studies in Jewish
Statistics*, p. 57.
[4] Fishberg, *The Jews*, p. 240 *sq.* See also Pearl and Salaman,
'Relative Time of Fertilization of the Ovum and the Sex Ratio
amongst Jews,' in *American Anthropologist*, N.S. xv. 670.

born males.[1]   E. Nagel attributes the excess of male births among Jews to the greater care which Jewish wives take of their health during pregnancy, as also to the smaller number of illegitimate births. But Mr. Jacobs believes that the ratio of male births is nevertheless greater among Jews than among non-Jewish Europeans.

On various islands, as we have noticed above,[2] there is said to be a considerable excess of males over females, and in some cases we know that there is a similar disproportion of the sexes among the children. At the settlement of Port Blair, in the Andaman Islands, there were among the locally born population 461 male children and only 376 female children. Yet female infanticide is unknown ; indeed, owing to the general shortage of women, female children have a higher marketable value than male, and are equally, if not more, desired. " There are no endogamous or exogamous groups, or prohibited degrees of relationship."[3] In the Nicobars the large surplus of males over females seems likewise to depend on a surplus of male births ; for even in Car Nicobar, where the adult females are in excess of the adult males, there are more boys than girls. Here also daughters are at any rate as welcome as sons. The prohibited degrees of relationship are confined to the actual members of a family, and do not extend to cousins, and there is a good deal of intermarrying in groups.[4]

Dr. Thurnwald found in Buin the proportion of boys to girls as 595 to 307, or almost as 2 to 1. He points out that the natives more readily remember males than females, but that on the other hand the mortality is much greater among the male than among the female children ; and he comes to the conclusion that the excess of boys in any case must be considerable.[5] On seven islands belonging to the Duke of York group there were, in 1898, 676 boys and 515 girls,

[1] v. Oettingen, op. cit. p. 57.   [2] Supra, iii. 56 sqq.

[3] Lowis, Census of India, 1911, vol. ii. (Andaman and Nicobar Islands), p. 66 sq.

[4] Ibid. p. 99 sq.

[5] Thurnwald, Forschungen auf den Salomo-Inseln und dem Bismarck-Archipel, iii. 80 sq.

and in 1900, 735 boys and 598 girls ; between September 1898 and May 1900, 131 boys and 122 girls were born, and 56 boys and 37 girls died.[1] In the Gazelle Peninsula of New Britain there were among the coast people, according to a census taken in 1912, 607 boys and 483 girls.[2] On the smaller islands the population must certainly be much in-bred. On those of the Duke of York group all marriages, so far as it could be ascertained, were concluded between relatives, even when emigrations took place from one island to another.[3] It would have been interesting to learn whether the striking excess of males among the Maori was connected with a similar disproportion of the sexes at birth ; for they were in the habit of marrying relatives.[4] Thomson says, " The whole of the present generation are closely intermingled ; chiefs living widely apart, and formerly hostile, can trace without difficulty blood-connections with each other, while among the lower orders of the people this breeding in and in is still more marked."[5] The preponderance of males in so many islands of the Pacific may, of course, be due to various causes ; but if future investigations should prove that there is a considerable excess of boys at birth, I think that its coexistence with close intermarrying would deserve careful consideration.

Concerning the inhabitants of Garah, an isolated village in the Libyan desert, Mr. St. John writes :—" It is said that there are only generally forty souls in the village. According to my guide's account, however, the numbers must have been greater at the particular moment at which we arrived ; as there were twenty-two children in the village, of which fifteen were male. This disproportion between the sexes always exists at Garah ; so that a great many men are com-

[1] ' Statistik der Eingeborenen-Bevölkerung der Neu-Lauenburg-Gruppe,' in *Mittheil. Deutsch. Schutzgeb.* xiv. 128.
[2] Burger, *Die Küsten- und Bergvölker der Gazellehalbinsel,* p. 29 n. 1.
[3] *Mittheil. Deutsch. Schutzgeb.* xiv. 127.
[4] Best, ' Maori Marriage Customs,' in *Trans. and Proceed. New Zealand Institute,* xxxvi. 20. Polack, *Manners and Customs of the New Zealanders,* i. 136.
[5] Thomson, *Story of New Zealand,* ii. 289.

pelled to lead a life of single-blessedness. Sometimes a fellaha girl is imported from the valley of the Nile, as was the custom of some of the desert tribes of old. . . . Occasionally they procure a female slave from Siwah. The people of the latter place are too proud to give their daughters in marriage to a Garah man, who is looked upon as an inferior being."[1]

Of the Samaritans, who nowadays are found only in their ancient holy city, Nablus, where they live crowded together, two gentlemen from Palestine told me that women are very scarce among them and that the men consequently, though in vain, have asked for permission to marry Jewesses. Dr. Montgomery gives us more detailed information on the subject. He writes :—" According to statistics of 1901 they number 152 souls, and the doom which confronts the community is presented in the proportion of males and females, the former numbering 97, the latter only 55. They do not marry outside of their own body, the Jews, the only race with whom they might intermingle, of course refusing alliances."[2] They must thus be a highly in-bred people. According to the Rev. John Mills, " they seem to be all of one type, and bear an unmistakable family likeness."[3]

With reference to the North-West Frontier Province of India, Mr. Latimer observes that the past history of the bulk of the inhabitants of the Province, as well as their present customs, point to a genuine deficiency of females. Indications given by other sources of information, namely, the vital statistics, also suggest that the males considerably outnumber the females, in showing that the proportion of females is very low at birth, and that they die in greater numbers than males. In the last decade the births of 819 girls were registered for 1,000 boys ; but these figures are not beyond suspicion, as female births seem not uncommonly to go unrecorded. The Chief Medical Officer of the Province writes :—" Personally I regard the excess of males in the North-West Frontier Province as exemplifying a provision of nature, to prevent over-population in

---

[1] St. John, *Adventures in the Libyan Desert*, p. 97 *sq.*
[2] Montgomery, *Samaritans*, p. 24.   [3] Mills, quoted *ibid*. p. 25.

a country unfitted by nature to support many inhabitants,
. . . Probably also there is, owing to blood feuds and the
poverty of the country, a good deal of in-breeding. This,
also, I think, tends to produce more males." Mr. Latimer
adds that the latter suggestion is an interesting one because
close marriages among Pathans and, indeed, among the
Muhammadans of the Province generally are very common.[1]
Mr. Hughes-Buller likewise considers the excess of males
over females in Baluchistan to give support to the theory
I am here advocating.   He observes that the defect in females
is greater with the Baloch, among whom marriage with
cousins is common, than among Afghans and Brahuis,
among whom the custom is not nearly so prevalent.[2]   It
seems to me quite possible that the unusually great
proportion of male births which has been found among
some highlanders is the result, not, as has been supposed,
of deficient nourishment, but of consanguineous marriages
due to comparative isolation.

When we now, after this somewhat lengthy discussion of
a biological hypothesis, come back to our subject, it is
interesting to note that if that hypothesis could be proved
to be true, it might perhaps throw some light on the origin
of polyandry by connecting it in a curious manner with
consanguineous marriages. As appears from what has
been said above, polyandrous marriage has been principally
found among highlanders or mountaineers and on islands.
In Tibet, to quote Baber once more, " polygamy obtains in
valleys, while polyandry prevails in the uplands ";[3] and
in the Himalayan region it has been noticed that polyandry
is practised in the upper and polygyny in the lower part of
the same valley.[4]   Of various polyandrous peoples we have
direct evidence that they are much addicted to marriages
between relatives. "Among the common Tibetans, so

[1] Latimer, *Census of India*, 1911, vol. xiii. (North-West Frontier
Province) Report, p. 132 *sq.*
[2] Hughes-Buller, *Census of India*, 1901, vol. v. (Baluchistan)
Report, p. 54.
[3] Baber, *loc. cit.* i. 97.
[4] Miss Gordon Cumming, *op. cit.* p. 405 *sq.*

long as the parties do not claim a common father, there is
no objection to the marriage,"[1] and marriages between
cousins are very frequent.[2] Among the Gilyak, as we have
seen, cross-cousin marriage is prescribed by custom,[3] and
the same is the case with many tribes and castes in South
India, some of whom practise polyandry.[4] The Todas of
the Nilgiri Hills seem to be one of the most in-bred people
of whom anything is known,[5] whereas the Kotas inhabiting
the same hill ranges, among whom women are not so scarce
as among the Todas and polyandry is not practised, always
avoid marrying within their own village.[6] It is interesting
to note that the number of males is considerably more
marked in the case of the Teivaliol Todas than in that of
the Târthârol tribe, who have more intercourse with the
external world than the former ; and although Mr. Punnett
thinks that the diminished proportion of males is due to the
check which this intercourse has imposed upon female
infanticide,[7] it is also exactly what might be expected if my
suggestion is correct. I have previously spoken of the cousin
marriages among the Sinhalese,[8] the Bantu mountaineers
of South Africa,[9] and the ancient Arabs.[10] In this connection I also wish to call attention to the fact that among the
Herero sexual communism, which will be dealt with in the
next chapter, occurs hand in hand with habitual marriages
between the children of a brother and a sister—it is indeed

[1] Sarat Chandra Das, *op. cit.* p. 326 *sq.*
[2] Desideri, in Puini, *op. cit.* p. 129.
[3] *Supra*, ii. 74.   [4] *Supra*, ii. 71 *sq.*
[5] *Supra*, ii. 48 *sq.* Marshall, *A Phrenologist amongst the Todas*,
p. 110 *sq.*
[6] Metz, *op. cit.* p. 131.
[7] Punnett, 'On the Proportion of the Sexes among the Todas,' in
Proceedings of the Cambridge Philosophical Society, xii. 481, 486 *sq.*
Mr. Punnett thinks (p. 482) that the balance of evidence is on the
whole against my hypothesis affording an adequate explanation of
the excessive preponderance of the male sex among the Todas, and
points out that on the islands of Mabuiag and Badu in Torres Straits,
as also in Murray Island, where there exists a considerable amount of
in-breeding, the males preponderate only to a small extent. I
cannot look upon this as evidence against my suggestion.
[8] *Supra*, ii. 73.   [9] *Supra*, ii. 71.   [10] *Supra*, ii. 69.

quite an unusual thing for a Herero to marry a woman who
is not related to him by blood ;[1] and at the same time we
are told that among them the female offspring are less
numerous than the male,[2] whilst infanticide is rare if not
unknown.[3]

It is true, however, that the coincidence of cousin-marriage
with fraternal polyandry allows of an explanation very
different from the one just suggested : instead of being
cause and effect they may both have their root in a desire
to keep property within the family. Nay, it may even be
said that the simultaneous occurrence of an excess of males
and polyandry does not necessarily imply that the latter
is an effect of the former. Dr. Shortt has argued that where
the disproportion of the sexes is caused by female infanticide, polyandry may have pre-existed and female infanticide
arisen in consequence as a means of doing away with superfluous females.[4] Or it may be said that if polyandry has
sprung from a desire to economise or to keep down the
population, a similar desire may have led to the destruction
of newborn girls. Yet however difficult or impossible it
may be to find out in every case the actual relation between
the paucity of women and polyandry, there are, among the
instances mentioned above, at least a few in which it undoubtedly is one of cause and effect, and others in which it
is probably so. On the other hand, polyandry also prevails
among peoples where the males are not known to outnumber
the females. Among the Vilkurups, who practise fraternal
polyandry, the proportion of the sexes was according to a
recent census almost exactly equal—there were 704 males
and 703 females.[5] Among the Orang Sakai the women are

---

[1] Schinz, *Deutsch-Süd-West-Afrika*, p. 177. Bensen, in Kohler,
'Das Recht der Herero,' in *Zeitschr. f. vergl. Rechtswiss.* xiv. 300.
Dannert, *Zum Rechte der Herero*, p. 33.

[2] v. François, *Nama und Damara Deutsch-Süd-West-Afrika*,
p. 195.

[3] *Ibid.* p. 197. Büttner, ' Sozialpolitisches aus dem Leben der
Herero,' in *Das Ausland*, lv. 852. Dannert, *op. cit.* p. 48.

[4] Shortt, in *Trans. Ethn. Soc.* N.S. vii. 265. See also Rivers, *op.
cit.* p. 521.

[5] Anantha Krishna Iyer, *op. cit.* i. 182.

considerably in excess of the men ;[1] and the same is the case at least in some Subanu communities.[2]   Those who maintain that nothing but a scarcity of women could have led to the unnatural practice of polyandry would perhaps argue that an institution may survive the cause from which it sprang. But we have every reason to believe that if a people began to practise polyandry only because the women were scarce, this practice would be abandoned if from some cause or another the disproportion between the sexes ceased —evidence of this has indeed been given above. We shall now look for other causes to which polyandry may be traced.

Besides an actual disproportion between the sexes, a scarcity of available women may lead to polyandry. M. Coudreau observes that among the Roucouyennes in French Guiana the lack of women for some of the men is the result of the polygyny of others ; but he adds that their polyandry is not a necessary consequence of their polygyny, since a man who has no wife can easily console himself with any woman he likes. He also mentions the following curious causes of polyandry among those Indians :—" La polyandrie se produit quand elle accomode à la fois une femme qui aime deux hommes plus que les autres, et ces deux hommes, qui veulent jouir de leur femme en paix, à l'exclusion des autres hommes. Ou bien parfois elle est établie par le tamouchi (i.e., the chief) qui, ayant deux Indiens fainéants à marier, ne leur donne qu'une seule femme pour eux deux. C'est ainsi qu'on châtie les fainéants en pays roucouyenne."[3] The sexual group-relations of the Australian aborigines, as will be shown in the next chapter, are presumably connected not only with the comparative scarcity of women but also with the polygyny of the old men ; and the same may be said of their unions of a polyandrous character. Wherever polyandry is due to a lack of women, it is obvious that it must become more frequent if some men take a plurality of wives each. But, generally speaking, polygyny

---

[1] Hagen, *Die Orang Kubu auf Sumatra,* p. 197 *sq.*
[2] Finley and Churchill, *op. cit.* p. 29.
[3] Coudreau, *Chez nos Indiens,* p. 132.

docs not seem to be very common among polyandrous peoples ; and it is doubtful whether it has anywhere been responsible for the first introduction of polyandry.

Among various peoples polyandry has been traced to economic motives. It has been said that in Tibet it obtains "as a necessary institution. Every spot of ground within the hills which can be cultivated, has been under the plough for ages ; the number of mouths must remain adapted to the number of acres, and the proportion is preserved by limiting each proprietary family to one giver of children."[1] Even one of the Moravian missionaries defended the poly-andry of the Tibetans "as good for the heathen of so sterile a country," since superabundant population in an unfertile country would be a great calamity and produce "eternal warfare or eternal want."[2] And not only does polyandry serve the end of checking the increase of population in regions from which emigration is difficult,[3] but it also keeps the family property together where the husbands are brothers, as they usually are in Tibet.[4] Rockhill observes :— " If at the death of the head of the family the property was divided among the sons, there would not be enough to supply the wants of all of them if each had a wife and family. Moreover, the paternal abode would not accommodate them. The secular experience of the whole human race showing that several families cannot live in peace and concord under the same roof, the only solution of the problem in this case was for the sons of a family to take one wife among them, by which means their ancestral estate remained undivided, and they also saved considerable money." This, however, refers to the agricultural districts only, whereas " among the

[1] Cunningham, *History of the Sikhs*, p. 18. See also Desideri, in Puini, *op. cit.* p. 131 ; *Hsi-Ts'ang Chienwen-lu*, ii. 7, quoted by Rockhill, in *Jour. Roy. Asiatic Soc.* N.S. xxiii. 231 n. 1 ; Ahmad Shah, *op. cit.* p. 52 ; Koeppen, *op. cit.* i. 476 ; Risley, *People of India*, p. 211 *sq.*

[2] Wilson, *op. cit.* p. 216.   [3] *Ibid.* p. 216.

[4] This has been mentioned as a motive for Tibetan polyandry by Desgodins, *op. cit.* p. 244 ; Waddell, *Among the Himalayas*, p. 197 ; Sarat Chandra Das, *op. cit.* p. 327 ; Kingdon Ward, *op. cit.* p. 57 ; Earle, quoted by Risley, *People of India*, p. 212.

nomads, where existence is not dependent on the produce
of the soil, where herds of yak and flocks of sheep and goats
are ever increasing and supply all their owner's wants, this
necessity of preserving the family property undivided can
never have existed. Hence we find polyandry unknown
among them ; monogamy, and perhaps a very few cases of
polygamy, is the rule where they are found."[1]

Similar reasons have been assigned for polyandry in
Ladakh.[2] " There can be no doubt," says Drew, " that the
practice of polyandry in Ladākh originated from the small-
ness of the extent of land that could be tilled and the
general inelasticity of the country's resources, while the
isolation from the rest of the world—isolation of manners,
language and religion, as well as geographical isolation—
hindered emigration. It was found impossible for the
younger ones either to marry and settle or to go out for their
living. They naturally became mere helpers in the household—farm-servants to the elder brother."[3] So also Mr.
Knight speaks of polyandry in Ladakh as a means adopted
to maintain the prosperity of the cultivator, despite the
natural poverty of the country, and as a substitute for
emigration, which is not a feasible relief to over-population
for a people like the Ladakhis, who, accustomed to high
elevations, succumb to bilious fever when they reach the
plains.[4] Now, as a consequence of the practice, the great
body of the people are in easy and comfortable circumstances, owing chiefly to the valuable fleeces of their goats,[5]
and present an " extremely well-to-do appearance."[6]

[1] Rockhill, *Land of the Lamas*, p. 211 *sq.* He adds that this
explanation is not offered as elucidating the origin of polyandry, but
rather its continuance in the country ; and he expresses the belief
that its remote origin has been rightly ascribed by Spencer as an
advance on the primitive unregulated state of savage tribes (*ibid.*
p. 212 n. 1). See also Grenard, *op. cit.* p. 256.

[2] See Cunningham, *Ladák*, p. 306 ; Bellew, *op. cit.* p. 118.; J. D.
Cunningham, ' Notes on Moorcroft's Travels in Ladakh,' in *Jour.
Asiatic Soc. Bengal*, vol. xiii. pt. i. 202 ; Matin-uz-Zaman Khan,
op. cit. p. 136 *sq.*

[3] Drew, *op. cit.* p. 250.   [4] Knight, *op. cit.* p. 137 *sq.*

[5] Moorcroft and Trebeck, *op. cit.* i. 320.

[6] Knight, *op. cit.* p. 137.

The origin of polyandry in Bhutan is attributed by Mr. Earle to the poverty of the country and the desire to prevent the division of property.[1] But in Kanawar and some other districts it is said to spring from the latter motive alone ; and the result is that all the brothers are enabled to live in comparative comfort.[2] The polyandry of the Gûjars, which was said to be mainly due to the scarcity of women in the tribe, had also an economic ground :—" It was to the benefit of the married brother and his wife that all the brothers should live together, and that the joint earnings should be enjoyed by the single wife and her children. It was through this feeling of self-interest that the wife and her real husband permitted the other brothers to share her favours."[3] In Southern India, also, fraternal polyandry is in various cases said to be connected either with poverty[4] or with a desire to keep family property together[5] or to be " regarded as strengthening the ties of fraternity."[6] Among the Sinhalese, according to Sir Emerson Tennent, the custom has in modern times been extenuated on the plea that it prevents the subdivision of estates ; [7] this view, as we have seen, was expressed by the compilers of the Níti-Nighaṇḍuva, though they also speak of a man taking a fellow-husband to obtain assistance. An old Kandyan chief said to Davy that " the apology of the poor is, that they cannot afford each to have a particular wife ; and of the wealthy and men of rank, that such a union is politic, as it unites families, con-

[1] Risley and Gait, op. cit. p. 448.

[2] Stulpnagel, in Indian Antiquary, vii. 134 sq. The Punjab Superintendent says that " the custom tends to prevent from partition the holdings which, from force of circumstances, are extremely small " (Pandit Harikishan Kaul, op. cit. p. 288).

[3] Râja Lachhman Sinh, quoted by Crooke, Tribes and Castes of the North-Western Provinces, ii. 445.

[4] Schlagintweit, Indien, i. 101. Vinson, in Bull. Soc. d'Anthr. Paris, ser. iii. vol. v. 229 (natives of Malabar). Thurston, Ethnographic Notes, p. 114 sq. (blacksmiths of Malabar). Nagam Aiya, op. cit. ii. 359 (fraternal polyandrists of Malabar).

[5] Zeen-ud-deen, op. cit. p. 65 (carpenters, &c., of Malabar). Moegling, Coorg Memoirs, p. 31.

[6] Conner, in Jour. Literature and Science Madras Literary Soc. i. 71.

[7] Tennent, op. cit. ii. 429. See also Perera, op. cit. p. 11.

centrates property and influence, and conduces to the interest of the children, who, having two fathers, will be better taken care of, and will still have a father though they may lose one." [1] With reference to Polybius' statement concerning the Spartans C. O. Müller observes that their polyandry was due to economic causes ; if the number of persons to be fed was too great as compared with the means of feeding them, the natural consequence was that the privileged eldest brother could afford to marry, while the younger brothers remained without wives or children. [2] But their polyandric practices may also have been connected with their warlike habits, which caused the husbands so often to be away from home. [3] The fraternal polyandry of the ancient Arabs has been traced to poverty in combination with female infanticide, Arabia being such a barren country outside the oases that the life of the people is practically bound up in these fertile spots. [4] Wellhausen remarks that ordinary individual marriage seems to have sometimes been looked upon as a luxury which poor people could not afford to indulge in. [5]

Although economic considerations may lead to polyandry both among the rich and the poor, it appears from various statements quoted above that it is often principally or exclusively practised by the latter, whilst those who can afford it take a wife for themselves alone or even indulge in polygyny. Sometimes polyandry is said to be due to the difficulty of raising the sum to be paid for a wife, which induces brothers or other men to club together and buy a common wife. Thus it sometimes happens among the poorer classes of the Miris that " two brothers will unite, and from the proceeds of their joint labour buy a wife

---

[1] Davy, *op. cit.* p. 286 *sq.*

[2] Müller, *History and Antiquities of the Doric Race*, ii. 204 *sq.* See also Schrader, *Reallexikon der indogermanischen Altertumskunde*, p. 634 ; Leist, *Graeco-italische Rechtsgeschichte*, p. 78 ; Delbrück, *loc. cit.* p. 545.

[3] *Cf.* Rose, ' On the alleged Evidence for Mother-right in Early Greece,' in *Folk-Lore*, xxii. 290.

[4] Barton, *Sketch of Semitic Origins*, p. 71 *sq.*

[5] Wellhausen, *loc. cit.* p. 463. *Cf. Homeritarum leges*, ch. vi. (Migne, *Patrologiæ cursus*, Ser. Graeca, lxxxvi. 583 *sq.*).

between them."[1] Fraser thinks that polyandry in Sirmur may in part have a similar origin ;[2] and some other instances have been mentioned before.[3] Or a poor man may ask a wealthier one to help him on condition that he will share his wife with the benefactor.[4] It is obvious that poverty and paucity of women easily may be a combined cause of polyandry : where women are scarce the difficulty in procuring a single wife must be particularly great for the poor. Râja Lachhman Sinh states that among the Gûjars " the custom prevailed only among the poorer families, the male members of which found it difficult to get married in consequence of the scarcity of girls in the caste, and also from the natural desire of parents to marry their daughters to as affluent persons as possible."[5] Breeks says of the Todas, whose polyandry is undoubtedly connected with scarcity of women, that " its practice depends now chiefly on the means of individuals," and that " it is considered desirable for each man to have his own wife if he can afford it."[6]

It has been noticed that in various cases polyandry is associated with pastoral habits of life. The Rev. John Roscoe points out that the Bahima, like some other African tribes who live chiefly on the milk of their herds, carefully abstain from a vegetable diet lest the contact of vegetables with milk in their stomachs should injure the milch kine and thereby endanger their principal means of subsistence. Accordingly among them a man who marries must have cows enough to enable him to support a wife and family, since he cannot hope to eke out a livelihood by tilling the ground. But a poor man cannot afford to keep so many cows ; hence he is under a strong temptation to club together with other poor men, whether his brothers or not, and put their cattle into a common stock to purchase and keep one wife in common between them.[7] But the connection between polyandry and a pastoral life may also have another

---

[1] Dalton, *op. cit.* p. 33.   [2] Fraser, *op. cit.* p. 206.
[3] Subanu, Bahima.   [4] Bantu mountaineers of South Africa.
[5] Crooke, *Tribes and Castes of the North-Western Provinces*, ii. 445.
[6] Breeks, *op. cit.* p. 10.
[7] Roscoe, quoted by Frazer, *Totemism and Exogamy*, ii. 539 *sq.*

ground. Speaking of the polyandry of the Gûjars and Jâts in the North-Western Provinces of India, Mr. Crooke remarks that the arrangement suits these pastoral people, who graze their herds in the river valleys. The brothers take it in turn to attend the cattle, and one remains at home in charge of the house-wife.[1] So also Talboys Wheeler thinks that the polyandry of the Tibetans " may have sprung up amongst a pastoral people, where men are frequently away from their homes for many months at a time, either to seek new pastures for their cattle, or to dispose of the cattle amongst the people of the plains."[2] Waddell likewise remarks that although polyandry in Tibet is also viewed as a device to keep the common property within the family in a country which cannot support a large population, " it is rather regarded in this pastoral country as an arrangement to protect the joint-family when its head is away for weeks, herding the cattle."[3] Mr. Kingdon Ward, again, maintains that the fundamental reason for the polyandry of the Tibetans is that they as a race are only halfway between a nomadic pastoral people and a settled agricultural people, and that the men consequently are great travellers who leave their wives behind for months at a time ; and as a negative evidence in favour of this theory he adds that the Lutzu, like other neighbouring tribes, who come much into contact with the Tibetans, are both monogamists and notorious stay-at-homes.[4] It is not only on account of their pastoral mode of life that the husbands are so often away from home. Turner observes that " different pursuits, either agricultural employments, or mercantile speculations, may occasionally cause the temporary absence of each " ;[5] and according to Rockhill, who much emphasises the prevalence of polyandry among the agricultural population of Tibet, it is not too much to say that more than half of the time of nearly every man in the country is spent away from his home,

[1] Crooke, _Tribes and Castes_, ii. 445.
[2] Talboys Wheeler, _op. cit._ i. 116.
[3] Waddell, _Among the Himalayas_, p. 197.
[4] Kingdon Ward, _op. cit._ p. 57 _sq._
[5] Turner, _op. cit._ p. 350.   See also Wilson, _op. cit._ p. 215.

which "renders the custom of one woman marrying several brothers less objectionable than it would be in a richer country where the conditions of life are different."[1]

It has been said that the Mongoloid people of the Himalayas, as well as their Tibetan kindred, find polyandry expedient not only on account of the poverty of their country, but also " because of the dangers and difficulties which would inevitably surround any woman left alone in her remote home, during the prolonged absence of her lord, whether he be engaged in traffic or in the chase."[2] Mr. Horne was told by a woman who was married to four brothers that " they were never at home together. One would be absent with sheep, bringing salt from Tibet ; another with a consignment for disposal in the Ram Serai valley ; a third attending to the cultivation of some distant outlying fields, or tending sheep on the far-off hill-side : so that all went on very amicably."[3] Fraser says that in Sirmur "of a family of four or five brothers, only one or two are in general at home at the same time : some are out on service as soldiers, or with the minor chiefs ; others are travelling : the elder usually remains at home."[4] Among the Coorgs of Southern India the men were absent from home for weeks and months, since their Rajahs were accustomed to keep a large number of soldiers constantly in attendance upon themselves, or because they had to accompany their Rajah on some hunting or fighting expedition ; and the brothers at home would then take the place of the absent one in house and family.[5] The Sinhalese maintain that their own polyandry originated in the so-called feudal times. They say that the enforced attendance of the people on the king and the higher chiefs would have led to the ruin of the rice lands, had not some interested party been left to look after the tillage ; hence, when several brothers on a farm were called out for the

---

[1] Rockhill, *Land of the Lamas*, p. 211.

[2] Miss Gordon Cumming, *op. cit.* p. 406.

[3] Horne, ' Notes on Villages in the Himâlayas, in Kumaon Garhwâl, and on the Satlej,' in *Indian Antiquary*, v. 164.

[4] Fraser, *op. cit.* p. 208. [5] Moegling, *op. cit.* p. 32.

corvée, the law allowed one of them to remain at home.[1]
Sir Emerson Tennent makes the objection that polyandry
is much more ancient than the system thus indicated—that
it is shown to have existed at a period long antecedent to
" feudalism."[2] But even though the exigencies of public
duty did not give rise to polyandry in Ceylon, they may have
helped to preserve it or increased its frequency. Among
the Kaniyans of the Cochin State the husbands are often
absent on account of poverty. They explain their practice
of polyandry by saying that their caste-men are very poor
and cannot afford the expenses of the large families that there
might be if the brothers married different women and had
separate families. The brothers cannot afford to live
together for a long time, and they very often go from place
to place to earn their livelihood by astrology. Each brother
is at home only for a few days in each month, and hence the
woman may practically have only one husband at a time.[3]
The frequent statement that the younger brothers have
access to the eldest brother's wife during his absence also
indicates that there is some connection between polyandrous
practices and the men's habit of being away from their
homes.

Sometimes polyandry is due to the desire for offspring.
Among the Punans of Borneo it generally occurs in cases in
which a woman married to an elderly man has no children
by him.[4] With reference to the Eskimo inhabiting the land
situated in the north-east corner of Baffin's Bay, Ross wrote,
" We learned that each man took one wife, when he was able
to maintain a family ; if she had children, he took no other,
nor was she permitted to have another husband ; but, if
otherwise, the man may take another wife, and so on a third,
until they have children ; the women having the same privilege."[5] This statement is not absolutely clear, but as there

---

[1] Tennent, op. cit. ii. 429. Perera, op. cit. p. 11.
[2] Tennent, op. cit. ii. 429.
[3] Anantha Krishna Iyer, op. cit. i. 209.
[4] Hose and McDougall, op. cit. ii. 183.
[5] Ross, Voyage of Discovery for the purpose of exploring Baffin's
Bay, i. 184.

is no mention of separation in either case, I understand its
meaning to be that childlessness might lead either to polygyny or polyandry. We have seen before that the latter,
also, occurs among the Eskimo ; and among the Greenlanders, at any rate, it seems to have been a matter of course
for a married man who had no offspring, and considered
himself to be the cause of it, to ask another man to have
intercourse with his wife. A young Greenlander whose wife
had given birth to no children once offered Nils Egede a
fox-skin either to come to his aid himself in the matter, or to
order one of his sailors to do so, and was much astonished to
find Egede indignant at the proposal. " There would be no
disgrace," he said, " for she is married, and she could have
one of your married sailors."[1] We have also seen that
among the Chukchee a married man who has no children
may be anxious to make a strong bachelor his " companion."[2]
The custom of a childless man introducing his brother or
some other man to his wife that he may have a child by her
has been mentioned above as existing among various African
tribes[3] and among Indo-European peoples in former
times.[4]

Where polyandry serves an economic object or prevents the
wife from being left alone or secures the production of offspring, it may be said to be useful not only to the husbands,
or the first husband, but to the wife as well ; and there may
be yet other reasons for her to approve of it. Among the
Tiyyans of Malabar, where property devolves through the
eldest brother's wife, " a girl will not be given to an only son,
for, they say, ' Where is the good ? He may die, and she
will have nothing. The more brothers, the better the
match.' "[5] Among the Kammālan women there seems to be
a belief that the more husbands they have, the greater will
be their happiness.[6] The women of Tibet have assured

---

[1] Nansen, *Eskimo Life*, p. 172. See also Dalager, *Grønlandske
Relationer*, p. 68.
[2] *Supra*, iii. 109 *sq.*   [3] *Supra*, iii. 153.   [4] *Supra*, iii. 144.
[5] Fawcett, quoted by Thurston, *Ethnographic Notes in Southern
India*, p. 112.
[6] Appadorai Iyer, quoted *ibid.* p. 114.

travellers " that they sincerely pity their Western sisters who are compelled to own but one husband, and cannot realise how it is possible for any woman to become rich and be well provided for without enjoying the luxury of several husbands, who all conspire to make their common wife comfortable and feel at home."[1] And when Sarat Chandra Das told a Tibetan lady that in India a husband had several wives, she answered him " that Tibetan women are happier than Indian ones, for they enjoy the privileges conceded in the latter country to the men."[2] There can be little doubt that the wishes of the women have been a contributing cause of polyandry ; nay, from statements quoted above it appears that they have in some cases been the principal, if not the only, cause. Notice the capable and intelligent Lengua woman who had two husbands contrary to the customs of her people ; the connection between polyandry and gynaicocracy among certain Iroquois (which, however, may be only Lafitau's own inference) ; the women of rank in the Marshall Islands who can take as many husbands as they like ; the right of the principal wife of a Marquesas Islander to take a secondary husband on her own account ; the rich Nukahiva women who had two husbands chosen by themselves, one of whom was generally handsome but poor ; the women in the families of Hawaian chiefs for whom it likewise was usual to marry two men ; the queens of Madagascar who were free to take several husbands according to their choice ; and the licence granted to the sisters of the king of Ashantee and the paramount female chief in Sierra Leone. We should also remember the right of a Ladakhi wife to select a man belonging to another family than the brother-husbands to be her *magpa* and to divorce him whenever she likes ; and the similar right of a Toda wife to choose · a gallant, to whom, according to the older accounts, the real husbands must give the precedence on all occasions. This institution, however, may also have in view the comfort of

---

[1] Ahmad Shah, *op. cit.* p. 53.

[2] Sarat Chandra Das, *Journey to Lhasa and Central Tibet*, p. 216.

the men ; for the *magpa* is a younger brother who is
excluded from all access to the family wife, and the
Toda gallants, according to one account, are "such
young men as, by the paucity of women among the
tribe, are prevented from obtaining a share in a wife."[1]
That female inclinations have played no insignificant
part in the history of polyandry is all the more probable
as among polyandrous peoples women generally enjoy
great sexual freedom[2] and the men are little addicted to
jealousy.

Polyandry of the fraternal type, however, could hardly
have its principal root in the free choice of the women ;
in those cases in which polyandry obviously in a large
measure depends on their wishes the husbands are not
brothers. On the other hand it is easy to see that where it is
a result of a disproportion between the sexes or of poverty
or of the frequent absence of the men from their homes, it
naturally tends to assume a fraternal character, even though
it does not do so in every case ; and if it is intended to keep
property together, it is necessary that the husbands should
be brothers or at all events near relatives. When it is
impossible for every man to get a wife for himself owing to
the paucity of women, fraternal feelings may induce a man
to give his younger brothers a share in his wife. When a man
is too poor to take or to maintain a wife for himself alone,
he would by preference choose his brother as his partner,
owing to the economic interests they have in common ; and
when a plurality of husbands is desirable in order that the
family and homestead shall not be left without a male
supporter and protector for any length of time, a brother
would generally be the most suitable substitute for the absent
husband. Brothers generally live at the same spot, there is
a feeling of solidarity and fellowship between them, and no
stranger is brought into the world through intercourse with
the same woman. But these circumstances would have
little force if the wife lives apart from her husbands and the

---

[1] King, *op. cit.* p. 23 *sq.*

[2] See, *e.g.*, Gait, *op. cit.* pp. 246, &c. (polyandrists of India) ;
Calvert, *op. cit.* p. 32 (Kulu) ; Wilson, *op. cit.* p. 210 (Tibetans).

children belong to their mother's kin—as is the case among the Nayars.

The polyandry of the Nayars has been traced to different causes. The popular belief is that the Nambuthiris, or Brahmans of Malabar, brought it about to accommodate their domestic habits.[1] Among these Brahmans only the eldest son is allowed to marry, except in cases where it is evident that he will have no male issue ; and his younger brothers in consequence very frequently indulge in concubinage with Nayar women without any obligation of supporting the children, who are looked after by the senior males of the women's families.[2] The restriction in question was imposed to keep the family property together, and perhaps also, in some degree, " to prevent the diminution of dignity by the increase of numbers."[3] The suggestion has been made that it is a survival of a system of fraternal polyandry.[4] One writer—of the seventeenth century—even states that although according to the law of the Brahmans only one of their sons takes a wife, all his brothers are afterwards allowed access to her ;[5] but this statement seems to be based upon suspicion rather than evidence. Now a result of the rule which prevents the younger males of a family from marrying is that a large number of Nambuthiri women must live and die unmarried,[6] whereas the Brahmans' alliances with Nayar women would have made it impossible for each Nayar to have a wife for himself, considering that he was not allowed to attach himself to any woman of a lower caste.[7] Barbosa says that the young Brahmans who cannot marry " sleep with the wives of the nobles, and these women hold

---

[1] Anantha Krishna Iyer, op. cit. ii. 39 sqq.

[2] Barbosa, op. cit. p. 121 sq. Zeen-ud-deen, op. cit. p. 63 sq. Jogendra Nath Bhattacharya, Hindu Castes and Sects, p. 107. Anantha Krishna Iyer, op. cit. ii. 183, 198.

[3] Conner, in Jour. Literature and Science, i. 63.

[4] Risley and Gait, op. cit. p. 449.

[5] Giuseppe di Santa Maria, op. cit. p. 160.

[6] Conner, loc. cit. p. 63. Anantha Krishna Iyer, op. cit. ii. 198. Cf. Fra Paolino da S. Bartolomeo, op. cit. p. 201.

[7] I ópez de Castanheda, op. cit. i. 47. Giuseppe di Santa Maria, op. cit. p. 160.

it as a great honour because they are Brahmans, and no woman refuses them."[1] Yet, although the influence of the Nambuthiris on the sexual relations of the Nayars may have been considerable, it is hard to believe that they are responsible for the first introduction of polyandry among the latter. Sir T. Muttusami Ayyar observes that a handful of Brahmans, who must have settled in Malabar in small groups from time to time, could not have succeeded in uprooting the national institution of marriage, if any, even if they had attempted to do so.[2] According to Moore, there appear to be valid reasons for holding that the Nayars entered the country under a military organisation before Nambuthiris were heard of in Malabar.[3]

It has, further, been suggested either that the Nayars brought polyandry with them when they entered Malabar— whether they did so after separating from their fellow Dravidians on the east coast[4] or they came from the north, as an early subdivision of the Newars of Nepal—or that they adopted it from the aborigines among whom they settled.[5] The architecture of the Malabar temples, it is said, suggests Mongolian influence. The faces of the demons carved on them are almost identical with those of Tibetan masks. The custom which allows only the eldest son of a Nambuthiri Brahman to marry has its counterpart in Tibet, though with this difference, that in that country the younger brothers share their elder brother's wife. The mock marriage (though a similar ceremony is often performed before a girl becomes a prostitute) is celebrated as a preliminary to a regular, though less formal, union nowhere nearer than Nepal, where it is in vogue amongst the Newars ; and these also,

---

[1] Barbosa, *op. cit.* p. 121 *sq.* According to Mr. Gopal Panikkar (*op. cit.* p. 37 *sq.*) there are even at the present day Nayar families, especially in the interior of the district, who look upon it as an honour to be thus united with Brahmans, although a reaction has begun to take place against this feeling. See also Sankara Menon, *op. cit.* p. 161 *sq.*

[2] Muttusami Ayyar, quoted by Moore, *op. cit.* p. 59.

[3] *Ibid.* p. 58 *sqq.* See also Anantha Krishna Iyer, *op. cit.* ii. 40

[4] Moore, *op. cit.* p. 68.

[5] Anantha Krishna Iyer, *op. cit.* i. 295 ; ii. 2.

until recently, allowed great liberty to their women.[1] The Newars have a recorded tradition uniting them with the Nayars—a name identical, they say, with Neyár or Newár, y and w being intercalary letters ;[2] whilst the Kallans of the Madura district have a tradition that they came from the north, and bury their dead with the face turned in that direction.[3]

These suggestions, however, completely fail to account for the important difference between the polyandry of the Nayars and that of other polyandrists of India : among the latter the husbands are regularly brothers, among the former they are not.   The immediate cause of this difference is, in my opinion, that among the Nayars the men do not live together with the women with whom they consort, and that, at the same time, inheritance runs through the mother. This is not the case among the other polyandrous peoples of India, nor among the Tibetans ; and, as we have noticed before, their system of fraternal polyandry seems to be intimately connected just with those conditions which are lacking among the Nayars.   If the men live apart from the woman to whom they are attached and their property is not inherited by their children, there is no strong reason on their part why they should be brothers ; and if the woman enjoys a great deal of independence, as she does among the Nayars, she is likely to select by preference men belonging to different families to be her husbands or paramours.[4] But why did the Nayars not live with their wives or mistresses and the children borne by them ?

The answer to this question most probably lies in the military organisation of the Nayars, which prevented them from living the ordinary life of a husband and father of a

[1] Gait, *op. cit.* p. 242 *sq.*   Anantha Krishna Iyer, *op. cit.* ii. 2. Oldham, *The Sun and the Serpent*, p. 158.   Kirkpatrick, *Account of the Kingdom of Nepaul*, p. 187.

[2] Hodgson, *Miscellaneous Essays*, ii. 129 *sq.*

[3] Gait, *op. cit.* p. 243.

[4] An English lady, to whom I spoke about different kinds of polyandry, emphatically declared that she would not like to be married to *brothers*.

family. Lopez de Castanheda writes that the law interdicting them to marry was established by their kings that they might have neither wives nor children on whom to fix their love and attachment, and that, being free from all family cares, they might the more willingly devote themselves to warlike service.[1] Speaking of their law of inheritance in particular, Barbosa says that it was made by the kings that the Nayars " should not be covetous, and should not abandon the king's service."[2] In a later time Mr. Warden, who was Collector of Malabar from 1804 to 1816, gave a similar explanation of the origin of polyandry and inheritance through the female line among the Nayars :—" The profession of arms by birth, subjecting the males of a whole race to military service from the earliest youth to the decline of manhood, was a system of polity utterly incompatible with the existence amongst them of the marriage state. Without matrimony the existence of the common Hindu laws of inheritance was equally incompatible."[3] The same opinion was expressed by Burton, who found it corroborated by the fact that when the Nayars ceased to be a military caste, the relations between the sexes among them gradually changed and the succession of nephews was practically broken through.[4] Among earlier writers on the subject, Montesquieu took the same view as Castanheda,[5] but in recent days this explanation has met with little approval.[6] Dr. Herbert Müller, in a monograph on polyandry in Southern India, admits that the military life of the Nayars may possibly have contributed a little to the preservation of an old custom, but maintains that the theory which traces the origin of their polyandrous unions to such a source is at least

[1] Lopez de Castanheda, op. cit. i. 48 :—" Esta ley de não poderem casar os Naires fizerão os reys : porque não tendo eles molheres nem filhos a que teuessem amor podessem aturar a guerra."
[2] Barbosa, op. cit. p. 127.
[3] Warden, quoted by Moore, op. cit. p. 65.
[4] Burton, Goa, p. 219 sq.
[5] Montesquieu, L'esprit des loix, xvi. 5.
[6] Cf., however, Subramhanya Aiyar, Census of India, 1901, vol. xxvi. (Travancore) Report, p. 330, who says that Montesquieu's explanation deserves to be noted.

as futile as that which ascribes it to the influence of the Brahmans.[1]

Montesquieu observes that in Europe soldiers are not encouraged to marry.[2] In Rome, as we have seen, they were even forbidden to do so, although they were allowed to live in concubinage ; and similar rules have been found elsewhere.[3] The Zaporog Cossacks, who occupied themselves with nothing but war and brigandage, are of particular interest in this connection. They lived in a fortified place, called *setcha*, which women were forbidden to enter upon pain of death. They were not permitted to marry if they wanted to remain Zaporogs, but every man had a right to carry off a girl and have intercourse with her in a hut outside the *setcha*. Boys who were born of these unions were educated in the *setcha*, whereas a girl was sent back with her mother to the homestead of the latter. If a man decided to marry he had to leave the *setcha* and support himself by agriculture or other work, and ceased to be a Zaporog for ever, unless he abandoned his wife.[4] On the authority of Sir John M'Neil these Cossacks were represented by McLennan as practising polyandry ;[5] but this could only have meant that several men might have intercourse with the same girl. In one account, for which no authority is stated, it is said that "each Zaporog had a right to go to the women when, and select those, he chose. When a woman was pregnant, no person gave himself any trouble to ascertain who was the father of the child, as it belonged to the nation at large."[6] In another account we read that if boys were born of the union between a Zaporog and his mistress, they were kept by the father.[7]

But although the military organisation of the Nayars gives

[1] Müller, *Untersuchungen über die Geschichte der polyandrischen Eheformen in Südindien*, p. 47 *sq.*

[2] Montesquieu, *op. cit.* xvi. 5.

[3] *Supra*, i. 369 *sq.*

[4] Lesur, *Histoire des Kosaques*, i. 290, 293. v. Kessel, ' Zur Geschichte der Kosaken,' in *Das Ausland*, xlv. 866. Lady Hamilton, *Marriage Rites*, p. 120 *sq.*

[5] McLennan, *Studies in Ancient History*, p. 98.

[6] Lady Hamilton, *op. cit.* p. 121.

[7] v. Kessel, *loc. cit.* p. 866.

us the most probable explanation of the unusual character
of their polyandrous habits, it hardly accounts for those
habits in full. We must also take into consideration the
strong polyandrous tendencies, the laxity of sexual morals,
and the freedom enjoyed by the women among the Dravidian
peoples ; to some extent, I believe, the great demand for
Nayar women among the younger Brahmans ; and possibly
economic circumstances as well. Pyrard observes that the
advantage the Nayars derive from the custom in question is
" that one who hath not means himself to maintain a wife,
may have a third part of one, and the cost of her maintenance
is only in this proportion."[1] Whether the Nayar rule of
inheritance through the mother, as has been generally
supposed, is a consequence of their non-fraternal polyandry
is difficult to say. According to some accounts the relations
between the men and the children of their mistress were of
such a nature as to make any other rule impossible ; but, on
the other hand, there are castes in the same tract who follow
the uterine system of descent and yet have never been known
to practise polyandry of the Nayar type.[2]

Dr. Müller argues that a marriage system similar to that of
the Nayars has been found among other castes or tribes in
Southern India.[3] He mentions the potters and workers of
clay, the washermen, the weavers, and the Tiver, whose
principal employment was to till the palm trees, gather their
fruits, and make wine ; and he gives Barbosa as his authority
with regard to the three first-mentioned castes. Now Barbosa says that they in their marriages follow the law of
the Nayars,[4] but by " marriage " he obviously means the
tāli kettu ceremony and not the polyandrous unions, which
he refuses to call marriages.[5] Of the weavers, however, we
are told that " their wives have the power of doing what
they please with themselves with the nairs (Nayars), or with
other weavers " ;[6] of the washermen, that only the Nayars
can have mistresses from amongst their women ;[7] and of the

---

[1] Pyrard, *op. cit.* p. 384 *sq.*   [2] Gait, *op. cit.* p. 241.
[3] Müller, *op. cit.* p. 50 *sq.*   [4] Barbosa, *op. cit.* p. 135 *sq.*
[5] See *ibid.* p. 124 *sq.*   [6] *Ibid.* p. 136.
[7] *Ibid.* p. 136.

Tiver, that their wives with the knowledge of their husbands give themselves both to the Moors, natives of the country, and to foreigners of all kinds, as also that " of this sect sometimes two brothers have one wife only and both of them live with her "[1]—in other words, that they practised fraternal polyandry, which we also know from more recent statements, the Tiver evidently being the same as the Tiyyans.[2] Among the three last-mentioned castes inheritance is, besides, said to run through the mother.[3] We further learn that the potters were only separated from the Nayars on account of a fault which they committed ;[4] that many of the weavers were sons of Nayars and bore arms and went to war ;[5] and that most of the Tiver were serfs of the Nayars and some of them learned the use of arms and fought in the wars when it was necessary.[6] From these statements it appears that the castes in question were so closely connected with the Nayars that if polyandrous unions similar to those of the latter really occurred among them, they may have been due to the influence of the Nayars. Dr. Müller further refers to Visscher's statement that neither the " Chetriahs " (Kshatriya) nor the Nayars were allowed to have lawful wives, that among both of them the children always belonged to the mother's family, and that their ceremonies and observances in a great measure coincided ;[7] but it should be remembered that the Kshatriya also were warriors and undoubtedly stood in close relations to the Nayars. Zeen-ud-deen states that among the Nayars " and the castes connected with them " two or four men live with one woman ;[8] he does not mention those castes by name, but the fact that they were connected with the Nayars makes it probable that their polyandrous habits had a common origin. From Harkness' information as regards the Irulas, that they " have no marriage contract, the sexes cohabiting almost indiscriminately,"[9] Dr. Müller draws the inference that the relations between the sexes

---

[1] Barbosa, *op. cit.* p. 138.   [2] *Supra*, iii. 128 *sq.*
[3] Barbosa, *op. cit.* pp. 136, 138.   [4] *Ibid.* p. 134.
[5] *Ibid.* p. 136.   [6] *Ibid.* p. 137.
[7] Visscher, *op. cit.* p. 122.   [8] Zeen-ud-deen, *op. cit.* p. 64.
[9] Harkness, *op. cit.* p. 92.

among them must have been very similar to those among the
Nayars ; but from what has been said previously about the
sexual peculiarities of the Irulas[1] it appears that there is no
ground for such a conclusion.   Finally Dr. Müller argues
that there are other castes besides the Nayars that have
a *tāli kettu* or mock marriage and a subsequent *sambandham*
union implying cohabitation, and also follow the uterine
system of descent.[2]   But this by no means proves that they
once were polyandrous like the Nayars ; it should particularly be remembered that the custom of tracing descent
through the mother does not imply that man and wife live
apart from each other as they did among the latter.   The
theory that the peculiar form of polyandrous unions which
prevailed among the Nayars was intimately connected with
their military habits of life would certainly lose much of its
probability if it could be shown that the same custom has
occurred among other castes of India who have neither been
military themselves nor may be supposed to have been
influenced by the practices of the Nayars.   But, so far as I
know, there is nothing to show that this has been the case.

Dr. Müller's own belief is that the polyandry of the Nayars
can only be explained as a late survival of an ancient marriage
system, which was perhaps the earliest in the whole history
of marriage.[3]   This was also the view of McLennan, who
looked upon polyandry of " the ruder sort," in which the
husbands are not kinsmen, as a modification of and advance
from promiscuity,[4] and considered fraternal polyandry to
have developed out of the ruder form.   Theories of this
kind, however, explain nothing and are of no value at all.
To explain polyandry is to trace it to its causes, and when
this is done it is found that certain circumstances lead to
unions in which the husbands are brothers and other circumstances to unions in which they are not so ; but I see no
reason whatever to assume that the former have developed
out of the latter.   It would indeed be rather surprising if

[1] *Supra*, i. 116 *sq.*
[2] See Francis, *Census of India*, 1901, vol. xv. (Madras) Report,
pp. 143, 162 ; Gait, *op. cit.* p. 241 *sq.*
[3] Müller, *op. cit.* p. 48 *sq.*   [4] McLennan, *op. cit.* p. 93 *sq.*

a people so cultivated as the Nayars had preserved the primitive form while lower castes living in the same neighbourhood had grown out of it and changed their polyandry into fraternal.

I certainly do not maintain that my discussion of the causes from which polyandry has sprung gives a full solution of the problem. There are many peoples among whom the males outnumber the females or to whom polyandry would be useful on account of poverty or as a method of keeping property together or for other reasons, and who all the same never practise it. A paucity of marriageable women, for example, may lead to celibacy, prostitution, or homosexual practices,[1] as well as to polyandry. To explain in full why certain factors in some cases give rise to polyandry and in other cases not is as impossible as it often is to say exactly why one people is monogamous and another people polygynous. But, generally speaking, there can be little doubt that the main reason why polyandry is not more commonly practised is the natural desire in most men to be in exclusive possession of their wives. Among many polyandrous peoples the men are expressly stated to be remarkably little addicted to jealousy. Bogle says this of the Tibetans,[2] and Wilson describes their whole race as one " of a peculiarly placid, unpassionate temperament."[3] The Ladakhis are " a mild and timid people,"[4] whose jealousy " takes no violent form."[5] The Kulu husbands are described as " très peu jaloux,"[6] although Calvert was told of one who committed suicide from jealousy.[7] Among the Todas[8] and Kurumbas[9] the

---

[1] See Westermarck, *Origin and Development of the Moral Ideas*, ii. 466 ; also Moncelon, in *Bull. Soc. d'Anthr. Paris*, ser. iii. vol. ix. 367 (New Caledonians).

[2] Bogle, *Narrative of Mission to Tibet*, p. 123.

[3] Wilson, *op. cit.* p. 212. See also Miss Gordon Cumming, *op. cit.* p. 406.

[4] Moorcroft and Trebeck, *op. cit.* i. 321.

[5] Knight, *op. cit.* p. 140.

[6] Ujfalvy, in *Bull. Soc. d'Anthr. Paris*, ser. iii. vol. v. 228. See also *Idem, Aus dem westlichen Himalaja*, p. 37.

[7] Calvert, *op. cit.* p. 32.   [8] Rivers, *Todas*, p. 529.

[9] Thurston, *Ethnographic Notes*, p. 113.

men do not seem to object to their women being open even to others than their fellow husbands. The male Sinhalese are not troubled with very jealous dispositions, and the infidelity of a woman is generally easily forgiven, unless she has intercourse with a man of lower caste.[1] Of some of the Marquesas Islanders Porter says that jealousy "is confined altogether to the females,"[2] although according to Roquefeuil there are married men among them who punish their wives for infidelity.[3] Among the Záparo Indians of Ecuador, who have polyandry, the men, entirely contrary to what is the case in neighbouring tribes, "are not at all jealous, but allow their women great liberty."[4] We also often hear how well the husbands in polyandrous families get on together,[5] though statements to the contrary are not entirely wanting.[6]

Although the number of peoples who are known to practise or to have practised polyandry as a regular custom is not large, it has been suggested by McLennan and his followers that in early times polyandry was the rule and monogamy and polygyny exceptions. According to his view, the only marriage law in which female kinship could have originated was polyandry of "the ruder sort," in which the husbands are not kinsmen. And it is, he says, impossible not to believe that the levirate, or practice of marrying a dead brother's widow, is derived from polyandry.[7] The first inference is

---

[1] Forbes, *Eleven Years in Ceylon*, i. 333. Davy, *op. cit.* p. 287. Sarasin, *Ergebnisse naturwissenschaftlicher Forschungen auf Ceylon*, iii. 464. Sirr, *op. cit.* ii. 167.

[2] Porter, *Journal of a Cruise made to the Pacific Ocean*, ii. 60.

[3] de Roquefeuil, *op. cit.* i. 309.

[4] Simson, *op. cit.* p. 173.

[5] Chaffanjon, *op. cit.* p. 283 (Maquiritarés). Ross, *Second Voyage*, p. 373 (Netchilirmiut). Bonvalot, *op. cit.* ii. 127 ; Sarat Chandra Das, *op. cit.* p. 286 (Tibetans). Fraser, *op. cit.* p. 208 (people of Sirmur). Ujfalvy, *Aus dem westlichen Himalaja*, p. 37 (Kulu). Rivers, *Todas*, p. 516. *Supra*, iii. 138 (Nayars). Vincendon-Dumoulin and Desgraz, *Iles Marquises ou Nouka-Hiva*, p. 287.

[6] Schlagintweit, *Indien*, i. 100.

[7] McLennan, *op. cit.* p. 112 *sq.* *Idem*, 'Levirate and Polyandry,' in *Fortnightly Review*, N.S. xxi. 703 *sqq.*

based on the assumption that the matrilineal system of descent is due to uncertainty as to fathers, and the illegitimacy of this assumption has been shown in a previous chapter. We shall now consider whether the second inference is more convincing.

The levirate is a very widespread custom,[1] and if it could

[1] The levirate has, for instance, been found among the following peoples :—Brazilian aborigines (v. Martius, *Beiträge zur Ethnographie Amerika's*, i. 117), Arawaks (*ibid*. i. 691), Warraus (Schomburgk, ' Natives of Guiana,' in *Jour. Ethn. Soc. London*, i. 275), Roucouyennes (Coudreau, *Chez nos Indiens*, p. 128), Mosquito Indians, Azteks, Mayas (Bancroft, *Native Races of the Pacific States of North America*, i. 730 ; ii. 466, 671), Pawnee (Grinnell, *Story of the Indian*, p. 46), Hidatsa (Matthews, *Ethnography and Philology of the Hidatsa Indians*, p. 53), Shawnee (Ashe, *Travels in America*, p. 250), Omaha (Dorsey, ' Omaha Sociology,' in *Ann. Rep. Bur. Ethn*. iii. 258 ; James, *Expedition from Pittsburgh to the Rocky Mountains*, i. 243), Miwok of California (Powers, *Tribes of California*, p. 256), Chimariko Indians of California (Dixon, *Chimariko Indians and Language*, p. 301), Stlatlumh (Hill Tout, ' Report on the Ethnology of the Stlatlumh of British Columbia,' in *Jour. Anthr. Inst*. xxxv. 133), Shuswap (Teit, ' Shuswap,' in *Publications of the Jesup North Pacific Expedition*, i. 591). For other American instances see Frazer, *Totemism and Exogamy*, iii. 85 (Blackfeet), 127 (Kansa), 246 (Apache), 249 (Mohave), 305 (Haida), 361 (Tsetsaut), 498 (Maidu of California), 562 (Goajiros).—Ainu (Dall, *Alaska*, p. 524 ; Dixon, ' Tsuishikari Ainos,' in *Trans. Asiatic Soc. Japan*, vol. xi. pt. i. 44), Kamchadal (Steller, *Beschreibung von dem Lande Kamtschatka*, p. 347), Koryak (Jochelson, *Koryak*, p. 748), Gilyak, Tungus, Buryat (Miss Czaplicka, *Aboriginal Siberia*, pp. 101, 106, 120), Turkomans (Grenard, *op. cit*. p. 253), Ossetes (v. Haxthausen, *Transcaucasia*, p. 403 ; Kovalewsky, *Coutume contemporaine et loi ancienne*, p. 178 *sqq*.), Arabs (*Alberuni's India*, i. 109 ; Burckhardt, *Notes on the Bedouins and Wahábys*, p. 64), Li of Hainan (Strzoda, ' Die Li auf Hainan,' in *Zeitschr. f. Ethnol*. xliii. 203), Kakhyens (Anderson, *Mandalay to Momien*, p. 142), Nagas (Hodson, *Nāga Tribes of Manipur*, p. 95), Bhotias of Almora and British Garhwal (Sherring, ' Notes on the Bhotias of Almora and British Garhwal,' in *Memoirs Asiatic Soc. Bengal*, i. 99), Mrús (Lewin, *op. cit*. p. 234), Pahárias (Dalton, *Descriptive Ethnology of Bengal*, p. 273), Bilúchis (Postans, ' Bilúchi Tribes inhabiting Sindh,' in *Jour. Ethn. Soc. London*, i. 105), Gonds of the Eastern Ghauts (Hayavadana Rao, ' Gonds of the Eastern Ghauts,' in *Anthropos*, v. 795), Katis in the province of Gujarāt (Chatterji, ' Origin and Traditions of Kathis,' in *Calcutta Review*, cxxxi. 389), Krishnavakkakars of Travancore (Thurston, *Ethnographic Notes in Southern India*, p. 113),

be proved to be a survival of polyandry we should certainly
be compelled to conclude that this form of marriage was
at one time very common.

It seems to me, however, that the levirate is so easily
explained by existing conditions that we have no right to

and various other tribes of India (Gait, *Census of India*, 1911,
vol. i. [India] Report, p. 247 *sq.* ; Crooke, *North-Western Provinces
of India*, p. 229 ; Kirkpatrick, ' Polyandry in the Panjâb,' in *Indian
Antiquary*, vii. 86 ; Frazer, *op. cit.* ii. 222, 236, 279–281, 296, 299,
313, 315).—Tribes in the Malay Archipelago (Wilken, *Over de
verwantschap en het huwelijks- en erfrecht bij de volken van het maleische
ras*, pp. 32, 39, 54, 57 *sqq.* ; Marsden, *History of Sumatra*, pp. 228,
229, 260 *sq.* ; Junghuhn, *Die Battaländer auf Sumatra*, ii. 134 ;
Zollinger, ' Lampong Districts,' in *Jour. Indian Archipelago*, v. 697)
and New Guinea (Wilken, *op. cit.* p. 66 ; Williamson, ' Customs of
the Mekeo People of British New Guinea,' in *Jour. Roy. Anthr. Inst.*
xliii. 277), natives of New Britain (Romilly, ' Islands of the New
Britain Group,' in *Proceed. Roy. Geo. Soc.* N.S. ix. 9 ; Burger, *Die
Küsten- und Bergvölker der Gazellehalbinsel*, pp. 31, 57), Banks
Islanders (Rivers, *History of Melanesian Society*, i. 48), Pentecost
Islanders (*ibid.* i. 206 ; Speiser, *Two Years with the Natives in the
Western Pacific*, p. 236), natives of East Mallicolo (Paton, quoted by
Serbelov, ' Social Position of Men and Women among the Natives
of East Malekula, New Hebrides,' in *American Anthropologist*, N.S.
xv. 279) ; Erromangans (Robertson, *Erromanga*, p. 397), New
Caledonians (Moncelon, in *Bull. Soc. d'Anthr. Paris*, ser. iii. vol. ix.
367 ; Lambert, *Mœurs et Superstitions des Néo-Calédoniens*, p. 95),
Fijians (Thomson, *Fijians*, p. 186 ; Rivers, *op. cit.* i. 296), Maori
(Colenso, *Maori Races of New Zealand*, p. 26 ; Best, ' Maori Marriage
Customs,' in *Trans. and Proceed. New Zealand Institute*, xxxvi. 29,
62 *sq.*), Samoans (Turner, *Samoa*, p. 98), Marshall Islanders (Herns-
heim, *Südsee-Erinnerungen*, p. 81 ; Kohler, ' Das Recht der Marshall-
insulaner,' in *Zeitschr. f. vergl. Rechtswiss.* xiv. 416 *sq.*), many or
most of the Australian tribes (Waitz-Gerland, *Anthropologie der
Naturvölker*, vi. 776 ; Curr, *The Australian Race*, i. 107 ; Malinowski,
The Family among the Australian Aborigines, p. 63 *sq.* ; Brough
Smyth, *Aborigines of Victoria*, i. 87 ; Howitt, *Native Tribes of South-
East Australia*, pp. 193, 217, 220, 224, 227, 236, 250, 258, 266, 281 ;
Schulze, ' Aborigines of the Upper and Middle Finke River,' in
Trans. and Proceed. Roy. Soc. South Australia, xiv. 239 ; Newland,
' Parkengees,' in *Proceed. Roy. Geograph. Soc. Australasia : South
Australian Branch*, ii. 21 ; Bonney, ' Customs of the Aborigines of
the River Darling,' in *Jour. Anthr. Inst.* xiii. 135 ; Palmer, ' Notes
on some Australian Tribes,' *ibid.* xiii. 298 ; Petrie, *Reminiscences of
Early Queensland*, p. 60 *sq.* ; Lumholtz, *Among Cannibals*, p. 164 ;

look upon it as a survival at all. Wives may be inherited like other belongings.[1] Mr. Crooke observes that in the North-Western Provinces of India, where the custom of marrying the elder brother's widow practically obtains in all the tribes, " the widow is regarded as a kind of property which has been purchased into the family by the payment of the brideprice."[2] In West Africa, says Dr. Nassau, " it is Salvado, *Mémoires historiques sur l'Australie*, p. 278 ; Brown, ' Three Tribes of Western Australia,' in *Jour. Roy. Anthr. Inst.* xliii. 158 ; Frazer, *op. cit.* i. 500, 501, 549, 552, 572 ; *Idem, Folk-Lore in the Old Testament*, ii. 303. There are, however, Australian tribes that prohibit or avoid marriage with a deceased brother's widow [Howitt, *op. cit.* pp. 199, 237, 248 ; Beveridge, *Aborigines of Victoria and Riverina*, p. 25]).—Malagasy (Sibree, *op. cit.* p. 246 ; Grandidier, *op. cit.* ii. 188) ; Barotse and Matabele (Decle, *Three Years in Savage Africa*, pp. 78, 160), Basuto (Minnie Martin, *Basutoland*, p. 88), Bechuanas and Zulus (Conder, ' Present Condition of the Native Tribes in Bechuanaland,' in *Jour. Anthr. Inst.* xvi. 85), Kafirs (Kropf, *Das Volk der Xosa-Kaffern im östlichen Südafrika*, p. 152 ; Kidd, *The Essential Kafir*, p. 226), Thonga (Junod, *Life of a South African Tribe*, i. 248, 272), Wahehe and Konde people (Fülleborn, *Das Deutsche Njassa- und Ruwuma-Gebiet*, pp. 229, 348), natives of Ruanda (Schumacher, ' Das Eherecht in Ruanda,' in *Anthropos*, vii. 8), Wapokomo (Gregory, *Great Rift Valley*, p. 343), Wanika (New, *Life, Wanderings, &c. in Eastern Africa*, p. 120), Wasania (Barrett, ' Customs and Beliefs of the Wa-Giriama, &c., British East Africa,' in *Jour. Roy. Anthr. Inst.* xli. 31), Bahima (Roscoe, *Northern Bantu*, p. 113 *sq.*), Manyema (Cunningham, *Uganda*, p. 322), Galla (Waitz, *op. cit.* ii. 516), Bogos (Munzinger, *Ueber die Sitten und das Recht der Bogos*, p. 64), Kûri (Nachtigal, *Sahara und Sudan*, ii. 375), Buduma of Lake Chad (Talbot, ' Buduma of Lake Chad,' in *Jour. Roy. Anthr. Inst.* xli. 248), people of Bouna and Séguéla (Clozel and Villamur, *Les coutumes indigènes de la Côte d'Ivoire*, pp. 309, 326), Yoruba (formerly ; Ellis, *Yoruba-speaking Peoples of the Slave Coast*, p. 185 *sq.*), some Western Equatorial Africans mentioned by Du Chaillu (*Journey to Ashango-Land*, p. 429), people of the Lower Congo (Weeks, *Among the Primitive Bakongo*, p. 148), Bambala (Torday, *Camp and Tramp in African Wilds*, p. 96). For other African instances see Frazer, *Totemism and Exogamy*, ii. 384 (Swazies, Pondos), 419 (Taveta), 428 (Suk), 630 (Awemba and Wahorohoro west of Lake Tanganyika).—Several other cases of the levirate will be given subsequently.

[1] *Cf.* Spencer, *Principles of Sociology*, ii. 649.
[2] Crooke, *Tribes and Castes*, i. p. cxc. *sq.* See also Hodson, *Nāga Tribes of Manipur*, p. 95 ; Codrington, *Melanesians*, p. 244.

preferred that widows shall be retained in the family circle because of the dowry that was paid for them, which is considered as a permanent instalment."[1] Among the Sango[2] and Bateso[3] a widow may refuse to marry one of her deceased husband's brothers or his heir, whoever it be, only on condition that she or her relatives pay back the price paid for her. Among the Herero, according to Dannert, the custom of marrying the elder brother's widow serves the purpose of keeping the property within the family ; and for the same reason it is customary for the heir to marry also the widow's growing daughters by her first husband, besides herself, in order to secure to himself the heiresses and with them the enjoyment of their substance.[4] In many cases it is simply said that widows pass into the possession of their deceased husband's heirs.[5] Often also the brother, or, in default of a brother, the nearest male relative, is expressly stated to be entitled to have the widow ; and if he does not marry her, he has nevertheless the guardianship over her and may give her away or sell her to some other man.[6]

McLennan lays stress on the fact that it is the deceased husband's *brother* who inherits his widow. " How came the right of succession," he says, " to open, as in the ruder cases, to the brother in preference to the son of the deceased ? We repeat, that the only explanation that can be given of

[1] Nassau, *Fetichism in West Africa*, p. 6.
[2] Heese, ' Sitte und Brauch der Sango,' in *Archiv f. Anthropologie*, N.S. xii. 140.
[3] Roscoe, *Northern Bantu*, p. 267.
[4] Dannert, *Zum Rechte der Herero*, p. 38 *sq.*
[5] Curr, *Recollections of Squatting in Victoria*, p. 248 (Bangerang). Ellis, *Ewe-speaking Peoples of the Slave Coast*, p. 205. Bufe, ' Die Bakundu,' in *Archiv f. Anthropologie*, N.S. xii. 236. Torday and Joyce, ' Ba-Huana,' in *Jour. Roy. Anthr. Inst.* xxxvi. 286. Roscoe, *Northern Bantu*, p. 263 (Bateso).
[6] v. Martius, *Beiträge zur Ethnographie Amerika's*, i. 117, 118, 691 (Brazilian aborigines and Arawaks). Gibbs, ' Tribes of Western Washington and Northwestern Oregon,' in *Contributions to North American Ethnology*, i. 199. Mathew, *Two Representative Tribes of Queensland*, p. 163 (Kabi and Wakka). Scott Robertson, *Káfirs of the Hindu-Kush*, p. 535. Munzinger, *Ostafrikanische Studien*, p 488 (Kunáma).

this is, that the law of succession was derived from poly-andry."[1] But among various peoples who have the custom of the levirate sons either inherit nothing or are preceded by brothers in succession.[2] Of the Maori we are told that, on the death of the elder brother, it was the established custom for the next in succession to take not only his wife but also his slaves.[3] Among some peoples the widow together with the other property of the dead man goes either to his brother or to his sister's son.[4] But it is more natural, where succession runs in the female line, that the widow should be married by the brother than by the nephew, because as a rule she is considerably older than the nephew and he in many cases is too young to marry and to maintain her properly. Among the Ewhe-speaking peoples of the Slave Coast " when a brother succeeds a brother it is more usual for the union to be consummated than when a nephew succeeds an uncle."[5]

Even when a son inherits the other property of his father it is easy to understand why he does not inherit the widow, apart from any considerations of age. To inherit her is, generally speaking, to marry her. But nowhere is a son allowed to marry his own mother ; hence it is natural, at least where monogamy prevails, that the right of succession in this case should belong to the brother. Even marriage

[1] McLennan, *Studies in Ancient History*, p. 112 *sq.*

[2] Samoans (Pritchard, *Polynesian Reminiscences*, p. 393), some Papuans of New Guinea (Finsch, *Neu-Guinea*, p. 77 ; Waitz-Gerland, *Anthropologie der Naturvölker*, vi. 661), Caroline Islanders (*ibid.* vol. v. pt. ii. 117 ; v. Kotzebue, *Voyage of Discovery*, iii. 209), Santals (Man, *Sonthalia and the Sonthals*, p. 100). Among many other peoples the right of succession belongs in the first place to the brother.

[3] Shortland, *Traditions and Superstitions of the New Zealanders*, p. 120.

[4] Tlingit (Holmberg, Ethnographische Skizzen über die Völker des russischen Amerika,' in *Acta Soc. Scientiarum Fennicae*, iv. 316, 325), Kunáma (Munzinger, *Ostafrikanische Studien*, pp. 484, 488), Ewhe-speaking Peoples of the Slave Coast (Ellis, *op. cit.* p. 205), Gold Coast natives (Cruickshank, *Eighteen Years on the Gold Coast*, ii. 199). In Loango men inherit the wives of their fathers, elder brothers, and uncles (Wilson, *Western Africa*, p. 310).

[5] Ellis, *op. cit.* p. 205.

with a step-mother may be looked upon as incestuous. Instances of this have been given above.[1]

Among many peoples, however, it is the rule that in polygynous families the eldest son, or all the sons, inherit the father's widows, the mother being in each case excepted.[2] Bosman wrote of the Negroes of Benin that if the mother of the eldest son, the only heir, was alive, he allowed her a proper maintenance, whereas he took home his father's other widows and used them as his wives, especially those who had not had children, if he liked them ; but if the deceased left no children the brother inherited all his property.[3] Among the Akikúyu a son " inherits his father's widows, but only takes as his wives any in excess of three, and these only if they have not borne more than one child."[4] Among the Ja-luo, or Nilotic Kavirondo, " the brothers of the deceased take his wives, but the eldest son probably takes the youngest wife of his deceased father."[5] Of the Bantu Kavirondo, again, it is said that if one of the widows has only small children the eldest son of her dead husband takes her as his wife, whereas the mother of a grown-up son

---

[1] *Supra*, ii. 153 *sq.*

[2] Mishmis (Rowlatt, ' Expedition into the Mishmee Hills,' in *Jour. Asiatic. Soc. Bengal*, vol. xiv. pt. ii. 488 ; Dalton, *op. cit.* p. 16), Miris (Rowney, *op. cit.* p. 154), Tartars (Marco Polo, *Kingdoms and Marvels of the East*, i. 253 ; de Rubruquis, ' Travels into Tartary and China,' in Pinkerton, *Collection of Voyages and Travels*, vii. 33 *sq.*), Akamba (Hildebrandt, ' Ethnographische Notizen über Wakámba,' in *Zeitschr. f. Ethnol.* x. 406), Baele (Nachtigal, *Sahara und Sudan*, ii. 176), Baganda (Felkin, ' Notes on the Waganda Tribe,' in *Proceed. Roy. Soc. Edinburgh*, xiii. 745), Bavuma, Yao, and Lendu (Cunningham, *Uganda*, pp. 130, 322, 324, 338), people of the ·Mahou (Clozel and Villamur, *Les coutumes indigènes de la Côte d'Ivoire*, p. 326), Yoruba (Ellis, *Yoruba-speaking Peoples of the Slave Coast*, p. 185), Egbas (Burton, *Abeokuta*, i. 208), Negroes of Fida (Bosman, *loc. cit.* p. 480), Boloki (Weeks, *Congo Cannibals*, p. 111), Zandehs (Junker, *Travels in Africa during the Years 1879-1883*, p. 189), Wanyamwezi (Decle, *Three Years in Savage Africa*, p. 348), some Bantu tribes south of the Zambesi (Theal, *Yellow and Dark-skinned People of Africa south of the Zambesi*, p. 234), &c.

[3] Bosman, *loc. cit.* p. 528.

[4] Routledge, *With a Prehistoric People*, p. 143.

[5] Johnston, *Uganda*, p. 794.

goes to live with him.[1] The rules of succession are thus modified according to circumstances, and they are not uniform even among the same people. It happens, for instance, that the brother succeeds to the chieftainship, whilst the son inherits the property of the dead man[2]—no doubt because the brother, being older and more experienced, is generally better fitted for command than the son.[3]

The levirate, however, is not only looked upon as a right belonging to the deceased husband's brother but in many cases as a duty incumbent upon him.[4] Among the Gournditch-mara in South-Western Victoria, " when a married man dies, his brother is bound to marry the widow if she has a family, as it is his duty to protect her and rear his brother's children."[5] Among the Tlingit the neglect of the obligation to marry a brother's or maternal uncle's widow has led to

---

[1] Hobley, *Eastern Uganda*, p. 25.

[2] McLennan, *Patriarchal Theory*, p. 89.

[3] *Cf.* Maine, *Ancient Law*, p. 241.

[4] Maynas of the Upper Marañon (Chantre y Herrera, *Historia de las Misiones en el Marañón español*, p. 73), Chippewa (Keating, *Expedition to the Source of St. Peter's River*, ii. 170 *sq.*), Cree (Waitz, *op. cit.* iii. 110), Omaha (Alice C. Fletcher and La Flesche, ' Omaha Tribe,' in *Ann. Rep. Bur. Ethn.* xxvii. 313), Takelma Indians (Sapir, ' Notes on the Takelma Indians of Southwestern Oregon,' in *American Anthropologist*, N.S. ix. 268), Thompson Indians (Teit, ' Thompson Indians of British Columbia,' in *Publications of the Jesup North Pacific Expedition*, i. 325), Atkha Aleut (Petroff, ' Report on the Population, &c. of Alaska,' in *Tenth Census of the United States*, p. 158), Eskimo (Klutschak, *op. cit.* p. 234; Bogoras, *op. cit.* p. 608 *sq.*), certain natives of Australia not mentioned by name (Purcell, ' Rites and Customs of Australian Aborigines,' in *Verhandl. Berliner Gesellsch. Anthrop.* 1893, p. 287), New Caledonians (de Rochas, *La Nouvelle-Calédonie*, p. 232 ; Brainne, *La Nouvelle Calédonie*, p. 240), natives of Nitendi and the New Hebrides (Waitz-Gerland, *op. cit.* vi. 634), Nufors of New Guinea (Guillemard, *op. cit.* p. 390), Battas of Sumatra (Brenner, *Besuch bei den Kannibalen Sumatras*, p. 250 ; Moszkowski, *Auf neuen Wegen durch Sumatra*, p. 241), Santals (Hertel, *Indisk Hjemmemission blandt Santalerne*, p. 74), Gonds (Forsyth, *Highlands of Central India*, p. 150), some Bedouins (Jennings-Bramley, ' Bedouin of the Sinaitic Peninsula,' in *Quarterly Statement of the Palestine Exploration Fund*, 1905, p. 218).

[5] Dawson, *Australian Aborigines*, p. 27. Howitt, *Native Tribes of South-East Australia*, p. 250,

bloody feuds.[1] Among the Chukchee, after the death of one
of several brothers, the next oldest takes care of the wife and
children of the deceased, finds for them a dwelling in his
camps, and acts as husband to the woman and as father to
the children ; and in the absence of brothers, the levirate
passes to cousins. It often, says Bogoras, " has the character
of a duty rather than that of a right. A woman left without
a husband, with her children and a herd to attend to, needs
a protection ; and the obligation to assist her falls on the
nearest relative."[2] In Dardistan it is considered disgraceful
to refuse to marry a brother's widow, so that it is not uncommon for a boy of ten to marry a woman more than twice
his age.[3] In Afghanistan, too, it is incumbent on the
brother of the deceased to marry his widow, although the
widow is not compelled to take a husband against her will.[4]
Among the Fingu Kafirs, according to Kropf, the object of
the levirate is to keep the family together after the death
of its head, " so that the wives shall not be scattered, and the
children not be left unsupported " ; but among them also
a widow cannot be forced to marry her brother-in-law.[5]
Of the Bechuanas we are told that " when a man dies and
leaves a widow, a relation of the husband must take her
home as his wife. Which of the relations shall do this, is
fixed at a meeting of friends, when she is generally assigned
to him who has the smallest family."[6] The Shambaa look
upon it as a great offence against the widow if none of her
deceased husband's relatives is willing to take her to him.[7]
Among a strictly monogamous people the compulsory
levirate may indeed be an extremely serious duty. Thus
the unmarried Kuki who is compelled to marry the widow
of his deceased elder brother will never be allowed to take
another wife as long as she remains alive.[8]

[1] Dall, op. cit. p. 416. [2] Bogoras, op. cit. p. 608.
[3] Biddulph, Tribes of the Hindoo Koosh, p. 76.
[4] Elphinstone, Account of the Kingdom of Kaubul, i. 236.
[5] Kropf, op. cit. p. 152.
[6] Campbell, Second Journey, ii. 212.
[7] Dahlgrün, ' Heiratsgebräuche der Schambaa,' in Mittheil.
Deutsch. Schutzgeb. xvi. 227.
[8] Soppitt, Account of the Kuki-Lushai Tribes, p. 15.

Among the ancient Hebrews it was the duty of a man to marry the widow of his brother if he died childless, and the firstborn should succeed in the brother's name " that his name be not put out of Israel."[1] To " raise up seed " to the dead brother was also the object of the Hindu *niyoga*, which, however, implied only cohabitation, not marriage.[2] In Madagascar the younger brother who performs the duty of marrying the elder brother's widow is said to " make to live the eye," and the children are considered the elder brother's heirs and descendants.[3] So also among the Yoruba-speaking peoples of the Slave Coast, if the deceased brother left no child, the son first born of the new union was named after him and considered to fill the place of a son.[4] Among the Dinka it is the duty of a widow " to raise children to her dead husband's name " by cohabiting with her husband's brother or other of his close male relations.[5] Charlevoix says that the reason which the Hurons and the Iroquois gave for the duty of a widow to marry her deceased husband's brother if he died childless was the same as that mentioned in Deuteronomy.[6]

Among certain other peoples all the children begotten by the brother are accounted the children of the first husband.[7]

[1] *Deuteronomy*, xxv. 5 *sqq.*

[2] *Laws of Manu*, ix. 59, 145. For a detailed discussion of the *niyoga* see Winternitz, in *Jour. Roy. Asiatic Soc.* 1897, p. 716 *sqq.* Mr. Gait says (*Census of India*, 1911, vol. i. [India] Report, p. 247 ; see also Crooke, *Tribes and Castes of the North-Western Provinces and Oudh*, i. p. cxc.) that " with one or two local exceptions, the idea of raising up seed to the deceased is entirely foreign to the custom of widow marriage as it now obtains in India. The woman is regarded as the permanent wife of the second husband whoever he may be, and the children are held to be his."   [3] Sibree, *op. cit.* p. 246.

[4] Ellis, *Yoruba-speaking Peoples*, p. 186.

[5] O'Sullivan, ' Dinka Laws and Customs,' in *Jour. Roy. Anthr. Inst.* xl. 184.

[6] Charlevoix, *Voyage to North-America*, ii. 36.

[7] Some Kafirs (Kropf, *op. cit.* p. 152 ; Kidd, *The Essential Kafir*, p. 226 ; Theal, *Yellow and Dark-skinned People of Africa south of the Zambesi*, p. 234), Bechuanas (Campbell, *Second Journey*, ii. 212 ; Livingstone, *Missionary Travels*, p. 185), Ossetes (v. Haxthausen, *op. cit.* p. 403 ; Kovalewsky, ' La famille matriarcale au Caucase,' in *L'Anthropologie*, iv. 274).

McLennan looks upon this also as evidence of the levirate being a survival of earlier polyandry. " It is obvious," he says, " that it could more easily be feigned that the children belonged to the brother deceased, if already, at a prior stage, the children of the brotherhood had been accounted the children of the eldest brother, *i.e.*, if we suppose the obligation to be a relic of polyandry."[1] Against this argument it may be said that the cases in question may also be quite easily explained otherwise. As Dr. Starcke justly observes, a man may from a juridical point of view be the father of a child, although he is not so in fact.[2] Concerning the Papuans of Geelvink Bay of Dutch New Guinea M. Bink states, " À la mort du père, c'est l'oncle (frère du père) qui se charge de la tutelle ; si l'enfant devient orphelin, il reconnaît son oncle comme son père."[3] And in Samoa the brother of a deceased husband considered himself entitled, not only to have his brother's widow, but to be regarded by the orphan children as their father.[4] Quite in accordance with these facts, the children of a widow may be considered to belong to her former husband. Indeed, where death without posterity is looked upon as a horrible calamity, the ownership of the children is a thing of the utmost importance for the dead man. It is only when the deceased has no offspring that the Jews, Hindus, and Malagasy prescribed that the brother should raise up seed to him. If the levirate really were a relic of polyandry, it might rather be expected that the issue should belong to the surviving man who was once a fellow-husband.[5]

A subsidiary motive for the levirate may in some cases be fear of the deceased husband's jealous ghost. Dr. Karsten informs us that the Jíbaros of Ecuador, among whom a man is obliged to marry his brother's widow, believe that if the widow unlawfully marries another man she may

[1] McLennan, *Studies in Ancient History*, p. 113.
[2] Starcke, *Primitive Family*, ch. iii.
[3] Bink, in *Bull. Soc. d'Anthr. Paris*, ser. iii. vol. xi. 395.
[4] Turner, *Samoa*, p. 98. See also Matthews, *Ethnography and Philology of the Hidatsa Indians*, p. 53.
[5] *Cf.* Mayne, *Treatise on Hindu Law and Usage*, p. 86.

give birth to a monstrous child and the man is in danger of dying soon. " The demon (*iguánchi*) operating in this case is the spirit of the dead husband, who is jealous of the wife he left behind and does not cede her to any other man than his brother, who together with himself forms as it were one personality and represents him in the most real sense of the word."[1] We have previously noticed that among various peoples a widow, before marrying another man than the brother of her deceased husband, must go through a ritual coitus with somebody else, lest her new husband or her children should die or she should become barren, and that among the Maori the dead husband's brother has to " free her from *tapu* " by first marrying her.[2] But the fact that the jealousy of the former husband's ghost is not aroused by his widow's marriage with his brother by no means implies that the living husband was willing to share his wife with his brother.

There is still one point which calls for our attention because it may possibly be supposed to give support to McLennan's theory. We have seen that where fraternal polyandry prevails it is generally the elder brother who marries first and the younger brothers get a share in his wife. On the other hand, the elder brother may be prohibited from marrying the wife of a younger brother ; and there is a similar restriction in cases where the younger brothers have access to the elder one's wife without being married to her. So also the levirate is frequently, especially in India, restricted to a younger brother marrying the elder one's widow, the elder brothers being prohibited from similarly marrying the widows of their younger brothers. But here again we must be on our watch against any hasty conclusion and see whether we cannot find a satisfactory explanation in existing conditions. I am of opinion that such an explanation has been found by Dr. Jochelson. He thinks that the restriction in question is due to the elder brother's position in the family. When the father dies or becomes too old to remain the head

[1] Karsten, *Contributions to the Sociology of the Indian Tribes of Ecuador* (*Acta Academiae Aboensis*, Humaniora, i. no. 3), p. 75.

[2] *Supra*, i. 327 *sqq.*

of the household, the eldest son takes his place ;[1] and sexual intercourse of the eldest brother with his sister-in-law " seems to be imagined to be the same kind of incest as the cohabitation of a father with his daughter-in-law."[2] This explanation is strongly corroborated by the following statement made by Mr. Hayavadana Rao with reference to the Gonds of the Eastern Ghauts :—" It is usual for a younger brother to marry his elder brother's widow. But an elder brother cannot marry his younger brother's widow, for the elder brother is held to stand in the position of the father of the family."[3] Now it seems highly probable that the rule which restricts polyandrous relations to marriage or intercourse between the younger brothers and the wife of the elder brother is due to a similar cause ;[4] so that the rules relating to polyandrous unions and the levirate, instead of being cause and effect, have only a common root. M. Grandidier says expressly that in Madagascar the elder brother is denied access to the wives of the younger brothers, but not *vice versâ*, " because he will one day be the head of the family and like their father."[5] Speaking of the levirate in the North-Western Provinces of India, where marriage with the elder brother of the late husband is rigidly prohibited, Mr. Crooke observes that " in fact all through the Hindu caste system any intercourse, even to the extent of speaking to, touching, or appearing unveiled in the presence of, her husband's *Jeth*, or elder brother, is strictly guarded by a special taboo."[6] A similar regard for a superior age and position is shown in the case of other relatives. Among the Chukchee, in case of need, even the

---

[1] *Cf.* Westermarck, *Origin and Development of the Moral Ideas*, i. 605, 606, 614.

[2] Jochelson, *Koryak*, p. 751.

[3] Hayavadana Rao, in *Anthropos*, v. 795.

[4] The reason given in India for the analogous prohibition of marrying the wife's elder sister is that she is in the position of mother to her younger sister (Crooke, ' Hill Tribes of the Central Indian Hills,' in *Jour. Anthr. Inst.* xxviii. 238).

[5] Grandidier, *op. cit.* ii. 155 n. (2).

[6] Crooke, *Tribes and Castes of the North-Western Provinces and Oudh*, i. p. cxci.

nephew marries his widowed aunt, but the uncle is forbidden
to do the same with the widow of his nephew.[1]

As to the supposed connection between the levirate and
polyandry, it may be of interest to notice some observations
made by Dr. Rivers among the Todas. He found a few
cases which seemed to show that when two brothers had
different wives and one brother died, the widow might be
taken by the surviving brother ; but in other cases the widow
of one brother did not become the wife of the others, and when
she married somebody else the buffaloes which the new husband paid for her were not given to them, but to the dead
man's children.[2] We have seen that in Ladakh, if the eldest
brother dies, the wife—provided she has no children—can
actually rid herself of his brothers, who are her minor
husbands, by a simple ceremony.[3] Again, among the
Chukchee, who have both the levirate and unions of a polyandrous character as well as group-relations, brothers do
not enter into such unions at all.[4] Facts of this kind
certainly show no special relation between polyandry and the
levirate.

I do not even believe that the right of access to the eldest
brother's wife which under certain circumstances is granted
to the younger ones can be assumed to be a survival of an
earlier marriage union on equal terms of all the brothers of
a family with one woman.[5] With reference to fraternal
polyandry in India Mr. Gait writes :—" It merges gradually
into monogamy by the steady growth of the rights of the
elder brother. The wife and children come gradually to
be regarded as his, until at last the younger brothers can
scarcely be regarded as husbands at all, but merely as the
casual recipients, at her discretion, of the wife's favours when
their elder brother is out of the way."[6] This evolutionary

---

[1] Bogoras, *op. cit.* p. 608.   [2] Rivers, *Todas*, p. 520.
[3] *Supra*, iii. 121.   [4] Bogoras, *op. cit.* p. 603.
[5] Nobody, I presume, would maintain that the custom found
among some tribes in Sierra Leone and Southern Nigeria which
allows sons to have connection with their father's wives (*supra*,
iii. 153 *sq.*) is the survival of actual polyandry or group-marriage.
[6] Gait, *op. cit.* p. 239.

process, however, is a mere construction for which there is no foundation in fact. The same circumstances as in certain cases lead to marriages in which all the brothers have an equal right to the woman may in other cases only lead to unions in which the younger brothers are husbands of secondary rank or nothing but "casual recipients of her favours." Considering how exceptional polyandry after all is, it seems to me much more reasonable to trace the superiority of the eldest husband or, generally, of the first husband—just as the higher position so commonly granted to the first married wife in polygynous families—to the persistent influence of monogamous habits, rather than to look upon it as a change towards monogamy.

If there are no widespread customs which can be legitimately interpreted as relics of an earlier state of general polyandry, the only condition on which we may conjecture the prevalence of such a state is that the causes to which polyandry is due may be assumed to have operated generally in the past. In a previous chapter we have noticed the groundlessness of McLennan's suggestion that in all, or nearly all, the primitive hordes female infanticide disturbed the balance between the sexes.[1] But even if the men had frequently been in the majority it does not follow that polyandry had been the result ; for, as has already been pointed out, an excess of males by no means always leads to polyandry. The like may be said of the other causes to which polyandry has been ascribed. We have every reason to believe that the jealousy of the men has always prevented its being general, also in primitive times. It is noteworthy that it has been mainly found, not among savages of the lowest type, but among peoples who have flocks and herds or who practise agriculture. Mr. Bridges wrote to me that the Yahgans of Tierra del Fuego consider it utterly abominable. With regard to the Veddas Mr. Bailey states :—" Polyandry is unknown among them. The practice is alluded to with genuine disgust. I asked a Veddah once what the consequence would be if one of their women were to live with two husbands, and the unaffected vehemence with which he

[1] *Supra*, ii. 163 *sqq.*

raised his axe, and said, ' A blow would settle it,' showed conclusively to my mind the natural repugnance with which they regard the national custom of their Kandyan neighbours."[1] These neighbours were certainly no savages ; and the same may be said of the Tibetans and various polyandrous tribes and castes in India. Mr. Anantha Krishna Iyer contrasts the loose polyandrous unions of the Nayars with the " regular system of marriage " among the jungle tribes and very low castes.[2] Speaking of the people of Sirmur, Mr. Fraser observes :—" It is remarkable that a people so degraded in morals, and many of whose customs are of so revolting a nature, should in other respects evince a much higher advancement in civilisation than we discover among other nations, whose manners are more engaging, and whose moral character ranks infinitely higher. Their persons are better clad and more decent ; their approach more polite and unembarrassed ; and their address is better than that of most of the inhabitants of the remote Highlands of Scotland ; . . . and their houses, in point of construction, comfort and internal cleanliness, are beyond comparison superior to Scottish Highland dwellings."[3] On the arrival of the Spaniards, the polyandrous inhabitants of Lancerote were distinguished from the other Canarians, who were strictly monogamous, by marks of greater civilisation.[4]

---

[1] Bailey, ' Account of the Wild Tribes of the Veddahs of Ceylon,' in *Trans. Ethn. Soc.* N.S. ii. 292.

[2] Anantha Krishna Iyer, *op. cit.* ii. 41.

[3] Fraser, *op. cit.* p. 209.   [4] *Cf.* v. Humboldt, *op. cit.* i. 83.

CHAPTER XXXI

GROUP-MARRIAGE AND OTHER GROUP-RELATIONS

GROUP-MARRIAGE has been found among many peoples who practise polyandry.

M. Grenard speaks of Tibetan households in which there are several husbands and several wives.[1] Ahmad Shah says of certain Tibetans, not specified by him, that " if a man and his brothers have in common three wives, and they all are childless, they are not allowed to marry a fourth wife, but another husband may be called in for help and, if this plan also fails, a fifth husband may be added."[2] In his description of polyandry in Sikkim, Tibet, and Bhutan Mr. White, late Political Agent in Sikkim, states that " three brothers can marry three sisters, and all the wives be in common, but this is not very often met with. In such a case the children of the eldest girl belong to the eldest brother, of the second to the second, and of the third to the third, if they each bear children. Should one or more not bear children, then the children are apportioned by arrangement."[3]

Among the Sissee Abors, according to Mr. Rowney, it is a common rule for two or three brothers to have a number of wives in common.[4] Speaking of polyandry among the Kanets of the higher hills, the Punjab Superintendent makes the statement that " the brothers may, if necessary, marry a second or a third joint wife or one of the brothers

[1] Grenard, *Tibet*, p. 257.
[2] Ahmad Shah, *Four Years in Tibet*, p. 54.
[3] White, *Sikhim and Bhutan*, p. 320. *Cf*. Landor, *In the Forbidden Land*, ii. 62.
[4] Rowney, *Wild Tribes of India*, p. 158 *sq*.

who may have gone out may marry a separate wife there. When he returns home, it depends on the choice of the wife whether she will remain the exclusive wife of the husband who married her or become the joint property of the family. Cases are known in which a family of three brothers has three or as many as four joint wives."[1] It is a matter of means and of land ; a large farm requires several women to look after it.[2] In Sarāj in Kulu there may be in one house " three brothers with one wife, and in the next three brothers with four wives, all alike in common ; in the adjoining house there will be an only son with four wives to himself."[3] In the Jounsar district, if much difference exists in the ages of the brothers of a family, as, for instance, when there are six brothers, and the elder are grown up while the younger are but children, " the three elder then marry a wife, and when the young ones come of age they marry another, but the two wives are considered equally the wives of all six."[4]

In 1869 Dr. Shortt wrote of the Todas :—" If there be four or five brothers, and one of them, being old enough, gets married, his wife claims all the other brothers as her husbands, and, as they successively attain manhood, she consorts with them ; or, if the wife has one or more younger sisters, they in turn, on attaining a marriageable age, become the wives of their sister's husband or husbands. . . . Owing, however, to the great scarcity of women in this tribe, it more frequently happens that a single woman is wife to several husbands, sometimes as many as six."[5]   In a more recent account, Dr. Rivers speaks of the " tendency for the poly-andry of the Todas to become combined with polygyny. Two brothers, who in former times would have had one wife between them, may now take two wives, but as a general rule the two men have the two wives in common. . . . When

[1] Pandit Harikishan Kaul, *Census of India*, 1911, vol. xiv. (Punjab) Report, p. 287.
[2] Gait, *Census of India*, 1911, vol. i. (India) Report, p. 241.
[3] Lyall, quoted by Harcourt, *Himalayan Districts of Kooloo, Lahoul, and Spiti*, p. 241.
[4] Dunlop, *Hunting in the Himalaya*, p. 181.
[5] Shortt, ' Account of the Hill Tribes of the Neilgherries,' in *Trans. Ethn. Soc.* N.S. vii. 240. *Cf.* Baierlein, *Nach und aus Indien*, p. 249.

a man or a group of men have more than one wife, the two
wives usually live together at the same village, but sometimes
they live at different villages, the husband or husbands
moving about from one village to the other." Dr. Rivers
thinks that polygyny is thus becoming associated with
polyandry because there are now a greater number of women
owing to the diminished female infanticide.[1] A similar
practice is said to have occurred among the Coorgs ; according to Moegling, they had a kind of marriage communism
within the family, the wives of the brothers of one house
being considered as common property, and the children
consequently being rather children of the family, or of the
mother, than of the acknowledged father.[2] Of the Kammālans of Malabar we read that if one of the brothers who have
a wife in common, on the ground of incompatibility of
temper, brings a new wife, she is privileged to cohabit with
the other brothers.[3] Among the Izhuvans or Tiyyans in
the northern part of the Cochin State, if the union of several
brothers with one woman proves to be unpleasant or incon-
venient, one of them takes a new wife and either keeps her for
himself or allows her to be the wife of others also.[4] Of the
carpenters, blacksmiths, and some other low castes of
Malabar, Duncan said that the men—evidently the brothers
of a family—lived promiscuously with one or more women.[5]
Among the Tottiyans in the Madura district there seem to be
not only polyandrous relations but group-relations as well :
Dubois wrote of them that " brothers, uncles, nephews and
other kindred, hold their wives in common."[6] Among the
Sinhalese, according to the Níti-Nighanduva, it was not
only frequently the custom for one man to have at the same
time a number of wives and for one woman to have at the
same time a number of husbands, but it was " also a frequent

---

[1] Rivers, *Todas*, pp. 521, 518 *sq.*
[2] Moegling, *Coorg Memoirs*, p. 29 *sq.*
[3] Thurston, *Ethnographic Notes in Southern India*, p. 114.
[4] Anantha Krishna Iyer, *Cochin Tribes and Castes*, i. 295.
[5] Duncan, ' Remarks on the Coast of Malabar,' in *Asiatick
Researches*, v. 14 n. *
[6] Dubois, *Description of the Character, Manners, and Customs of the
People of India*, p. 3.

custom for two or three men to have two or three wives in common."[1] There can be no doubt that in these cases group-marriage has arisen as a combination of polygyny with polyandry. This is implied or even directly said in several of the statements just quoted, and may in other cases be inferred from the facts that both in Tibet and India polyandry is much more prevalent than group-marriage ; that the latter occurs there nowhere except side by side with polyandry ; and that the occasional combination of polygyny with polyandry, when the circumstances permit it, is easy to explain, whereas no satisfactory reason has been given for the opinion held by some sociologists that polyandry has developed out of an earlier stage of group-marriage. We are told that the Todas, the Sinhalese, and the Himalayans, or their ancestors—like every other people—originally practised group-marriage, and that polyandry arose among them when they fell into the habit of killing off so many female infants that only one was left in each family ; the sons in one family, who had formerly married all the daughters of another family, had thenceforth to be content with a single wife between them.[2] Bernhöft and Kohler seem to look upon this process as self-evident since they produce no proof of it. I never heard that the Sinhalese and Himalayans have been in the habit of destroying all female infants but one in each family, and a statement to that effect referring to the Todas in 1871[3] is obviously incorrect—to say nothing of the bold assumption that all peoples practising polyandry formerly lived in group-marriage.

It is possible that Caesar's well-known statement about the marriages of the ancient Britons likewise refers to a combination of polygyny with polyandry. He says :—" In their domestic life they practise a form of community of

---

[1] *Niti-Nighaṇḍuva*, p. 22.

[2] Bernhöft, ' Altindische Familienorganisation,' in *Zeitschr. f. vergl. Rechtswiss.* ix. 6. Kohler, ' Rechtsphilosophie und Universalrechtsgeschichte,' in v. Holtzendorff, *Enzyklopädie der Rechtswissenschaft*, i. 28. See also Bloch, *Sexual Life of Our Time*, p. 193 *sq.*

[3] [Madame Janssen,] ' Die Todas,' in *Globus*, xliii. 371.

wives, ten or twelve combining in a group, especially brothers
with brothers and fathers with sons. The children born of
such wedlock are then reckoned to belong to that member
of the partnership who was the first to receive the mother
as a bride into the household."[1] The latter passage almost
suggests that the community of wives spoken of—provided
that it really existed—had a polyandric origin. So far as the
Celtic population of Britain is concerned, the accuracy of
Caesar's statement has been doubted or denied. Sir John
Rhys observes that " in the first place, one might suppose
that he had heard and misunderstood some description of the
families of the Britons to the effect, that it was usual for
ten or twelve men, with their wives and children, to live
together under the *patria potestas* or power of one father and
head, a kind of undivided family well known to the student
of early institutions, and marking a particular stage in the
social development of most Aryan nations. In the next
place it is probable that the Britons of the south-east of the
island, and some of the Gauls of the Continent, had heard of
tribes in the remoter parts of Britain, whose view of matrimony was not the one usual among Aryan nations."[2] Professor Zimmer has no doubt that Caesar's statement refers
to the non-Aryan inhabitants of Britain ;[3] but Professor
Ridgeway maintains that " the theory of a non-Aryan
population in the British Isles rests on no other evidence,
historical, social, or linguistic, than a few rash assumptions."[4] Statements more or less similar to Caesar's
were subsequently made by Strabo with reference to the
Irish,[5] by Dio Cassius[6] and St. Jerome[7] with reference to

[1] Caesar, *De bello Gallico*, v. 14.   [2] Rhys, *Celtic Britain*, p. 55 *sq.*
[3] Zimmer, ' Das Mutterrecht der Pikten und seine Bedeutung für
die arische Alterthumswissenschaft,' in *Zeitschr. d. Savigny-Stiftung f.
Rechtsgeschichte*, xv. 224 *sqq.* See also Schrader, *Reallexikon der
indogermanischen Altertumskunde*, p. 634.
[4] Ridgeway, ' Who were the Romans ? ' in *Proceed. British
Academy*, 1907-1908, p. 58.   [5] Strabo, *Geographica*, iv. 6. 4, C. 201.
[6] Dio Cassius, *Historia Romana*, Xiphilini Epitome, lxxvi. 12.
[7] ' Ex Hieronymo,' in *Monumenta Historica Britannica*, i. p. xcix.
For a discussion of polyandry in the British Isles see Gomme,
'Exogamy and Polyandry,' in *Archæological Review*, i. 388 *sqq.*

the people of Scotland, and by the Irish interpolator of Solinus with reference to the pauper king of the Hebrides and the inhabitants of Shetland Mainland.[1]

Genuine group-marriage has, so far as I know, been found only side by side with polyandry. But there are peoples who have a kind of sex communism, in which several men have the right of access to several women, although none of the women is properly married to more than one of the men. The fact that some of our authorities apply the term " group marriage " to relations of this sort should not deceive us as regards their true nature.

Thus Dr. Bogoras states that " marriage among the Chukchee does not deal with one couple only, but extends over an entire group." The men belonging to such a " marriage-union " are called " companions in wives." " Each ' companion ' has a right to all the wives of his ' companion,' but takes advantage of his right comparatively seldom, namely, only when he visits for some reason the camp of one of the ' companions.' Then the host cedes him his place in the sleeping-room. If possible, he leaves the house for the night ; goes to his herd, for instance. After such a call, the companion visited generally looks for an occasion to return the visit, in order, in his turn, to exercise his rights." The union sometimes includes up to ten married couples, but a man may have several " companions," who do not stand in a similar relation to one another. The companions are mostly persons who are well acquainted, especially neighbours and relatives, but seldom inmates of one and the same camp ; and although second and third cousins are almost invariably united by ties of this kind, brothers do not enter into such unions. On the other hand, there are unions with inhabitants of other districts, with chance acquaintances during temporary trading-relations, and even with individuals belonging to a different people—Tungus, Russians, or American Eskimo. Indeed, " wherever the Chukchee and the Tungus live in one locality, numerous families of one of these peoples are united by group-marriages to those of the other." But in these cases there is no strict reci-

1 Solinus, *Collectanea rerum memorabilium*, rec. Mommsen, p. 219.

procity ; for, while the Chukchee have marital rights to the
greater part of married Tungus women, it is among the
Tungus only the most skilful hunters, or those most friendly
with the Chukchee, who have similar rights to women belonging to the latter. The " companions " are generally
persons of about the same age, the older people being reluctant to enter into unions with young people, especially if the
latter are single ; but, as we have noticed in another place,
if a married man has no children and desires to have some,
he may nevertheless be anxious to make a union with a strong
single man. Persons become " companions " by making
sacrifices and anointing themselves with blood, first in one
camp, and then in the other, after which they are considered as belonging to one fireside, as do the relatives in the
male line. Yet " at present group-marriages are often concluded without any rite. One man simply says to another,
' Let us be companions in wives.' After this they both
exercise their rights." The children born in the families
of any of these unions are regarded as cousins, or even as
brothers and sisters, and cannot marry each other, as is
natural considering that they may easily have a common
father. Rupture of a group-union is regarded as possible,
but Bogoras knows of no cases where it has occurred except
those mentioned in accounts concerning syphilitics.[1]

Dr. Bogoras seems to believe that the sex communism of
the Chukchee is a survival of a kind of group-marriage which
many anthropologists consider to be the most primitive form
of marriage. He says that in ancient times it " was obviously a union between the members of a related group,"
and that it was only in course of time that other friendly
persons began to be included in the union ; " the rite accom-
panying the formation of group-marriages reflects such an
origin, for it is intended to give the union the character of
a tie between relatives."[2] This opinion is shared by Sir
James G. Frazer, who remarks:—"That the partners in these
connubial unions are theoretically deemed to be blood
relations, even when they are not so in fact, is plainly indicated by the ceremony of smearing themselves with the blood

---

[1] Bogoras, *Chukchee*, p. 602 *sqq.*   [2] *Ibid.* p. 603.

of sacrificial victims in the camps of both the partners ;
for this is nothing but a form of the widespread blood-
covenant whereby two persons are supposed to unite themselves artificially by a tie of consanguinity."[1] For my own
part I cannot attach any such meaning either to the
ceremony in question or to the rite of blood-covenant generally, which has for its main object to impose duties on both
parties and also, in many cases at least, contains the potential
punishment for their transgression.[2] If the so-called group-
marriage of the Chukchee were in the first place a union
between relatives, how is it that brothers, who among so
many peoples have their wife or wives in common, are
expressly excluded from it, whereas perfect strangers are
not ? That the access granted to strangers is not a modern
innovation is obvious from some of the tales referring to
ancient times in which mention is made of unions with
American Eskimo. When the Eskimo traders from the
opposite shore arrived at the maritime Asiatic villages of the
Chukchee they found their temporary wives in the houses of
their friends, and similarly the Chukchee traders had their
temporary wives on the American shore.[3] From facts like
these, as well as from the important statements that " the
inmates of one and the same camp are seldom willing to
enter into a group-marriage,"[4] and that a man takes advantage of his right of access only when he visits the camp of
one of his " companions,"[5] I draw the conclusion that one
object at least of the sex communism of the Chukchee has
been to provide men with bedfellows during their absence
from home.[6] Another object may be mutual protection.
" Not to be connected with such a union," says Bogoras,
" means to have no friends and good-wishers, and no pro-

[1] Frazer, *Totemism and Exogamy*, ii. 350 *sq.*
[2] See Westermarck, *Origin and Development of the Moral Ideas*, ii.
208.
[3] Bogoras, *op. cit.* p. 606.   [4] *Ibid.* p. 603.
[5] *Ibid.* p. 602.
[6] According to Erman (*Travels in Siberia*, ii. 530 n. *), the Chukchee
offer their wives and daughters to travellers who chance to visit
them, and " observe the same custom with men of their own race,
and expect as much in return."

tectors in case of need ; for the members of a marriage-group stand nearer to one another than even relations in the male line." Hence at the present time the unions through group-marriage embrace practically all Chukchee families.[1] The taste for change and variety has also in all probability something to do with the custom. Extreme sensuality is characteristic of the Chukchee, both male and female ; everybody was ready to tell Bogoras that sexual intercourse was the "best thing in the world."[2] It occurs that a man takes his companion's wife, lives with her for several months, and then returns her ; and sometimes " the exchanged wives stay with their new husbands for a longer period, or even permanently."[3] On the other hand, there is no reason to suppose that the group-unions of the Chukchee have been connected with any disproportion of the sexes. As we have seen, according to the data in a census for 1897 the whole number of women as compared to that of men formed 102 per cent.[4]

Although these unions are well recognised by the customs of the people, they can certainly not be styled " group-marriages," if by marriage is meant something more than a right to sexual intercourse.[5] They may, besides, give rise to certain rights and duties commonly connected with blood-brotherhood, but there is no indication that they have the slightest influence upon the social constitution of the family, which, as Dr. Bogoras says, " usually consists of a husband, with one or several wives and their children." Generally the parents of the men live near by in a lodging of their own ; and with them may live younger daughters who are not yet married, or, if married, have no children.[6] But " the house with those living in it forms the real basis of the Chukchee family " ;[7] and the husband's " companions in wives " do not belong to them. They live, as a rule, in another camp, often far away. Dr. Bogoras has been told that poor people,

---

[1] Bogoras, *op. cit.* p. 604.   [2] *Ibid.* p. 571.
[3] *Ibid.* p. 604.   [4] *Ibid.* p. 550.
[5] *Cf.* Miss Czaplicka, *Aboriginal Siberia*, p. 78 *sqq*., who more appropriately speaks of " supplementary unions."
[6] Bogoras, *op. cit.* p. 544.   [7] *Ibid.* p. 540.

on entering the group-union, are sometimes so friendly that they live in one tent and even in the same sleeping-room, and there are descriptions of similar conditions in the tales ;[1] but the cases of this kind must be altogether exceptional. It should be remembered that even sexual intercourse with the wife of a " companion " is said to be comparatively rare.[2]

On the whole it seems that the so-called group-marriages of the Chukchee do not essentially differ from practices found among their neighbours on the other side of the sea and among Eskimo farther east.   As regards those about Bering Strait, Nelson writes that " it is a common custom for two men living in different villages to agree to become bond fellows, or brothers by adoption.   Having made this agreement, whenever one of the men goes to the other's village he is received as the bond brother's guest and is given the use of his host's bed with his wife during his stay.   When the visit is returned the same favour is extended to the other, consequently neither family knows who is the father of the children." [3]   As we have noticed above, exchange of wives is probably practised all over the area inhabited by Eskimo.[4] Nobody, I suppose, would call this temporary exchange of wives " group-marriage " ; nor can we regard as a relic of earlier group-marriage a practice the causes of which are easy to trace among a people so little addicted to jealousy as are the Eskimo.   It is noteworthy that the men who exchange their wives are nowhere said to be brothers.

We are told that the Herero in South-West Africa sometimes practise " a form of group-marriage," for which the native name is *oupánga*.[5]   This word, according to Brincker, was originally the right word for " friendship," but came to be used by the heathen Herero for a custom consisting in a community of women and, to a certain extent, of property.[6]

---

[1] Bogoras, *op. cit.* p. 603.   [2] *Ibid.* p. 602.
[3] Nelson, ' Eskimo about Bering Strait,' in *Ann. Rep. Bur. Ethn.* xviii. 292.   See also *supra*, iii. 109.   [4] *Supra*, i. 230 *sqq.*
[5] Frazer, *Totemism and Exogamy*, ii. 366.   Kohler (' Das Recht der Herero,' in *Zeitschr. f. vergl. Rechtswiss.* xiv. 301) calls it a revival of the group-marriage idea.
[6] Brincker, *Wörterbuch und kurzgefasste Grammatik des Otji-Hérero*, p. 227.

" Two men," he says, " who are each *epánga* to the other,
bind themselves by mutual presents of cattle and other
things to an intimate friendship, which makes accessible to
every *epánga* the wives of his *epánga*, and on the other hand
confers the right to take anything from his herd at pleasure."[1]
In another place Dr. Brincker observes that the community
of property exists only in so far as the *omapanga*, or members
of such a community, may not refuse each other anything.[2]
Hahn also speaks of the *oupánga* as a custom through which
a few men agree to have property and wives in common.[3]
Bensen tells us that three men unite together and hold
their wives and cattle in common, that is, they use their
wives mutually and slaughter their cattle among each
other.[4] According to von François, the *oupánga* gives
those who conclude it a right to each other's assistance in
critical cases, during a famine and in war, and secures each
of them a hospitable reception at the other's farm and even
access to one or several of his wives.[5] Dr. Dannert expressly denies that the community of wives among the
Herero carries with it a community of goods, in spite of the
strong communistic tendencies otherwise prevalent among
them.[6] The partners may not even ask anything directly
of each other, but if they want to make a request they have
to send it through a messenger, who delivers his message
in veiled language and roundabout phrases. But, on the
other hand, a man is considered to be by honour bound to
give to his *epánga* the best piece of meat at a feast and the
best ram of his flock if the *epánga* in travelling passes one
of his stock-stations. The same writer also informs us that

---

[1] *Idem*, ' Character, Sitten und Gebräuche speciell der Bantu
Deutsch-Südwestafrikas,' in *Mittheil. d. Seminars f. orientalische
Sprachen*, iii. 3. 86.

[2] *Idem, Wörterbuch*, p. 227.

[3] Hahn, ' Die Ovahereró,' in *Zeitschr. d. Gesellsch. f. Erdkunde*, iv.
490.

[4] Bensen, in Kohler, *loc. cit.* p. 298.

[5] v. François, *Nama und Damara Deutsch-Süd-West-Afrika*
p. 198 *sq.*

[6] On this point see Büttner, Sozialpolitisches aus dem Leben der
Herero,' in *Das Ausland*, lv. 828 *sqq.*

a man who lives in polygyny may conclude an *oupánga*-union with reference to one of his wives only, although he may give other men a share in his other wives.[1] The *oupánga* is concluded by a verbal agreement without any religious or other formalities, and it may be dissolved at any time, which commonly happens through a quarrel caused by one of the women concerned.[2]

As regards the persons who form an *oupánga* our authorities disagree. Schinz[3] and von François[4] state that they are often brothers, but Dannert tells us that it is strictly forbidden (*ku zera*) for brothers to become *omapanga*, nay that the male partners must not be related to each other by blood at all, whereas two men not thus related who have married sisters may conclude an *oupánga* with reference to those wives.[5] According to one of our informants, an agreement of this kind may also be made between a man and a woman, though, if the latter is married, only with the permission of her husband ;[6] but the accuracy of this statement has been questioned.[7] On the other hand, there can be no doubt that an *oupánga* may be formed by two unmarried women, who thereby not only promise to stand by each other in all circumstances, but also enter into sexual relations with one another.[8] This alone is sufficient to show that the Herero *oupánga* is not equivalent to group-marriage. Nor can the *oupánga* concluded by men be regarded as a marriage-union. It is a contract of friendship and intimacy extended to access to the partner's wife, but it does not give rise to family life or family duties. Viehe says that he has never heard of a case of several men living together with several women in group-marriage as members of the same household.[9] The children remain with the husband of the

---

[1] Dannert, *Zum Rechte der Herero*, p. 41 *sq.*   [2] *Ibid.* p. 39 *sq.*

[3] Schinz, *Deutsch-Süd-West-Afrika*, p. 173.

[4] v. François, *op. cit.* p. 199.   [5] Dannert, *op. cit.* p. 40.

[6] v. François, *op. cit.* p. 198 *sq.*   [7] Dannert, *op. cit.* p. 40.

[8] Brincker, in *Mittheil. d. Seminars f. orientalische Sprachen*, iii. 3. 86.   *Idem, Wörterbuch*, p. 16.   Fritsch, *Die Eingeborenen Süd-Afrika's*, p. 227.

[9] Viehe, in Steinmetz, *Rechtsverhältnisse von eingeborenen Völkern in Afrika und Ozeanien*, p. 307.

woman who bore the child, even though it can be proved that another man is its real father ;[1] and the children belonging to the families of different husbands are not, like the children of brothers or of sisters, regarded, juridically, as brothers and sisters to each other.[2]

As to the origin of the *oupánga* formed by men different opinions have been expressed. Kohler looks upon it as a relic of an earlier group-marriage in which the husbands were brothers ;[3] but this is nothing but an arbitrary interpretation made to suit a certain evolutionary scheme for which there is no foundation in fact. Dannert not only denies that brothers, and blood-relatives generally, are allowed to form an *oupánga*, but even refutes Kohler's assumption that the *oupánga* is a kind of blood-brotherhood.[4] Fritsch attributes this institution to poverty.[5] But I should imagine that poverty would lead to polyandry rather than to group-unions, and so far as I can gather from the information available, the men who conclude an *oupánga* are married men who mutually agree to give each other a share in their wives. It may, however, be a substitute for polygyny, resorted to either from economic motives or from lack of women, especially as the female offspring among the Herero are said to be less numerous than the male.[6] Dr. Dannert suggests that the *oupánga* may be due to the fact that a young man is not at liberty to choose his wife himself but has to marry the girl selected for him by his parents, and therefore is anxious to form new connections after his own taste. Or it may be that a man enters into such a union with one or several other men in order not to lack female companionship when he visits their houses or when he goes to his stock-station and is unable to take his wife with him.[7] The *oupánga* of the Herero may thus serve the same purpose as the group-unions of the Chukchee. It should be added that there are similar relations among neighbouring tribes.[8]

[1] Bensen, in Kohler, *loc. cit.* p. 298. [2] Dannert, *op. cit.* p. 41.
[3] Kohler, *loc. cit.* p. 299. [4] Dannert, *op. cit.* p. 39.
[5] Fritsch, *op. cit.* p. 227.
[6] v. François, *op. cit.* p. 195. [7] Dannert, *op. cit.* p. 41.
[8] Fritsch, *op. cit.* p. 227. Brincker, in *Mittheil. d. Seminars f. orientalische Sprachen,* iii. 3. 86

A relation of the same kind also exists between " friends "
(*tafi*) among the Maty Islanders off the coast of New
Guinea.[1] In the Bartle Bay communities of British New
Guinea, according to Messrs. Seligman and Giblin, all the
individuals of the same sex who are of approximately the
same age are respectively considered as members of a class
called a *kimta*. The members of a *kimta* form a sort of association having certain rights to each other's fellowship and
help ; and the relations are particularly intimate between
a man and his *kimta* mates in his own settlement, who are
called *eriam*. Messrs. Seligman and Giblin state that at
Wedau and some other communities, at least, each member
of the *eriam* fellowship has marital rights over the wives
of his fellow *eriam*, the only bar to these rights being those
laws of clan-group and totem or individual consanguinity
which would have prevented the man himself from marrying these women. " A man who wished to have connection
with the wife of one of his *eriam* would see her and arrange
to meet her at an appointed spot in the bush, where he
would prepare a small clearing if there were not one already.
It was not bad form or unusual for a man to avail himself
frequently of this privilege even when his own wife was
able to receive him, but when she was pregnant he naturally
resorted to the wives of his *eriam* more frequently." According to Mr. Newton, a man cannot have as an *eriam* a man of
his own clan, or one whose wife is of his own clan, nor can
two men whose wives are of the same clan be *eriam* to each
other ; a man may be *eriam* to a man of a younger *kimta*,
although he would more often be *eriam* to men of his own
kimta ; the *eriam* relationship is hereditary ; and if a man
with one wife is *eriam* to a man with several wives, his
rights only extend to the first or one wife, whereas he has no
rights over the others.[2] The custom is said to have come to
Wedau from Boianai, where the word for *eriam* is *rikam*.
" In this district, as throughout the greater part of south-
eastern New Guinea, a man abstains from connection with

[1] Dempwolff, ' Über aussterbende Völker,' in *Zeitschr. f. Ethnol.*
xxxvi. 403 *sq.*

[2] Seligman, *Melanesians of British New Guinea*, p. 470 *sqq.*

his wife from the time pregnancy is diagnosed until the child is weaned, and during this period as at other times this abstinence is rendered easier by his ready access to the wives of any of his *rikam* who are not themselves pregnant, or forbidden to him on account of their clan."[1] Perhaps we may conjecture that the main object of the sexual rights implied in the *eriam* relationship was to give men an opportunity to gratify their desires by intercourse with the wives of their friends at times when they had to abstain from intercourse with their own. Such rights, however, do not always seem to form part of the *eriam* relationship. At Wamira, which also belongs to the Bartle Bay communities, " a man having connection with the wife of his *eriam* would be punished as an ordinary adulterer."[2]

We are told that a sort of sexual communism between persons of the same age exists among the Masai— that it is no offence if a man commits adultery or fornication with a woman or girl of his own age, and that a woman may cohabit with any man of her husband's age grade, provided that they are not of the same sub-clan or too nearly related.[3] It seems, however, that a man has access to another man's wife chiefly when he comes as a guest. For it is said that when a Masai goes to another kraal to pay a visit he enters a hut of a man of his own age and is left there alone with the wife, or one of the wives, of the owner, who himself goes to search for a place to sleep in elsewhere. " A Masai cannot refuse hospitality to a stranger (of his own age) for he is afraid that the other members of his age will curse him, and he will die."[4] Weiss speaks of the sexual communism of the Masai only as a form of hospitality, frequently practised on account of their travelling habits ; when a man comes to a friendly village, he thrusts his spear into the ground outside one of the huts, with the result that its owner has

---

[1] Seligman, *op. cit.* p. 474.
[2] *Ibid.* p. 477.
[3] Hollis, *Masai*, p. 312. *Idem*, ' Note on the Masai System of Relationship,' in *Jour. Roy. Anthr. Inst.* xl. 480. Merker, *Die Masai*, p. 118.   [4] Hollis, *Masai*, p. 287 *sq.*

to spend the night in another hut.[1] Among the Akamba, also, " a married woman can quite lawfully have relations with other men, her husband often placing her at the disposal of a man of the same clan, or of a friend, who comes on a visit and stays over night " ; but although such relations are considered lawful by the Akamba, the man who indulges in them must be purified before he can enter his own hut again. The same people have also the following custom, for which our authority, Dr. Lindblom, has been unable to find any explanation :—" If a man has several wives (A, B, and C), and they have sons who are married, every man has a right to have sexual intercourse with the wife of the half-brother corresponding to him in age ; that is to say, A's eldest son can sleep with the wife of the eldest son of B or C ; A's second son with the wife of the second son of B or C ; and so on. A *kimwemwe, i.e.*, a man who has no true brothers or sisters, has the right to sleep with all his half-brothers' wives—presumably because he is, in a way, at the same time his mother's eldest, youngest, and middle son."[2]

In certain savage tribes blood-brothers are said to have access to each other's wives.[3] There is also some reason to believe that among the ancient Semites blood-brotherhood sometimes implied community of women. In a Syro-Roman law-book of the fifth century, the various forms of which have been collected and illustrated by Sachau and Bruns, it is said, " If a man desires to write a compact of brotherhood with another man that they shall be as brothers and have all things in common that they possess or may acquire, then the law forbids them and annuls their compact ; for their wives are not common, and their children cannot

---

[1] Weiss, *Die Völkerstämme im Norden Deutsch-Ostafrikas*, p. 386. See also *ibid.* p. 407.

[2] Lindblom, *Akamba*, p. 78 *sq.*

[3] Waitz-Gerland, *Anthropologie der Naturvölker*, vi. 130 *sq.* (some Polynesians). v. Kotzebue, *Voyage of Discovery into the South Sea*, iii. 172 (natives of Radack). Grandidier, *Ethnographie de Madagascar*, ii. 155. Post, *Studien zur Entwicklungsgeschichte des Familienrechts*, p. 32. *Idem, Grundriss der ethnologischen Jurisprudenz*, i. 56, 95.

be common."[1] This suggests that attempts were actually
made to form compacts of brotherhood in which wives as
well as goods were in common.[2] A reminiscence of such a
practice may perhaps also be found in a story related by
Bukhārī, in which we are told that when the Prophet made
'Abd al-Raḥmān ibn 'Auf and Sa'd ibn Rabī'a take each
other as brothers, the latter, who had two wives, proposed
that they should go halves in his goods and his women, in
consequence of which 'Abd al-Raḥmān got one of Sa'd's
wives. Robertson Smith argues that a state of things in
which this seemed a natural consequence of brotherhood
can most naturally be regarded as a relic of Tibetan
polyandry, similar to what Strabo describes ;[3] but this inference is inconclusive. We must not look upon the so-
called blood-brotherhood as an exact image of the real
brotherhood. It is a covenant by which two men impose
upon themselves mutual duties, which may even be more
sacred than those of brothers towards one another ; and
the community of women may serve to make the ties between
them as intimate and binding as possible. If blood-brotherhood with sexual communism had been a mere imitation
of actual brotherhood, why should that communism have
ceased long ago in the case of real brothers and still survive
in the case of blood-brothers ?

In the cases of group-unions which we have hitherto
considered, apart from group-marriages which have arisen
by a combination of polygyny with polyandry, the male
partners are not necessarily or generally, or may not even be,
brothers or relatives, and the female partners are not necessarily or generally sisters. We now come to another type
of group-unions, where a group of brothers are represented
as married or having access to a group of sisters ; and since
these groups are said to consist of brothers and sisters in
the classificatory sense, they would be of considerable size.

---

[1] Bruns and Sachau, *Syrisch-römisches Rechtsbuch aus dem fünften
Jahrhundert*, § 86, p. 24.

[2] *Cf. ibid.* p. 255 ; Wellhausen, Die Ehe bei den Arabern,' in
Nachrichten Königl. Gesellsch. Wissensch. Göttingen, 1893, p. 461.

[3] Robertson Smith, *Kinship and Marriage in Early Arabia*, p. 160.

The classical instance of this sort of group-unions is the *punalua* system of the Sandwich Islanders. Judge Lorin Andrews wrote in 1860 to Morgan :—" The relationship of *pŭnalŭa* is rather amphibious. It arose from the fact that two or more brothers with their wives, or two or more sisters with their husbands, were inclined to possess each other in common ; but the modern use of the word is that of *dear friend* or *intimate companion.*"[1] The Rev. A. Bishop, who sent Morgan a schedule of the Hawaian system of relationship terms, observed that the " confusion of relationships " was " the result of the ancient custom among relatives of the living together of husbands and wives in common." Dr. Bartlett wrote, " Husbands had many wives and wives many husbands, and exchanged with each other at pleasure."[2] Dr. Rivers remarks that side by side with the presence of individual marriage as a social institution there existed among the Sandwich Islanders much laxity, and also " a definite system of cicisbeism in which the paramours had a recognised status. Of these paramours those who would seem to have had the most definite status were certain relatives, viz. the brothers of the husband and the sisters of the wife. These formed a group within which all the males had marital rights over all the females " ; and Dr. Rivers was told that even now, nearly a century after the general acceptance of Christianity, the rights of *punalua* " are still sometimes recognised, and give rise to cases which come before the law courts where they are treated as cases of adultery. In addition to these *punalua* who had a recognised status owing to their relationship to the married couple, there were often other paramours apparently chosen freely at the will of the husband and wife."[3]

That the Sandwich Islanders have had individual marriage as long as they have been known to us is certain. Ellis, who wrote his account nearly a hundred years ago, speaks of nothing else, and says that polygyny was practised only

[1] Morgan, *Ancient Society*, p. 427.
[2] *Ibid.* p. 427 *sq.*
[3] Rivers, *History of Melanesian Society*, ii. 386 *sq.*

by the chiefs.[1] That the *punalua* system was not group-marriage, but at most, as Dr. Rivers puts it, " a definite system of cicisbeism," is also more than probable. Whether the right of a *punalua* belonged to him as a matter of course or on account of his relationship to the married couple, or was specially granted to him in each case, is not clear ; although Mr. Andrews' statement that brothers with their wives and sisters with their husbands " were inclined to possess each other in common " rather speaks in favour of the latter alternative. The *punalua* custom is certainly full of obscurity. The accounts of it are so meagre and indefinite and so much mixed up with reference to the terms of relationship that one cannot help asking oneself whether there may not have been some confusion between the habits of life and the terms of relationship similar to that which has led to the statement that in Australian tribes all the males in one division of a tribe were married to all the females of the same generation in another division. As to the origin of the *punalua* system no other conjecture has, to my knowledge, been made than Morgan's that it developed out of " the consanguine family."[2] The males are said to have outnumbered the females among the Sandwich Islanders,[3] and this disproportion of the sexes may, of course, have influenced the sexual relations of the people.

Dr. Rivers states that in some parts of Melanesia there are, side by side with definite individual marriage, sexual relations between a group of men formed by the husband's brothers and a group of women formed by the wife's sisters— brothers and sisters understood in the classificatory sense. He observes that now, at any rate, such group-relations are merely sexual, and that it therefore seems better in these cases not to speak of group-marriage but of sexual communism associated with individual marriage.[4] This statement, however, seems to be based not on direct

[1] Ellis, *Tour through Hawaii*, p. 414. *Cf.* Lisiansky, *Voyage round the World*, p. 128.

[2] See *supra*, ch. vii.   [3] *Supra*, iii. 57 n. 2.

[4] Rivers, ' Marriage (Introductory and Primitive),' in Hastings, *Encyclopædia of Religion and Ethics*, viii. 428.

evidence but on inference. In dealing with the subject of
sexual communism in Melanesia in his book ' The History
of Melanesian Society,' Dr. Rivers considers any evidence
for communism which may seem to be derived from the
terms of relationship, and then passes on to the evidence
of actual communistic relations in Melanesia at the present
time or in the recent past. He observes that certain
features of the classificatory system of relationship have
often been regarded as evidence in favour of sexual communism. In the systems of many peoples in different parts
of the world the wife's sisters and the brothers' wives (male
speaking) are classed in nomenclature with the wife, and,
reciprocally, the sisters' husbands (woman speaking) and
the husband's brothers are classed with the husband ; and
it has been supposed that this nomenclature is a survival
from a time when the persons so classed with the wife and
husband respectively were actually treated as such. Now
there are correspondences of this kind in Melanesia ; but
Dr. Rivers maintains that they lend no support to the
hypothesis that they are survivals of sexual communism,
since they are more naturally explained as the result of the
status of certain men and women as potential husbands and
wives.[1] In his book on the Melanesians Dr. Codrington
remarks :—" Speaking generally, it may be said that to a
Melanesian man all women, of his own generation at least,
are either sisters or wives, to the Melanesian woman all
men are either brothers or husbands. . . . It must not be
understood that a Melanesian regards all women who are
not of his own division as, in fact, his wives, or conceives
himself to have rights which he may exercise in regard to
those women of them who are unmarried ; but the women
who may be his wives by marriage and those who cannot
possibly be so, stand in a widely different relation to him."[2]

There are other features of nomenclature, Dr. Rivers
continues, that may possibly have arisen in a communistic
condition. One of these features is the use of the expression

[1] Rivers, *History of Melanesian Society*, ii. 128 *sq.* See *supra*, i.
271.
[2] Codrington, *Melanesians*, p. 22 *sq.*

wunu mumdal in Rowa (in the Banks group), which was translated " the wife of all of us." But he says that this is an isolated statement, and that it would be dangerous to attach too much importance to it until it has been confirmed.[1] The other features of nomenclature I shall not consider in detail, since Dr. Rivers himself admits that the most that can be said for them is that they suggest the probability of an origin in an ancient condition of sexual communism ;[2] to me they seem to carry no weight at all. He says that it is only " when we turn to the duties and restrictions associated with Melanesian terms of relationship that we meet with definite evidence for the existence of sexual communism, not merely in the past, but even at the present time."

We are told that the most conclusive evidence of this kind comes from the Torres Islands. " In these islands a man must not address any of his wife's relatives by name, and when speaking to them he must not use a word *cha* or *ja* which he uses when addressing his wife, and these are only special instances of a general regulation that he must not talk to these relatives familiarly. If a man is heard to address his wife's sister by name or to say *cha* to her, it is at once concluded that sexual relations have taken place between the pair. Further, if there have been such relations, the man may no longer use the proper term of relationship for the woman with whom the relations have occurred. Thus, if a man has had sexual relations with his wife's mother, whom in Loh he normally calls *kwiliga*, he must no longer use this term, but to the day of his death must address her and speak of her by her personal name." It would be interesting to know whether this is meant as a penalty for his offence ; for it is obvious from the account just quoted that a man is not allowed to have sexual relations with any of his wife's relatives, nor even to talk familiarly to them. The reader wonders how this can be looked upon as evidence of sexual communism, being the very reverse of it. But Dr. Rivers argues that there is a connection between the avoidance of personal names and the *potentiality* of sexual

---

[1] Rivers, *op. cit.* ii. 130.   [2] *Ibid.* ii. 132.

relations. It is evident, he says, that the possibility of such
relations between a group of men and a group of women is
constantly present in the minds of the Torres Islanders,
and these groups must be of considerable size, since the restrictions do not apply merely to the wife's mother and sister
and to the daughter's and sister's husband in our limited
sense, but in that of the classificatory system. Hence,
" these practices with their associated beliefs furnish the
strongest evidence in favour of the existence of a condition
of communism which even now has not wholly disappeared."[1]

I quite agree with Dr. Rivers that the prohibition of undue
familiarity with certain women—like the prohibition of
anything else—implies that the prohibited mode of conduct
is possible. It even presupposes, I should say, that such
conduct has actually occurred or is considered more or less
likely to occur, at least occasionally ; we may reverse the
words of the Apostle and say that where there is no transgression there is no law.[2] But neither the possibility nor the
actual occurrence of sexual relations between a group of
men and a group of women is sexual communism in the
meaning Dr. Rivers gives to the term when he defines it as
" a social condition in which it is recognised as legitimate
that sexual relations shall take place between a group of
men and a group of women."[3] If Dr. Rivers means that the
restrictions in question prove the earlier existence of such
communism, implying sexual rights, he is certainly mistaken. We might as well say that the prohibitions of our
criminal law prove that all the forbidden acts were in former
days recognised as legitimate. It is also worth noticing
that if Dr. Rivers were right in his assumptions, the groups
of men and women between whom sexual relations were
allowed would not have been restricted to real and classificatory brothers on one side and to real and classificatory
sisters on the other, as " a man must not address any of his
wife's relatives by name." He expressly says that the

---

[1] Rivers, *op. cit.* ii. 132 *sq.*
[2] I have dealt with this point in my book *The Origin and Development of the Moral Ideas*, i. 135.
[3] Rivers, *op. cit.* ii. 127.

restrictions also apply to the wife's mother, in the classificatory sense of the term.

After being told that in the Torres Islands a man must not address any of his wife's relatives by name, we cannot help feeling puzzled when we shortly after read the following sentences :—" Since it is clear that the application of the personal name to a female relative of the wife in the Torres group signifies the actual occurrence of sexual relations, it is very significant that in these islands, especially in Hiw, and in Rowa in the Banks group, the wife's sister is still addressed by her personal name. In Hiw this is almost certainly habitual, and we may therefore conclude that in this island sexual relations are habitual also ; in other words, that sexual communism is still in existence in this island."[1] As for the inhabitants of Rowa, Dr. Rivers does not seem, after all, to be certain whether among them the use of the personal name in the case of a wife's sister and a brother's wife implies the occurrence of sexual relations ; for he says in another place that there is evidence that it " perhaps " does so in some of the Banks Islands.[2] Among the people of Hiw sexual communism—that is, a social condition in which sexual relations between a group of men and a group of women are recognised as legitimate— is said to exist because it is " almost certainly habitual " to address the wife's sister by her personal name ; although we have just before been told that he must not do so in the group of islands to which Hiw belongs. Perhaps Dr. Rivers means that in this island, contrary to what is the rule in the other Torres Islands, the men not only habitually apply the personal name to the wife's sister but are actually allowed to do so by custom. But if this is the case, it may be asked if he is really certain that in Hiw also, as in the other islands of the group, the use of the personal name signifies the actual occurrence of sexual relations. If he is, why does he not directly say that there is sexual communism in Hiw instead of inferring its existence from the use of the personal name ?

An account in which there are so many obscurities and ambiguities, where possibilities, occurrences, and recognised

---

[1] Rivers, *op. cit.* ii. 133 *sq.*   [2] *Ibid.* ii. 129.

rights are mixed up in a way which makes it hardly possible
to find out what the author really means, and where statements of great importance for the argument are modified by
a "perhaps" or an "almost certainly"—such an account
cannot, in my opinion, provide us with "definite evidence
for the existence of sexual communism" in Melanesia.
But even if the evidence were conclusive, it would only
prove the existence of sexual communism in a very
small part of Melanesia. And Dr. Rivers' final conclusion that "in the earliest state of Melanesian society
of which we have evidence there was a condition
of sexual communism," [1] would, to my mind, require
much stronger arguments than he has been able to
produce.

Dr. Codrington is also inclined to believe that sexual
communism once existed in Melanesia. He admits that the
people have no memory of a time when all the women of
one division were in fact common wives to the men of
another division, and that "there is no occasion on which
the women become common to the men who are not of their
kin. The licence of a gathering at a feast is confessed to be
great, but is disorderly and illegitimate, and is not defended
on the ground of prescription. . . . The stories also of the
creation of mankind, and particularly of woman, represent
individual marriage." When Qat made men, male and
female, he assigned to each man his wife. But on the other
side, Dr. Codrington argues, "is to be set the testimony,
the strong testimony, of words." In the Mota language the
terms for mother and for husband and wife are used in
the plural form. *Veve* is the term for division or kin, *ra* is
the plural prefix, and mother is *ra-veve*. *Soai* is a word
which means "a member, as of a body, or a component part
of a house or of a tree," and *ra-soai* is the term for either
husband or wife. Thus "in Mota a man does not call his
wife a member of him, a component part of him, but his
members, his component parts ; and so a wife speaks of
her husband."[2]

A linguistic testimony of this kind seems to me to be of

[1] Rivers, *op. cit.* ii. 326.   [2] Codrington, *op. cit.* p. 27 *sq.*

extremely doubtful value. The Mota language has a so-called *pluralis majestatis*. Dr. Rivers was told that the prefix *ra* in the case of the mother and certain other relatives was a sign of respect and of especial nearness of relationship ;[1] and that the people themselves, as Dr. Codrington says,[2] definitely recognised its expression of plurality is not surprising considering that the term *ra-veve* is formally a plural. If it were the plural of *veve* not only with regard to its form but with regard to its sense it would mean " divisions " or " groups of kindred." *Ra-soai*, again, is a reciprocal term, and its plural may simply be due to the fact that husband and wife together make up a composite body.[3] According to Dr. Codrington it meant that they were parts of a composite body of married persons ; and he says that this was acknowledged by the people themselves " with a Melanesian blush," although they protested that the word did not represent a fact.[4] The blush evidently showed that they were ashamed at the very idea of group-marriage, or at least at the suspicion that they ever practised it. Generally speaking, I must confess that I am suspicious of socio-logical deductions from words and grammar ; and I have never found it very profitable to discuss linguistic niceties with uneducated people of any race.

Group-marriage has particularly been the subject of much discussion in connection with Australian ethnology. It is said actually to exist among some Australian tribes, whilst its former prevalence among others has been conjectured from certain practices which have been represented as social survivals.

The best known of the tribes that are still said to practise group-marriage are the Dieri—inhabiting part of the Barcoo delta on the east and south-east of Lake Eyre, in Central Australia—whose marriage customs have been most fully described by Dr. Howitt, largely on the authority of Mr. Gason and the Rev. Otto Siebert. The Dieri are divided into two exogamous moieties, whose members may freely intermarry, subject only to restrictions dependent on kin-

---

[1] Rivers, *op. cit.* ii. 131.   [2] Codrington, *op. cit.* p. 28.
[3] *Cf.* Rivers, *op. cit.* ii. 131.   [4] Codrington, *op. cit.* p. 29.

ship,   We are told that they have two kinds of marriages :
the *tippa-malku* or individual marriage, and the *pirrauru* or
group-marriage.   As regards the individual marriage Dr.
Howitt informs us in his latest book that it is usually brought
about by betrothal in infancy or childhood, and that the
arrangement is made by the mothers with the concurrence
of the girl's maternal uncles.[1] The *pirrauru* relation, on
the other hand, " arises through the exchange by brothers
of their wives.   When two brothers are married to two
sisters, they commonly live together in a group-marriage
of four.   When a man becomes a widower (*Topula*) he has
his brother's wife as *Pirrauru*, making presents to his brother.
A man being a visitor, and being of the proper class (*Murdu*),
is offered his host's *Tippa-malku* wife as a temporary
Pirrauru."   Moreover, if a man is in great favour with the
women, " a woman might even ask her husband to give her
such or such a man as a *Pirrauru*.   Should he refuse to do
this, she must put up with it ; but if he agrees to do so, the
matter is arranged."   In order to make the *pirrauru* relation legal a ceremony is performed by the head of the totem,
or heads when there are more than one totem concerned.
This ceremony is performed for batches of people at the same
time ; for " commonly it is not merely two pairs of *Pirrauru*
who are allotted to each other, but the whole of the marriageable or married people, even those who have already
Pirraurus, are re-allotted."[2] The re-allotment, however,
does not mean that the pre-existing conditions of *pirrauru*
are abolished, because " once a *pirrauru* always a *pirrauru*."[3]
A man may have several *pirrauru* wives and a woman
several *pirrauru* husbands, but no woman can have more

---

[1] Howitt, *Native Tribes of South-East Australia*, p. 177.   This
cancels a different statement made by the same writer in his article
' The Diery and other kindred Tribes of Central Australia,' in
Jour. Anthr. Inst. xx. 55.

[2] *Idem, Native Tribes*, p. 181 *sq.*   See also *Idem*, ' Australian
Group Relationships,' in *Jour. Roy. Anthr. Inst.* xxxvii. 279, where
allocation by the elders is mentioned as one source of the *pirrauru*
relation (*cf. Idem*, in *Jour. Anthr. Inst.* xx. 56).

[3] *Idem*, ' Native Tribes of South-East Australia,' in *Jour. Roy.
Anthr. Inst.* xxxvii. 272 *sqq.*

than one *tippa-malku* husband at the same time,[1] although a man can have more than one *tippa-malku* wife. The *tippa-malku* wife takes precedence over the *pirrauru* wife ;[2] and the rights granted to a *pirrauru* husband are much inferior to those possessed by the *tippa-malku* husband. He has marital rights over the wife only if the *tippa-malku* husband is absent ; " but he cannot take her away from him, unless by his consent, excepting at certain ceremonial times, as for instance at the initiation ceremonies, or at one of the marriages arranged between a man and a woman of two different tribes." Whilst the *tippa-malku* husband and his wife form a real household, it is only in his absence that she lives with any of her *pirraurus*, enjoying his protection.[3] And from a statement made by Mr. Gason it appears that the *tippa-malku* husband recognises all the children of his wife as his own and treats them with the same kindness and affection.[4]

Dr. Howitt says that these particulars are applicable with slight variations to neighbouring Lake Eyre tribes and even to various Queensland tribes,[5] of which he mentions the Kurnandaburi and the Wakelbura. Among the Kurnandaburi there is, besides the *nubaia* or individual marriage, the *dilpa-malli* or " group-marriage," in which " a group of men who are own or tribal brothers, and a group of women who are own or tribal sisters, cohabit when the tribe assembles, or indeed at any time when the *Dilpa-malli* group are all together."[6] The husband (*nubaia*) raises no objection to his wife having as many *dilpa-mallis* as she likes, so long as she does not transgress the class laws,

[1] *Idem, Native Tribes*, pp. 179, 181. In his book Dr. Howitt says that a woman becomes a *tippa-malku* wife before she becomes a *pirrauru* ; but this statement is somewhat qualified in a subsequent article (' Native Tribes of South-East Australia,' in *Folk-Lore*, xvii. 177), and expressly declared to be incorrect in a still later article (in *Jour. Roy. Anthr. Inst.* xxxvii. 268).

[2] *Idem, Native Tribes*, p. 184.

[3] *Ibid.* p. 184.

[4] Gason, ' Of the Tribes, Dieyerie, Auminie, &c.,' in *Jour. Anthr. Inst.* xxiv. 169.

[5] Howitt, *ibid.* xx. 58 *sq.*   [6] *Idem, Native Tribes*, p. 193.

and he receives a present from each of them as his due.
There is, however, no permanency in these relations, the
dilpa-mallis being constantly changed.[1] In addition to
these relations there are others between men and their
brothers' wives and between women and their sisters'
husbands, but they are *sub rosa* and not recognised as lawful
like the *dilpa-malli* relations.[2] Among the Wakelbura,
again, a man's unmarried brothers (own or tribal) have
access to his wife, and have to protect the children borne
by her. Dr. Howitt calls this group-marriage—" a form
of the *Pirrauru* marriage of the Lake Eyre tribes" ;[3] but,
as has been pointed out before, the relations between the
parties are merely of a polyandric character.

In the Urabunna tribe, whose territory adjoins that of
the Dieri on the north, Messrs. Spencer and Gillen have
found an institution very similar to the *pirrauru* relation.
A man can only marry women who stand to him in the
relationship of *nupa*, that is, are the children of his mother's
elder brothers (own or tribal), or, what is the same thing,
of his father's elder sisters. But whilst he has one or
perhaps two of these *nupa* women who are specially attached
to him and live with him in his own camp, he has in addition
to them certain other *nupa* women to whom he stands in
the relationship of *piraungaru*. To the latter he has access
under certain conditions only : " if the first man be present,
with his consent or, in his absence, without any restriction
whatever."[4] A woman's elder brothers will give one man
a preferential right to her and other men of the same group
a secondary right, but in the case of the *piraungaru* the
arrangement must receive the sanction of the old men of the
group before it can take effect. This relationship is usually
established at times when considerable numbers of the tribe
are gathered together to perform important ceremonies,
and when these and other matters of importance which

---

[1] Howitt, in *Jour. Anthr. Inst.* xx. 61.

[2] *Ibid.* p. 62. Howitt, *Native Tribes*, p. 192.

[3] *Idem, Native Tribes*, p. 224.

[4] These conditions are mentioned by Spencer and Gillen, *Native Tribes of Central Australia*, p. 110.

require the consideration of the old men are discussed and settled. A woman may also be *piraungaru* to a number of men, and " as a general rule men and women who are *Piraungaru* to one another are to be found living grouped together." Occasionally, though rarely, it happens that a man attempts to prevent his wife's *piraungaru* from having access to her, but this leads to a fight and the husband is looked upon as churlish.[1]

It may be seriously questioned whether the *pirrauru* or *piraungaru*—not to speak of the *dilpa-malli*—relation should be called marriage at all. It almost exclusively implies sexual licence, and is therefore essentially different from the *tippa-malku* relation or the ordinary Australian marriage, which, as Dr. Malinowski observes, cannot be detached from family life, but is defined by " the problems of the economic unity of the family, of the bonds created by common life in one wurley, through the common rearing of, and affection towards, the offspring."[2] But, as we have seen, even from the purely sexual point of view, there is no comparison between the rights of the individual husband and those of a *pirrauru*.

The *pirrauru* or *piraungaru* relation is of particular interest on account of the support it is considered to give to the hypo-thesis of ancient group-marriage in Australia, according to which the men of one division or class had as wives the women of another division or class. Marriages of this sort do not exist anywhere in Australia at the present time, hence I have, in the earlier editions of this book, spoken of them as " pretended group-marriages " ;[3] but this expression has been criticised by Messrs. Spencer and Gillen, who observe that in the case of the Urabunna " there is no pretence of any kind," and that exactly the same remark holds true of

---

[1] Spencer and Gillen, *op. cit.* p. 61 *sqq.*

[2] Malinowski, *The Family among the Australian Aborigines*, p. 119. Mr. Thomas (*Kinship Organisations and Group Marriage in Australia*, p. 135 *sq.*) likewise objects to the use of the term " marriage " for the *pirrauru* relation. Mr. Gason simply says (*Dieyerie Tribe of Australian Aborigines*, p. 24 n. *) that among the Dieri " each married woman is permitted a paramour."

[3] P. 95 n 1.

the Dieri.[1] This implies a curious confusion of terms, as
has been rightly pointed out by Mr. Thomas :[2] in the case
of the so-called group-marriage of the Urabunna and Dieri
the term " group " only means a number of persons who
stand in a certain relationship to another number of persons,
whereas in the theory of group-marriage the same term is
applied to a portion of a tribe distinguished by a class name
and term of relationship. Nor is this the only difference
between the two kinds of " group-marriages." No person
becomes a *pirrauru* or *piraungaru* as a matter of course on
account of his, or her, status. According to Howitt's later
account, an agreement must be made with the *tippa-malku*
husband, the *pirrauru* may have to pay for it (in the case of
a widower), and in spite of the rule " once a *pirrauru* always
a *pirrauru*," the relation may even be of very short duration
(in the case of a visitor) ; whilst the *piraungaru* requires
the consent of the woman's elder brothers. Considering,
further, that the *tippa-malku* spouse in every respect takes
precedence over the *pirrauru*, I find no reason to accept
Dr. Howitt's view that the *tippa-malku* marriage is an
innovation and " an encroachment upon the *pirrauru* group-
right."[3] On the contrary, it seems to me much more probable that the *pirrauru* relation is an engraftment on individual marriage, and that, partly at least, it owes its origin
to circumstances not unlike those which have led to more or
less similar customs in other parts of the world.

From various parts of Australia we hear of the difficulty
the young native has in getting a wife on attaining manhood.[4]

---

[1] Spencer and Gillen, *op. cit.* p. 109.
[2] Thomas, *op. cit.* p. 128.   [3] Howitt, in *Folk-Lore,* xvii. 187.
[4] Brough Smyth, *Aborigines of Victoria,* ii. 291. Dawson,
Australian Aborigines, p. 35. Ridley, *Kamilaroi, Dippil, and Turru-
bul,* p. 157. Hodgkinson, *Australia, from Port Macquarie to
Moreton Bay,* p. 230. Henderson, *Excursions and Adventures in
New South Wales,* ii. 110. Eylmann, *Die Eingeborenen der Kolonie
Südaustralien,* p. 131. Schulze, ' Aborigines of the Upper and
Middle Finke River,' in *Trans. Roy. Soc. South Australia,* xiv. 224.
Palmer, ' Notes on some Australian Tribes,' in *Jour. Anthr. Inst.*
xiii. 281. Mathew, *Two Representative Tribes of Queensland,* p. 162.
Lumholtz, *Among Cannibals,* p. 184.

In the Bangerang tribe, says Curr, few men under thirty years had wives ;[1] in the Kimberley district of West Australia it is rare to find a married man under thirty or forty.[2] Among the Victorian tribes described by Beveridge young men who had no female relatives under their control " must necessarily live all their lives in single blessedness, unless they chance to take up with withered old hags whom nobody owns, merely to have their fires cared for, their water-vessels filled, and their baggage carried from camp to camp."[3] One cause of the large number of bachelors is the comparative scarcity of women, of which I have spoken before,[4] and another cause is the polygyny of the old men, who have no scruple of appropriating to themselves a plurality of women, though many of the younger men have no wife at all. Among the Victorian tribes just referred to, where no man can get a wife unless he be the possessor of a sister or ward, " fathers of grown up sons frequently exchange their daughters for wives to themselves, even although they had two or three before, instead of allowing their sons to do so."[5] It is, as a rule, the young girls that the old men secure for themselves, whereas the boys or young men, whenever they are allowed to marry, get old lubras as wives. We have statements to this effect with regard to tribes scattered all over the continent.[6] In the Central tribes, according to Spencer and Gillen, a man and his mother-in-law are very often of about the same age,[7] and, speaking of the Dieri and neighbouring tribes, Howitt says that wives of old men are

---

[1] Curr, *Recollections of Squatting in Victoria*, pp. 141, 249.

[2] Hardman, ' Notes on some Habits and Customs of the Natives of the Kimberley District,' in *Proceed. Roy. Irish Academy*, ser. iii. vol. i. 71.

[3] Beveridge, *Aborigines of Victoria and Riverina*, p. 23.

[4] *Supra*, iii. 164.

[5] Beveridge, *op. cit.* p. 22 *sq.*

[6] Oberländer, ' Die Eingeborenen der australischen Kolonie Victoria,' in *Globus*, iv. 279. Ridley, *op. cit.* p. 157 (Wailwun). Lang, *Aborigines of Australia*, pp. 7, 10. Petrie, *Reminiscences*, p. 60 (Brisbane blacks). Hardman, *loc. cit.* p. 71 (Kimberley natives). Other references are found in Malinowski, *op. cit.* pp. 260–262, 309.

[7] Spencer and Gillen, *op. cit.* p. 558.

handed over to young boys.[1] It should also be noticed that the peculiar marriage rules which only allow marriages between members of certain small groups of people must increase the difficulties in securing a suitable wife.[2]

Whilst many men are thus compelled to remain unmarried for a considerable length of time or are married to women who must be more or less distasteful to them, tribal custom may provide them with certain means of gratifying their sexual desires outside the ordinary marriage relation. Among the natives of the Kimberley district, if a young man on reaching a marriageable age can find no wife, he is presented with a boy-wife, known as *chookadoo*—a boy of five years to about ten, when he is initiated ; and so common are these unions that it is the rule for a boy to be given to one of the young men when he becomes five years old.[3] Strehlow mentions the prevalence of a similar custom among the Western Loritja in Central Australia and various tribes living north of the Macdonnell range ; but among them the boy is from twelve to fourteen years when he is allotted to the young man, and he remains with him until the latter is married, often for several years, without being subject either to circumcision or subincision so as not to be looked upon as a man.[4] In all these cases the ordinary exogamic rules are observed, and Hardman says that among the Kimberley natives the " husband " has to avoid his " mother-in-law," just as if he were married to a woman. In the Dieri tribe, again, the *pirrauru* custom may serve as a substitute for regular marriage in the case of unmarried young men. Howitt expressly says that they may have *pirraurus*, nay

---

[1] Howitt, in *Jour. Anthr. Inst.* xx. 55.

[2] *Cf.* Schulze, *loc. cit.* p. 224 ; Strehlow, *Die Aranda- und Loritja-Stämme in Zentral-Australien*, vol. iv. pt. i. 98 ; Schurtz, *Altersklassen und Männerverbünde*, p. 186 *sq.*

[3] Hardman, *loc. cit.* p. 73 *sq.* *Cf.* Purcell, ' Rites and Customs of Australian Aborigines,' in *Verhandl. Berliner Gesellsch. Anthrop.* 1893, p. 287.

[4] Strehlow, *op. cit.* vol. iv. pt. i. 98. " On the Tully River, a husband, during the absence of his wife, has bestial rights over her younger brothers, but such conduct is despised " (Roth, *North Queensland Ethnography : Bulletin No. 8*, p. 7).

that there is no bachelor without one.[1] " The *Pirrauru* of an unmarried young man looks after him strictly, warns him perpetually, and makes secret inquiry of his doings from the other women. She requires him to camp near at hand, so that she can keep an eye upon him."[2] It is, moreover, obvious that the *pirrauru* relation must give comfort to many a young man who is married to an old woman. But it is equally evident that the old and influential men largely make use of it to their own advantage. Among the Urabunna " the number of a man's *Piraungaru* depends entirely upon the measure of his power and popularity ; if he be what is called ' ūrkū,' a word which implies much the same as our word ' influential,' he will have a considerable number, if he be insignificant or unpopular, then he will meet with scanty treatment."[3] Among the Dieri the leading men in the tribe have likewise more *pirraurus* than other men ; Howitt knew one who had over a dozen allotted to him, in addition to whom " honorary " *pirraurus* were assigned to him in neighbouring tribes.[4] We are told that the elders do not look favourably upon a youth having either a *tippa-malku* wife or a *pirrauru* early, and that when a man has a number of *pirraurus* the old men may recommend him to confine himself to one ; in the former case, it is said, the young people might otherwise be too much taken up with each other, and in the latter there might be strife between the women.[5] But there may be other reasons as well.

Dr. Eylmann was told by members of the Dieri and other tribes that the *pirrauru* custom chiefly benefited the old men, because it gave them an excellent opportunity to have sexual intercourse with young women without transgressing the rules of tribal morality, though it was only with the greatest reluctance that the younger men let them have access to their wives.[6] Nor is the sexual gratification the

---

[1] Howitt, in *Jour. Anthr. Inst.* xx. 57.
[2] *Idem, Native Tribes*, p. 183.
[3] Spencer and Gillen, *op. cit.* p. 63.
[4] Howitt, in *Jour. Anthr. Inst.* xx. 57. *Idem, Native Tribes*, p. 184.   [5] *Idem, Native Tribes*, p. 182 *sq.*
[6] Eylmann, *op. cit.* p. 136 *sq.*

only benefit a man derives from having many *pirraurus*.
Howitt observes that " it is an advantage to a man to have
as many *Pirraurus* as possible. He has then less work to
do in hunting, as when they are with him they supply him
with a share of the food they procure, their own *Tippa-malku*
husbands being absent. He also obtains great influence in
the tribe by lending his *Pirraurus* occasionally, and receiv-
ing presents from the younger men who have no *Pirraurus*
with them, or to whom none has yet been allotted."[1] It
should be remembered that the Australian natives are ruled
by a system of customs the tendency of which is to give
everything to the strong and old to the prejudice of the
young and weak.[2] If the old men keep for themselves the
best and fattest pieces and marry the most attractive women,
it is only natural that they also should favour an institution
like the *pirrauru* relation, which gives them sexual enjoyment and at the same time increases their influence.[3] I am
therefore inclined to believe that the *pirrauru* custom is a
consequence of the comparative scarcity of women and of
the selfish tyranny of the old men. But we must also remember another fact, which we have often before met with
in connection with polyandry and group-relations, namely,
the necessity of a married woman to have a protector and
guardian during the temporary absence of her husband.
It is significant that a man has sexual rights over a woman
who is *pirrauru* or *piraungaru* to him chiefly, if not exclusively,while her husband is away, and on such occasions only
does she live with him, enjoying his protection. That the
need of protection and guardianship has something to do
with the *pirrauru* custom is also suggested by a statement
for which I am indebted to Mr. Frank P.(" Bulman ") Brown.
He tells me that among the Kacoodja, on the South Alligator
River in the Northern Territory, if a man goes away for some
time he hands over his wife to some other man of his own

---

[1] Howitt, *Native Tribes*, p. 184 *sq.*

[2] See, *e.g.*, Lang, *Aborigines of Australia*, p. 7 *sq.* ; Krichauff,
' Further Notes on the " Aldolinga," &c.' in *Proceed. Roy. Geograph.
Soc. Australasia, South Australian Branch*, ii. 78.

[3] *Cf.* Eylmann, *op. cit.* p. 136 *sq.* ; Schurtz, *op. cit.* p. 179.

class, who during his absence is entitled to have sexual intercourse with her. In case she were left alone she would probably be seized by somebody else, or she might herself invite somebody to have connection with her. If the husband has received her as his wife from some old man he will most probably give her in charge to him.

I cannot, then, regard the *pirrauru* custom as evidence of a prior state of group-marriage ;[1] and the same is the case with various other customs which have been supposed to give support to the group-marriage theory, such as the lending or exchange of wives, the sexual intercourse to which a girl is regularly subject before her marriage, and the licence allowed at the performance of certain ceremonies when the ordinary rules of morality are more or less suspended. I have dealt with these customs in previous chapters, in my criticism of the hypothesis of promiscuity,[2] and the explanations of them which I offered give no more support to the hypothesis of group-marriage than to that of general communism. Spencer and Gillen attach much importance to the fact that the native to whom a man lends his wife must belong to the proper class : such a loan, they say, is radically different from the lending of a wife to a white man, which is sometimes done merely as an act of hospitality.[3] Of course the native must belong to the proper class, since otherwise he is forbidden by tribal law to have intercourse with the woman. If the lending of the wife really implied the recognition of a group-right, Spencer and Gillen themselves have certainly represented it very inadequately when they say that a man " may always " lend his wife to another man,[4] or may do so " of his own free will,"[5] or that when strangers visit a distant group they are

---

[1] Mr. Thomas (*op. cit.* p. 140) is likewise of opinion that the *pirrauru* custom affords no evidence whatever of earlier group-marriage. A similar view has been expressed by Crawley (*Mystic Rose*, p. 478 *sqq.*), Andrew Lang (*Secret of the Totem*, p. 51), and Malinowski (*op. cit.* p. 119). [2] *Supra*, i. ch. v. *sq.*

[3] Spencer and Gillen, *op. cit.* p. 101 *sq.*

[4] *Ibid.* p. 63. Spencer and Gillen, *Northern Tribes of Central Australia*, p. 141.

[5] Spencer and Gillen, *Native Tribes*, p. 74.

" usually " offered the use of lubras.[1]   Among the Kamilaroi,
according to Mr. Doyle, the men could lend their wives to
friends or to friendly visitors from a distance only with the
consent of the woman.[2]

We finally come to a set of facts to which the hypothesis
of Australian group-marriage practically owes its origin,
namely, the terms of relationship, which are classificatory.
Imbued with Morgan's ideas, the Rev. L. Fison concluded
from the prevalence of the classificatory system among the
South Australian Kamilaroi that their marriage was still
in theory communal, being " based upon the marriage of
all the males in one division of a tribe to all the females of
the same generation in another division."[3]   He admitted
that he was not aware of any tribe in which the actual
practice was to its full extent what the terms of relationship
implied as of former occurrence : " present usage," he
said, " is everywhere in advance of the system so implied,
and the terms are survivals of an ancient right, not precise
indications of custom as it is."[4]   Yet in spite of this admission various writers have asserted on Fison's authority that
among the Australian natives groups of males are actually
found united to groups of females.[5]   The belief in a close
connection between the terms of relationship and previous
group-marriage was shared by Howitt and by Spencer and
Gillen. " The classificatory terms of relationship," says
Howitt, " show that the ancestors of the tribes of the
Eastern half of this continent were at one time in the status
of group-marriage. To this I may add that the examples
which I have seen of the terms in use in the Western half
point to the same conclusion as I have indicated for those
of the Eastern."[6]   So, too, according to Spencer and Gillen,

[1] Iidem, Northern Tribes, p. 140.

[2] Doyle, quoted by Howitt Native Tribes, p. 208.

[3] Fison and Howitt, Kamilaroi and Kurnai, p. 50.

[4] Ibid. p. 159 sq.

[5] Avebury, Origin of Civilisation, p. 84 sqq. Morgan, in his
' Introduction ' to Fison and Howitt, Kamilaroi and Kurnai, p. 10.
Kohler, ' Ueber das Recht der Australneger,' in Zeitschr. f. vergl.
Rechtswiss. vii. 344.   Kovalewsky, Tableau des origines de la famille,
p. 13 sq. ; &c.   [6] Howitt, in Folk-Lore, xvii. 189.

it is the former existence of group-marriage that "has of necessity given rise to the terms of relationship used by the Australian natives."[1] "Each tribe has one term applied indiscriminately by the man to the woman or women whom he actually marries and to all the women whom he might lawfully marry—that is, who belong to the right group ; one term to his actual mother and to all the women whom his father might lawfully have married ; one term to his actual brother and to all the sons of his father's brothers, and so on right through the whole system."[2]

In an earlier chapter I have criticised the view that the classificatory system of relationship has originated in communism in women, whether group-marriage or any other kind of sexual communism ; and I tried to show that this view is not only unfounded but inconsistent with plain facts.[3] Spencer and Gillen tell us that in order to understand the native it is essential to lay aside all ideas of relationship as counted amongst ourselves ;[4] and yet they assume themselves that the classificatory terms of the Australian savages are founded on exactly the same principle as are our own " descriptive " terms. They lay particular stress on the fact that the term applied to the " special wife " is also applied to all the other women of her group " whom it is lawful for a man to marry and outside of whom he may not marry."[5] But, as I have said before, there is no reason whatever to look upon the common term as a relic of group-marriage, as it is easily explained by the fact that the women who may be a man's wives and those who cannot possibly be so stand in a widely different relation to him. Like Fison and Howitt, Spencer and Gillen are only too apt to confound present marriageability with actual marriage in the past, and, as Dr. Malinowski puts it, " describe the facts of sexual life to-day in terms of hypothetical assumptions."[6] They constantly apply the term " lawful

[1] Spencer and Gillen, *Native Tribes*, p. 59.
[2] *Ibid.* p. 57 *sq.*   [3] *Supra*, i. ch. vii.
[4] Spencer and Gillen, *Native Tribes*, p. 58.
[5] *Ibid.* pp. 95, 96, 106. Spencer and Gillen, *Northern Tribes*, p. 140.   [6] Malinowski, *op. cit.* p. 90

husbands " to men for whom it is merely lawful to marry a certain woman. If this is a correct use of the term, we may say that an English girl has millions of lawful husbands.

I must admit, therefore, that the facts produced by Messrs. Spencer and Gillen, and the severe criticism they have passed on my sceptical attitude towards Mr. Fison's group-marriage theory in earlier editions of this work, have not been able to convince me that among the Australian aborigines individual marriage has evolved out of a previous system of marriage between groups of men and women. Nor has Dr. Howitt in his various publications on the native tribes of South-East Australia in my opinion proved that such an evolution has taken place. He blames certain " ethnologists of the study " for not being willing " to take the opinion of men who have first-hand knowledge of the natives " ;[1] but I think we do well in distinguishing between statements based on direct observation and the observer's interpretation of the stated facts.

Dr. Howitt even ventures to forecast that the practice of group-marriage will be ultimately accepted as one of the primitive conditions of mankind.[2] He asks, " If the primitive aborigines of Australia had group-marriage, what is to be said of the former condition of other savage tribes, which also have classificatory systems which may include the same or analogous terms to those I have shown to have so momentous a significance ? "[3] The view that the pre-valence of the classificatory system is everywhere an indica-tion of group-marriage or sexual communism in the past is also held by other anthropologists ;[4] and combined with the idea that the classificatory system has once prevailed among all the races of the world, this view inevitably leads to the conclusion that group-marriage or sexual communism has been equally universal. Now there is no evidence that the classificatory system has prevailed everywhere ;[5] nor can the hypothesis that it is an indication of group-marriage

---

[1] Howitt, in *Folk-Lore*, xvii. 185.   [2] *Idem, Native Tribes*, p. 281.
[3] *Idem*, in *Folk-Lore*, xvii. 189.   [4] See *supra*, i. 239 *sqq*.
[5] See *supra*, i. 274.

or sexual communism be accepted as even probably correct. In addition to what was said on this subject before I shall deal here only with one point, which could not be fully discussed in the chapter on the classificatory system. If this system is found side by side with group-marriage or sexual communism among the same people a causal connection between them can be supposed to exist only in cases where a group of brothers, real and classificatory, are married or have a right of access to a group of sisters, real and classificatory.[1] So far as I know, however, there is no clear case of the actual existence of such group-marriages or group-relations anywhere. With regard to the Melanesians it may be said that even if Dr. Rivers' " definite evidence " in favour of sexual communism among them possessed the weight he ascribes to it, it would give no support to the general theory that the classificatory system is most readily accounted for by group-marriage. As we have noticed, the group of women would consist not only of the wife's sisters but of her mother and indeed of all her female relatives ; and I fail to see how this fact could be brought into harmony with the classificatory nomenclature. Among the Australian tribes, on the other hand, the groups of men and women between whom there is sexual communism are much smaller than what the nomenclature would indicate. Those men and women must of course belong to classes between which sexual relations are allowed, but the groups only consist of a few members of these classes and the right of access must be specially granted to each of them. Hence although there may be agreement between classificatory terms and potential husbands and wives, fathers, mothers, and children, and so forth, those terms certainly do not express the actual facts of Australian communism in women.

Another supposed survival of previous group-marriage

---

[1] Herr Cunow's argument (*Zur Urgeschichte der Ehe und Familie*, p. 59) that there is no connection of this sort because the Chukchee have group-marriage but not the classificatory system is not to the point, since their group-unions are of an entirely different type, brothers even being expressly said never to form such unions with each other.

is the levirate.[1] In the last chapter I discussed the origin of this custom and tried to show how unfounded is the view that it is a relic of polyandry. I think there is, if possible, even less reason for regarding it as a relic of group-marriage. Sir James G. Frazer is of a different opinion. Opposing McLennan's theory of the polyandric origin of the levirate, he argues that " whereas both the Levirate and the classificatory system, with its plain testimony to group-marriage, occur very widely over the world, the custom of polyandry appears to have been comparatively rare and exceptional " ; hence, he concludes, it is more reasonable to look for the origin of the levirate in group-marriage than in polyandry.[2] This argument, based as it is on the assumption that group-marriage has been at one time very widely diffused, falls to the ground if deprived of the support of the classificatory system.

Frazer admits that the current view of the levirate in Africa and Melanesia appears to be that a widow, having been bought and paid for, cannot be allowed to pass out of the family but must go to the heir. Again, " wherever it came to be supposed that a man's eternal welfare in the other world depends on his leaving children behind him, who will perform the rites necessary for his soul's salvation, it naturally became the pious duty of the survivors to remedy, as far as they could, the parlous state of a kinsman who had died without offspring, and on none would that duty appear to be more incumbent than on the brother of the deceased." But he argues that neither the mercenary nor the religious aspect of the custom can be original and fundamental, because the levirate is practised by the aborigines of Australia, and " these people neither buy their wives and transmit them like chattels to their heirs, nor do they believe in a heaven in which the dead can only secure and keep a footing through the good offices of their living

---

[1] Kohler, 'Zur Urgeschichte der Ehe,' in *Zeitschr. vergl. Rechtswiss.* xii. 321. Kovalewsky, *Coutume contemporaine et loi ancienne*, p.181. Howitt, *Native Tribes of South-East Australia*, p. 281.

[2] Frazer, *Totemism and Exogamy*, i. 501 *sq.* See also *Idem, Folk-Lore in the Old Testament*, ii. 341 note.

descendants. Accordingly we must look for another explanation of their custom of handing over a widow to her
deceased husband's brother, and such an explanation lies
to our hand in the old custom, of group marriage."[1] This
argument is the more surprising as Frazer has himself
pointed out that " on account of the extreme poverty of the
Australian aborigines a wife is among them a man's most
valuable possession," and that, " having no equivalent in
property to give for a wife, an Australian aboriginal is
generally obliged to get her in exchange for a female relative,
usually a sister or daughter."[2] Considering, further, the
unusual difficulties these natives often experience in procuring
a wife, it seems to me that the prevalence of the levirate in
Australia, as well as anywhere else, can be easily explained
without conjecturing an earlier custom of group-marriage
as its cause.

Frazer, moreover, draws attention to the widespread
custom of the sororate, or marrying a living or deceased
wife's sister, and argues that as the levirate points to
the marriage of women to a group of brothers, so the
sororate points to the marriage of men to a group of sisters.
" Taken together," he says, " the two customs seem to
indicate the former prevalence of marriage between a
group of husbands who were brothers to each other and
a group of wives who were sisters to each other."[3] But
the sororate, like the levirate, can be so naturally interpreted
as the outcome of existing conditions that there is no need
whatever for regarding it as the survival of an hypothetical
marriage system in the past. Nor can I find any reason
for the assumption that " the custom of marrying a deceased
wife's sister is doubtless derived from the custom of marrying
her other sisters in her lifetime " ;[4] why should the
remarriage of a widower be looked upon as an indication

---

[1] *Idem, Folk-Lore in the Old Testament,* ii. 339 *sqq. Idem, Totemism
and Exogamy,* i. 502 *sq.*

[2] *Idem, Folk-Lore in the Old Testament,* ii 194 *sq.*

[3] *Idem, Totemism and Exogamy,* ii. 144. *Idem, Folk-Lore in the
Old Testament,* ii. 304.

[4] *Idem, Totemism and Exogamy,* iv. 143. See also *Idem, Folk-
Lore in the Old Testament,* ii. 264.

of earlier polygyny ? Frazer attaches much importance
to the fact that the levirate and the sororate are often found
among the same people.[1] But this is only to be expected
in the case of two customs which are evidently more or less
akin to each other. They may both be a consequence of
marriage by consideration ; as a woman for whom a price
has been paid may be kept in the family after the death of
her first husband, so she may also have to be replaced if
she dies herself.[2] Moreover, as the children of a widow
are best cared for if their step-father is their uncle, so the
children of a widower are best cared for if their step-mother
is their aunt.[3] And, above all, both the levirate and the
sororate preserve the union between the two families.
With reference to the Koryak, among whom the widow
must be married to the younger brother, younger cousin,
or nephew (son of sister or brother) of her deceased husband,
and a widower must marry the younger sister, younger
cousin, or niece (daughter of sister or brother) of his deceased
wife, Dr. Jochelson observes that he looks upon this two-
sided custom as " an institution having for its object the
continuation of the union between families related by
affinity."[4] Yet though the levirate and the sororate are
often combined, there are also many peoples among whom
they are not found together. Among the Australian tribes,
for instance, the levirate is very widespread, whereas the
sororate is apparently rare.[5] This is distinctly unfavourable
to Frazer's hypothesis, which is based on the assumption
that the Australian levirate is the most primitive now
existing.

After trying to show that the two customs of the sororate
and the levirate are traceable to a common source in a form
of group-marriage, in which all the husbands were brothers
and all the wives were sisters, Frazer observes that we are
not left entirely to conjecture the former existence of such

---

[1] *Idem, Folk-Lore in the Old Testament*, ii. 265 *sqq.*
[2] See *supra*, ii. 392 ; iii. 94 *sq.* n. 3.
[3] See *supra*, iii. 96 ; Seligman, *Veddas*, p. 69.
[4] Jochelson, *Koryak*, pp. 748, 750.
[5] Frazer, *Folk-Lore in the Old Testament*, ii. 303.

group-marriages : " instances of them have been noted by
modern observers in several parts of the world."[1] He
mentions three instances. One is the occasional combination
of polyandry with polygyny among the Todas, of which I
have spoken before.[2] The two other cases refer to the
natives of the Tully River in North Queensland and to the
Santals of Bengal. Among the former, says Frazer, " a
group of men, who are blood brothers, have marital
relations with a group of women who are blood sisters.
This is exactly the form of group marriage in which, on my
hypothesis, both the sororate and the levirate took their
rise."[3] Among the Santals, he says, " the communal
groups consist of an elder married brother and a number of
unmarried younger brothers on the one hand, and an elder
married sister and a number of unmarried younger sisters
on the other hand."[4] But, so far as I can see, these statements differ essentially from those made by his authorities.
Mr. Roth speaks of the right of marital relationship between
a husband and his wife's blood sisters and between a wife
and her husband's blood brothers on the Tully River ;[5] and
of the Santals we are likewise told that a husband's younger
brothers are allowed to share his wife's favours and that
the husband in his turn has access to his wife's younger
sisters.[6] But in neither case is it said that the brothers, or
younger brothers, of the husband have access to the sisters,
or younger sisters, of the wife ; hence we cannot speak here
of conjugal relations between a group of brothers and a
group of sisters. If among the Tully River natives not
only unmarried brothers have access to their married
brother's wife, but married brothers also have access to

---

[1] Frazer, *Folk-Lore in the Old Testament*, ii. 304 *sq.*
[2] *Supra*, iii. 224 *sq.*
[3] Frazer, *Folk-Lore in the Old Testament*, ii. 305.
[4] *Ibid.* ii. 309.
[5] Roth, *North Queensland Ethnography, Bulletin No. 10, Marriage
Ceremonies and Infant Life*, p. 3, quoted by Frazer, *op. cit.* ii. 305.
[6] Craven, ' Traces of Fraternal Polyandry amongst the Santāls,'
in *Jour. Asiatic Soc. Bengal*, vol. lxxii. pt. iii. 89. Skrefsrud, ' Traces
of Fraternal Polyandry amongst the Santāls,' *ibid.* vol. lxxii. pt. iii.
90. Gait, *Census of India*, 1911, vol. i. (India) Report, p. 240.

each other's wives—which is not clear,—there are certainly group relations ; but we do not know that the brothers of one family are in the habit of marrying sisters of another family.

Most of the customs which have been represented as relics of promiscuity have also, chiefly by more modern writers, been regarded as survivals of group-marriage ; this is the case even with the liberty granted to unmarried women.[1] Hence I need say nothing more about them. The group-marriage has in certain quarters been made the residuary legatee of the old promiscuity, or has at any rate been proclaimed the earliest form of marriage out of which the others have gradually developed. Professor Kohler has recently declared that the theory of group-marriage is so firmly established that the futile criticism which has been passed on it does not even need refutation[2]—a convenient manner of dealing with troublesome opponents. For my own part I only want to add that even if the various customs which—in my opinion without sufficient reason—have been represented as relics of group-marriage really were so, its former universality would still have to be proved. To assume it would be a mere guess unsupported by the knowledge we possess of many of the lowest races now existing.

[1] Kohler, in *Zeitschr. vergl. Rechtswiss.* xii. 326. *Idem,* ' Das Banturecht in Ostafrika,' *ibid.* xv. 14. For a similar interpretation of the lending or exchange of wives see Bloch, *Sexual Life of Our Time*, p. 194.

[2] Kohler, in Holtzendorff, *Enzyclopädie der Rechtswissenschaft*, ed. by Kohler, i. 27.

CHAPTER XXXII

THE DURATION OF MARRIAGE AND THE RIGHT TO DISSOLVE IT

It is the general rule that marriage is contracted for an indefinite length of time or for life, although even in the latter case it may very frequently be dissolved, for some reason or other, during the lifetime of the partners. But we also hear of marriages being entered into for a fixed period of shorter duration.

Among the Eskimo of the Ungava district, for instance, " wives are often taken for a period."[1] The same is said to be the case among some North American Indians[2] and West African Negroes.[3] In several of the islands of the Indian Archipelago the parties are regularly " betrothed to each other for a longer or shorter time, sometimes not for more than a month, and at others for a period of years."[4] Among the ancient Arabs, according to Ammianus Marcellinus, marriages were often contracted for a limited period of definite length, after which the wife might withdraw if she pleased.[5] Somewhat of the same character is a temporary form of marriage which still exists in certain parts of Arabia.[6] In Mecca marriages of short duration are concluded by

[1] Turner, 'Ethnology of the Ungava District, Hudson Bay Territory,' in *Ann. Rep. Bur. Ethnol.* xi. 189.

[2] Waitz, *Anthropologie der Naturvölker*, iii. 105.   [3] *Ibid.* ii. 114.

[4] Crawfurd, *History of the Indian Archipelago*, i. 88.

[5] Ammianus Marcellinus, *Res gestae*, xiv. 4. 4.

[6] Barton, *Sketch of Semitic Origins*, p. 47 *sq.*

pilgrims who tarry there for longer or shorter spaces of time, and women go thither from Egypt with the avowed purpose of entering into such alliances.[1] The Shī'ah Moslems recognise as legal temporary marriages contracted for a fixed period of time—a day, a month, or a year, or any other specified period. Such a temporary contract of marriage, which is called *mut'ah*, creates no right of inheritance in either party, although the children born of the union are legitimate and inherit from their parents like the issue of a permanent contract. The wife is not entitled to any maintenance unless it is expressly stipulated ; the husband is entitled to refuse procreation, which he cannot do in ordinary marriages ; and there is also this difference between a permanent and a temporary contract of marriage, that in the case of the latter the husband has no power to divorce his wife, although the marriage may be dissolved by the mutual consent of the parties before the stipulated period has expired.[2] This temporary form of marriage exists in Persia to the present day,[3] but it is held to be unlawful by the Sunnīs.[4] Temporary marriages are recognised throughout Tibet, " whether contracted for six months, a month, or perhaps a week, and . . . these unions are not held immoral."[5] In Abyssinia, also, there are marriages entered into for a fixed period, at the end of which husband and wife separate.[6] We have previously spoken of " marriages upon trial."[7]

Among a few uncivilised peoples marriage is said to be indissoluble or divorce unknown. The Veddas of Ceylon have a proverb that " death alone separates husband and wife " ; and Mr. Bailey assures us that they faithfully act

[1] Snouck Hurgronje, *Mekka*, ii. 5, 109 *sq.*
[2] Ameer Ali, *Mahommedan Law*, ii. 438 *sqq.*
[3] Polak, *Persien*, i. 207 *sq.* Hughes, *Dictionary of Islam*, p. 424. Cf. *supra*, ii. 59.
[4] Ameer Ali, *op. cit.* ii. 438.
[5] Rockhill, *Land of the Lamas*, p. 212.
[6] Lobo, ' Voyage to Abyssinia,' in Pinkerton, *Collection of Voyages and Travels*, xv. 26. Barton, *op. cit.* p. 48 *sq.*
[7] *Supra*, i. 135.

on this principle.[1] According to Messrs. Sarasin there is probably no divorce among them ;[2] and Professor and Mrs. Seligman say that " anything like a formal divorce is unknown," although they heard of one instance, occurring three generations ago, in which a woman left her husband and returned to her parents, and of another instance in which a wife went to her parents for food and was kept by them because her lazy husband took no trouble to support her.[3] Of the Andamanese Mr. Portman states that " divorce is rare, and unknown after a child has been born to the married couple ";[4] while, according to Mr. Man, " no incompatibility of temper or other cause " is allowed to dissolve a marriage among them.[5] Divorces are said to be unknown among several tribes in the Indian Archipelago who have remained in their native-state and continue to follow ancient custom.[6] Among the " pure " tribes of the Malay Peninsula divorce

[1] Bailey, ' Account of the Wild Tribes of the Veddahs of Ceylon,' in *Trans. Ethn. Soc. London*, N.S. ii. 293.

[2] Sarasin, *Ergebnisse naturwissenschaftlicher Forschungen auf Ceylon*, iii. 458 *sq.*

[3] Seligman, *Veddas*, p. 100.

[4] Portman, *History of Our Relations with the Andamanese*, i. 39. See also *ibid.* i. 42.

[5] Man, ' On the Aboriginal Inhabitants of the Andaman Islands,' in *Jour. Anthr. Inst.* xii. 135. Kloss says (*In the Andamans and Nicobars*, p. 188) that divorce is unknown among the Andamanese, and (*ibid.* p. 220) that the Shom Pen of the interior of Great Nicobar, who must be regarded as the aborigines of the island, " marry for life."

[6] Wilken, *Over de verwantschap en het huwelijks- en erfrecht bij de volken van het maleische ras*, p. 58 (natives of Lampong ; Wilken thinks [*ibid.* p. 46 *sq.*] that the same was formerly the case among the Battas and in Nias). Hagen, *Die Orang Kubu auf Sumatra*, p. 164 (Orang Mamaq). Moszkowski, *Auf neuen Wegen durch Sumatra*, p. 40 (Orang Akit ; if divorce occurs at all, it is extremely rare). Hollander-van Eck, *Handleiding bij de beoefening der land- en volkenkunde van Nederlandsch Oost-Indië*, i. 615 ; v. Rosenberg, *Der malayische Archipel*, p. 199 (Mentawi Islanders). Riedel, *De sluik- en kroesharige rassen tusschen Selebes en Papua*, p. 206 (Watubela Islanders). Arzaga, quoted by Mozo, *Noticio histórico natural de los gloriosos triumphos por los religiosos del orden de N.P.S. Agustin en las islas Philipinas*, p. 19 (Italons of Luzon).

is unknown or, if it occurs at all, disapproved of ;[1] that the case is different among the Benua[2] and some of the Mantra[3] is due to Malay influence.[4] Of the Lisu tribes of Kuyung Kai, on the Burma-China frontier, we are told that there is " no divorce, even for a childless wife."[5] Among the Moriori of the Chatham Islands " there does not appear to have been anything equivalent to divorce, other than the neglect shown to the unfavoured wife when the husband was possessed of more than one."[6] " There is no divorce among the Mang-bettou," says Mr. Burrows. " A man simply takes another wife when he is tired of the first."[7] Among the Bahuana of Congo " divorce is not known, but if a woman becomes very ill, she returns to her parents until she has recovered."[8] Among the Gês or Crans of Matto Grosso in Brazil marriage is said to be indissoluble, any attempt to bring about a divorce being opposed by the whole community.[9]

[1] Swettenham, ' Comparative Vocabulary of the Dialects of some of the Wild Tribes inhabiting the Malayan Peninsula, Borneo, &c.,' in *Jour. Straits Branch Roy. Asiatic Soc.* no. v. 156 (Semang of Ijoh). Knocker, ' Aborigines of Sungei Ujong,' in *Jour. Roy. Anthr. Inst.* xxxvii. 293 (Orang Bukit, or Mantra). Stevens, ' Mittheilungen aus dem Frauenleben der Ôrang Bĕlendas, der Ôrang Djâkun und der Ôrang Lâut,' in *Zeitschr. f. Ethnol.* xxviii. 179 (Orang Laut ; formerly). Martin, *Die Inlandstämme der Malayischen Halbinsel*, p. 873.

[2] Favre, ' Account of the Wild Tribes inhabiting the Malayan Peninsula, &c.,' in *Jour. Indian Archipelago*, ii. 264, 269. Newbold, *Account of the British Settlements in the Straits of Malacca*, ii. 408.

[3] Bourien, ' Wild Tribes of the Interior of the Malay Peninsula,' in *Trans. Ethn. Soc. London*, N.S. vol. iii. 80.

[4] Martin, *op. cit.* p. 873. See also Stevens, in *Zeitschr. f. Ethnol.* xxviii. 179, with reference to the Orang Laut, who nowadays look upon divorce with indifference owing to contact with Malays.

[5] Rose and Brown, ' Lisu (Yawyin) Tribes of the Burma-China Frontier,' in *Memoirs Asiatic Soc. Bengal*, iii. 263.

[6] Shand, ' Moriori People of the Chatham Islands,' in *Jour. Polynesian Soc.* vi. 148 n.*

[7] Burrows, *Land of the Pigmies*, p. 86.

[8] Torday and Joyce, ' Notes on the Ethnography of the Ba-Huana,' in *Jour. Anthr. Inst.* xxxvi. 286.

[9] Pohl, quoted by v. Martius, *Beiträge zur Ethnographie und Sprachenkunde Amerika's*, i. 290.

Among many uncivilised peoples divorce is said to be
rare or marriage, as a rule, to be concluded for life. This
is the case with a great number of American tribes.[1] Among
the Yahgans of Tierra del Fuego, as I was informed by Mr.
Bridges, there had at any rate been many instances of
husband and wife living together until separated by death.
Among the Patagonians[2] and the Charruas of Uruguay[3]
marriage is as a rule a union for life if there are children.
Among the Choroti and Ashluslay, Baron Nordenskiöld
heard only of one marriage which had been dissolved.[4] If
an Uaupés Indian takes a new wife the elder one is not
turned away but remains the mistress of the house.[5] The
Caribs of the Antilles very rarely divorced their first wives,
especially if they had children with them.[6] Among the

---

[1] Azara (*Voyages dans l'Amérique méridionale*, ii. 32, 44, 114, 132
(Minuanes, Pampas, Mbayas, Payaguas). do Prado, ' Historia dos
Indios Cavalleiros, da Nação Guaycurú,' in *O Patriota*, 1814, no. iv.
21 ; v. Martius, *op. cit.* p. 233 (Guaycurûs ; statements of an opposite
character, however, are made by Lozano, *Descripcion chorographica
del terreno de las Provincias del Gran Chaco, Gualamba*, p. 70, and
Sanchez Labrador, *El Paraguay Católico*, ii. 24). v. Koenigswald,
' Die Cayuás,' in *Globus*, xciii. 381. Waitz, *op. cit.* iii. 391 (Macusis).
Pelleprat, *Relation des missions des PP. de la Compagnie de Jesus
dans les Isles, et dans la terre ferme de l'Amerique Meridionale*, ii. 60
(Indians of French Guiana). Lumholtz, *Unknown Mexico*, i. 465
(Tepehuane). Dunbar, ' Pawnee Indians,' in *Magazine of American
History*, iv. 267 ; Grinnell, ' Marriage among the Pawnees,' in
American Anthropologist, iv. 280. Bossu, *Travels through that Part
of North America formerly called Louisiana*, i. 128, 231 (Illinois,
Alibamu). Marston, ' Letter to Jedidiah Morse,' in Emma Helen
Blair, *Indian Tribes of the Upper Mississippi Valley and Region of the
Great Lakes*, ii. 167 (Sauk and Foxes). Ashe, *Travels in America*,
p. 249 (Shawnee). Keating, *Narrative of an Expedition to the Source
of St. Peter's River*, ii. 157 (Ojibway). Mackenzie, *Voyages from
Montreal to the Frozen and Pacific Oceans*, p. cxxiii. (Chipewyan).
Bancroft, *Native Races of the Pacific States of North America*, i. 241
(Chinook).

[2] Falkner, *Description of Patagonia*, p. 126.

[3] Azara, *op. cit.* ii. 23.

[4] Nordenskiöld, *Indianliv i El Gran Chaco* (*Syd-Amerika*), p. 83.

[5] Wallace, *Travels on the Amazon*, p. 497.

[6] de Poincy, *Histoire naturelle et morale des Iles Antilles de
l'Amérique*, p. 545.

Mosquito Indians, although either man or woman can leave each other at choice, the constancy of married life " is about on a par with that of any other people, Europeans included."[1] Among the Natchez, according to Le Page du Pratz, separation between man and wife was so rare that during the eight years he lived in their neighbourhood he knew but one instance of it.[2] The Iroquois in ancient times regarded separation as discreditable to both man and woman, hence it was not frequently practised.[3] Speaking of some tribes on the eastern side of the Rocky Mountains, Harmon observes that if man and wife part they generally after a few days' absence come together again.[4] Among the Naudowessies, in the region of the Great Lakes, divorce is so rare that Carver had no opportunity of learning how it was accomplished.[5] Among the Californian Wintun it is very uncommon for a man to expel his wife ; " in a moment of passion he may strike her dead, or . . . ignominiously slink away with another, but the idea of divorcing and sending away a wife does not occur to him."[6] The Greenlanders seldom repudiated wives with whom they had children ;[7] and Dalager says of those of Frederikshaab that if man and wife had been married for some years and had offspring together they never separated.[8] Parry states that among the Eskimo of the Melville Peninsula the men sometimes repudiate their wives without ceremony in case of real or supposed bad behaviour, but that this does not often occur.[9]

[1] Bell, *Tangweera*, p. 261 *sq.*

[2] Le Page du Pratz, *History of Louisiana*, p. 343.

[3] Morgan, *League of the Iroquois*, p. 324.

[4] Harmon, *Journal of Voyages and Travels in the Interior of North America*, p. 342.

[5] Carver, *Travels through the Interior Parts of North America*, p. 375.

[6] Powers, *Tribes of California*, p. 239.

[7] Cranz, *History of Greenland*, i. 148. *Cf.* Holm, ' Konebaads-Expeditionen til Grønlands Østkyst,' in *Geografisk Tidskrift*, viii. 90 *sqq.* (Angmagsalik).

[8] Dalager, *Grønlandske Relationer*, p. 8.

[9] Parry, *Journal of a Second Voyage for the Discovery of a North-West Passage*, p. 528.

Of several peoples belonging to the former Russian empire we are told that their marriages as a rule lasted for life.[1] Among the Koryak, for instance, divorces are very rare.[2] Among the uncivilised tribes of India the marriage tie is generally loose, but among some of them divorce is said to be rare. This is the case with the Chukmas of Chittagong [3] and various tribes in Assam, such as the Nagas,[4] the Mikirs,[5] the Kukis,[6] and the Hajongs inhabiting the southern slope of the Garo Hills.[7] The Garos, according to Colonel Dalton, " will not hastily make engagements, because, when they do make them, they intend to keep them."[8] Dr. Bunker informed me that among the Karens of Burma separations, save by death, are rare. Among the Nayars, although a husband or wife may effect divorce at any time, more than ninety per cent. of the marriages are said to remain undissolved.[9] In many of the islands of the Indian Archipelago, even where divorce may be readily obtained, it is rarely practised.[10] The Bontoc Igorot say that " they never knew a man and woman to separate if a child was born to the pair and it lived and they had recognised themselves married."[11] Among the savages of Formosa the relationship between husband and wife seems in nearly all cases to continue until death, although divorce is possible with the

---

[1] Sauer, *Expedition to the Northern Parts of Russia performed by Joseph Billings*, p. 129 (Yakut). Georgi, *Beschreibung aller Nationen des russischen Reichs*, p. 42 (Chuvash, Votyak, Cheremiss, Mordvin, Vogul). v. Haxthausen, *Transcaucasia*, p. 404 (Ossetes).

[2] Jochelson, *Koryak*, p. 747.

[3] Lewin, *Wild Races of South-Eastern India*, p. 187.

[4] Hodson, *Nāga Tribes of Manipur*, p. 97.

[5] Stack, *Mikirs*, p. 20.

[6] Soppitt, *Short Account of the Kuki-Lushai Tribes*, p. 15.

[7] Endle, *Kacháris*, p. 86. See also *ibid.* pp. 85, 89, 95 (Rábhás, Moráns, Ahom Chutiyas).

[8] Dalton, *Descriptive Ethnology of Bengal*, p. 68.

[9] Kannan Nayar, ' Matrimonial Customs of the Nayars,' in *Malabar Quarterly Review*, vii. 190 *sq. Cf. supra* iii. 140.

[10] Crawfurd, *op. cit.* i. 78. Tauern, ' Ceram,' in *Zeitschr. f. Ethnol.* xlv. 172. Blumentritt, *Versuch einer Ethnographie der Philippinen*, p. 41 (Catalanganes).

[11] Jenks, *Bontoc Igorot*, p. 69.

consent of the tribe.[1] In certain parts of New Guinea,[2] in the island of Mabuiag in Torres Straits,[3] among some of the natives of the Gazelle Peninsula of New Britain,[4] and among some Solomon Islanders[5] divorce seems to be, or to have been, rare. Among the Maori the majority of marriages were apparently lifelong.[6] In Tonga, according to Mariner, more than half of the number of married women were parted from their husbands only by death;[7] and in Tahiti the birth of children generally prevented the dissolution of marriage.[8] Speaking of marriage among the Australian aborigines, Dr. Malinowski observes that " it is impossible to find a direct answer in the evidence to the question whether the general rule was duration for life, or whether, after the wife became useless both sexually and economically, she was repudiated "; but his discussion of the subject is rather in favour of the former alternative.[9] Of some Queensland natives, the Kabi and Wakka, Mr. Mathew states that " the conjugal band generally held out for a lifetime."[10] Among some of the Bushmen divorce is said to be rare.[11]

[1] Davidson, *Island of Formosa Past and Present*, p. 583. Müller, ' Über die Wildenstämme der Insel Formosa,' in *Zeitschr. f. Ethnol.* xlii. 230.

[2] Lawes, ' Notes on New Guinea and its Inhabitants,' in *Proceed. Roy. Geo. Soc.* N.S. ii. 614 (Port Moresby and Hood Bay). Bink, in *Bull. Soc. d'Anthr. Paris*, ser. iii. vol. xi. 397 (Geelvink Bay).

[3] Rivers, in *Reports of the Cambridge Anthropological Expedition to Torres Straits*, v. 246.

[4] Hahl, ' Ueber die Rechtsanschauungen der Eingeborenen eines Theiles der Blanchebucht und des Innern der Gazelle Halbinsel,' in *Nachrichten über Kaiser Wilhelms-Land und den Bismarck-Archipel*, 1897, p. 77. Cf. Pfeil, *Studien und Beobachtungen aus der Südsee*, p. 30 (natives of the Bismarck Archipelago).

[5] Elton, ' Notes on Natives of the Solomon Islands,' in *Jour. Anthr. Inst.* xvii. 95.

[6] Dieffenbach, *Travels in New Zealand*, ii. 40. Tregear, *The Maori Race*, p. 297.

[7] Mariner, *Account of the Natives of the Tonga Islands*, ii. 167.

[8] Waitz-Gerland, *Anthropologie der Naturvölker*, vi. 129.

[9] Malinowski, *The Family among the Australian Aborigines*, p. 65.

[10] Mathew, *Two Representative Tribes of Queensland*, p. 153.

[11] Kaufmann, ' Die Auin,' in *Mittheil. Deutsch. Schutzgeb.* xxiii. 157. See also Trenk, ' Die Buschleute der Namib,' *ibid.* xxiii. 168.

Of the Kafirs we are told that " the least cause may lead to divorce " ;[1] but various writers assert that divorces do not frequently occur or are even very rare among them,[2] and Mr. Cousins informed me that among the Cis-Natalian Kafirs marriage in the majority of cases was contracted for life. Separation between man and wife is infrequent among the Wafipa,[3] the Madi tribe,[4] the Southern Galla,[5] and the Masai.[6] Mr. Hollis even states that divorce is almost unknown among the Masai ;[7] and the same is said to be the case among the Banyankole or Bahima.[8] Among the Warega of Congo divorce, although very frequent at present, formerly occurred only in quite exceptional circumstances.[9] We shall soon find that among many of the simpler peoples marriage can be dissolved only on certain conditions which must make it in the majority of instances a lifelong union.

On the other hand there are also many tribes in which divorce is said to be of frequent occurrence or marriage often of very short duration.[10] Father Chomé states that

[1] Kidd, *The Essential Kafir*, p. 226.

[2] Alberti, *De Kaffers aan de Zuidkust van Afrika*, p. 140. Lichtenstein, *Travels in Southern Africa*, i. 264. Maclean, *Compendium of Kafir Laws and Customs*, p. 70. Nauhaus, ' Familienleben, Heirathsgebräuche und Erbrecht der Kaffern,' in *Verhandl. Berliner Gesellsch. Anthr.* 1882, p. 210.

[3] Fromm, ' Ufipa,' in *Mittheil. Deutsch. Schutzgeb.* xxv. 98.

[4] Felkin, ' Notes on the Madi or Moru Tribe of Central Africa,' in *Proceed. Roy. Soc. Edinburgh*, xii. 322.

[5] Wakefield, ' Marriage Customs of the Southern Gallas,' in *Folk-Lore*, xviii. 324.

[6] Merker, *Die Masai*, p. 50.

[7] Hollis, ' Note on the Masai System of Relationship,' in *Jour. Roy. Anthr. Inst.* xl. 481. See also *Idem, Masaï*, p. 304 n. 1.

[8] Roscoe, *Northern Bantu*, p. 114.

[9] Delhaise, *Les Warega*, pp. 171, 183.

[10] Keane, ' On the Botocudos,' in *Jour. Anthr. Inst.* xiii. 206. Kumlien, *Contributions to the Natural History of Arctic America*, p. 17 (Eskimo). Miss Czaplicka, *Aboriginal Siberia*, p. 104 (Ainu). Laufer, ' Preliminary Notes on Explorations among the Amoor Tribes,' in *American Anthropologist*, N.S. ii. 321 (Gold). Jellinghaus, ' Sagen, Sitten und Gebräuche der Munda-Kolhs in Chota Nagpore,' in *Zeitschr. f. Ethnol.* iii. 370. Yule, ' Notes on the Kasia Hills,'

among the Chiriguanos of Bolivia married people usually remained together for two years, after which time the husband settled down in another village and took a new wife.[1] Among the Creeks marriage was considered "only as a temporary convenience, not binding on the parties more than one year," the consequence being that a large portion of the old and middle-aged men had had many different wives and that their children, scattered around the country, were unknown to them.[2] Among the Eskimo of the Ungava district "it is seldom that a man keeps a wife for a number of years," and only in rare instances the pair remain together for life.[3] Many a Kalmuck changes his wife two or three or four times within a short period.[4] Among the Yendalins of Indo-China it is rare for any woman to arrive at middle age without having a family by two or more husbands.[5] With the Koravas—a tribe of vagabonds, thieves, quack doctors, and fortune-tellers, who are scattered all over India—a woman who has had seven husbands, whether she lost them by death or by divorce, is much esteemed and takes the lead in marriages

in Jour. Asiatic Soc. Bengal, vol. xiii. pt. ii. 624 ; Gurdon, Khasis, p. 79. Raffles, History of Java, i. 357. Hagen, op. cit. p. 133 (Kubus of Sumatra). Moszkowski, Auf neuen Wegen durch Sumatra, p. 106 (Sakai). Idem, ' Die Völkerstämme am Mamberamo in Holländisch-Neuguinea und auf den vorgelagerten Inseln,' in Zeitschr. f. Ethnol. xliii. 339. Safford, ' Guam and its People,' in American Anthropologist, N.S. iv. 716. Dahlgren, ' Om Palau-öarna,' in Ymer, iv. 328 (Pelew Islanders). Wilkes, Narrative of the United States Exploring Expedition, v. 101 (Kingsmill Islanders). Turner, Samoa, p. 97. Burton, First Footsteps in East Africa, p. 122 (Somal). Delafosse, ' Les Agni,' in L'Anthropologie, iv. 429. ' Negersitten,' in Das Ausland, liv. 1027 (Negroes of Bondo). Cruickshank, Eighteen Years on the Gold Coast of Africa, ii. 197. Zöller, Das Togoland und die Sklavenküste, p. 180 (natives of the Povo countries). Torday and Joyce, ' Notes on the Ethnography of the Ba-Mbala,' in Jour. Anthr. Inst. xxxv. 411.

[1] Chomé, ' Dritter Brief an Rev. Patrem Vanthiennen,' in Stoecklein, Der Neue Welt-Bott, vol. iv. pt. xxix. 72.

[2] Schoolcraft, Archives of Aboriginal Knowledge, v. 272 sq.

[3] Turner, in Ann. Rep. Bur. Ethnol. xi. 188 sq.

[4] Bergmann, Nomadische Streifereien unter den Kalmüken, iii. 152.

[5] Colquhoun, Amongst the Shans, p. 75.

and religious ceremonies generally.[1]   The Maldive Islanders
are said to be so fond of change that many a man marries
and divorces the same woman three or four times in the
course of his life.[2]   Among some of the Dyaks there are
few middle-aged men who have not had several wives, and
instances have been known of young women of seventeen
or eighteen who had already lived with three or four husbands.[3]   Speaking of the Southern Massim of British New
Guinea, Professor Seligman says "there is no doubt that
formerly many perfectly valid marriages lasted only a
short time, being dissolved by mutual agreement or without
any strong opposition, and where government and missionary influence has not been exerted this is still the
case."[4]   Among the Kiwai Papuans many men have had
some twenty wives in the course of their lives.[5]   In Nauru,
one of the Marshall Islands, Senfft knew a man, at most
twenty-four years of age, who had already had eleven
wives ; some of them had deserted him and others had
been divorced by him.[6]   Sometimes it is the young people
who are said to be particularly addicted to divorce.[7]
Among certain American Eskimo " a great many changes
take place before a permanent choice is made," whereas
" a union once apparently settled between parties grown up
is rarely dissolved."[8]   Among the Chukchee the marriage
tie is broken very easily, and for a variety of reasons,
advanced by either the wife's or the husband's family ;
but if a couple have lived together for a year or a year and
a half it is no longer regarded as proper for the husband's
family to send the wife back.[9]

[1] Gait, *Census of India*, 1911, vol. i. (India) Report, p. 245.

[2] Rosset, ' On the Maldive Islands,' in *Jour. Anthr. Inst.* xvi. 169

[3] St. John, ' Wild Tribes of the North-West Coast of Borneo,'
in *Trans. Ethn. Soc. London*, N.S. ii. 237.

[4] Seligman, *Melanesians of British New Guinea*, p. 510.

[5] Landtman, *Nva Guinea färden*, p. 81.

[6] Senfft, ' Die Insel Nauru,' in *Mittheil. Deutsch. Schutzgeb.* ix. 106.

[7] Cardús, *Las Misiones Franciscanas entre los infieles de Bolivia*,
p. 254 (Matacos).

[8] Simpson, quoted with approval by Murdoch, ' Ethnological
Results of the Point Barrow Expedition,' in *Ann. Rep. Bur. Ethnol.*
ix. 412.   [9] Bogoras, *Chukchee*, p. 597.

Owing to the defective character of the information at our disposal it is impossible to say anything definite about the comparative prevalence of lifelong unions and of divorce among the lower races in general, or about the duration of marriage at the different grades of economic culture compared with one another. But the durability of marriage among some of the lower hunters and incipient agriculturists is certainly very striking.[1]

Somewhat more definite than the information we possess of the actual prevalence of divorce among the simpler peoples are the statements as to the circumstances in which their customs allow it to be practised. Among a large number of tribes the husband is said to be able to dissolve the marriage at will or on the slightest grounds or pretexts, and in the majority of these cases a similar right is granted to the wife. This is borne out by my own materials as well as by the figures given by Messrs. Hobhouse, Wheeler, and Ginsberg.[2] Of certain tribes we are only told explicitly that the wife can leave at will. In some, or most, of these tribes the husband presumably possesses the same power; [3] but this is not the case among all of them.

Among the Jíbaros of Ecuador the husband is said to be at liberty not only to repudiate but to kill his wife;[4] the Apache warrior may at any time dissolve his marriage; [5] and among the Caribs of the Lesser Antilles, while a married

---

[1] See also Schmidt, *Die Stellung der Pygmäenvölker in der Entwicklungsgeschichte des Menschen*, p. 162.

[2] Hobhouse, Wheeler, and Ginsberg, *Material Culture and Social Institutions of the Simpler Peoples*, p. 164 *sq.* Out of 271½ cases of divorce there are 61½ in which divorce is at the will of the husband and 131½ which are classed under the heading "divorce at will of the parties." The latter include cases in which divorce is said to be simple, easy, or frequent; cases in which the only condition to be observed is the repayment of the bride price, unless we are specially told that the price is so heavy as to make divorce difficult; cases in which incompatibility, neglect, or ill-treatment on either side is sufficient to break the union; and cases of mutual consent (*ibid.* p. 146 *sq.*). The last-mentioned cases are not very numerous.

[3] *Cf. ibid.* p. 147.

[4] Rivet, 'Les Indiens Jibaros,' in *L'Anthropologie*, xviii. 608.

[5] Cremony, *Life among the Apaches*, p. 249.

man could abandon his wife at will, the latter could leave her husband only with his consent.[1] But the general custom of the American Indians seems to have been that the marriage tie could be broken with the greatest facility by either party.[2] Among the Pima Indians of Arizona the woman usually took the initiative, by either going to the home of her parents or going away with another man.[3] Among the Guarayos of Bolivia it was nearly always the wife who abandoned her husband.[4] Among the Witoto and Boro of the North-West Amazons a man who divorces his wife lays himself open to severe tribal censure should the consensus of opinion be that he had no good

[1] Du Tertre, *Histoire générale des Antilles*, ii. 379. Among the Sauk and Foxes a deserted husband could oblige his wife to return to him if he pleased (Forsyth, ' Account of the Manners and Customs of the Sauk and Fox Nations of Indians Tradition,' in Emma Helen Blair, *op. cit.* ii. 215).

[2] Lozano, *op. cit.* p. 70 ; Charlevoix, *History of Paraguay*, i. 91 *sq.* ; Sánchez Labrador, *op. cit.* ii. 24 ; do Prado, in *O Patriota*, 1814, no. iv. 21 (Guaycurûs). Kohler, *Pater Florian Bauche*, p. 316 (Mocobis). Azara, *op. cit.* ii. 93 (Guanas). Church, *Aborigines of South America*, p. 106 *sq.* (Mojos of South-West Amazonia). von den Steinen, *Unter den Naturvölkern Zentral-Brasiliens*, p. 332 (Bakaïrí). Bell, *op. cit.* p. 261 (Mosquito Indians). Bossu, *op. cit.* i. 128 (Illinois). Anho, *op. cit.* p. 249 (Shawnee). Speck, *Family Hunting Territories and Social Life of Various Algonkian Bands of the Ottawa Valley*, p. 24 (Timagami band of the Ojibway ; formerly). *Idem, Ethnology of the Yuchi Indians*, p. 95. Parkman, *Jesuits in North America in the Seventeenth Century*, p. xxxiv. (Hurons). Harrington, ' Preliminary Sketch of Lenápe Culture,' in *American Anthropologist*, N.S. xv. 215 (Delaware Indians). Turner, ' Ethnology of the Ungava District, Hudson Bay Territory,' in *Ann. Rep. Bur. Ethnol.* xi. 270 (Nenenot). Lahontan, *New Voyages to North America*, ii. 453, 457 *sq.* (Canadian Indians). Bancroft, *op. cit.* i. 277 (Inland Columbians). Schoolcraft, *op. cit.* iv. 223 *sq.* (Bonak of California). McCoy, *History of Baptist Indian Missions*, p. 25 *sq.* Kohler, ' Die Rechte der Urvölker Nordamerikas,' in *Zeitschr. f. vergl. Rechtswiss.* xii. 387 *sq.* Hodge, *Handbook of American Indians north of Mexico*, i. 810.

[3] Russell, ' Pima Indians,' in *Ann. Rep. Bur. American Ethnol.* xxvi. 184.

[4] Cardús, *op. cit.* p. 72. Among the Guanas " le divorce est libre aux deux sexes, comme tout le reste, et les femmes y sont très-portées " (Azara, *op. cit.* ii. 93).

reason for doing so ; but " a woman is never blamed for deserting her husband, on the presumption that such unnatural procedure would alone be due to the fact that she had been not only ill-treated but grossly ill-treated by him."[1] Among the Eskimo divorce is practically unrestricted, and wives are in this respect as free to suit themselves as are their husbands.[2] Among the Ainu " it was just as easy, and considered just as possible for a woman to cast off her husband as for a man to divorce his wife. . . . A woman might dissolve her connection with her husband for the reason of adultery, dislike to him, idleness, inability to keep the larder supplied with fish and animal food."[3] Among the Gold of the Amoor, on the other hand, though a man can send his wife back to her parents, the wife has no right to part from her husband.[4] Among the Mongols a husband can divorce his wife at will, but a wife may also desert a husband who is not affectionate.[5]

Among many of the tribes and low castes of India marriage may be dissolved at the will of the husband, but in nearly all such cases known to me it may also be dissolved at the will of the wife.[6] In several instances it is the woman's

---

[1] Whiffen, North-West Amazons, p. 166.

[2] Murdoch, loc. cit. p. 411 sq. Boas, ' Central Eskimo,' in Ann. Rep. Bur. Ethnol. vi. 579. Turner, loc. cit. p. 189 (Koksoagmiut of the Ungava district ; " the one who so desires leaves with little ceremony, but is sometimes sought for and compelled to return "). Hodge, op. cit. i. 809. Gilbertson, Some Ethical Phases of Eskimo Culture, p. 69 sq.

[3] Batchelor, Ainu and their Folk-Lore, p. 233. We are told, however, that the matter is settled by the eldest of the clan (Miss Czaplicka, op. cit. p. 104).

[4] Laufer, in American Anthropologist, N.S. ii. 321.

[5] Prejevalsky, Mongolia, i. 70.

[6] Hodgson, Miscellaneous Essays relating to Indian Subjects, i. 402 (Kirántis). White, Sikhim and Bhutan, p. 321. Shakespear, Lushei Kuki Clans, p. 52. Hutchinson, Account of the Chittagong Hill Tracts, p. 156 (Tipperahs). Carey and Tuck, Chin Hills, i. 210. Hayavadana Rao, ' Gonds of the Eastern Ghauts,' in Anthropos, v. 795. Dahmen, ' Paliyans, a Hill-Tribe of the Palni Hills (South India),' ibid. iii. 27. Hough, Letters on the Climate, Inhabitants, Productions, &c. of the Neilgherries, p. 108 ; Ward, in Grigg, Manual of the Nílagiri District, Appendix, p. lxxvii. (Kotas). Cox, Madras

right to desert her husband at pleasure that is particularly mentioned.[1] Among the Badagas of the Nilgiris, for example, a woman " can change husbands as often as she pleases by a simple system of divorce " ;[2] and among the Irulas, living in the same neighbourhood, the option of remaining in union or of separating is expressly said to rest principally with the wife.[3] Among many tribes in the Indian Archipelago and the islands of the Pacific Ocean the marriage bond may be severed at the will of either party.[4] Sometimes,

District Manuals : North Arcot, i. 235 (Paraiyans, the agricultural labourers of the Tamil districts of North Arcot), 250 (Yánádis). Nelson, *Madura Country*, ii. 51 (Kallans). Kannan Nayar, in *Malabar Quarterly Review*, vii. 190 *sq.* ; Gopal Panikkar, *Malabar and its Folk*, p. 22 ; Anantha Krishna Iyer, *Cochin Tribes and Castes*, ii. 42 (Nayars ; the last-mentioned writer, however, also says that marriage can be dissolved only with the consent of the elders of the family). Gait, *op. cit.* p. 245.

[1] Ward, in Grigg, *op. cit.* Appendix, p. lxxvii. (Kotas). Cox, *op. cit.* i. 213 (Malayális of North Arcot). Nelson, *op. cit.* ii. 34 (Kunnuvans in the Madura country). Gait, *op. cit.* p. 245.

[2] Thurston, *Castes and Tribes of Southern India*, i. 105. See also Hough, *op. cit.* p. 92 ; Ward, in Grigg, *op. cit.* Appendix, p. lxxi.

[3] Harkness, *Description of a Singular Race inhabiting the Neilgherry Hills*, p. 92.

[4] Hornaday, *Two Years in the Jungle*, p. 453 (Hill Dyaks). Gomes, *Seventeen Years among the Sea Dyaks of Borneo*, pp. 69, 128 ; Brooke Low, quoted by Ling Roth, *Natives of Sarawak*, i. 128 (Sea Dyaks ; if there are no children). Hagen, *Die Orang Kubu auf Sumatra*, p. 134 ; Volz, ' Zur Kenntniss der Kubus in Südsumatra,' in *Archiv f. Anthrop.* N.S. vii. 104. Moszkowski, *op. cit.* p. 106 (Sakai of Sumatra). Mallat, *Les Philippines*, ii. 121 (Negritos of the Philippines ; *cf.* Bowring, *Visit to the Philippine Islands*, p. 173, and Mozo, *op. cit.* p. 108). Jenks, *Bontoc Igorot*, p. 69 ; *cf.* de Mas, *Informe sobre el estado de las Islas Filipinas en* 1842, ii. Poblacion, p. 18 (Igorot). *Ibid.* i. 20 (Tagals at the time of the arrival of the Spaniards). Worcester, *Philippine Islands and their People*, p. 108 (Tagbanuas of Palawan). Bink, in *Bull. Soc. d'Anthr. Paris*, ser. iii. xi. 397 (natives of Dorey) ; Moszkowski, ' Die Völkerstämme am Mamberamo in Holländisch-Neuguinea,' in *Zeitschr. f. Ethnol.* xliii. 339 ; Chalmers, *Pioneering in New Guinea*, p. 167 ; Guise, ' On the Tribes inhabiting the mouth of the Wanigela River, New Guinea,' in *Jour. Anthr. Inst.* xxviii. 209 (the wife may desert a husband who is distasteful to her) ; Williamson, ' Some unrecorded Customs of the Mekeo People of British New Guinea,' in *Jour. Roy.*

though rarely, only the husband's right of sending away his
wife whenever he pleases is spoken of ;[1] and in Samoa a
husband can dissolve the marriage without the consent of
the wife, although the wife cannot do so without the consent
of the husband, unless she be his superior in rank.[2] Among
the Mekeo people of British New Guinea,[3] and in various
Melanesian islands,[4] where divorce is easily effected by either
husband or wife, it is easier for the former than for the
latter ; but among the Sakai of Sumatra the reverse is the
case,[5] and among the Inland Papuans of Dutch New Guinea[6]

Anthr. Inst. xliii. 277 ; *Idem, Mafulu Mountain People of British
New Guinea*, p. 174 (though formal divorce or separation does not
exist, a dissatisfied husband or wife can easily dissolve the marriage) ;
Vetter, ' Papuanische Rechtsverhältnisse, wie solche namentlich bei
den Jabim beobachtet wurden,' in *Nachrichten über Kaiser Wilhelms-
Land und den Bismarck-Archipel*, 1897, p. 91 (as among the Mafulu).
Parkinson, *Dreissig Jahre in der Südsee*, p. 267 (natives of New
Hanover and New Ireland). Hahl, *loc. cit.* p. 77 (some natives of
the Gazelle Peninsula of New Britain ; *cf.* Schnee, *Bilder aus der
Südsee*, p. 99). Codrington, *Melanesians*, p. 244. Christian,
Caroline Islands, p. 73 (natives of Ponapé). Senfft, ' Die Marshall-
Insulaner,' in Steinmetz, *Rechtsverhältnisse von eingeborenen Völkern
in Afrika und Ozeanien*, p. 436 ; *Idem*, ' Die Insel Nauru,' in *Mittheil.
Deutsch. Schutzgeb.* ix. 106. Waitz-Gerland, *op. cit.* vol. v. pt. ii.
106 *sq.* (Ladrone Islanders). Jarves, *History of the Hawaiian Islands*,
p. 42 ; Lisiansky, *Voyage round the World*, p. 127 *sq.* (Hawaians).
Mangeret, *Mgr Bataillon et les missions de l'Océanie Centraie*, i. 243
(natives of Futuna). Ellis, *Polynesian Researches*, i. 256 ; Turnbull,
Voyage round the World, p. 338 (Tahitians). Geiseler, *Die Oster-
Insel*, p. 29 *sq.* (Easter Islanders).

[1] v. Brenner, *Besuch bei den Kannibalen Sumatras*, p. 250 (Battas ;
according to Junghuhn [*Die Battaländer auf Sumatra*, ii. 134], the
wife can also dissolve the marriage, but the payment which has to
be made to the divorced husband makes it difficult or almost
impossible for her to avail herself of this right). Kubary, ' Die
Palau-Inseln in der Südsee,' in *Jour. d. Museum Godeffroy*, iv. 54
(if the wife is poor). Burger, *Die Küsten- und Bergvölker der Gazellehalbinsel*, p. 55 (mountaineers of the Gazelle Peninsula of New
Britain). Mariner, *op. cit.* ii. 173 (Tonga Islanders).

[2] v. Bülow, ' Die Ehegesetze der Samoaner,' in *Globus*, lxxiii. 185.

[3] Williamson, in *Jour. Roy. Anthr. Inst.* xliii. 277 *sq.*

[4] Codrington, *op. cit.* p. 244.

[5] Moszkowski, *Auf neuen Wegen durch Sumatra*, p. 106.

[6] *Idem*, in *Zeitschr. f. Ethnol.* xliii. 339.

and the Mafulu mountain people of British New Guinea[1] it is also mostly the wife who leaves the husband. Among the Australian natives marriage is looked upon as a privilege acquired by the man and as an obligation binding on the woman.[2] It seems that the husband is generally allowed to send away his wife at pleasure,[3] although this is not a rule which is quite without exceptions ;[4] but I am aware of no case in which the wife can dissolve the marriage at will, unless it be by eloping with another man.[5]

Among many African peoples—apart from those having Muhammadan law—a man can repudiate his wife whenever he pleases,[6] and of some of them it is expressly said that the corresponding right is denied the wife.[7] In Madagascar, where the man was generally at perfect liberty to divorce his wife, the latter could only in rare cases claim divorce ; but she could separate from her husband without being permitted to marry anybody else.[8] Among the Herero a man may at any time send away his wife ; but the wife can also desert her husband, and although he in theory is

---

[1] Williamson, *Mafulu Mountain People of British New Guinea,* p. 174.   [2] See Malinowski, *op. cit.* p. 62 *sq.*

[3] See, *e.g.*, Beveridge, *Aborigines of Victoria and Riverina*, p. 22 ; Hill and Thornton, *Notes on the Aborigines of New South Wales*, p. 7.

[4] See *infra*, p. 287 *sq.*   [5] See *supra*, ii. 324 *sqq.*

[6] Schinz, *Deutsch-Süd-West-Afrika*, p. 311 (Ovambo). Decle, *Three Years in Savage Africa*, p. 233 (natives of the Portuguese Zambesi). Fraser, *Winning a Primitive People*, p. 155 (Tumbuka of British Central Africa). Baumann, *Durch Massailand zur Nilquelle*, p. 190 (Wanyaturu). Tessmann, *Die Pangwe*, ii. 263. Sarbah, *Fanti Customary Laws*, p. 52 ; Connolly, 'Social Life in Fanti-Land,' in *Jour. Anthr. Inst.* xxvi. 145. Torday and Joyce, 'Notes on the Ethnography of the Ba-Mbala,' in *Jour. Anthr. Inst.* xxxv. 411. *Iidem,* 'Notes on the Ethnography of the Ba-Yaka,' *ibid.* xxxvi. 45. Johnston, *George Grenfell and the Congo*, ii. 676 (unless the wife has borne two or more children to her husband; see *infra*, p. 288). de Espinosa, *Guanches of Tenerife*, p. 35.

[7] Magyar, *Reisen in Süd-Afrika*, p. 284 (Kimbunda). Decle, *op. cit.* p. 160 (Matabele). Kraft, 'Die Wapokomo,' in Steinmetz, *op. cit.* p. 287 *sq.* Desoignies, 'Die Msalala,' *ibid.* p. 274. Nassau, *Fetichism in West Africa*, p. 10 ("marriage can be dissolved by divorce at almost any time, and for almost any reason, by the man— by a woman rarely ").

[8] Grandidier, *Ethnographie de Madagascar*, ii. 230, 231, 236.

entitled to fetch her back he does not avail himself of this right in practice.[1] Among the Bogos of North-Eastern Africa the ordinary divorce depends on the free decision of the husband ; but if the wife three times runs away to her father's house, he can no longer claim her back and she is at liberty to marry again.[2] In Africa, also, the same right to dissolve the marriage at will as belongs to the husband is frequently granted to the wife ;[3] and in various cases her right to divorce herself is particularly emphasised,[4] whilst

[1] Brincker, ' Charakter, Sitten und Gebräuche speciell der Bantu Deutsch-Südwestafrikas,' in *Mittheil. d. Seminars f. orientalische Sprachen an der Universität zu Berlin*, vol. iii. pt. iii. 85. Kohler, ' Das Recht der Herero,' in *Zeitschr. f. vergl. Rechtswiss.* xiv. 302.

[2] Munzinger, *Ueber die Sitten und das Recht der Bogos*, pp. 60, 61, 64.

[3] Theal, *Yellow and Dark-skinned People of Africa south of the Zambesi*, p. 47 (Bushmen ; " any disagreement was sufficient to cause the separation of the man and woman "). Le Vaillant, *Travels from the Cape of Good-Hope, into the Interior Parts of Africa*, ii. 69 *sq.* (Hottentots). Stow, *Native Races of South Africa*, p. 260 (Mountain Damara). Richter, ' Der Bezirk Bukoba,' in *Mittheil. Deutsch. Schutzgeb.* xii. 85. Baumann, *Usambara*, p. 47 *sq.* (natives of the Tanga coast). Volkens, *Der Kilimandscharo*, p. 252 (Wadshagga). New, *Life, Wanderings, &c. in Eastern Africa*, p. 120 (Wanika). Condon, ' Contribution to the Ethnography of the Basoga-Batamba, Uganda Protectorate,' in *Anthropos*, vi. 372 ; Avon, ' Vie sociale des Wabende au Tanganika,' *ibid.* x.–xi. 102. Munzinger, *Ostafrikanische Studien*, p. 489 (Kunáma). Tellier, ' Kreis Kita, Französischer Sudan,' in Steinmetz, *op. cit.* p. 156. Clozel and Villamur, *Les coutumes indigènes de la Côte d'Ivoire*, p. 103 (Baoulé). Delafosse, ' Les Agni,' in *L'Anthropologie*, iv. 429. Ruelle, ' Notes sur quelques populations noires du 2ᵉ territoire militaire de l'Afrique occidentale française,' *ibid.* xv. 662 (Lobi). Poupon, Étude ethnographique des Baya de la circonscription du M'Bimou,' *ibid.* xxvi. 127. Torday and Joyce, *Les Bushongo*, pp. 114, 116. Delhaise, *Les Warega*, p. 183. Hutereau, *Notes sur la Vie familiale et juridique de quelques populations du Congo Belge*, p. 4 (Batua).

[4] Dundas, ' Wawanga and other Tribes of the Elgon District, British East Africa,' in *Jour. Roy. Anthr. Inst.* xliii. 55. Roscoe, *Northern Bantu*, p. 211 (Basoga). Cunningham, *Uganda and its Peoples*, pp. 140 (Bavuma), 266 (Bakonjo, inhabiting the slopes of Mount Ruwenzori). Hobley, *Eastern Uganda*, p. 29 (Nilotic Kavirondo). Talbot, ' Buduma of Lake Chad,' in *Jour. Roy. Anthr. Inst.* xli. 247. Cruickshank, *op. cit.* ii. 197 *sq.* (Gold Coast natives).

in some of them the husband evidently is not equally free
to effect a divorce.[1]   Among the Bakene, a Bantu tribe of
Busoga, the bride holds the right to break off the marriage
and refuse to remain with the man, should she during the
first four to ten days discover any reason for disliking him.[2]
In Garenganze in Central Africa a wife " may leave her
husband at any time, if she cares to do so."[3]   In the Nouaer
tribes in the Upper Nile basin, should the wife be unhappy
and unable to live with her husband, she goes to her parents
or her nearest relative ; and in case her husband refuses
to support her she is given in marriage to another.[4]   Among
the Cross River natives, if husband and wife disagree and
perhaps come to blows and the latter runs away to another
man, she cannot be forced to return, but the first husband
must be repaid all his courting expenses.[5]   We shall subsequently see that, especially where a price has been paid for
the bride, the liberty to dissolve the marriage tie is frequently restricted by the economic loss suffered by the party
who dissolves it or, if the wife deserts her husband, by her
family.[6]

The liberty may also in other respects be less than it
appears to be.   In Tonga, where a man divorced his wife
by simply telling her that she might go,[7] and in Hawaii,
where either party could separate at will,[8] it was considered
disgraceful to separate after the marriage had lasted for
some time.[9]   Among the Káfirs of the Hindu-Kush,
" although divorce is theoretically simple, and usually is
so in practice, yet with well-born wives the woman's family
and public opinion have sometimes to be considered. . . .
If the husband simply tired of her and wanted to get rid of
her out of the village, there might be obstacles raised by

---

[1] Baumstark, ' Die Warangi,' in *Mittheil. Deutsch. Schutzgeb.*
xiii. 54. O'Sullivan, ' Dinka Laws and Customs,' in *Jour. Roy.
Anthr. Inst.* xl. 182.

[2] Roscoe, *Northern Bantu*, p. 150.   [3] Arnot, *Garenganze*, p. 194.

[4] Petherick, *Travels in Central Africa*, i. 320.

[5] Partridge, *Cross River Natives*, p. 255 sq.   [6] *Infra*, pp. 293–295.

[7] Mariner, *op. cit.* ii. 173.   [8] Jarves, *op. cit.* p. 42.

[9] West, *Ten Years in South-Central Polynesia*, p. 270 (Tonga).
Jarves, *op. cit.* p. 43 (Hawai).

her family against his doing so."[1]   Among the Muduvars
of South India, though "in theory a man may divorce his
wife at will, . . . it is scarcely etiquette to do so, except
for infidelity, or in the case of incompatibility of temper " ;
on the other hand, " a woman cannot divorce her husband
at all in theory, but she can make his life so unbearable
that he gladly allows her to palm herself off on somebody
else."[2]   Divorce is thus in some cases easier in theory than
in practice, but in other cases easier in practice than in
theory.   To the latter cases also belong those in which
divorce can be effected " on the slightest pretext."   We
thus gradually pass to peoples whose customs permit
divorce only under certain conditions, apart from such
economic measures as the forfeiture or the returning of the
bride price or the payment of a fine.

Among many of the simpler peoples marriage can only be
dissolved by mutual consent, unless it be for some very
cogent reason, or one of the parties cannot effect divorce
against the will of the other ; and although in such cases
the husband's consent is probably more often required than
the wife's, there are also many cases in which the wife's
wishes have to be consulted.[3]   Among the Santals divorce
is said to be easy, but cannot take place without the consent
of both husband and wife.[4]   Although divorce is common
among the Khasis, the rule is that both parties must agree.[5]
Among the Garos divorce is permitted when the husband
and wife disagree and the separation is by mutual consent,
when either party is guilty of adultery, or when either the
husband or the wife refuses to work for the support of the

---

[1] Scott Robertson, *Káfirs of the Hindu-Kush*, p. 536 *sq.*
[2] Thurston, *op. cit.* v. 94.
[3] Wilken, *Over de verwantschap en het huwelijks- en erfrecht bij
de volken van het maleische ras*, p. 54 (Timorese).   Bourien, in *Trans.
Ethn. Soc. London*, N.S. iii. 80 (Mantra).   Lewin, *Wild Races of
South-Eastern India*, p. 194 (Toungtha).   Cunningham, ' Notes on
Moorcroft's Travels in Ladakh,' in *Jour. Asiatic Soc. Bengal*,
vol. xiii. pt. i. 204.   See also Post, *Grundriss der ethnologischen
Jurisprudenz*, ii. 118.
[4] Hertel, *Indisk Hjemmemission blandt Santalerne*, p. 83 *sq.*
[5] Gurdon, *op. cit.* p. 79.

household.[1] In the Nicobar Islands, according to Mr. Lowis, divorce is effected simply by mutual consent when there are no children, whereas, when there are children, it is a matter for arbitration.[2] Among the Warangi of the former German East Africa a wife who is tired of her husband can return to her father's house, but no wife can be compelled to leave her husband against her will.[3]

The birth of a child may make the marriage indissoluble. Among the Lengua Indians of the Paraguayan Chaco, if the wife does not become a mother within a reasonable time, the couple are justified in separating ; " but when once a child is born to them, even should the child die or be put to death, they are considered to be bound to each other for life."[4] So also among the Illinois a man could not separate from his wife when he had had children by her.[5] The Red Karens in Indo-China allow divorce if there are no children ; " but should there be one child, the parents are not permitted to separate."[6] Among the Mikirs "divorce is rare, but permissible if there is no offspring, or if the girl goes home after marriage and refuses to return to her husband."[7] Among the Kukis, " if a woman has a son by her husband, the marriage is indissoluble," although if they do not agree and have no son the husband can cast off his wife and take another.[8] In the tribes of Western Victoria described by Mr. Dawson a man can divorce a childless wife for serious misconduct, though in every case the charge against her

[1] Playfair, *Garos*, p. 70.

[2] Lowis, *Census of India*, 1911, vol. ii. (Andaman and Nicobar Islands), p. 100. According to Bille (*Beretning om Corvetten Galatheas's Reise omkring Jorden*, i. 447), divorce is by mutual consent. Kloss says (*op. cit.* p. 237 *sq.*) that it " is a matter for the two most concerned only," and that the woman as often divorces her husband as *vice versâ*. According to Chopard (' A few Particulars respecting the Nicobar Islands,' in *Jour. Indian Archipelago*, iii. 273), a man dismisses his wife for the slightest motive and takes another.

[3] Baumstark, in *Mittheil. Deutsch. Schutzgeb.* xiii. 54.

[4] Grubb, *An Unknown People in an Unknown Land*, p. 214.

[5] Perrot, ' Memoir on the Manners, Customs, and Religion of the Savages of North America,' in Emma Helen Blair, *op. cit.* i. 66 n. 42.

[6] Colquhoun, *op. cit.* p. 64.

[7] Stack, *op. cit.* p. 20.

[8] Lewin, *op. cit.* p. 276.

must first be laid before the chiefs of his own and his wife's tribes and their consent to her punishment obtained ; but if the wife has children she cannot be divorced.[1] Among the Masai, according to Mr. Hollis, it is only barren women who may be divorced.[2] The Nandi permit a man to divorce a barren wife who is a bad woman but not a wife who has had a child, though the husband and wife may live apart.[3] Speaking of certain tribes along the Upper Wele and Bomokandi and Upper Rubi Rivers, Mr. Grenfell states that a woman who has borne two or more children to her husband cannot be divorced.[4]

We are frequently told that a man must not divorce his wife and a wife not separate from her husband without just or good cause.[5] The ideas as to what constitutes such a cause vary among different tribes. The most generally recognised ground for divorce is probably adultery on the part of the wife. In many cases it seems to be the only, or almost the only, ground.[6] On the other hand, we also hear of uncivilised

---

[1] Dawson, *Australian Aborigines*, p. 33.

[2] Hollis, in *Jour. Roy. Anthr. Inst.* xl. 481. See, however, *infra*, pp. 292 n. 9, 295 n.

[3] *Idem, Nandi*, p. 69.

[4] Johnston, *George Grenfell and the Congo*, ii. 676.

[5] Charlevoix, *Voyage to North-America*, ii. 37 (Algonkin). Goddard, *Life and Culture of the Hupa*, p. 56. Hodson, *Nāga Tribes of Manipur*, p. 97 (Tangkhuls). Best, ' Maori Marriage Customs,' in *Trans. and Proceed. New Zealand Institute*, xxxvi. 62. Alberti, *op. cit.* p. 140 (Kafirs).

[6] Dunbar, in *Magazine of American History*, iv. 267 ; Grinnell, in *American Anthropologist*, iv. 280 (Pawnee). Perrot, *loc. cit.* p. 64 *sq.* (Ottawa). Soppitt, *op. cit.* p. 15 (Kukis). Endle, *op. cit.* pp. 85 (Rábhás), 86 (Hajongs), 95 (Ahom Chutiyas). Bainbridge, ' Saorias of the Rajmahal Hills,' in *Memoirs Asiatic Soc. Bengal*, ii. 58. Anantha Krishna Iyer, *op. cit.* i. 32 (Nattu Malayans, a jungle tribe in the Cochin State). Riedel, *op. cit.* pp. 134, 263, 325, 351, 448 (natives of Ceram, Aru Islands, Sermatta Islands, Babber, and Wetter, in the Indian Archipelago). Wilken, *op. cit.* p. 51 (natives of Buru). Reed, *Negritos of Zambales*, p. 61 (if a man divorces his wife for any other reason than desertion or unfaithfulness her relatives are likely to cause trouble). Trenk, in *Mittheil. Deutsch. Schutzgeb.* xxiii. 168 (Namib Bushmen ; marriage can be dissolved only if the wife commits adultery or is barren).

peoples who do not consider a man justified in repudiating his wife on account of adultery, even though he may do so for some other cause. Dr. Rivers was told among the Todas that a man divorces his wife for two reasons only, the first being that she is a fool and the second that she will not work ; whereas intercourse with another man is not regarded as a reason for divorce, but rather as a perfectly natural occurrence.[1] Among the Mikirs the village council inflicts a fine on the man who commits adultery with another man's wife ; but after the fine is paid the husband has to take his wife back, unless there are no children, when he may refuse to do so.[2] Among the Moráns of Assam divorce is only permitted when the wife is guilty of adultery with a man of lower caste-standing than her own.[3] In the island of Mabuiag in Torres Straits the chief reasons for divorce appear to have been sterility and infidelity, and sometimes incompatibility of temper was regarded as sufficient ground for it ; but a native stated that a first wife could be divorced only for sterility.[4] Among the Dinka the husband may for various causes sue for " breaking of marriage," but his wife's unfaithfulness is not one of them, provided she be willing to remain in his enclosure.[5] Among the Basuto " sterility is the only cause of divorce which is not subject to litigation."[6] The Herero[7] and the Shambaa of East Africa[8] allow a man to divorce his wife on account of " repeated adultery " ; whereas in some tribes of Sierra Leone not even continuous adultery is alone sufficient cause for the man driving away his wife and claiming back what he has paid for her.[9] Among the Mossi of the Western Sudan a husband can send back his wife to her

---

[1] Rivers, *Todas*, p. 526 *sq.*   [2] Stack, *op. cit.* p. 19.

[3] Endle, *op. cit.* p. 89.

[4] Rivers, in *Reports of the Cambridge Anthropological Expedition to Torres Straits*, v. 246.

[5] O'Sullivan, in *Jour. Roy. Anthr. Inst.* xl. 182.

[6] Casalis, *Basutos*, p. 184 *sq.*   [7] Dannert, *Zum Rechte der Herero*, p. 46

[8] Dahlgrün, ' Heiratsgebräuche der Schambaa,' in *Mittheil. Deutsch. Schutzgeb.* xvi. 227.

[9] Vergette, *Certain Marriage Customs of some of the Tribes in the Protectorate of Sierra Leone*, p. 27.

parents if she is thievish or lazy or, especially, if she is
unfaithful to him, but even in the last-mentioned case his
action is disapproved of ; " he who repudiates his wife will
find all doors closed for him, and he will be unable to procure
new wives."[1] Among some peoples the wife is said to have
a right to divorce a husband who is guilty of adultery.[2]
A very frequent cause of divorce is barrenness in the
wife ;[3] and it is so not only where the husband may repudiate
his wife at will, but also where his right of divorcing her is
restricted. Among some peoples a childless wife is exchanged

---

[1] Mangin, ' Les Mossi,' in *Anthropos*, ix. 481.
[2] Lumholtz, *op. cit.* i. 465 (Tepehuane of Mexico). Playfair,
Garos, p. 70. Riedel, *op. cit.* pp. 134, 448 (natives of Ceram and
Wetter). Seligman, *Melanesians of British New Guinea*, p. 511
(Southern Massim). Fülleborn, *Das Deutsche Njassa- und Ruwuma-
Gebiet*, p. 61 (Wamuera).
[3] Whiffen, *North-West Amazons*, p. 168 (Witoto and Boro).
de Lodi, ' Extrait d'une lettre au *P.* André d'Arezzo,' in *Annales
de la propagation de la Foi*, xvii. 415 (Botocudos). Forsyth, in
Emma Helen Blair, *op. cit.* ii. 215 (Sauk and Foxes). Dixon, ' Notes
on the Achomawi and Atsugewi Indians of Northern California,' in
American Anthropologist, N.S. x. 217. Egede, *Description of Greenland*, p. 143. Dall, *Alaska and its Resources*, p. 139 (Western
Eskimo). Laufer, in *American Anthropologist*, N.S. ii. 321 (Gold of
the middle portion of the Amoor). Rossillon, Mœurs et coutumes
du peuple *Kui*, Indes Anglaises,' in *Anthropos*, vii. 100 (Kandhs).
Kloss, *op. cit.* p. 237 (Nicobarese). Strzoda, ' Die Li auf Hainan,'
in *Zeitschr. f. Ethnol.* xliii. 203. Jenks, *Bontoc Igorot*, p. 69. Gomes,
op. cit. p. 128 (Sea Dyaks). Seligman, *op. cit.* p. 511 (Southern
Massim of British New Guinea). Trenk, in *Mittheil. Deutsch.
Schutzgeb.* xxiii. 168 (Namib Bushmen). Casalis, *Basutos*, p. 184 *sq.*
Kidd, *The Essential Kafir*, p. 226. Tyler, *Forty Years among the
Zulus*, p. 119. v. François, *Nama und Damara Deutsch-Süd-West-
Afrika*, p. 200 (Herero). Gouldsbury and Sheane, *Great Plateau
of Northern Rhodesia*, p. 170 (Awemba). v. Rosen, *Träskfolket*,
p. 421 (Balenge of Northern Rhodesia). Junod, *Life of a South
African Tribe*, i. 188 (Thonga of South-Eastern Africa). Fülleborn,
op. cit. p. 350 (Konde people). Beverley, ' Die Wagogo,' in Steinmetz, *op. cit.* p. 210. Lang, ' Die Waschambala,' *ibid.* p. 231
(Shambaa). Wilson and Felkin, *Uganda and the Egyptian Soudan*,
ii. 48 (Banyoro). Roscoe, *Northern Bantu*, p. 174 (Bagesu).
O'Sullivan, in *Jour. Roy. Anthr. Inst.* xl. 182 (Dinka). Sarbah,
op. cit. p. 52 (Fanti). Cruickshank, *op. cit.* ii. 196 (Gold Coast
natives). Buchner, *Kamerun*, p. 31 (Dualla). See also Post,

for a marriageable sister.¹ Again, the wife can effect
divorce if the husband proves to be impotent.² Among the
people on the Lower Congo, if the bridegroom is unable to
consummate the marriage it is broken off and the money
returned, though sometimes he finds a substitute, a suitable
young man, who is permitted to have intercourse with his
wife ; and if a childless wife can prove that her husband is
to blame, she can procure a divorce from him, and he then
becomes the butt of the village wits.³

There are other recognised grounds for divorce. A man
may divorce his wife if she is lazy and neglects her household
duties or other work incumbent upon her ;⁴ if she does not
cook his food properly ;⁵ if she neglects her children⁶ or all

Grundriss der ethnologischen Jurisprudenz, ii. 114 *sq.*—On the other
hand, barrenness is not recognised as sufficient ground of divorce,
for example, among the Todas (Rivers, *op. cit.* p. 526), the Koita
of British New Guinea (Seligman, *op. cit.* p. 80), the Xosa Kafirs
(Kropf, *Das Volk der Xosa-Kaffern im östlichen Südafrika*, p. 154),
and the Wanyamwezi (Decle, *op. cit.* p. 347).

¹ Koslowski, quoted by Schmidt, ' Die Guató,' in *Verhandl.
Berliner Gesellsch. Anthr.* 1902, p. 88. Theal, *op. cit.* p. 220 (Bantu
people south of the Zambesi). Cunningham, *Uganda*, p. 267
(Bakonjo). Schuster ' Die sozialen Verhältnisse des Banjange-
Stammes (Kamerun),' in *Anthropos*, ix. 952. Weeks, *Among the
Primitive Bakongo*, p. 147 (people on the Lower Congo).

² Riedel, *op. cit.* p. 134 (Ceramese). Magyar, *op. cit.* p. 284
(Kimbunda). Dahlgrün, in *Mittheil. Deutsch. Schutzgeb.* xvi. 227
(Shambaa). Fromm, *ibid.* xxv. 98 (Wafipa). Velten, *Sitten und
Gebräuche der Suaheli*, p. 136. Torday and Joyce, *Les Bushongo*,
p. 114.   ³ Weeks, *op. cit.* pp. 146, 107.

⁴ Whiffen, *op. cit.* p. 166 (Witoto and Boro). Hutchinson,
op. cit. p. 23 (Chittagong hill tribes). Playfair, *op. cit.* p. 70 (Garos).
de Morgan, ' Mœurs, coutumes et langages des Négritos de l'intérieur
de la presqu'île Malaise,' in *Société normande de Géographie, Bulletins*,
vii. 422 (Sakai). Seligman, *op. cit.* pp. 80, 511 (Koita, Southern
Massim). Kropf, *op. cit.* p. 154 (Xosa Kafirs). Duff, *Nyasaland
under the Foreign Office*, p. 318. Beverley, in Steinmetz, *op. cit.*
p. 210 (Wagogo). Lang, *ibid.* p. 231 ; Dahlgrün, *loc. cit.* p. 227
(Shambaa). Vergette, *op. cit.* p. 27 (some tribes of Sierra Leone).

⁵ Seligman, *op. cit.* p. 511 (Southern Massim). Decle, *op. cit.*
p. 347 (Wanyamwezi). Fülleborn, *op. cit.* pp. 343, 350 (Konde
people).

⁶ Dahlgrün, *loc. cit.* p. 227 ; Lang, in Steinmetz, *op. cit.* p. 231
(Shambaa).

her children die ;[1] if she is bad-tempered or quarrelsome,[2] or there is an incompatibility of temper on her part ;[3] if she is disobedient,[4] thievish,[5] or suspected of witchcraft ;[6] if she suffers from a foul or incurable disease ;[7] if she becomes too old ;[8] and, of course, if she deserts her husband. The wife, again, may dissolve the marriage if the husband neglects or ill-treats her or is guilty of gross misconduct ;[9] if he is

[1] Duff, *Nyasaland*, p. 318.   v. Rosen, *op. cit.* p. 421 (Balenge).

[2] Whiffen, *op. cit.* p. 166 (Witoto and Boro).   Beverley, in Steinmetz, *op. cit.* p. 210 (Wagogo).   Seligman, *op. cit.* p. 80 (Koita). Duff, *Nyasaland*, p. 318.   v. Rosen, *op. cit.* p. 421 (Balenge).   Decle, *op. cit.* p. 347 (Wanyamwezi).   Schuster, ' Die sozialen Verhältnisse des Banjange-Stammes (Kamerun),' in *Anthropos*, ix. 952.

[3] Ehrenreich, *Beiträge zur Völkerkunde Brasiliens*, p. 27 (Karayá). Hutchinson, *op. cit.* p. 23 (Chittagong hill tribes).   Stow, *op. cit.* p. 95 (Bushmen).   Hinde, *Last of the Masai*, p. 106.

[4] Whiffen, *op. cit.* p. 166 (Witoto and Boro).   Laufer, in *American Anthropologist*, N.S. ii. 321 (Gold).

[5] Pfeil, *op. cit.* p. 30 (natives of the Bismarck Archipelago). Schuster, in *Anthropos*, ix. 952 (Banjange of Kamerun).

[6] Junod, *op. cit.* i. 196 (Thonga).   Beverley, in Steinmetz, *op. cit.* p. 210 (Wagogo).

[7] Whiffen, *op. cit.* p. 166 (Witoto and Boro).   de Lodi, in *Annales de la propagation de la Foi*, xvii. 415 (Botocudos).   Laufer, in *American Anthropologist*, N.S. ii. 321 (Gold).   Kloss, *op. cit.* p. 237 (Nicobarese).   Seligman, *op. cit.* p. 511 (Southern Massim).

[8] Krause, *In den Wildnissen Brasiliens*, p. 325 *sq.* (Karayá). Kloss, *op. cit.* p. 237 (Nicobarese).   Kaufmann, ' Die Auin,' in *Mittheil. Deutsch. Schutzgeb.* xxiii. 157.

[9] Whiffen, *op. cit.* p. 166 (Witoto and Boro).   Hutchinson, *op. cit.* p. 23 (Chittagong hill tribes).   de Morgan, in *Société normande de Géographie, Bulletins*, vii. 422 (Sakai of the Malay Peninsula).   Riedel, *op. cit.* p. 263 (Aru Islanders).   Worcester, *op. cit.* p. 492 (Tagbanuas of Culion and Busuanga).   Seligman, *op. cit.* p. 80 (Koita).   Mrs. Langloh Parker, *Euahlayi Tribe*, p. 58. Kidd, *op. cit.* pp. 222, 223, 226 (Kafirs).   Minnie Martin, *Basutoland*, p. 87.   Dahlgrün, *loc. cit.* p. 227 (Shambaa).   Heese, ' Sitte und Brauch der Sango,' in *Archiv f. Anthrop.* N.S. xii. 138.   Last, ' Visit to the Masai People living beyond the Borders of the Nguru Country,' in *Proceed. Roy. Geo. Soc.* N.S. v. 533.   Johnston, *Uganda Protectorate*, pp. 747, 790 (Bantu and Nilotic Kavirondo).   Pallme, *Travels in Kordofan*, p. 82.   Ellis, *Ewe-speaking Peoples of the Slave Coast*, p. 206.   *Idem, Yoruba-speaking Peoples of the Slave Coast*, p. 187.   *Idem, Tshi-speaking Peoples of the Gold Coast*, p. 284.

lazy and will not do his fair share of the work ;[1] if he deserts her[2] or is long absent from home ;[3] and, sometimes, if she has a strong repugnance to him.[4] Among some natives of Eastern Central Africa the wife may divorce a husband who neglects to sew her clothes.[5] Among the Shans of Burma, should the husband take to drinking or otherwise misconduct himself, the wife has the right to turn him adrift and to retain all the goods and money of the partnership.[6]

A divorce without good reason very frequently entails economic loss for the party who effects it, whereas a divorce for good reason entails loss for the party who is at fault. Thus a husband who puts away or abandons his wife without satisfactory cause forfeits the price he paid or the presents he gave for her,[7] or he has to pay a fine or give up some portion of his property ; [8] but if he divorces her because she

---

[1] Playfair, *op. cit.* p. 70 (Garos). Gomes, *op. cit.* p. 128 (Sea Dyaks). Seligman, *op. cit.* p. 511 (Southern Massim).

[2] Hutchinson, *op. cit.* p. 23 (Chittagong hill tribes).

[3] Taupin, reviewed in *L'Anthropologie*, ii. 489 (Laose). Dennett, *At the Back of the Black Man's Mind*, p. 40 (Bavili).

[4] Theal, *op. cit.* p. 221 (Bantu south of the Zambesi).

[5] Macdonald, *Africana*, i. 140.   [6] Colquhoun, *op. cit.* p. 295.

[7] Holmberg, ' Ethnographische Skizzen über die Völker des russischen Amerika,' in *Acta Soc. Scientiarum Fennicae*, iv. 315 (Tlingit). Samokvasoff, quoted by Miss Czaplicka, *Aboriginal Siberia*, p. 121 (Buryat). Prejevalsky, *op. cit.* i. 70 (Mongols). Harkness, *op. cit.* p. 117 (Badagas). Rossillon, in *Anthropos*, vii. 100 (Kandhs). Shakespear, *Lushei Kuki Clans*, p. 52. Endle, *Kachāris*, p. 31. Crawfurd, *op. cit.* iii. 101 (Malays). de Morga, *Philippine Islands*, p. 301 (Tagals). Baumstark, in *Mittheil. Deutsch. Schutzgeb.* xiii. 54 (Warangi). Baumann, *Usambara*, p. 47 (natives of the Tanga coast). Condon, in *Anthropos*, vi. 372 (Batamba). Poupon, in *L'Anthropologie*, xxvi. 127 (Baya). Delafosse, ' Le peuple Siéna ou Sénoufo,' in *Revue des études ethnographiques et sociologiques*, i. 483. Connolly, in *Jour. Anthr. Inst.* xxvi. 145 (Fanti). ' Negersitten,' in *Das Ausland*, liv. 1026 (Negroes of Bondo). Merolla da Sorrento, ' Voyage to Congo,' in Pinkerton, *Collection of Voyages and Travels*, xvi. 235 (Negroes of Sogno). Torday and Joyce, *Les Bushongo*, p. 116. See also Post, *Grundriss der ethnologischen Jurisprudenz*, ii. 110 *sq.*

[8] Hutchinson, *op. cit.* p. 156 (Tipperahs). Gomes, *op. cit.* p. 69 (Sea Dyaks). Riedel, *op. cit.* p. 134 (Ceramese). Worcester, *op. cit.* p. 492 (Tagbanuas of Culion and Busuanga). Among the

has been unfaithful or proved barren or otherwise affords sufficient cause for divorce, the price paid for her is returned.[1] So also it is generally returned if the wife dissolves the marriage ;[2] but if she does so for some fault of

Manipuris, according to Dalton (*op. cit.* p. 51), a wife who is put away without fault on her part takes all the personal property of the husband, except one drinking cup and the cloth round his loins. Hutchinson (*op. cit.* p. 138) says almost the same of a Kuki wife who is abandoned by her husband.

　[1] Holmberg, in *Acta Soc. Scientiarum Fennicae*, iv. 315 (Tlingit). Goddard, *Life and Culture of the Hupa*, p. 56 (the man received the money he had paid if there were no children ; if only one child was living he might get half of his money back). Sauer, *op. cit.* p. 129 (Yakut). Miss Czaplicka, *op. cit.* p. 125 (Samoyed). Shakespear, *Lushei Kuki Clans*, p. 52. Riedel, *op. cit.* p. 263 (Aru Islanders). *Idem*, 'Galela und Tobeloresen,' in *Zeitschr. f. Ethnol.* xvii. 78. Pfeil, *op. cit.* p. 30 (natives of the Bismarck Archipelago). Dannert, *op. cit.* p. 46 (Herero). Kidd, *op. cit.* p. 226 ; Maclean, *op. cit.* p. 70 (Kafirs ; if there are no children). Rosen, *op. cit.* p. 421 (Balenge). Fülleborn, *op. cit.* p. 349 (Konde people). Heese, in *Archiv f. Anthrop.* N.S. xii. 138 (Sango). Hildebrandt, ' Ethnographische Notizen über Wakámba,' in *Zeitschr. f. Ethnol.* x. 401. Cunningham, *Uganda*, p. 267 (Bakonjo). Felkin, ' Notes on the Madi or Moru Tribe of Central Africa,' in *Proceed. Roy. Soc. Edinburgh*, xii. 322 (the greater part of the cattle paid for her is refunded). Sarbah, *op. cit.* p. 53 *sq.* (Fanti). Tessmann, *op. cit.* ii. 263 (Pangwe). Ellis, *Yoruba-speaking Peoples of the Slave Coast*, p. 186. Merolla da Sorrento, *loc. cit.* p. 235 (Negroes of Sogno). Weeks, *Among the Primitive Bakongo*, p. 147. See al o Post, *Grundriss der ethnologischen Jurisprudenz*, ii. 112 *sq.* Among some African peoples another woman may be given to the ma instead of the restitution of the bride price. Among the Ceramese (Riedel, *op. cit.* p. 134) and the Tagbanuas of Culion and Busuanga (Worcester, *op. cit.* p. 492) a fine is said to be paid to the husband.

　[2] Samokvasoff, quoted by Miss Czaplicka, *op. cit.* p. 121 (Buryat). Prejevalsky, *op. cit.* i. 70 (Mongols). Ward, in Grigg, *op. cit.* Appendix, pp. lxxi. (Badagas), lxxvii. (Kotas). Hodgson, *op. cit.* i. 402 (Kirántis). Carey and Tuck, *op. cit.* i. 210 (tribes of the northern Chin Hills). Taupin, reviewed in *L'Anthropologie*, ii. 489 (Laose). Favre, in *Jour. Indian Archipelago*, ii. 264, 269 (Benua). Junghuhn, *op. cit.* ii. 134 (Battas). Marsden, *History of Sumatra*, p. 235 (Rejangs). de Morga, *op. cit.* p. 301 (Tagals). Williamson, *Mafulu Mountain People of British New Guinea*, p. 174. Vetter, *loc. cit.* p. 91 (Jabim). Hahl, *loc. cit.* p. 77 ; Burger, *op. cit.* p. 30 ;

her husband the bride price is in many cases not given back to him.[1] Among the Rejangs of Sumatra, if the husband has settled down with the family of his wife without paying a price for her, her father can divorce him from her whenever he thinks proper, and in this case he is not entitled to any effects other than the clothes on his back nor to any of the children ; but this rule does not hold good if the wife is willing still to live with her husband and he is able to redeem her and the children by paying her father one hundred dollars.[2]

cf. Schnee, *op. cit.* p. 98 *sq.* (natives of the Gazelle Peninsula of New Britain). Maclean, *op. cit.* p. 69 *sq.* (Kafirs). Theal, *op. cit.* p. 221 (Bantu tribes south of the Zambesi). Junod, *op. cit.* i. 263 *sq.* (Thonga). Richter, ' Der Bezirk Busoga,' in *Mittheil. Deutsch. Schutzgeb.* xii. 85. Baumstark, ' Die Warangi,' *ibid.* xiii. 54. Baumann, *Usambara,* p. 47 *sq.* (natives of the Tanga coast). Condon, in *Anthropos,* vi. 372 (Batamba). Avon, *ibid.* x.–xi. 102 (Wabende ; the woman cannot marry before the bride price has been returned). Last, ' Visit to the Masai People living beyond the Borders of the Nguru Country,' in *Proceed. Roy. Geo. Soc.* N.S. v. 533 ; Hinde, *op. cit.* p. 106 (Masai). Cunningham, *Uganda,* pp. 140 (Bavuma), 266 (Bakonjo). Hobley, *Eastern Uganda,* p. 29 (Nilotic Kavirondo). O'Sullivan, in *Jour. Roy. Anthr. Inst.* xl. 182 (Dinka). Dundas, *ibid.* xliii. 55 (Wawanga and other tribes of the Elgon district of East Africa). Poupon, in *L'Anthropologie,* xxvi. 127 (Baya ; only if she has not given birth to a child). Clozel and Villamur, *op. cit.* p. 104 (Baoulé). Delafosse, ' Siéna ou Sénoufo,' in *Revue des études ethnographiques et sociologiques,* i. 483. Partridge, *Cross River Natives,* p. 256. Cruickshank, *op. cit.* ii. 197 *sq.* (Gold Coast natives). Wilson, *Western Africa,* p. 268 (people of Southern Guinea). Hutereau, *op. cit.* p. 4 (Batua). Delhaise, *Les Warega,* p. 183. See also Post, *Grundriss der ethnologischen Jurisprudenz,* ii. 112 *sq.*

[1] Carey and Tuck, *op. cit.* i. 210 (tribes of the northern Chin Hills). Kidd, *The Essential Kafir,* pp. 222, 223, 226. Minnie Martin, *Basutoland,* p. 87. Magyar, *op. cit.* p. 284 (Kimbunda ; the husband may even have to pay the bride price a second time for the benefit of the wife, if she demands divorce because no child has been born within two years after the conclusion of the marriage or because the husband has proved to be impotent). Sarbah, *op. cit.* p. 53 (Fanti). Cruickshank, *op. cit.* ii. 197 (Gold Coast natives). Ellis, *Ewe-speaking Peoples of the Slave Coast,* p. 206. Torday and Joyce, *Les Bushongo,* p. 114.

[2] Marsden, *op. cit.* p. 236.

Sometimes the party whose conduct affords good cause for divorce loses the children in consequence. Among the Sakai of the Malay Peninsula, if the dissolution of a marriage is caused by grave misconduct on the part of the husband, the children are kept by their mother, but if it is due to the wife's neglect of her duties they are retained by their father.[1] Among the Ainu they are either divided between the two parents or all are given to the one who is considered innocent.[2] Among the Madi of Central Africa the father keeps the child of a wife who has been divorced for adultery, but is not allowed to keep the child of one whom he has divorced for any other reason.[3] Of some tribes in India we are told that the father retains all the children if he is divorced or deserted by his wife,[4] nothing being said as to what happens in other cases of divorce. The general rule, however, seems to be that the fate of the children is little influenced by the question which of the parents is to blame. If they are very young they naturally remain with the mother ; but they may afterwards have to be given to the father, who among very many peoples is considered to have a right to his children.[5] This is particularly often said to

---

[1] de Morgan, in *Société normande de Géographie, Bulletins*, vii. 422.

[2] Pilsudski, quoted by Miss Czaplicka, *op. cit.* p. 104. According to Mr. Batchelor (*op. cit.* p. 233 *sq.*), the father takes the sons and the mother the daughters.

[3] Felkin, in *Proceed. Roy. Soc. Edinburgh*, xii. 323.

[4] Hough, *op. cit.* p. 92 (Badagas). Ward, in Grigg, *op. cit.* Appendix, pp. lxxi. (Badagas), lxxvii. (Kotas). Cox, *Madras District Manuals : North Arcot*, i. 213 (Malayális). Nelson, *Madura Country*, ii. 34 (Kunnuvans). The same is the case among the Rejangs of Sumatra if a price has been paid for the bride (Marsden, *op. cit.* p. 235).

[5] Krause, *op. cit.* p. 326 (Karayá). Lumholtz, *Unknown Mexico*, i. 465 (Tepehuane). Speck, *Family Hunting Territories and Social Life of Various Algonkian Bands of the Ottawa Valley*, p. 24 (Timagami band of Ojibway). Bogoras, *Chukchee*, p. 598. Hodgson, *op. cit.* i. 402 (Kirántis). Jellinghaus, ' Sagen, Sitten und Gebräuche der Munda-Kolhs in Chota Nagpore,' in *Zeitschr. f. Ethnol.* iii. 370. Bainbridge, ' Saorias of the Rajmahal Hills,' in *Memoirs Asiatic Soc. Bengal*, ii. 59 (the children by the first marriage). Marshall, *A Phrenologist amongst the Todas*, p. 218. Carey and Tuck, *op. cit.*

be the case in Africa, where marriage by purchase is so prominent. Among some peoples, however, a nursling is apparently not only taken by its mother but also kept by her in the future, while the older children remain with their father.[1] We are often told that the children are divided between the parents,[2] and in such cases the boys may be taken by the father and the girls by the mother.[3] But among a large number of peoples all the children generally

i. 210 (tribes of the northern Chin Hills). Riedel, *op. cit.* p. 263 (Aru Islanders). Mrs. Langloh Parker, *Euahlayi Tribe*, p. 58. Dannert, *op. cit.* p. 47 (Herero). Kaufmann, in *Mittheil. Deutsch. Schutzgeb.* xxiii. 157 (Auin). Trenk, *ibid.* xxiii. 168 (Namib Bushmen). Kropf, *op. cit.* p. 155 ; Kidd, *op. cit.* p. 226 (Kafirs). Junod, *op. cit.* i. 265 (Thonga). Heese, in *Archiv f. Anthrop.* N.S. xii. 138 (Sango). Fromm, 'Ufipa,' in *Mittheil. Deutsch. Schutzgeb.* xxv. 98. Condon, in *Anthropos*, vi. 371 *sq.* (Batamba). Hurel, 'Religion et Vie domestique des Bakerewe,' *ibid.* vi. 293. Avon, *ibid.* x.–xi. 102 (Wabende). Burton, *Lake Regions of Central Africa*, ii. 333. Dundas, in *Jour. Roy. Anthr. Inst.* xliii. 55 (Wawanga and other tribes of the Elgon district in East Africa). Baumann, *Durch Massailand zur Nilquelle*, p. 190 (Wanyaturu). Johnston, *Uganda Protectorate*, p. 790 (Nilotic Kavirondo). Mangin, 'Les Mossi' (of the Western Sudan), in *Anthropos*, ix. 482. Partridge, *Cross River Natives*, p. 257. Ellis, *Yoruba-speaking Peoples of the Slave Coast*, p. 186 *sq.* Nassau, *Fetichism in West Africa*, p. 10. Delhaise, *Les Warega*, p. 183. See also Post, *Grundriss der ethnologischen Jurisprudenz,* ii. 126.

[1] Turner, *Samoa*, p. 97. Vetter, *loc. cit.* p. 91 (Jabim of New Guinea). Ruelle, in *L'Anthropologie*, xv. 662 (Lobi in French West Africa). Munzinger, *Ueber die Sitten und das Recht der Bogos*, p. 60 *sq.*

[2] Ashe, *op. cit.* p. 249 (Shawnee). Lahontan, *op. cit.* ii. 458 (some Canadian Indians). Hodge, *op. cit.* i. 809 (Salish). Gilhodes, 'Mariage et Condition de la Femme chez les Katchins (Birmanie),' in *Anthropos*, viii. 372. Tauern, 'Ceram,' in *Zeitschr. f. Ethnol.* xlv. 172. Delafosse, 'Siéna ou Sénoufo,' in *Revue des études ethnographiques et sociologiques*, i. 484 (sometimes ; in other cases they are kept by the father). See also Post, *Grundriss der ethnologischen Jurisprudenz*, ii. 126 *sq.*

[3] Bossu, *op. cit.* i. 231 (Alibamu). Jochelson, *Koryak*, p. 746. Batchelor, *op. cit.* p. 233 *sq.* (Ainu ; see, however, *supra*, iii. 296). Le Vaillant, *op. cit.* ii. 70 (Hottentots ; at least the younger girls follow the mother). Dennett, *At the Back of the Black Man's Mind*, p. 40 (Bavili). Pallme, *op. cit.* p. 82 (natives of Kordofan).

follow the mother.[1]   This is especially the case where descent
is matrilineal,[2] and among the native tribes of North
America it seems to be the general rule.[3]   Among various
West African tribes, where the mother retains her children,
she is liable to her husband for a certain sum to compensate
him for what he has paid for their maintenance ;[4] but this
arrangement is often compromised by the mother allowing
her sons to remain with their father.[5]   Among some peoples
the children may themselves choose whether they will go
with their mother or remain with their father.[6]

[1] Azara, *Voyages dans l'Amérique méridionale*, ii. 132 (Payaguas).
Kohler, *Pater Florian Baucke*, p. 316 (Mocobis). Du Tertre, *Histoire
générale des Antilles*, ii. 376.   Speck, *Ethnology of the Yuchi Indians*,
p. 95. Hennepin, *New Discovery of a Vast Country in America*,
ii. 480 ; Loskiel, *History of the Mission of the United Brethren among
the Indians in North America*, i. 61 ; Buchanan, *Sketches of the
History, Manners, and Customs of the North American Indians*,
p. 338 *sq.* (Iroquois and some neighbouring tribes).   Powers, *Tribes
of California*, p. 178 (Gallinomero). Bancroft, *op. cit.* i. 277 (Spokan),
513 (Indians of New Mexico). Dalager, *op. cit.* p. 8 ; Cranz, *op. cit.*
i. 148 (Greenlanders). Waitz, *op. cit.* iii. 105, 328 ; Hodge, *op. cit.*
i. 809 *sq.* (various North American tribes). Gurdon, *Khasis*, p. 81 ;
Steel, ' On the Kasia Tribe,' in *Trans. Ethn. Soc. London*, N.S. vii.
308 ; Dalton, *op. cit.* p. 57 (Khasis). Moszkowski, *Auf neuen Wegen
durch Sumatra*, p. 106 (Sakai). Brainne, *La Nouvelle-Calédonie*,
p. 251 (the children of a first marriage). Parkinson, *Dreissig Jahre
in der Südsee*, p. 267 (natives of New Ireland and New Hanover).
Mariner, *op. cit.* ii. 179 (Tonga Islanders). Waitz-Gerland, *op. cit.* vol. v.
pt. ii. 107 (Ladrone Islanders). Magyar, *op. cit.* p. 284 (Kimbunda).
See also Post, *Grundriss der ethnologischen Jurisprudenz*, ii. 125 *sq.*

[2] *Cf.* Post, *op. cit.* ii. 125 *sq.* Hodge says (*op. cit.* i. 810) that in
North America the children always stay with their mother " in
tribes having maternal clans."   [3] *Cf.* Hodge, *op. cit.* i. 809 *sq.*

[4] Ellis, *Tshi-speaking Peoples of the Gold Coast*, p. 284. *Idem*,
Ewe-speaking Peoples of the Slave Coast, p. 206.

[5] *Idem, Tshi-speaking Peoples*, p. 284. Cruickshank, *op. cit.* ii. 198.

[6] Favre, in *Jour. Indian Archipelago*, ii. 264 (Benua of Malacca ;
according to Newbold [*Account of the British Settlements in the
Straits of Malacca*, ii. 408], however, the children generally go with
the mother). Hagen, *Die Orang Kubu auf Sumatra*, p. 134. Kloss,
op. cit. p. 237 *sq.* (Nicobarese). Shaw, ' Betsileo,' in *Antananarivo
Annual and Madagascar Magazine*, iv. 9 (to a certain extent,
although the father has full authority over all his children). Rosen,
op. cit. p. 421 (Balenge).

Sometimes one of the parties, or even both, are prohibited from remarrying ; in such cases there is no divorce in our sense of the term, but something corresponding to our " judicial separation." Among the Tepehuane of Mexico, if either husband or wife should prove unfaithful, they immediately separate, the guilty one is severely punished, and neither of them is permitted to marry again.[1] Among the Bayaka a wife who has been repudiated for adultery must remain unmarried ;[2] and among the Bambala, another Congo tribe, the same is the case with every wife who has been divorced by her husband.[3] So also among the Kandhs of India, according to Sir W. W. Hunter, " a wife separated on any grounds whatsoever from her husband cannot marry again."[4] In Samoa, in former times, " a discarded wife of a chief, or one who had voluntarily left her husband, was prohibited from marrying another man, unless the latter were powerful enough to set this prohibition at defiance."[5] Among the Brazilian Karayá, again, a man who has divorced his wife cannot take another, although he is allowed to engage a woman to keep house for him.[6] Among the Khasis of Assam parties who have been divorced cannot afterwards remarry one another.[7]

Certain formalities may have to be observed at the dissolution of a marriage. The consent or assistance of relatives or the elders of the parties,[8] or of clansmen, villagers, or the village elders,[9] or of the

---

[1] Lumholtz, *Unknown Mexico*, i. 465 *sq.*

[2] Torday and Joyce, ' Notes on the Ethnography of the Ba-Yaka,' in *Jour. Anthr. Inst.* xxxvi. 45.

[3] *Iidem*,' Notes on the Ethnography of the Ba-Mbala,' *ibid.* xxxv. 411.

[4] Hunter, *Annals of Rural Bengal*, iii. 83.   [5] Stair, *Old Samoa*, p. 175.

[6] Ehrenreich, *Beiträge zur Völkerkunde Brasiliens*, p. 27.

[7] Gurdon, *op. cit.* p. 79.

[8] Anantha Krishna Iyer, *op. cit.* ii. 42 (Nayars).   Sarat Chandra Roy, *Mundas*, p. 455.   de Morga, *Philippine Islands*, p. 301 (Tagals). Worcester, *Philippine Islands*, p. 492 (Tagbanuas of Culion and Busuanga).

[9] Hunter, *Annals of Rural Bengal*, i. 208 ; Hertel, *op. cit.* p. 83 (Santals).   Lewin, *op. cit.* p. 276 (Tipperahs).   Kolbe, *Present State of the Cape of Good-Hope*, i. 157 (Hottentots).   Gouldsbury and Sheane, *Great Plateau of Northern Rhodesia*, p. 170 (Awemba).

tribe,[1] may be required for the purpose. Among the
Bagobo of Mindanao, "if a couple cannot agree, a
separation can be arranged by applying to the local
head-man, who, after listening to their troubles, decides
which one is at fault, and whether or no the marriage gifts must be returned."[2] Among the Tumbuka
of British Central Africa, if a man wanted to repudiate
his wife, "the divorce did not take place in private,
but before the assembled villagers and their chief. The
husband repudiated his wife by taking an arrow and sticking
it into the ground. An arrow was his sign of jealous possession of his wife. Should any one wrong her, he was at
liberty to shoot the culprit. Now, when he repudiated the
woman, he stuck the arrow upright in the ground, as a sign
that whosoever would might have her, and he would take
no revenge."[3] As marriages are concluded with rites
which symbolise, or are intended to strengthen, the union,
so they are sometimes dissolved with rites of a contrary
character, such as the tearing of a leaf or a piece of grass[4] or
the breaking of a straw.[5] Among the Kacháris of Assam,
for instance, man and wife appear before the village elders,
state their case, and conclude by tearing a betel-leaf into
two pieces, "a symbolic act indicating that, as the sundered
leaf can never reunite, so their own married life is severed
for ever."[6] Among the Hajongs, living on the southern
slope of the Garo Hills, the parties not only tear a betel-leaf
in the presence of the village elders, but formally address
each other as father and mother, thus showing that the
relation of husband and wife has ceased.[7] Among the

[1] Müller, in *Zeitschr. f. Ethnol.* xlii. 230 (savage tribes of Formosa).

[2] Cole, 'Wild Tribes of Davao District, Mindanao,' in *Field
Museum of Natural History, Anthropological Series*, xii. 103. See
also Finley and Churchill,' *Subanu of Mindanao*, p. 41.

[3] Fraser, *Winning a Primitive People*, p. 155 *sq.*

[4] Crooke, ' Hill Tribes of the Central Indian Hills,' in *Jour. Anthr.
Inst.* xxviii. 243. Sarat Chandra Roy, *Mundas*, p. 455. Hertel,
op. cit. p. 83 (Santals). Endle, *op. cit.* p. 96 (Ahom Chutiyas of
Assam).

[5] Bainbridge, in *Memoirs Asiatic Soc. Bengal*, ii. 58 (Saorias of the
Rajmahal Hills).

[6] Endle, *op. cit.* p. 31.   [7] *Ibid.* p. 86.

Bagobo of Mindanao, " when a couple parts, plates, bowls, and jars are sometimes broken as a sign that they will never live together again and the spirits are thus called to witness."[1] Among the Khasis " the husband gives the woman five cowries (the small shells in use as currency in India), and the woman throws them away ; they are then free to be married again."[2] Among some Canadian Indians the couple, at the marriage ceremony, held a rod between them, which they afterwards broke into as many pieces as there were relatives present ; these pieces were distributed among the latter, but if the marriage was dissolved they were again brought into the hut where it had been celebrated and were burnt in the presence of the relatives.[3] Rites of this sort are probably not mere symbols, but, like most of the rites performed at the conclusion of a marriage, they may be supposed to have a magical significance. We are told that the Maori of New Zealand had " a charm to be uttered as a divorce-spell."[4]

Among the peoples who have reached a higher culture the stability of marriage is not less variable than it is among the lower races. There are in this respect very marked differences among the different nations of ancient civilisation, in the New World as well as in the Old.

The Aztecs of Mexico looked upon marriage as a solemn and binding tie which should be dissolved by death only. Divorce was permitted, but as a general rule discouraged. In the event of discord arising between man and wife so that they could not live together peacefully, or if one or the other of the parties considered that he, or she, had just cause of complaint, an application was made to a judge for permission to separate.[5] Not even a " less legitimate

---

[1] Cole, in *Field Museum of Natural History, Anthropological Series*, xii. 103.   [2] Steel, in *Trans. Ethn. Soc. London*, N.S. vii. 308.

[3] Lahontan, *op. cit.* ii. 457 *sq.* *Cf.* Ashe, *op. cit.* p. 249 (Shawnee).

[4] Tregear, *op. cit.* p. 297.

[5] Bancroft, *Native Races of the Pacific States of North America*, ii. 262 *sq.* Torquemada, *Monarchia Indiana*, ii. 442. Gomara. ' Primera y segunda parte de la historia general de las Indias,' in *Biblioteca de autores españoles*, xxii. 440.

wife," or concubine, could be repudiated without good cause and the sanction of a court.[1] We are told that a man was permitted to divorce his chief, or real, wife only for malevolence, dirtiness, or sterility ; an adulteress was not divorced but punished with death.[2] In the case of separation the parties divided their goods according to the portion which each of them had brought when they married ; and the daughters went with the mother, while the sons remained with the father.[3] The divorce once effected, the man and woman were forbidden to unite again, according to Acosta on pain of death.[4] Among the Maya nations, on the other hand, divorce was obtained with great facility.[5] In Yucatan it was frequently practised ; but it was not unusual for the husband to return to the wife after a while if she was free, regardless of the fact that she had belonged to another man in the meantime. If the children were still of tender age at the time the parents separated, they were left with the mother ; if they were grown up, the boys followed the father and the girls the mother.[6] In Nicaragua an adulteress was discarded and could not marry again ; but if the wife deserted her husband, she was neither punished nor reproved, and he usually refrained from fetching her back.[7] In Guatemala the wife could leave her husband on the same slight grounds as the man could leave his wife ; if she refused to return to him after being requested to do so, he was allowed to take another wife and she was then considered free.[8]

According to Chinese law a husband can divorce his wife, but only on certain conditions. It is said in the Penal Code that if he repudiates her " without her having broken the matrimonial connection by the crime of adultery or otherwise, and without her having furnished him with any of the

---

[1] Bancroft, *op. cit.* ii. 265.   [2] Gomara, *loc. cit.* p. 440.

[3] Acosta, *Natural and Moral History of the Indies*, ii. 370.

[4] *Ibid.* ii. 370.

[5] Landa, *Relacion de las cosas de Yucatan*, p. 138 *sq.* Bancroft, *op. cit.* ii. 672 *sq.*

[6] Landa, *op. cit.* p. 138 *sqq.* de Herrera, *General History of the Vast Continent and Islands of America*, iv. 171.

[7] Gomara, *loc. cit.* p. 283.   [8] Bancroft, *op. cit.* ii. 672.

seven justifying causes of divorce," he shall in every such case be punished with eighty blows. The seven causes in question are : barrenness, lasciviousness, disregard of the husband's parents, talkativeness, thievish propensities, envious and suspicious temper, and inveterate infirmity. Yet none of these causes will justify a divorce if the wife has mourned three years for her husband's parents, if the family has become rich since the marriage after being poor previously, or if the wife has no parents living to receive her back again ;[1] the first two provisions are due to the idea that the wife has suffered privation enough with her husband to give her a claim to his lasting regard.[2] A wife who has been convicted of adultery is not protected by any of these saving clauses ; indeed, the husband is liable to punishment if he retains such a wife.[3] Marriage can, moreover, be dissolved by mutual consent : it is expressly said in the code that " when the husband and wife do not agree, and both parties are desirous of separation, the law limiting the right of divorce shall not be enforced to prevent it."[4] The same prescriptions also apply to the " inferior wives," or lawful concubines, with the difference, however, that if the husband transgresses the law his punishment is reduced.[5] In practice the husband's power of divorce was no doubt greater than it was according to the letter of the law.   Sir R. K. Douglas observes that even on occasions when the seven legal plaints are in question " a decree without any *nisi* is generally granted by a court composed of the elders of the neighbourhood, and not by the mandarins.   In this and similar matters local social pressure takes the place of a wider public opinion."[6]   On the other hand, it does not seem that either law or public opinion justified a wife in deserting her husband or demanding a separation from him. " The idea of a wife divorcing her husband for adultery, or for any reason whatever," says Mr. Doolittle, " is one

[1] *Ta Tsing Leu Lee*, sec. cxvi. p. 120.

[2] Medhurst, ' Marriage, Affinity, and Inheritance in China,' in *Trans. Roy. Asiatic Soc. China Branch*, iv. 26.

[3] *Ibid.* p. 26 n.†   *Ta Tsing Leu Lee*, sec. cxvi. p. 120.

[4] *Ta Tsing Leu Lee*, sec. cxvi. p. 120.

[5] *Ibid.* sec. cxvi. p. 121.   [6] Douglas, *Society in China*, p. 206.

which excites a smile, as absurd and preposterous, whenever
mentioned to the Chinese."[1]   As to the actual prevalence
of divorce in China, Mr. Medhurst remarks that, apart from
the legal check on it, " the sex possesses an effectual safe-
guard in the peculiarly indulgent and forgiving disposition
of the Chinese character, which no doubt tends to make
such an extreme measure as repudiation one of very rare
occurrence."[2]

The divorce law of the Japanese Taihō Code was substan-
tially the same as that in China.[3] Professor Hozumi,
however, remarks that the seven grounds for divorce recognised by it were not limitative, but only mentioned as just
grounds for abandoning a wife ; practically, a wife could
be divorced at the pleasure of her husband, under any slight
or flimsy pretext, the most usual being that she did not
" conform to the usage of the family."[4]   Indeed, in the case
of barrenness—which according to the commentators
meant the failure of male offspring,—of adultery, or of
hereditary disease, divorce was a duty which the husband
owed to his ancestors : barrenness was an obstacle to the
perpetuation of ancestor-worship, adultery caused a confusion of blood whereby a person not in reality related to
the ancestors might succeed to the worship, and hereditary
disease led to a pollution of the ancestral blood.[5]   To obtain
a divorce no legal procedure was necessary beyond the
husband's writ with his signature, countersigned by the
nearest ascendants.[6]   As in China, the wife had no legal
right to demand divorce from her husband on any ground.
This was the case till the year 1873, when a law was enacted

---

[1] Doolittle, *Social Life of the Chinese*, i. 106.

[2] Medhurst, *loc. cit.* p. 26 *sq.*

[3] Küchler, ' Marriage in Japan,' in *Trans. Asiatic Soc. Japan,*
xiii. 130. Hozumi, *Ancestor-Worship and Japanese Law*, p. 144.
Idem, Lectures on the New Japanese Civil Code, p. 70.

[4] Hozumi, *Lectures on the New Japanese Civil Code*, p. 70 *sq.*

[5] *Idem, Ancestor-Worship and Japanese Law*, p. 145 *sq. Idem,
Lectures on the New Japanese Civil Code*, p. 70 *sq.*

[6] Nakajima, ' Marriage (Japanese and Korean),' in Hastings,
Encyclopædia of Religion and Ethics, viii. 460. Hozumi, *Ancestor-
Worship and Japanese Law*, p. 145.

which for the first time allowed the wife to bring an action
of divorce against the husband.[1] The new Civil Code,
promulgated in 1896–1898, went further in the same direction. It recognises two forms of divorce : by mutual
arrangement and by judicial decree. In order to effect a
divorce by mutual arrangement, however, a person who has
not reached the age of twenty-five years must obtain the
consent of those persons whose consent would be necessary
for his or her contracting a marriage.[2] The latter form of
legal divorce, which requires an act of the court upon the
contested request of one of the parties, must be for some one
of certain causes recognised by law. Thus a husband or a
wife, as the case may be, can bring an action for divorce if
either party contracts a second marriage, if the wife commits
adultery, if the husband is sentenced to punishment for an
offence involving criminal carnal intercourse, if one party
is so ill-treated or grossly insulted by the other that it makes
further living together impracticable, or if one party is
deserted by the other.[3] Professor Hozumi, in his commentaries on the new Civil Code, says that it places husband
and wife on an equal footing with regard to the right of
divorce ;[4] but I fail to see that mere adultery on the part
of the husband gives the wife a right to divorce him, although
he can divorce an unfaithful wife. Divorces are very
frequent in Japan, but since the new code came into force
their number has rapidly decreased. In 1897 the proportion
of divorces to marriages was 34 per cent. ; in 1899, 22·3
per cent. ; in 1900, 18·5 per cent.[5] Professor Rein remarks
that the Japanese husbands seldom made use of their
privilege of divorcing their wives, especially when the
marriage was blessed with children, as training and public
opinion required that in such cases the wife should be
treated with kindness and respect.[6] And Küchler wrote in
1885 :—" It must not be supposed either that divorce in
Japan is the easy matter which most residents in, and visitors

---

[1] Hozumi, *Lectures on the New Japanese Civil Code*, p. 71 *sq.*
[2] *Civil Code of Japan*, § 808 *sq.*   [3] *Ibid.* § 813.
[4] Hozumi, *Lectures on the New Japanese Civil Code*, p. 72.
[5] Rein, *Japan*, i. 586.   [6] *Ibid.* i. 585.

to, this country suppose it to be. A solemn conclave of the relations of both parties is held, and the question argued with as much care and regard to justice as would be found in any court of law. An improper divorce by a husband of his wife has often been the cause of a life-long feud between the two families."[1] It is probable that these statements chiefly refer to the upper classes, who, according to Professor Chamberlain, rarely resort to divorce, the immense majority of cases occurring among the lower ranks of society.[2]

Among Semitic peoples the husband has had, or still has, the legal right of repudiating his wife at will. In Babylonia, according to the Laws of Ḫammurabi, however, the wife, and even the concubine, had certain pecuniary guarantees against arbitrary divorce. It is said :—" If a man has set his face to put away his concubine who has borne him children or his wife who has granted him children, to that woman he shall return her her marriage portion and shall give her the usufruct of field, garden and goods, and she shall bring up her children. From the time that her children are grown up, from whatever is given to her children they shall give her a share like that of one son, and she shall marry the husband of her choice."[3] Again, " if a man has put away his bride who has not borne him children, he shall give her money as much as her dowry (bride price), and shall pay her the marriage portion which she brought from her father's house."[4] If there was no bride price he shall give her one mina of silver for a divorce, unless he be a poor man, in which case he shall give her one-third of a mina.[5] But if the wife " has set her face to go out and has acted the fool, has wasted her house, has belittled her husband," then she may be divorced without compensation or be retained in the house as a maid-servant.[6] In case of adultery on the part of the wife both she and the adulterer shall be drowned,

[1] Küchler, *loc. cit.* p. 132.

[2] Chamberlain, *Things Japanese*, p. 314.

[3] *Laws of Ḫammurabi*, § 137 (Johns' translation, p. 26 *sq.* ; Winckler's translation, p. 39).

[4] *Ibid.* § 138 (Johns' trans. p. 27 ; Winckler's trans. p. 41).

[5] *Ibid.* § 139 *sq.* (Johns' trans. p. 27 ; Winckler's trans. p. 41).

[6] *Ibid.* § 141 (Johns' trans. p. 27 *sq.* ; Winckler's trans. p. 41).

unless the king pardons his servant or " the owner " his wife.[1] On the other hand, the wife may also in certain circumstances claim a divorce, or at least separation.[2] " If a woman hates her husband and has said ' Thou shalt not possess me,' one shall enquire into her past what is her lack, and if she has been economical and has no vice, and her husband has gone out and greatly belittled her, the woman has no blame, she shall take her marriage portion and go off to her father's house."[3] But if on investigation it turns out that " she has not been economical, and goes about, has wasted her house, has belittled her husband, that woman one shall throw her into the waters."[4] From the few marriage contracts and records of divorce which have been studied the conclusion has been drawn that divorce was not uncommon in Babylonia.[5] Peiser has pointed out that two tablets in the British Museum reveal upon comparison that a woman who had been married to one man was within eight months married to another, while the first was still living.[6]

The right of the husband to divorce his wife at his pleasure is the central thought in the entire system of Jewish divorce law ; and the Rabbis neither did nor could set it aside, although they gradually tempered its severity by numerous restrictive measures. Two restrictions are already found in the Deuteronomic Code—the husband shall not put his wife away all his days if he has falsely accused her of ante-nuptial incontinence[7] or if he has ravished her before marriage ;[8] but his loss of the right to divorce her in these cases was really a penalty inflicted upon him on account of his own

---

[1] *Ibid.* § 129 (Johns' trans. p. 24 *sq.* ; Winckler's trans. p. 37).

[2] Nothing is said of her being allowed to marry again (*cf.* Hobhouse, *Morals in Evolution*, p. 181 n. 1).

[3] *Laws of Ḫammurabi*, § 142 (Johns' trans. p. 28). According to Winckler's translation (p. 41), " if she is in the right, there is no fault on her part, her husband goes about, and greatly neglects her."

[4] *Laws of Ḫammurabi*, § 143 (Johns' trans. p. 28). *Cf.* Winckler's translation, p. 41.

[5] Barton, *Sketch of Semitic Origins*, p. 45 *sq.*

[6] Kohler and Peiser, *Aus dem Babylonischen Rechtsleben*, ii. 13 *sqq.*

[7] *Deuteronomy*, xxii. 13 *sqq.*   [8] *Ibid.* xxii. 28 *sq.*

offensive behaviour. To these restrictions the Mishnah added three others by providing that the husband could not divorce his wife if she had become insane, if she was in captivity, or if she was a minor too young to take care of her bill of divorce, the so-called *get*.[1] The Mishnah also checked the husband's exercise of his right to divorce by prescribing formalities which made the divorce procedure difficult ; the numerous rules and regulations incident to it compelled him to seek the help of one learned in the law to assist him in divorcing his wife, and this person was expected to use every effort to reconcile the parties, unless sufficient reason appeared for the divorce. Other checks were the law compelling the husband to pay the divorced wife the dowry fixed in the *kethūbhāh*[2] and the decree which deprived him of the power of annulling the bill of divorce.[3]

In the period of the Mishnah the very theory of the law was challenged by the school of Shammai, who held that according to Deuteronomy the husband cannot divorce his wife unless he has found her guilty of sexual immorality. The ancient doctrine was strongly supported by the school of Hillel, who went so far as to say that a man can divorce his wife even for the most trivial reason, for instance, for spoiling his food or if he sees another woman who pleases him better. Both schools based their opinions on the same passage in the Deuteronomic text :—" When a man hath taken a wife, and married her, and it come to pass that she find no favour in his eyes, because he hath found some uncleanness in her : then let him write her a bill of divorcement, and give it in her hand, and send her out of his house."[4] But the school of Shammai maintained that the expression " some uncleanness " (lit. " the nakedness of a thing ") signified sexual immorality ; whereas the school of Hillel interpreted it to mean anything offensive to the husband and, besides, pressed the clause " if she find no favour in

[1] Amram, *Jewish Law of Divorce*, p. 45 *sq.*

[2] See *supra*, ii. 417.

[3] Amram, *op. cit.* p. 46 *sqq.* Mielziner, *Jewish Law of Marriage and Divorce*, p. 119 *sq.*

[4] *Deuteronomy*, xxiv. 1.

his eyes."[1]   In legal respects the opinion of Hillel prevailed, but at the same time divorce without good cause was morally disapproved of by the rabbis in general.   The theoretical right of the husband to divorce his wife whenever it pleased him to do so ceased to exist in practice, and was at last, in the earlier part of the eleventh century, formally abolished by a decree issued by Rabbi Gershom ben Yehudah, who presided over a Sanhedrin convened at Mayence.   In this decree it is ordained " that even as the man does not put away his wife except of his own free will, so shall the woman not be put away except by her own consent."   This, however, did not imply that the right of divorce was abolished in cases where good cause could be shown.[2]   According to Jewish law the husband is entitled to divorce his wife if she is guilty of adultery or even strongly suspected of having committed this crime, if she publicly violates moral decency, if she changes her religion or shows disregard of the ritual law in the management of the household, thereby causing him to transgress the religious precepts against his will, if she obstinately refuses to have connubial intercourse with him during a whole year, if she without good cause refuses to follow him to another domicile, if she insults her father-in-law in the presence of her husband or insults the husband himself, or if she suffers from some incurable disease which renders cohabitation impracticable or dangerous.[3]

In the Old Testament it is nowhere said that a marriage could be dissolved at the will of the wife, and the Jewish law has never given her a right to divorce her husband. But the Mishnah allowed her to sue for divorce, and if the court decided that she was entitled to be divorced the husband was forced to give her a *get*, although he was supposed to give it of his own free will and accord.[4]   When the right of the wife to demand a divorce had once been established, the causes for which it could be exercised

---

[1] Amram, *op. cit.* p. 32 *sqq.*   Mielziner, *op. cit.* p. 118 *sq.*   Bergel, *Die Eheverhältnisse der alten Juden*, p. 29.   Driver, *Critical and Exegetical Commentary on Deuteronomy*, p. 270
[2] Amram, *op. cit.* pp. 24, 52 *sq.*   [3] Mielziner, *op. cit.* p. 122.
[4] *Ibid.* p. 118.   Amram, *op. cit.* p. 57 *sqq.*

gradually became more numerous. At Jewish law the wife
may demand a bill of divorce from her husband if he
repeatedly illtreats her—for example, beating her or turning
her out of doors, or prohibiting her from visiting her parental
home,—if he changes his religion, if he after marriage engages
in a disgusting trade, if he is guilty of notorious dissoluteness
of morals, if he wastes his property and refuses to support
her, if he commits a crime which compels him to flee from
the country, if he suffers from some loathsome chronic
disease contracted after marriage, if he is physically
impotent, or, according to some authorities, if he persistently refuses to have matrimonial intercourse with her.[1]
When the causes of the complaining wife are found to be
sufficient to entitle her to divorce, the husband is compelled
not only to give her a *get* but also to pay her dowry ;
whereas she, as the guilty party, forfeits her dowry when
the court grants a divorce enforced upon the wife on the
petition of the husband.   She is also entitled to receive her
dowry in case of divorce by mutual agreement.   For such
a divorce no specific causes are required ; according to a
principle of Rabbinical law, the court has no right to interfere
when both parties declare that their marriage is a failure
and they desire to dissolve it.[2]

But though liberal in permitting divorce, the Jewish law
favoured remarriage of the parties, except in certain cases :
Deuteronomy prohibited them from remarrying if the wife
had married another man after her divorce,[3] and the Mishnah
added five other cases, forbidding, for example, a man to
remarry a wife who had been divorced upon suspicion of
adultery or because of her barrenness.[4]   According to the
earlier law, the children of the divorced woman remained
in her custody at least until they were weaned, and after
that time it was optional with her to retain the custody of
them ; but the custody of the boys could be claimed by the
father after their sixth year.   The later law seems to have
gone back to the old rule of the Roman law, giving the court

---

[1] Mielziner, *op. cit.* p. 123 *sq.*   Amram, *op. cit.* p. 63 *sqq.*
[2] Mielziner, *op. cit.* p. 120 *sq.*
[3] *Deuteronomy*, xxiv. 1 *sqq.*   [4] Amram, *op. cit.* p. 81 *sqq.*

the power in the first instance to award the custody of the children of the divorced couple according to its discretion.[1]

As the ancient Hebrews, so the pagan Arabs permitted the husband to repudiate his wife whenever he pleased ; but we also hear of many Arab women of noble families who divorced their husbands.[2] Subsequently the unlimited customary right of the husband was crystallised in Muhammad's law, which allowed him to repudiate his wife without any misbehaviour on her part or without assigning any cause for his action. The Prophet is said to have pronounced *ṭalāq*, that is, divorce effected by the husband, to be the most detestable before God of all permitted things, as preventing conjugal happiness and interfering with the proper bringing-up of children ;[3] but the ancient privilege of the husband was too thoroughly fixed in Arabic custom and too congenial to the natures of the Prophet and his followers to be changed.[4] There are, however, certain conditions essential to the capacity of effecting a valid divorce. The husband must be adult and sane ; according to the Shāfi'ī and Mālikī doctrines he must also act of his own free will, and the Shī'ahs require as a fourth condition that he shall have a distinct intention to dissolve the marriage tie. But among the Hanafīs, as the Ālamgīrī puts it, "a *ṭalāq* pronounced by any husband who is of mature age and possessed of understanding is effective, whether he be free or slave, willing or acting under compulsion ; and even though it were muttered in sport or jest, or inadvertently by a mere slip of the tongue." Intoxication does not generally make a *ṭalāq* invalid ; but the husband must be awake when he pronounces it.[5] As regards the formalities necessary for a divorce there are also differences between different schools. According to the Sunnī doctrines a *ṭalāq* may be effected either by express terms, as when the husband says "Thou art divorced," or by the use of

---

[1] *Ibid.* p. 130.　　　　[2] Perron, *Femmes arabes*, p. 127.
[3] Ameer Ali, *Mahommedan Law*, ii. 511.
[4] *Cf.* Barton, *op. cit.* p. 46 *sq.*
[5] Hughes, *op. cit.* p. 88.　Ameer Ali, *op. cit.* ii. 516 *sqq.*　Sautayra and Cherbonneau, *Droit musulman*, i. 279 *sqq.*　Sachau, *Muhammedanisches Recht nach Schafiitischer Lehre*, p. 12.

ambiguous or implicative expressions ; whereas the Shī'ahs recognise it as valid only if it is pronounced in express terms and not made dependent upon or subjected to any condition.[1] The Sunnīs hold that a *ṭalāq* may be effected by writing as well as spoken words ; whereas the Shī'ahs do not allow it to be given in writing nor in any other language than the Arabic when the husband is able to pronounce the words necessary for its validity.[2] The Sunnīs do not require the presence of witnesses but regard the repudiation as valid in law so long as it comes to the knowledge of the wife ; whereas the Shī'ah law lays down the rule that there shall be two reliable witnesses present at the time of repudiation to hear the words in which it is pronounced.[3] In every case where a *ṭalāq* is pronounced on the initiation of the husband he has to render the wife an account of the administration of her estate during their marriage and to make over to her all her property together with the ante-nuptial settlement, or *mahr* ; and on failing to do so he is liable to a suit for damages as well as for payment of the dower.[4] According to a Koranic decree, a husband may take a divorced wife back again twice, but if he give sentence of divorce to her a third time it is not lawful for him to take her back until she shall have married another man.[5]

At Muhammadan, as at Jewish, law the wife can never divorce her husband, but she may take steps leading to the dissolution of her marriage. When she desires a divorce, she may obtain from him a release from the marriage contract by giving up either her settled dower or some other property ; such a divorce is called *ḥula'*.[6] When the married couple have a mutual aversion to each other due to incompatibility of temper, want of sympathy, or the like, they can dissolve the marriage tie by mutual agreement ; such a dissolution is called *mubārāt*.[7] Finally, when the husband

---

[1] Ameer Ali, *op. cit.* ii. 516. Sautayra and Cherbonneau, *op. cit.* i. 284 *sqq.*   [2] Ameer Ali, *op. cit.* ii. 523 *sq.*   [3] *Ibid.* ii. 524 *sq.*
[4] *Ibid.* ii. 531.   [5] *Koran*, ii. 229 *sq.*
[6] Ameer Ali, *op. cit.* ii. 513, 546. Sautayra and Cherbonneau, *op. cit.* i. 236 *sq.*
[7] Ameer Ali, *op. cit.* ii. 513, 546, 560. Sautayra and Cherbonneau, *op. cit.* i. 253 *sqq.*

is guilty of conduct which makes the matrimonial life
intolerable to the wife, when he neglects to perform the
duties which the law imposes on him as obligations resulting
from marriage, or when he fails to fulfil the engagements
voluntarily entered into at the time of the matrimonial
contract, she has the right of preferring a complaint before
the judge and demanding a divorce by authority of justice.
The power of the judge to pronounce a divorce is founded
on the express words of Muhammad, " If a woman be
prejudiced by a marriage, let it be broken off." Such a
divorce may be claimed on various grounds : if the husband
is impotent and the wife was unaware of it prior to the
marriage, if he does not give the stipulated dowry when
demanded, if he falsely charges his wife with adultery, if he
takes a vow to abstain from her for four months and keeps
the vow inviolate, or if he wilfully neglects her, habitually
illtreats her, or makes her life miserable by cruelty of
conduct in some way or other.[1] The facility with which
Muhammadan women can dissolve their marriage is influenced by local custom. Among some Berber tribes of
Morocco, as said above, a married woman can not only
get rid of her husband by taking refuge to another man's
house or tent, but she can actually compel the latter to
marry her.[2] In Persia, if a woman wishes to leave her
husband, she can do so by going to the *gazi*, or judge, and
turning up her slipper ; but this remedy is rarely resorted
to as she must go out penniless.[3] Among the Bedouins of
the Euphrates the wife is said to have the same right to
leave her husband, with or without reason, as he has to send
her back to her parents.[4]

The frequency of divorce also differs considerably among
the Muhammadans of different countries. Among some of
them it is practised to an extent which is almost without
a parallel.[5] This is the case in Morocco, or some parts of

[1] Ameer Ali, *op. cit.* ii. 560 *sqq.* Sautayra and Cherbonneau,
op. cit. i. 254 *sqq.* Hughes, *op. cit.* p. 88.
[2] *Supra*, ii. 319.   [3] Wilson, *Persian Life and Customs*, p. 265.
[4] Lady Blunt, *Bedouin Tribes of the Euphrates*, ii. 226.
[5] Pischon, *Der Einfluss des Islâm auf das häusliche, sociale und
politische Leben seiner Bekenner*, p. 13. Chavanne, *Die Sahara*, p. 603.

that country. Dr. Churcher wrote to me from Tangier
that one of the servants there was reported to have had
nineteen wives although he was still only middle-aged ;
and I had myself in my service a Berber from Sūs, in
the south of Morocco, who told me that he had divorced
twenty-two wives. In Cairo, according to Lane, there
are not many men who have not divorced one wife,
if they have been married for a long time, and not
a few men in Egypt have in the course of two
years married as many as twenty, thirty, or more
wives ; while there are women, not far advanced in age,
who have been wives to a dozen or more men successively. Lane even heard of men who had been in the habit
of taking a new wife almost every month.[1] Burckhardt
knew Arabs about forty-five years old who had had more
than fifty different wives.[2] Snouck Hurgronje states, on
the other hand, that separation is rare in Acheh, in Sumatra,
as compared with other Muhammadan countries ; [3] and
among the Muhammadans of India, according to Mr. Gait,
the husband seldom exercises his right to divorce his wife
without any special reason.[4] This may be due to Hindu
influence.

With orthodox Hindus marriage is a religious sacrament
which cannot be revoked. A woman convicted of adultery
may be deprived of her status and turned out of her caste,
but even in this case divorce in the ordinary sense is an
impossibility ; she cannot form a new connection and,
often at least, remains in her husband's house on the footing
of a slave.[5] Again, the only remedy which a blameless
wife has against an offending husband is to obtain a decree
for her separate maintenance, such decree being practically
equivalent to a decree for judicial separation.[6] The law,
however, was not always equally stringent. In the Smriti

---

[1] Lane, *Manners and Customs of the Modern Egyptians*, i. 247, 251.
[2] Burckhardt, *Notes on the Bedouins and Wahábys*, p. 64.
[3] Snouck Hurgronje, *Achehnese*, i. 367.
[4] Gait, *Census of India*, 1911, vol. i. (India) Report, p. 245 *sq.*
[5] *Ibid.* p. 245. Mayne, *Treatise on Hindu Law and Usage*, p. 112.
Steele, *Law and Custom of Hindoo Castes*, p. 171 *sq.*
[6] Trevelyan, *Hindu Family Law*, p. 59.

literature cases are recognised in which divorce with the
possibility of the wife contracting a new marriage during
her husband's lifetime is allowed, and the occasions for
divorce (*tyāga*), that is, abandoning a wife and leaving her
without maintenance on the part of the husband, are set
out.[1] According to Nārada, a married woman "who
wastes the entire property of her husband under the pretence
that it is (her own) Strîdhana, or who procures abortion, or
who makes an attempt on her husband's life, he shall
banish from the town"; and "one who always shows
malice to him, or who makes unkind speeches, or eats before
her husband, he shall quickly expel from his house."[2] But
"if a man leaves a wife who is obedient, pleasant-spoken,
skilful, virtuous, and the mother of (male) issue, the king
shall make him mindful of his duty by (inflicting) severe
punishment (on him)."[3] The same authority, moreover,
lays down that there are five cases of legal necessity in which
a woman may be justified in taking another husband,
namely, "when her husband is lost or dead, when he has
become a religious ascetic, when he is impotent, and when
he has been expelled from caste"; and it is stipulated how
many years women of the three higher castes shall wait for
the return of their absent husbands until they can contract
a new marriage, whereas no such definite period is prescribed
for a Śūdra woman whose husband is gone on a journey.[4]
Manu admits that a wife "who drinks spirituous liquor, is
of bad conduct, rebellious, diseased, mischievous, or wasteful,
may at any time be superseded by another wife. A barren
wife may be superseded in the eighth year; one whose
children all die, in the tenth; one who bears only daughters,
in the eleventh; but one who is quarrelsome, without
delay."[5] But this was not divorce in our sense of the term;
for Manu declares that "neither by sale nor by repudiation
is a wife released from her husband,"[6] and that a man may
only marry a virgin.[7] This, however, is evidently one of

[1] Keith, 'Marriage (Hindu),' in Hastings, *op. cit.* viii. 453.
[2] *Nârada*, xii. 92 *sq.*   [3] *Ibid.* xii. 95.
[4] *Ibid.* xii. 97 *sqq.*   [5] *Laws of Manu*, ix. 80 *sq.*
[6] *Ibid.* ix. 46.   [7] *Ibid.* viii. 226.   See also *Âpastamba*, ii. 6. 13. 4.

the many instances in which the existing text has suffered from interpolations and omissions, as Nārada had an earlier text of Manu before him.[1]

The orthodox Hindu law of divorce is more or less disregarded by certain low castes in the north of India and by many castes, both high and low, in the south, among whom usage has superseded texts.[2] Agreeably to such usage, says Mandlik, " the granting of a divorce, or the recognition of a divorce as one properly made, is the duty of the caste. In some cases the mere will of either party or of both parties suffices, and there the caste can do very little, except to accept what has been done."[3] Where it is allowed by custom, a divorce by mutual agreement is also recognised by law.[4] It may be said that, as a rule, the degree in which divorce prevails in India is in direct ratio to the degree in which the respective castes have imitated Brahman habits.[5]

The Buddhists of Burma regard marriage merely as a civil contract which can be annulled by either side without much difficulty.[6] Homicide, stealing, heresy, and adultery are grounds of divorce, and so is desertion. In the case of the husband it must be proved that a period of three years has elapsed during which time he has failed to support his wife in any way, while in the case of the wife it is sufficient that she has deserted her husband for one year, during which no support must have been given her by the husband. Repeated ill-treatment of a wife will entitle her to a divorce. Marriage may always be dissolved by the consent of the parties ; in such a case it is the ordinary rule that the father is given the sons and the mother the daughters, though a son of very tender age also remains with the mother.[7] If one of the parties wishes to separate without good reason, he or she must suffer in property, more or less severely according to the nature of the plea ;[8] and in some

[1] Mayne, op. cit. p. 113 sq.
[2] Gait, op. cit. p. 245.   Steele, op. cit. p. 173.   Mandlik, Vyavahára Mayúkha, p. 428 sqq.   [3] Mandlik, op. cit. p. 434.
[4] Trevelyan, op. cit. p. 58.   [5] Mayne, op. cit. p. 116.
[6] Gait, op. cit. p. 246.   Fytche, Burma Past and Present, ii. 73.
[7] Burge, Commentaries on Colonial and Foreign Laws, iii. 901 sq.
[8] Shway Yoe, The Burman, p. 60.

instances the party not at fault may receive the whole of
the property possessed by both.[1]   Yet in spite of the facility
with which a divorce may be obtained in Burma, we are
told that " unless there is good known cause for a separation
the divorced parties are not by any means looked upon with
a favourable eye";[2] and divorce is said to be very uncommon among the great mass of the people.[3]   In Siam mutual
consent is likewise a good and valid ground for divorce ;[4]
the wife then takes away all the property she brought to
the husband on her marriage and all she may have since
acquired either by trade or purchase, and she retains possession of the first, third, and fifth children.[5]   But marriage
may also be dissolved on such grounds as ill-treatment,
failure to maintain a wife in the position she ought to occupy,
desertion for a statutory period, adultery on the part of the
wife, serious crimes committed by a husband and probably
by a wife, assault on and serious abuse of a wife's parents,
or the husband becoming a priest.[6]

According to Sinhalese law, a marriage publicly contracted
according to proper custom or by the mere consent of the
parties themselves can be dissolved either by the husband
or by the wife.   On the dissolution of such a marriage all
lands, goods, and cattle belonging to the wife, acquired by
right of inheritance, by dowry or by gift, or earned by her
own exertions during marriage, shall revert to her, and
similarly all property belonging to the husband shall revert
to him.   Property acquired by the husband and wife in
common shall be equally divided between them ; but if
the divorce is effected in accordance with the wishes of the
husband for no fault on the part of the wife, he must give
her a proper suit of clothes before discarding her.   As to
the disposal of the children it is laid down that if a *díga*
married woman—that is, a wife who was conducted to,
and lives in, the husband's house—is divorced at the

[1] Burge, *op. cit.* iii. 902.   [2] Shway Yoe, *op. cit.* p. 61.
[3] Fielding, *The Soul of a People*, p. 218 *sq.*
[4] Burge, *op. cit.* iii. 904.
[5] Young, *Kingdom of the Yellow Robe*, p. 99.   *Cf.* Bowring,
Kingdom and People of Siam, i. 119.
[6] Burge, *op. cit.* iii. 903 *sq.*

pleasure of the husband for no fault on her part, she is at
liberty to make over all the children, if there be any, to
the father's care and to refuse to bring up even one of
them ; whereas if such a wife is divorced by the husband
on account of her bad conduct, and if there are several
children, the father may take his choice of them as his
share and commit the others to the care of the mother.
Again, if a *bíni* married husband—that is, one living in
the wife's home or family residence—is sent away by his
wife or by the members of her family, or if he departs in
displeasure, he cannot claim the charge of the children and
has no power over them.[1] An old writer says of the
Sinhalese that if husband or wife dislike one another they
part without disgrace, and that " both women and men
do commonly wed four or five times before they can settle
themselves to their contentation."[2]

When passing to the so-called Aryan peoples of Europe
we find that among the Greeks and Romans in early days,
as among the Hindus, marriage evidently was a union of
great stability, although in later times, contrary to what
was the case among the Aryans of India, it became extremely
easy and frequent. Among the Greeks of the Homeric
age divorce seems to have been almost unknown ;[3] but
afterwards it became an everyday event in Greece.[4]
According to Attic law the husband could repudiate his
wife whenever he liked and without stating any motives.[5]
It is possible that the repudiation generally took place
before witnesses,[6] but this does not seem to have been a
legal necessity. The husband, however, was compelled to
send his divorced wife back to her father's house with her

---

[1] *Níti-Nighanḍuva*, p. 22 *sqq.*

[2] Knox, *Historical Relation of the Island of Ceylon*, p. 188 *sq.*
See also Forbes, *Eleven Years in Ceylon*, i. 332.

[3] Meier and Schömann, *Der attische Process*, p. 510. Hruza,
Beiträge zur Geschichte des griechischen und römischen Familienrechtes,
ii. 24 *sq.* Beauchet, *Histoire du droit privé de la République Athénienne*, i. 376.

[4] Meier and Schömann, *op. cit.* p. 510. Beauchet, *op. cit.* i. 376 *sq.*

[5] Beauchet, *op. cit.* i. 378, 380.

[6] See Lysias, *Oratio contra Alcibiadem*, i. 28.

dowry, and there is no evidence that he could claim the dowry even though the woman had been guilty of adultery or was repudiated for some other fault on her part.[1] If the wife had been convicted of adultery it was necessary for the husband to divorce her, condonation of the offence being visited by *atimia*, or infamy.[2] To repudiate a barren wife was also a sort of duty, both on religious and patriotic grounds, since one of the principal reasons for marriage was to assure the continuation of the family and the perpetuation of the State.[3] The dissolution of marriage could, further, take place by mutual consent, probably without any formalities, except perhaps that, according to usage, the parties made a declaration to the Archon about their divorce.[4] The wife could demand a divorce by appealing to the Archon and stating the motives for her demand.[5] When a marriage was dissolved, the children remained with the father, even though the divorce had been effected by the wife on account of the misconduct of her husband.[6]

A Roman marriage was perhaps at no time indissoluble, but the specifically patrician kind of marriage, by *confarreatio*, was at any rate very nearly so.[7] It could only be dissolved by a formal act, modelled on the principle of *contrarius actus*, a so-called *diffarreatio*, consisting of a counter-sacrifice

[1] Beauchet, *op. cit.* i. 318, 319, 380 *sq.* According to the code of Gortyn, in Crete, if the husband was to blame for the dissolution of marriage, the wife returned to her own family, taking with her her dowry, together with half the increase thereof, half the fruits of her own labour, and five *staters* paid by the husband as fine (Bücheler and Zitelmann, *Das Recht von Gortyn,* p. 118 *sq.*).

[2] *Oratio contra Neæram,* § 87, in Demosthenes, *Opera.*

[3] Beauchet, *op. cit.* i. 379. According to Herodotus (v. 39), barrenness was good ground for divorce at Sparta, at any rate for the royal house (*cf. ibid.* vi. 61).

[4] Beauchet, *op. cit.* i. 387 *sq.*

[5] *Ibid.* i. 381 *sqq.* Meier and Schömann, *op. cit.* p. 512. According to the code of Gortyn marriage could likewise be dissolved by the wife, but we do not know under what conditions (Bücheler and Zitelmann, *op. cit.* p. 118).

[6] Beauchet, *op. cit.* i. 397.

[7] According to Dionysius of Halicarnassus (*Antiquitates Romanæ,* ii. 25) it could not be dissolved.

offered with certain " contrary " words.[1] But as *diffarreatio*
is said to have been a very awful rite,[2] it has been assumed
that it was used only for penal purposes ;[3] while Karlowa
believes that it was a later invention of the priesthood.[4]
The other forms of marriage, not being of the same mystical
and sacramental character as marriage by *confarreatio*,
could be dissolved without difficulty, and the legal form of
divorce is as old as the Twelve Tables and therefore probably
earlier than the fifth century.[5] The divorced wife had to
surrender the keys of the store-rooms, which had been
given to her when newly-married, hence the formula
claves adimere, exigere.[6] Marriages by *coëmtio* and *usus*
were dissolved by *remancipatio*, which corresponded exactly
with the *emancipatio* of a daughter. A husband might
discharge, that is, emancipate, his wife from his power in
the same way as he might discharge his child. " In its
formal aspect," says Sohm, " a *remancipatio* was not so
much an act of divorce as an act of discharge or repudiation."
In the old law a wife *in manu* was as little a free party to
the act of divorce as a child was a free party to that of
emancipation. She had neither the power to require, nor
the power to prevent, a divorce ; and the husband's legal
authority in regard to the dissolution of a marriage with
manus was as absolute as it was in regard to the other
incidents of such a marriage.[7] Yet in practice the husband's
right was no doubt more or less checked by public opinion
and, as it seems, even by the Censors, who probably
exercised their authority when a husband made an unjustifiable use of his power.[8] There was a tradition that
Romulus had forbidden the repudiation of wives unless

[1] Festus, *De significatione verborum*, *s.v.* ' Diffarreatio,' p. 74.
Karlowa, *Römische Rechtsgeschichte*, ii. 186. Sohm, *Institutes*,
p. 474.

[2] Plutarch, *Questiones Romanae*, 50.

[3] Fowler, ' Marriage (Roman),' in Hastings, *op. cit.* viii. 466.

[4] Karlowa, *op. cit.* ii. 186.

[5] Fowler, in Hastings, *op. cit.* viii. 466.

[6] Cicero, *In M. Antonium oratio Philippica*, ii. 28.

[7] Sohm, *op. cit.* p. 475.

[8] Hunter, *Exposition of Roman Law*, p. 691.

they were guilty of adultery or drinking wine, on pain of
forfeiture of all the offender's property, one-half to go to
the wife and the other to Ceres ;[1] and it was also said that
for five hundred years no one took advantage of the liberty
of divorce until Spurius Carvilius put away his wife for
barrenness by order of the Censor.[2] The actual meaning
of this statement is not clear,[3] but it at any rate shows
that in earlier times divorce must have been rare in Rome.

The rule of divorce was very different in regard to a
" free " marriage, which implied that the wife did not fall
under the *manus* of her husband. The dissolution of such
a marriage could be brought about either by mutual agreement between both parties or by the will of one party only.
Besides the intention to separate, however, the Roman
law required what was called a *repudium,* that is, an act
by which one spouse notified the other of his or her intention
to dissolve the marriage, which, in fact, was required in
all cases of divorce.[4] Such a notification might be conveyed
either by word of mouth or through a messenger ; the *Lex
Julia de adulteriis* prescribed that a *libellus repudii* should
be given in the presence of seven Roman citizens above
the age of puberty as witnesses.[5] As far as the right to
bring about a divorce was concerned, the legal position of
the wife was the same as that of the husband.[6] It should
be noticed, however, that when the wife remained in the
potestas of her father, the latter could, in the exercise of

---

[1] Dionysius of Halicarnassus, *op. cit.* ii. 25.   Plutarch, *Romulus,*
xxii. 4 *sq.*

[2] Dionysius of Halicarnassus, *op. cit.* ii. 25.

[3] See Rein, *Das Römische Privatrecht,* p. 208 ; Marquardt, *Das
Privatleben der Römer,* p. 70 *sq.*

[4] That this was the meaning of the term *repudium* has been
shown by Zeumer (' Geschichte der westgothischen Gesetzgebung,'
in *Neues Archiv der Gesellschaft für ältere deutsche Geschichtskunde,*
xxiv. 620 *sqq.*), contrary to the earlier opinion (held, for example, by
Dernburg, *Pandekten,* iii. 18) that *repudium* was a divorce by unilateral act while *divortium* meant a divorce by mutual consent.
Divortium was the general name for any kind of divorce, whether
effected by agreement or by the act of one party only.

[5] *Digesta,* xxiv. 2. 9.

[6] Sohm, *op. cit.* p. 475 *sq.*   Hunter, *op. cit.* p. 691.

his power, take his daughter from her husband against the wishes of both.[1]   And it may be presumed that this power was not unexercised, as we find that a constitution of Antoninus Pius prohibited a father from disturbing a harmonious union, and Marcus Aurelius afterwards limited this prohibition by allowing the interference of a father for a " strong and just cause."[2]

The rules of divorce which were recognised in the case of a free marriage were afterwards extended to marriages with *manus*. A wife *in manu* could not, it is true, directly effect the extinction of the *manus* by means of a *repudium* ; but according to the view of the later times, the wife's *repudium* operated indirectly to dissolve even marriages with *manus*, by compelling the husband in his turn to take all necessary steps for the purpose of extinguishing the *manus*. And in the end marriages with *manus* fell into disuse altogether.[3]

As to the settlement of children after the divorce of their parents the earliest legal provision seems to be a constitution of Diocletian and Maximian, which stated that there was no law compelling the judge in such a case to give the male children to the father and the female children to the mother, but that he could act according to his discretion.[4] Justinian enacted that if the father was guilty of an offence justifying his wife in divorcing him and she remained unmarried, the children were to be given into her custody but maintained at the cost of the father ; whereas, if the mother was guilty, the father had the right of custody. If he was poor and unable to support the children and the mother was rich, she was obliged to take them and maintain them.[5]

In pagan times Roman law was thus as liberal as possible so far as the husband's right of divorce was concerned, and in the case of marriage without *manus*, and in later days in practically all cases, equally liberal with regard to the wife's. Though in early times seldom taken advantage of,

[1] *Cf.* Hunter, *op. cit.* p. 689.
[2] *Ibid.* p. 689. *Codex Justinianus*, v. 17. 5.
[3] Sohm, *op. cit.* p. 476. Karlowa, *op. cit.* ii. 189.
[4] *Codex Justinianus*, v. 24. 1.   [5] *Novellae*, cxvii. 7.

this freedom was subsequently exercised on a large scale, at least among the upper classes. By the second century B.C., when marriage was becoming unpopular in high social circles, divorce was becoming common, and its frequency increased towards the end of the Republican era and during the Empire.[1] Almost all the well-known ladies of the Ciceronian age were divorced at least once,[2] and Seneca said that some women counted their years, not by consuls, but by their husbands.[3] Ovid and Pliny the Younger married three times, Cæsar and Antony four, Sulla and Pompey five; and such cases must have been frequent. On the stone erected to a certain Turia by her husband in the early days of the Empire it is said, " Seldom do marriages last until death undivorced."[4]

In the law-books of Celtic peoples we find various rules relating to divorce, from which we may draw the conclusion that separation of married couples was by no means an uncommon occurrence. In ancient Ireland separation might take place either by mutual consent or as the outcome of legal proceedings. As we have seen above, if the couple separated by mutual consent the woman took away with her all she had brought on the marriage day, while the man retained what he had contributed; and in case the joint property had gone on increasing during married life the couple divided the whole in proportion to the original contributions, though special circumstances were also carefully taken into account, such as if the man or the woman had been a " great " worker or a " small " worker.[5] With reference to the latter kind of separation it is said in one of the Brehon law tracts :—" There are with the Feine seven women, who, though bound by son and security, are competent to separate from cohabitation,

---

[1] Fowler, *Social Life at Rome in the Age of Cicero*, p. 147. Marquardt, *op. cit.* p. 71 *sq.*

[2] Fowler, in Hastings, *op. cit.* viii. 466.

[3] Seneca, *De beneficiis*, iii. 16. 2.

[4] Friedländer, *Darstellungen aus der Sittengeschichte Roms in der Zeit von August bis zum Ausgang der Antonine*, i. 284.

[5] *Supra*, ii. 427. Joyce, *Social History of Ancient Ireland*, ii. 9 *sqq.*

whatever day they like ; and whatever has been given them as their dowry, is theirs by right : a woman of whom her husband circulates a false story ; a woman upon whom her husband gives circulation to a satire until she is laughed at ; a woman upon whom a check-blemish is inflicted ; a woman who is sent back and repudiated for another ; a woman who is cheated of bed-rites, so that her husband prefers to lie with servant-boys when it was not necessary for him ; a woman to whom her mate has administered a philtre when entreating her, so that he brings her to fornication ; a woman who is not able to receive her desire in the community of marriage,—for every woman among the Feine on whom there is this bond, and who gives her proper co-operation for it, is entitled to her desire."[1]

In ancient Wales either husband or wife might, practically, separate whenever one or both chose. There seems to have been no legal method of bringing the parties again together ; but the time and circumstances of the separation entailed different consequences in regard to the division of the household goods.[2] If the separation was voluntary on both sides and took place before the union had lasted seven years less three nights, the wife was only entitled to take away from the house her marriage portion and morning gift,[3] whereas in the case of separation by agreement at a later date everything belonging to the couple was divided into two portions. The law set out minutely the things that were to go to the wife and to the husband respectively, and as to those which the law did not specifically allot, the wife had the right to divide them and the husband chose which portion he would take.[4] Of the children two shares went to the father and one to the mother—the eldest and the youngest to the former, and the middlemost to the mother.[5] If a wife was " guilty of an odious deed along

---

[1] *Ancient Laws and Institutes of Ireland*, v. 293.

[2] Rhys and Brynmor-Jones, *The Welsh People*, p. 212 *sq.*

[3] *Venedotian Code*, ii. 1. 9 (*Ancient Laws and Institutes of Wales*, p. 39).

[4] *Ibid.* ii. 1. 1, 2, 4 *sqq.* (p. 38 *sq.*).

[5] *Ibid.* ii. 1. 3 (p. 38). *Gwentian Code*, ii. 29. 13 (*Ancient Laws and Institutes of Wales*, p. 364).

with another man, whether by kiss, *aut coitu aut palpando,*"
the husband could repudiate her, and she forfeited all her
property rights.[1] She also lost all her property, with the
exception of her morning gift and her right to any fine due
from the husband for having committed adultery, in case
she left him before the seventh year less three nights without
good cause.[2] But if the husband was affected with leprosy
or had a fetid breath or was impotent, she might repudiate
him without any loss of property.[3]

According to the old customary law of the Teutonic
peoples outlawry of either husband or wife put an end to
the marriage. It could be dissolved by agreement between
the husband and the woman's kin ; and the husband was
entitled to repudiate his wife if she was sterile or guilty of
conjugal infidelity and perhaps for some other offences.
If he did so without good cause, the marriage was dissolved, but he exposed himself to the revenge of her
kindred or had to pay a fine or suffered some other loss
in property.[4] The wife had originally no right to dis-

---

[1] *Dimetian Code,* ii. 18. 31 (*Ancient Laws and Institutes of Wales,*
p. 257).

[2] *Venedotian Code,* ii. 1. 9 (*Ancient Laws and Institutes of Wales,*
p. 39).

[3] *Ibid.* ii. 1. 10 (p. 39). *Gwentian Code,* ii. 29. 26 (*Ancient Laws
and Institutes of Wales,* p. 365). For the method of deciding whether
the husband was impotent or not, see *Venedotian Code,* ii. 1. 66
(*Ancient Laws and Institutes of Wales,* p. 47).

[4] Brunner, *Grundzüge der deutschen Rechtsgeschichte,* p. 224.
Idem, ' Die Geburt eines lebenden Kindes und das eheliche Vermögensrecht,' in *Zeitschr. d. Savigny-Stiftung f. Rechtsgeschichte,*
xvi. 105 *sqq.* Schroeder, *Lehrbuch der deutschen Rechtsgeschichte,*
p. 305 *sq.* Freisen, *Geschichte des Canonischen Eherechts,* p. 778
sq. Loening, *Geschichte des deutschen Kirchenrechts,* ii. 617 *sqq.*
Pollock and Maitland, *History of the English Law before the Time of
Edward I.,* ii. 392 *sq.* Gudmundsson and Kålund, ' Sitte. Skandinavische Verhältnisse,' in Paul, *Grundriss der germanischen Philologie,* iii. 422. According to Tacitus (*Germania,* ch. 19), the husband
could disgrace a wife who had committed adultery and turn her
out of his house. Brunner (*Grundzüge der deutschen Rechtsgeschichte,*
p. 226 n. 2) points out that if the wife had given birth to a living
child, even if it died shortly afterwards, one of the main grounds
for divorce was lacking.

solve the marriage ;[1] but in the Frankish period she could, according to some law-books, effect a divorce in certain cases, as if the husband was convicted of adultery or sodomy.[2] This innovation has been traced to the influence of Christian ideas.[3]

[1] Brunner, *Grundzüge der deutschen Rechtsgeschichte*, p. 224. *Idem*, in *Zeitschr. d. Savigny-Stiftung f. Rechtsgeschichte*, xvi. 106. Loening, *op. cit.* ii. 618.

[2] Brunner, *Grundzüge der deutschen Rechtsgeschichte*, p. 224. Loening, *op. cit.* ii. 619, 622 *sq.* Freisen, *op. cit.* p. 780. Freisen observes (*ibid.* p. 780 *sq.*) that the wife could never divorce her husband, because she was unable to annul his power (*mundium*) over her, but that the law in certain cases deprived him of his *mundium*, with the result that the wife could leave him if she pleased.

[3] Freisen, *op. cit.* p 780.

CHAPTER XXXIII

THE DURATION OF MARRIAGE AND THE RIGHT TO DISSOLVE IT

(*Concluded*)

CHRISTIANITY revolutionised European legislation with regard to divorce. In the New Testament there are various passages bearing upon the question.[1] A man who puts away his wife and marries another commits adultery against her, and a woman who puts away or deserts her husband and is married to another is guilty of the same crime. A man shall cleave to his wife, " they twain shall be one flesh"; and "what God hath joined together, let not man put asunder." There are, however, two exceptions to this rule. Like Shammai and his school, Christ taught, according to St. Matthew, that a man might put away his wife for fornication, but for no other reason;[2] and St. Paul lays down the rule that if a Christian is married to an unbeliever and the latter departs, the Christian " is not under bondage in such cases."[3] A man who married the divorced adulteress was himself guilty of adultery, but there is no indication whatever that the innocent husband was prohibited from remarrying. Yet, in accordance with the ascetic tendencies of early Christianity, it seems to have been the general opinion among the Fathers of the first three centuries that no such remarriage was allowed ; if a second marriage was disapproved of as adultery even in the case of a widower

---

[1] *St. Matthew*, v. 32 ; xix. 3 *sqq.* *St. Mark*, x. 2 *sqq.* *St. Luke*, xvi. 18. *Romans*, vii. 2. 1 *Corinthians*, vii. 10-15, 39.
[2] *St. Matthew*, v. 32 ; xix. 9. [3] 1 *Corinthians*, vii. 15.

or widow, how could it be permitted while the first spouse was still alive ? Subsequently laxer views were expressed, but, largely under the influence of St. Augustine, the Church gradually made up her mind to deny the dissolubility of a valid Christian marriage, at least if it had been consummated.[1] Her doctrine on the subject was in the twelfth century definitely fixed by Gratian and Peter Lombard ;[2] it was dogmatically asserted by the Council of Trent,[3] and was in the nineteenth century reaffirmed by Pius IX and Leo XIII.[4] A consummated Christian marriage is a sacrament and must as such remain valid for ever. It represents the union between Christ and the Church, and is consequently as indissoluble as that union.[5] It is also permanent according to the law of nature, because only as permanent can marriage fulfil its object. And God made it so at the very beginning of our race, when He decreed[6] that a man shall leave his father and his mother and shall cleave unto his wife, and they shall be one flesh.[7]

On the other hand, a Christian marriage which has not been consummated is not indissoluble ; it is only by consummation that such a marriage becomes a sacrament and a symbol of the union between Christ and the Church.[8] The Council of Trent expressly decreed that " matrimony

---

[1] Loening, op. cit. ii. 607 sqq. v. Moy, Das Eherecht der Christen, p. 11 sqq. Freisen, op. cit. p. 770 sqq. Esmein, Le mariage en droit canonique, ii. 49 sqq.

[2] Esmein, op. cit. ii. 73 sqq. Gratian, Decretum, ii. 32. 7. 2 :— " Nulla ratione dissolvitur conjugium, quod semel initum probatur."

[3] While the indissolubility of marriage on the ground of adultery was expressed in somewhat guarded terms (Canones et decreta Concilii Tridentini, sess. xxiv. can. 7) out of consideration for the Eastern Church (see Esmein, op. cit. ii. 305), the other causes for divorce were expressly condemned in the fifth canon, where it is said :—" Si quis dixerit, propter haeresim, aut molestam cohabitationem, aut affectatam absentiam a coniuge dissolvi posse matrimonii vinculum : anathema sit." This condemnation was particularly directed against the Protestants (see Esmein, op. cit. ii. 305 sq.).

[4] Esmein, op. cit. ii. 307.

[5] Freisen, op. cit. p. 802 sq. Loening, op. cit. ii. 610 sq.

[6] Genesis, ii. 24. [7] Esmein, op. cit. i. 64 sqq.

[8] Gratian, op. cit. ii. 27. 2. 39. Freisen, op. cit. p. 802 sq.

contracted but not consummated" might be dissolved by
"the solemn profession of religion by one of the married
parties";[1] and it may also be dissolved for other reasons
by an act of Papal authority.[2] Non-Christian marriage is
not a sacrament, even though consummated;[3] hence it
is in certain circumstances dissoluble, in accordance with
St. Paul's dictum that a Christian married to an infidel
is not under bondage if the latter depart. Innocent III
declared authoritatively that if, in the case of a marriage
between two infidels, one of them became a Christian, the
convert was justified in entering into another marriage,
provided that either the non-Christian was unwilling to
live with the other or such cohabitation would cause the
blasphemy of the Divine name or be an incentive to mortal
sin.[4] It was argued that this so-called *privilegium Paulinum*
is no exception to the rule that Christian marriage is indissoluble, because in the case in question the marriage is
dissolved not by the Christian but by the infidel, and the
Church has nothing to do with the marriages of infidels.[5]

While asserting the indissolubility of Christian marriage,
the Church admitted a *divortium imperfectum* or *separatio
quoad thorum et mensam*, a "separation from bed and
board," which discharged the parties from the duty of
living together but at the same time left them husband and
wife and consequently unable to marry any other person.
According to the Council of Trent, such separation may
take place "for many causes," either for a determinate or
for an indeterminate period.[6] The chief cause is adultery
or other carnal sin, equivalent to it; but already St.
Augustine had spoken of a *fornicatio spiritualis* as a ground

---

[1] *Canones et decreta Concilii Tridentini*, xxiv. 6.
[2] Ballerini-Palmieri, *Opus theologicum morale*, vi. 367 *sq.* Freisen,
op. cit. pp. 212, 213, 826 *sq.* Walter, *Lehrbuch des Kirchenrechts
aller christlichen Confessionen*, p. 714 *sq.* Friedberg, *Lehrbuch des
katholischen und evangelischen Kirchenrechts*, p. 503.
[3] Friedberg, *op. cit.* p. 503. Esmein, *op. cit.* i. 222.
[4] Ballerini-Palmieri, *op. cit.* vi. 325. See also Friedberg, *op. cit.*
p. 503.
[5] Freisen, *op. cit.* p. 806 *sqq.*
[6] *Canones et decreta Concilii Tridentini*, xxiv. 8.

for separation,[1] and this view was accepted by Gratian, who regarded as such apostasy,[2] heresy,[3] and incitement to evil deeds.[4] Subsequently a distinction was made between permanent and temporary separation.[5] According to some writers, perpetual separation may be granted only for *fornicatio carnalis*, unless it has been condoned or unless both parties have been guilty of it.[6] According to others, it may also be granted for defection from the Faith whether by the rejection of Christianity or by heresy, and on account of entrance into the state of Christian perfection, that is, entrance into religious life on the part of the wife or of the husband or by the reception of Holy Orders on the part of the husband ;- but in such cases there are required both mutual consent and some arrangement on the part of ecclesiastical authority. Besides these special cases of separation many other cases may arise justifying temporary separation. They may be summed up under the general notion of " danger to body or soul."[7]

Yet in spite of the theory of the indissolubility of Christian marriage, the Roman Catholic doctrine gives ecclesiastics a large practical power of dissolving marriages which may have appeared perfectly valid. The Church recognised a legal process which was popularly, though incorrectly, called a divorce *a vinculo matrimonii*, " from the bond of matrimony," in case the union had been unlawful from the beginning on the ground of some canonical impediment, such as relationship or earlier engagement of marriage. This only implied that a marriage which never had been valid would remain invalid ; but practically it led to the possibility of dissolving marriages which in theory were indissoluble. For, as Lord Bryce observes, " the rules regarding impediments were so numerous and so intricate that it was easy, given a sufficient motive, whether political

[1] Freisen, *op. cit.* p. 836. [2] Gratian, *op. cit.* ii. 28. 1. 6.
[3] *Ibid.* ii. 28. 2. 2. [4] *Ibid.* ii. 28. 1. 5.
[5] Freisen, *op. cit.* p. 837.
[6] *Ibid.* p. 830 *sqq.* Friedberg, *op. cit.* p. 508. Walter, *op. cit.* p. 716.
[7] Ballerini-Palmieri, *op. cit.* vi. 381 *sqq.* Lehmkuhl, ' Divorce,' in *Catholic Encyclopedia,* v. 63 *sq.*

or pecuniary, to discover some ground for declaring almost any marriage invalid."[1]

The doctrine of the Western Church profoundly influenced the secular legislation of the countries in which she was established. For a long time, however, it was not accepted in full by the legislators. The Christian emperors laid down certain grounds on which a husband could divorce his wife and a wife her husband without blame. According to Constantine, a man was allowed to dissolve the marriage if his wife was an adulteress, a preparer of poisons, or a procuress ; and the wife could do so if her husband was guilty of murder, prepared poisons, or violated tombs.[2] After some further legislation on the subject by later emperors,[3] Justinian repealed the earlier constitutions and resettled the grounds of divorce. A man may repudiate his wife if, she knows of any plots against the Empire and does not disclose them to him ; if she commits adultery ; if she makes an attempt on his life or conceals any plots against it ; if she frequents banquets or baths with men against his orders ; if she remains from home against his wishes unless with her own parents or unless he drives her out ; or if she goes to the circus, theatre, or amphitheatre without the knowledge or after the express prohibition of her husband.[4] A woman may divorce her husband if he engages in or is privy to any plots against the Empire ; if he makes an attempt on her life or conceals any plots against it of which he is aware ; if he attempts to induce her to commit adultery ; if he accuses her of adultery and fails to substantiate the charge ; if he takes a woman to live in the same house with his wife ; or if he persists in frequenting any other house in the same town with any woman after being warned more than once by his wife or her parents or other persons of respectability.[5] At the

---

[1] Bryce, *Studies in History and Jurisprudence*, ii. 434. Lecky, *Democracy and Liberty*, ii. 193 *sq.* Pollock and Maitland, *op. cit.* ii. 393.

[2] *Codex Theodosianus*, iii. 16. 1.

[3] *Ibid.* iii. 16. 2 (Honorius and Theodosius). *Codex Justinianus*, v. 17. 8. 2 (Theodosius and Valentinian).

[4] *Novellae*, cxvii. 8.   [5] *Ibid.* cxvii. 9.

same time the right of either party to dissolve the marriage at will by simple notice to the other party was not formally abolished even by the legislation of the Christian Empire ; however causeless the *repudium*, its effect was to terminate the marriage. But it was provided that, when a marriage was dissolved without any statutory ground of divorce, the offending party should suffer certain penalties. Thus when a wife repudiated the marriage without sufficient cause she forfeited her dowry, whereas when the husband was the offender he was deprived of his *donatio propter nuptias*, in other words, he was required actually to pay over the *donatio* he had covenanted to pay. On the conclusion of every marriage the husband was required to contribute a *donatio ante (propter) nuptias* corresponding to the *dos* contributed on the part of the wife, and in the Christian Empire it was the primary purpose of this *donatio* to confer on a wife who was divorced without just cause a positive proprietary benefit at the expense of her husband.[1] Justinian also prohibited divorce by mutual consent—which until then seems to have taken place without any legal check whatever—except when the husband was impotent, when either he or the wife desired to enter a monastery, and when either of them was in captivity for a certain length of time.[2] Subsequently Justinian even enacted that persons dissolving a marriage by mutual consent should forfeit all their property and be confined for life in a monastery.[3] But his nephew and successor, Justin the Second, repealed his uncle's prohibitions relating to this kind of divorce.[4]

The facility of divorce by mutual consent also remained in the Roman codes of the German kings, and, as under the older Roman legislation, a man might further divorce his wife for certain offences.[5] Those subjects of the Western rulers who elected to live under the old Teutonic systems of law seem to have had an equal facility.[6] Thus the dooms

---

[1] Sohm, *Institutes*, p. 476.   Hunter, *op. cit.* p. 692 *sq.*
[2] *Novellae*, cxvii. 12.   [3] *Ibid.* cxxxiv. 11.   [4] *Ibid.* cxl. 1.
[5] Freisen, *op. cit.* p. 776 *sqq.*   Watkins, *Holy Matrimony*, p. 380 *sq.*   [6] Freisen, *op. cit.* p. 778 *sqq.*

of Aethelbirht, Christian though they be, suggest that the marriage might be dissolved at the will of both parties or even at the will of one of them.[1] Even the Anglo-Saxon and Frankish penitentials allow a divorce in various cases.[2] According to Theodore's Penitential the husband may divorce an adulterous wife and marry another, and she too may marry again, though only after five years of penance ;[3] but a wife cannot dissolve the marriage on account of the adultery of her husband.[4] The husband may also marry another woman if the wife is carried into captivity [5] or if she deserts him, but in the latter case only after five years have elapsed and with the bishop's consent.[6] Since the days of Charlemagne, however, the canonical doctrine of the indissolubility of marriage entered the secular legislation of German peoples, and in the tenth century the ecclesiastical rules and courts gained exclusive control of this branch of law in Germany.[7] At a somewhat earlier date the provisions of the Roman law had been superseded by new rules enforced by the Church in the regions where the imperial law had been observed.[8]

While the Western Church in the matter of divorce at last completely triumphed in the countries under her sway, the Eastern Church, instead of shaping the secular law, was on the contrary greatly influenced by it. It is true that the Council of Trullo in 692 expressly condemned divorce by mutual consent and that largely in consequence of this condemnation the emperor Leo III (the Isaurian) in 740 put a stop to the legality of consensual divorces ; and at the end of the ninth century the prohibition against them was reinforced, never again to be relaxed.[9] But of the whole long list of specified grounds of divorce which were

---

[1] *Laws of Aethelbirht,* 79 *sqq.   Cf.* Pollock and Maitland, *op. cit.* ii. 393.   [2] Freisen, *op. cit.* p. 785 *sqq.*

[3] *Pœnitentiale Theodori,* ii. 12. 5 (in Haddan and Stubbs, *Councils and Ecclesiastical Documents relating to Great Britain and Ireland,* iii. 199).   [4] *Ibid.* ii. 12. 6. (vol. iii. 199).

[5] *Ibid.* ii. 12. 23 (vol. iii. 200 *sq.*).   [6] *Ibid.* ii. 12. 19 (vol. iii. 200).

[7] Brunner, *Grundzüge der deutschen Rechtsgeschichte,* p. 224.

[8] Bryce, *op. cit.* ii. 433.

[9] Zhishman, *Das Eherecht der Orientalischen Kirche,* p. 104 *sqq.*

admitted by the secular law none, except that of absence
without tidings, appears even to have been questioned by
the Eastern Church. " The enactments of the emperors
and princes as to the grounds of divorce," says Zhishman,
"never met with an ecclesiastical contradiction. No
Council, no patriarch, no bishop of the East has ever in
that matter called the emperors to account, assigned
penalties to them, or forced them to the repeal of their
enactments."[1] The grounds of divorce with the right of
remarriage are those admitted by the laws of Justinian
with certain modifications introduced in later times. In
the Eastern Churches of the present day divorce is permitted
on the following grounds, with penalty attached : high
treason, designs of either of the partners on the life of the
other, adultery, circumstances affording presumption of
adultery or equivalent to adultery, the procuring of abortion,
difference of religion arising from the conversion to
Christianity of one of the partners, and the acting as
sponsor for one's own child in baptism. There are further
grounds for divorce, without penalty attached, namely :
impotence, absence without tidings received, captivity and
slavery, insanity and imbecility, the undertaking of monastic
obligations, and episcopal consecration.[2]

The canonical doctrines that marriage is a sacrament and
that it is indissoluble save by death were rejected by the
Reformers. They all agreed that divorce, with liberty for
the innocent party to remarry, should be granted for
adultery, and most of them regarded malicious desertion as
a second legitimate cause for the dissolution of marriage.[3]
The latter opinion was based on St. Paul's dictum that a
Christian married to an unbeliever " is not under bondage "
if the unbeliever depart, which was broadened by Luther
so as to include malicious desertion even without a religious

[1] *Ibid.* p. 115.
[2] *Ibid.* pp. 107 *sqq.*, 729 *sqq.* A summary of Zhishman's account
is given by Watkins, *op. cit.* p. 353 *sqq.*
[3] Friedberg, *op. cit.* p. 514 *sq.* Walter, *op. cit.* p. 719 *sq.* For
the opinions of the continental Reformers see particularly Richter,
*Beiträge zur Geschichte des Ehescheidungsrechts in der evangelischen
Kirche*, p. 6 *sqq.*

motive.[1] The same reformer admits that the worldly authorities may allow divorce also on other strong grounds,[2] and mentions himself obstinate refusal of conjugal intercourse as sufficient cause for it.[3] Several reformers went farther than Luther.[4] Lambert of Avignon argues that if a wife leaves her husband because she is constantly ill-treated by him without cause, this should be counted as repudiation by the man and not as desertion by the woman ;[5] and Melanchton likewise justifies divorce in the case of ill-treatment.[6] The views of the Reformers exercised a lasting influence upon the Protestant legislators both in Germany and other continental countries. Thus the Danish law-book issued by Christian V in 1684 mentions as sufficient grounds for divorce desertion for at least three years, impotence which has lasted for the same period,[7] and leprosy which has been concealed and communicated to the other party.[8] The Swedish code of 1734 allows divorce for malicious desertion after the judge has caused a notice to be read from the pulpits of the churches within his jurisdiction citing the absconding party to return within a year and a night to his or her home and this notice has been neglected ;[9] for long absence without tidings ;[10] and for bodily incapacity or incurable contagious disease deliberately concealed.[11]

The Fathers of English Protestantism as a body were more conservative than the brethren across the Channel. But they were unanimous in allowing the husband to put away an unfaithful wife and contract another marriage ; and prevailing opinion appears also to have accorded a similar privilege to the wife on like provocation, although there were undoubtedly some in the Protestant ranks who were not so liberal in her behalf.[12] A general revision of the ecclesiastical code, with special attention directed to the

---

[1] v. Strampff, *Dr. Martin Luther : Ueber die Ehe*, pp. 381, 393.

[2] *Ibid.* pp. 354, 399.   [3] *Ibid.* p. 394.

[4] See Richter, *op. cit.* p. 31 *sqq.*   [5] Richter, *op. cit.* p. 32.

[6] *Ibid.* p. 33 *sq.* Friedberg, *op. cit.* p. 514 *sq.*

[7] *Kong Christian den Femtis Danske Lov*, iii. 16. 15. 2 *sq.*

[8] *Ibid.* iii. 16. 16. 4.   [9] *Sveriges Rikes Lag*, Giftermåls-Balk, xiii. 4.

[10] *Ibid.* Giftermåls-Balk, xiii. 6.   [11] *Ibid.* Giftermåls-Balk, xiii. 8.

[12] Howard, *History of Matrimonial Institutions*, ii. 71 *sqq.*

law of divorce, was contemplated in the earlier days of the
Reformation. A commission of leading ecclesiastics was for
this purpose appointed by Henry VIII and Edward VI.
The commissioners drew up the elaborate report known as
Reformatio Legum, in which they recommended that
" divorces from bed and board," which had been rejected
by nearly all the English reformers of the sixteenth century
as a papist innovation,[1] should be abolished, and in their
place complete divorce, with liberty for the innocent party
to marry again, should be allowed in cases of adultery,
desertion, and cruelty, as also in cases where a husband not
guilty of deserting his wife had been for several years absent
from her in circumstances which justified her in considering
that he was dead, and in cases of such violent hatred as
rendered it in the highest degree improbable that the
husband and wife would survive their animosities and again
love one another. The whole scheme, however, fell to the
ground, partly in consequence of King Edward's premature
death.[2] Yet the principle represented by it was carried
out in practice. Already in 1548, some years before the
commission had completed its report, the new doctrine had
been in a measure sustained by the well-known case of Lord
Northampton, whose second marriage was declared valid
by an Act of Parliament. Under Elizabeth this decision
seems to have been deemed good law until 1602, when, in
the Foljambe case, it was decided that remarriage after
judicial separation was null and void.[3] After this revival
of the old canon law, says Jeaffreson, " our ancestors lived
for several generations under a matrimonial law of un-
exampled rigour and narrowness. The gates of exit from
true matrimony had all been closed, with the exception of
death. Together with the artificial impediments to wedlock,
the Reformation had demolished the machinery for annulling

---

[1] *Ibid.* ii. 73.

[2] Macqueen, *Practical Treatise on the Appellate Jurisdiction of the
House of Lords and Privy Council*, p. 467. Morgan, *Doctrine and
Law of Marriage, Adultery, and Divorce*, ii. 227 *sqq.* Jeaffreson,
Brides and Bridals, ii. 319 *sqq.*

[3] Howard, *op. cit.* ii. 79 *sqq.* Jeaffreson, *op. cit.* ii. 323 *sq.* Morgan,
op. cit. ii. 229 *sqq.*

marriages on fictitious grounds.   Henceforth no man could
slip out of matrimonial bondage by swearing that he was
his wife's distant cousin, or had loved her sister in his
youth, or had before his marriage stood godfather to one of
her near spiritual kindred."[1]

In the latter part of the seventeenth century a practice
arose in England which in a small degree mitigated the
rigour of the law.   While a valid English marriage could
not be dissolved by mere judicial authority, it might be
so by a special Act of Parliament.   Such a parliamentary
divorce, however, was granted only for adultery : to a
husband whose own conduct had been free from reproach, if
he had previously obtained a " divorce from bed and board "
in the ecclesiastical court, but to a wife only in aggravated
cases, such as incestuous intercourse of her husband with
some of her relations.[2]   Moreover, it was a remedy within
the reach of the wealthier classes only : owing to the triple
cost of the law action, the ecclesiastical decree, and the
legislative proceedings, it could be obtained only through
the expenditure of a fortune sometimes amounting to
thousands of pounds.[3]   As a matter of fact, up to and
including the year 1857, no more than 317 divorce bills
passed,[4] and the practice had already been in operation
for a hundred and thirty years when, in 1801, a married
woman for the first time obtained a divorce of this kind.[5]

In the civil divorce law of 1857 the legal principle of the
indissolubility of marriage was at last abandoned, though
only after stubborn resistance.   For the dilatory and
expensive proceedings of three tribunals was substituted
one inquiry by a court specially constituted to exercise this
jurisdiction, a new " Court for Divorce and Matrimonial
Causes."   On this court was conferred all the authority of
the ecclesiastical courts in matrimonial causes, as also power
to grant a " divorce from the bond of matrimony," as a

[1] Jeaffreson, *op. cit.* ii. 339.

[2] Blackstone-Kerr, *Commentaries on the Laws of England*, i. 416
sq. Macqueen, *op. cit.* p. 471 *sqq.* Morgan, *op. cit.* ii. 237 *sqq.*
Jeaffreson, *op. cit.* ii. 341 *sqq.*

[3] Howard, *op. cit.* ii. 107 *sq.*   Blackstone-Kerr, *op. cit.* i. 417.

[4] Burge, *op. cit.* iii. 862   [5] Macqueen, *op. cit.* p. 474 *sq.*

right, not as a privilege. Such a divorce, however, could only be granted to a husband whose wife had been guilty of adultery and to a wife whose husband had been guilty of incestuous adultery, bigamy with adultery, rape, sodomy, bestiality, or adultery coupled with cruelty or with desertion without reasonable excuse for two years and upwards. " Cruelty " has been defined as " conduct of such a character as to have caused danger to life, limb, or health (bodily or mental), or as to give rise to a reasonable apprehension of such danger."[1] Since the Judicature Act, 1873, the powers of that tribunal to which the jurisdiction in matrimonial matters was transferred are vested in the Probate and Divorce Division of the High Court of Justice, but the grounds on which divorce can be granted have remained unchanged.[2] The Matrimonial Causes Act, 1857, does not extend to Ireland, where the complete dissolution of the marriage tie can still be obtained only by an Act of Parliament.[3] In Scotland the courts began to grant divorces very soon after the Roman connection had been repudiated, and in 1573 a statute added desertion to adultery of the husband or the wife as a ground for divorce.[4]

On the Continent a fresh impetus to a more liberal legislation on divorce was given in the eighteenth century by the new philosophy with its conceptions of human freedom and natural rights. If marriage is a contract entered into by mutual consent it ought also to be dissolvable if both parties wish to annul the contract. In the Prussian ' Project des Corporis Juris Fridericiani ' of 1749, " founded on reason and the constitutions of the country," it is admitted that married people may demand with common consent the dissolution of their marriage. The procedure in the affair, however, shall be only gradual. First, endeavours shall be made to reconcile the parties, and, if it be necessary, a

[1] Earl of Halsbury, *Laws of England*, xvi. 473 *sq.*

[2] Blackstone-Kerr, *op. cit.* i. 417. Geary, *Law of Marriage and Family Relations*, p. 239 *sqq.* Howard, *op. cit.* ii. 109 *sq.* Burge, *op. cit.* iii. 862 *sq.* Earl of Halsbury, *op. cit.* xvi. 481, 500.

[3] Burge, *op. cit.* iii. 863, 877.

[4] Bryce, *op. cit.* ii. 435. Erskine-Rankine, *Principles of the Law of Scotland*, p. 77.

clergyman shall be called to give them a suitable exhortation. If these steps prove ineffectual, they shall be separated from bed and board for one year ; but if after this period they still persist in their petition and there remain no more hopes of reconciling them, the marriage may be dissolved.[1] The ' Project ' never became law ; but in practice divorce was freely granted by Frederick II *ex gratia principis* at the common request of husband and wife.[2]   In the Prussian ' Landrecht ' of 1794 divorce by mutual consent is admitted if the couple have no children and there is no reason to suspect levity, precipitation, or compulsion ;[3] and power is given to the judge to dissolve a marriage in cases in which he finds a dislike so strong and deeply rooted that there is no prospect of reconciliation and the marriage consequently will fail to fulfil its aim.[4]   The code contains a long list of other grounds of divorce,[5] such as an illicit intimacy for which a presumption of adultery may arise,[6] obstinate refusal of the rights of marriage, incapacity to perform the conjugal duties even if arising subsequent to the marriage, other incurable bodily defects that excite disgust and horror, lunacy if after a year there is no reasonable hope of recovery, attempt on the life of one spouse by the other or gross and unlawful attack on the honour or personal liberty,[7] incompatibility of temper and quarrelsome disposition if rising to the height of endangering life or health, opprobrious crime for which either spouse has suffered imprisonment, a knowingly false accusation of such crime made by one spouse with regard to the other,[8] and change of religion.[9]

In France the new ideas led to the law on divorce of 20th September 1792.   Previous to that date the Roman canon law prevailed : marriage was indissoluble and only a separation from bed and board, known as *la séparation d'habitation*, was permitted.   In the preamble of the new law it is said that marriage is merely a civil contract, and

---

[1] *Project des Corporis Juris Fridericiani,* i. 2. 3. 1. 35, p. 56.
[2] Roguin, *Traité de droit civil comparé.   Le mariage,* p. 334.
[3] *Allgemeines Landrecht für die Preussischen Staaten,* § 716.
[4] *Ibid.* § 718.   [5] *Ibid.* § 669 *sqq.*   [6] *Ibid.* § 673.
[7] *Ibid.* § 694 *sqq.*   [8] *Ibid.* § 703 *sqq.*   [9] *Ibid.* § 715.

that facility in obtaining divorce is the natural consequence of the individual's right of freedom, which is lost if engagements are made indissoluble.[1] Divorce is granted on the mutual desire of the two parties,[2] and even at the wish of one party on the ground of incompatibility of temper, subject only to a short period of delay and to the necessity of appearing before a family council who are to endeavour to arrange the dispute.[3] It may also be demanded on such grounds as insanity, condemnation to a punishment which is either *afflictive* or *infamante*, ill-treatment or serious injury, notorious immorality, desertion for at least two years, absence without tidings for at least five years, and emigration contrary to the law.[4] And while divorce was introduced, separation from bed and board was abolished.[5] Great benefits were expected from the reform. It was said that divorce was instituted in order to preserve in marriage " cette quiétude heureuse qui rend les sentiments plus vifs."[6] Marriage would no longer be a yoke or a chain, but " l'acquit d'une dette agréable que tout citoyen doit à la patrie. . . . Le divorce est le dieu tutélaire de l'hymen. . . . Libres de se séparer, les époux n'en sont que plus unis."[7] The new law was certainly very popular : in the year VI. the number of divorces in Paris exceeded the number of marriages.[8]

Six years later, in 1804, the law of 1792 was superseded by the new provisions in Napoleon's 'Code Civil des Français.' Divorce was made more difficult. Mere incompatibility of temper is no longer recognised as a cause for it   Marriage may still be dissolved on the ground of mutual consent, but on certain conditions only : the husband must be at least twenty-five years of age and the wife twenty-one ; they must have been married for at least two years and not more

---

[1] *Loi sur le divorce.* 20 *septembre* 1792 (in *Lois civiles intermédiaires,* i. 325).

[2] *Ibid.* i. 2 ; ii. 1 *sqq.* (vol. i. 326 *sqq.*).

[3] *Ibid.* i. 3 ; ii. 8 *sqq.* (vol. i. 326, 328 *sqq.*).

[4] *Ibid.* i. 4 (vol. i. 326).   [5] *Ibid.* i. 7 (vol. i. 326).

[6] Taine, *Les origines de la France contemporaine,* iii. 102.

[7] Mortimer-Ternaux, *Histoire de la Terreur* 1792–1794, iv. 408.

[8] Glasson, *Le mariage civil et le divorce,* p. 261.

than twenty years, and the wife must not be over forty-five years of age ; the parents or the other living ascendants of both parties must give their approval ;[1] and the mutual and unwavering consent of the married couple must sufficiently prove " that their common life is insupportable to them, and that there exists in reference to them a peremptory cause of divorce."[2]   A husband can always obtain a divorce from his unfaithful wife, but a wife from her unfaithful husband only " when he has kept his mistress in the common house."[3]   Other grounds of divorce are *excès* (defined by Locré as " a generic expression comprising all acts tending to compromise the safety of the person, . . . attempts upon life as well as simple woundings "[4]), *sévices* (" acts of ill-treatment, less grave in character, which, while not endangering life, render existence in common intolerable "[5]), or *injures graves* (which have been described as " acts, writings, or words which reflect upon the honour or the reputation of the party against whom they are directed "[6]),[7] and condemnation to a degrading punishment.[8]   Separation from bed and board is again introduced.   Such a separation can be obtained on the same grounds as a divorce, except that it cannot be obtained by mutual consent ;[9] and if the separation has continued in force for three years, the defendant party can claim a divorce, unless the cause of the separation was the adultery of the wife.[10]   At the Restoration in 1816 divorce was abolished in France ;[11] but it was re-enacted by a law of 1884, the provisions of which were simplified by later laws.   The divorce law of the Napoleonic Code was again introduced, but with important changes : divorce by mutual consent has disappeared, and a wife can in all circumstances obtain a divorce for the adultery of her husband.[12]   In the Belgian

---

[1] *Code civil des Français,* art. 275 *sqq.*

[2] *Ibid.* art. 233.   [3] *Ibid.* art. 229 *sq.*

[4] Locré, quoted by Kelly-Bodington, *French Law of Marriage, Marriage Contracts and Divorce,* p. 122.

[5] *Ibid.* p. 122.   [6] *Ibid.* p. 122.

[7] *Code civil des Français,* art. 231.   [8] *Ibid.* art. 232.

[9] *Ibid.* art. 306 *sq.*   [10] *Ibid.* art. 310.

[11] Glasson, *op. cit.* p. 266.   [12] *Code civil,* art. 230.

code, on the other hand, no such changes have been made.[1]

In the course of the nineteenth century divorce was made legal in several Roman Catholic countries even in the case of marriage between Catholics. In Germany the possibility of obtaining a divorce became universal in 1876, when the Personal Status Act came in force ; before that year Bavaria only knew separation from bed and board, and Würtemberg and Saxony had one law for Catholics and another law for Protestants.[2] This was also formerly the case in Hungary, as is still in Austria, where only non-Catholics can obtain a divorce ;[3] but by a law of 1894 Hungary granted the right of divorce to all its citizens.[4] In the same year divorce was introduced in Guatemala and Salvador, and a few years previously in Costa Rica.[5] In Portugal divorce was permitted by a law of 1910.[6] In the United States South Carolina stands alone in granting no divorces whatsoever,[7] which is the more remarkable as no state has fewer Roman Catholic citizens.[8] It is the only Protestant community in the world which nowadays holds marriage indissoluble.

From the history of the subject we shall now pass to a

[1] Belgian *Code civil*, arts. 230, 233.

[2] Schuster, *Principles of German Civil Law*, p. 524. Roguin, *op. cit.* p. 264.

[3] In Austria divorce is prohibited even if one of the parties belonged to the Catholic creed at the time of marriage (*Das allgemeine bürgerliche Gesetzbuch für das Kaisertum Oesterreich*, § 111), but if one of them has become a Catholic subsequently the other party may, for valid reason, obtain a divorce (*ibid.* § 116).

[4] Roguin, *op. cit.* pp. 251, 266. Lehr, *Le mariage, le divorce et la séparation de corps dans les principaux pays civilisés*, p. 122.

[5] Roguin, *op. cit.* p. 272.

[6] *Royal Commission on Divorce and Matrimonial Causes. Appendices to the Minutes of Evidence and Report*, p. 152.

[7] *Reports on the Laws on Marriage and Divorce in the Colonies and in Foreign Countries presented to the House of Commons*, 1893, ii. 157. Bishop says (*New Commentaries on Marriage, Divorce, and Separation*, i. 24) that in South Carolina, with the exception of six years following the Secession War and Reconstruction (from 1872 to 1878), no divorces, even for adultery, are or have ever been granted either by the courts or by the legislature.   [8] Bryce, *op. cit.* ii. 440.

brief consideration of the chief grounds on which divorce
may be obtained according to the existing laws of those
European and American states in which it is permitted.
As this branch of legislation, however, is particularly subject
to changes, it is possible that some of the statements, though
derived from the best sources available to me, have become
antiquated in the course of the last few years.

The most general grounds for divorce are offences of
some kind or other committed by either husband or wife
and entitling the other party to demand a dissolution of
the marriage.   In this respect the two spouses are as a
rule on a footing of perfect equality ; but there are some
exceptions to the rule.   While any act of adultery in the
wife is everywhere a sufficient cause for dissolving the
marriage, there are countries in which adultery on the part
of the husband only in certain circumstances gives the
wife a right to demand a divorce.   We have already noticed
the English and Belgian laws on the subject, the latter of
which has preserved the provision of the Napoleonic Code.[1]
In Belgium, however, any adultery on the part of the
husband which causes public scandal is, as a matter of
fact, regarded as an *injure grave* justifying a suit for divorce.[2]
In Victoria the wife may obtain a divorce if her husband is
guilty of adultery in the conjugal residence or with circumstances of aggravation, or of repeated adultery.[3]   In some
of the commonwealths of the United States proof must be
made that the husband is " living in adultery " at the time
of the suit.   In Texas the husband may have a dissolution
of the marriage " where his wife shall have been taken in
adultery," and the wife " where he shall have abandoned
her and lived in adultery with another woman."[4]   In
Kentucky the husband must have been living in adultery
for six months ; while not only adultery by the wife but
even " such lewd, lascivious behaviour on her part as proves
her to be unchaste, without actual proof of an act of

---

[1] *Code civil*, art. 230.   [2] Roguin, *op. cit.* p. 291.
[3] Burge, *op. cit.* iii. 885.
[4] Bishop, *op. cit.* i. 623.   North Carolina has a similar law (*Reports
on the Laws on Marriage and Divorce*, ii. 157 ; Wright, *Report on
Marriage and Divorce in the United States*, 1867 to 1886, p. 105).

adultery," will sustain a divorce in favour of the husband.[1] In Louisiana the husband must have kept a concubine either openly or in the common dwelling.[2] In Greece, where the legal grounds of divorce established in the *Novellae* of Justinian are still in force with certain amendments, a marriage may be dissolved on account of adultery committed by the husband in the house in which he lives with his wife or in another house in the same town, notwithstanding repeated warnings given him by his relatives, as also if he is convicted of adultery with a married woman.[3] In some law-books bigamy or unnatural crime is especially mentioned as a ground of divorce.[4] In Serbia a marriage may be dissolved not only in the case of proved adultery, but if the wife without her husband's consent visits the baths, beer-gardens, or other suspicious places, with other men, or spends the night in a strange house ; or if the husband brings strange women into his house or keeps them elsewhere. A husband also gives sufficient cause for divorce if he accuses his wife of infidelity and is unable to prove the charge, or if he urges his innocent and virtuous wife to sacrifice her honour.[5]

Desertion, or " malicious " desertion, or desertion " without just cause or excuse," is very frequently mentioned as a ground of divorce, especially in Protestant law-books.[6] In Germany [7] and among non-Catholics in Austria[8] the term of desertion must be at least one year ; in Switzerland,[9] Sweden,[10] and Norway,[11] two ; in Denmark,[12] Portugal,[13]

---

[1] *Reports on the Laws on Marriage and Divorce*, ii. 157.   Bishop, *op. cit.* i. 623.

[2] *Reports on the Laws on Marriage and Divorce*, ii. 157.

[3] *Ibid.* ii. 81.   [4] Roguin, *op. cit.* p. 301.

[5] *Reports on the Laws on Marriage and Divorce*, ii. 135 *sq.*

[6] *Cf.* Roguin, *op. cit.* p. 304 *sqq.*

[7] *Bürgerliches Gesetzbuch*, art. 1567.

[8] *Das allgemeine bürgerliche Gesetzbuch für das Kaisertum Oester-reich*, § 115.

[9] *Schweizerisches Zivilgesetzbuch vom 10. Dezember* 1907, art. 140.

[10] *Lag om äktenskaps ingående och upplösning* (of 1915), vi. 5.

[11] *Lov om adgang til opløsning av egteskap* (of 20th August, 1909), § 6.

[12] Burge, *op. cit.* iii. 853.

[13] *Royal Commission on Divorce and Matrimonial Causes. Appendices*, p. 152.

Victoria,[1] and New South Wales,[2] three ; in Scotland,
four ; [3] in Holland [4] and New Zealand,[5] five ; in Serbia,
according to ecclesiastical law, seven.[6] In the United
States, where the courts may everywhere grant " divorce"—
usually " absolute," sometimes "from bed and board," and
sometimes one or the other at their own discretion—if either
party deserts the other without good cause, the term is in
fifteen of the commonwealths one year, in eleven two years,
in twelve three years, in three five years, and in Arizona
six months.[7] In several countries divorce is obtained only
after a judicial order to return has remained unheeded.   It
should be noticed that desertion may be a ground of divorce
even where it is not expressly mentioned as such by the

[1] Burge, *op. cit.* iii. 885.   [2] *Ibid.* iii. 882.
[3] Erskine-Rankine, *op. cit.* p. 77 *sq.*
[4] *Burgerlijk Wetboek*, art. 266.
[5] *Papers relating to the Laws of Marriage and Divorce in Self-governing British Colonies. Presented to both Houses of Parliament,*
1903, p. 16.
[6] *Reports on the Laws on Marriage and Divorce*, ii. 136.   Burge,
op. cit. iii. 842.   Under the Civil Code of Serbia the wife may obtain
a divorce earlier, namely, after three years' desertion if the husband
has left the country without the knowledge or permission of the
Government and cannot be traced, and after four years on proof
that the desertion is wilful (Burge, *op. cit.* iii. 842).—In Hungary a
divorce may be obtained for wilful and unjustifiable desertion if the
deserting spouse fails, after six months' absence, to re-establish the
conjugal home within the period allowed for that purpose by judicial
decree, or if the deserting spouse, whose residence is unknown, does
not return within a year from an official citation to do so (*ibid.*
iii. 847 *sq.*).   In the Union of South Africa, where the law of Holland
as it was at the beginning of the nineteenth century is still in force,
" malicious " desertion is a ground of divorce, but what length of
absence amounts to desertion is a matter in the discretion of the
court granting the order (*Papers relating to the Laws of Marriage and
Divorce*, p. 22), except in Natal, where the desertion must have lasted
at least for eighteen months (*Reports on the Laws of Marriage and
Divorce*, i. 12 ; Kitchin, *History of Divorce*, p. 238).   It is not necessary, however, " that the desertion should be originally malicious,
it is sufficient if the one party, being away unreasonably, refuses to
return to or to receive the other " (*Papers relating to the Laws of
Marriage and Divorce*, p. 22 ; *cf.* Kitchin, *op. cit.* p. 238 *sq.*).
[7] *Reports on the Laws on Marriage and Divorce*, ii. 158.   See also
Bishop, *op. cit.* i. 686 *sqq.*

law—as in France, Belgium, and Rumania—in so far as it may be regarded as an *injure grave* justifying dissolution of the marriage.[1] In the Russian code five years' absence is spoken of.[2] In the Portuguese law of 1910 absence for not less than four years during which the absentee gives no tidings of himself or herself is mentioned side by side with abandonment of home as a legitimate cause for divorce,[3] and in the Swedish law of 1915 absence without tidings for three years.[4]

In the laws of various countries attempt on the life of one spouse by the other is mentioned as a ground on which the latter is entitled to obtain a divorce.[5] The Dutch code speaks of the infliction of serious wounds or injurious treatment endangering life as a cause for dissolving the marriage.[6] In other law-books such grounds fall under some more comprehensive heading. In most countries in which divorce is allowed ill-treatment of some kind is a sufficient reason for it. The provisions of the Code Napoléon in the case of *excès*, *sévices*, or *injures graves* remain in the present civil codes of France[7] and Belgium[8] and have passed into the Rumanian code.[9] We have previously seen how those terms have been defined.[10] With reference to the *injures graves* it may be added that publicity is not a necessary character-

[1] Roguin, *op. cit.* p. 304.   Kelly-Bodington, *op. cit.* p. 123 (France).
[2] *Zivilkodex*, art. 54 (Klibansky, *Handbuch des gesamten russischen Zivilrechts*, i. 26).   When speaking of Russian law I mean this code, although the legislation on marriage and divorce has been changed by the Soviet government (see *infra*, p. 354).
[3] *Royal Commission on Divorce and Matrimonial Causes.   Appendices*, p. 152.   [4] *Lag om äktenskaps ingående och upplösning*, vi. 6.
[5] *Bürgerliches Gesetzbuch*, art. 1566 (Germany).   *Schweizerisches Zivilgesetzbuch*, art. 138 (Switzerland).   *Lag om äktenskaps ingående och upplösning*, vi. 10 (Sweden).   *Das allgemeine bürgerliche Gesetzbuch für das Kaisertum Oesterreich*, § 115 (Austria ; " dem Leben oder der Gesundheit gefährliche Nachstellungen "). Lehr, *op. cit.* pp. 122 (Hungary), 266 (Greece).   *Codicele civile*, art. 215 (Rumania). *Reports on the Laws on Marriage and Divorce*, ii. 135 (Serbia).   Burge, *op. cit.* iii. 882 *sq.* (New South Wales).
[6] *Burgerlijk Wetboek*, art. 264.   [7] *Code civil*, art. 231.
[8] Belgian *Code civil*, art. 231.
[9] *Codicele civile*, art. 212 (" escese, cruḑimĭ saŭ insulte grave ").
[10] *Supra*, iii. 341.

istic of the offence, although it aggravates it ; a letter from
one spouse to the other may constitute a cause for divorce.
The courts consider themselves entitled to exercise a wide
discretion in the interpretation of that term. *Injures graves*
have been held to include refusal to accomplish the conjugal
act if habitual and with intent to offend, communication of
venereal disease, refusal to consent to a religious ceremony
of marriage, and habitual drunkenness.[1] In Germany
" gross ill-treatment " (*grobe Misshandlung*) is a " relative "
ground of divorce, which implies that it is left to judicial
discretion whether, in the special circumstances of the case,
divorce ought to be granted.[2] This offence is deemed a
grave breach of duty within the meaning of that section of
the code which lays down as relative grounds of divorce
any faults by which the marital relation, owing to any
grave breach of marital duty or dishonourable or immoral
conduct on the respondent's part, is disturbed to such an
extent that the petitioner cannot fairly be expected to
continue the marriage.[3] The Swiss law speaks of grave
ill-treatment and gross insults (*schwere Ehrenkränkung*)[4] ;
the Austrian law, of repeated acts of grave ill-treatment[5] ;
the Hungarian law, of ill-treatment endangering body or
health ;[6] the Norwegian law, of the infliction of bodily
injury or other offence that is injurious to the health of the
spouse ;[7] the Swedish law, of gross ill-treatment ;[8] the
Portuguese law, of ill-treatment ;[9] the law of New South
Wales, of assault with intent to cause grievous bodily harm
and of repeated assaults ;[10] the law of Victoria, of violent
assault.[11] In almost all of the commonwealths of the United

---

[1] Kelly-Bodington, *op. cit.* p. 122 *sq.*

[2] For the distinction between " absolute " and " relative "
grounds of divorce in the German code see *Bürgerliches Gesetzbuch*,
' Siebenter Titel. Scheidung der Ehe.'

[3] *Ibid.* art. 1568.   [4] *Schweizerisches Zivilgesetzbuch*, art. 138.

[5] *Das allgemeine bürgerliche Gesetzbuch für das Kaisertum Oesterreich*, § 115.   [6] Lehr, *op. cit.* p. 122.

[7] *Lov om adgang til opløsning av egteskap*, § 4.

[8] *Lag om äktenskaps ingående och upplösning*, vi. 10.

[9] *Royal Commission on Divorce and Matrimonial Causes. Appen-
dices*, p. 152.   [10] Burge, *op. cit.* iii. 882 *sq.*   [11] *Ibid.* iii. 885.

States " divorce "—generally " from the bond of matrimony," but in some of them " from bed and board " only—is obtainable for cruelty.   The degree of cruelty necessary is usually actual and repeated violence endangering life, limb, or health, or giving reasonable grounds to apprehend such danger ; but some jurisdictions add to this intolerable indignities to the person, public and false accusations of adultery, habitual manifestations of hatred, or violent and ungovernable temper (Florida).[1]

An extremely frequent ground of divorce is the condemnation of one of the parties to a certain punishment or his or her being convicted of a certain crime.   The present French code requires a punishment which is both *afflictive* and *infamante*,[2] that is to say, a punishment involving both corporal confinement and moral degradation.[3]   The Belgian code, on the other hand, has preserved the provision of the Code Napoléon, which only requires that the punishment shall be *infamante* ;[4] but as this term has been abolished by the criminal code, the word *criminelle* should be substituted for it.[5]   The Russian code recognises as a ground for divorce a punishment involving loss of civil rights or deportation to Siberia ;[6] the Swedish law, penal servitude or hard labour for three years, or for a shorter period exceeding six months at the discretion of the court ;[7] the Norwegian law, imprisonment for three years ;[8] the Dutch code, imprisonment for four years ;[9] the Austrian code[10] and the Hungarian law of 1894,[11] imprison-

---

[1] *Reports on the Laws on Marriage and Divorce*, ii. 159.   Bishop, *op. cit.* i. 629 *sqq.*   Personal indignities rendering condition intolerable or life burdensome constitute a ground of " divorce from the bond of matrimony " in favour of the wife in Pennsylvania and in favour of either spouse in Arkansas, Louisiana, Missouri, Oregon, Vermont, and Wyoming (Burge, *op. cit.* iii. 895).

[2] *Code civil*, art. 232.   [3] Kelly-Bodington, *op. cit.* p. 124.

[4] Belgian *Code civil*, art. 232.   [5] *Codes Belges*, p. 59 n. 2.

[6] *Zivilkodex*, arts. 45, 50 (Klibansky, *op. cit.* i. 20, 24).

[7] *Lag om äktenskaps ingående och upplösning*, vi. 11.

[8] *Lov om adgang til opløsning av egteskap*, § 5.

[9] *Burgerlijk Wetboek*, art. 264.

[10] *Das allgemeine bürgerliche Gesetzbuch für das Kaisertum Oesterreich*, § 115.   [11] Burge, *op. cit.* iii. 848.

ment for five years ; the Danish law, penal servitude for
seven years[1] ; the Serbian code, imprisonment for a
term of more than seven years or hard labour.[2] In
the United States divorces are granted throughout the
greater part of the country against those who after marriage
have been convicted of felony or of infamous or unnatural
crimes, against those who have fled from justice, and
against those who have been sentenced to the penitentiary
for life or for a term of years.[3] In Portugal conviction of
one of the major crimes, such as murder, assaults, robbery,
and offences against morality, is a ground of divorce ;[4]
in Switzerland, a degrading crime or a dishonourable life.[5]
The German code speaks neither of punishment nor of
crime, but, as we have seen, regards dishonourable or
immoral conduct generally as a " relative " ground of divorce.

There are yet some special offences that in some law-
books are mentioned as causes for divorce. In the United
States a husband who is able to support his wife but for a
certain time neglects to do so may according to twenty-two
jurisdictions (out of forty-nine) be divorced on that account ;
and according to thirty-eight jurisdictions divorce may be
obtained on proof of the habitual drunkenness of either party
for varying terms.[6] In Sweden the court may in extreme
cases grant a divorce for drunkenness.[7] In Victoria,[8]

---

[1] *Ibid.* iii. 853.

[2] *Reports on the Laws on Marriage and Divorce*, ii. 136. In
Rumania the condemnation of either spouse to hard labour or
seclusion is a ground of divorce (*Codicele civile*, art. 213). The laws
of New South Wales and Victoria contain rather elaborate stipu-
lations as regards divorce obtainable for the conviction for crime
(Burge, *op. cit.* iii. 882, 883, 885). In South Africa lifelong imprisonment amounts to " malicious " desertion (*ibid.* iii. 825).

[3] *Reports on the Laws on Marriage and Divorce.* ii. 159. *Cf.* Bishop,
op. cit. i. 748 *sq.*

[4] *Royal Commission on Divorce and Matrimonial Causes. Appendices*, p. 152.

[5] *Schweizerisches Zivilgesetzbuch*, art. 139.

[6] Willcox, ' Divorce,' in *Encyclopædia Britannica*, viii. 345. See
also *Reports on the Laws on Marriage and Divorce*, ii. 158 *sq.* ; Bishop,
op. cit. i. 740, 741, 743 *sqq.*

[7] *Lag om äktenskaps ingående och upplösning*, vi. 12.

[8] *Reports on the Laws of Marriage and Divorce*, i. 19.

New South Wales,[1] and New Zealand[2] habitual drunkenness, with cruelty or leaving the wife without the means of support in the case of the husband and with neglect of domestic duties in the case of the wife, is recognised as a ground of divorce. In Texas the wife may obtain a divorce if her husband is a vagrant, and in North Carolina a husband may obtain a divorce if his wife has without good reason refused sexual intercourse to him for the space of twelve months.[3] The refusal of sexual intercourse was a ground of divorce according to various German law-books previous to the imperial code, and, though not specially mentioned in that code, it is considered to be included among the " relative " grounds of divorce.[4] In England the mere wilful refusal of a wife to submit to her husband's embraces is not *per se* a ground for annulling a marriage, but if she refuses to submit to inspection the court will presume her impotence, being averse to a husband using excessive force ; and so also, if a husband refuses to consummate his marriage, the court may draw the inference that such refusal arises from impotence and may annul the marriage.[5] In the Portuguese law inveterate gambling habits are specified as a cause for dissolving the marriage.[6] In Norway a divorce is obtainable for ill-treatment of the children or punishable behaviour towards them ;[7] in Hungary, for inciting or attempting to incite a child belonging to the family to an immoral or criminal act ; [8] and in New Zealand, for murdering, or for an attempt to murder, a child of either spouse.[9]

There are certain other circumstances recognised as

---

[1] *Papers relating to the Laws of Marriage and Divorce in Self-governing British Colonies*, p. 13 sq.

[2] *Ibid.* p. 16.

[3] *Reports on the Laws on Marriage and Divorce*, ii. 160.

[4] Roguin, *op. cit.* p. 318 sq.

[5] Hall, *Law and Practice in Divorce*, p. 583.   Dixon, *Law and Practice in Divorce*, p. 37.

[6] *Royal Commission on Divorce and Matrimonial Causes. Appendices*, p. 152.   [7] *Lov om adgang til opløsning av egteskap*, § 4.

[8] Burge, *op. cit.* iii. 848.   [9] *Ibid.* iii. 886.

grounds of divorce, which may or may not involve guilt in one of the parties but in all cases are supposed to make marriage a burden for the other spouse. Impotence in the husband or wife, existing at the time of marriage and afterwards but unknown to the other party, is specially mentioned as a cause for divorce in the laws of Norway,[1] Denmark,[2] Finland,[3] and Russia.[4] In England it has long been a ground for pronouncing an otherwise valid marriage invalid ;[5] and in the United States, also, divorce is commonly granted for incurable physical incapacity if the plaintiff was ignorant of the defendant's condition.[6] In Norway epilepsy, leprosy, and contagious venereal disease,[7] in Denmark leprosy which has been communicated to the other party,[8] in Finland " incurable contagious disease,"[9] and in Sweden the exposing of the other spouse to the danger of venereal contagion,[10] are in similar circumstances grounds for divorce. The Portuguese law speaks of incurable contagious disease or any disease which induces sexual aberration.[11] In Kentucky loathsome diseases, whether concealed at marriage or contracted afterwards, justify a dissolution of the marriage.[12] So does in Norway[13] and Denmark insanity, or incurable insanity,[14] which existed at the time of marriage or prior to it without the knowledge of the other party ;

---

[1] *Lov om forandringer i lov om adgang til opløsning av egteskap av* 20 *august* 1909 (of 10th April, 1915), § 3.

[2] *Reports on the Laws on Marriage and Divorce*, ii. 53.

[3] *Finlands rikes lag*, Giftermåls Balk, xiii. 8.

[4] *Zivilkodex*, arts. 45, 48 *sq.* (Klibansky, *op. cit.* i. 20, 24).

[5] Hall, *op. cit.* p. 581. Dixon, *op. cit.* pp. 27, 34.

[6] *Reports on the Laws on Marriage and Divorce*, ii. 158. Burge, *op. cit.* iii. 894.

[7] *Lov om forandringer i lov om adgang til opløsning av egteskap,* § 3.

[8] Burge, *op. cit.* iii. 853.

[9] *Finlands rikes lag*, Giftermåls Balk, xiii. 8.

[10] *Lag om äktenskaps ingående och upplösning*, vi. 9.

[11] *Royal Commission on Divorce and Matrimonial Causes. Appendices*, p. 152.

[12] *Reports on the Laws on Marriage and Divorce*, ii. 158.

[13] *Lov om forandringer i lov om adgang til opløsning av egteskap,* § 3.

[14] Burge, *op. cit.* iii. 853.

and in Norway,[1] Sweden,[2] Germany,[3] Switzerland,[4] and
Portugal [5] divorce is obtainable for insanity which has been
pronounced incurable or gives no reasonable hope of
recovery after three years' duration, and in Utah for
insanity regarded as hopeless after five years.[6]
In Serbia divorce may be obtained if one of the parties
forsakes the Christian faith, and even secession from the
Orthodox Church to any other branch of the Christian
faith would, according to the interpretation of the ' Canons
of the Church ' by Bishop Nicanor, furnish grounds for a
divorce.[7] Among non-Catholics in Austria divorce is
permitted, after separation or repeated separations have
been tried and found useless, on the ground of "uncon-
querable aversion " of the parties for each other ;[8] and even
unilateral aversion has been considered a sufficient cause
for divorce if both parties apply for it.[9] The Swiss code
contains a provision to the effect that, even though none of
the specified causes for divorce exists, a marriage may be
dissolved if there are circumstances seriously affecting the
maintenance of the conjugal tie.[10] In Iowa divorce is
granted if the court decides that it is impossible for the
couple to live together in peace and happiness,[11] and in

---

[1] *Lov om adgang til opløsning av egteskap*, § 7 (by royal decree
[*ibid*. § 9]).

[2] *Lag om äktenskaps ingående och upplösning*, vi. 13.

[3] *Bürgerliches Gesetzbuch*, art. 1569. The law says that the
insanity shall be of a kind so severe that the intellectual community
between the spouses has ceased and that there is no hope of its
re-establishment.

[4] *Schweizerisches Zivilgesetzbuch*, art. 141.

[5] *Royal Commission on Divorce and Matrimonial Causes. Appendices*, p. 152.

[6] Burge, *op. cit.* iii. 894. Hopeless insanity is also a ground of
divorce in Denmark (*ibid*. iii. 853) and Washington (*ibid*. iii. 894) and,
under certain conditions, in New Zealand (*ibid*. iii. 886).

[7] *Reports on the Laws on Marriage and Divorce*, ii. 135.

[8] *Das allgemeine bürgerliche Gesetzbuch für das Kaisertum Oesterreich*, § 115.

[9] Geller, *Österreichische Justizgesetze*, i. 138 n.

[10] *Schweizerisches Zivilgesetzbuch*, art. 142.

[11] *Reports on the Laws on Marriage and Divorce*, ii. 160. Howard,
op. cit. iii. 126.

Washington [1] it may be obtained at the general discretion of the court.

We have seen that divorce by mutual consent, which had been permitted in the Roman Empire even in Christian times but not been recognised by the Reformers, was reintroduced as a legal practice by the French law of 1792 and, though with important limitations, by the Prussian code of 1794. At the beginning of the nineteenth century, however, a reaction against it set in, and at present consensual divorce is recognised by a few law-books only, unless it be preceded by judicial separation. It is allowed in Belgium[2] and Rumania,[3] but is in both countries surrounded by the old barriers of the Code Napoléon, which makes it very rare in practice ; it is said that in Rumania only about one divorce out of a hundred takes place by mutual consent.[4] In Austria consensual divorce is permitted to Jews,[5] but to no other citizens. In Portugal a divorce may be obtained after a separation *de facto* by mutual consent for ten years.[6] In Wisconsin and one or two other North American states there is the provision that when married parties have voluntarily lived separate five years the court may dissolve the marriage bond, and the interpretation of this provision is that " the separation must be mutual.''[7] In Norway [8] and Guatemala[9] a marriage may be dissolved upon the common application of the parties after one year's living apart in accordance with a decree of separation, and such a decree may itself have been obtained by mutual consent.[10] The laws of Sweden,[11]

---

[1] Howard, *op. cit.* iii. 135. Wright, *op. cit.* p. 111.

[2] Belgian *Code civil*, arts. 233, 275 *sqq.*

[3] *Codicele civile*, arts. 214, 254 *sqq.*

[4] Roguin, *op. cit.* p. 335 *sq.*

[5] *Das allgemeine bürgerliche Gesetzbuch für das Kaisertum Oester-reich,* § 133.

[6] *Royal Commission on Divorce and Matrimonial Causes. Appendices,* p. 152.   [7] Bishop, *op. cit.* i. 752.

[8] *Lov om adgang til opløsning av egteskap,* § 8 (by royal decree [*ibid.* § 9]).   [9] Roguin, *op. cit.* p. 336.

[10] *Lov om adgang til opløsning av egteskap,* § 1 (Norway). Roguin, *op. cit.* p. 336 (Guatemala).

[11] *Lag om äktenskaps ingående och upplösning,* vi. 1.

Greece, and Costa Rica[1] likewise admit consensual separation ; and a judicial separation may, upon the application of either husband or wife, be converted into a divorce, in Costa Rica and apparently in Greece,[2] as also in Norway,[3] after two years, and in Sweden after one year.[4] In the new Russian ' Soviet Law of Marriage and the Family ' no such formalities are required. It goes in fact even further than the French law of 1792 by simply stating that " the grounds for divorce may be either the mutual consent of the parties or the desire of one of them." The demand for a dissolution of marriage may be made either in writing or verbally, although in the latter case it must be reduced to writing.[5] Demands for divorce shall be adjudicated by the local judge, publicly and without assessors ;[6] but there is no indication that the applicant is obliged to state any ground for his or her demand.[7]

A large number of law-books that permit divorce also permit judicial separation—formerly called in England divorce *a mensâ et thoro* and nowadays called in France *séparation de corps*—either for life or for a definite or an indefinite period, which implies that neither party can contract another marriage before the death of the other or before the marriage is dissolved by divorce. In France judicial separation was abolished by the law of 1792, but was reintroduced by the Code Napoléon ; it remained, of course, when divorce was prohibited, in 1816, and exists since 1884 side by side with divorce.[8] In Germany it was prohibited by the Personal Status Act, 1875, for Protestants and Catholics alike, as it had previously been in Prussia ; but, under the pressure of the Roman Catholic party, the code which became law in 1896 and came into force in 1900 introduced an exactly similar institution called *Aufhebung*

---

[1] Roguin, *op. cit.* p. 334. [2] *Ibid.* p. 342 *sq.*

[3] *Lov om adgang til opløsning av egteskap*, § 8 (by royal decree [*ibid.* § 9]).

[4] *Lag om äktenskaps ingående och upplösning*, vi. 3.

[5] *Soviet Law of Marriage and the Family*, § 87 *sq.* (in *Contemporary Review*, cxvii. 574). [6] *Ibid.* § 93 (vol. cxvii. 575).

[7] *Cf.* Hoichbarg, ' Soviet Law of Marriage and the Family,' in *Contemporary Review*, cxvii. 410. [8] Roguin, *op. cit.* pp. 258, 262 *sq.*

der ehelichen Gemeinschaft, "dissolution of the conjugal community."[1] In Switzerland judicial separation was abolished in 1874, likewise under anti-Catholic influence,[2] but was again permitted by the code of 1910.[3] Both divorce and judicial separation exist in Belgium, Holland, England, Scotland, the Scandinavian countries, Hungary, Greece, and Portugal, in twenty-four of the commonwealths of the United States, and in all those Central American states which now permit divorce.[4] The Austrian code grants both divorce and judicial separation to non-Catholics, but to Catholics the latter alone.[5] According to the Russian code, again, there is divorce but no judicial separation for members of the Russo-Greek Church. In Serbia, Montenegro, Rumania, and various North American commonwealths there is divorce only ; but in Serbia the guilty party is not allowed to remarry, and neither party is allowed to do so if both are guilty.[6]

In some of the countries which allow both divorce and judicial separation the parties cannot in every case choose one or the other just as they like, the grounds for divorce being more or less different from the grounds for separation. Thus in Belgium divorce by mutual consent is permissible, though difficult, whereas separation by mutual consent is prohibited.[7] In Holland the case is exactly the reverse : consensual divorce is prohibited but consensual separation allowed.[8] In England a husband or wife may petition for a decree of judicial separation on the ground of adultery, or cruelty, or desertion without cause for two years and

---

[1] *Ibid.* p. 264. Schuster, *Principles of German Civil Law,* p. 524. *Bürgerliches Gesetzbuch,* art. 1575.   [2] Roguin, *op. cit.* p. 258.

[3] *Schweizerisches Zivilgesetzbuch,* art. 146.

[4] Roguin, *op. cit.* pp. 262, 263, 265 *sqq.* For Portugal see *Royal Commission on Divorce and Matrimonial Causes. Appendices,* p. 153 ; for the United States, Burge, *op. cit.* iii. 893 ; for Norway, *Lov om adgang til oplǿsning av egteskap,* § 1 *sq.* ; for Sweden, *Lag om äktenskaps ingående och upplösning,* vi. 1 *sq.*

[5] *Das allgemeine bürgerliche Gesetzbuch für das Kaisertum Oesterreich,* § 111.

[6] Roguin, *op. cit.* p. 259 *sqq.* For Rumania and Serbia see also Lehr, *op. cit.* pp. 351, 383.

[7] Belgian *Code civil,* arts. 233, 307.   [8] *Burgerlijk Wetboek,* art. 291.

upwards ;[1] in Scotland, on the ground of adultery or cruelty.[2] In Norway separation from bed and board is to be granted, after a previous attempt at reconciliation, when both parties are agreed thereon ; and it may also be granted upon the requirement of either party if the other fails in the obligation of maintenance, or otherwise is guilty of breach of matrimonial duties, or has fallen a victim to the abuse of alcoholic liquors, or leads a scandalous life, or has been convicted with loss of civil rights, or when such disagreement has arisen between husband and wife that it cannot reasonably be required that they shall continue to live together.[3] The Swedish law of 1915 contains very similar provisions, but allows the court in particular circumstances to refuse the demand unless both parties are agreed on separation.[4] On the other hand, under German law a judicial separation cannot be obtained on any ground which would not be sufficient to establish a cause for a divorce, and a spouse who is entitled to petition for a divorce may in every case claim judicial separation in lieu of it.[5]   Thus separation is not, as it is in England, intended as a minor remedy for minor offences, but as an alternative enabling petitioners to obtain universal relief without a complete severance of the marriage tie.[6]   The same system is followed in France,[7] Switzerland,[8] Portugal,[9] Hungary,[10] Greece,[11] and many North American commonwealths,[12] if exception is made for cases in which previous separation is itself a ground for subsequent divorce.

A judicial separation may very frequently be converted into a divorce.   In most countries which have both, divorce is regarded as the normal remedy, whereas separation has only with some reluctance been admitted by the legislators ;

[1] Earl of Halsbury, *op. cit.* xvi. 500.
[2] Erskine-Rankine, *op. cit.* p. 70.
[3] *Lov om adgang til opløsning av egteskap*, § 1 sq.
[4] *Lag om äktenskaps ingående och upplösning*, vi. 1 sq.
[5] *Bürgerliches Gesetzbuch*, art. 1575.   [6] *Cf.* Schuster, *op. cit.* p. 524.
[7] *Code civil*, art. 306.   [8] *Schweizerisches Zivilgesetzbuch*, art. 146.
[9] *Royal Commission on Divorce and Matrimonial Causes. Appendices*, p. 153   [10] Lehr, *op. cit.* p. 127.
[11] *Ibid.* p. 266.   [12] Roguin, *op. cit.* p. 272.

and where the grounds on which they may be obtained are the same, there is no reason to prevent separation from being turned into divorce.[1] The Belgian code, like the Code Napoléon, allows the defendant party to claim divorce after three years' separation unless the ground for it was adultery on the part of the wife.[2] According to the present French code either party may do so in all cases, whatever was the reason for the separation.[3] In some countries a judicial separation can upon the application of either party be transformed into a divorce after two years[4] or one year[5] or, in Germany, at any time.[6] In Norway the husband or the wife may obtain a divorce if they have lived apart for three years consecutively although they have done so without a decree of separation.[7] There is a similar provision in the Swedish law, though discretion is left to the court if only one of the parties desires a dissolution of the marriage.[8]

In those Roman Catholic countries which still prohibit divorce the grounds for judicial separation are generally very similar to, though not infrequently somewhat more extensive than, the grounds for which divorce may be obtained in other countries. The chief cause for separation is adultery, but according to some codes the adultery of the husband is not in all circumstances a sufficient cause for it. In Italy the wife may obtain separation from an unfaithful husband only if he has a concubine whom he maintains in his house or " notoriously " in some other place, or if he is guilty of adultery in circumstances that make it a grave insult to the wife.[9] In Spain separation— or *divorcio*, as it is called by Spanish-speaking peoples—may

---

[1] *Cf.* Roguin, *op. cit.* p. 338 *sq.*   [2] Belgian *Code civil*, art. 310.
[3] French *Code civil*, art. 310.
[4] *Supra*, iii. 354 (Norway, Greece, Costa Rica).   Roguin, *op. cit.* p. 343 (Hungary).   [5] *Supra*, iii. 354 (Sweden).
[6] *Bürgerliches Gesetzbuch*, art. 1576.   With reference to the United States, Bishop says (*op. cit.* i. 752), " In exceptional States, after a divorce *nisi*, or when the parties have lived apart for a given number of years under a divorce from bed and board, the separation may be transmuted to, or be made ground for, a dissolution of the marriage."
[7] *Lov om adgang til opløsning av egteskap*, § 8 (by royal decree, [*ibid.* § 9]).   [8] *Lag om äktenskaps ingående och upplösning*, vi. 4.
[9] *Codice civile*, art. 150.

be obtained if the adultery of the husband has given rise
to public scandal and he has completely abandoned his
wife, or if he keeps the other woman in his house ;[1] and in
Mexico, if the adultery of the husband has taken place in
the common dwelling, if he has had continuous illicit intercourse either in the joint home or elsewhere, if his behaviour
has caused public scandal, if he has insulted his wife, or if
his accomplice has maltreated her by word or deed.[2]   In
Portugal, before divorce was introduced there by the law
of 1910, the adultery of the husband was a ground for
separation if it caused public scandal, if it was coupled with
complete desertion of the wife, or if it was committed with
a paramour living and maintained by the husband under
the conjugal roof.[3]   Desertion is mentioned as a cause for
separation in the Italian,[4] Austrian,[5] and Mexican [6] and
several South American[7] codes ; grave ill-treatment or insults, in the same[8] and the Spanish[9] and former Portuguese[10]
codes.   Condemnation to punishment is another ground for
separation.[11]   In Italy a judicial separation can be demanded

[1] *Código civil de España*, art. 164.   [2] Mexican *Código civil*, art. 228.
[3] *Codigo civil portuguez*, art. 1204.   [4] *Codice civile*, art. 150.
[5] *Das allgemeine bürgerliche Gesetzbuch für das Kaisertum Oesterreich*, § 109.
[6] Mexican *Código civil*, art. 227.
[7] de la Grasserie, *Code Civil du Vénézuéla*, p. 8.   *Idem, Code Civil
Péruvien*, p. 14.   Burge, *op. cit.* iii. 840 (Brazil, Argentina, Chili).
[8] Italian *Codice civile*, art. 150 (" eccessi, sevizie, minacce e
ingiurie gravi ").   *Das allgemeine bürgerliche Gesetzbuch für das
Kaisertum Oesterreich*, § 109 (acts of grave ill-treatment or " sehr
empfindliche, wiederholte Kränkungen ").   Mexican *Código civil*,
art. 227 (" la sevicia, las amenazas ó las injurias graves de un cónyuge
para con el otro ").   de la Grasserie, *Code civil de Vénézuéla*, p. 8.
Idem, Code Civil Péruvien, p. 14.   *Idem, Code Civil Chilien*, p. 17.
Lehr, *op. cit.* p. 138 (Brazil).   *Código civil de la república Argentina*,
art. 204 (" ofensas físicas ó malos tratamientos ").
[9] *Código civil de España*, art. 164 (" malos tratamientos graves de
obra ó de palabra inferidos por el marido á la mujer ").
[10] *Codigo civil portuguez*, art. 1204 (" sevicias e injurias graves ").
[11] Italian *Codice civile*, art. 151 (" pena criminale ").   *Código civil
de España*, art. 164 (" cadena ó reclusion perpetua ").   *Codigo civil
portuguez*, art. 1204 (" pena perpetua ").   de la Grasserie, *Code
Civil Péruvien*, p. 14.   *Reports on the Laws on Marriage and Divorce*,
ii. 51 (Chili).

by the wife if her husband without good cause refrains from
fixing his residence or, although he has the means, refuses
to fix it in a way that befits his position.[1]   In Spain she may
do so if the husband exercises moral or physical violence to
compel her to change her religion, or if he attempts or
proposes to prostitute her ;   and a separation may also
take place if either party endeavours to corrupt the sons
or to prostitute the daughters or connives in their corruption
or prostitution.[2]   Attempts to prostitute the wife or to
prostitute or corrupt the children are likewise admitted as
grounds for separation in the Mexican[3] and some South
American[4] law-books ;   and other causes mentioned in
some of these codes are the instigation of one of the parties
by the other to commit a crime,[5] incorrigible gambling
habits or drunkenness,[6] and contagious disease.[7]   Separation by mutual consent is permitted by the Italian[8] and
Austrian[9] codes, in Poland and Bolivia,[10] and in Mexico[11]

[1] *Codice civile*, art. 152.   [2] *Código civil de España*, art. 164.
[3] Mexican *Código civil*, art. 227.
[4] de la Grasserie, *Code Civil du Vénézuéla*, p. 8.   *Idem, Code Civil
Chilien*, p. 17.
[5] Mexican *Código civil*, art. 227.   *Reports on the Laws on Marriage
and Divorce*, ii. 9 (Argentina).
[6] Mexican *Código civil*, art. 227.   de la Grasserie, *Code Civil Péruvien*, p. 14.   *Reports on the Laws on Marriage and Divorce*, ii. 51
(Chili).
[7] Mexican *Código civil*, art. 227.   de la Grasserie, *Code Civil Péruvien*, p. 14.   *Reports on the Laws on Marriage and Divorce*, ii. 51
(Chili).   There is a similar provision in the Austrian code (§ 109).
[8] *Codice civile*, art. 158.
[9] *Das allgemeine bürgerliche Gesetzbuch für das Kaisertum Oesterreich*, § 103 *sqq.*
[10] Roguin, *op. cit.* p. 333.
[11] Mexican *Código civil*, arts. 227, 233.   When this chapter was
already in type I became aware of the fact that divorce was introduced in Mexico some years ago.   The grounds on which it may be
obtained are very similar to those on which judicial separation was
granted according to the *Código civil* of 1884.   The adultery of the
wife is in any case a sufficient reason for divorce, but the adultery
of the husband only in the circumstances mentioned above (*Ley
sobre relaciones familiares*, art. 76 *sq.*).   Other grounds of divorce
are : attempts to prostitute the wife or to corrupt the children, or
connivance in their corruption ;   the instigation of one of the parties

and Brazil[1] after the marriage has lasted for two years.

In the countries of Western civilisation, as elsewhere, a dissolution of marriage entails certain economic consequences. " Selon la plupart des législations," says M. Roguin, " le divorce provoque une liquidation des intérêts nuptiaux, qui s'opère en appliquant les règles ordinaires de chaque régime. En d'autres termes, il y a séparation de biens obéissant aux règles du régime légal ou conventionnel."[2] Thus in Germany, where the husband is entitled to the management and usufruct of the wife's non-privileged property,[3] he is deprived of this right when the marriage is dissolved, whether he or the wife be at fault.[4] But an innocent spouse may claim from the spouse declared to have been the exclusively guilty party a restitution of all the gifts made during the marriage or in contemplation of the marriage.[5] In France the spouse against whom the divorce has been pronounced loses all the benefits accruing to him or her from the other spouse either by the marriage contract or since the marriage ; whereas the spouse at whose instance the divorce has been pronounced preserves all such benefits although they were stipulated to be reciprocal and reciprocity has not in fact ensued.[6] In England, if a divorce or judicial separation is pronounced against a wife on the ground of her adultery and

by the other to commit a crime ; physical incapacity, syphilis, tuberculosis, incurable insanity, or other incurable disease which is either contagious or hereditary ; unjustified abandonment of the conjugal domicile by either party for six consecutive months ; absence of the husband for more than one year with neglect of the duties incumbent upon him ; ill-treatment or insults of such a kind as to make married life impossible ; condemnation to more than two years' imprisonment ; incurable drunkenness (*ibid*. art. 76). The marriage may also be dissolved, after the observance of certain formalities, by the mutual consent of the parties when they have been married for at least a year (*ibid*. arts. 76, 82 *sqq*.). I am indebted to Consul Y. de A. Fernández in London for making me acquainted with the law in question.

[1] Burge, *op. cit.* iii. 840. [2] Roguin, *op. cit.* p. 358.
[3] *Bürgerliches Gesetzbuch*, art. 1363. Schuster, *op. cit.* pp. 500, 503
[4] *Cf.* Roguin, *op. cit.* p. 359.
[5] *Bürgerliches Gesetzbuch*, art. 1584. [6] *Code civil*, art. 299 *sq*.

she has property, either in possession or reversion, a settlement may be ordered out of such property for the benefit of
the innocent party and of the children of the marriage.[1]

It seems that according to all modern laws on divorce a
guilty husband, or a guilty wife as well, may, in certain
circumstances at least, be compelled to furnish an innocent
spouse with a maintenance.[2] In England, on a decree for
dissolution of marriage, the court may order the husband to
secure to the wife such gross sum of money or such annual
sum of money for any term not exceeding her life as it shall
deem reasonable, having regard to her fortune, if any, to
the ability of the husband to earn, and to the conduct of the
parties. There is no fixed rule as to what proportion of
the joint incomes of the husband and wife should be allowed
to the innocent wife, but it has usually been one-third. As for
a wife who has been found guilty of adultery, although there
is nothing to prevent her from petitioning for maintenance,
it is not the practice to permit her to do so ; but where it is
clear that she is practically unable to earn her living or to
obtain any support, the court's discretion is properly exercised in requiring the husband to provide a small maintenance for her, so that at least she may not be turned out
destitute on the streets to starve.[3] According to French
law, where either there is no property available or it is
insufficient as a subsistence, an alimentary pension, not
exceeding a third of the revenues of the guilty spouse, may
be accorded to the innocent one ; but this allowance may be
withdrawn should it cease to be required.[4] In Germany,
after a divorce or judicial separation declaring the husband
to be the exclusively guilty party, he must supply the divorced
or separated wife with maintenance suitable to her station
in life, in so far as she is unable to obtain it out of her income
or her earnings ; and if the wife is declared to be the exclusively guilty party, she is bound to maintain the divorced
or separated husband in accordance with his station in life,

---

[1] Hall, *op. cit.* p. 688.   Lord Halsbury, *op. cit.* xvi. 569 *sq.*
[2] Roguin, *op. cit.* p. 364 *sqq.*
[3] Lord Halsbury, *op. cit.* xvi. 564 *sqq.*   Hall, *op. cit.* pp. 682, 683,
686 *sq.*   [4] *Code civil*, art. 301.

in so far as he is unable to maintain himself.[1] The duty to furnish maintenance, however, is extinguished on the remarriage of the person entitled to it.[2] According to Austrian law, an innocent spouse may demand a pension from the guilty, and if both parties are guilty the court may, according to the circumstances, allot a pension to the wife.[3] But in Hungary, although a wife for whose benefit divorce has been pronounced may obtain a fixed maintenance, a similar right is not granted to a husband.[4]

The question of innocence or guilt may also influence the disposal of the children, although in this respect more or less discretion is generally given to the court.[5] In France the custody of the children is entrusted to the spouse who has obtained the divorce, unless the tribunal, in the interests of the children and upon the application of the family or the *ministère public*, commits the custody of all or some of them to the other parent or to a third party;[6] but in every case both parents are bound to contribute to the maintenance and education of the children.[7] According to the German code, if either spouse is declared the exclusively guilty party, the custody and care of the children belong to the innocent party ; if both parties are declared to be guilty, the mother has the custody of the daughters and of the sons who have not attained the age of six years, whereas the infant sons who have attained that age are given to the father. The Guardianship Court, however, may provide differently if a modification of the ordinary rule appears

---

[1] *Bürgerliches Gesetzbuch*, arts. 1578, 1586.
[2] *Ibid.* art. 1581. If a marriage has been dissolved on account of the insanity of one of the spouses, the other spouse shall furnish maintenance to him or her in the same manner as a spouse declared to be the exclusively guilty party (*ibid.* art. 1583).
[3] Roguin, *op. cit.* p. 365.   [4] Burge, *op. cit.* iii. 848.
[5] Roguin, *op. cit.* p. 352. In Portugal the children shall by preference be confided to the parent in whose favour divorce has been pronounced (*Royal Commission on Divorce and Matrimonial Causes, Appendices*, p. 152 *sq.*), and in Sweden to the parent who is not chiefly responsible for the divorce in case both are considered to be equally fit to take care of them (*Lag om äktenskaps ingående och upplösning*, vi. 23).
[6] *Code civil*, art. 302.   [7] *Ibid.* art. 303.

GN 480

F67

AB/
121/3
C/3

GN
6
L4

HQ
510
L3

HQ
665
M3.

the fine is $5.00.

If not returned by ~~DEC 08 1988~~
at the end of the business day
the fine is $10.00.

The fine for any book not returned by the end of the business day, the last day of the
semester, is $10.00.

THANK YOU
FOR RETURNING THE
BOOK ON TIME.

COLLEGE OF MARIN LIBRARY

desirable in the interests of the child.[1]   The duties of the
spouses as to the maintenance of their children are not
modified by the divorce ; where such duty falls on the
husband and the maintenance cannot be supplied out of
the children's own income, the wife has to contribute a
reasonable part of her income and earnings.[2]   In England
great discretion is given to the court.   It is the first duty of
the court to tend the welfare of the children, and, subject
to that principle, if it is not to be anticipated that the giving
of the custody of a child to a guilty parent will be the cause
of its being injured morally, the court may award custody
both to a guilty husband and, in extremely rare circumstances, even to a guilty wife.[3]   For a long time the court
considered that it ceased to have jurisdiction over children
when they attained the age of sixteen, but the Court of
Appeal in 1894 held that the Divorce Court might make
orders for custody, maintenance, and education of
children until they attained the age of twenty-one.[4]
In Austria[5] and Hungary[6] the law favours an amicable
agreement between the divorced spouses as to the custody
of the children.   In the absence of such agreement sons
up to four years of age and daughters up to seven years
are in Austria entrusted to the mother and thereafter
to the father even if he is responsible for the divorce ;[7]
while in Hungary all children up to seven years of age are
entrusted to the mother and thereafter to the innocent
spouse.   If both spouses have been declared guilty, the
sons are, in the latter country, given into the custody of
the father and the daughters into that of the mother ; but
the tribunal may, in the interests of the children and notwithstanding any agreement by the parents, commit them to the
care of a third person.[8]   In the case of judicial separation
the rules relating to the custody of children follow very
similar principles to those adopted in the case of divorce.[9]
According to the Italian code the court decides which

[1] *Bürgerliches Gesetzbuch*, art. 1635.   [2] *Ibid.* art. 1585.
[3] Hall, *op. cit.* p. 389 *sq.*   [4] *Ibid.* p. 391.
[5] *Das allgemeine bürgerliche Gesetzbuch für das Kaisertum Oesterreich*, § 117.   [6] Roguin, *op. cit.* p. 354.   [7] *Ibid.* p. 355.
[8] Burge, *op. cit.* iii. 848.   [9] See Roguin, *op. cit.* p. 374 *sqq.*

parent is to keep the children ;[1] whereas in Spain they are entrusted to the custody of the innocent parent,[2] and it does not seem that the court can decide otherwise.

When we pass from laws to practice we find that the divorce-rate varies greatly in the different countries of the West. In Europe it is highest in Switzerland, but in the United States it is higher than in any European country and the number of divorces probably exceeds that in all European countries put together.[3] In nearly all the countries for which statistics are available divorce has been steadily increasing during recent years. In Switzerland there were 242 divorces per 100,000 married couples in 1906–1915 and 188 in 1886–1891 ; in Denmark, 153 in 1906–1915 and 96 in 1896–1905 ; in Hungary, 152 in 1906–1915 and 32 in 1876–1885 ; in Germany, 133 in 1907–1914 and 80 in 1886–1895 ; in France, 115 in 1908–1913 and 69 in 1886–1895 ; in Holland, 91 in 1905–1914 and 25 in 1875–1884 ; in Belgium, 80 in 1909–1912 and 21 in 1876–1885 ; in Sweden, 68 in 1908–1913 and 28 in 1876–1885 ; in Norway, 61 in 1906–1915 and 20 in 1887–1894 ; in Finland, 44 in 1906–1915 and 13 in 1876–1885 ; in Luxemburg, 41 in 1909–1912 and 21 in 1896–1905 ; in Scotland, 31 in 1906–1915 and 13 in 1876–1885 ; in England and Wales, 10 in 1907–1914 and 7 in 1876–1885 ; in Austria, 8 in 1909–1912 and 3 in 1886–1895 ; in Ireland, 0·17 in 1896–1905 and 0·01 in 1876–1885. Serbia is, according to available statistics, the only European country in which the divorce-rate has remained stationary ; it was there 65 both in 1887–1894 and in 1896–1905.[4] In the United States there were in 1906–1915 626 divorces per 100,000 married couples, and in 1896–1905 406. The following list gives the names of the states in which the proportion of divorces in 1906–1915 exceeded 1,000, as also the figures both for that period and, in parentheses, for the years 1896–1905 :—Nevada, 4,016

---

[1] *Codice civile*, art. 154.   [2] *Código civil de España*, art. 167.

[3] Willcox, ' Study in Vital Statistics,' in *Political Science Quarterly*, viii. 78. *Idem, Divorce Problem*, p. 11.

[4] *Annuaire international de statistique publié par l'office permanent de l'Institut international de statistique*, 1917, ii. Mouvement de la population (Europe), p. 30 *sq.*

(725) ; Montana, 2,141 (996) ; Arizona, 1,606 (745) ; Oregon, 1,578 (799) ; Washington, 1,547 (1,145) ; Idaho, 1,296 (755) ; Arkansas, 1,280 (810) ; Texas, 1,189 (77) ; California, 1,167 (519) ; Oklahoma, 1,155 (753) ; Wyoming, 1,123 (742). The lowest divorce rates were, in 1906–1915, found in the district of Columbia (72 ; in 1896–1905, 279), North Carolina (174 ; 161), New York (180 ; 120), New Jersey (227 ; 121), Georgia (295 ; 159), Pennsylvania (328 ; 198), West Virginia (342 ; 385), Massachusetts (359 ; 262), Wisconsin (391 ; 358). Contrary to the general rule, the proportion of divorces has decreased in Colorado, the district of Columbia, North and South Dakota, Maine, and West Virginia.[1] Both in Europe[2] and America there are, comparatively speaking, more divorces in towns than in the country. With reference to the United States, Dr. Willcox observes that in about 95 per cent. of the cases the divorce-rate of a large city is greater than that in the other counties of the state.[3]

The duration of marriage and the customs or laws by which it is regulated depend on such a variety of circumstances that our explanation of the facts stated above must necessarily be very incomplete. All that I can do is to make some general observations as to the influences which tend either to prolong or to shorten the unions between the sexes, and as to the rules which either prevent or control their dissolution.

Marriage, as we have seen, is by its very nature a relation which lasts beyond the mere act of propagation. It seems to be based upon a primeval habit. We have found reasons to believe that even in primitive times it was the habit for a man and a woman, or several women, to remain together till after the birth of the offspring, and that they were induced to do so by an instinct which had been acquired through natural selection because the offspring were in need of both maternal and paternal care. In other species having the same habit the period during which the union

---

[1] *Ibid.* 1920, iv. Mouvement de la population (Amérique), p. 21 *sq.*
[2] v. Oettingen, *Die Moralstatistik*, p. 163.
[3] Willcox, in *Political Science Quarterly*, viii. 83 *sqq.*

lasts varies greatly. Among many birds it lasts for life,[1] whereas among the mammals the same male and female very seldom seem to live together longer than a year.[2] Among the man-like apes family groups containing young ones of different ages have been found ; [3] but we cannot, of course, be certain that in such cases the latter have the same father. It is remarkable that among some of the lowest races of men marriage is regularly a lifelong union ; but this by no means proves that it was so among our earliest human ancestors. We may assume that if man originally made love at a certain season only, but subsequently began to pair throughout the year, there came a new inducement for the mates to remain with one another, which must have had the tendency to make their union more durable. But apart from the purely sexual instinct, conjugal affection may keep man and wife together even after their marriage has fulfilled its original aim. And conjugal affection has certainly become more durable in proportion as love has been influenced by mental qualities.

Parental feelings exercise a similar influence, and they do so longer than is necessary for the rearing of the progeny. Marriage not only came into existence for the sake of the offspring but often becomes a lasting union through the presence of children. Among many of the lower races the birth of offspring is the best guarantee for the continuance of the marriage tie.[4] Speaking of some North American Indians, Schoolcraft observes, " The best protection to married females arises from the ties of children, which, by bringing into play the strong natural affections of the

---

[1] Brehm, *Thierleben*, iv. 20.   [2] *Ibid.* i. 33.   [3] *Supra*, i. 32, 34.

[4] See, besides various statements given above, Chantre y Herrera, *Historia de las Misiones de la Compañia de Jesús en el Marañón español*, p. 71 *sq.* (Maynas) ; Appun, ' Die Indianer von Britisch-Guayana,' in *Das Ausland*, xliv. 447 (Macusis) ; Bell, *Tangweera*, p. 261 *sq.* (Mosquito Indians) ; Isabella Bird, *Unbeaten Tracks in Japan*, ii. 100 (Ainu) ; Brooke Low, quoted by Ling Roth, *Natives of Sarawak and British North Borneo*, i. 128, and St. John, *Life in the Forests of the Far East,* i. 66 (Sea Dyaks) ; Stephan and Graebner, *Neu-Mecklenburg (Bismarck-Archipel)*, p. 110 ; Lambert, *Mœurs et Superstitions des Néo-Calédoniens*, p. 92 ; Jarves, *op. cit.* p. 43 (Hawaians) ; Lichtenstein, *op. cit.* ii. 48 (Bushmen).

heart, appeal at once to that principle in man's original organisation which is the strongest."[1]   The influence which the presence of children exercises on the duration of marriage also shows itself in the fact that childless marriages are often dissolved.   We have seen that among the lower races barrenness in the wife is a frequent cause of divorce, and that it is so also where the husband's right to divorce his wife is restricted.   The same is the case among many peoples who have reached a higher degree of civilisation. Even among modern civilised nations, who do not recognise barrenness as a sufficient ground for repudiating a wife, divorces are more frequent in cases where there are no children.   Dr. Willcox thinks it fair to conclude that in the United States childless marriages are between three and four times as likely to end in divorce as marriages with children, and statistics from the middle of the last century showed a similar tendency in France.[2]   It has been noticed that in Switzerland two-fifths of the total number of divorces take place between married people who have no children, while the sterile marriages only amount to one-fifth of the number of marriages.[3]

The marriage tie is further strengthened by economic considerations.   The dissolution of it deprives the woman of a supporter and the man of a helpmate and in many cases of a drudge.   It is true that considerations of this sort may be of slight importance where the man or the woman can without difficulty contract a new marriage, and they may even be a cause of divorce ; we are told that the Dyak husbands " coolly dismiss their helpmates when too lazy or too weak to work, and select partners better qualified to undergo the toils of life."[4]   But to find another partner is not always an easy matter, and the contraction of a new marriage may entail fresh expense.   Among the Tamulians, says Baierlein, a marriage costs such a lot of money that it often takes a man's whole lifetime to pay off the debts incurred at one, and this alone is a reason, at

[1] Schoolcraft, *Indian in his Wigwam*, p. 73.
[2] Willcox, *Divorce Problem*, p. 34.   [3] Glasson, *op. cit.* p. 470.
[4] St. John, in *Trans. Ethn. Soc. London*, N.S. ii. 237.

all events in respectable families, why the tie should not be loosened.[1] The man may have to provide his divorced wife with the means of subsistence,[2] and very frequently he is obliged to give her what she brought with her into the house, and even a certain proportion of the common wealth.[3] If the marriage is dissolved the husband may lose the price he paid for his wife, or her family may on the other hand have to return the price received for her. Both the custom of providing a daughter with a marriage portion and the purchase of wives undoubtedly tend to make marriage more durable. Leighton Wilson states that among the natives of Southern Guinea the relatives of a woman who runs away from her husband are seldom able to return the money paid for her, and that, consequently, " it is their policy to have her remain quietly with her husband whether he is kind to her or not."[4] We are told that among the Kafirs a man does not often divorce his wife, partly because by so doing he deprives himself of her labour as his servant, and partly because he finds it very difficult to recover the bride price even when he is entitled to demand it.[5] In his book on the Basuto, Casalis remarks that " cases of divorce are very frequent where the price of the wife is of small value. Among the Basutos, where it is of considerable amount, the dissolution of marriage is attended with much difficulty."[6] It is said that among the eastern tribes of Northern Rhodesia " the introduction of cattle into the dowry makes divorce in many cases more difficult to obtain ; and, indeed, among the Wiwa very few cases are brought to court, as the cattle and wives are scarce and must be retained at all costs."[7] Speaking of divorce in Melanesia, Dr. Codrington observes, " The great difficulty is the property given for the wife ; a man does not wish to lose this, and will try

[1] Baierlein, *Land of the Tamulians*, p. 36.

[2] For instances of this among some of the lower races see *supra*, i. 53.

[3] For the lower races see, *e.g.*, Bancroft, *op. cit.* i. 197 (Nootka), 277 (Inland Columbians) ; Colquhoun, *Amongst the Shans*, p. 295 ; McNair, *Perak and the Malys*, p. 236 ; Munzinger, *Ostafrikanische Studien*, pp. 320 *sq.* (Beni-Amer), 489 (Kunáma).

[4] Wilson, *Western Africa*, p. 268.   [5] Maclean, *op. cit.* p. 70.

[6] Casalis, *op. cit.* p. 184   [7] Gouldsbury and Sheane, *op. cit.* p. 171

many times to get back a runaway wife before he gives her up, giving presents to her relations."[1]   Dr. Finsch ascribes the frequency of divorce in Ponapé, one of the Caroline Islands, to the fact that wife-purchase does not exist there.[2]

The economic factor has in various ways proved an obstacle to divorce in civilised communities.   In the United States depressions in trade have had a tendency to decrease divorces as well as marriages.   " In the great mass of the population," says Dr. Willcox, " they have discouraged change, have compelled men and women ' in whatsoever state they were, therewith to be content,' or at least to abandon or postpone the idea of change."[3]   He adds that in England, on the other hand, the number of divorces has not fallen off, but rather increased, in the years in which the number of marriages has been diminished by hard times ; and in explanation of this he conjectures that the expense and delay involved in procuring a divorce in England are so great that only somewhat wealthy persons, who do not feel so severely the burden of a financial crisis, can afford to go into court.[4]   There can be no doubt that the cost of carrying a suit through has been a very important reason for the remarkably small number of divorces in England and Wales ; we have seen that in the days of parliamentary divorce, which was exceedingly expensive, the number of divorces was infinitesimal.   In France a law passed in 1851, which allowed those unable to pay the expense of a suit for separation to plead without cost, resulted in a distinct increase in the number of applications ;[5]   and the present remarkable frequency of divorce in England, while very largely a consequence of certain circumstances arising from the war, is also undoubtedly connected with the fact that a divorce may now be obtained more cheaply than before.[6]

---

[1] Codrington, *op. cit.* p. 244.
[2] Finsch, ' Ueber die Bewohner von Ponapé,' in *Zeitschr. f. Ethnol.* xii. 317.   [3] Willcox, in *Political Science Quarterly*, viii. 79 *sqq.*
[4] *Ibid.* p. 82.   [5] Willcox, *The Divorce Problem*, p. 58.
[6] According to Lord Birkenhead, the social upheaval of war has in nineteen cases out of twenty been responsible for the increased number of petitions for the dissolution of the marriage bond.   But, as was pointed out in an article in *The Times* for June 2nd, 1921,

While there are thus various factors that tend to make marriage durable, there are others that have the very opposite tendency. To these belong certain peculiarities of the sexual instinct. The physical qualities in men and women which act as sexual stimulants are not imperishable, and the loss of the attractive quality may put an end to the union. We often hear of men repudiating wives who grow old or ugly.[1] According to Cook, it was much more common for a Tahitian to cast off his first wife and take a more youthful partner than to live with both.[2] A Malay in many cases turns away his wife as soon as she becomes ugly from hard work and maternal cares.[3] Among the Aleut, " when a wife ceases to possess attractions or value in the eyes of her proprietor, she is sent back to her friends."[4] Among the Abipones, according to Dobrizhoffer, " should the husband cast his eyes upon any handsomer woman, the old wife must remove merely on this account, her fading form or advanced age being her only accusers."[5] In Switzerland marriage is much more frequently dissolved through divorce when the wife is the husband's senior than when the reverse is the case.[6] Moreover, the sexual desire is dulled by long companionship and excited by novelty. Dr. Bérenger-Féraud observes that the Moors of Senegambia " divorcent avec une facilité extrême, non seulement sous le prétexte le plus futile, mais souvent, et même uniquement, pour le plaisir de changer."[7] According to von Oettingen,

the facilities afforded to suitors under the Poor Persons Rules must also have something to do with the increase in question, since " the figures which are published day by day indicate that a considerable proportion of the work of the Divorce Court is the hearing of such suits."

[1] *Supra*, iii. 292. Barth, *Reisen und Entdeckungen in Nord- und Central-Afrika*, i. 258 (Touareg of Rhāt).

[2] Cook, *Voyage to the Pacific Ocean*, ii. 157.

[3] Bock, *Head-Hunters of Borneo*, p. 315.

[4] Bancroft, *op. cit.* i. 92.

[5] Dobrizhoffer, *Account of the Abipones*, ii. 211.

[6] Glasson, *op. cit.* p. 469.

[7] Bérenger-Féraud, ' Le mariage chez les nègres Sénégambiens,' in *Revue d'Anthropologie*, ser. ii. vol. vi. 290. *Cf.* Keane, ' On the Botocudos,' in *Jour. Anthr. Inst.* xiii. 206 ; Krauss, *Sitte und Brauch der Südslaven*, p. 568.

the statistics of divorce and remarriage in Europe show
that the taste for variety is often the chief cause of the
dissolution of marriage.[1] It does not appear from the
statistics that divorced men and women are more disposed
to remarry than widowers and widows ;[2] but this does not
disprove the contention, supported by ordinary experience
in countries where divorce is of common occurrence, that
sexual indifference and a desire for new gratifications of
the sexual instinct are potent causes of it.

The custom of marrying without previous knowledge of
the partner must also, of course, be injurious to the stability
of marriage. The facility of Muhammadan divorce, as
Mr. Bosworth Smith points out, is the necessary consequence
of the separation of the sexes. " A man," says Mr. Stanley
Lane-Poole, " would never embark in the hazardous lottery
of Eastern marriage, if he had not the escape of divorce
from the woman whom he has never seen, and who may be
in every way uncongenial to him."[3] The frequency of
divorce in ancient Athens[4] and among some of the simpler
peoples[5] has been attributed to a similar cause. Influences
of this sort and others just mentioned may, however, to
some extent be counteracted by the prevalence of polygyny
or concubinage. Speaking of the rarity of divorce among
the upper classes in Japan, Professor Chamberlain asks,
" Why, indeed, should a man take the trouble to get
separated from an uncongenial wife, when any wife occupies
too inferior a position to be able to make herself a serious
nuisance, and when society has no objection to his keeping
any number of mistresses ? "[6]

[1] v. Oettingen, *op. cit.* p. 150.

[2] Mayo-Smith, *Science of Statistics*, i. 119

[3] Lane-Poole, in a review of Bosworth Smith's *Mohammed and
Mohammedanism*, in *Academy*, v. 684.   [4] Beauchet, *op. cit.* i. 376 *sq.*

[5] Bourien, ' Wild Tribes of the Interior of the Malay Peninsula,'
in *Trans. Ethn. Soc. London*, N.S. iii. 80 (Mantra). St. John, *ibid.*
ii. 237 (Dyaks). Mason, in *Jour. Asiatic Soc. Bengal*, vol. xxxv.
pt. ii. 20 (Karens). On the other hand it is said that on Ugi and
San Cristoval, in the Solomon Group, divorce is comparatively rare
because " when a man chooses his wife he knows her well and has
been living with her before marriage " (Elton, in *Jour. Anthr. Ins*
xvii. 95).   [6] Chamberlain, *op. cit.* p. 314.

However carefully the partner is selected, marriage is always something of an adventure. Where two persons are brought into so close contact with, and into such constant dependence on, each other it would be little short of a miracle if their wills always acted in complete unison. In modern civilisation, where life is becoming richer in interests and individual differences are getting more accentuated, the causes of disagreement are multiplied and the frictions are apt to become more serious and, consequently, more likely to end in a rupture of the marriage tie. The idea that it is a right, or even a duty, to assert one's own individuality is characteristic of our age. As Lord Bryce observes, " the desire of each person to do what he or she pleases, to gratify his or her tastes, likings, caprices, to lead a life which shall be uncontrolled by another's will—this grows stronger. So, too, whatever stimulates the susceptibility and sensitiveness of the nervous system tends to make tempers more irritable, and to produce causes of friction between those who are in constant contact. . . It is temper rather than unlawful passion that may prove in future the most dangerous enemy to the stability of the marriage relation."[1] There is also the spread of a spirit of dissatisfaction in our time, which has been called " the age of discontent." It has been noticed that the rates of divorce and of suicide—the highest expression of discontent—show a close and constant relation. Both are much more common among Protestants than among Catholics, among the Teutons than among the Celts, and in cities than in the country ; both are rapidly increasing, and the proportion of suicides among divorced persons is abnormally large.[2] The emancipation of women, too, has its share in the increasing instability of marriage. It is natural to find divorce most frequent where a woman finds it most easy to earn her bread. In the United States nearly two-thirds of the divorces are granted on demand of the wife.[3]

It is impossible to doubt that the number of divorces is also influenced by the rules laid down by custom or law.

[1] Bryce, *op. cit.* ii. 463.   [2] Willcox, *Divorce Problem*, p. 70.
[3] *Ibid.*, pp. 66, 68, 69, 34.

although the effect of legal restrictions may often have
been exaggerated. Dr. Willcox even maintains that "the
immediate, direct and measurable influence of legislation is
subsidiary, unimportant, almost imperceptible."[1] In support
of this opinion he points out that in New York, in spite of
its more stringent divorce law, the rate of divorces was
higher than in New Jersey and only a little lower than in
Pennsylvania.[2] This means that more divorces for adultery
were granted in New York, in proportion to the population,
than for adultery and desertion in New Jersey, and almost
as many as for adultery, desertion, cruelty, and imprisonment in Pennsylvania. From this he draws the conclusion
that "limiting the causes increases the number of divorces
in those which remain, but without materially affecting the
total number. A certain proportion of the married couples
in the three states desired divorce and were willing to offer
the evidence required in order to obtain the decree."[3]   In
Europe, also, the rates of divorces are certainly not proportionate to the facility with which divorce may be obtained
according to law ; Norway, for instance, has a more liberal
divorce law, but at the same time fewer divorces, than
several other continental countries. Yet I believe that
Dr. Willcox has somewhat underrated the influence of legal
obstacles. He argues that restrictions on divorce and on
remarriage after divorce have been tried in various places
and at various times and have proved of little effect.[4] This
contention is by no means borne out by recent experience
in Japan, where the introduction of the new Civil Code,
which made divorce considerably more difficult than it had
been before, was accompanied with a sudden and great
decrease in the number of divorces.[5] Much depends, of
course, on the manner in which the law is administered. It
seems that the exceptionally great divorce-rates in the
United States are largely due to the laxity of procedure

[1] *Ibid.* p. 61.

[2] This statement is based on earlier figures than those quoted
above.

[3] Willcox, *Divorce Problem*, p. 45 *sq.*   [4] *Ibid.* pp. 49, 50, 72.

[5] *Supra*, iii. 305. Professor Rein (*Japan*, i. 586) expressly attributes this decrease to the influence of the new code.

which has grown up there. One wife alleges that her husband has never offered to take her out "riding" (= driving); another, that he does not come home till ten o'clock at night, and when he does return he keeps plaintiff awake talking.[1] On the other hand, Dr. Willcox admits that the public sentiment of a community has much to do with its rate of divorce, and that the law is a register of the public sentiment. He observes that this sentiment changes much more rapidly in new and small communities than in old and large ones ; and he illustrates his observation by pointing out that the highest divorce rate in Europe is found in Switzerland, which until 1876 had separate laws for each canton, and Denmark, and that in North America there are marked differences between the laws of the eastern and the western belts of states.[2]

Laws and rules of custom, while undoubtedly influencing conduct, are themselves influenced by it, and have largely originated in behaviour which has been habitual in the community. Hence the circumstances which tend either to preserve or to dissolve the unions of men and women have also made themselves felt in the establishing of rules relating to divorce. But there are other influences that have been at work as well. The dissolution of a marriage is not a matter which concerns the interests of one person alone, and individual desires may for this reason also be checked by the public sentiment of the community.

Among many peoples there is said to be no such check, either with regard to the husband or with regard to the wife. This is the case with a large number of uncivilised tribes, but with no people of ancient civilisation at least in the Old World. Among other peoples, again, the husband but not the wife is allowed to dissolve the marriage at will, or, though the husband has perfect liberty in this respect, the wife may even be denied the right of effecting a divorce on any ground whatever. To this class of peoples belong many civilised nations in the earlier days of their history, the peoples following Muhammadan law, and also many savage

[1] Bryce, *op. cit.* ii. 441 *sqq.*   [2] Willcox, *Divorce Problem*, p. 65.

tribes. These facts tend to confirm a conclusion at which
I have arrived in another work, namely, that the position
of married women is more favourable in a large part of the
uncivilised world than it has been among peoples of archaic
culture.[1] This may be explained by the facts that among
these peoples the higher civilisation was almost exclusively
the prerogative of the men, which widened the gulf between
the sexes ; that the great religions of the East regarded
woman as an unclean and inferior being, which naturally
affected the estimation in which she was held ;[2] and that
in the ancient State the father assumed an extraordinary
power over his children, which by marriage was transferred
to the husband.

The nature of the restrictions to which divorce is subject
generally discloses the causes from which they have sprung.
They are in the first place intended to prevent the infliction
of an injury on a spouse who does not desire to dissolve the
marriage. But in certain circumstances this regard for his
or her interests ceases to act as a check, namely, if the
spouse is guilty of offensive behaviour, or if the preservation
of the marriage tie for some other reason—such as impotence
or insanity or disease—would entail considerable suffering
for the party who is desirous of dissolving it. The rules
relating to divorce have thus in a large measure originated
in the tendency of the community to sympathise with the
sufferings of its members as long as they behave without
reproach. This tendency, as I have tried to show elsewhere,
is the main cause of moral rules as expressed in customs or
laws. On the one hand, marriage is a contract which
grants rights and imposes duties, but on the other hand it
" gives either party an extraordinary power of injuring the
other." The community tries to protect the interests of
both parties, or at least of one of them, and provides divorce
as a remedy if the marriage proves a failure. It may
certainly be anything but impartial in laying down its rules

---

[1] *Origin and Development of the Moral Ideas,* ch. xxvi. ' The
Subjection of Wives.'   See particularly i. 647.

[2] *Ibid.* i. 663 *sqq.*

of divorce ; but this is only another instance of that inequality of rights which so often characterises the legal
relations between the sexes.

Husband and wife are not the only persons whose interests
are affected by a divorce. The welfare of the offspring has
also been considered in the rules controlling the dissolution of
marriage. There are not only provisions for safeguarding
the children's future, but in some cases, as we have seen,
the birth of a child makes the marriage indissoluble. Among
ourselves the interests of children are often appealed to by
those who oppose changes in the existing laws on divorce,
however little the children may have been thought of when
the laws were framed.

In many cases the rules of divorce have been greatly
influenced by religion. We have seen that in some countries,
as Japan and ancient Greece, this influence has been in
favour of divorce in certain circumstances, particularly in
the case of a barren wife. In other instances religion has,
on the other hand, acted as a bar to divorce in all circumstances. Although Jesus, like the school of Shammai,
simply prohibited a man from putting away his wife for any
other reason than adultery and a woman from deserting her
husband, the Christian Church established the dogma that
a valid marriage can never be dissolved, and that in the case
of adultery on the part of the wife the innocent husband
is not allowed to take another wife. This draconic legislation
is undoubtedly due to the ascetic tendencies of the Church,
which made her insensible to the misery caused by unhappy
marriages. So thoroughly did she succeed in impressing
her views upon the minds of Christian legislators that to this
day even many Roman Catholic countries which have introduced civil marriage obstinately refuse to permit divorce
in any circumstances whatsoever. In other countries,
where the principle of the indissolubility of marriage has
broken down long ago and even the express injunctions of
Christ are no longer followed, the rigid attitude of the
Church has left behind sentiments which put obstacles in
the way of the most needful reforms. Legislators are still

imbued with the idea that a marriage must inevitably end in a catastrophe, either by the death or some great misfortune of one of the consorts or by the commission of a criminal or immoral act.   New motives are found for old restrictions, new wine is poured into the old bottles.   It would seem that a contract entered into by mutual consent also should be dissolvable by mutual consent.[1]   But it is argued that marriage cannot be treated as an ordinary contract, and that its dissolution should only be permitted on very serious grounds.   It is said that few things can be more harmful to the moral well-being of the offspring than the divorce of their parents.   This is perfectly true, but constitutes no valid argument against divorce.   The interests of children are obviously out of the question where the marriage is childless, and where it is not so, there is every reason to believe that it is rather better than worse for the child to live peacefully with one parent alone than to live with two parents who cannot agree or who, for some reason or other, wish to break up their home.   Moreover, if the regard for the children's welfare were the real cause of the prohibition of consensual divorce, why should it be prohibited in so many countries which allow consensual separation ?   We have seen that divorce by mutual consent has already been introduced by some modern law-books, and it is not known that any evils have resulted from this concession.   Where such divorce is not allowed by law it is nevertheless easily obtained in practice ; and it is strange that any legislator should persist in regarding crime or immoral conduct on the part of one of the spouses as a more proper ground or excuse for dissolving the marriage than the mutual agreement of both.

It is a widespread idea that divorce is the enemy of marriage and, if made too easy, might prove destructive to the very institution of the family.   This view I cannot share.   I look upon divorce as the necessary remedy for a misfortune and as a means of preserving the dignity of

---

[1] For a recent discussion of divorce by mutual consent see Haynes, *Divorce as it might be*, p. 42 *sqq.*

marriage by putting an end to unions which are a disgrace to its name. The existence of marriage does not depend on laws. If the main thesis of this work is correct, if marriage is not an artificial creation but an institution based on deep-rooted sentiments, conjugal and parental, it will last as long as these sentiments last. And should they ever cease to exist, no laws in the world could save marriage from destruction.

AUTHORITIES QUOTED

Abd-er-Razzak, 'Narrative of the Journey of'; in *India in the Fifteenth Century*, trans. and ed. by R. H. Major. London, 1857.

Abdullah al-Māmūn al-Suhrawardy, *The Sayings of Muhammad.* Ed. by. London, 1910.

—— See Russell (A. D.) and Abdullah al-Ma'mun Suhrawardy.

Abeghian (Manuk), *Der armenische Volksglaube.* (*Inaugural-Dissertation.*) Leipzig, 1899.

Abercromby (John), 'Marriage Customs of the Mordvins'; in *Folk-Lore*, vol. i. London, 1890.

Abhandlungen der Königlichen Sächsischen Gesellschaft der Wissenschaften. Leipzig.

—— *und Berichte des Königlichen Zoologischen und Anthropologisch-Ethnographischen Museums zu Dresden.* Berlin.

Åbo Tidningar. Åbo.

Abrahams (Israel), *Jewish Life in the Middle Ages.* London, 1896.

—— 'Marriage (Jewish)'; in Hastings, *Encylopædia of Religion and Ethics*, vol. viii. Edinburgh, 1915.

Abreu de Galindo (Juan de), *The History of the Discovery and Conquest of the Canary Islands.* Trans. by G. Glas. London, 1764.

Abulfeda, *Historia anteislamica arabice.* Ed. and trans. into Latin by H. O. Fleischer. Lipsiae, 1831.

Academy (The). London.

Acosta (Joseph de), *The Natural and Moral History of the Indies.* Trans. ed. by C. R. Markham. 2 vols. London, 1880.

Acta Academiæ Aboensis. Åbo.

—— *Societatis Scientiarum Fennicæ.* Helsingfors.

Actes de l'Académie nationale des sciences, belles lettres et arts de Bordeaux. Paris.

Adair (James), *The History of the American Indians.* London, 1775.

Adam (W.), 'Consanguinity in Marriage'; in *The Fortnightly Review*, vols. ii.–iii. London, 1865–66.

Adams (John), *Sketches taken during Ten Voyages to Africa, between the Years 1786 and 1800.* London, [1825].

Addison (Lancelot), *The Present State of the Jews.* London, 1676.

Adriani (N.) and Kruijt (A. C.), *De Bare'e-sprekende Toradja's van Midden-Celebes.* 3 vols. 's-Gravenhage, 1912–14.

Aelian, *De natura animalium, Varia historia, &c.* Ed. by R. Hercher. Parisiis, 1858.

Aeschylus, *Tragœdiæ et fragmenta*. Ed. by E. A. J. Ahrens. Parisiis, 1842.
Aethelbirht (*King*), ' The Laws of ' ; in *Ancient Laws and Institutes of England*. London, 1840.
Agassiz (L. J. R.), *A Journey in Brazil*. Boston, 1868.
Ahlqvist (A.), *Die Kulturwörter der westfinnischen Sprachen*. Helsingfors, 1875.
—— ' Unter Wogulen und Ostjaken ' ; in *Acta Societatis Scientiarum Fennicæ*, vol. xiv. Helsingfors, 1885.
Ahmad Shah (*Rev.*), *Four Years in Tibet*. Benares, 1906.
Aigremont (*Dr.*), *Fuss- und Schuh-Symbolik und -Erotik*. Leipzig, 1909.
Albericus, *Visio*. Ed. by Catello de Vivo. Ariano, 1899.
Alberti (L.), *De Kaffers aan de Zuidkust van Afrika*. Amsterdam, 1810.
Albertis (L. M. d'), *New Guinea*. Trans. 2 vols. London, 1880.
Alberuni's India. An Account of the Religion, &c. of India about A.D. 1030. English edition by E. C. Sachau. 2 vols. London, 1910.
Alcedo (A. de), *The Geographical and Historical Dictionary of America and the West Indies*. Trans. ed. by G. A. Thompson. 5 vols. London, 1812–15.
Äldre Västgötalagen. See *Västgötalagen, Äldre*.
Alexander (*Sir* James E.), *An Expedition of Discovery into the Interior of Africa*. 2 vols. London, 1838.
Allardt (Anders), *Nyländska folkseder och bruk, vidskepelse m.m.* (*Nyland. Samlingar utgifna af Nyländska Afdelningen*, vol. iv.) Helsingfors, 1889.
Allen (W.) and Thomson (T. R. H.), *A Narrative of the Expedition sent by Her Majesty's Government to the River Niger, in 1841*. 2 vols. London, 1848.
Allgemeine bürgerliche Gesetzbuch für das Kaisertum Oesterreich (*Das*). Ed. by J. von Schey. Wien, 1916.
Allgemeines Landrecht für die Preussischen Staaten. 4 vols. and *Register*. Berlin, 1828–32.
Almindelig norsk lovsamling. Ed. by P. I. Paulsen, J. E. Thomle, and C. S. Thomle. Kristiania.
Alvares Cabral (Pedro), ' Navigation del captino P. A.' Trans. from the Portuguese ; in Ramusio, *Navigationi et viaggi*, vol. i. Venetia, 1554.
Am Urquell. Monatsschrift für Volkskunde. Ed. by F. S. Krauss. Lunden.
Ambrose (*Saint*), *Opera omnia*. (Migne, *Patrologiæ cursus*, vols. xiv.–xvii.) Parisiis, 1845.
Ameer Ali (*Syed*), *Mahommedan Law compiled from Authorities in the Original Arabic. Vol. II. Containing the Law relating to Succession and Status*. Calcutta, 1908.
American Anthropologist (*The*). Washington, New York, Lancaster.
American Naturalist (*The*). New York.
Amira (Karl von), ' Recht ' ; in Paul, *Grundriss der germanischen Philologie*, vol. iii. Strassburg, 1900.
Ammianus Marcellinus. See Marcellinus (Ammianus).
Amram (D. W.), *The Jewish Law of Divorce according to Bible and Talmud*. London, 1897.
Anales de la Universidad de Chile. Santiago de Chile.

Anantha Krishna Iyer (L. K.), *The Cochin Tribes and Castes*. 2 vols. Madras, 1909–12.
Anatomische Hefte. Ed. by Fr. Merkel and R. Bonnet. Wiesbaden.
Ancient Laws and Institutes of England. London, 1840.
Ancient Laws and Institutes of Ireland. Dublin and London, 1865–79.
Ancient Laws and Institutes of Wales. London, 1841.
Andagoya (Pascual de), *Narrative of the Proceedings of Pedrarias Davila in the Province of Tierra Firme or Castilla del Oro*. Trans. and ed. by C. R. Markham. London, 1865.
Anderson (John), *Mandalay to Momien*. London, 1876.
Anderson (John W.), *Notes of Travel in Fiji and New Caledonia*. London, 1880.
Andersson (C. J.), *Lake Ngami*. London, 1856.
—— *The Okavango River*. London, 1861.
Andree (Richard), ' Die Beschneidung ' ; in *Archiv für Anthropologie* vol. xiii. Braunschweig, 1881.
—— *Ethnographische Parallelen und Vergleiche*. Stuttgart, 1878.
—— *Ethnographische Parallelen und Vergleiche*. *Neue Folge*. Stuttgart, 1889.
—— *Zur Volkskunde der Juden*. Bielefeld & Leipzig, 1881.
Angas (G. F.), *Polynesia*. London, [1866].
—— *Savage Life and Scenes in Australia and New Zealand*. London, 1850.
—— *South Australia Illustrated*. London, 1847.
Angus (—), ' " Chensamwali " or Initiation Ceremony of Girls, as performed in Azimba Land, Central Africa ' ; in *Verhandl. Berliner Gesellsch. f. Anthr.* 1898. Berlin.
Ankermann (B.), ' Kulturkreise und Kulturschichten in Afrika ' ; in *Zeitschr. f. Ethnol.* vol. xxxvii. Berlin, 1905.
Annales de démographie internationale. Paris.
—— *de la propagation de la Foi*. Lyon.
—— *du Musée du Congo Belge*. *Ethnographie et Anthropologie*. Bruxelles.
Annandale (Nelson) and Robinson (H. C.), *Fasciculi Malayenses*. *Anthropology*. 2 pts. London, 1903–04.
Année sociologique (L'). Ed. by É. Durkheim. Paris.
Annuaire international de statistique publié par l'office permanent de l'Institut International de Statistique. La Haye.
Annual Reports of the Board of Regents of the Smithsonian Institution. Washington.
Annual Reports of the Bureau of American Ethnology. Washington.
Annual Reports of the Registrar-General of Births, Deaths, and Marriages in England and Wales. London.
Antananarivo Annual and Madagascar Magazine. Antananarivo.
Ante-Nicene Christian Library. Ed. by A. Roberts and J. Donaldson. 24 vols. Edinburgh, 1867–72.
Anthropological Essays presented to E. B. Tylor. Oxford, 1907.
Anthropological Review (The). London.
Anthropologie (L'). Paris.
Anthropos. Ed. by P. W. Schmidt. Salzburg, Wien.
' Anugîtâ(The),' trans. by K. T. Telang ; in *The Sacred Books of the East*, vol. viii. Oxford, 1898.
' Âpastamba,' trans. by G. Bühler ; in *The Sacred Books of the East*, vol. ii. Oxford, 1897.

Apocrypha and Pseudepigrapha of the Old Testament in English.
Ed. by R. H. Charles. 2 vols. Oxford, 1913.
Apocrypha translated out of the Greek and Latin Tongues (The).
The version set forth A.D. 1611 and revised A.D. 1894.
Cambridge, 1895.
Apollodorus Atheniensis, *Bibliotheca.* Ed. by I. Bekker. Lipsiae,
1854.
Apollonius Rhodius, *Argonautica.* Ed. by F. S. Lehrs.
Appun (K. F.), ' Die Indianer von Britisch-Guayana ' ; in *Das
Ausland,* vol. xliv. Augsburg, 1871.
Arago (J.), *Narrative of a Voyage round the World.* Trans. 2 parts.
London, 1823.
Arbois de Jubainville (H. d'), *Cours de littérature celtique.* 12 vols.
Paris, 1883-1902.
—— ' Le droit du roi dans l'épopée irlandaise ' ; in *Revue archéo
logique,* vol. xlii. Paris, 1881.
—— *L'épopée celtique en Irlande,* vol. i. (*Cours de littérature celtique,*
vol. v.) Paris, 1892.
—— *La famille celtique.* Paris, 1905.
Arbousset (T.) and Daumas (F.), *Narrative of an Exploratory Tour
to the North-East of the Colony of the Cape of Good Hope.*
Trans. London, 1852.
Archæological Review (The). London.
Archiv für Anthropologie. Braunschweig.
—— *für Mikroskopische Anatomie und Entwicklungsgeschichte.* Bonn.
—— *für Rassen- und Gesellschafts-Biologie.* München, Leipzig
& Berlin.
—— *für Religionswissenschaft.* Leipzig.
Archives marocaines. Paris.
Archivio per l'antropologia e la etnologia. Firenze.
—— *per lo studio delle tradizioni popolari.* Palermo & Torino.
Arendt (C.), ' Stray Notes ' [on Chinese Marriage Ceremonies],
in *Folk-Lore,* vol. i. London, 1890.
Aristotle, *Opera omnia.* 5 vols. Parisiis, 1848-74.
Armstrong (Alex.), *A Personal Narrative of the Discovery of the
North-West Passage.* London, 1857.
Arner (G. B. L.), *Consanguineous Marriages in the American Popu-
lation.* (*Studies in History, Economics, and Public Law
edited by the Faculty of Political Science of Columbia University,*
vol. xxxi. no. 3.) New York, 1908.
Arnesen (M. E.), ' Från Gyda-viken till Obdorsk' ; in *Ymer,* vol. iii.
Stockholm, 1883.
Arnobius, ' Disputationum adversus gentes libri septem ' ; in
Migne, *Patrologiæ cursus,* vol. v. Parisiis, 1844.
Arnot (Fred.), *Garenganze ; or, Seven Years' Pioneer Mission Work
in Central Africa.* London, [1889].
Arvieux (*Chevalier* d'), *Travels in Arabia the Desart.* Trans. London,
1718.
Ashe (Thomas), *Travels in America, performed in the Year* 1806.
London, 1809.
Ashton-Rigby (L. E.), ' Marriage Customs in Cromarty ' ; in *Folk-
Lore,* vol. xxvii. London, 1916.
Asiatick Researches. Calcutta.
Atharva-Veda, *Hymns of the.* Trans. by M. Bloomfield. (*The
Sacred Books of the East,* vol. xlii.) Oxford, 1897.

Athenaeus, *Deipnosophistarum libri quindecim.* Ed. by G. Kaibel. 3 vols. Lipsiae, 1887–90.
Athenagoras, ' Legatio pro Christianis ' ; in Migne, *Patrologiæ cursus,* Ser. Graeca, vol. vi. Parisiis, 1857.
Atkinson (E. T.), ' Notes on the History of Religion in the Himálaya of the N.W. Provinces ' ; in *Jour. Asiatic Soc. Bengal,* vol. liii. pt. i. Calcutta, 1884.
Atkinson (J. J.), ' The Natives of New Caledonia ' ; in *Folk-Lore,* vol. xiv. London, 1903.
—— ' Primal Law ' ; in Lang and Atkinson, *Social Origins and Primal Law.* London, 1903.
Atkinson (James), *Customs and Manners of the Women of Persia,* trans. by. London, 1832.
Augustine *(Saint), Opera omnia.* 16 vols. (Migne, *Patrologiæ cursus,* vols. xxxii.–xlvii.) Parisiis, 1845–49.
—— *De civitate Dei.* Ed. by B. Dombart. 2 vols. Lipsiae, 1905–09.
Aus allen Welttheilen. Familienblatt für Länder- und Völkerkunde. Leipzig.
' Aus dem Wanderbuche eines Weltreisenden' ; in *Das Ausland,* vol. liv. Stuttgart, 1881.
Ausland (Das). Stuttgart, Augsburg, München.
Avebury *(Sir* John Lubbock, *Lord), Marriage, Totemism, and Religion.* London, 1911.
—— ' Note on the Macas Indians ' ; in *Jour. Anthr. Inst.* vol. iii. London, 1874.
—— ' On the Customs of Marriage and Systems of Relationship among the Australians ' ; in *Jour. Anthr. Inst.* vol. xiv. London, 1885.
—— *The Origin of Civilisation.* London, 1912.
Avesta. French trans. by C. de Harlez. Paris, 1881.
Avon (—), ' Vie sociale des Wabende au Tanganika ' ; in *Anthropos,* vols. x.–xi. Wien, 1915–16.
Aymonier (Étienne), *Le Cambodge.* 3 vols. Paris, 1900–04.
Ayrton (E. R.), Currelly (C. T.), and Weigall (A. E. P.), *Abydos.* 3 parts. London, 1902–04.
Azara (F. de), *Voyages dans l'Amérique méridionale.* 4 vols. Paris, 1809.

Baber (E. C.), ' Travels and Researches in the Interior of China ' ; in *Roy. Geo. Soc. Supplementary Papers,* vol. i. London, 1886.
Bacci (Orazio), *Usanze nuziali del contado della Valdelsa.* Castelfiorentino, 1893.
Bachofen (J. J.), *Antiquarische Briefe.* Strassburg, 1880.
—— *Das Mutterrecht.* Stuttgart, 1861.
Backhouse (James), *A Narrative of a Visit to the Australian Colonies.* London, 1843.
Bächtold (H.), *Die Gebräuche bei Verlobung und Hochzeit mit besonderer Berücksichtigung der Schweiz,* vol. i. Basel & Strassburg i. E. 1914.
Baegert (Jacob), ' An Account of the Aboriginal Inhabitants of the Californian Peninsula.' Trans. ; in *Smithsonian Report,* 1863-64. Washington.

Baessler-Archiv. Beiträge zur Völkerkunde. Ed. by P. Ehrenreich. Leipzig & Berlin.

Baierlein (E. R.), *The Land of the Tamulians and its Missions.* Trans. [Madras,] 1875.

—— *Nach und aus Indien.* Leipzig, 1873.

Baikie (R.), *The Neilgherries.* Calcutta, 1857.

Bailey (John), ' An Account of the Wild Tribes of the Veddahs of Ceylon ' ; in *Trans. Ethn. Soc. London,* new ser. vol. ii. London, 1863.

Bain (Alex.), *The Emotions and the Will.* London, 1880.

Bainbridge (R. B.), ' The Saorias of the Rajmahal Hills ' ; in *Memoirs Asiatic Soc. Bengal,* vol. ii. 1907–1910. Calcutta, 1911.

Baines (*Sir* J. Athelstane), ' The Recent Trend of Population in England and Wales ; ' in *Jour. Roy. Statistical Soc.* new ser. vol. lxxix. London, 1916.

Baker (*Sir* Samuel W.), *The Albert N'yanza.* 2 vols. London, 1867.

—— *The Nile Tributaries of Abyssinia.* London, 1868.

Balbi (Gasparo), *Viaggio dell' Indie Orientali.* Venetia, 1590.

Baldaeus (Philip), ' A True and Exact Description of the most celebrated East-India Coasts of Malabar and Coromandel ; as also of the Isle of Ceylon.' Trans. ; in Churchill, *Collection of Voyages and Travels,* vol. iii. London, 1732.

Balfour (Edward), *The Cyclopædia of India, and Eastern and Southern Asia.* 3 vols. London, 1885.

Balfour (Marie Clothilde), *County Folk-Lore. Vol. IV. Examples of printed Folk-Lore concerning Northumberland.* Collected by M. C. B. and edited by N. W. Thomas. London, 1904.

Ball (J. Dyer), *The Chinese at Home.* London, 1911.

—— *Things Chinese.* London, 1904.

Ballerini (Antonius), *Opus theologicum morale.* Ed. by D. Palmieri. 7 vols. Prati, 1889–94.

Bancroft (H. H.), *The Native Races of the Pacific States of North America.* 5 vols. New York, 1875–76.

Bancroft (T. L.), ' Note on Mutilations practised by Australian Aborigines ' ; in *Jour. and Proceed. Roy. Soc. New South Wales,* vol. xxxi. Sydney, 1897.

Barbosa (Duarte), *A Description of the Coasts of East Africa and Malabar in the beginning of the Sixteenth Century.* Trans. by H. E. J. Stanley. London, 1866.

Bargy (*Dr.*), ' Notes ethnographiques sur les Birifons ' ; in *L'Anthropologie,* vol. xx. Paris, 1909.

Barrett (W. E. H.), ' Notes on the Customs and Beliefs of the Wa-Giriama, etc., British East Africa' ; in *Jour. Roy. Anthr. Inst.* vol. xli. London, 1911.

Barrington (George), *The History of New South Wales.* London, 1810.

Barros (S. Giovanni di), *L'Asia.* Trans. from the Portuguese. 2 vols. Venetia, 1562.

Barrow (John), *An Account of Travels into the Interior of Southern Africa, in the Years* 1797 *and* 1798. 2 vols. London, 1801–04.

Bartels (Max), ' Isländischer Brauch und Volksglaube in Bezug auf die Nachkommenschaft' ; in *Zeitschr. f. Ethnol.* vol. xxxii. Berlin, 1900.

Barth (Heinrich), *Reisen und Entdeckungen in Nord- und Central-Afrika.* 5 vols. Gotha, 1857–58.

Barth (Heinrich), *Sammlung und Bearbeitung central-afrikanischer Vokabularien.—Collection, &c.* Gotha, 1862.
Barth (Hermann von), *Ost-Afrika vom Limpopo bis zum Somalilande.* Leipzig, 1875.
Barthema (Ludovico de), *Itinerario nello Egypto, nella Surria, nella Arabia deserta & felice, nella Persia, nella India, & nella Ethiopia.* Roma, 1510.
—— *Travels of L. di Varthema.* Trans. by J. W. Jones, ed. by G. P. Badger. London, 1863.
Barton (G. A.), ' Marriage (Semitic) ' ; in Hastings, *Encyclopædia of Religion and Ethics*, vol. viii. Edinburgh, 1915.
—— *A Sketch of Semitic Origins Social and Religious.* New York, 1902.
Bartram (William), ' Observations on the Creek and Cherokee Indians ' ; in *Trans. American Ethn. Soc.* vol. iii. pt. i. New York, 1853.
Bartsch (Karl), *Sagen, Märchen und Gebräuche aus Mecklenburg.* 2 vols. Wien, 1879–80.
Barua (H. C.), *Notes on the Marriage Systems of the Peoples of Assam.* Sibsagar, 1909.
Baskerville (G. K.), ' Die Waganda ' ; in Steinmetz, *Rechtsver-hältnisse von eingeborenen Völkern in Afrika und Ozeanien.* Berlin, 1903.
Bastian (A.), *Afrikanische Reisen. Ein Besuch in San Salvador.* Bremen, 1859.
—— *Allerlei aus Volks- und Menschenkunde.* 2 vols. Berlin, 1888.
—— *Die Culturländer des alten America.* 2 vols. Berlin, 1878.
—— *Die deutsche Expedition an der Loango-Küste.* 2 vols. Jena, 1874–75.
—— *Der Mensch in der Geschichte.* 3 vols. Leipzig, 1860.
—— *Die Rechtsverhältnisse bei verschiedenen Völkern der Erde.* Berlin, 1872.
—— ' Ueber die Eheverhältnisse ' ; in *Zeitschr. f. Ethnol.* vol. vi. Berlin, 1874.
Batchelor, *The Ainu and their Folk-Lore.* London, 1901.
—— ' Notes on the Ainu ' ; in *Trans. Asiatic Soc. Japan*, vol. x. Yokohama, 1882.
Bates (H. W.), *The Naturalist on the River Amazon.* 2 vols. London, 1863.
Baucke (*Pater* Florian). See Kohler (A.).
' Baudhâyana,' trans. by G. Bühler ; in *The Sacred Books of the East*, vol. xiv. Oxford, 1882.
Baumann (Oscar), *Durch Massailand zur Nilquelle.* Berlin, 1894.
—— *Usambara.* Berlin, 1891.
Baumstark (*Lieutenant*), ' Die Warangi ' ; in *Mittheil. Deutsch. Schutzgeb.* vol. xiii. Berlin, 1900.
Baur (Erwin), *Einführung in die experimentelle Vererbungslehre.* Berlin, 1914.
Bayle (Pierre), *Dictionnaire historique et critique.* 16 vols. Paris, 1820[–24].
Beardmore (E.), ' The Natives of Mowat, Daudai, New Guinea ' ; in *Jour. Anthr. Inst.* vol. xix. London, 1890.
Beauchet (L.), *Histoire du droit privé de la République Athénienne.* 4 vols. Paris, 1897.

C C

Beauregard (O.), 'En Asie; Kachmir et Tibet'; in *Bull. Soc. d'Anthr. Paris*, ser. iii. vol. v. Paris, 1882.
Bebel (August), *Woman in the Past, Present, and Future*. Trans. London, 1885.
Becker (W. A.), *Charikles*. Ed. by H. Göll. Berlin, 1877–78.
Beecham (John), *Ashantee and the Gold Coast*. London, 1841.
Beechey (F. W.), *Narrative of a Voyage to the Pacific and Beering's Strait*. 2 vols. London, 1831.
Begbie (P. J.), *The Malayan Peninsula*. Madras, 1834.
Behr (H. F. v.), 'Die Völker zwischen Rufiyi und Rovuma'; in *Mittheil. Deutsch. Schutzgeb*. vol. vi. Berlin, 1893.
Belcher (*Sir* Edward), 'Notes on the Andaman Islands'; in *Trans. Ethn. Soc. London*, new ser. vol. v. London, 1867.
Bell (C. Napier), *Tangweera*. London, 1899.
Bell (J. S.), *Journal of a Residence in Circassia during the Years* 1837, 1838, *and* 1839. 2 vols. London, 1840.
Bell (Thomas), *The History of Improved Short-Horn, or Durham Cattle*. Newcastle, 1871.
Bellew (H. W.), *Kashmir and Kashghar*. London, 1875.
Belly (Félix), *À travers l'Amérique Centrale*. 2 vols. Paris, 1867.
Belt (Thomas), *The Naturalist in Nicaragua*. London, 1874.
Beltrame (A. G.), *Il Fiume Bianco e i Dénka*. Verona, 1881.
Benedict (*Diaconus*), 'Capitularium collectio'; in Migne, *Patrologiæ cursus*, vol. xcvii. Parisiis, 1862.
Benhazera (Maurice), *Six mois chez les Touareg du Ahaggar*. Alger, 1908.
Bentham (Jeremy), *Theory of Legislation*. Trans. from the French of E. Dumont. London, 1882.
Benzinger (I.), *Hebräische Archäologie*. Tübingen, 1907.
Berchon (—), in *Actes de l'Académie nationale des sciences, belles-lettres et arts de Bordeaux*, ser. iii. vol. xlvii. Paris, 1885.
Bérenger-Féraud, 'Le mariage chez les Nègres Sénégambiens'; in *Revue d'Anthropologie*, ser. ii. vol. vi. Paris, 1883.
—— 'Note sur la fécondité des mulâtres au Sénégal'; in *Revue d'Anthropologie*, ser. ii. vol. ii. Paris, 1879.
Bergel (Joseph), *Die Eheverhältnisse der alten Juden im Vergleiche mit den Griechischen und Römischen*. Leipzig, 1881.
Bergmann (B.), *Nomadische Streifereien unter den Kalmüken*. 4 vols. Riga, 1804–05.
Berichte der Naturforschenden Gesellschaft zu Freiburg i. B.
Bernau (J. H.), *Missionary Labours in British Guiana*. London, 1847.
Bernhöft (Franz), 'Altindische Familienorganisation'; in *Zeitschr. f. vergl. Rechtswiss*. vol. ix. Stuttgart, 1890.
Bertholon (L.) and Chantre (E.), *Recherches anthropologiques dans la Berbérie orientale—Tripolitaine, Tunisie, Algérie*. 2 vols. Lyon, 1912–13.
Bertillon, 'Natalité (démographie)'; in *Dictionnaire encyclopédique des sciences médicales*, ser. ii. vol. xi. Paris, 1875.
Besse (P. L.), 'Un ancien document inédit sur les Todas'; in *Anthropos*, vol. ii. Salzburg, 1907.
Best (Elsdon), 'The Lore of the Whare-Kohanga'; in *Jour. Polynesian Soc*. vols. xiv.–xv. Wellington, 1905–06.
—— 'Maori Beliefs concerning the Human Organs of Generation'; in *Man*, vol. xiv. London, 1914.

Best (Elsdon), ' Maori Marriage Customs ' ; in *Trans. and Proceed. New Zealand Institute*, 1903, vol. xxxvi. Wellington, 1904.
—— ' Notes on the Art of War, as conducted by the Maori of New Zealand ' ; in *Jour. Polynesian Soc.* vols. xi.–xii. Wellington, 1902–03.
Beukemann (Wilhelm), *Ein Beitrag zur Untersuchung über die Vertheilung der Geburten nach Monaten.* Göttingen, 1881.
Beveridge (Peter), *The Aborigines of Victoria and Riverina.* Melbourne, 1889.
Beverley (J. E.), ' Die Wagogo ' ; in Steinmetz, *Rechtsverhältnisse von eingeborenen Völkern in Afrika und Ozeanien.* Berlin, 1903.
Bible (*The Holy*). Appointed to be read in Churches.
Biblia sacra cum glossa interlineari, ordinaria. 6 vols. Venetiis, 1588.
Biblioteca de autores españoles. Madrid.
—— *delle tradizioni popolari siciliane.* Palermo.
Bibliothèque Anthropos. Münster i. W.
—— *de l'École des Hautes Études. Sciences religieuses.* Paris.
Bickmore (A. S.), ' Some Notes on the Ainos ' ; in *Trans. Ethn. Soc. London*, new ser. vol. vii. London, 1869.
—— *Travels in the East Indian Archipelago.* London, 1868.
Biddulph (J.), *Tribes of the Hindoo Koosh.* Calcutta, 1880.
Bidrag till vår odlings häfder. Ed. by Artur Hazelius. Stockholm.
Bijdragen tot de taal-, land- en volkenkunde van Nederlandsch-Indië. 's-Gravenhage.
Bille (Steen), *Beretning om Corvetten Galathea's Reise omkring Jorden 1845, 46 og 47.* 2 vols. Kjøbenhavn, 1849–50.
Billington (Mary Frances), *Woman in India.* London, 1895.
Bingham (J.), *Works.* Ed. by R. Bingham. 10 vols. Oxford, 1855.
Bink (G.–L.), ' Réponses faites au Questionnaire de sociologie et d'ethnographie de la Société ' ; in *Bull. Soc. d'Anthr. Paris*, ser. iii. vol. xi. Paris, 1888.
Biologisches Centralblatt. Leipzig.
Bird (Isabella L.), *Unbeaten Tracks in Japan.* 2 vols. London, 1880.
Birlinger (Anton), *Volksthümliches aus Schwaben.* 2 vols. Freiburg i. B., 1861–62.
Bischofs (*P.* Jos.), ' Die Niol-Niol, ein Eingeborenenstamm in Nordwest-Australien ' ; in *Anthropos*, vol. iii. Wien, 1908.
Bishop (J. P.), *New Commentaries on Marriage, Divorce, and Separation.* 2 vols. Chicago, 1891.
Black (G. F.), *County Folk-Lore. Vol. III. Examples of printed Folk-Lore concerning the Orkney and Shetland Islands.* Collected by G. F. B. and edited by N. W. Thomas. London, 1903.
Blackstone (William), *The Commentaries on the Laws of England.* Adapted to the present State of the Law by R. M. Kerr. 4 vols. London, 1876.
Blair (Emma Helen), *The Indian Tribes of the Upper Mississippi Valley and Region of the Great Lakes as described by Nicolas Perrot, &c.* 2 vols. Cleveland, 1911–12.
Blake (T. P. U.), ' Matrimonial Customs in the West of Ireland ' in *Folk-Lore*, vol. xviii. London, 1907.

Blau (O.), ' Nachrichten über kurdische Stämme ' ; in *Zeitschr. Deutsch. Morgenl. Gesellsch.* vol. xvi. Leipzig, 1862.
Bleyer (*Dr.*), ' Die wilden Waldindianer Santa Catharinas : die " Schokléng " ' ; in *Zeitschr. f. Ethnol.* vol. xxxvi. Berlin, 1904.
Bloch (Iwan), *The Sexual Life of Our Time in its Relations to Modern Civilization.* Trans. by M. Eden Paul. London, 1908.
Blochmann (H.), ' Koch Bihár, Koch Hájo, and A'sám, in the 16th and 17th Centuries, according to the Akbarnámah, the Padishahnámah, and the Fathiyah i 'Ibriyah ' ; in *Jour. Asiatic Soc. Bengal,* vol. xli. pt. i. Calcutta, 1872.
Blümner (Hugo), *The Home Life of the Ancient Greeks.* Trans. London, 1893.
Blumentritt (Ferd.), *Versuch einer Ethnographie der Philippinen.* (Petermann's *Mittheilungen, Ergänzungsheft No. 67.*) Gotha, 1882.
Blunt (*Lady* Anne), *Bedouin Tribes of the Euphrates.* 2 vols. London, 1879.
Bluntschli (J. C.), *Staats- und Rechtsgeschichte der Stadt und Landschaft Zürich.* 2 vols. Zürich, 1838.
Boas (Franz), ' The Central Eskimo ' ; in *Ann. Rep. Bur. Ethnol.* vi., 1884–85. Washington, 1888.
—— *Changes in Bodily Form of Descendants of Immigrants.* Washington, 1910.
—— ' Changes in the Bodily Form of Descendants of Immigrants ' ; in *American Anthropologist,* new ser. vol. xiv. Lancaster, 1912.
—— ' First General Report on the Indians of British Columbia ' ; in *Fifth Report on the North-Western Tribes of Canada.* (Reprinted from the Report of the British Association for 1889.) London.
—— ' The Half-blood Indian. An Anthropometric Study ' ; in *Popular Science Monthly,* vol. xlv. New York, 1894.
—— ' The Mythology of the Bella Coola Indians ' ; in *Publications of the Jesup North Pacific Expedition,* vol. i. New York, 1900.
—— ' Second General Report on the Indians of British Columbia,' in ' Sixth Report of the Committee . . . appointed to investigate the Physical Characters, etc. of the North-Western Tribes of the Dominion of Canada ' ; in *Report of the Sixtieth Meeting of the British Association held at Leeds in September* 1890. London, 1891.
—— ' The Social Organization and the Secret Societies of the Kwakiutl Indians ' ; in *Smithsonian Report,* 1895. Washington, 1897.
Bock (Carl), *The Head-Hunters of Borneo.* London, 1881.
—— *Temples and Elephants.* London, 1884.
Bode (C. A. de), ' On the Yamúd and Goklán Tribes of Turkomania ' ; in *Jour. Ethn. Soc. London,* vol. i. Edinburgh (printed), 1848.
Bodin (Jean), *De Republica.* Ursellis, 1601.
Boece. See Boethius.
Boecler (J. W.), *Der Ehsten abergläubische Gebräuche, Weisen und Gewohnheiten.* Ed. by Fr. K. Kreutzwald. St. Petersburg, 1854.

Boethius (Hector), *Scotorum historiæ a prima gentis origine.* Parisiis, 1575.

Bogle (George), *Narrative of the Mission of, to Tibet, &c.* Ed. by C. R. Markham. London, 1876.

Bogoras (Waldemar), *The Chukchee.* (*Publications of the Jesup North Pacific Expedition,* vol. vii.) Leiden & New York, 1904–09.

Bolinder (Gustaf), *Ijca-indianernas kultur.* Alingsås, 1918.

Boller (H. A.), *Among the Indians.* Philadelphia, 1868.

Bombet (L. A. C.), *The Lives of Haydn and Mozart.* Trans. London, 1818.

Bonney (F.), ' On some Customs of the Aborigines of the River Darling ' ; in *Jour. Anthr. Inst.* vol. xiii. London, 1884.

Bontier (Pierre) and Le Verrier (Jean), *The Canarian, or, Book of the Conquest and Conversion of the Canarians in the Year* 1402, *by Messire Jean de Bethencourt.* Trans. ed. by R. H. Major. London, 1872.

Bonvalot (Gabriel), *Across Thibet.* Trans. 2 vols. London, 1891.

Bonwick (James), ' The Australian Natives ' ; in *Jour. Anthr. Inst.* vol. xvi. London, 1887.

—— *Daily Life and Origin of the Tasmanians.* London, 1870.

—— *The Last of the Tasmanians.* London, 1870.

Book of Leinster (The). See *Leinster, The Book of.*

Book of Tobit (The). See *Tobit, The Book of.*

Borheck (A. C.), *Erdbeschreibung von Asien.* 3 vols. Düsseldorf, 1792–94.

Born (*Dr.*), ' Einige Beobachtungen ethnographischer Natur über die Oleaï-Inseln ' ; in *Mittheil. Deutsch. Schutzgeb.* vol. xvii. Berlin, 1904.

Bory de St. Vincent (J. B. G. M.), *Essais sur les Isles Fortunées.* Paris, 1803.

Bos (Ritzema), ' Untersuchungen über die Folgen der Zucht in engster Blutsverwandtschaft ' ; in *Biologisches Centralblatt,* vol. xiv. Leipzig, 1894.

Bosman (W.), ' A New Description of the Coast of Guinea.' Trans. ; in Pinkerton, *Collection of Voyages and Travels,* vol. xvi. London, 1814.

Bossu (——), *Travels through that Part of North America formerly called Louisiana.* Trans. 2 vols. London, 1771.

Boston Journal of Natural History. Boston.

Bouche (P.), *Sept ans en Afrique occidentale. La Côte des Esclaves et Le Dahomey.* Paris, 1885.

Boudinhon (A.), ' Impediments, Canonical ' ; in *The Catholic Encyclopedia,* vol. vii. New York, 1910.

Bourien (*le Père*), ' On the Wild Tribes of the Interior of the Malay Peninsula ' ; in *Trans. Ethn. Soc. London,* new ser. vol. iii. London, 1865.

Bourke (J. G.), ' Notes upon the Gentile Organization of the Apaches of Arizona ' ; in *Jour. American Folk-Lore,* vol. iii. Boston & New York, 1890.

—— *The Snake-Dance of the Moquis of Arizona.* London, 1884.

Bovallius (Carl), *Resa i Central-Amerika,* 1881–1883. 2 vols. Upsala, 1887.

Bove (Giacomo), *Patagonia. Terra del Fuoco. Mari Australi.* Genova, 1883.

Bowdich (T. E.), *Mission from Cape Coast Castle to Ashantee.* London, 1819.
Bowring (*Sir* John), *The Kingdom and People of Siam.* 2 vols. London, 1857.
—— *A Visit to the Philippine Islands.* London, 1859.
Boyle (Frederick), *Adventures among the Dyaks of Borneo.* London, 1865.
Bradbury (John), *Travels in the Interior of America, in the Years 1809–1811.* Liverpool, 1817.
Bradley-Birt (F. B.), *Chota Nagpore.* London, 1910.
Brailsford (H. N.), ' The Macedonian Revolt ' ; in *The Fortnightly Review,* new ser. vol. lxxiv. London, 1903.
Brainne (Ch.), *La Nouvelle-Calédonie.* Paris, 1854.
Brand (John), *Observations on Popular Antiquities.* With the additions of Sir Henry Ellis. London, 1888.
Bray (Denys), *Census of India,* 1911. *Vol. IV. Baluchistan,* pt. i. Report. Calcutta, 1913.
Breasted (J. H.), *Ancient Records of Egypt.* 5 vols. Chicago, 1906–07.
Breeks (J. W.), *An Account of the Primitive Tribes and Monuments of the Nilagiris.* London, 1873.
Brehm (A. E.), *Bird-Life.* Trans. London, 1874.
—— *Thierleben.* 10 vols. Leipzig, 1877–80.
Brenchley (J. L.), *Jottings during the Cruise of H.M.S. Curaçoa among the South Sea Islands in 1865.* London, 1873.
Brenner (J. von), *Besuch bei den Kannibalen Sumatras.* Würzburg, 1894.
Bresciani (Antonio), *Dei costumi dell' isola di Sardegna comparati cogli antichissimi popoli orientali.* 2 vols. Napoli, 1850.
Breton (W. H.), *Excursions in New South Wales, Western Australia, and Van Dieman's Land.* London, 1833.
Brett (W. H.), *The Indian Tribes of Guiana.* London, 1868.
Bridges (Thomas), Letter to the author, dated Downeast, Tierra del Fuego, August 28th, 1888.
—— ' Manners and Customs of the Firelanders ' ; in *A Voice for South America,* vol. xiii. London, 1866.
' Brihaspati,' trans. by J. Jolly ; in *The Sacred Books of the East,* vol. xxxiii. Oxford, 1889.
Brincker (P. H.), ' Charakter, Sitten und Gebräuche speciell der Bantu Deutsch-Südwestafrikas ' ; in *Mittheilungen des Seminars für orientalische Sprachen an der Königl. Friedrich Wilhelms-Universität zu Berlin,* vol. iii. pt. iii. Berlin & Stuttgart, 1900.
—— *Wörterbuch und kurzgefasste Grammatik des Otji-Hérero.* Ed. by C. G. Büttner. Leipzig, 1886.
Broca (Paul), *On the Phenomena of Hybridity in the Genus Homo.* Trans. ed. by C. C. Blake. London, 1864.
Brooke (Charles), *Ten Years in Saráwak.* 2 vols. London, 1866.
Brooke (James), *Narrative of Events in Borneo and Celebes . . . from the Journals of.* Ed. by R. Mundy. 2 vols. London, 1848.
Brown (A. R.), ' Three Tribes of Western Australia ' ; in *Jour. Roy. Anthr. Inst.* vol. xliii. London, 1913.
Brown (G.), ' Notes on the Duke of York Group, New Britain, and New Ireland ' ; in *Jour. Roy. Geo. Soc.* vol. xlvii. London, 1877.

Brown (J. Macmillan), *Maori and Polynesian.* London, 1907.
Browne (James), ' Die Eingebornen Australiens, ihre Sitten und Gebräuche ' ; in Petermann's *Mittheilungen,* 1856. Gotha.
Bruce (James), *Travels to discover the Source of the Nile, in the Years 1768–1773.* 5 vols. Edinburgh, 1790.
Brunner (Heinrich), *Deutsche Rechtsgeschichte.* 2 vols. Leipzig, 1887–92.
—— ' Die Geburt eines lebenden Kindes und das eheliche Vermögensrecht,' in *Zeitschr. der Savigny-Stiftung für Rechtsgeschichte,* vol. xvi. Weimar, 1895.
—— *Grundzüge der deutschen Rechtsgeschichte.* München & Leipzig, 1913.
Bruns (C. G.), *Fontes juris romani antiqui.* Ed. by Th. Mommsen and O. Gradenwitz. Friburgi i. B. & Lipsiae, 1893.
—— and Sachau (E.), *Syrisch-römisches Rechtsbuch aus dem fünften Jahrhundert.* Leipzig, 1880.
Bry (Theodor de), *Narrative of Le Moyne, an Artist who accompanied the French Expedition to Florida under Laudonnière,* 1564. Trans. Boston, 1875.
Bryce (James, *Lord*), *Studies in History and Jurisprudence.* 2 vols. Oxford, 1901.
Buch (Max), *Die Wotjäken.* Stuttgart, 1882.
—— ' Die Wotjäken ' ; in *Acta Societatis Scientiarum Fennicæ,* vol. xii. Helsingfors, 1883.
Buchanan (Francis), ' A Journey from Madras through the Countries of Mysore, Canara, and Malabar ' ; in Pinkerton, *Collection of Voyages and Travels,* vol. viii. London, 1811.
Buchanan (George), *Rerum Scoticarum historia.* Edinburgi, 1583.
Buchanan (James), *Sketches of the History, Manners, and Customs of the North American Indians.* London, 1824.
Buchner (Max), *Kamerun.* Leipzig, 1887.
Bücheler (Franz) and Zitelmann (Ernst), *Das Recht von Gortyn.* (*Rheinisches Museum für Philologie. Neue Folge,* vol. xl. *Ergänzungsheft.*) Frankfurt a.M., 1885.
Büchner (Ludwig), *Liebe und Liebes-Leben in der Thierwelt.* Leipzig, 1885.
Bühler (J. G.), *Grundriss der indo-arischen Philologie und Altertumskunde.* Ed. by. Strassburg, 1896, &c. *In progress.*
Bülow (W. von), ' Die Ehegesetze der Samoaner ' ; in *Globus,* vol. lxxiii. Braunschweig, 1898.
Bürgerliches Gesetzbuch. Berlin, 1916.
Büttner (C. G.), ' Sozialpolitisches aus dem Leben der Herero in Damaraland ' ; in *Das Ausland,* vol. lv. Stuttgart, 1882.
Bufe (*Missionary*), ' Die Bakundu ' ; in *Archiv f. Anthropologie,* new ser. vol. xii. Braunschweig, 1913.
Bukhārī (El-), *Les traditions islamiques.* French translation by O. Houdas and W. Marçais. 4 vols. (*Publications de l'École des langues orientales,* ser. iv. vols. iii.–vi.) Paris, 1903–14.
Bulletins (et mémoires) de la Société d'Anthropologie de Paris.
——— *de la Société de Géographie.* Paris.
—— *de la Société de Géographie commerciale de Paris.*
—— *of the U.S. National Museum.* Washington.
· —— See *Société normande de Géographie, Bulletins.*
Burbridge (F. W.), *The Gardens of the Sun.* London, 1880.

Burchell (W. J.), *Travels in the Interior of Southern Africa*. 2 vols. London, 1822–24.

Burckhardt (J. L.), *Arabic Proverbs*. London, 1830.

—— *Notes on the Bedouins and Wahábys*. London, 1830.

Burdach (C. F.), *Die Physiologie als Erfahrungswissenschaft*. 6 vols. Leipzig, 1832–40.

Burge (William), *Commentaries on Colonial and Foreign Laws*. Ed. by A. Wood Renton and G. Grenville Phillimore. London, 1907, &c. *In progress*.

Burger (Friedrich), *Die Küsten- und Bergvölker der Gazellehalbinsel*. Stuttgart, 1913.

Burgerlijk Wetboek'; in *De Nederlandsche Wetboeken zooals zij tot op 31 Maart van het jaar 1918 zijn gewijzigd en aangevuld*. Ed. by J. A. Fruin. 's-Gravenhage, 1918.

Burne (Charlotte Sophia), *The Handbook of Folklore*. New edition revised and enlarged by. London, 1914.

—— *Shropshire Folk-Lore*. Ed. by, from the Collections of Georgina F. Jackson. London, 1883.

—— 'Wedding Custom'; in *Folk-Lore*, vol. xix. London, 1908.

Burnes (Alex.), *Travels into Bokhara*. 3 vols. London, 1834.

Burrows (Guy), *The Land of the Pigmies*. London, 1898.

Burton (*Sir* Richard F.), *Abeokuta and the Camaroons Mountains*. 2 vols. London, 1863.

—— *The City of the Saints and across the Rocky Mountains to California*. London, 1861.

—— 'Ethnological Notes on M. du Chaillu's " Explorations and Adventures in Equatorial Africa "'; in *Trans. Ethn. Soc. London*, new ser. vol. i. London, 1861.

—— *First Footsteps in East Africa*. London, 1856.

—— *Goa, and the Blue Mountains*. London, 1851.

—— *The Highlands of the Brazil*. 2 vols. London, 1869.

—— *The Lake Regions of Central Africa*. 2 vols. London, 1860.

—— *A Mission to Gelele, King of Dahome*. 2 vols. London, 1864.

—— 'Notes on certain Matters connected with the Dahoman'; in *Memoirs Anthr. Soc. London*, vol. i. 1863–64. London, 1865.

—— *Personal Narrative of a Pilgrimage to Al-Madinah and Mekkah*. 2 vols. London, 1898.

—— *Two Trips to Gorilla Land and the Cataracts of the Congo*. 2 vols. London, 1876.

Burton (Robert), *The Anatomy of Melancholy*. London, 1845.

Buschmann (J. C. E.), 'Ueber den Naturlaut'; in *Philologische und historische Abhandlungen der Königl. Akademie der Wissenschaften zu Berlin*, 1852.

Bustico (Guido), 'Il matrimonio nel Bellunese'; in Provenzal, *Usanze e feste del popolo italiano*. Bologna, 1912.

Butler (John), *Travels and Adventures in the Province of Assam*. London, 1855.

Byskomakaren Jonas Stolts minnen från 1820-talet. Anteckningar från Högsby socken i Småland, utgifna från Nordiska museet. (Bidrag till vår odlings häfder, ed. by Artur Hazelius, vol. v.) Stockholm, 1892.

Cadamosto (Alvise), 'Delle navigationi'; in Ramusio, *Navigationi et viaggi*, vol. i. Venetia, 1554.

Caesar (C. J.), *Opera omnia.* 5 vols. London, 1819.
Caillié (Réné), *Travels through Central Africa to Timbuctoo.* 2 vols. London, 1830.
Cain (John), ' The Bhadrachellam and Rekapalli Taluqas ' ; in *The Indian Antiquary*, vol. viii. Bombay, 1879.
Calcutta Review (The). Calcutta.
Calder (J. E.), ' Some Account of the Wars of Extirpation, and Habits of the Native Tribes of Tasmania ' ; in *Jour. Anthr. Inst.* vol. iii. London, 1874.
Calonne Beaufaict (A. de), ' Zoolâtrie et Totémisme chez les peuplades septentrionales du Congo Belge ' ; in *Revue des études ethnographiques et sociologiques*, vol. ii. Paris, 1909.
Calvert (A. F.), *The Aborigines of Western Australia.* London, 1894.
Calvert (J.), *Vazeeri Rupi, the Silver Country of the Vazeers, in Kulu.* London, 1873.
Calvör (Caspare), *Rituale ecclesiasticum.* 2 vols. Jena, 1705.
Cambridge Natural History. Ed. by S. F. Harmer and A. E. Shipley. 10 vols. London, 1895–1909.
Cameron (A. L. P.), ' Notes on some Tribes of New South Wales ' ; in *Jour. Anthr. Inst.* vol. xiv. London, 1885.
Cameron (V. L.), *Across Africa.* 2 vols. London, 1877.
Campbell (A.), ' Note on the Limboos, and other Hill Tribes hitherto undescribed ' ; in *Jour. Asiatic Soc. Bengal*, vol. ix. pt. i. Calcutta, 1840.
Campbell (F. A.), *A Year in the New Hebrides, Loyalty Islands, and New Caledonia.* Geelong & Melbourne, [1873].
Campbell (J.), Short summary of a paper ' On Polygamy : its Influence in determining the Sex of our Race and its Effects on the Growth of Population ' read by ; in *The Anthropological Review*, vol. viii. London, 1870.
Campbell (John), *A Personal Narrative of Thirteen Years' Service amongst the Wild Tribes of Khondistan.* London, 1864.
Campbell (John), *Travels in South Africa.* London, 1815.
—— *Travels in South Africa, being a Narrative of a Second Journey in the Interior of that Country.* 2 vols. London, 1822.
Canada and its Provinces. Ed. by A. Shortt and A. G. Doughty. Toronto, 1913 &c.
Canada Department of Mines. Geological Survey. Memoirs. Ottawa.
—— *Geological Survey. Museum Bulletins.* Ottawa.
Candelier (H.), *Rio-Hacha et les Indiens Goajires.* Paris, 1893.
Canones et decreta Concilii Tridentini ex editione Romana a. MDCCCXXXIV. Ed. by E. L. Richter. Lipsiae, 1853.
Canziani (Estella), ' Courtship, Marriage and Folk-Belief in Val d'Ossola (Piedmont) ' ; in *Folk-Lore*, vol. xxiii. London, 1912.
Captivity of Hans Stade (The). See Stade, Hans.
Cardús (P. José), *Las Misiones Fransiscanas entre los infieles de Bolivia.* Barcelona, 1886.
Carey (B. S.) and Tuck (H. N.), *The Chin Hills.* 2 vols. Rangoon, 1896.
[Carli (G. R.),] *Le lettere Americane.* 2 vols. Cremona, 1781–82.
Carnegie Institution of Washington Publications.
' Carolinen (Die) ' ; in *Deutsche Rundschau für Geographie und Statistik*, vol. viii. Wien, Pest, & Leipzig, 1886.

Carr (William), *The History of the Rise and Progress of the Killerby, Studley, and Warlaby Herds of Shorthorns*. London, 1867.
Cartwright (Minnie), ' Scraps of Scottish Folklore, I.' ; in *Folk-Lore*, vol. xxi. London, 1910.
Carver (J.), *Travels through the Interior Parts of North America*. London, 1781.
Casalis (E.), *The Basutos*. London, 1861.
Casati (G.), *Ten Years in Equatoria*. Trans. 2 vols. London, 1891.
Castañeda de Naçera (Pedro de), ' Relacion de la Jornada de Cibola ' ; in *Ann. Rep. Bur. Ethnol.* xiv. pt. i. Washington, 1896.
Castelnau (François de), *Expédition dans les parties centrales de l'Amérique du Sud*. 7 vols. Paris, 1850–59.
Castle (W. E.), Carpenter (F. W.), Clark (A. H.), Mast (S. O.), and Barrows (W. M.), ' The Effects of Inbreeding, Cross-breeding, and Selection upon the Fertility and Variability of Drosophila ' ; in *Proceedings of the American Academy of Arts and Sciences*, vol. xli. Boston, 1906.
Castrén (M. A.), *Nordiska resor och forskningar*. 5 vols. Helsingfors, 1852–58.
—— ' Reseminnen ' ; in *Helsingfors Morgonblad*, 1843. Helsingfors.
—— in *Litterära Soiréer i Helsingfors under hösten* 1849. Helsingfors, 1849.
Catholic Encyclopedia. 17 vols. New York, 1907–18.
Catlin (George), *Illustrations of the Manners, Customs, and Condition of the North American Indians*. 2 vols. London, 1876.
—— *Last Rambles amongst the Indians of the Rocky Mountains and the Andes*. Edinburgh & London, 1877.
Catullus (G. V.), *Carmina*. Ed. by Joh. P. Postgate. Londini, 1889.
Caussin de Perceval (A. P.), *Essai sur l'histoire des Arabes*. 3 vols. Paris, 1847–48.
Cauvet (J.), ' De l'organisation de la famille à Athènes ' ; in *Revue de législation et de jurisprudence*, vol. xxiv. Paris, 1845.
Census of India, 1891. Calcutta &c.
—— 1901. Calcutta &c.
—— 1911. Calcutta &c.
Chaffanjon (J.), *L'Orénoque et le Caura*. Paris, 1889.
Chalmers (James), ' Notes on the Natives of Kiwai Island, Fly River, British New Guinea ' : in *Jour. Anthr. Inst.* vol. xxxiii. London, 1903.
—— *Pioneer Life and Work in New Guinea* 1877–1894. London, 1895.
—— *Pioneering in New Guinea*. London, 1887.
—— ' Report on the Australasian, Papuan, and Polynesian Races. (I.) New Guinea. Toaripi and Koiari Tribes ' ; in *Report of the Second Meeting of the Australasian Association for the Advancement of Science held at Melbourne, Victoria, in January*, 1890. Sydney, 1890.
Chamberlain (B. H.), *Things Japanese*. London, 1905.
Chanler (W. A.), *Through Jungle and Desert*. London & New York, 1896.
Chantre y Herrera (P. José), *Historia de las Misiones de la Compañia de Jesús en el Marañón español*. Madrid, 1901.
Chapeaurouge (— de). See Roemer (Th.).

Chapman (J.), *Travels in the Interior of South Africa*. 2 vols. London, 1868.
Charax of Pergamus, ' Hellenica ' ; in *Fragmenta Historicorum Græcorum*, ed. by C. Müller, vol. iii. Parisiis, 1849.
Charles (R. H.). See *Apocrypha and Epigrapha of the Old Testament in English ;* and *Testaments of the Twelve Patriarchs* (*The*).
Charlevoix (P. F. X. de), *Histoire et description generale de la Nouvelle France*. 6 vols. Paris, 1744.
—— *The History of Paraguay*. Trans. 2 vols. London, 1769.
—— *A Voyage to North-America*. Trans. 2 vols. Dublin, 1766.
Chatterji (J. L.), ' The Origin and Traditions of Kathis ' ; in *The Calcutta Review*, vol. cxxxi. Calcutta, 1910.
Chavanne (Joseph), *Reisen und Forschungen im alten und neuen Kongostaate*. Jena, 1887.
—— *Die Sahara*. Wien, Pest, & Leipzig, 1879.
Chen (I.), *The Patriarchal System in China* (The China Society, 9th December, 1909). *S.l.*
Chénier (Louis de), *The Present State of the Empire of Morocco*. Trans. 2 vols. London, 1788.
Cherbonneau (Eugène). See Sautayra (Édouard) and Cherbonneau (Eugène).
Chervin (N.), *Recherches médico-philosophiques sur les causes physiques de la polygamie dans les pays chauds*. Paris, 1812.
Cheyne (Andrew), *A Description of Islands in the Western Pacific Ocean*. London, 1852.
Cheyne (T. K.), ' Blessings and Cursings ' ; in *Encyclopædia Biblica*, vol. i. London, 1899.
—— ' Harlot ' ; in *Encyclopædia Biblica*, vol. ii. London, 1901.
—— and Black (J. S.), *Encyclopædia Biblica*. 4 vols. London, 1899–1903.
China Review (*The*). Hongkong.
Chisholm (James A.), ' Notes on the Manners and Customs of the Winamwanga and Wiwa ' ; in *Jour. African Soc*. vol. ix. London, 1910.
Chitty (S. C.), *The Ceylon Gazetteer*. Ceylon, 1834.
Chomé (*P. I.*), ' Dritter Brief an Rev. Patrem Vanthiennen.' Trans. ; in Stoecklein, *Der Neue Welt-Bott*, vol. iv. pt. xxix. Wien, 1755.
Chopard (J. M.), ' A few Particulars respecting the Nicobar Islands ' ; in *Jour. Indian Archipelago*, vol. iii. Singapore, 1849.
Christian (F. W.), *The Caroline Islands*. London, 1899.
—— *Eastern Pacific Lands*. London, 1910.
Chronique dite de Nestor. See Nestor.
Chunder Dey (Shumbhoo), ' An Account of the Garos ' ; in *The Calcutta Review*, vol. cxxviii. Calcutta, 1909.
Church (G. E.), *Aborigines of South America*. Ed. by C. R. Markham. London, 1912.
Churchill (Awnsham and John), *A Collection of Voyages and Travels*. 6 vols. London, 1704–32.
Cicero (M. Tullius), *Scripta quæ manserunt omnia*. Ed. by R. Klotz and C. F. W. Müller. 4 parts. Lipsiae, 1876–1917.
Cieza de Leon (P. de), ' La Crónica del Perú [parte primera] ' ; in *Biblioteca de autores españoles*, vol. xxvi. Madrid, 1853.
Civil Code of Japan (*The*). Trans. by Ludwig Lönholm. Bremen & Tokyo. *S.d.*

Clarke (Samuel R.), *Among the Tribes in South-West China.* London, 1911.
Claus (Heinrich), *Die Wagogo. Ethnographische Skizze eines ost-afrikanischen Bantustammes.* (*Baessler-Archiv. Beiheft II.*) Leipzig & Berlin, 1911.
Clavigero (F. S.), *The History of Mexico.* Trans. 2 vols. London, 1807.
Clement of Alexandria, *Opera omnia.* (Migne, *Patrologiæ cursus,* Ser. Graeca, vols. viii.–ix.) Parisiis, 1857.
Clement I. of Rome (*Saint*), *Opera omnia.* (Migne, *Patrologiæ cursus,* Ser. Graeca, vols. i.–ii.) Parisiis, 1857.
Clercq (F. S. A. de), *Bijdragen tot de kennis der residentie Ternate.* Leiden, 1890.
Clot-Bey (A.-B.), *Aperçu général sur l'Égypte.* 2 vols. Paris, 1840.
Clozel (F.-J.) and Villamur (R.), *Les coutumes indigènes de la Côte d'Ivoire.* Paris, 1902.
Cnut (*King*), ' The Laws of ' ; in *Ancient Laws and Institutes of England.* London, 1840.
' Code civil ' ; in *Codes Belges.* Bruxelles, 1914.
' Code civil ' ; in *Les codes Français collationnés sur les textes officiels,* by L. Tripier and H. Monnier. Paris, 1910.
Code civil des Français (*Code Napoléon*). Paris, An XII.–1804.
Codes Belges et lois usuelles en vigeur en Belgique. Ed. by J. de Le Court. Bruxelles, 1914.
Codes Néerlandais (*Les*). French trans. by Gustave Tripels. Maestricht, 1886.
Codex des Civilrechts (*Russisches Civilgesetzbuch*). German trans. by Klibanski. Berlin, 1902.
Codex Justinianus. See Justinian.
Codex Theodosianus. Ed. by G. Haenel. Bonnae, 1842.
' Codice civile ' ; in *Codici e leggi del regno d'Italia,* ed. by L. Franchi, vol. i. Milano, 1908.
Codicele civile. Ed. by I. C. Codrescu. Bucuresci, 1866.
Código civil de España, ed. by M. Navarro Amandi. Madrid, 1880.
Código civil de la república Argentina. Buenos Aires, 1889.
Codigo civil portuguez. Lisboa, 1879.
Código civil promulgado en Marzo de 1884. México, 1901.
Codrington (R. H.), *The Melanesians.* Oxford, 1891.
Cojazzi (A.), *Los indios del Archipiélago Fueguino.* Santiago de Chile, 1914.
Colberg (H.), *Ueber das Ehehinderniss der Entführung.* Halle, 1869.
Cole (Fay-Cooper), ' The Wild Tribes of Davao District, Mindanao ' ; in *Field Museum of Natural History, Anthropological Series,* vol. xii. Chicago, 1913.
Colebrooke (T. E.), *Miscellaneous Essays.* 3 vols. London, 1873.
Coleman (E. H.), ' Sawdust Wedding ' ; in *Notes and Queries,* ser. v. vol. v. London, 1876.
Colenso (William), *On the Maori Races of New Zealand. S.l.,* [1865].
Collection de monographies ethnographiques. Ed. by Cyr. van Overbergh. Bruxelles, 1907 &c. *In progress.*
—— *of Modern Contemporary Voyages and Travels* (*A*). 10 vols. London, 1805–09.
Collections of the Minnesota Historical Society. Saint Paul (Minn.).
—— *of the New York Historical Society.*

Collins (David), *An Account of the English Colony in New South Wales*. 2 vols. London, 1798–1802.
Colquhoun (A. R.), *Amongst the Shans*. London, 1885.
Columbus (Ferdinand), 'The History of the Life and Actions of Admiral Christopher Colon'; in Pinkerton, *Collection of Voyages and Travels*, vol. xii. London, 1812.
'Concilium Carthaginense quartum'; in Migne, *Patrologiæ cursus*, vol. lxxxiv. Parisiis, 1850.
Conder (C. R.), *Heth and Moab*. London, 1885.
—— 'The Present Condition of the Native Tribes in Bechuanaland'; in *Jour. Anthr. Inst.* vol. xvi. London, 1887.
Condon (*Father* M. A.), 'Contribution to the Ethnography of the Basoga-Batamba, Uganda Protectorate'; in *Anthropos*, vols. v.–vi. Wien, 1910–11.
Conner (P. E.), 'Extract from the General Memoir of the Survey of Travancore'; in *The Journal of Literature and Science, published under the Auspices of the Madras Literary Society*, vol. i. Madras, 1834.
Connolly (R. M.), 'Social Life in Fanti-Land'; in *Jour. Anthr. Inst.* vol. xxvi. London, 1897.
Contemporary Review (The). London.
Conti (Nicolò), 'The Travels of, in the Early Part of the Fifteenth Century'; in *India in the Fifteenth Century*, trans. and ed. by R. H. Major. London, 1857.
Conybeare (F. C.), 'A Brittany Marriage Custom'; in *Folk-Lore*, vol. xviii. London, 1907.
Cook (Alice Carter), 'The Aborigines of the Canary Islands'; in *American Anthropologist*, new ser. vol. ii. New York, 1900.
Cook (F. C.), *The Holy Bible*, ed. by. 10 vols. London, 1871–81.
Cook (James), *A Journal of a Voyage round the World . . . in the Years* 1768–1771. London, 1771.
—— *A Voyage to the Pacific Ocean . . . in the Years* 1776–1780. 3 vols. London, 1785.
—— *A Voyage towards the South Pole, and round the World.* 2 vols. London, 1777.
Cooke (G. H.), 'Te Pito Te Henua, known as Rapa Nui ; commonly called Easter Island, South Pacific Ocean'; in *Smithsonian Report*, 1897, pt. i. Washington, 1899.
Cooper (T. T.), *The Mishmee Hills*. London, 1873.
Coreal (François), *Voyages aux Indes Occidentales*. Trans. 3 vols. Amsterdam, 1722.
Corin (James), *Mating, Marriage, and the Status of Woman*. London & Felling-on-Tyne, 1910.
Cornelius Nepos, *Vitæ*. Ed. by C. Halm. Lipsiae, 1881.
Corpus inscriptionum Semiticarum. Parisiis, 1881 &c. *In progress*.
Corpus Juris Sueo-Gotorum antiqui. Samling af Sveriges Gamla Lagar. Ed. by H. S. Collin and C. J. Schlyter. 13 vols. Stockholm, Lund, 1827–77.
Cosmas of Prague, 'Chronica Bohemorum'; in Migne, *Patrologiæ cursus*, vol. clxvi. Parisiis, 1854.
Co m os. Ed. by Guido Cora. Torino.
Co dreau (Henri), *Chez nos Indiens. Quatre années dans la Guyane Française* (1887–1891). Paris, 1893.
—— *La France équinoxiale.* 2 vols. Paris, 1887.

Coulter (Thomas), ' Notes on Upper California ' ; in *Jour. Roy. Geo. Soc. London*, vol. v. London, 1835.
County Folk-Lore. Published by the Folk-Lore Society. London, 1895 &c. *In progress.*
Couto de Magalhães (J. V.), *Trabalho preparatorio para aproveitamento do selvagem e do solo por elle occupado no Brazil. O selvagem.* Rio de Janeiro, 1876.
Cowburn (J. B.), ' Roping the Wedding ' ; in *Gloucestershire Notes and Queries*, vol. ii. London, 1884.
Cox (A. F.), *Madras District Manuals : North Arcot.* New edition revised by H. A. Stuart. 2 vols. Madras, 1894-95.
Cox (M. R.), *An Introduction to Folk-Lore.* London, 1897.
Coxe (William), *Account of the Russian Discoveries between Asia and America.* London, 1804.
Coxhead (J. C. C.), *The Native Tribes of North-Eastern Rhodesia : their Laws and Customs.* London, 1914.
Craelius (M. G.), *Försök till Ett Landskaps Beskrifning, uti en Berättelse om Tuna Läns, Sefwedes och Aspelands Häraders Fögderie, uti Calmar Höfdinge Döme.* Calmar, 1774.
Craigie (W. A.), ' Nephew ' and ' Niece ' ; in *A New English Dictionary on Historical Principles*, ed. by James A. H. Murray, vol. vi. pt. 4. Oxford, 1903.
Crampe (*Dr.*), ' Untersuchungen über die Vererbung der Farbe und über die Beziehungen zwischen der Farbe und dem Geschlecht bei Pferden ' ; in *Landwirthschaftliche Jahrbücher*, vol. xiii. Berlin, 1884.
Cranz (David), *The History of Greenland.* Trans. 2 vols. London, 1820.
Crasselt (F.), ' Die Stellung der Ehefrau in Japan ' ; in *Anthropos*, vol. iii. Wien, 1908.
Craven (C. H.), ' Traces of Fraternal Polyandry amongst the Santāls '; in *Jour. Asiatic Soc. Bengal*, vol. lxxii. pt. iii. Calcutta, 1904.
Crawfurd (John), *History of the Indian Archipelago.* 3 vols. Edinburgh, 1820.
―― ' On the Classification of the Races of Man ' ; in *Trans. Ethn. Soc. London*, new ser. vol. i. London, 1861.
Crawley (A. E.), ' Exogamy and the Mating of Cousins ' ; in *Anthropological Essays presented to E. B. Tylor.* Oxford, 1907.
―― *The Mystic Rose.* London, 1902.
Creagh (James), *Armenians, Koords, and Turks.* London, 1880.
Cremony (J. C.), *Life among the Apaches.* San Francisco, 1868.
Crespigny (C. de), ' On Northern Borneo ' ; in *Proceed. Roy. Geo. Soc.* vol. xvi. London, 1872.
Crevaux (J.), *Voyages dans l'Amérique du Sud.* Paris, 1883.
Crisp (John), ' An Account of the Inhabitants of the Poggy, or, Nassau Islands, lying off Sumatra ' ; in *Asiatick Researches*, vol. vi. Calcutta, 1799.
Crocker (W. M.), ' Notes on Saràwak and Northern Borneo ' ; in *Proceed. Roy. Geo. Soc.* new ser. vol. iii. London, 1881.
Crooke (W.), ' The Hill Tribes of the Central Indian Hills ' ; in *Jour. Anthr. Inst.* vol. xxviii. London, 1899.
―― ' The Holi : a Vernal Festival of the Hindus ' ; in *Folk-Lore*, vol. xxv. London, 1914.
―― ' The Lifting of the Bride ' ; in *Folk-Lore*, vol. xiii. London, 1902.

Crooke (W.), *The North-Western Provinces of India.* London, 1897.
—— *The Popular Religion and Folk-Lore of Northern India.* 2 vols. Westminster, 1896.
—— *Things Indian.* London, 1906.
—— *The Tribes and Castes of the North-Western Provinces and Oudh.* 4 vols. Calcutta, 1896.
Cross (D. Kerr), ' Notes on the Country lying between Lakes Nyassa and Tanganyika ' ; in *Proceed. Roy. Geo. Soc.* new ser. vol. xiii. London, 1891.
Crozet (—), *Voyage to Tasmania, &c. in the Years* 1771–2. Trans. London, 1891.
Cruickshank (B.), *Eighteen Years on the Gold Coast of Africa.* 2 vols. London, 1853.
Cumming (*Miss* C. F. Gordon), *In the Himalayas and on the Indian Plains.* London, 1884.
Cummins (S. L.), ' Sub-tribes of the Bahr-el-Ghazal Dinkas ' ; in *Jour. Anthr. Inst.* vol. xxxiv. London, 1904.
Cumont (Franz), *Les religions orientales dans le paganisme romain.* Paris, 1906.
Cunningham (Alex.), *Ladák.* London, 1854.
Cunningham (J. D.), *A History of the Sikhs.* London, 1849.
—— ' Notes on Moorcroft's Travels in Ladakh, &c.' ; in *Jour. Asiatic Soc. Bengal,* vol. xiii. pt. i. Calcutta, 1844.
Cunningham (J. F.), *Uganda and its People.* London, 1905.
Cunow (Heinrich), *Die Verwandtschafts-Organisationen der Australneger.* Stuttgart, 1894.
—— *Zur Urgeschichte der Ehe und Familie.* (*Ergänzungshefte zur Neuen Zeit,* no. 14.) Stuttgart, 1912.
Curr (E. M.), *The Australian Race.* 4 vols. Melbourne & London, 1886–87.
—— *Recollections of Squatting in Victoria.* Melbourne, &c., 1883.
Curtiss (S. I.), *Primitive Semitic Religion To-day.* London, 1902.
Customs and Manners of the Women of Persia. See Atkinson (James).
Cyprian (*Saint*), *Opera omnia.* (Mignc, *Patrologiæ cursus,* vol. iv.) Parisiis, 1844.
Czaplicka (*Miss* M. A.), *Aboriginal Siberia. A Study in Social Anthropology.* Oxford, 1914.
—— *My Siberian Year.* London, *s.d.*
Czekanowski (Jan), ' Die anthropologisch-ethnographischen Arbeiten der Expedition S.H. des Herzogs Adolf Friedrich zu Mecklenburg für den Zeitraum vom 1. Juni 1907 bis 1. August 1908 ' ; in *Zeitschr. f. Ethnol.* vol. xli. Berlin, 1909.

Dahl (L. V.), *Bidrag til Kundskab om de Sindssyge i Norge.* Christiania, 1859.
Dahlgren (E. W.), ' Om Palau-öarna ' ; in *Ymer,* vol. v. Stockholm, 1885.
Dahlgrün (H.), ' Heiratsgebräuche der Schambaa ' ; in *Mittheil. Deutsch. Schutzgeb.* vol. xvi. Berlin, 1903.
Dahlmann (Joseph), *Das Mahābhārata als Epos und Rechtsbuch.* Berlin, 1895.
Dahmen (*Father*), ' The Kunnuvans or Mannadis, a Hill-Tribe of the Palnis, South India ' ; in *Anthropos,* vol. v. Wien, 1910.
—— ' The Paliyans, a Hill-Tribe of the Palni Hills (South India) ' : in *Anthropos,* vol. iii. Wien, 1908.

Dalager (Lars), Grønlandske Relationer. Kiøbenhavn, s.d.
Dale (G.), ' An Account of the Principal Customs and Habits of the Natives inhabiting the Bondei Country ' ; in Jour. Anthr. Inst. vol. xxv. London, 1896.
Dale (J. H. van), Groot Woordenboek der nederlandsche taal. Ed. by P. J. van Malssen. 's-Gravenhage & Leiden, 1914.
Dall (W. H.), Alaska and its Resources. London, 1870.
Dalton (E. T.), Descriptive Ethnology of Bengal. Calcutta, 1872.
—— ' The " Kols " of Chota-Nagpore ' ; in Trans. Ethn. Soc. London, new ser. vol. vi. London, 1868.
Dalyell (J. G.), The Darker Superstitions of Scotland, illustrated from History and Practice. Edinburgh, 1834.
Daniell (W. F.), ' On the Ethnography of Akkrah and Adampé, Gold Coast, Western Africa ' ; in Jour. Ethn. Soc. London, vol. iv. London, 1856.
Danks (Benj.), ' Marriage Customs of the New Britain Group ' ; in Jour. Anthr. Inst. vol. xviii. London, 1889.
Dannert (Missionary), ' Soziale Verhältnisse der Ovaherero ' ; in Mitteilungen der Geographischen Gesellschaft (für Thüringen) zu Jena, vol. vi. Jena, 1888.
—— ' Ueber die Sitte der Zahnverstümmelung bei den Ovaherero ' ; in Zeitschr. f. Ethnol. vol. xxxix. Berlin, 1907.
Dannert (E.), Zum Rechte der Herero, insbesondere über ihr Familien- und Erbrecht. Berlin, 1906.
Dapper (O.), Description de l'Afrique. French trans. Amsterdam, 1686.
Darab Dastur Peshotan Sunjana, Next-of-kin Marriages in Old Irân. London, 1888.
—— The Position of Zoroastrian Women in Remote Antiquity. Bombay, 1892.
Dargun (L.), Mutterrecht und Raubehe und ihre Reste im germanischen Recht und Leben. Breslau, 1883.
—— Mutterrecht und Vaterrecht. Leipzig, 1892.
Darinsky (A.), ' Die Familie bei den kaukasischen Völkern ' ; in Zeitschr. f. vergl. Rechtswiss. vol. xiv. Stuttgart, 1899.
Darmesteter (James), ' Introduction to the Vendîdâd ' ; in The Sacred Books of the East, vol. iv. Oxford, 1880.
—— Ormazd et Ahriman. Paris, 1877.
Darwin (Charles), The Descent of Man. 2 vols. London, 1888.
—— The Effects of Cross and Self Fertilisation in the Vegetable Kingdom. London, 1876.
—— Journal of Researches into the Geology and Natural History of the various Countries visited by H.M.S. Beagle. London, 1839.
—— On the Origin of Species. 2 vols. London, 1888.
—— The Variation of Animals and Plants under Domestication. 2 vols. London, 1868.
Darwin (G. H.), ' Marriages between First Cousins in England and their Effects ' ; in The Fortnightly Review, new ser. vol. xviii. London, 1875.
—— ' Marriages between First Cousins in England and their Effects ' ; in Jour. Statistical Soc. vol. xxxviii. London, 1875.
—— ' Note on the Marriages of First Cousins ' ; in Jour. Statistical Soc. vol. xxxviii. London, 1875.
Das (S. C.). See Sarat Chandra Das.

David (J.), ' Notizen über die Pygmäen des Ituriwaldes ' ; in *Globus*, vol. lxxxvi. Braunschweig, 1904.

Davids (T. W. Rhys), *Buddhist India*. London, 1903.

—— *Hibbert Lectures on the Origin and Growth of Religion as illustrated by some Points in the History of Indian Buddhism*. London, 1881.

Davidson (J. W.), *The Island of Formosa Past and Present*. London & New York, 1903.

Davis (*Sir* John Francis), *China : a general Description of the Empire and its Inhabitants*. 2 vols. London, 1857.

Davis (W. W. H.), *El Gringo ; or, New Mexico and her People*. New York, 1857.

Davy (John), *An Account of the Interior of Ceylon*. London, 1821.

Dawson (James), *Australian Aborigines*. Melbourne, &c., 1881.

Déchelette (Joseph), ' La peinture corporelle et le tatouage ' ; in *Revue archéologique*, ser. iv. vol. ix. Paris, 1907.

Decle (Lionel), *Three Years in Savage Africa*. London, 1898.

Deecke (W.), *Die deutschen Verwandtschaftsnamen*. Weimar, 1870.

Dehon (*Father*), ' Religion and Customs of the Uraons ' ; in *Memoirs Asiatic Soc. Bengal*, vol. i. 1905–07. Calcutta, 1907.

Delafosse (Maurice), ' Les Agni (Pai-Pi-Bri) ' ; in *L'Anthropologie*, vol. iv. Paris, 1893.

—— *Haut-Sénégal-Niger (Soudan Français). Le Pays, les Peuples, les Langues, l'Histoire, les Civilisations*. 3 vols. Paris, 1912.

—— ' Le peuple Siéna ou Sénoufo ' ; in *Revue des études ethnographiques et sociologiques*, vol. i. Paris, 1908.

Delaunay (—), ' Sur la beauté ' ; in *Bull. Soc. d'Anthr. Paris*, ser. iii. vol. viii. Paris, 1885.

Delbrück (B.), ' Die indogermanischen Verwandtschaftsnamen ' ; in *Abhandlungen der Königl. Sächsischen Gesellsch. der Wissenschaften*, vol. xxv. (*Abhandlungen der philologisch-historischen Classe*, vol. xi.) Leipzig, 1890.

Delepierre (J. O.), *L'enfer décrit par ceux qui l'ont vu*. 2 pts. London, [1864–65].

Delhaise (—), *Les Warega (Congo Belge)*. (*Collection de monographies ethnographiques*, ed. by Cyr. van Overbergh, vol. v.) Bruxelles, 1909.

Delisle (F.), Review of M.-J. Taupin's article ' Relation d'un voyage d'exploration et d'études au Laos ' in *Soc. normande de Géographie, Bull*. 1890 ; in *L'Anthropologie*, vol. ii. Paris, 1891.

De-Marchi (Attilio), *Il culto privato di Roma antica. I. La religione nella vita domestica*. Milano, 1896.

Demosthenes, *Opera*. Ed. by J. Th. Voemel. Parisiis, 1843.

Dempwolff (*Dr.*), ' Ueber aussterbende Völker. (Die Eingeborenen der " westlichen Inseln " in Deutsch-Neu-Guinea) ' ; in *Zeitschr. f. Ethnol*. vol. xxxvi. Berlin, 1904.

Denkschriften der kaiserlichen Akademie der Wissenschaften. Wien.

Dennett (R. E.), *At the Back of the Black Man's Mind or Notes on the Kingly Office in West Africa*. London, 1906.

—— *Nigerian Studies or the Religious and Political System of the Yoruba*. London, 1910.

—— *Notes on the Folklore of the Fjort (French Congo)*. London, 1898.

Dernburg (Heinrich), *Pandekten*. 3 vols. Berlin, 1902–03.

Deschamps (É.), *Carnet d'un voyageur—Au pays des Veddas.* Paris, 1892.
—— 'Les Veddas de Ceylan'; in *L'Anthropologie*, vol. ii. Paris, 1891.
Desgodins (C. H.), *Le Thibet d'après la correspondance des missionaires.* Paris, 1885.
Desideri (Ippolito). See Puini (Carlo).
Desoignies (P.), 'Die Msalala'; in Steinmetz, *Rechtsverhältnisse von eingeborenen Völkern in Afrika und Ozeanien.* Berlin, 1903.
Destaing (E.), *Étude sur le dialecte berbère des Beni-Snous.* Paris, 1907.
Deutsch (E.), *Literary Remains.* London, 1874.
Deutsche Jahrbücher für Politik und Literatur. Berlin.
Deutsche Rundschau für Geographie und Statistik. Ed. by Friedrich Umlauft. Wien, Pest, & Leipzig.
Devay (Francis), *Du danger des mariages consanguins au point de vue sanitaire.* Paris & Lyon, 1857.
Dhammapada (The). Trans. by F. Max Müller. (*The Sacred Books of the East*, vol. x.) Oxford, 1898.
Dhorme (P.), *La religion assyro-babylonienne.* Paris, 1910.
Dickinson (G. Lowes), *The Greek View of Life.* London, 1896.
Dictionnaire encyclopédique des sciences médicales. Paris.
Dictionnaire universel d'histoire naturelle. Paris.
Dieffenbach (E.), *Travels in New Zealand.* 2 vols. London, 1843.
Digesta. See Justinian.
Dijk (P. A. L. E. van), 'Eenige aanteekeningen omtrent de verschillende stammen (margas) en de stamverdeeling bij de Battaks'; in *Tijdschrift voor indische taal-, land- en volkenkunde*, vol. xxxviii. Batavia & 's Hage, 1895.
'Dimetian Code (The)'; in *Ancient Laws and Institutes of Wales.* London, 1841.
'Dînâ-î Maînôg-î Khirad,' trans. by E. W. West; in *The Sacred Books of the East*, vol. xxiv. Oxford, 1885.
Dio Cassius, *Historia Romana.* 4 vols. Lipsiae, 1863–64.
Diodorus Siculus, *Bibliotheca historica.* Ed. by C. Müller. 2 vols. Parisiis, 1842–44.
Dionysius of Halicarnassus, *Antiquitatum Romanarum quæ supersunt.* Parisiis, 1886.
Distant (W. L.), 'The Inhabitants of Car Nicobar'; in *Jour. Anthr. Inst.* vol. iii. London, 1874.
Dithmar of Merseburg, 'Chronicon'; in Pertz, *Monumenta Germaniæ historica*, vol. v. Hannoverae, 1839.
Dittmar (C. von), 'Ueber die Koräken und die ihnen sehr nahe verwandten Tschuktschen'; in *Mélanges russes tirés du bulletin historico-philologique de l'Académie impériale des sciences de St.-Pétersbourg*, vol. iii. St.-Pétersbourg, 1856.
Dixon (G.), *A Voyage round the World.* London, 1789.
Dixon (J. M.), 'The Tsuishikari Ainos'; in *Trans. Asiatic Soc. Japan*, vol. xi. pt. i. Yokohama, 1883.
Dixon (R. B.), *The Chimariko Indians and Language.* (*University of California Publications in American Archæology and Ethnology*, vol. v. no. 5.) Berkeley, 1910.
—— 'Notes on the Achomawi and Atsugewi Indians of Northern California'; in *American Anthropologist*, new ser. vol. x. Lancaster, 1908.

Dixon (W. J.), *Law and Practice in Divorce and other Matrimonial Causes*. London, 1908.

Djurklou (G.), *Ur Nerikes folkspråk och folklif*. Örebro, 1860.

Dobell (Peter), *Travels in Kamtschatka and Siberia*. 2 vols. London, 1830.

Dobrizhoffer (M.), *An Account of the Abipones*. Trans. 3 vols. London, 1822.

Dodge (R. Irving), *Our Wild Indians*. Hartford, 1882.

Döllinger (J. J. I.), *The Gentile and the Jew in the Courts of the Temple of Christ*. Trans. 2 vols. London, 1862.

Domenech (E.), *Seven Years' Residence in the Great Deserts of North America*. 2 vols. London, 1860.

Domis (H. I.), *De Residentie Passoeroeang op het eiland Java*. 's-Gravenhage, 1836.

Doncaster (L.), *The Determination of Sex*. Cambridge, 1914.

Donner (Kai), *Bland samojeder i Sibirien åren 1911–1913*, 1914. Helsingfors, 1915.

Doolittle (J.), *Social Life of the Chinese*. 2 vols. New York, 1867.

Dorman (R. M.), *The Origin of Primitive Superstitions*. Philadelphia, 1881.

Dornan (S. S.), ' The Tati Bushmen (Masarwas) and their Language ' ; in *Jour. Roy. Anthr. Inst*. vol. xlvii. London, 1917.

Dorsey (J. Owen), ' Omaha Sociology ' ; in *Ann. Rep. Bur. Ethnol*. vol. iii. Washington, 1884.

—— ' Siouan Sociology ' ; in *Ann. Rep. Bur. Ethnol*. vol. xv. Washington, 1897.

Dottin (G.), ' Marriage (Celtic) ' ; in Hastings, *Encyclopædia of Religion and Ethics*, vol. viii. Edinburgh, 1915.

Douce (Francis), *Illustrations of Shakspeare*. London, 1839.

Douglas (R. K.), *Confucianism and Taouism*. London, 1889.

—— *Society in China*. London, 1894.

Doutté (Edmond), *Magie et religion dans l'Afrique du Nord*. Alger, 1909.

—— *Merrâkech*. Paris, 1905.

Dove (T.), ' Moral and Social Characteristics of the Aborigines of Tasmania ' ; in *The Tasmanian Journal of Natural Science, &c*. vol. i. Hobart Town, 1842.

Drechsler (Paul), *Sitte, Brauch und Volksglaube in Schlesien. I.* Leipzig, 1903.

Drew (Frederic), *The Jummoo and Kashmir Territories*. London, 1875.

Driver (S. R.), *A Critical and Exegetical Commentary on Deuteronomy*. Edinburgh, 1895.

Dubois (J. A.), *A Description of the Character, Manners, and Customs of the People of India*. Trans. ed. by G. U. Pope. Madras, 1862.

—— *Mœurs, institutions et cérémonies des peuples de l'Inde*. 2 vols. Paris, 1825.

Du Chaillu (P. B.), *Explorations and Adventures in Equatorial Africa*. London, 1861.

—— *A Journey to Ashango-Land*. London, 1867.

—— ' Observations on the People of Western Equatorial Africa ' ; in *Trans. Ethn. Soc. London*, new ser. vol. i. London, 1861.

Düben (G. von), *Om Lappland och Lapparne*. Stockholm, 1873.

Düringsfeld (Ida von) and Reinsberg-Düringsfeld (Otto von), *Hochzeitsbuch. Brauch und Glaube der Hochzeit bei den christlichen Völkern Europa's.* Leipzig, 1871.

Düsing (Carl), *Die Regulierung des Geschlechtsverhältnisses bei der Vermehrung der Menschen, Tiere und Pflanzen.* Jena, 1884.

Duff (H. L.), *Nyasaland under the Foreign Office.* London, 1906.

Du Halde (J. B.), *Description de l'Empire de la Chine et de la Tartarie Chinoise.* 4 vols. Le Hague, 1736.

Du Maurier (George), *Trilby.* 3 vols. London, 1894.

Dumont (Arsène), ' L'âge au mariage ' ; in *Bull. et mém. Soc. d'Anthr. Paris,* ser. v. vol. iii. Paris, 1902.

Dumont d'Urville (J. S. C.), *Voyage au Pole Sud et dans l'Océanie.* 23 vols. Paris, 1841–54.

Dunbar (J. B.), ' The Pawnee Indians ' ; in *The Magazine of American History,* vols. iv., v., viii. New York & Chicago, 1880, 1882.

Duncan (John), *Travels in Western Africa, in 1845 and 1846.* 2 vols. London, 1847.

Duncan (Jonathan), ' Historical Remarks on the Coast of Malabar ' ; in *Asiatick Researches* (printed verbatim from the Calcutta edition), vol. v. London, 1799.

Dundas (Charles), ' The Organization and Laws of some Bantu Tribes in East Africa ' ; in *Jour. Roy. Anthr. Inst.* vol. xlv. London, 1915.

Dundas (Kenneth R.), ' Notes on the Tribes inhabiting the Baringo District, East Africa Protectorate ' ; in *Jour. Roy. Anthr. Inst.* vol. xl. London, 1910.

—— ' The Wawanga and other Tribes of the Elgon District, British East Africa ' ; in *Jour. Roy. Anthr. Inst.* vol. xliii. London, 1913.

Dunlop (R. H. W.), *Hunting in the Himalaya.* London, 1860.

Dunnill (E. J.), ' Welsh Folklore Items, I.' ; in *Folk-Lore,* vol. xxiv. London, 1913.

Durga Singh (Mian), ' A Report on the Panjab Hill Tribes ' ; in *The Indian Antiquary,* vol. xxxvi. Bombay, 1907.

Durham (M. Edith), *High Albania.* London, 1909.

—— ' High Albania and its Customs in 1908 ' ; in *Jour. Roy. Anthr. Inst.* vol. xl. London, 1910.

—— ' Some Montenegrin Manners and Customs ' ; in *Jour. Roy. Anthr. Inst.* vol. xxxix. London, 1909.

Durkheim (Émile), *Les formes élémentaires de la vie religieuse.* Paris, 1912.

—— ' La prohibition de l'inceste et ses origines ' ; in *L'année sociologique,* vol. i. 1896–1897. Paris, 1898.

Du Tertre (J. B.), *Histoire générale des Antilles.* 4 vols. Paris, 1667–71.

Dutt (R. C.), ' The Social Life of the Hindus in the Rig-Veda Period ' ; in *The Calcutta Review,* vol. lxxxv. Calcutta, 1887.

Duvernoy (G. L.), ' Propagation ' ; in *Dictionnaire universel d'histoire naturelle,* vol. x. Paris, 1847.

Duveyrier (Henri), *Exploration du Sahara.* Paris, 1864.

Dyer (T. F. Thiselton), *Folk Lore of Shakespeare.* London, [1883].

Earl (G. W.), *Papuans.* London, 1853.

' East Greenland Eskimo ' ; in *Science,* vol. vii. New York, 1886.

Eastman (*Mrs.* Mary), *Dahcotah ; or, Life and Legends of the Sioux around Fort Snelling.* New York, 1849.

Eberstein (— von), 'Ueber die Rechtsanschauungen der Küstenbewohner des Bezirkes Kilwa'; in *Mittheil. Deutsch. Schutzgeb.* vol. ix. Berlin, 1896.

Eccius (—), 'Dotationspflicht'; in F. von Holtzendorff, *Encyclopädie der Rechtswissenschaft,* pt. ii. vol. i. Leipzig, 1873.

'Ecclesiasticus'; in *Apocrypha translated out of the Greek and Latin Tongues.* Cambridge, 1895.

Eckardt (M.), 'Der Archipel der Neu-Hebriden'; in *Verhandlungen des Vereins für naturwissenschaftliche Unterhaltung zu Hamburg,* 1877, vol. iv. Hamburg, 1879.

Edinburgh Medical Journal. Edinburgh.

Edwards (H. Milne), *Leçons sur la physiologie et l'anatomie comparée de l'homme et des animaux.* 8 vols. Paris, 1857–63.

Egede (Hans), *A Description of Greenland.* Trans. London, 1745.

Ehrenfels (Christian von), 'Erwiderung auf Dr. A. Ploetz' Bemerkungen zu meiner Abhandlung über die konstitutive Verderblichkeit der Monogamie'; in *Archiv f. Rassen- und Gesellschafts-Biologie,* vol. v. München, 1908.

—— 'Die konstitutive Verderblichkeit der Monogamie und die Unentbehrlichkeit einer Sexualreform'; in *Archiv f. Rassen- und Gesellschafts-Biologie,* vol. iv. München, 1907.

Ehrenreich (Paul), *Beiträge zur Völkerkunde Brasiliens. I. Die Karayastämme am Rio Araguaya (Goyaz). II. Über einige Völker am Rio Purus (Amazonas).* (*Veröffentlichungen aus dem königl. Museum für Völkerkunde,* vol. ii. fasc. 1–2.) Berlin, 1891.

—— 'Materialien zur Sprachenkunde Brasiliens'; in *Zeitschr. f. Ethnol.* vol. xxvi. Berlin, 1894.

—— 'Ueber die Botocudos der brasilianischen Provinzen Espiritu Santo und Minas Geraes'; in *Zeitschr. f. Ethnol.* vol. xix. Berlin, 1887.

Eichhorn (K. F.), *Einleitung in das deutsche Privatrecht.* Göttingen, 1825.

Eicken (H. von), *Geschichte und System der mittelalterlichen Weltanschauung.* Stuttgart, 1887.

Einszler (Lydia), 'Das böse Auge'; in *Zeitschr. des Deutschen Palaestina-Vereins,* vol. xii. Leipzig, 1889.

Eliot (*Sir* Charles), *The East Africa Protectorate.* London, 1905.

Elliot (*Sir* H. M.), *The History of India, as told by its own Historians.* Ed. by John Dawson. 8 vols. London, 1867–77.

—— *Memoirs on the History, Folk-Lore, and Distribution of the Races of the North Western Provinces of India.* 2 vols. London, 1869.

Elliott (H. W.), 'Report on the Seal Islands of Alaska'; in *Tenth Census of the United States.* Washington, 1884.

Ellis (A. B.), *The Ewe-speaking Peoples of the Slave Coast of West Africa.* London, 1890.

—— *The Tshi-speaking Peoples of the Gold Coast of West Africa.* London, 1887.

—— *The Yoruba-speaking Peoples of the Slave Coast of West Africa.* London, 1894.

Ellis (Havelock), *Man and Woman.* Fifth Edition. London & Felling-on-Tyne, [1914].

Ellis (Havelock), *Studies in the Psychology of Sex. Vol. I. The Evolution of Modesty. The Phenomena of Sexual Periodicity. Auto-erotism.* Philadelphia, 1910.
—— *Studies in the Psychology of Sex. Vol. II. Sexual Inversion.* Philadelphia, 1915.
—— *Studies in the Psychology of Sex. [Vol. III.] Analysis of the Sexual Impulse. Love and Pain. The Sexual Impulse in Women.* Philadelphia, 1908.
—— *Studies in the Psychology of Sex. [Vol. IV.] Sexual Selection in Man.* Philadelphia, 1906.
Ellis (William), *History of Madagascar.* 2 vols. London, 1838.
—— *Narrative of a Tour through Hawaii.* London, 1826.
—— *Polynesian Researches.* 4 vols. London, 1859.
Elmslie (W. A.), *Among the Wild Ngoni.* Edinburgh & London, 1899.
Elphinstone (Mountstuart), *An Account of the Kingdom of Kaubul.* 2 vols. London, 1839.
Elton (F.), ' Notes on Natives of the Solomon Islands ' ; in *Jour. Anthr. Inst.* vol. xvii. London, 1888.
Emily, Shareefa of Wazan, *My Life Story.* London, 1911.
Emin Pasha in Central Africa. Trans. London, 1888.
Encyclopædia Britannica. 29 vols. Cambridge, 1910–11.
Encyclopédie Méthodique. 167 vols. Paris, 1782–1832.
Endemann (K.), ' Mittheilungen über die Sotho-Neger ' ; in *Zeitschr. f. Ethnol.* vol. vi. Berlin, 1874.
Endle (Sidney), *The Kachúris.* London, 1911.
Eneström (F. J. E.), *Finvedsbornas seder och lif.* Halmstad, 1911.
Engels (Fr.), *Der Ursprung der Familie, des Privateigenthums und des Staats.* Hottingen-Zürich, 1884.
Erdland (A.), ' Die Stellung der Frauen in den Häuptlingsfamilien der Marshallinseln (Südsee) ' ; in *Anthropos,* vol. iv. Wien, 1909.
Erman (Adolf), *Life in Ancient Egypt.* Trans. London, 1894.
Erman (Georg Adolph), ' Ethnographische Wahrnehmungen und Erfahrungen an den Küsten des Berings-Meeres ' ; in *Zeitschr. f. Ethnol.* vol. iii. Berlin, 1871.
—— *Travels in Siberia.* Trans. 2 vols. London, 1848.
Erskine (J. E.), *Journal of a Cruise among the Islands of the Western Pacific.* London, 1853.
Erskine of Carnock (John), *Principles of the Law of Scotland.* Ed. by J. Rankine. Edinburgh, 1890.
Escayrac de Lauture (— d'), *Die afrikanische Wüste.* German trans. Leipzig, 1867.
Escherich (K.), *Die Ameise.* Braunschweig, 1917.
Eschwege (W. C. von), *Journal von Brasilien.* 2 vols. Weimar, 1818.
Esmein (A.), *Le mariage en droit canonique.* 2 vols. Paris, 1891.
Espinas (A.), *Des sociétés animales.* Paris, 1878.
Espinosa (Alonso de), *The Guanches of Tenerife.* Trans. and ed. by Sir Clements Markham. London, 1907.
Ethelred (*King*), ' The Laws of ' ; in *Ancient Laws and Institutes of England.* London, 1840.
Ethnographical Survey of India. Burma. Rangoon, 1906, &c. *In progress.*
Euripides, *Fabulæ.* Ed. by T. Fix. Parisiis, 1843.

Eusebius, *Opera.* 6 vols. (Migne, *Patrologiæ cursus*, Ser. Graeca, vols. xix.–xxiv.) Parisiis, 1857.
Ewald (G. H. A. von), *The Antiquities of Israel.* Trans. by H. S. Solly. London, 1876.
Ewart (J. C.), *The Penycuik Experiments.* London, 1899.
Ewers (J. Ph. G.), *Das älteste Recht der Russen in seiner geschichtlichen Entwickelung.* Dorpat & Hamburg, 1826.
Eylmann (Erhard), *Die Eingeborenen der Kolonie Südaustralien.* Berlin, 1908.
Eyre (E. J.), *Journals of Expeditions of Discovery into Central Australia.* 2 vols. London, 1845.

Fabre (J. H.), *The Life and Love of the Insect.* Trans. by A. Teixeira de Mattos. London, 1911.
Faggiani (Gina), ' Feste ed usanze della Sardegna ' ; in *Provenzal, Usanze e feste del popolo italiano.* Bologna, 1912.
Fahlbeck (Pontus E.), *Sveriges adel.* 2 vols. London, 1898–1902.
Falkner (Thomas), *A Description of Patagonia, and the Adjoining Parts of South America.* Hereford, 1774.
Fanning (W.), ' Marriage, Mixed ' ; in *The Catholic Encyclopedia*, vol. ix. New York, 1910.
Faria y Sousa (Manuel de), *Asia Portoguesa.* 3 vols. Lisboa, 1666–1675.
Farler (J. P.), ' The Usambaia Country in East Africa ' ; in *Proceed. Roy. Geo. Soc.* new ser. vol. i. London, 1879.
Farnell (L. R.), *The Cults of the Greek States.* 5 vols. 1896–1909.
—— *Greece and Babylon.* Edinburgh, 1911.
—— ' Sociological Hypotheses concerning the Position of Women in Ancient Religion ' ; in *Archiv für Religionswissenschaft*, vol. vii. Leipzig, 1904.
Farrand (L.), ' Notes on the Alsea Indians of Oregon ' ; in *American Anthropologist*, new ser. vol. iii. New York, 1901.
Farrer (J. A.), *Primitive Manners and Customs.* London, 1879.
Fataburen. Kulturhistorisk tidskrift. Ed. by Nordiska museet. Stockholm.
Favre (P.), ' An Account of the Wild Tribes inhabiting the Malayan Peninsula, Sumatra and a few Neighbouring Islands ' ; in *Jour. Indian Archipelago*, vol. ii. Singapore, 1848.
—— *An Account of the Wild Tribes inhabiting the Malayan Peninsula, Sumatra and a few Neighbouring Islands.* Paris, 1865.
Fawcett (F.), ' The Nâyars of Malabar ' ; in the Madras Government Museum's *Bulletin*, vol. iii. Madras, 1901.
—— ' On the Saoras (or Savaras) ' ; in *Jour. Anthr. Soc. Bombay*, vol. i. Bombay, 1888.
—— ' On some of the Earliest existing Races of the Plains of South India ' ; in *Folk-Lore*, vol. v. London, 1894.
Fay (E. A.), *Marriages of the Deaf in America.* Washington, 1898.
Fed[e]rici (Cesare), *Viaggio nell' India orientale, et oltra l'India.* Venetia, 1587.
Feer (—). See Rüdin (E.).
Fehlinger (Hans), ' Kreuzungen beim Menschen ' ; in *Archiv f. Rassen- und Gesellschafts-Biologie*, vol. viii. Leipzig & Berlin, 1911.

Fehrle (E.), *Die kultische Keuschheit im Altertum.* Giessen, 1910.
Feilberg (H. F.), *Bidrag til en ordbog over jyske almuesmäl.* 3 vols. and *Tillæg og rettelser.* Kjøbenhavn, 1911–12.
—— ' Hochzeitsschüsse, Neujahrsschüsse ', in *Archiv für Religions-wissenschaft,* vol. iv. Tübingen & Leipzig, 1901.
Felkin (R. W.), ' Contribution to the Determination of Sex, derived from Observations made on an African Tribe ' ; in *Edinburgh Medical Journal,* vol. xxxii. pt. i. July to December 1886. Edinburgh, 1887.
—— ' Introductory Address to a Course of Lectures on Diseases of the Tropics and Climatology ' ; in *Edinburgh Medical Journal,* vol. xxxi. pt. ii. Edinburgh, 1886.
—— ' Notes on the For Tribe of Central Africa ' ; in *Proceed. Roy. Soc. Edinburgh,* vol. xiii. Edinburgh, 1886.
—— ' Notes on the Madi or Moru Tribe of Central Africa ' ; in *Proceed. Roy. Soc. Edinburgh,* vol. xii. Edinburgh, 1884.
—— ' Notes on the Waganda Tribe of Central Africa ' ; in *Proceed. Roy. Soc. Edinburgh,* vol. xiii. Edinburgh, 1886.
Féraud (L.), ' Mœurs et coutumes kabiles ' ; in *Revue africaine,* vol. vi. Constantine, 1862.
Ferishta (Mahomed Kasim), *History of the Rise of the Mahomedan Power in India, till the Year* A.D. 1612. Trans. from the original Persian by John Briggs. 4 vols. London, 1829.
Fernandez (J. P.), *Relacion historial de las missiones de los Indios, que llaman Chiquitos.* Madrid, 1726.
Fernow (Erik), *Beskrifning öfver Wärmeland.* Götheborg, 1773–79.
Festschrift für Adolf Bastian zu seinem 70. Geburtstage. Berlin, 1896.
Festschrift für Otto Benndorf. Wien, 1898.
Festskrift til H. F. Feilberg fra nordiske sprog og folkemindeforskere. Stockholm, København, & Kristiania, 1911.
Festus (S. Pompejus), *De verborum significatione quæ supersunt.* Ed. by C. O. Müller. Lipsiae, 1839.
Fewkes (J. W.), ' The Aborigines of Porto Rico and Neighboring Islands ' ; in *Ann. Rep. Bur. American Ethnol.* vol. xxv. 1903–04. Washington, 1907.
ffoulkes (Arthur), ' The Fanti Family System ' ; in *Jour. African Soc.* vol. vii. London, 1908.
Field Museum of Natural History, Anthropological Series. Chicago.
Fielding Hall (H.), *The Soul of a People.* London, 1902.
Finck (H. T.), *Primitive Love and Love-Stories.* New York, 1899.
—— *Romantic Love and Personal Beauty.* 2 vols. London, 1887.
Finlands rikes lag. Ed. by A. Hernberg. Helsingfors, 1920.
Finley (John) and Churchill (William), *The Subanu. Studies of a Sub-Visayan Mountain Folk of Mindanao.* (*Carnegie Institute of Washington Publication No.* 184.) Washington, 1913.
Finsch (Otto), *Neu-Guinea und seine Bewohner.* Bremen, 1865.
—— *Reise nach West-Sibirien im Jahre* 1876. Berlin, 1879.
—— *Ueber Bekleidung, Schmuck und Tätowirung der Papuas der Südostküste von Neu-Guinea.* (Reprinted from *Mittheilungen der Anthropologischen Gesellschaft in Wien,* vol. xv. [new ser. vol. v.]) Wien, 1885.
—— ' Ueber die Bewohner von Ponapé (östl. Carolinen) ' ; in *Zeitschr. f. Ethnol.* vol. xii. Berlin, 1880.
Fischer (Eugen), *Die Rehobother Bastards und das Bastardierungs-problem beim Menschen.* Jena, 1913.

Fishberg (Maurice), *The Jews*. London & Felling-on-Tyne, 1911.
Fisher *(Captain)*, ' Memoir of Sylhet, Kachar, and the Adjacent Districts ' ; in *Jour. Asiatic Soc. Bengal*, vol. ix. pt. ii. Calcutta, 1840.
Fiske (John), *Outlines of Cosmic Philosophy*. 2 vols. London, 1874.
Fison (Lorimer), ' The Classificatory System of Relationship ' ; in *Jour. Anthr. Inst.* vol. xxiv. London, 1895.
—— ' Fijian Burial Customs ' ; in *Jour. Anthr. Inst.* vol. x. London, 1881.
—— and Howitt (A. W.), *Kamilaroi and Kurnai*. Melbourne & Sydney, 1880.
Flachs (Adolf), *Rumänische Hochzeits- und Totengebräuche*. Berlin, 1899.
Fletcher (Alice C.) and La Flesche (Francis), ' The Omaha Tribe ' ; in *Ann. Rep. Bur. American Ethnol.* vol. xxvii. 1905–1906. Washington, 1911.
Fleury (C.), *An Historical Account of the Manners and Behaviour of the Christians*. Trans. London, 1698
Foley (W. M.), ' Marriage (Christian) ' ; in Hastings, *Encyclopædia of Religion and Ethics*, vol. viii. Edinburgh, 1915.
Folk-Lore. London.
Folk-Lore Journal (The). London.
Forbes (Anna), *Insulinde*. Edinburgh & London, 1887.
Forbes (C. J. F. S.), *British Burma and its People*. London, 1878.
Forbes (H. O.), *A Naturalist's Wanderings in the Eastern Archipelago*. London, 1885.
—— ' On the Ethnology of Timor-laut ' : in *Jour. Anthr. Inst.* vol. xiii. London, 1884.
—— ' On the Kubus of Sumatra ' ; in *Jour. Anthr. Inst.* vol. xiv. London, 1885.
—— ' On some Tribes of the Island of Timor ' ; in *Jour. Anthr. Inst.* vol. xiii. London, 1884.
Forbes (James), *Oriental Memoirs*. 4 vols. London, 1813.
Forbes (Jonathan), *Eleven Years in Ceylon*. 2 vols. London, 1840.
Foreman (John), *The Philippine Islands*. London, 1890.
Forster (Ch. Thornton) and Daniell (F. H. Blackburne), *The Life and Letters of Ogier Ghiselin de Busbecq*. 2 vols. London, 1881.
Forster (George), *Sketches of the Mythology and Customs of the Hindoos*. London, 1785.
Forster (J. G. A.), *A Voyage round the World*. 2 vols. London, 1777.
Forsyth (J.), *The Highlands of Central India*. London, 1871.
Forsyth (Thomas), ' An Account of the Manners and Customs of the Sauk and Fox Nations of Indians Tradition ' · in Emma Helen Blair, *The Indian Tribes of the Upper Mississippi Valley and Region of the Great Lakes*, vol. ii. Cleveland, 1912.
Fortnightly Review (The). London.
Foucart (P.), *Des associations religieuses chez les Grecs*. Paris, 1873.
Fowler (W. Warde), ' Marriage (Roman) ' ; in Hastings, *Encyclopædia of Religion and Ethics*, vol. viii. Edinburgh, 1915.
—— *The Religious Experience of the Roman People from the Earliest Times to the Age of Augustus*. London, 1911.
—— *The Roman Festivals of the Period of the Republic*. London, 1899.

Fowler (W. Warde), *Social Life at Rome in the Age of Cicero.* London, 1908.
Fox (C. E.), ' Social Organization in San Cristoval, Solomon Islands ' ; in *Jour. Roy. Anthr. Inst.* vol. xlix. London, 1919.
Fraenkel (S.), ' Aus orientalischen Quellen ' ; in *Mitteilungen der Schlesischen Gesellschaft für Volkskunde,* vol. xix. Breslau, 1908.
Fragmenta Historicorum Græcorum. Ed. by C. Müller. 5 vols. Parisiis, 1841–84.
Framjee A. Ráná. *Parsi Law.* Bombay, 1902.
Francis (W.), *Census of India,* 1901. *Vol. XV. Madras,* pt. i. Report. Madras, 1902.
Francisci (E.), *Neu-polirter Geschicht- Kunst- und Sitten-Spiegel ausländischer Völcker.* Nürnberg, 1670.
François (H. von), *Nama und Damara Deutsch-Süd-West-Afrika.* Magdeburg, [1896].
Franklin (John), *Narrative of a Journey to the Shores of the Polar Sea.* London, 1823.
—— *Narrative of a Second Expedition to the Shores of the Polar Sea.* London, 1828.
Franzisci (Franz), *Cultur-Studien über Volksleben, Sitten und Bräuche in Kärnten.* Wien, 1879.
Fraser (Donald), *Winning a Primitive People.* London, 1914.
Fraser (George), ' Sexual Selection ' ; in *Nature,* vol. iii. London & New York, 1871.
Fraser (J. B.), *Journal of a Tour through Part of the Snowy Range of the Himālā Mountains.* London, 1820.
Fraser (John), *The Aborigines of New South Wales.* Sydney, 1892.
Frazer (*Sir* James G.), *Adonis Attis Osiris.* 2 vols. London, 1914.
—— *Balder the Beautiful.* 2 vols. London, 1913.
—— ' Certain Burial Customs as illustrative of the Primitive Theory of the Soul ' ; in *Jour. Anthr. Inst.* vol. xv. London, 1886.
—— *The Dying God.* London, 1911.
—— *Folk-Lore in the Old Testament.* 3 vols. London, 1919.
—— ' Folk-Lore in the Old Testament ' ; in *Anthropological Essays presented to E. B. Tylor.* Oxford, 1907.
—— *The Magic Art and the Evolution of Kings.* 2 vols. London, 1911.
—— *Pausanias's Description of Greece.* 6 vols. London, 1898.
—— *Psyche's Task.* First edition. London, 1909.
—— *Psyche's Task.* Second edition. London, 1913.
—— *Taboo and the Perils of the Soul.* London, 1911.
—— *Totemism.* Edinburgh, 1887.
—— *Totemism and Exogamy.* 4 vols. London, 1910.
Freisen (Joseph), *Geschichte des Canonischen Eherechts bis zum Verfall der Glossenlitteratur.* Tübingen, 1888.
French-Sheldon (*Mrs.*), ' Customs among the Natives of East Africa, from Teita to Kilimegalia ' ; in *Jour. Anthr. Inst.* vol. xxi. London, 1892.
Frescura (Bernardino), ' Fra i Cimbri dei Sette Comuni Vicentini ' ; in *Archivio per lo studio delle tradizioni popolari,* vol. xvii. Palermo & Torino, 1898.
Freud (Sigm.), *Three Contributions to the Theory of Sex.* Trans. by A. A. Brill. New York & Washington, 1918.

Freud (Sigm.), *Totem und Tabu. Einige Übereinstimmungen im Seelenleben der Wilden und der Neurotiker.* Leipzig & Wien, 1913.
Freycinet (Louis de), *Voyage autour du monde.* 9 vols. Paris, 1824–44.
Freytag (G. W.), *Einleitung in das Studium der Arabischen Sprache.* Bonn, 1861.
Frič (V.) and Radin (P.), ' Contribution to the Study of the Bororo Indians ' ; in *Jour. Anthr. Inst.* vol. xxxvi. London, 1906.
Friedberg (Emil), *Lehrbuch des katholischen und evangelischen Kirchenrechts.* Leipzig, 1909.
—— *Das Recht der Eheschliessung in seiner geschichtlichen Entwicklung.* Leipzig, 1865.
Friedlaender (Benedict), ' Notizen über Samoa ' ; in *Zeitschr. f. Ethnol.* vol. xxxi. Berlin, 1899.
Friedländer (Ludwig), *Darstellungen aus der Sittengeschichte Roms in der Zeit von August bis zum Ausgang der Antonine.* Ed. by G. Wissowa. Leipzig, 1919, &c. *In progress.*
Friedrichs (Karl), ' Ueber den Ursprung des Matriarchats ' ; in *Zeitschr. f. vergl. Rechtswiss.* vol. viii. Stuttgart, 1889.
Fries (Th. M.), *Grönland, dess natur och innevånare.* Upsala, 1872.
Fritsch (Gustav), *Die Eingeborenen Süd-Afrika's.* Breslau, 1872.
Fromm (P.), ' Ufipa—Land und Leute ' ; in *Mittheil. Deutsch. Schutzgeb.* vol. xxv. Berlin, 1912.
Fryer (G. E.), *The Khyeng People of the Sandoway District, Arakan.* (Reprinted from *Jour. Asiatic Soc. Bengal.*) Calcutta, 1875.
Fryer (John), *A New Account of East-India and Persia.* London, 1698.
Fülleborn (Friedrich), *Das Deutsche Njassa- und Ruwuma-Gebiet, Land und Leute, nebst Bemerkungen über die Schire-Länder.* Berlin, 1906.
Fustel de Coulanges (N. D.), *The Ancient City.* Trans. by W. Small. Boston, 1874.
—— *La cité antique.* Paris, 1864.
Fytche (A.), *Burma Past and Present.* 2 vols. London, 1878.

Gabelentz (H. C. von der), *Die melanesischen Sprachen.* 2 vols. Leipzig, 1861–73.
Gait (E. A.), *Census of India,* 1891. *Assam,* vol. i. Report. Shillong, 1892.
—— *Census of India,* 1911. *Vol. I. India,* pt. i. Report. Calcutta, 1913.
—— See Risley (*Sir* Herbert) and Gait (E. A.).
Gaius, *Institutionum juris civilis commentarii quattuor.* Ed. and trans. by E. Poste. Oxford, 1890.
Galindo (Don Juan), ' On Central America ' ; in *Jour. Roy. Geo. Soc.* vol. vi. London, 1836.
Gallardo (C. R.), *Tierra del Fuego—Los Onas.* Buenos Aires, 1910.
Galton (Francis), *Hereditary Genius.* London, 1869.
—— *The Narrative of an Explorer in Tropical South Africa.* London, 1853.
Gans (E.), *Das Erbrecht in weltgeschichtlicher Entwickelung.* 4 vols. Berlin, Stuttgart, & Tübingen, 1824–35.

Garcilasso de la Vega, *First Part of the Royal Commentaries of the Yncas.* Trans. ed. by C. R. Markham. 2 vols. London, 1869–71.

Gardiner (Alan H.), ' Ethics and Morality (Egyptian) ' ; in Hastings, *Encyclopædia of Religion and Ethics,* vol. v. Edinburgh, 1912.

—— ' The Goddess Nekhbet at the Jubilee Festival of Rameses III.' ; in *Zeitschr. für Ägyptische Sprache und Altertumskunde,* vol. xlviii. Leipzig, 1911.

Gardiner (J. Stanley), ' The Natives of Rotuma ' ; in *Jour. Anthr. Inst.* vol. xxvii. London, 1898.

Garnett (Lucy M. J.), *The Women of Turkey and their Folk-Lore.* 2 vols. London, 1890–91.

Gartenlaube (Die). Leipzig.

Gaslander (*Kyrckoherden*), ' Beskrifning, Om Allmogens Sinnelag, Seder vid de årliga Högtider, Frierier, Bröllop . . . m.m. i *Jönköpings Lähn och Wässbo Härad* ' ; in *Nyare bidrag till kännedom om de svenska landsmålen ock svenskt folklif, Bihang I.* Stockholm & Uppsala, 1883–95.

Gason (Samuel), *The Dieyerie Tribe of Australian Aborigines.* Adelaide, 1874.

—— ' The Manners and Customs of the Dieyerie Tribe of Australian Aborigines ' ; in Woods, *The Native Tribes of South Australia.* Adelaide, 1879.

—— ' Of the Tribes, Dieyerie, Auminie, Yandrawontha, Yarawu-arka, Philladapa ' ; in *Jour. Anthr. Inst.* vol. xxiv. London, 1895.

Gatschet (A. S.), *A Migration Legend of the Creek Indians.* Vol. I. Philadelphia, 1884.

Gaudefroy-Demombynes (—), *Les Cérémonies du mariage chez les indigènes de l'Algérie.* Paris, 1901.

—— ' Coutumes de mariage ' ; in *Revue des traditions populaires,* vol. xxii. Paris, 1907.

' Gautama,' trans. by G. Bühler ; in *The Sacred Books of the East,* vol. ii. Oxford, 1897.

Gaya (Louis de), *Ceremonies nuptiales de toutes les nations.* Paris, 1681.

Geary (Nevill), *The Law of Marriage and Family Relations. A Manual of Practical Law.* London & Edinburgh, 1892.

Geddes (P.) and Thomson (J. A.), *The Evolution of Sex.* London, 1901.

Geiger (Wilhelm), *Civilization of the Eastern Irānians in Ancient Times.* Trans. 2 vols. London, 1885–86.

Geijer (E. G.), *Samlade skrifter.* 8 vols. Stockholm, 1873–75.

Geiseler (—), *Die Oster-Insel.* Berlin, 1883.

Geller (Leo), *Osterreichische Justizgesetze.* Wien, 1900, &c. *In progress.*

Gellius (Aulus), *Noctes Atticæ.* Ed. by A. Lion. 2 vols. Gottingae, 1824.

Gemelli-Careri (G. F.), *Giro del mondo.* 9 vols. Venezia, 1728.

Gennep (A. van), *Mythes et légendes d'Australie.* Paris, [1906].

—— *Les rites de passage.* Paris, 1911.

—— *Tabou et totémisme à Madagascar.* (*Bibliothèque de l'École des Hautes Études. Sciences religieuses,* vol. xvii.) Paris, 1904.

Geoffroy Saint-Hilaire (I.), *Histoire générale et particulière des anomalies de l'organisation chez l'homme et les animaux.* 3 vols. Paris, 1832-37.
—— *Histoire naturelle générale des règnes organiques.* 3 vols. Paris, 1854-62.
Geografisk Tidskrift, udgivet af Bestyrelsen for det kongelige danske geografiske Selskab. Kjøbenhavn.
Geographi Græci minores, ed. by C. Müller. 3 vols. Parisiis, 1855-61.
Georgi (J. G.), *Beschreibung aller Nationen des russischen Reichs.* St. Petersburg, 1776.
Gerland (Georg). See Waitz (Th.).
Ghani (M. A.), ' Social Life and Morality in India ' ; in *International Journal of Ethics,* vol. vii. London, 1897.
Gibbon (Edward), *The History of the Decline and Fall of the Roman Empire.* Ed. by W. Smith. 8 vols. London, 1854-55.
Gibbs (George), ' Tribes of Western Washington and Northwestern Oregon ' ; in *U.S. Geographical and Geological Survey of the Rocky Mountain Region—Contributions to North American Ethnology,* vol. i. Washington, 1877.
Giddings (F. H.), *The Principles of Sociology.* New York, 1896.
Gids (De). Amsterdam.
Gierke (Otto von), ' Grundzüge des deutschen Privatrechts ' ; in v. Holtzendorff, *Enzyklopädie der Rechtswissenschaft,* ed. by J. Kohler, vol. i. München, Leipzig, & Berlin, 1915.
—— *Der Humor im deutschen Recht.* Berlin, 1871.
Gieseler (J. C. L.), *Text-Book of Ecclesiastical History.* Trans. by F. Cunningham. 3 vols. Philadelphia, 1836.
Gilbertson (A. N.), *Some Ethical Phases of Eskimo Culture.* (Reprinted from the *Journal of Religious Psychology,* vols. vi.–vii. 1913-14.) *S.l.*
Gilder (W. H.), *Schwatka's Search.* London, [1882].
Giles (H. A.), *Strange Stories from a Chinese Studio.* 2 vols. London, 1880.
Gilhodes (P. Ch.), ' Mariage et Condition de la Femme chez les Katchins (Birmanie) ' ; in *Anthropos,* vol. viii. Wien, 1913.
Gill (W. W.), *Life in the Southern Isles.* London, [1876].
—— ' Report on the Australasian, Papuan, and Polynesian Races. (2.) Mangaia (Hervey Islands) ' ; in *Report of the Second Meeting of the Australasian Association for the Advancement of Science held at Melbourne, Victoria, in January,* 1890. Sydney, 1890.
Gillen (F. J.), ' Notes on some Manners and Customs of the Aborigines of the McDonnell Ranges belonging to the Arunta Tribe ' ; in *Report on the Work of the Horn Scientific Expedition to Central Australia,* pt. iv. London & Melbourne, 1896.
—— See Spencer (*Sir* Walter Baldwin) and Gillen (F. J.).
Gilmour (James), *Among the Mongols.* London, 1888.
Ginoulhiac (Ch.), *Histoire du régime dotal.* Paris, 1842.
Giraldus de Barri, Cambrensis, *The Itinerary of Archbishop Baldwin through Wales, A.D. MCLXXXVIII.* Trans. by Sir Richard Colt Hoare. 2 vols. London, 1806.
Giraud-Teulon (A.), *La Mère chez certains peuples de l'antiquité.* Paris, 1867.
—— *Les origines de la famille.* Genève, 1874.
—— *Les origines du mariage et de la famille.* Genève & Paris, 1884.

Gisborne (Lionel), *The Isthmus of Darien in* 1852. London, 1853.
Gisborne (William), *The Colony of New Zealand.* London, 1888.
Giuseppe di Santa Maria, *Prima speditione all' Indie Orientali.* Roma, 1666.
Glasson (Ernest), *Le mariage civil et le divorce.* Paris, 1880.
Giobus. *Illustrirte Zeitschrift für Länder- und Völkerkunde.* Hild-burghausen, Braunschweig.
Gloucestershire Notes and Queries. Ed. by Beaver H. Blacker. London.
Goar (Jacobus), *Euchologion sive Rituale Græcorum.* Lutetiæ Parisiorum, 1647.
Gobineau (A. de), *The Moral and Intellectual Diversity of Races.* Trans. ed. by H. Hotz. Philadelphia, 1856.
Goddard (P. E.), *Life and Culture of the Hupa.* (*University of California Publications in American Archaeology and Ethnology,* vol. i. no. 1.) Berkeley, 1903.
Godden (Gertrude M.), ' The False Bride ' ; in *Folk-Lore,* vol. iv. London, 1893.
Godron (D. A.), *De l'espèce et des races dans les êtres organisés.* 2 vols. Paris, 1859.
Goehlert (V.), ' Ueber die Vererbung der Haarfarben bei den Pferden ' ; in *Zeitschr. f. Ethnol.* vol. xiv. Berlin, 1882.
Goertz (Carl von), *Reise um die Welt in den Jahren* 1844–1847. 3 vols. Stuttgart & Tübingen, 1852–54.
Goethe (J. W. von), *Zur Farbenlehre.* 2 vols. Tübingen, 1810.
Götte (W.), *Das Delphische Orakel.* Leipzig, 1839.
Göttingische gelehrte Anzeigen. Göttingen.
Goguet (A. Y.), *The Origin of Laws, Arts, and Sciences.* Trans. 3 vols. Edinburgh, 1761.
Goldenweiser (A. A.), Review of Hartland's *Primitive Paternity ;* in *American Anthropologist,* new ser. vol. xiii. Lancaster, 1911.
Golder (F. A.), ' The Songs and Stories of the Aleuts, with Translations from Veniaminov ' ; in *Jour. American Folk-Lore,* vol. xx. Boston & New York, 1907.
Goldschmidt (Richard), ' Erblichkeitsstudien an Schmetterlingen I. 1. Untersuchungen über die Vererbung der sekundären Geschlechtscharaktere und des Geschlechts' ; in *Zeitschr. f. induktive Abstammungs- und Vererbungslehre,* vol. vii. Berlin, 1912.
—— and Pappelbaum (Hermann), ' Erblichkeitsstudien an Schmetterlingen II. 2. Weitere Untersuchungen über die Vererbung der sekundären Geschlechtscharaktere und des Geschlechts ' ; in *Zeitschr. f. induktive Abstammungs- und Vererbungslehre,* vol. xi. Berlin, 1914.
Goldziher (Ignaz), ' Endogamy and Polygamy among the Arabs ' ; in *The Academy,* vol. xviii. London, 1880.
—— ' Wasser als Dämonen abwehrendes Mittel ' ; in *Archiv für Religionswissenschaft,* vol. xiii. Leipzig, 1910.
Gomara (F. Lopez de), ' Primera y segunda parte de la historia general de las Indias ' ; in *Biblioteca de autores españoles,* vol. xxii. Madrid, 1852.
Gomes (E. H.), *Seventeen Years among the Sea Dyaks of Borneo.* London, 1911.
Gomme (*Sir* G. Laurence), ' Exogamy and Polyandry ' ; in *The Archæological Review,* vol. i. London, 1888.

Goncourt (E. L. A. and J. A. de), *La Femme au dix-huitième siècle*. Paris, 1862.
—— *Journal des Goncourt*. 9 vols. Paris, 1887-96.
Gopal Panikkar (T. K.), *Malabar and its Folk*. Madras, 1900.
Gopalan Nair (C.), *Wynad : its Peoples and Traditions*. Madras, 1911.
Gopčević (S.), *Oberalbanien und seine Liga*. Leipzig, 1881.
Gordon (E. M.), *Indian Folk Tales*. London, 1908.
' Gospel of the Nativity of Mary (The) ' ; in *Ante-Nicene Christian Library*, vol. xvi. Edinburgh, 1870.
' Gospel of Pseudo-Matthew (The) ' ; in *Ante-Nicene Christian Library*, vol. xvi. Edinburgh, 1870.
Gottschling (E.), ' The Bawenda : a Sketch of their History and Customs ' ; in *Jour. Anthr. Inst.* vol. xxxv. London, 1905.
Gould (B. A.), *Investigations in the Military and Anthropological Statistics of American Soldiers*. New York, 1869.
Gould (John), *Handbook to the Birds of Australia*. 2 vols. London, 1865.
Gouldsbury (Cullen), ' Notes on the Customary Law of the Awemba and Kindred Tribes ' ; in *Jour. African Soc.* vol. xv. London, 1915-16.
—— and Sheane (Hubert), *The Great Plateau of Northern Rhodesia*. London, 1911.
Graafland (A. F. P.), ' De verbreiding van het matriarchaat in het landschap Indragiri ' ; in *Bijdragen tot de taal-, land- en volkenkunde van Nederlandsch-Indië*, vol. xxxix. (ser. v. vol. v.). 'sGravenhage, 1890.
Graebner (Fritz), *Methode der Ethnologie*. Heidelberg, 1911.
—— See Stephan (Emil) and Graebner (Fritz).
Grandidier (Alfred and Guillaume), *Ethnographie de Madagascar*. 3 pts. (*Histoire physique, naturelle et politique de Madagascar*, ed. by A. and G. Grandidier, vol. iv.) Paris, 1908-17.
Grant (Charles), *The Gazetteer of the Central Provinces of India*. Na'gpu'r, 1870.
Grant (William), ' Magato and his Tribe ' ; in *Jour. Anthr. Inst.* vol. xxxv. London, 1905.
Grath (G. F.), *Svenska kyrkans brudvigsel*. Upsala, 1904.
Gratian, *Decretum*. (Migne, *Patrologiæ cursus*, vol. clxxxvii.) Parisiis, 1855.
Graul (K.), *Reise nach Ostindien über Palästina und Egypten*. 5 vols. Leipzig, 1854-56.
Gray (J. H.), *China : a History of the Laws, Manners, and Customs of the People*. 2 vols. London, 1878.
Gray (Louis H.), ' Circumcision, Introductory ' ; in Hastings, *Encyclopædia of Religion and Ethics*, vol. iii. Edinburgh, 1910.
—— ' Marriage (Iranian).—Next-of-kin marriage ' ; in Hastings, *Encyclopædia of Religion and Ethics*, vol. viii. Edinburgh, 1915.
Gray (William), ' Some Notes on the Tannese ' ; in *Report of the Fourth Meeting of the Australasian Association for the Advancement of Science held at Hobart, Tasmania, in January, 1892*. Tasmania, 1893.
Greenstone (J. H.), ' Polygamy ' ; in *Jewish Encyclopedia*, vol. x. New York & London, *s.d.*

Gregor (Walter), *Notes on the Folk-Lore of the North-East of Scotland.* London, 1881.
—— ' Some Marriage Customs in Cairnbulg and Inverallochy ' ; in *The Folk-Lore Journal*, vol. i. London, 1883.
Gregory I. (*Saint*), surnamed *the Great, Opera omnia.* 5 vols. (Migne, *Patrologiæ cursus*, vols. lxxv.–lxxix.) Parisiis, 1849.
Gregory III., ' Judicia congrua poenitentibus ' ; in Labbe-Mansi, *Sacrorum Conciliorum collectio*, vol. xii. Florentiae, 1766.
Gregory (J. W.), *The Great Rift Valley.* London, 1896.
Grenard (F.), *Tibet.* Trans. London, 1904.
Grey (*Sir* George), *Journals of Two Expeditions of. Discovery in North-West and Western Australia.* 2 vols. London, 1841.
—— *Polynesian Mythology.* Auckland, 1885.
Grézel (*le Père*), *Dictionnaire Futunien-Français avec notes grammaticales.* Paris, 1878.
Grierson (G. A.), *Bihār Peasant Life.* Calcutta, 1885.
Griffis (W. E.), *Corea.* London, 1905.
—— *The Religions of Japan.* London, 1895.
Griffith (F. L.), *The Inscriptions of Siûṭ and Dêr Rîfeh.* London, 1889.
—— ' Marriage (Egyptian) ' ; in Hastings, *Encyclopædia of Religion and Ethics*, vol. viii. Edinburgh, 1915.
Griffith (William), ' Journal of a Visit to the Mishmee Hills in Assam ' ; in *Jour. Asiatic Soc. Bengal*, vol. vi. Calcutta, 1837.
—— *Journals of Travels in Assam, Burma, Bootan, Affghanistan and the Neighbouring Countries.* Calcutta, 1847.
Grigg (H. B.), *A Manual of the Nílagiri District in the Madras Presidency.* Madras, 1880.
Grihya-Sûtras (*The*). Trans. by H. Oldenberg. 2 vols. (*The Sacred Books of the East*, vols. xxix.–xxx.) Oxford, 1886–92.
Grimm (Jacob), *Deutsche Mythologie.* 2 vols. Göttingen, 1844.
—— *Deutsche Rechtsalterthümer.* Ed. by A. Heusler and R. Hübner. 2 vols. Leipzig, 1899.
—— *Teutonic Mythology.* Trans. by J. S. Stallybrass. 4 vols. London, 1880–88.
Grinnell (G. B.), ' Marriage among the Pawnees ' ; in *American Anthropologist*, vol. iv. Washington, 1891.
—— *The Story of the Indian.* London, 1896.
Groos (Karl), *The Play of Animals.* Trans. by Elizabeth L. Baldwin. London, 1898.
—— *The Play of Man.* Trans. by Elizabeth L. Baldwin. New York, 1901.
—— *Die Spiele der Tiere.* Jena, 1907.
Groot (J. J. M. de), *The Religious System of China.* Leyden, 1892 &c. *In progress.*
Grose (J. H.), *A Voyage to the East-Indies ; Began in 1750 ; With Observations continued till 1764.* 2 vols. London, 1766.
Grosier (C. B. G. A.), *A General Description of China.* Trans. 2 vols. London, 1788.
Grosse (Ernst), *The Beginnings of Art.* [Trans.] New York, 1897.
—— *Die Formen der Familie und die Formen der Wirthschaft.* Freiburg i.B. & Leipzig, 1896.
Grubb (W. Barbrooke), *Among the Indians of the Paraguayan Chaco.* London, 1904.

Grubb (W. Barbrooke), *An Unknown People in an Unknown Land.*
*An Account of the Life and Customs of the Lengua Indians of
the Paraguayan Chaco.* Ed. by H. F. Morrey Jones. London,
1911.
Gruenhagen (A.), *Lehrbuch der Physiologie.* 3 vols. Hamburg &
Leipzig, 1885–87.
Grünwedel (Albert), ' Die Reisen des Hrn. Vaughan Stevens in
Malacca ' ; in *Verhandl. Berliner Gesellsch. Anthr.* 1891.
Berlin.
Grunwald (M.), ' Marriage Ceremonies ' ; in *The Jewish Encyclopedia,*
vol. viii. New York & London, *s.d.*
Grupen (Christian Ulrich), *De uxore theotisca, Von der Teutschen Frau.*
Göttingen, 1748.
Gruppe (Otto), *Griechische Mythologie und Religionsgeschichte.*
München, 1906.
Gryse (R. P. de), ' Les premiers habitants de Bengale ' ; in *Les
Missions Catholiques,* 1897. Lyon.
Guaita (Georg von), ' Versuche mit Kreuzungen von verschiedenen
Rassen der Hausmaus ' ; in *Berichte der Naturforschenden
Gesellschaft zu Freiburg I.B.* vol. x. Freiburg, 1898.
Gubernatis (Angelo de), *Memoria intorno ai viaggiatori italiani
nelle Indie Orientali dal secolo XIII a tutto il XVI.* Firenze,
1867.
—— *Storia comparata degli Usi Nuziali in Italia e presso gli altri
popoli indo-europei.* Milano, 1878.
Gudmundsson (V.) and Kålund (Kr.), ' Sitte. Skandinavische Ver-
hältnisse ' ; in Paul, *Grundriss der germanischen Philologie,*
vol. iii. Strassburg, 1900.
Guenther (A. C. L. G.), *An Introduction to the Study of Fishes.*
Edinburgh, 1880.
Guétat (J.-E.), *Histoire élémentaire du droit français.* Paris, 1884.
Guevara (Tomas), ' Folklore Araucano ' ; in *Anales de la Universidad
de Chile,* vol. cxxvii. Santiago de Chile, 1910.
—— *Historia de la Civilizacion de Araucanía.* 3 vols. Santiago de
Chile, 1898–1902.
—— See Rivet (*Dr.*).
Guillemard (F. H. H.), *The Cruise of the " Marchesa " to Kamschatka
and New Guinea.* London, 1889.
Guinnard (A.), *Three Years' Slavery among the Patagonians.* Trans.
London, 1871.
Guise (R. E.), ' On the Tribes inhabiting the mouth of the Wanigela
River, New Guinea ' ; in *Jour. Anthr. Inst.* vol. xxviii.
London, 1899.
Gumilla (Joseph), *El Orinoco ilustrado, y defendido, historia natural,
civil, y geographica de este gran rio.* 2 vols. Madrid, 1745.
Gumplowicz (L.), *Grundriss der Sociologie.* Wien, 1885.
Guppy (H. B.), *The Solomon Islands.* London, 1887.
Gurdon (P. R. T.), *The Khasis.* London, 1907.
Gutch (*Mrs.*), *County Folk-Lore. Vol. II. Examples of printed
Folk-Lore concerning the North Riding of Yorkshire, York
and the Ainsty.* London, 1901.
—— *County Folklore. Vol. VI. Examples of printed Folk-Lore
concerning the East Riding of Yorkshire.* London, 1912.
—— and Peacock (Mabel), *County Folk-Lore. Vol. V. Examples
of printed Folk-Lore concerning Lincolnshire.* London, 1908.

Guyon (C. M.), *A New History of the East-Indies, Ancient and Modern.*
    Trans. 2 vols. London, 1757.
Guys (Henri), *Un Dervich algérien en Syrie.* Paris, 1854.
' Gwentian Code (The) ' ; in *Ancient Laws and Institutes of Wales.*
    London, 1841.

Haas (E.), ' Die Heirathsgebräuche der alten Inder ' ; in Weber,
    Indische Studien, vol. v. Berlin, 1862.
Haberlandt (Michael), *Ethnology.* Trans. by J. H. Loewe. London,
    1900.
Haddan (A. W.) and Stubbs (William), *Councils and Ecclesiastical
    Documents relating to Great Britain and Ireland.* 3 vols.
    Oxford, 1869–78.
Haddon (A. C.), ' The Ethnography of the Western Tribe of Torres
    Straits ' ; in *Jour. Anthr. Inst.* vol. xix. London, 1890.
—— *Head-Hunters.* London, 1901.
—— ' Notes on Mr. Beardmore's Paper ' [on the Natives of Mowat,
    Daudai, New Guinea] ; in *Jour. Anthr. Inst.* vol. xix.
    London, 1890.
—— in *Reports of the Cambridge Anthropological Expedition to
    Torres Straits,* vol. v. Cambridge, 1904.
Haeckel (Ernst), *Indische Reisebriefe.* Berlin, 1884.
Haecker (Valentin), *Allgemeine Vererbungslehre.* Braunschweig,
    1911.
—— *Der Gesang der Vögel.* Jena, 1900.
Härtter (G.), ' Sitten und Gebräuche der Angloer (Ober-Guinea) ' ;
    in *Zeitschr. f. Ethnol.* vol. xxxviii. Berlin, 1906.
Hagen (A.), ' Les indigènes des îles Salomon ' ; in *L'Anthropologie,*
    vol. iv. Paris, 1893.
Hagen (B.), *Die Orang Kubu auf Sumatra.* (*Veröffentlichungen aus
    dem städtischen Völker-Museum Frankfurt am Main, II.*)
    Frankfurt am Main, 1908.
—— *Unter den Papua's.* Wiesbaden, 1899.
Hagman (Lucina), ' Från samskolan ' ; in *Humanitas,* vol. ii.
    Helsingfors, 1897.
Hahl (Albert), ' Ueber die Rechtsanschauungen der Eingeborenen
    eines Theiles der Blanchebucht und des Innern der Gazelle
    Halbinsel ' ; in *Nachrichten über Kaiser Wilhelms-Land und
    den Bismarck-Archipel,* 1897. Berlin.
Hahn (J. G. von), *Albanesische Studien.* 3 vols. Jena, 1854.
Hahn (Josaphat), ' Die Ovahereró ' ; in *Zeitschrift der Gesellschaft
    für Erdkunde zu Berlin,* vol. iv. Berlin, 1869.
Hahn (Theophilus), *Tsuni-Goam. The Supreme Being of the Khoi-
    Khoi.* London, 1881.
Hailes (*Sir* David Dalrymple, *Lord*), *Annals of Scotland, from the
    Accession of Malcolm III. to the Accession of the House of
    Stewart.* 3 vols. Edinburgh, 1797.
Hale (Abraham), ' On the Sakais ' ; in *Jour. Anthr. Inst.* vol. xv.
    London, 1886.
Hale (Horatio), *The Iroquois Book of Rites.* Philadelphia, 1883.
—— ' The Klamath Nation ' ; in *Science,* vol. xix. New York,
    1892.
—— *U.S. States Exploring Expedition under the Command of Ch.
    Wilkes. Vol. VI. Ethnography and Philology.* Philadelphia,
    1846.

Hall (A. G. J.), *The Law and Practice in Divorce and Matrimonial Causes.* London, 1905.

Hall (C. F.), *Arctic Researches and Life among the Esquimaux.* New York, 1865.

Hallam (Henry), *View of the State of Europe during the Middle Ages.* 2 vols. Paris, 1840.

Halphen (A.-E.), *Recueil des lois &c. concernant les Israélites depuis la Révolution de 1789.* Paris, 1851.

Halsbury (H. S. Giffard, *Earl of*), *The Laws of England.* 31 vols. London, 1907–17.

Hämäläinen (Albert), *Mordvalaisten, tseremissien ja votjakkien kosinta- ja häätavoista.* Helsinki, 1913.

Hamilton (Alex.), ' A New Account of the East Indies ' ; in Pinkerton, *Collection of Voyages and Travels,* vol. viii. London, 1811.

Hamilton (*Lady* Augusta), *Marriage Rites, Customs, and Ceremonies, of the Nations of the Universe.* London, 1824.

Hammarstedt (N. E.), ' Kvarlevor av en Frös-ritual i en svensk bröllopslek ' ; in *Festskrift til H. F. Feilberg.* Stockholm, København, & Kristiania, 1911.

Hammurabi (*King of Babylon*), *The Code of Laws promulgated by.* Trans. by C. H. W. Johns. Edinburgh, 1903.

—— *Die Gesetze Hammurabis in Umschrift und Übersetzung.* Ed. by Hugo Winckler. Leipzig, 1904.

Hanauer (*l'Abbé*), *Les paysans de l'Alsace au moyen-âge.* Paris & Strasbourg, 1865.

Hanoteau (A.) and Letourneux (A.), *La Kabylie et les coutumes Kabyles.* 3 vols. Paris, 1872–73.

Harcourt (A. F. P.), *The Himalayan Districts of Kooloo, Lahoul, and Spiti.* London, 1871.

Hardenburg (W. E.), *The Putumayo.* London, 1912.

Hardisty (W. L.), ' The Loucheux Indians ' ; in *Smithsonian Report,* 1866. Washington, 1867.

Hardman (E. T.), ' Notes on some Habits and Customs of the Natives of the Kimberley District, Western Australia ' ; in *Proceed. Roy. Irish Academy,* ser. iii. vol. i. Dublin, 1889–91.

Hardouin (E.) and Ritter (W. L.), *Java.* Leiden, 1876.

Harkness (H.), *A Description of a Singular Aboriginal Race inhabiting the Neilgherry Hills.* London, 1832.

Harmon (D. W.), *A Journal of Voyages and Travels in the Interior of North America.* Andover, 1820.

Harper (Andrew), *The Song of Solomon.* With Introduction and Notes by. Cambridge, 1902.

Harper (C. H.) and Others, ' Notes on the Totemism of the Gold Coast ' ; in *Jour. Anthr. Inst.* vol. xxxvi. London, 1906.

Harrington (J. P.), ' Tewa Relationship Terms ' ; in *American Anthropologist,* new ser. vol. xiv. Lancaster, 1912.

Harrington (M. R.), ' A Preliminary Sketch of Lenápe Culture ' ; in *American Anthropologist,* new ser. vol. xv. Lancaster, 1913.

Harris (John), *Navigantium atque Itinerantium Bibliotheca.* 2 vols. London, 1744–48.

Harris (W. Cornwallis), *The Highlands of Aethiopia.* 3 vols. London, 1844.

Harrison (J. Park), ' On the Artificial Enlargement of the Earlobe ' ; in *Jour. Anthr. Inst.* vol. ii. London, 1873.

Harrison (Jane Ellen), *Prolegomena to the Study of Greek Religion.*
Cambridge, 1908.
Hartknoch (Christ.), *Alt- und Neues Preussen.* 2 vols. Franckfurt
& Leipzig, 1684.
Hartland (E. Sidney), ' Concerning the Rite at the Temple of
Mylitta ' ; in *Anthropological Essays presented to E. B. Tylor.*
Oxford, 1907.
—— *The Legend of Perseus.* 3 vols. London, 1894–96.
—— ' Matrilineal Kinship and the Question of its Priority ' ; in
Memoirs of the American Anthropological Association, vol. iv.
Lancaster, 1917.
—— *Primitive Paternity.* 2 vols. London, 1909.
—— *Ritual and Belief. Studies in the History of Religion.* London,
1914.
—— ' Totemism and Exogamy ' ; in *Folk-Lore,* vol. xxii. London,
1911.
—— ' Travel Notes in South Africa ' ; in *Folk-Lore,* vol. xvii.
London, 1906.
—— in the Discussion on Dr. Winternitz's paper ' On a Comparative
Study of Indo-European Customs ' ; in *Transactions of the
International Folk-Lore Congress,* 1891. London, 1892.
Hartley (C. Gasquoine ; Mrs. Walter M. Gallichan), *The Position of
Woman in Primitive Society.* London, 1914.
Hartley (David), *Observations on Man.* 2 vols. London, 1810.
Hartmann (Robert), *Die menschenähnlichen Affen.* Leipzig, 1883.
Hartshorne (B. F.), ' The Weddas ' ; in *The Indian Antiquary,*
vol. viii. Bombay, 1879.
Harvard African Studies. Cambridge (Mass.).
Haseman (J. D.), ' Some Notes on the Pawumwa Indians of South
America ' ; in *American Anthropologist,* new ser. vol. xiv.
Lancaster, 1912.
Hasselt (A. L. van), *Volksbeschrijving van Midden-Sumatra.* Leiden,
1882.
Hasselt (F. J. F. van), ' De Huwelijksregeling voor de Papoesche
Christenen, op Noord-Nieuw-Guinea ' ; in *Mededeelingen van
wege het Nederlandsche Zendelinggenootschap,* vol. lviii.
Rotterdam, 1914.
Hasselt (J. B. van), ' Die Noeforezen ' ; in *Zeitschr. f. Ethnol.* vol.
viii. Berlin, 1876.
Hastings (J.), *A Dictionary of the Bible.* 5 vols. Edinburgh,
1899–1904.
—— *Encyclopædia of Religion and Ethics.* Edinburgh, 1908, &c.
In progress.
Haushofer (Max), *Lehr- und Handbuch der Statistik.* Wien, 1882.
Hawkes (E. W.), *The Labrador Eskimo.* (*Canada Department of
Mines, Geological Survey, Memoir* 91. *No.* 14 *Anthropological
Series.*) Ottawa, 1916.
Hawkesworth (John), *An Account of Voyages in the Southern Hemi-
sphere.* 3 vols. London, 1773.
Hawkins (—), ' Notes on the Creek System of Government ' ; in
Trans. American Ethn. Soc. vol. iii. pt. i. New York,
1853.
Haxthausen (A. von), *The Russian Empire.* Trans. 2 vols.
London, 1856.
—— *Transcaucasia.* Trans. London, 1854.

Hay (*Captain*), ' Report on the Túran Mall Hill ' ; in *Jour. Asiatic Soc. Bengal*, vol. xx. Calcutta, 1852.
Hayavadana Rao (C.), ' The Gonds of the Eastern Ghauts, India ' ; in *Anthropos*, vol. v. Wien, 1910.
—— ' The Irulans of the Gingee Hills ' ; in *Anthropos*, vol. vi. Wien, 1911.
—— ' The Kasubas, a Forest Tribe of the Nilgiris ' ; in *Anthropos*, vol. iv. Wien, 1909.
Haycraft (J. B.), ' On some Physiological Results of Temperature Variations ' ; in *Trans. Roy. Soc. Edinburgh*, vol. xxix. Edinburgh, 1880.
Haynes (E. S. P.), *Divorce as it might be.* Cambridge, 1915.
Hazelius (Artur). See *Bidrag till vår odlings häfder.*
Heape (Walter), ' Abortion, Barrenness, and Fertility in Sheep ' ; in *Jour. Roy. Agricultural Soc. England*, ser. iii. vol. x. London, 1899.
—— ' The Menstruation and Ovulation of *Macacus Rhesus* ' ; in *Philosophical Transactions Roy. Soc. London*, ser. B. vol. clxxxviii. London, 1897.
—— ' The Menstruation of *Semnopithecus entellus* ' ; in *Philosophical Transactions Roy. Soc. London*, ser. B. vol. clxxxv. pt. i. London, 1894.
—— ' The Proportion of the Sexes produced by Whites and Coloured Peoples in Cuba ' ; in *Philosophical Transactions Roy. Soc. London*, ser. B. vol. cc. London, 1909.
—— *Sex Antagonism.* London, 1913.
—— ' The " Sexual Season " of Mammals and the Relation of the " Pro-œstrum " to Menstruation ' ; in *Quarterly Jour. Microscopical Science*, new ser. no. 173 (vol. xliv. pt. i.). London, 1900.
Hearn (W. E.), *The Aryan Household.* London & Melbourne, 1879.
Hearne (S.), *A Journey from Prince of Wales's Fort to the Northern Ocean.* Dublin, 1796.
Hedin (Sven), *Central Asia and Tibet.* 2 vols. London, 1903.
Heese (*Missionary*), ' Sitte und Brauch der Sango ' ; in *Archiv f. Anthropologie*, new ser. vol. xii. Braunschweig, 1913.
Hefele (C. J. von), *Conciliengeschichte.* 9 vols. Freiburg i.B., 1873–90.
Heikel (E.), *Sandalion. Beiträge zu antiken Zauberriten bei Geburt, Hochzeit und Tod.* Helsingfors, 1915.
Heimskringla. See Snorri Sturluson.
Helfer (J. W.), ' Note on the Animal Productions of the Tenasserim Provinces ' ; in *Jour. Asiatic Soc. Bengal*, vol. vii. Calcutta, 1838.
Hellwald (F. von), *Die menschliche Familie.* Leipzig, 1889.
—— ' Das Volk der Aleuten ' ; in *Das Ausland*, vol. liv. Stuttgart, 1881.
Helsingfors Morgonblad. Helsingfors.
Hembygden. Tidskrift för svensk folkkunskap och hembygdsforskning i Finland (Tidskrift utgiven av Samfundet för svensk folklivsforskning i Finland). Helsingfors.
Henderson (John), *Excursions and Adventures in New South Wales.* 2 vols. London, 1854.
Henderson (William), *Notes on the Folk-Lore of the Northern Counties of England and the Borders.* London, 1879.

Hennepin (*Father* Louis), *A New Discovery of a Vast Country in America* . . . . *between New France and New Mexico.* Trans. ed. by R. G. Thwaites. 2 vols. Chicago, 1903.
Henry (A.), ' The Lolos and other Tribes of Western China ' ; in *Jour. Anthr. Inst.* vol. xxxiii. London, 1903.
Henry (Jos.), *L'âme d'un peuple africain. Les Bambara.* (*Bibliothèque Anthropos*, vol. i. fasc. 2.) Münster i.W., 1910.
Hensel (Reinhold), ' Die Coroados der brasilianischen Provinz Rio Grande do Sul ' ; in *Zeitschr. f. Ethnol.* vol. i. Berlin, 1869.
Hensen (V.), *Physiologie der Zeugung.* (Hermann, *Handbuch der Physiologie*, vol. vi. pt. ii.) Leipzig, 1881.
—— ' Wachstum und Zeugung ' ; in *Schriften des Naturwissenschaftlichen Vereins für Schleswig-Holstein*, vol. xv. Kiel, 1913.
Hepding (Hugo), ' Die falsche Braut ' ; in *Hessische Blätter für Volkskunde*, vol. v. Leipzig, 1906.
Herbert (*Sir* Thomas), *Some Years Travels into Divers Parts of Africa, and Asia the Great.* London, 1677.
Heriot (George), *Travels through the Canadas.* London, 1807.
Hermann (K. F.), *Lehrbuch der griechischen Privatalterthümer.* Ed. by H. Blümner. Freiburg i.B. & Tübingen, 1882.
Hermann (L.), *Handbuch der Physiologie*, ed. by. 6 vols. Leipzig, 1879–81.
Hernandez (P. Pablo), *Organización social de las doctrinas Guaranies de la Compañía de Jesús.* 2 vols. Barcelona, 1913.
Hernsheim (Franz), *Südsee-Erinnerungen* (1875–1880). Berlin, [1883].
Herodotus, *Historiarum libri IX.* Ed. by G. Dindorf. Parisiis, 1844.
—— The same work. English version, ed. by G. Rawlinson, Col. Rawlinson, and Sir J. G. Wilkinson. 4 vols. London, 1875.
Herport (Albrecht), *Eine kurtze Ost-Indianische Reiss-Beschreibung.* Bern, 1669.
Herrera (Antonio de), *The General History of the Vast Continent and Islands of America, commonly call'd the West-Indies.* Trans. by J. Stevens. 6 vols. London, 1725–26.
Herrmann (Wilhelm), ' Die ethnographischen Ergebnisse der Deutschen Pilcomayo-Expedition ' ; in *Zeitschr. f. Ethnol.* vol. xl. Berlin, 1908.
Hertel (Ludvig), *Indisk Hjemmemission blandt Santalerne ved H. P. Børresen og L. O. Skrefsrud.* Kolding, 1877.
Hertz (Wilhelm), *Gesammelte Abhandlungen.* Ed. by F. von der Leyen. Stuttgart & Berlin, 1905.
Hervé (Georges), ' Noirs et blancs ' ; in *Revue de l'École d'anthropologie de Paris*, vol. xvi. Paris, 1906.
Herzen (A.), *Le Peuple russe et le socialisme. Lettre à M. J. Michelet.* Paris, 1852.
Herzog (J. J.), *Realencyklopädie für protestantische Theologie und Kirche.* Ed. by Albert Hauck. 24 vols. Leipzig, 1896–1913.
Hesiod, *Carmina.* Ed. by F. S. Lehrs. Parisiis, 1840.
Hesse (G.). See Hilzheimer.
Hessische Blätter für Volkskunde. Leipzig.
Heusler (Andreas), *Institutionen des Deutschen Privatrechts.* 2 vols. Leipzig, 1885–86.
Heuzey (L.), *Le Mont Olympe et l'Acarnanie.* Paris, 1860.

Heyl (J. A.), *Volkssagen, Bräuche und Meinungen aus Tirol.* Brixen, 1897.

Heyting (Th. A. L.), 'Beschrijving der onder-afdeeling Groot-Mandeling en Batang-Natal'; in *Tijdschrift van het Koninklijk Nederlandsch Aardrijkskundig Genootschap,* ser. ii. vol. xiv. Leiden, 1897.

Hibbert (Samuel), *A Description of the Shetland Islands.* Edinburgh, 1822.

Hickson (S. J.), *A Naturalist in North Celebes.* London, 1889.

Hieronimo di Santo Stefano, 'Account of the Journey of'; in *India in the Fifteenth Century,* trans. and ed. by R. H. Major. London, 1857.

Hieu (von), in Harper and Others, 'Notes on the Totemism of the Gold Coast'; in *Jour. Anthr. Inst.* vol. xxxvi. London, 1906.

Hildebrand (Richard), *Recht und Sitte auf den verschiedenen wirtschaftlichen Kulturstufen.* Vol. I. Jena, 1896.

Hildebrandt (J. M.), 'Ethnographische Notizen über Wakámba und ihre Nachbaren'; in *Zeitschr. f. Ethnol.* vol. x. Berlin, 1878.

Hilhouse (William), 'Notices of the Indians settled in the Interior of British Guiana'; in *Jour. Roy. Geo. Soc. London,* vol. ii. London, 1832.

Hill (Richard) and Thornton (George), *Notes on the Aborigines of New South Wales.* Sydney, 1892.

Hill (S. A.), 'The Life Statistics of an Indian Province'; in *Nature,* vol. xxxviii. London & New York, 1888.

Hillebrandt (Alfred), 'Eine Miscelle aus dem Vedaritual'; in *Zeitschr. der Deutschen Morgenländischen Gesellschaft,* vol. xl. Leipzig, 1886.

—— Rituallitteratur. Vedische Opfer und Zauber. (Bühler, *Grundriss der Indo-arischen Philologie und Altertumskunde,* vol. iii. pt. ii.) Strassburg, 1897.

Hill-Tout (C.). See Tout (C. Hill).

Hilzheimer (—), Review of G. Hesse's article 'Inzucht- und Vererbungsstudien bei Rindern der Westpreussischen Herdbuchgesellschaft,' in *Arbeiten der deutschen Gesellschaft für Züchtungskunde,* fasc. 18, Berlin, 1913; in *Archiv f. Rassen- und Gesellschafts-Biologie,* vol. xi. Leipzig & Berlin, 1916.

Hinde (S. L. and Mrs. Hildegarde), *The Last of the Masai.* London, 1901.

Hirn (Yrjö), *The Origins of Art.* London, 1900.

Hirsch (E.), Review of R. Müller's article 'Inzuchtsversuch mit vierhörnigen Ziegen,' in *Zeitschrift für induktive Abstammungs- und Vererbungslehre,* vol. vii.; in *Archiv f. Rassen- und Gesellschafts-Biologie,* vol. ix. Leipzig & Berlin, 1912.

Hirth (F.), 'The Peninsula of Lei-chou'; in *The China Review,* vol. ii. Hongkong, 1873–74.

Hislop (S.), *Papers relating to the Aboriginal Tribes of the Central Provinces.* Ed. by R. Temple. *S.l.,* 1866.

Hitopadesa. Trans. by F. Pincott. London, 1880.

Hobhouse (L. T.), *Morals in Evolution.* London, 1915.

—— Wheeler (G. C.), and Ginsberg (M.), *The Material Culture and Social Institutions of the Simpler Peoples. An Essay in Correlation.* London, 1915.

Hobley (C. W.), *Eastern Uganda. An Ethnological Survey.* London, 1902.

Hobley (C. W.), *Ethnology of A-Kamba and other East African Tribes.* Cambridge, 1910.
—— ' Kikuyu Customs and Beliefs ' ; in *Jour. Roy. Anthr. Inst.* vol. xl. London, 1910.
Hocart (A. M.), ' Early Fijians ' ; in *Jour. Roy. Anthr. Inst.* vol. xlix. London, 1919.
Hodge (F. W.), *Handbook of American Indians north of Mexico.* 2 vols. (*Smithsonian Institution, Bureau of American Ethnology, Bulletin* 30.) Washington, 1907–10.
—— *Handbook of Indians of Canada. Reprinted . . . . from Handbook of American Indians north of Mexico.* Ottawa, 1913.
Hodgkinson (Clement), *Australia, from Port Macquarie to Moreton Bay ; with Descriptions of the Natives.* London, 1845.
Hodgson (B. H.), *Miscellaneous Essays relating to Indian Subjects.* 2 vols. London, 1880.
—— ' On the Origin, &c. of the Kócch, Bodo, and Dhimál People ' ; in *Jour. Asiatic Soc. Bengal,* vol. xviii. pt. ii. Calcutta, 1850.
Hodgson (C. P.), *Reminiscences of Australia.* London, 1846.
Hodson (T. C.), ' The " Genna " amongst the Tribes of Assam ' ; in *Jour. Anthr. Inst.* vol. xxxvi. London, 1906.
—— ' Head-Hunting among the Hill Tribes of Assam ' ; in *Folk-Lore,* vol. xx. London, 1909.
—— *The Meitheis.* London, 1908.
—— *The Nāga Tribes of Manipur.* London, 1911.
—— ' The Native Tribes of Manipur ' ; in *Jour. Anthr. Inst.* vol. xxxi. London, 1901.
Hoëvell (G. W. W. C. van), ' Iets over 't oorlogvoeren der Batta's ' ; in *Tijdschrift voor Nederlandsch Indië,* new ser. vol. vii. pt. ii. Zalt-Bommel, 1878.
Hofberg (Herm.), *Nerikes gamla minnen.* Örebro, 1868.
Hoffmann (F. L.), *Race Traits and Tendencies of the American Negro.* (*Publications of the American Economic Association,* vol. xi. nos. 1–3.) New York, 1896.
Hoichbarg (Alex.), ' Soviet Law of Marriage and the Family ' ; in *The Contemporary Review,* vol. cxvii. London, 1920.
Hollander (J. J. de), *Handleiding bij de beoefening der land- en volkenkunde van Nederlandsch Oost-Indië.* 2 vols. Te Breda, 1861–64.
—— The same work. Fifth edition, ed. by R. van Eck. 2 vols. Te Breda, 1895–98.
Hollis (A. C.), *The Masai. Their Language and Folklore.* Oxford, 1905.
—— *The Nandi. Their Language and Folk-Lore.* Oxford, 1909.
—— ' A Note on the Masai System of Relationship and other Matters connected therewith ' ; in *Jour. Roy. Anthr. Inst.* vol. xl. London, 1910.
—— ' Notes on the History and Customs of the People of Taveta, East Africa ' ; in *Jour. African Soc.* vol. i. London, 1901–02.
Holm (G.), ' Ethnologisk Skizze af Angmagsalikerne ' ; in *Meddelelser om Grönland,* vol. x. Kjøbenhavn, 1888.
—— ' Konebaads-Expeditionen til Grønlands Østkyst 1883–85' ; in *Geografisk Tidskrift, udgivet af Bestyrelsen for det kongelige danske geografiske Selskab,* vol. viii. 1885–86. Kjøbenhavn, 1886.

Holmberg (A. E.), *Bohusläns historia och beskrifning*. Ed. by G. Brusewitz. 2 vols. Örebro, 1867.
Holmberg (H. J.), ' Ethnographische Skizzen über die Völker des russischen Amerika ' ; in *Acta Societatis Scientiarum Fennicæ*, vol. iv. Helsingfors, 1856.
Holsti (Rudolf), *The Relation of War to the Origin of the State*. Helsingfors, 1913.
Holtzendorff (Franz von), *Encyclopädie der Rechtswissenschaft*. 2 parts. Leipzig, 1873-76.
—— The same work. Ed. by J. Kohler. 5 vols. München, Leipzig, & Berlin, 1913-15.
Holub (E.), *Seven Years in South Africa*. Trans. 2 vols. London, 1881.
Homer, *Carmina*. Parisiis, 1838.
' Homeritarum leges ' ; in Migne, *Patrologiæ cursus*, Ser. Graeca, vol. lxxxvi. Parisiis, 1860.
Homme (L'). Ed. by G. de Mortillet. Paris.
Hommel (Fritz), *Die semitischen Völker und Sprachen*. Vol. I. Leipzig, [1881-]83.
Hooker (J. D.), *Himalayan Journals*. 2 vols. London, 1855.
Hooker (R. H.), ' Correlation of the Marriage-Rate with Trade ' ; in *Jour. Roy. Statistical Soc.* vol. lxiv. London, 1901.
Hooper (W. H.), *Ten Months among the Tents of the Tuski*. London, 1853.
Hoops (Johannes), *Reallexikon der Germanischen Altertumskunde*. 4 vols. Strassburg, 1911-19.
Hopkins (E. W.), *The Religions of India*. London, 1896.
—— ' The Social and Military Position of the Ruling Caste in Ancient India, as represented by the Sanskrit Epic ' ; in *Jour. American Oriental Soc.* vol. xiii. New Haven, 1889.
Hornaday (W. T.), *Two Years in the Jungle*. New York, 1885.
Horne (C.), ' Notes on Villages in the Himâlayas, in Kumaon Garhwâl, and on the Satlej ' ; in *The Indian Antiquary*, vol. v. Bombay, 1876.
Hose (Charles) and McDougall (William), *The Pagan Tribes of Borneo*. 2 vols. London, 1912.
Hough (James), *Letters on the Climate, Inhabitants, Productions, &c. of the Neilgherries*. London, 1829.
Hough (Walter), ' Korean Clan Organization ' ; in *American Anthropologist*, new ser. vol. i. New York, 1899.
Hourst (É. A. L.), *Sur le Niger et au pays des Touaregs*. Paris, 1898.
Houzeau (J. C.), *Études sur les facultés mentales des animaux comparées à celles de l'homme*. 2 vols. Mons, 1872.
Hovorka (Oskar), ' Verstümmelungen des männlichen Gliedes bei einigen Völkern des Alterthums und der Jetztzeit ' ; in *Mittheil. Anthrop. Gesellsch. Wien*, vol. xxiv. (new ser. vol. xiv.). Wien, 1894.
—— ' Verzierungen der Nase ' ; in *Mittheil. Anthrop. Gesellsch. Wien*, vol. xxv. (new ser. vol. xv.). Wien, 1895.
Howard (B. Douglas), *Life with Trans-Siberian Savages*. London, 1893.
Howard (G. E.), *A History of Matrimonial Institutions*. 3 vols. Chicago & London, 1904.
Howitt (A. W.), ' Australian Group Relations ' ; in *Smithsonian Report*, 1883. Washington, 1885.

Howitt (A. W.), ' Australian Group-Relationships ' ; in *Jour. Roy. Anthr. Inst.* vol. xxxvii. London, 1907.
—— ' The Diery and other kindred Tribes of Central Australia ' ; in *Jour. Anthr. Inst.* vol. xx. London, 1891.
—— *The Native Tribes of South-East Australia.* London, 1904.
—— ' The Native Tribes of South-East Australia ' ; in *Folk-Lore*, vol. xvii. London, 1906.
—— ' The Native Tribes of South-East Australia ' ; in *Jour. Roy. Anthr. Inst.* vol. xxxvii. London, 1907.
—— ' Notes on the Australian Class Systems ' ; in *Jour. Anthr. Inst.* vol. xii. London, 1883.
—— ' On the Organisation of Australian Tribes ' ; in *Transactions Roy. Soc. Victoria*, vol. i. pt. ii. Melbourne, 1889.
Hozumi (Nobushige), *Ancestor-Worship and Japanese Law.* Tokyo, Osaka, & Kyoto, 1913.
—— *Lectures on the New Japanese Civil Code.* Tokyo, 1912.
Hrdlička (Aleš), ' Notes on the Indians of Sonora, Mexico ' ; in *American Anthropologist*, new ser. vol. vi. Lancaster, 1904.
Hruza (Ernst), *Beiträge zur Geschichte des griechischen und römischen Familienrechtes.* 2 vols. Erlangen & Leipzig, 1892–94.
' Hsiâo King (The),' trans. by J. Legge ; in *The Sacred Books of the East*, vol. iii. Oxford, 1879.
Huc (E. R.), *Travels in Tartary, Thibet, and China, during the Years 1844–1846.* Trans. 2 vols. London, [1852].
Hübbe-Schleiden (W.), *Ethiopien. Studien über West-Afrika.* Hamburg, 1879.
Hübschmann (H.), ' Ueber die persische Verwandtenheirath ' ; in *Zeitschr. Deutsch. Morgenländischen Gesellsch.* vol. xliii. Leipzig, 1889.
Hughes (T. P.), *A Dictionary of Islam.* London, 1896.
Hughes-Buller (R.), *Census of India*, 1901. *Vol. V. Baluchistan*, pt. i. Report. Bombay, 1902.
Humanitas. Helsingfors.
Humboldt (A. von), *Personal Narrative of Travels to the Equinoctial Regions of the New Continent.* Trans. 7 vols. London, 1814–29.
—— *Political Essay on the Kingdom of New Spain.* Trans. 2 vols. London, 1811.
Hume (David), *Philosophical Works.* Ed. by T. H. Green and T. H. Grose. 4 vols. London, 1874–75.
Hunter (John), *An Historical Journal of the Transactions at Port Jackson and Norfolk Island, &c.* London, 1793.
Hunter (W. A.), *A Systematical and Historical Exposition of Roman Law.* London, 1903.
Hunter (W. W.), *The Annals of Rural Bengal.* 3 vols. London, 1868–72.
—— *A Comparative Dictionary of the Non-Aryan Languages of India and High Asia.* London, 1868.
Hurel (P. Eugène), ' Religion et Vie domestique des Bakerewe ' ; in *Anthropos*, vol. vi. Wien, 1911.
Hurgronje (C. Snouck), *The Achehnese.* Trans. by A. W. S. O'Sullivan. 2 vols. Leyden & London, 1906.
—— *Het Gajōland en zijne Bewoners.* Batavia, 1903.
—— *Mekka.* 2 vols. Haag, 1888–89.
—— *Mekkanische Sprichwörter und Redensarten.* Haag, 1886.

Hutchinson (R. H. Sneyd), *An Account of the Chittagong Hill Tracts.* Calcutta, 1906.
Hutchinson (Th. J.), 'The Tehuelche Indians of Patagonia'; in *Trans. Ethn. Soc. London,* new ser. vol. vii. London, 1869.
Hutereau (A.), *Notes sur la Vie familiale et juridique de quelques populations du Congo Belge.* (*Annales du Musée du Congo Belge. Ethnographie et Anthropologie.—Ser. III. Documents ethnographiques concernant les populations du Congo Belge,* vol. i. fasc. 1.) Bruxelles, 1909.
Huth (A. H.), *The Marriage of Near Kin considered with respect to the Laws of Nations, &c.* London, 1875.
—— The same work. Second edition. London, 1887.
Hutter (Franz), *Wanderungen und Forschungen im Nord-Hinterland von Kamerun.* Braunschweig, 1902.
Hutton (S. K.), *Among the Eskimos of Labrador.* London, 1912.
Huxley (T. H.), *Evidence as to Man's Place in Nature.* London, 1863.
Hyades (P.), 'Ethnographie des Fuégiens'; in *Bull. Soc. d'Anthr. Paris,* ser. iii. vol. x. Paris, 1887.
—— and Deniker (J.), *Mission scientifique du Cap Horn,* 1882–1883. *Tome VII. Anthropologie, Ethnographie.* Paris, 1891.
Hyltén-Cavallius (G. O.), *Wärend och Wirdarne.* 2 vols. Stockholm, 1863–68.

Ibn Batuta, *The Travels of.* Trans. by the Rev. S. Lee. London, 1829.
Iden-Zeller (Oskar), 'Ethnographische Beobachtungen bei den Tschuktschen'; in *Zeitschr. f. Ethnol.* vol. xliii. Berlin, 1911.
Ignace (*l'Abbé*), 'Les Capiekrans'; in *Anthropos,* vol. v. Wien, 1910.
Iguchi, 'Wenig bekannte japanische Hochzeitsbräuche'; in *Globus,* vol. lxviii. Braunschweig, 1895.
Im Thurn (*Sir* E. F.), *Among the Indians of Guiana.* London, 1883.
Imperial Gazetteer of India (The). 26 vols. Oxford, 1907–09.
India in the Fifteenth Century. See Major (R. H.)
Indian Antiquary (The), a Journal of Oriental Research. Bombay.
Indische Gids (De). Amsterdam.
Indische Studien. See Weber (Albrecht).
Indo-Chinese Gleaner (The). 3 vols. Malacca, 1818–21.
Inglis (John), *In the New Hebrides.* London, 1887.
—— 'Report of a Missionary Tour in the New Hebrides'; in *Jour. Ethn. Soc. London,* vol. iii. London, 1854.
Institutes of Vishnu (The). Trans. by J. Jolly. (*The Sacred Books of the East,* vol. vii.) Oxford, 1880.
Institutiones. See Justinian.
International Journal of Ethics. London & Philadelphia.
Internationales Archiv für Ethnographie. Ed. by J. D. E. Schmeltz. Leiden.
Irenaeus (*Saint*), *Contra hæreses libri quinque.* (Migne, *Patrologiæ cursus,* Ser. Graeca, vol. vii.) Parisiis, 1857.
Isaeus, 'Orationes'; in *Oratores Attici,* ed. by C. Müller, vol. i. Parisiis, 1847.

Jacobs (Joseph), 'Intermarriage'; in *The Jewish Encyclopedia,* vol. vi. New York & London, s.d.

Jacobs (Joseph), ' On the Racial Characteristics of Modern Jews ' ; in *Jour. Anthr. Inst.* vol. xv. London, 1886.
—— *Studies in Jewish Statistics.* London, 1891.
Jacobs (Julius), *Eenigen Tijd onder de Baliërs.* Batavia, 1883.
Jaffur Shurreef, *Qanoon-e-Islam, or the Customs of the Mussulmans of India.* Trans. by G. A. Herklots. Madras, 1863.
Jagor (F.), *Reisen in den Philippinen.* Berlin, 1873.
Jahrbuch der internationalen Vereinigung für vergleichende Rechtswissenschaft und Volkswirtschaftslehre zu Berlin.
—— *des Vereins für niederdeutsche Sprachforschung.* Bremen.
Jahrbücher für classische Philologie. Ed. by A. Fleckeisen. Leipzig.
Jamblichus, *De mysteriis liber.* Ed. by G. Parthey. Berolini, 1857.
James (Edwin), *Account of an Expedition from Pittsburgh to the Rocky Mountains, performed in the Years 1819 and '20, under the Command of S. H. Long.* 2 vols. Philadelphia, 1823.
James (G. W.), *The Indians of the Painted Desert Region.* London, 1903.
Jamieson (E.), *Description of Habits and Customs of the Muhsös (Black and Red) also known as Lahus.* (*Ethnographical Survey of India.* Burma, No. 3.) Rangoon, 1909.
Jamieson (G.), ' Translations from the General Code of Laws of the Chinese Empire ; vii.—Marriage Laws ' ; in *The China Review*, vol. x. Hongkong, 1881–82.
Jansen (H.), ' Mitteilungen über die Juden in Marroko ' ; in *Globus*, vol. lxxi. Braunschweig, 1897.
[Janssen (*Madame*),] ' Die Todas ' ; in *Globus*, vol. xliii. Braunschweig, 1883.
Jarves (J. J.), *History of the Hawaiian Islands.* Honolulu, 1872.
Jaussen (A.), *Coutumes des Arabes au pays de Moab.* Paris, 1908.
Jeaffreson (J. C.), *Brides and Bridals.* 2 vols. London, 1872.
Jellinghaus (Th.), ' Sagen, Sitten und Gebräuche der Munda-Kolhs in Chota Nagpore ' ; in *Zeitschr. f. Ethnol.* vol. iii. Berlin, 1871.
Jenks (A. E.), *The Bontoc Igorot.* (*Philippine Islands.—Department of the Interior. Ethnological Survey Publications*, vol. i.) Manila, 1905.
—— ' Bulu Knowledge of the Gorilla and Chimpanzee ' ; in *American Anthropologist*, new ser. vol. xiii. Lancaster, 1911.
Jennings-Bramley (W. E.), ' The Bedouin of the Sinaitic Peninsula ' ; in *Palestine Exploration Fund. Quarterly Statement for* 1905. London.
Jeremias (A.), *Izdubar-Nimrod. Eine altbabylonische Heldensage.* Leipzig, 1891.
Jeremy, ' Epistle of ' ; in *Apocrypha and Pseudepigrapha of the Old Testament*, ed. by R. H. Charles, vol. i. Oxford, 1913.
Jerome (*Saint*), *Opera omnia.* 11 vols. (Migne, *Patrologiæ cursus*, vols. xxii.–xxx.) Parisiis, 1845–46.
—— ' Ex Hieronymo ' ; in *Monumenta Historica Britannica*, vol. i. London, 1848.
Jesuit Relations (The) and Allied Documents. Travels and Explorations of the Jesuit Missionaries in New France, 1610–1791. The Original Texts, with English Translations and Notes. Ed. by R. G. Thwaites. 73 vols. Cleveland, 1896–1901.
Jesup North Pacific Expedition (The). See *Publications of the Jesup North Pacific Expedition.*

Jewish Encyclopedia (The). Ed. by Isidore Singer and Joseph Jacobs. 12 vols. New York & London, *s.d.*

Jhering (Hermann von), ' Die künstliche Deformierung der Zähne ' ; in *Zeitschr. f. Ethnol.* vol. xiv. Berlin, 1882.

Jivanji Jamshedji Modi, ' Marriage (Iranian).—Zoroastrian ' ; in Hastings, *Encyclopædia of Religion and Ethics*, vol. viii. Edinburgh, 1915.

Jochelson (W.), *The Koryak*. (*Publications of the Jesup North Pacific Expedition*, vol. vi.) Leiden & New York, 1908.

—— *The Yukaghir and the Yukaghirized Tungus*. (*Publications of the Jesup North Pacific Expedition*, vol. ix. pt. i.) Leiden & New York, 1910.

Joest (W.), ' Bei den Barolong ' ; in *Das Ausland*, vol. lvii. München, 1884.

—— ' Reise in Afrika im Jahre 1883 ' ; in *Verhandl. Berliner Gesellsch. Anthrop.* 1885. Berlin.

—— *Tätowiren, Narbenzeichnen und Körperbemalen*. Berlin, 1887.

Jogendra Nath Bhattacharya, *Hindu Castes and Sects*. Calcutta, 1896.

John of Antioch, ' Historia ' ; in *Fragmenta Historicorum Græcorum*, ed. by C. Müller, vol. iv. Parisiis, 1851.

Johnston (*Sir* Harry H.), *British Central Africa*. London, 1897.

—— *George Grenfell and the Congo*. 2 vols. London, 1908.

—— *The Kilima-njaro Expedition*. London, 1886.

—— *The River Congo*. London, 1884.

—— *The Uganda Protectorate*. 2 vols. London, 1902.

Johnstone (J. C.), *Maoria*. London, 1874.

Joinville ( ), ' On the Religion and Manners of the People of Ceylon ' ; in *Asiatick Researches*, vol. vii. Calcutta, 1801.

Jolly (J.), ' Beiträge zur indischen Rechtsgeschichte ' ; in *Zeitschr. Deutsch. Morgenländischen Gesellsch.* vol. xliv. Leipzig, 1890.

—— *Recht und Sitte*. (Bühler, *Grundriss der indo-arischen Philologie und Altertumskunde*, vol. ii. fasc. 8.) Strassburg, 1896.

Jones (Owen), *The Grammar of Ornament*. London, [1865].

Jones (Peter), *History of the Ojebway Indians*. London, 1861.

Jones (S.), ' The Kutchin Tribes ' ; in *Smithsonian Report*, 1866. Washington, 1867.

Josephus, *Opera*. Ed. by G. Dindorf. 2 vols. Parisiis, 1845–47.

Journal and Proceedings of the Royal Society of New South Wales. Sydney & London.

Journal Asiatique. Paris.

—— *de la Société Finno-ougrienne*. Helsingfors.

—— *des Museum Godeffroy*. Hamburg.

—— *of the African Society*. London.

—— *of American Folk-Lore (The)*. Boston & New York.

—— *of the American Oriental Society*. New York, New Haven.

—— *of the (Royal) Anthropological Institute of Great Britain and Ireland (The)*. London.

—— *of the Asiatic Society of Bengal*. Calcutta.

—— *of the Ceylon Branch of the Royal Asiatic Society*. Colombo.

—— *of the Ethnological Society of London*.

—— *of the Gypsy Lore Society*. New Series. Liverpool.

—— *of Hellenic Studies (The)*. London.

—— *of the Indian Archipelago and Eastern Asia*. Singapore.

Journal of Literature and Science, published under the Auspices of the Madras Literary Society (The). Madras.
—— *of the Polynesian Society.* Wellington.
—— *of the Royal Agricultural Society of England.* London.
—— *of the Royal Asiatic Society.* London.
—— *of the Royal Geographical Society of London.*
—— *of the (Royal) Statistical Society.* London.
—— *of the Straits Branch of the Royal Asiatic Society.* Singapore.
Joustra (M.), ' Het leven, de zeden en gewoonten der Bataks ' ; in *Mededeelingen van wege het Nederlandsche Zendelinggenootschap,* vol. xlvi. Rotterdam, 1902.
Joyce (P. W.), *A Social History of Ancient Ireland.* 2 vols. London, 1903.
Juan (George) and Ulloa (A. de), ' A Voyage to South America.' Trans ; in Pinkerton, *Collection of Voyages and Travels,* vol. xiv. London, 1813.
Jullian (Camille), *Histoire de la Gaule.* Paris, 1908 &c. *In progress.*
Jung (—), ' Aufzeichnungen über die Rechtsanschauungen der Eingeborenen von Nauru ' ; in *Mittheil. Deutsch. Schutzgeb.* vol. x. Berlin, 1897.
Jung (C. E.), ' Aus dem Seelenleben der Australier ' ; in *Mittheilungen des Vereins für Erdkunde zu Leipzig,* 1877.
Jung (C. G.), *Collected Papers on Analytical Psychology.* Trans. London, 1917.
—— *Psychology of the Unconscious.* Trans. London, 1916.
Junghuhn (Franz), *Die Battaländer auf Sumatra.* German trans. 2 vols. Berlin, 1847.
Junker (Wilhelm), *Travels in Africa during the Years* 1879–1883. Trans. by A. H. Keane. London, 1891.
—— *Travels in Africa during the Years* 1882–1886. Trans. by A. H. Keane. London, 1892.
Junod (H. A.), *Les Ba-Ronga.* Neuchâtel, 1898.
—— ' Les Conceptions psychologiques des bantou sud-africains et leurs tabous ' ; in *Revue d'ethnographie et de sociologie,* vol. i. Paris, 1910.
—— *The Life of a South African Tribe.* 2 vols. London & Neuchâtel, 1912.
Justi (Ferd.), ' Die Weltgeschichte des Tabari ' ; in *Das Ausland,* vol. xlviii. Stuttgart, 1875.
Justin, *Historiæ Philippicæ.* Ed. by F. Duebner. Lipsiae, 1831.
Justin Martyr (*Saint*), ' Apologia prima pro Christianis ' ; in *Patrologiæ cursus,* Ser. Graeca, vol. vi. Parisiis, 1857.
Justinian (*Emperor*), *Codex Justinianus.* Ed. by P. Krueger. (*Corpus juris civilis,* vol. ii.) Berolini, 1888.
—— ' Digesta,' ed. by Th. Mommsen ; in *Corpus juris civilis,* vol. i. Berolini, 1889.
—— ' Institutiones,' ed. by P. Krueger ; in *Corpus juris civilis,* vol. i. Berolini, 1889.
—— *Novellæ.* Ed. by R. Schoell and G. Kroll. (*Corpus juris civilis,* vol. iii.) Berolini, 1895.

Kaegi (Adolf), *The Rigveda : the Oldest Literature of the Indians.* Trans. Boston, 1886.
Kaindl (R. F.), ' Ruthenische Hochzeitsgebräuche in der Bukowina ' ; in *Zeitschr. des Vereins für Volkskunde,* vol. xi. Berlin, 1901.

Kames (Henry Home, *Lord*), *Sketches of the History of Man.* 3 vols. Edinburgh, 1813.
Kanakasabhai [Pillai] (V.), *The Tamils Eighteen hundred Years ago.* Madras & Bangalore, 1904.
Kane (E. K.), *Arctic Explorations.* 2 vols. Philadelphia, 1856.
Kanjilal (K. C.), ' Hindu Early Marriage ' ; in *The Calcutta Review,* vol. cxxviii. Calcutta, 1909.
Kannan Nayar (K.). *See* Nayar (K. Kannan).
Karasek (A.), ' Beiträge zur Kenntnis der Waschambaa ; nach hinterlassenen Aufzeichnungen von A. K., 'ed. by August Eichhorn ; in *Baessler-Archiv,* vol. i. Leipzig & Berlin, 1911.
Karlowa (Otto), *Römische Rechtsgeschichte.* 2 vols. Leipzig, 1885–1901.
Karsten (Rafael), *Contributions to the Sociology of the Indian Tribes of Ecuador.* (*Acta Academiæ Aboensis. Humaniora,* vol. i. no. 3.) Åbo, 1920.
—— *Indian Dances in the Gran Chaco* (*S. America*). (*Öfversigt af Finska Vetenskaps-Societetens Förhandlingar. Bd. LVII.* 1914–1915. *Afd. B. N:o.* 6.) Helsingfors, 1915.
—— *Studies in South American Anthropology, I.* (*Översigt av Finska Vetenskaps-Societetens Förhandlingar. Bd. LXII.* 1919–1920. *Avd. B. N:o.* 2.) Helsingfors, 1920.
Karutz (*Dr.*), ' Volksthümliches aus den baskischen Provinzen ' ; in *Verhandl. Berliner Gesellsch. Anthr.* 1899. Berlin.
Kasteren (J. P. van), ' Aus dem " Buche der Weiber " ' ; in *Zeitschr. des Deutschen Palaestina-Vereins,* vol. xviii. Leipzig, 1895.
Kate (H. F. C. ten), *Reizen en onderzoekingen in Noord-Amerika.* Leiden, 1885.
Kater (C.), ' De Dajaks van Sidin ' ; in *Tijdschrift voor indische taal-, land- en volkenkunde,* vol. xvi. Batavia & 's Hage, 1867.
Katscher (Leopold), *Bilder aus dem chinesischen Leben.* Leipzig & Heidelberg, 1881.
Kaufmann (Hans), ' Die Auin. Ein Beitrag zur Buschmannforschung'; in *Mittheil. Deutsch. Schutzgeb.* vol. xxiii. Berlin, 1910.
Kautsky (Carl), ' Die Entstehung der Ehe und Familie ' ; in *Kosmos,* vol. xii. Stuttgart, 1882.
Kealy (E. H.), *Census of India,* 1911. *Vol. XXII. Rajputana and Ajmer-Merwara,* pt. i. Report. Ajmer, 1913.
Keane (A. H.), *Ethnology.* Cambridge, 1901.
—— ' On the Botocudos ' ; in *Jour. Anthr. Inst.* vol. xiii. London, 1884.
Kearns (J. F.), *Kalyán'a Shat'anku, or the Marriage Ceremonies of the Hindus of South India.* Madras, 1868.
—— *The Tribes of South India.* [London, 1865].
Keate (George), *An Account of the Pelew Islands.* London, 1788.
Keating (W. H.), *Narrative of an Expedition to the Source of St. Peter's River.* 2 vols. Philadelphia, 1824.
Keil (C. F.), *Manual of Biblical Archæology.* Trans. 2 vols. Edinburgh, 1887–88.
Keith (A. Berriedale), ' Marriage (Hindu) ' ; in Hastings, *Encyclopædia of Religion and Ethics,* vol. viii. Edinburgh, 1915.
—— See Macdonell (A. A.) and Keith (A. B.).
Keith (Arthur), *The Antiquity of Man.* London, 1915.
Kelly (Edmond), *The French Law of Marriage, Marriage Contracts and Divorce.* Ed. by O. E. Bodington. London, 1895.

Kennan (George), *Tent Life in Siberia*. London, 1871.
Keppel (H.), *The Expedition to Borneo of H.M.S. Dido*. 2 vols. London, 1847.
Kern (H.), *Manual of Indian Buddhism*. Strassburg, 1896.
Kerry-Nicholls (J. H.), ' The Origin, Physical Characteristics, and Manners and Customs of the Maori Race ' ; in *Jour. Anthr. Inst.* vol. xv. London, 1886.
Kessel (Karl von), ' Zur Geschichte der Kosaken ' ; in *Das Ausland*, vol. xlv. Augsburg, 1872.
Kessler (Ernst), *Plutarchs Leben des Lykurgos*. (*Quellen und Forschungen zur alten Geschichte und Geographie*, ed. by W. Sieglin, fasc. 23.) Berlin, 1910.
Ketjen (E.), ' De Kalangers ' ; in *Tijdschrift voor indische taal-, land- en volkenkunde*, vol. xxiv. Batavia, 1877.
Keyser (Arthur), *Our Cruise to New Guinea*. London, 1885.
Kicherer (—), *An Extract from the Rev. Mr. K.'s Narrative of his Mission in South Africa*. Wiscasset, 1805.
Kidd (Dudley), *The Essential Kafir*. London, 1904.
Kikuchi (*Baron* Dairoku), *Japanese Education*. London, 1909.
Kincaid (*Colonel*), ' On the Bheel Tribes of the Vindhyan Range ' ; in *Jour. Anthr. Inst.* vol. ix. London, 1880.
King (P. Parker) and Fitzroy (R.), *Narrative of the surveying Voyages of the " Adventure " and " Beagle."* 3 vols. London, 1839.
King (Richard), ' On the Intellectual Character of the Esquimaux ' ; in *Jour. Ethn. Soc. London*, vol. i. Edinburgh (printed), 1848.
King (W. Ross), *The Aboriginal Tribes of the Nilgiri Hills*. London, 1870.
Kingsley (Mary H.), *Travels in West Africa*. London, 1897.
—— *West African Studies*. London, 1901.
Kirby (W. W.), ' A Journey to the Youcan, Russian America ' ; in *Smithsonian Report*, 1864. Washington, 1865.
Kirke (Henry), *Twenty-five Years in British Guiana*. London, 1898.
Kirkpatrick (*Colonel*), *An Account of the Kingdom of Nepaul*. London, 1811.
Kirkpatrick (C. S.), ' Polyandry in the Panjâb ' ; in *The Indian Antiquary*, vol. vii. Bombay, 1878.
Kitchin (S. B.), *A History of Divorce*. London, 1912.
Klaproth (H. J. von), *Asia Polyglotta*. 2 pts. Paris, 1831.
—— See *Magasin asiatique*.
Klein (F. A.), ' Mittheilungen über Leben, Sitten und Gebräuche der Fellachen in Palästina ' ; in *Zeitschr. des Deutschen Palaestina-Vereins*, vol. vi. Leipzig, 1883.
Kleinpaul (Rudolf), *Sprache ohne Worte*. Leipzig, 1888.
Klemm (G.), *Allgemeine Cultur-Geschichte der Menschheit*. 10 vols. Leipzig, 1843–52.
Klibansky (*Justizrat*), *Handbuch des gesamten russischen Zivilrechts*. 3 vols. Berlin, [1911–18].
Klose (Heinrich), *Togo unter deutscher Flagge*. Berlin, 1899.
Kloss (C. B.), *In the Andamans and Nicobars*. London, 1903.
Klugmann (N.), *Die Frau im Talmud*. Wien, 1898.
Klunzinger (C. B.), *Upper Egypt*. Trans. London, 1878.
Klutschak (H. W.), *Als Eskimo unter den Eskimos*. Wien, Pest, & Leipzig, 1881.
Knight (E. F.), *Where Three Empires meet*. London, 1893.

Knoche (Walter), ' Einige Beobachtungen über Geschlechtsleben und Niederkunft auf der Osterinsel ' ; in *Zeitschr. f. Ethnol.* vol. xliv. Berlin, 1912.

Knocker (F. W.), ' The Aborigines of Sungei Ujong ' ; in *Jour. Roy. Anthr. Inst.* vol. xxxvii. London, 1907.

—— ' Notes on the Wild Tribes of the Ulu Plus, Perak ' ; in *Jour. Roy. Anthr. Inst.* vol. xxxix. London, 1909.

Knox (Robert), *An Historical Relation of the Island of Ceylon.* London, 1817.

Königliche Museen zu Berlin. Veröffentlichungen aus dem königlichen Museum für Völkerkunde.

Königliches Ethnographisches Museum zu Dresden.

Koenigswald (G. von), ' Die Cayuás,' in *Globus,* vol. xciii. Braunschweig, 1908.

Koenigswarter (L. J.), *Études historiques sur le développement de la société humaine.* Paris, 1850.

—— *Histoire de l'organisation de la famille en France.* Paris, 1851.

Koeppen (C. F.), *Die Religion des Buddha und ihre Entstehung.* 2 vols. Berlin, 1857–59.

Köstlin (Julius), *Martin Luther. Sein Leben und seine Schriften.* Ed. by G. Kawerau. 2 vols. Berlin, 1903.

Kohl (J. G.), ' Bemerkungen über die Bekehrung canadischer Indianer zum Christenthum und einige Bekehrungsgeschichten ' ; in *Das Ausland,* vol. xxxii. Stuttgart & Augsburg, 1859.

—— *Kitchi-Gami. Wanderings round Lake Superior.* Trans. London, 1860.

Kohlbrugge (J. H. F.), ' Der Einfluss des Tropenklimas auf den blonden Europäer ' ; in *Archiv f. Rassen- und Gesellschafts-Biologie,* vol. vii. München, 1910.

Kohler (A.), *Pater Florian Baucke, ein Jesuit in Paraguay.* (1748–1766.) *Nach dessen eigenen Aufzeichnungen.* Regensburg, 1870.

Kohler (Josef), ' Das Banturecht in Ostafrika ' ; in *Zeitschr. f. vergl. Rechtswiss.* vol. xv. Stuttgart, 1901.

—— ' Ein Beitrag zur ethnologischen Jurisprudenz ' ; in *Zeitschr. f. vergl. Rechtswiss.* vol. iv. Stuttgart, 1883.

—— ' Indische Gewohnheitsrechte ' ; in *Zeitschr. f. vergl. Rechtswiss.* vol. viii. Stuttgart, 1889.

—— ' Indisches Ehe- und Familienrecht ' ; in *Zeitschr. f. vergl. Rechtswiss.* vol. iii. Stuttgart, 1882.

—— *Nachwort zu Shakespeare vor dem Forum der Jurisprudenz.* Würzburg, 1884.

—— ' Das Recht der Australneger ' ; in *Zeitschr. f. vergl. Rechtswiss.* vol. vii. Stuttgart, 1887.

—— ' Das Recht der Herero ' ; in *Zeitschr. f. vergl. Rechtswiss.* vol. xiv. Stuttgart, 1900.

—— ' Das Recht der Hottentotten ' ; in *Zeitschr. f. vergl. Rechtswiss.* vol. xv. Stuttgart, 1901.

—— ' Das Recht der Marschallinsulaner ' ; in *Zeitschr. f. vergl. Rechtswiss.* vol. xiv. Stuttgart, 1900.

—— ' Das Recht der Papuas ' ; in *Zeitschr. f. vergl. Rechtswiss.* vol. xiv. Stuttgart, 1900.

—— ' Das Recht der Papuas auf Neu-Guinea ' ; in *Zeitschr. f. vergl. Rechtswiss.* vol. vii. Stuttgart, 1887.

Kohler (Josef), ' Die Rechte der Urvölker Nordamerikas ' ; in *Zeitschr. f. vergl. Rechtswiss.* vol. xii. Stuttgart, 1897.
—— ' Rechtsphilosophie und Universalrechtsgeschichte ' ; in F. von Holtzendorff, *Enzyklopädie der Rechtswissenschaft in systematischer Bearbeitung*, ed. by J. Kohler, vol. i. München, Leipzig, & Berlin, 1915.
—— ' Studien über Frauengemeinschaft, Frauenraub und Frauenkauf ' ; in *Zeitschr. f. vergl. Rechtswiss.* vol. v. Stuttgart, 1884.
—— ' Zur Urgeschichte der Ehe ' ; in *Zeitschr. f. vergl. Rechtswiss.* vol. xii. Stuttgart, 1897.
—— and Peiser (F. E.), *Aus dem Babylonischen Rechtsleben.* 4 vols. Leipzig, 1890–98.
Kohler (Kaufmann), ' Intermarriage ' ; in *Jewish Encyclopedia*, vol. vi. New York & London, s.d.
Kolbe (Peter), *The Present State of the Cape of Good Hope.* Trans. 2 vols. London, 1731.
Kollmann (J.), ' Neue Gedanken über das alte Problem von der Abstammung des Menschen ' ; in *Globus*, vol. lxxxvii. Braunschweig, 1905.
Kollmann (Paul), *The Victoria Nyanza.* Trans. London, 1899.
Kong Christian den Femtis Danske Lov. Ed. by V. A. Secher. Kjøbenhavn, 1878.
Kongliga Vetenskaps-academiens Handlingar. Stockholm.
Kongliga Vitterhets, Historie och Antiquitets Academiens Handlingar. Stockholm.
Koppenfels (H. von), ' Meine Jagden auf Gorillas ' ; in *Die Gartenlaube*, 1877. Leipzig.
Korân (The). Trans. by J. M. Rodwell. London, 1876.
—— See *Qur'ân (The)*.
Koschaker (Paul), *Rechtsvergleichende Studien zur Gesetzgebung Hammurapis.* Leipzig, 1917.
Kosmos. Zeitschrift für die gesamte Entwickelungslehre. Stuttgart.
Kotzebue (Otto von), *A Voyage of Discovery into the South Sea and Beering's Straits.* Trans. 3 vols. London, 1821.
Kovalewsky (Maxime), *Coutume contemporaine et loi ancienne.* Paris, 1893.
—— ' La famille matriarcale au Caucase ' ; in *L'Anthropologie*, vol. iv. Paris, 1893.
—— ' Marriage among the Early Slavs ' ; in *Folk-Lore*, vol. i. London, 1890.
—— *Modern Customs and Ancient Laws of Russia.* London, 1891.
—— *Tableau des origines et de l'évolution de la famille et de la propriété.* Stockholm, 1890.
Krämer (Augustine), *Die Samoa-Inseln.* 2 vols. Stuttgart, 1902.
—— ' Studienreise nach den Zentral- und Westkarolinen ' ; in *Mittheil. Deutsch. Schutzgeb.* vol. xxi. Berlin, 1908.
Kraft (August), ' Die Wapokomo ' ; in Steinmetz, *Rechtsverhältnisse von eingeborenen Völkern in Afrika und Ozeanien.* Berlin, 1903.
Krapf (J. L.), *Reisen in Ost-Afrika.* 2 vols. Kornthal & Stuttgart, 1858.
—— *Travels, Researches and Missionary Labours, during an Eighteen Years' Residence in Eastern Africa.* London, 1860.

Krasheninnikoff (S. P.), *The History of Kamschatka, and the Kurilski Islands, with the Countries adjacent.* Trans. by J. Grieve. London & Gloucester, 1764.

Kraus (F.) and Döhrer (H.), ' Blutsverwandtschaft in der Ehe und deren Folgen für die Nachkommenschaft '; in v. Noorden and Kaminer, *Krankheiten und Ehe.* Leipzig, 1916.

Krause (Fritz), ' Bericht über seine ethnographische Forschungsreise in Zentralbrasilien '; in *Zeitschr. f. Ethnol.* vol. xli. Berlin, 1909.

—— *In den Wildnissen Brasiliens.* Leipzig, 1911.

Krauss (F. S.), *Sitte und Brauch der Südslaven.* Wien, 1885.

—— Review of the German translation of the first edition of the present work, in *Am Urquell,* vol. iv. Lunden, 1893.

Krauss (Samuel), *Talmudische Archäologie.* 3 vols. Leipzig, 1910–12.

Kraut (W. Th.), *Die Vormundschaft nach den Grundsätzen des deutschen Rechts.* 3 vols. Göttingen, 1835–59.

Kreemer (J.), ' Die Loeboes in Mandailing '; in *Bijdragen tot de taal-, land- en volkenkunde van Nederlandsch-Indië,* vol. lxvi. 's-Gravenhage, 1911.

Krek (Gregor), *Einleitung in die slavische Literaturgeschichte.* Graz, 1887.

Kretzschmar (Eduard), *Südafrikanische Skizzen.* Leipzig, 1873.

Krichauff (F. E. H. W.), ' The Customs, Religious Ceremonies, &c., of the " Aldolinga " or " Mbenderinga " Tribe of Aborigines in Krichauff Ranges, South Australia '; in *Proceed. Roy. Geo. Soc. Australasia : South Australian Branch,* vol. ii. Session 1886–7. Adelaide, 1890.

—— ' Further Notes on the " Aldolinga," or " Mbenderinga " Tribe of Aborigines '; in *Proceed. Roy. Geo. Soc. Australasia : South Australian Branch,* vol. ii. Session 1886–7. Adelaide, 1890.

Krieger (Eduard), *Die Menstruation.* Berlin, 1869.

Krieger (Maximilian), *Neu-Guinea.* Berlin, [1899].

Kristensen (E. T.), *Gamle folks fortællinger om det jyske almueliv.* 6 parts. Kolding, 1891–94.—*Tillægsbind I—IV.* Århus, 1900.

Kroeber (A. L.), ' Classificatory Systems of Relationship '; in *Jour. Roy. Anthr. Inst.* vol. xxxix. London, 1909.

—— ' A Mission Record of the California Indians '; in *University of California Publications in American Archæology and Ethnology,* vol. viii. Berkeley, 1908.

—— ' Preliminary Sketch of the Mohave Indians '; in *American Anthropologist,* new ser. vol. iv. New York, 1902.

Kropf (A.), *Das Volk der Xosa-Kaffern im östlichen Südafrika.* Berlin, 1889.

Kropotkin (P.), *Mutual Aid.* London, 1902.

Kruijt (J. A.), *Atjeh en de Atjehers.* Leiden, 1877.

Krusenstern (A. J. von), *Voyage round the World in the Years 1803, 1804, 1805 & 1806.* 2 vols. Trans. London, 1813.

Kubary (J.), ' Die Bewohner der Mortlock Inseln '; in *Mittheilungen der Geographischen Gesellschaft in Hamburg,* 1878–79.

—— *Ethnographische Beiträge zur Kenntnis der Karolinischen Inselgruppe und Nachbarschaft. Heft I. : Die socialen Einrichtungen der Pelauer.* Berlin, 1885.

—— ' Die Palau-Inseln in der Südsee '; in *Journal des Museum Godeffroy,* pt. iv. Hamburg, 1873.

Kubary (J.), ' Die Religion der Pelauer ' ; in Bastian, *Allerlei aus Volks- und Menschenkunde*, vol. i. Berlin, 1888.

—— ' Die Verbrechen und das Strafverfahren auf den Pelau-Inseln ' ; in *Original-Mittheilungen aus der ethnologischen Abtheilung der königlichen Museen zu Berlin*, vol. i. Berlin, 1886.

Kuechler (L. W.), ' Marriage in Japan ' ; in *Trans. Asiatic Soc. Japan*, vol. xiii. Yokohama, 1885.

Kuhn (A.), *Märkische Sagen und Märchen nebst einem Anhange von Gebräuchen und Aberglauben*. Berlin, 1843.

—— und Schwartz (W.), *Norddeutsche Sagen, Märchen und Gebräuche*. Leipzig, 1848.

Kulischer (M.), ' Die communale " Zeitehe " und ihre Ueberreste ' ; in *Archiv f. Anthropologie*, vol. xi. Braunschweig, 1879.

—— ' Die geschlechtliche Zuchtwahl bei den Menschen in der Urzeit ' ; in *Zeitschr. f. Ethnol.* vol. viii. Berlin, 1876.

—— ' Intercommunale Ehe durch Raub und Kauf ' ; in *Zeitschr. f. Ethnol.* vol. x. Berlin, 1878.

Kultur der Gegenwart, ihre Entwickelung und ihre Ziele (Die). Ed. by P. Hinneberg. Berlin & Leipzig, 1905 &c. *In progress.*

Kumlien (L.), *Contributions to the Natural History of Arctic America*. (*Bulletin of the United States National Museum, No. 15.*) Washington, 1879.

Kupczanko (G.), ' Hochzeitsgebräuche der Weissrussen ' ; in *Am Urquell*, vol. ii. Lunden, 1891.

Laband (Paul), ' Die rechtliche Stellung der Frauen im altrömischen und germanischen Recht ' ; in *Zeitschr. für Völkerpsychologie und Sprachwissenschaft*, vol. iii. Berlin, 1865.

Labat (J. B.), *Relation historique de l'Éthiopie occidentale*. 5 vols. Paris, 1732.

Labbé (Paul), ' L'île de Sakhaline ' ; in *Bulletins de la Société de géographie commerciale de Paris*, vol. xxiii. Paris, 1901.

Labbe (Ph.), *Sacrorum Conciliorum collectio*. Ed. by J. D. Mansi. 31 vols. Florentiae, Venetiis, 1759–98.

Labillardière (J. J. Houtou de), *An Account of a Voyage in Search of La Pérouse in the Years 1791–1793.* Trans. 2 vols. London, 1800.

La Borde (— de), ' Relation de l'origine, moeurs, coustumes, religion, guerres et voyages des Caraibes, sauvages des isles Antilles de l'Amerique ' ; in *Recueil de divers voyages faits en Afrique et en l'Amerique*, ed. by H. Justel. Paris, 1674.

Laboulaye (Édouard), *Histoire du droit de propriété foncière en Occident*. Paris, 1839.

Lacassagne (A.), *Les tatouages*. Paris, 1881.

La Croix (J. Errington de), ' Étude sur les Sakaies de Perak ' ; in *Revue d'ethnographie*, vol. i. Paris, 1882.

Lactantius (L. C. F.), *Opera omnia*. 2 vols. (Migne, *Patrologiæ cursus*, vols. vi–vii.) Parisiis, 1844.

Ladbury (E. J.), ' Scraps of English Folklore, III. Worcestershire ' ; in *Folk-Lore*, vol. xx. London, 1909.

Laet (J. de), *Novus orbis seu descriptionis Indiæ Occidentalis libri XVIII.* Lugd. Batav., 1633.

Lafitau (J. F.), *Moeurs des sauvages ameriquains comparées aux moeurs des premiers temps*. 2 vols. Paris, 1724.

La Flesche (Francis), ' Osage Marriage Customs ' ; in *American Anthropologist*, new ser. vol. xiv. Lancaster, 1912.
—— See Fletcher (Alice C.) and La Flesche (Francis).
' Lag om äktenskaps inagende och upplösning av den 12 november 1915 ' ; in Stjernstedt, *Den nya äktenskapslagen.* Stockholm, 1916.
La Girondière (Paul Proust de). See Proust de la Girondière (Paul).
La Grasserie (Raoul de), *Code Civil Chilien.* (*Résumés analytiques des principaux codes civils de l'Europe et de l'Amérique, III.*) Paris, 1896.
—— *Code Civil du Vénézuéla. Lois civiles du Brésil.* (*Résumés &c. IV.–V.*) Paris, 1897.
—— *Code Civil Péruvien.* (*Résumés &c. II.*) Paris, 1896.
Lahontan (L. A. de Lom d'Arce, Baron de), *New Voyages to North-America.* Trans. ed. by R. G. Thwaites. 2 vols. Chicago, 1905.
Laing (A. Gordon), *Travels in the Timannee, Kooranko, and Soolima Countries in Western Africa.* London, 1825.
Laisnel de la Salle (—), *Croyances et légendes du centre de la France.* 2 vols. Paris, 1875.
Lala (R. Reyes). See Reyes Lala (R.).
Laloy (L.), ' Déformations des organes génitaux chez les Japonais ' ; in *L'Anthropologie*, vol. xiv. Paris, 1903.
Lambert (*le Père*), *Mœurs et Superstitions des Néo-Calédoniens.* Nouméa, 1900.
Lamont (E. H.), *Wild Life among the Pacific Islanders.* London, 1867.
Lamouroux (R.), ' La région du Toubouri. Notes sur les populations de la subdivision de Fianga ' ; in *L'Anthropologie*, vol. xxiv. Paris, 1913.
Landa (Diego de), *Relacion de las cosas de Yucatan.* Ed. with French translation by *l'Abbé* Brasseur de Bourbourg. Paris, 1864.
Landolphe (J. F.), *Mémoirs contenant l'histoire de ses voyages pendant trente-six ans, aux côtes d'Afrique et aux deux Amériques.* Ed. by J. S. Quesné. 2 vols. Paris, 1823.
Landon (Perceval), *Lhasa.* London, 1906.
Landor (A. H. Savage), *In the Forbidden Land.* 2 vols. London, 1898.
Landtman (Gunnar), *Kulturens ursprungsformer.* Helsingfors, 1918.
—— *Nya Guinea färden.* Helsingfors, 1913.
—— *The Origin of Priesthood.* Ekenaes (printed), 1905.
—— *Papuan Magic in the Building of Houses.* (*Acta Academiæ Aboensis. Humaniora*, vol. i. no. 5.) Åbo, 1920.
—— *The Primary Causes of Social Inequality.* (*Öfversigt af Finska Vetenskaps-Societetens Förhandlingar. LI.* 1908–1909. *Afd. B. N:o* 2.) Helsingfors, 1909.
Landwirthschaftliche Jahrbücher. Berlin.
Lane (E. W.), *An Account of the Manners and Customs of the Modern Egyptians.* 2 vols. London, 1849.
—— The same work. London, 1896.
—— *Arabian Society in the Middle Ages.* Ed. by Stanley Lane-Poole. London, 1883.
Lane-Poole (Stanley), Review of Bosworth Smith's *Mohammed and Mohammedanism*, in *The Academy*, vol. v. London, 1874.

Lang (Andrew), ' The Origin of Terms of Human Relationship ' ;
    in *Proceedings of the British Academy*, vol. iii. 1907–1908.
    London.
—— ' Quæstiones Totemicæ ' ; in *Man*, vol. vi.   London, 1906.
—— *The Secret of the Totem*.   London, 1905.
—— ' Theory of the Origin of Exogamy and Totemism ' ; in *Folk-
    Lore*, vol. xxiv.   London, 1913.
—— ' Totemism and Exogamy ' ; in *Folk-Lore*, vol. xxii.   London,
    1911.
—— and Atkinson (J. J.), *Social Origins and Primal Law*.   London,
    1903.
Lang (F. H.), ' Die Waschambala ' ;   in Steinmetz, *Rechtsverhält-
    nisse von eingeborenen Völkern in Afrika und Ozeanien*.
    Berlin, 1903.
Lang (Gideon S.), *The Aborigines of Australia*.   Melbourne, 1865.
Lang (J. D.), *Cooksland in North-Eastern Australia*.   London, 1847.
—— *Queensland*.   London, 1861.
Langsdorf (G. H. von), *Voyages and Travels in various Parts of the
    World, during the Years* 1803–1807.   2 vols.   London,
    1813–14.
Lansdell (Henry), *Through Siberia*.   2 vols.   London, 1882.
La Pérouse (J. F. G. de), *A Voyage round the World, in the Years*
    1785–88.   Trans. 3 vols.   London, 1799.
La Salle (R. R. de), ' An Account of Monsieur de la Salle's Last
    Expedition and Discoveries in North America ' ; in *Collections
    of the New-York Historical Society, for the Year* 1814, vol. ii.
    New-York, 1814.
Lasaulx (Ernst von), *Der Fluch bei Griechen und Römern*.   Würz-
    burg, 1843.
Lasch (Richard), ' Einige besondere Arten der Verwendung des Eies
    im Volksglauben und Volksbrauch ' ; in *Globus*, vol. lxxxix.
    Braunschweig, 1906.
—— ' Der Selbstmord aus erotischen Motiven bei den primitiven
    Völkern ' ; in *Zeitschr. f. Socialwissensch.* vol. ii.   Berlin,
    1899.
—— ' Über Sondersprachen und ihre Entstehung ' ; in *Mitteil.
    Anthrop. Gesellsch. Wien*, vol. xxxvii.   Wien, 1907.
Lassen (Christian), *Indische Alterthumskunde*.   2 vols.   Leipzig,
    Bonn, & London, 1867–74.
Last (J. T.), ' A Visit to the Masai People living beyond the Borders
    of the Nguru Country ' ; in *Proceed. Roy. Geo. Soc.* new ser.
    vol. v.   London, 1883.
Latcham (R. E.), ' Ethnology of the Araucanos ' ; in *Jour. Roy.
    Anthr. Inst.* vol. xxxix.   London, 1909.
Latimer (C.), *Census of India*, 1911. *Vol. XIII.   North-West
    Frontier Province*.   Peshawar, 1912.
Laufer (Berthold), ' Preliminary Notes on Explorations among the
    Amoor Tribes ' ; in *American Anthropologist*, new ser. vol. ii.
    New York, 1900.
' Law of the Northumbrian Priests ' ; in *Ancient Laws and Institutes
    of England*.   London, 1840.
Lawes (W. G.), ' Notes on New Guinea and its Inhabitants ' ; in
    Proceed. Roy. Geo. Soc. new ser. vol. ii.   London, 1880.
Lawrence (W.), *Lectures on Physiology, Zoology, and the Natural
    History of Man*.   London, 1823.

Laws of Manu (The). Trans. by G. Bühler. *(The Sacred Books of the East,* vol. xxv.) Oxford, 1886.
Lea (H. C.), *An Historical Sketch of Sacerdotal Celibacy in the Christian Church.* Boston, 1884.
Leabhar na h-Uidhri. See Mac Ceileachair (Moelmuiri).
Le Bon (Gustave), *La civilisation des Arabes.* Paris, 1884.
—— *L'homme et les sociétés.* 2 vols. Paris, 1881.
Lecky (W. E. H.), *Democracy and Liberty.* 2 vols. London, 1899.
—— *History of European Morals from Augustus to Charlemagne.* 2 vols. London, 1890.
Leden (Christian), ' Unter den Indianern Canadas ' ; in *Zeitschr. f. Ethnol.* vol. xliv. Berlin, 1912.
Lees (G. Robinson), *The Witness of the Wilderness.* London, 1909.
Leggatt (T. Watt), ' Malekula, New Hebrides ' ; in *Report of the Fourth Meeting of the Australasian Association for the Advancement of Science held at Hobart, Tasmania, in January,* 1892. Tasmania, 1893.
Leguével de Lacombe (B. F.), *Voyage à Madagascar et aux Iles Comores.* 2 vols. Paris, 1840.
Le Herissé (A.), *L'Ancien Royaume du Dahomey. Mœurs, Religion, Histoire.* Paris, 1911.
Lehmann (Carl), *Verlobung und Hochzeit nach den nordgermanischen Rechten des früheren Mittelalters.* München, 1882.
Lehmkuhl (Aug.), ' Divorce ' ; in *The Catholic Encyclopedia,* vol. v. New York, 1909.
Lehr (E.), *Le mariage, le divorce et la séparation de corps dans les principaux pays civilisés.* Paris, 1899.
Leinster, The Book of, sometime called The Book of Glendalough. A collection of pieces (prose and verse) in the Irish language, compiled in part about the middle of the twelfth century. Ed. by Robert Atkinson. Dublin, 1880.
Leist (B. W.), *Alt-arisches Jus Civile.* 2 vols. Jena, 1892–96.
—— *Alt-arisches Jus Gentium.* Jena, 1889.
—— *Græco-italische Rechtsgeschichte.* Jena, 1884,
Leitner (G. W.), *Results of a Tour in ' Dardistan, Kashmir, Little Tibet, Ladak, Zanskar, &c.'* Vol. i. pts. i–iii. Lahore & London, [1868–]73.
Lejeune (Ch.), in the Discussion on Maupetit's paper ' La pudeur ' ; in *Bull. et mém. Soc. d'Anthr. Paris,* ser. vi. vol. v. Paris, 1914.
Le Jeune (Paul), ' Relation de ce qui s'est passé en la Nouvelle France, en l'année 1635 ' ; in *The Jesuit Relations,* vols. vii.–viii. Cleveland, 1897.
Le Mesurier (C. J. R.), ' The Veddás of Ceylon ' ; in *Jour. Roy. Asiatic Soc. Ceylon Branch,* vol. ix. Colombo, 1887.
Leo Africanus, *The History and Description of Africa.* Trans. ed. by R. Brown. 3 vols. London, 1896.
Leong (Y. K.) and Tao (L. K.), *Village and Town Life in China.* London, 1915.
Le Page du Pratz (—), *The History of Louisiana, or of the Western Parts of Virginia and Carolina.* Trans. London, 1774.
Leroy-Beaulieu (Anatole), *The Empire of the Tsars and the Russians.* Trans. by Z. A. Ragozin. 3 vols. New York & London, 1893–96.

Lery (Jean de), ' Extracts out of the Historie of John Lerius.'
Trans. ; in Purchas, *Purchas his Pilgrimes*, vol. xvi. Glasgow,
1906.
—— *Histoire d'un voyage faict en la terre du Bresil.* [Paris ?] 1585.
Leslie (David), *Among the Zulus and Amatongas.* Edinburgh, 1875.
Leslie (John), *De origine moribus, et rebus gestis Scotorum libri decem.*
Romae, 1578.
Lesur (Charles Louis), *Histoire des Kosaques.* 2 vols. Paris, 1814.
Letherman (Jona.), ' Sketch of the Navajo Tribe of Indians, Territory
of New Mexico ' ; in *Smithsonian Report*, 1855. Washington,
1856.
Letourneau (Ch.), *L'évolution de la morale.* Paris, 1887.
—— *L'évolution du mariage et de la famille.* Paris, 1888.
—— *Sociology based upon Ethnography.* Trans. London, 1881.
Leuckart (Rud.), ' Zeugung ' ; in Rud. Wagner, *Handwörterbuch der
Physiologie*, vol. iv. Braunschweig, 1853.
Le Vaillant (François), *Travels from the Cape of Good-Hope, into the
Interior Parts of Africa.* Trans. 2 vols. London, 1790.
Levick (G. Murray), *Antarctic Penguins. A Study of their Social
Habits.* London, 1914.
Lewin (T. H.), *Wild Races of South-Eastern India.* London, 1870.
Lewis (C. J. and J. Norman), *Natality and Fecundity.* Edinburgh,
1905.
Lewis (Hubert), *The Ancient Laws of Wales.* London, 1889.
Lewis (J. P.), ' On the Terms of Relationship in Sinhalese and Tamil ' ;
in *The Orientalist*, vols. i.–ii. Kandy, Bombay, 1884–86.
Lewis (M.) and Clarke (W.), *Travels to the Source of the Missouri
River, and across the American Continent to the Pacific Ocean.*
London, 1814.
Ley sobre relaciones familiares. Ed. by E. Pallares. Paris &
México, 1917.
Lî Kî (The). Trans. by James Legge. 2 vols. (*The Sacred Books
of the East*, vols. xxvii.–xxviii.) Oxford, 1885.
' Liber Tobiæ ' ; in *Biblia sacra cum glossa interlineari, ordinaria*,
vol. ii. Venetiis, 1588.
Lichtenstein (H.), *Travels in Southern Africa.* Trans. 2 vols.
London, 1812–15.
Lichtschein (L.), *Die Ehe nach mosaisch-talmudischer Auffassung.*
Leipzig, 1879.
Liddell (H. C.) and Scott (R.), *Greek-English Lexicon.* Oxford, 1901.
Liebich (R.), *Die Zigeuner.* Leipzig, 1863.
Liebrecht (Felix), *Zur Volkskunde.* Heilbronn, 1879.
Lindblom (Gerhard), *The Akamba in British East Africa.* Uppsala,
1916.
Lindroos (A.) and Andersson (J.), ' Ett bröllop i Pellinge, Borgå
skärgård, för 100 år tillbaka'; in *Hembygden*, [vol. i.] Hel-
singfors, 1910.
Linschoten (J. H. van), *The Voyage of, to the East Indies.* Trans.
ed. by A. C. Burnell and P. A. Tiele. 2 vols. London, 1885.
Lippert (Julius), *Die Geschichte der Familie.* Stuttgart, 1884.
—— *Kulturgeschichte der Menschheit.* 2 vols. Stuttgart, 1886–87.
Lisiansky (U.), *A Voyage round the World.* London, 1814.
Lith (P. A. van der), Spaan (A. J.), Fokkens (F.), and Snelleman
(J. F.), *Encyclopædie van Nederlandsch-Indië.* 4 vols.
'sGravenhage & Leiden, [1895–1905].

Lithberg (Nils), ' Bröllopsseder på Gottland ' ; in *Fataburen*, 1906–
    1908, 1911. Stockholm.
Litterära Soiréer i Helsingfors under hösten 1849. Helsingfors, 1849.
Livingstone (David), *The Last Journals of, in Central Africa*. Ed.
    by H. Waller. 2 vols. London, 1874.
——— *Missionary Travels and Researches in South Africa*. London,
    1857.
——— and Livingstone (Charles), *Narrative of an Expedition to the
    Zambesi and its Tributaries*. London, 1865.
Livius (Titus), *Ab urbe condita libri*. Ed. by W. Weissenborn. 5
    vols. Lipsiae, 1858–63.
Lloyd (G. Thomas), *Thirty-three Years in Tasmania and Victoria*.
    London, 1862.
Lloyd (L.), *Peasant Life in Sweden*. London, 1870.
Lobo (Jerome), ' A Voyage to Abyssinia.' Trans. ; in Pinkerton,
    Collection of Voyages and Travels, vol. xv. London, 1814.
Lodi (P. Samuel de), ' Extrait d'une lettre au *P*. André d' Arezzo ' ;
    in *Annales de la propagation de la Foi*, vol. xvii. Lyon,
    1845.
Loebel (D. Th.), *Hochzeitsbräuche in der Türkei*. Amsterdam, 1897.
Loening (Edgar), *Geschichte des deutschen Kirchenrechts*. 2 vols.
    Strassburg, 1878.
Löw (Leopold), *Gesammelte Schriften*. 5 vols. Szegedin, 1889–
    1900.
Logan (J. R.), ' The Biduanda Kallang of the River Pulai in Johore ' ;
    in *Jour. Indian Archipelago*, vol. i. Singapore, 1847.
——— ' Five Days in Naning ' ; in *Jour. Indian Archipelago*, vol. iii.
    Singapore, 1849.
[———] ' The Manners and Customs of the Malays ' ; in *Jour. Indian
    Archipelago*, vol. iii. Singapore, 1849.
——— ' The Orang Binua of Johore ' ; in *Jour. Indian Archipelago*,
    vol. i. Singapore, 1847.
——— ' The Orang Muka Kuning ' ; in *Jour. Indian Archipelago*,
    vol. i. Singapore, 1847.
——— ' The Orang Sabimba of the Extremity of the Malay Peninsula ' ;
    in *Jour. Indian Archipelago*, vol. i. Singapore, 1847.
Logan (William), *Malabar*. 3 vols. Madras, 1887–91.
' Loi sur le divorce. 20 septembre 1792 ' ; in *Lois civiles* (*inter-
    médiaires*), *ou collection des lois rendues sur l'État des per-
    sonnes, et la transmission des biens, depuis le* 4 *août* 1789,
    jusques au 30 *ventose an* 12 (*mars* 1804), vol i. Ed. by J. B.
    S[irey] and G. S. L. 4 vols. Paris, 1806.
Lombroso (Cesare) and Ferrero (Guglielmo), *La donna delinquente,
    la prostituta e la donna normale*. Milano, Torino, & Roma,
    1915.
Long (John), *Voyages and Travels of an Indian Interpreter and
    Trader*. Ed. by R. G. Thwaites. (Thwaites, *Early Western
    Travels* 1748–1846, vol. ii.) Cleveland, 1904.
Loon (Gerard van), *Beschryving der aloude Regeeringwyze van
    Holland*. 5 vols. Leiden, 1744–50.
Lopez Cogolludo (Diego), *Historia de Yucathan*. Madrid, 1688.
Lopez de Castanheda (Fernão), *Historia do descobrimento e conqvista
    da India pelos Portugueses*. 7 vols. Lisboa, 1833.
Lord (J. K.), *The Naturalist in Vancouver Island and British
    Columbia*. 2 vols. London, 1866.

Loskiel (G. H.), *History of the Mission of the United Brethren among the Indians in North America.* Trans. 3 vols. London, 1794.
' Lov om adgang til opløsning av egteskap ' ; in *Almindelig norsk lovsamling, I. Supplementsbind,* 1908–1911. Ed. by P. I. Paulsen. Kristiania, 1912.
' Lov om forandringer i lov om adgang til opløsning av egteskap av 20 august 1909 ' ; in *Almindelig norsk lovsamling, II. Supplementsbind,* 1912–1915. Kristiania, 1916.
Lovisato (Domenico), ' Appunti etnografici con accenni geologici sulla Terra del Fuoco ' ; in *Cosmos,* ed. by Guido Cora, vol. viii. Torino, 1884–85.
Low (David), *On the Domesticated Animals of the British Islands.* London, 1845.
Low (Hugh), *Sarawak.* London, 1848.
Low (James), ' The Karean Tribes or Aborigines of Martaban and Tavai, with Notices of the Aborigines in Keddah and Perak ' ; in *Jour. Indian Archipelago,* vol. iv. Singapore, 1850.
Lowis (C. C.), *A Note on the Palaungs of Hsipaw and Tawnpeng. (Ethnographical Survey of India. Burma, No.* 1.) Rangoon, 1906.
Lowis (R. F.), *Census of India,* 1911. *Vol. II. The Andaman and Nicobar Islands.* Calcutta, 1912.
Loysel (Antoine), *Institutes coutumières.* Ed. by M. Dupin and Éd. Laboulaye. 2 vols. Paris, 1846.
Lozano (Pedro), *Descripcion chorographica del terreno . . . de las . . . Provincias del Gran Chaco, Gualamba.* Cordoba, 1733.
Lubbock (*Sir* John). See Avebury (*Lord*).
Lucian, *Opera.* Ed. by G. Dindorf. Parisiis, 1867.
Ludlow (J. M.), ' Consent to Marriage ' ; in Smith and Cheetham, *A Dictionary of Christian Antiquities,* vol. i. London, 1875.
Lumholtz (Carl), *Among Cannibals.* London, 1889.
—— *Unknown Mexico.* 2 vols. London, 1903.
Lynch (W. F.), *Narrative of the United States' Expedition to the River Jordan and the Dead Sea.* London, 1850.
Lyon (G. F.), *The Private Journal during the Voyage of Discovery under Captain Parry.* London, 1824.
Lysias, ' Orationes ' ; in *Oratores Attici,* ed. by C. Müller, vol. i. Parisiis, 1847.

Maass (Alfred), ' Durch Zentral-Sumatra ' ; in *Zeitschr. f. Ethnol.* vol. xli. Berlin, 1909.
MacCauley (Clay), ' The Seminole Indians of Florida ' ; in *Ann. Rep. Bur. Ethnol.* vol. v. Washington, 1887.
Mac Ceileachair (Moelmuiri), *Leabhar na h-Uidhri.* A Collection of pieces in prose and verse, in the Irish Language, compiled and transcribed about A.D. 1100, by. Dublin, 1870.
McCoy (Isaac), *History of Baptist Indian Missions : embracing Remarks on the former and present Condition of the Aboriginal Tribes.* Washington, 1840.
Macdonald (D.), *Oceania : Linguistic and Anthropological.* Melbourne & London, 1889.
Macdonald (Duff), *Africana.* 2 vols. London, 1882.
Macdonald (J. R. L.), ' Notes on the Ethnology of Tribes met with during Progress of the Juba Expedition of 1897–99 ' ; in *Jour. Anthr. Inst.* vol. xxix. London, 1899.

Macdonald (James), ' East Central African Customs ' ; in *Jour. Anthr. Inst.* vol. xxii. London, 1893.

Macdonell (A. A.), *Vedic Mythology.* (Bühler, *Grundriss der indoarischen Philologie und Altertumskunde,* vol. iii. fasc. i.) Strassburg, 1897.

—— and Keith (A. B.), *Vedic Index of Names and Subjects.* 2 vols. London, 1912.

Macfie (M.), *Vancouver Island and British Columbia.* London, 1865.

McGee (W. J.), ' The Seri Indians ' ; in *Ann. Rep. Bur. Ethnol.* vol. xvii. pt. i. Washington, 1898.

Macgillivray (John), *Narrative of the Voyage of H.M.S. " Rattlesnake."* 2 vols. London, 1852.

Máchal (J.), ' Marriage (Slavic) ' ; in Hastings, *Encyclopædia of Religion and Ethics,* vol. viii. Edinburgh, 1915.

Macieiowski (W. A.), *Slavische Rechtsgeschichte.* German trans. 4 vols. Stuttgart & Leipzig, 1835–39.

Mackenzie (Alex.), *Voyages from Montreal . . . to the Frozen and Pacific Oceans.* London, 1801.

Mackenzie (George), *The Lives and Characters of the most Eminent Writers of the Scots Nation.* 3 vols. Edinburgh, 1708–22.

Mackenzie (Thomas), *Studies in Roman Law.* Ed. by John Kirkpatrick. Edinburgh, 1886.

McKiernan (B.), ' Some Notes on the Aborigines of the Lower Hunter River, New South Wales ' ; in *Anthropos,* vol. vi. Wien, 1911.

Maclean (John), *A Compendium of Kafir Laws and Customs.* Mount Coke, 1858.

McLennan (J. F.), ' The Levirate and Polyandry ' ; in *The Fortnightly Review,* new ser. vol. xxi. London, 1877.

—— *The Patriarchal Theory.* London, 1885.

—— *Studies in Ancient History.* London, 1886.

—— *Studies in Ancient History. The Second Series. Comprising an Inquiry into the Origin of Exogamy.* Ed. by his widow and A. Platt. London, 1896.

MacMahon (A. R.), *Far Cathay and Farther India.* London, 1893.

McMahon (E. O.), ' The Sakalava and their Customs ' ; in *Antananarivo Annual and Madagascar Magazine,* vol. iv. Antananarivo, 1889–92.

Macmillan (D. A.), ' The Bhuiyas ' ; in *The Calcutta Review,* vol. ciii. Calcutta, 1896.

Macnaghten (W. H.), *Principles of Hindu Law.* Calcutta, 1880.

McNair (F.), *Perak and the Malays.* London, 1878.

Macphail (J. M.), ' The Cycle of the Seasons in a Santal Village ' ; in *The Calcutta Review,* new ser. vol. i. Calcutta, 1913.

Macpherson (John), *Critical Dissertations on the Origin, Antiquities, Language, Government, Manners, and Religion, of the Antient Caledonians, their Posterity the Picts, and the British and Irish Scots.* Dublin, 1768.

Macpherson (S. Ch.), *Memorials of Service in India.* London, 1865.

Macqueen (John), *A Practical Treatise on the Appellate Jurisdiction of the House of Lords and Privy Council. Together with the Practice on Parliamentary Divorce.* London, 1842.

Macrae (John), ' Account of the Kookies ' ; in *Asiatick Researches,* vol. vii. Calcutta, 1831.

Madras District Manuals. See Cox (A. F.), Nicholson (F. A.), Stuart (H. A.), Sturrock (J.).
Madras Government Museum's *Bulletins* (The). Madras.
Madras Journal of Literature and Science. New Series. Madras.
Magasin asiatique. Ed. by H. J. von Klaproth. Paris.
Magazine of American History (*The*). New York & Chicago.
Magnus (Olaus). See Olaus Magnus.
Magyar (L.), *Reisen in Süd-Afrika.* Pest & Leipzig, 1859.
Mahabharata (*The*). Translated into English prose by Protap Chandra Roy. Calcutta, 1883–96.
Maine (*Sir* Henry Sumner), *Ancient Law.* London, 1885.
—— *Dissertations on Early Law and Custom.* London, 1883.
—— *Lectures on the Early History of Institutions.* London, 1875.
Majerus (—), ' Brautwerbung und Hochzeit bei den Wabende (Deutsch-Ostafrika) ' ; in *Anthropos,* vol. vi. Wien, 1911.
Major (R. H.), *India in the Fifteenth Century,* trans. and ed. by. London, 1857.
Malabar Quarterly Review (*The*). Trivandrum.
Malcolm (J.), ' Essay on the Bhills ' ; in *Trans. Roy. Asiatic Soc.* vol. i. London, 1827.
Malinowski (Bronislaw), ' Baloma ; the Spirits of the Dead in the Trobriand Islands ' ; in *Jour. Roy. Anthr. Inst.* vol. xlvi. London, 1916.
—— *The Family among the Australian Aborigines.* London, 1913.
—— ' The Natives of Mailu ' ; in *Trans. Roy. Soc. South Australia,* vol. xxxix. Adelaide, 1915.
Mallat (J.), *Les Philippines.* 2 vols. Paris, 1846.
Mallery (Garrick), ' Picture-Writing of the American Indians ' ; in *Ann. Rep. Bur. Ethnol.* vol. x. 1888–'89. Washington, 1893.
Mallet (*Sir* Bernard), ' Vital Statistics as affected by the War ' ; in *Jour. Roy. Statistical Soc.* vol. lxxxi. London, 1918.
Malo (David), *Hawaiian Antiquities* (*Moolelo Hawaii*). Trans. from the Hawaiian by N. B. Emerson. Honolulu, 1903.
Man. A Monthly Record of Anthropological Science. London.
Man (E. G.), *Sonthalia and the Sonthals.* London, [1867].
Man (E. H.), ' A Brief Account of the Nicobar Islanders ' ; in *Jour. Anthr. Inst.* vol. xv. London, 1886.
—— ' On the Aboriginal Inhabitants of the Andaman Islands ' ; in *Jour. Anthr. Inst.* vol. xii. London, 1883.
Mandelslo (J. A. von), *Morgenländische Reise-Beschreibung.* Ed. by Adam Olearius. Hamburg, 1696.
—— ' The Remarks and Observations made by J. A. de Mandelsloe, in his Passage from the Kingdom of Persia through several Countries of the Indies ' ; in Harris, *Navigantium atque Itinerantium Bibliotheca,* vol. i. London, 1744.
Mandlik (Vishvanáth Náráyan). See Vishvanáth Náráyan Mandlik.
Mangeret (*le Père*), *Mgr Bataillon et les missions de l'Océanie Centrale.* 2 vols. Lyon, 1895.
Mangin (E.), ' Les Mossi. Essai sur les us et coutumes du peuple Mossi au Soudan Occidental ' ; in *Anthropos,* vol. ix. Wien, 1914.
Mannerheim (C. G. E.), *A Visit to the Sarö and Shera Yögurs.* (Reprinted from *Journal de la Société Finno-Ougrienne,* vol. xxvii.) Helsingfors, 1911.

Mannhardt (Wilhelm), *Mythologische Forschungen*. Ed. by H. Patzig. Strassburg & London, 1884.
—— *Wald- und Feldkulte*. 2 vols. Berlin, 1875–77.
Mantegazza (Paolo), *Rio de la Plata e Tenerife*. Milano, 1867.
Manu, The Laws of. See *Laws of Manu (The)*.
Marcellinus (Ammianus), *Rerum gestarum libri qui supersunt*. Ed. by V. Gardthausen. 2 vols. Lipsiae, 1874–75.
Marche (Alfred), *Trois voyages dans l'Afrique Occidentale*. Paris, 1879.
Marchesi (G. B.), ' In Capitanata ' ; in *Archivio per lo studio delle tradizioni popolari*, vol. xx. Palermo & Torino, 1901.
—— ' In Valtellina ' ; in *Archivio per lo studio delle tradizioni popolari*, vol. xvii. Palermo & Torino, 1898.
Marcuse (Adolf), *Die Hawaiischen Inseln*. Berlin, 1894.
Margolis (M. L.), ' Celibacy ' ; in *The Jewish Encyclopedia*, vol. iii. New York & London, *s.d.*
Mariner (William), *An Account of the Natives of the Tonga Islands compiled . . . from the Communications of*, by John Martin. 2 vols. London, 1817.
Markham (A. H.), ' A Visit to the Galapagos Islands in 1880 ' in *Proceed. Roy. Geo. Soc.* new ser. vol. ii. London, 1880.
Marmol Caravajal (Luis del), *La descripcion general de Affrica*. 3 vols. Granada & Malaga, 1573–99.
Marquardsen (H. von), *Handbuch des Oeffentlichen Rechts der Gegenwart in Monographien*. Ed. by, [and others]. Freiburg i.B. & Tübingen, 1887 &c. *In progress*.
Marquardt (Carl), *Die Tätowirung beider Geschlechter in Samoa*. Berlin, 1899.
Marquardt (J.), *Das Privatleben der Römer*. Vol. I. Ed. by A. Mau. Leipzig, 1886.
Marques (A.), ' The Population of the Hawaiian Islands ' ; in *Jour. Polynesian Soc.* vol. ii. Wellington, 1893.
Marquordt (F.), ' Bericht über die Kavirondo ' ; in *Zeitschr. f. Ethnol.* vol. xli. Berlin, 1909.
Marsden (W.), *The History of Sumatra*. London, 1811.
Marshall (F. H. A.), *The Physiology of Reproduction*. London, 1910.
Marshall (W. E.), *A Phrenologist amongst the Todas*. London, 1873.
Marston (Morrell), ' Letter to Reverend Dr. Jedidiah Morse ' ; in Emma Helen Blair, *The Indian Tribes of the Upper Mississippi Valley and Region of the Great Lakes*, vol. ii. Cleveland, 1912.
Martène (Edmond), *De antiquis ecclesiæ ritibus*. 3 vols. Antuerpiae, 1736–37.
Martin (K.), *Reisen in den Molukken, in Ambon, den Uliassern, Seran (Ceram) und Buru*. Leiden, 1894.
Martin (Minnie), *Basutoland : its Legends and Customs*. London, 1903.
Martin (Rudolf), *Die Inlandstämme der Malayischen Halbinsel*. Jena, 1905.
Martineau (James), *Types of Ethical Theory*. 2 vols. Oxford, 1889.
Martinengo-Cesaresco (*Countess* Evelyn), ' American Songs and Games' ; in *Folk-Lore Journal*, vol. ii. London, 1884.
Martius (C. F. Ph. von), *Beiträge zur Ethnographie und Sprachenkunde Amerika's zumal Brasiliens*. 2 vols. Leipzig, 1867.
—— See Spix (J. B. von) and Martius (C. F. Ph. von).

Martrou (*P.* Louis), ' Les " Eki " des Fang ' ; in *Anthropos*, vol. i. Salzburg, 1906.
Marx (L.), ' Die Amahlubi' ; in Steinmetz, *Rechtsverhältnisse von eingeborenen Völkern in Afrika und Ozeanien.* Berlin, 1903.
[Mas (S. de),] *Informe sobre el estado de las Islas Filipinas en* 1842. 2 vols. Madrid, 1843.
Mason (F.), ' On Dwellings, Works of Art, Laws, &c. of the Karens ' ; in *Jour. Asiatic Soc. Bengal*, vol. xxxvii. pt. ii. Calcutta, 1868.
—— ' Physical Character of the Karens ' ; in *Jour. Asiatic Soc. Bengal*, vol. xxxv. pt. ii. Calcutta, 1867.
Mason (J. Alden), *The Ethnology of the Salinan Indians.* (*University of California Publications in American Archæology and Ethnology*, vol. x. no. 4.) Berkeley, 1912.
Masson (Charles), *Narrative of various Journeys in Balochistan, Afghanistan, and the Panjab.* 3 vols. London, 1842.
Massoudi, ' Description du Caucase.' Trans. ; in Klaproth, *Magasin asiatique*, vol. i. Paris, 1825.
Mathew (John), ' The Australian Aborigines ' ; in *Jour. and Proceed. Roy. Soc. New South Wales.* vol. xxiii. London & Sydney, 1889.
—— *Eaglehawk and Crow.* London & Melbourne, 1899.
—— ' The Origin of the Australian Phratries and Explanations of some of the Phratry Names ' ; in *Jour. Roy. Anthr. Inst.* vol. xl. London, 1910.
—— *Two Representative Tribes of Queensland.* London, 1910.
Mathews (R. H.), ' Beiträge zur Ethnographie der Australier ' ; in *Mitteil. Anthrop. Gesellsch. Wien*, vol. xxxvii. Wien, 1907.
—— *Ethnological Notes on the Aboriginal Tribes of N.S. Wales and Victoria.* Sydney, 1905.
Matin-uz-Zaman Khan (Md), *Census of India*, 1911. *Vol. XX. Kashmir*, pt. i. Report. Lucknow, 1912.
Mattans (J.), ' Bröllopsseder i Korsnäs ' ; in *Hembygden*, vol. vi. Helsingfors, 1915.
Matthes (B. F.), *Bijdragen tot de Ethnologie van Zuid-Celebes.* 's Gravenhage, 1875.
Matthews (John), *A Voyage to the River Sierra-Leone, on the Coast of Africa.* London, 1788.
Matthews (Washington), *Ethnography and Philology of the Hidatsa Indians.* (*U.S. Geological and Geographical Survey, Miscellaneous Publications*, no. 7.) Washington, 1877.
—— ' The Gentile System of the Navajo Indians ' ; in *Jour. American Folk-Lore*, vol. iii. Boston & New York, 1890.
—— *Navaho Legends.* (*Memoirs of the American Folk-Lore Society*, vol. v.) Boston & New York, 1897.
Mauch (Carl), *Reisen im Inneren von Süd-Afrika* 1865–1872. (Petermann's *Mittheilungen, Ergänzungsheft No.* 37.) Gotha, 1874.
Maundeville (*Sir* John), *The Voiage and Travaile of Sir J. M.* Reprinted from the Edition of A.D. 1725. With an Introduction, &c. by J. O. Halliwell. London, 1839.
Maung Tet Pyo, *Customary Law of the Chin Tribe.* Text, Translation, and Notes, with a Preface by John Jardine. Rangoon, 1884.
Maupetit (G.), ' La pudeur ' ; in *Bull. et mém. Soc. d'Anthr. Paris*, ser. vi. vol. v. Paris, 1914.

Maurer (G. L. von), *Geschichte der Dorfverfassung in Deutschland*. 2 vols. Erlangen, 1865–66.

[Maxwell,] ' The Semang and Sakei Tribes of the Districts of Kedah and Perak bordering on Province Wellesley ' ; in *Jour. Straits Branch Roy. Asiatic Soc.* no. i. Singapore, 1878.

Maya Das, ' Marriage Custom, &c.' ; in *Panjab Notes and Queries*, vol. i. Allahabad, 1883.

Mayer (J. R.), *Die Mechanik der Wärme*. Stuttgart, 1874.

Mayer (Samuel), *Die Rechte der Israeliten, Athener und Römer*. 2 vols. Leipzig, 1862–66.

Mayet (P.), ' Die Verwandtenehe und die Statistik ' ; in *Jahrbuch der internationalen Vereinigung für vergleichende Rechtswissenschaft und Volkswirtschaftslehre zu Berlin*, vols. vi.–vii. Berlin, 1903–04.

Mayne (J. D.), *A Treatise on Hindu Law and Usage*. Madras, 1914.

Mayne (R. C.), *Four Years in British Columbia and Vancouver Island*. London, 1862.

Mayo-Smith (Richmond), *Science of Statistics*. 2 vols. New York, 1895–99.

Mayr (Aurel), *Das indische Erbrecht*. Wien, 1873.

Mayr (Georg von), *Bevölkerungsstatistik*. (*Handbuch des Oeffentlichen Rechts der Gegenwart*, ed. by H. von Marquardsen and others. *Einleitungsband* [ed. by M. von Seydel], *Sechste Abtheilung*.) Freiburg i.B., 1897.

—— *Die Gesetzmässigkeit im Gesellschaftsleben*. München, 1877.

Meade (Herbert), *A Ride through the disturbed Districts of New Zealand ; together with some Account of the South Sea Islands*. London, 1870.

Meares (John), *Voyages made in the Years 1788 and 1789 from China to the North-West Coast of America*, London, 1790.

Meddelelser om Grönland. Kjøbenhavn.

Mededeelingen van wege het Nederlandsche Zendelinggenootschap. Rotterdam.

Medhurst (W. H.), ' Marriage, Affinity, and Inheritance in China ' ; in *Trans. Roy. Asiatic Soc. China Branch*, vol. iv. Hongkong, 1855.

Meier (M. H. E.) and Schömann (G. F.), *Der attische Process*. Ed. by J. H. Lipsius. Berlin, 1883–87.

Meiners (C.), *Allgemeine kritische Geschichte der Religionen*. 2 vols. Hannover, 1806–07.

—— *Vergleichung des ältern, und neuern Russlandes*. 2 vols. Leipzig, 1798.

Meinicke (C. E.), *Die Inseln des Stillen Oceans*. 2 vols. Leipzig, 1875–76.

Meissner (B.), *Beiträge zum altbabylonischen Privatrecht*. Leipzig, 1893.

Mela (Pomponius), *De chorographia* (*situ orbis*) *libri tres*. Ed. by C. Frick. Lipsiae, 1880.

Mélanges tirés du bulletin historico-philologique de l'Académie impériale des sciences de St.-Pétersbourg. St.-Pétersbourg.

Meletius (J.), *De religione et sacrificiis veterum Borussorum, epistola*. S.l., 1582.

Melnikow (N.), ' Die Burjäten (Burjaten) des Irkutskischen Gouvernements ' ; in *Verhandl. Berliner Gesellsch. Anthr.* 1899. Berlin.

Mélusine. Revue de mythologie, littérature populaire, traditions et usages. Ed. by H. Gaidoz. Paris.

Melville (H.), *Typee.* London, [1892].

Mémoires de la Société d'Anthropologie de Paris.

Memoirs of the American Anthropological Association. Lancaster.

—— *of the American Folk-Lore Society.* Boston & New York.

—— *of the American Museum of Natural History.* New York.

——*of the Asiatic Society of Bengal.* Calcutta.

—— *read before the Anthropological Society of London.*

'Memoirs of Malays'; in *Jour. Indian Archipelago,* vol. ii. Singapore, 1848.

Memorie della Società Geographica Italiana. Roma.

Mendiarov (——). See Volkov (Th.).

Menouillard (——), 'Un Mariage dans le Sud Tunisien (Matmata)'; in *Revue tunisienne,* vol. ix. Tunis, 1902.

Méray (Antony), *La vie au temps des Trouvères.* Paris & Lyon, 1873.

Merker (M.), *Die Masai.* Berlin, 1904.

Merolla da Sorrento (Jerome), 'A Voyage to Congo and several other Countries.' Trans.; in Pinkerton, *Collection of Voyages and Travels,* vol. xvi. London, 1814.

Methodius (*Saint*), 'Opera omnia'; in Migne, *Patrologiæ cursus,* Ser. Graeca, vol. xviii. Parisiis, 1857.

Metz (F.), *The Tribes inhabiting the Neilgherry Hills.* Mangalore, 1864.

Meyer (A. B.), *Die Philippinen. II. Negritos.* (*Königliches Ethnographisches Museum zu Dresden, IX.*) Dresden, 1893.

Meyer (E. H.), *Badisches Volksleben im neunzehnten Jahrhundert.* Strassburg, 1900.

—— *Deutsche Volkskunde.* Strassburg, 1898.

Meyer (H. E. A.), 'Manners and Customs of the Aborigines of the Encounter Bay Tribe'; in Woods, *Native Tribes of South Australia.* Adelaide, 1879.

Meyer (Hans), 'Die Igorrotes von Luzon (Philippinen)'; in *Verhandl. Berliner Gesellsch. Anthr.* 1883. Berlin.

Meyer (Paul), *Der römische Konkubinat nach den Rechtsquellen und den Inschriften.* Leipzig, 1895.

Michaelis (J. D.), *Commentaries on the Laws of Moses.* Trans. 4 vols. London, 1814.

Michaux-Bellaire (E.), 'Quelques tribus de montagnes de la région du Habt'; in *Archives marocaines,* vol. xvii. Paris, 1911.

Mielziner (M.), *The Jewish Law of Marriage and Divorce in Ancient and Modern Times.* Cincinnati, 1884.

Migne (J. P.), *Patrologiæ cursus completus.* 221 vols. Parisiis, 1844–64.

—— *Patrologiæ cursus completus. Series Græca.* 162 vols. Parisiis, 1857–66.

Miklucho-Maclay (N. von), 'Anthropologische Bemerkungen über die Papuas der Maclay-Küste in Neu-Guinea'; in *Natuurkundig Tijdschrift voor Nederlandsch Indie,* vol. xxxiii. Batavia, 1873.

—— 'Ethnological Excursions in the Malay Peninsula'; in *Jour. Straits Branch Roy. Asiatic Soc.* 1878, no. 2. Singapore.

—— 'Ethnologische Bemerkungen über die Papuas der Maclay-Küste in Neu-Guinea'; in *Natuurkundig Tijdschrift voor Nederlandsch Indie,* vols. xxxv.–xxxvi. Batavia, 1875–76.

Miklucho-Maclay (N. von), ' Ueber die künstliche Perforatio Penis bei den Dajaks auf Borneo ' ; in *Verhandl. Berliner Gesellsch. Anthr.* 1876. Berlin.
—— ' Über die Mika-Operation in Central-Australien ' ; in *Verhandl. Berliner Gesellsch. Anthr.* 1880. Berlin.
Miler (E.), ' Die Hauskommunion der Südslaven ' ; in *Jahrbuch der internationalen Vereinigung für vergleichende Rechtswissenschaft und Volkswirtschaftslehre zu Berlin*, vol. iii. Berlin, 1897.
Milliot (L.), *La Femme musulmane au Maghreb.* Paris, 1910.
Milman (H. H.), *History of Latin Christianity.* 9 vols. London, 1867.
Mindeleff (Cosmos), ' Localization of Tusayan Clans ' ; in *Ann. Rep. Bur. Ethnol.* vol. xix. Washington, 1900.
Mireur (H.), *La prostitution à Marseille.* Paris & Marseille, 1882.
Missions Catholiques (Les). Lyon.
Mitchell (Arthur), ' Blood-Relationship in Marriage considered in its Influence upon the Offspring '; in *Memoirs Anthr. Soc. London*, vol. ii. London, 1866.
Mitchell (T. L.), *Three Expeditions into the Interior of Eastern Australia.* 2 vols. London, 1839.
Mitt(h)eilungen aus dem embryologischen Institute der K.K. Universität in Wien.
—— *aus den Deutschen Schutzgebieten.* Berlin.
—— *der Anthropologischen Gesellschaft in Wien.*
—— *der Geographischen Gesellschaft (für Thüringen) zu Jena.*
—— *der Geographischen Gesellschaft in Hamburg.*
—— *der Schlesischen Gesellschaft für Volkskunde.* Ed. by Th. Siebs. Breslau.
—— *der Vorderasiatischen Gesellschaft.* Berlin.
—— *des Seminars für orientalische Sprachen an der Königl. Friedrich Wilhelms-Universität zu Berlin.* Berlin & Stuttgart.
—— *des Vereins für Erdkunde zu Leipzig.*
Mitteis (Ludwig), *Reichsrecht und Volksrecht in den östlichen Provinzen des römischen Kaiserreichs.* Leipzig, 1891.
Mittermaier (C. J. A.), *Grundsätze des gemeinen deutschen Privatrechts.* 2 vols. Regensburg, 1847.
Mockler-Ferryman (A. F.), *British Nigeria.* London, 1902.
Mocquet (John), *Travels and Voyages into Africa, Asia, and America, the East and West-Indies ; Syria, Jerusalem, and the Holy-Land.* Trans. London, 1696.
Modigliani (Elio), *Un viaggio a Nías.* Milano, 1890.
Moegling (H.), *Coorg Memoirs ; an Account of Coorg, and of the Coorg Mission.* Bangalore, 1855.
Mökern (Ph. van), *Ostindien.* 2 vols. Leipzig, 1857.
Moerenhout (J. A.), *Voyages aux îles du Grand Océan.* 2 vols. Paris, 1837.
Moffat (Robert), *Missionary Labours and Scenes in Southern Africa.* London, 1842.
Moffet (Thomas), *Health's Improvement.* London, 1745.
Mohnike (O.), ' Die Affen auf den indischen Inseln ' ; in *Das Ausland*, vol. xlv. Augsburg, 1872.
Molina (J. J.), *The Geographical, Natural, and Civil History of Chili.* Trans. 2 vols. London, 1809.
Möller (P.), Pagels (G.), and Gleerup (E.), *Tre år i Kongo.* 2 vols. Stockholm, 1887–88.

Moloni (J. Ch.), *Census of India*, 1911. *Vol. XII. Madras*, pt. i. Report. Madras, 1912.

Mommsen (Theodor), *The History of Rome*. Trans. by W. P. Dickson. 5 vols. London, 1908.

—— *Römische Forschungen*. 2 vols. Berlin, 1864–79.

—— *Römisches Strafrecht*. Leipzig, 1899.

Monatsschrift für Geburtskunde und Frauenkrankheiten. Berlin.

Moncelon (Léon), ' Réponse alinéa par alinéa, pour les Néo-Calédoniens, au Questionnaire de sociologie et d'ethnographie de la Société '; in *Bull. Soc. d'Anthr. Paris*, ser. iii. vol. ix. Paris, 1886.

Mondières (*Dr.*), ' Renseignements ethnographiques sur la Cochinchine '; in *Bull. Soc. d'Anthr. Paris*, ser. ii. vol. x. Paris, 1875.

Monier-Williams (Monier), *Brāhmanism and Hindūism*. London, 1887.

—— *Buddhism*. London, 1890.

—— *Indian Wisdom*. London, 1893.

Monrad (H. C.), *Bidrag til en Skildring af Guinea-Kysten og dens Indbyggere*. Kjøbenhavn, 1822.

Montagu (*Lady* Mary Wortley), *The Letters and Works of*. 2 vols. London, 1861.

Montaigne (Michel de), *The Essays of*. Trans. by Charles Cotton. 3 vols. London, 1905.

Montano (J.), *Voyage aux Philippines et en Malaisie*. Paris, 1886.

Montefiore (C. G.), *Hibbert Lectures on . . . the Religion of the Ancient Hebrews*. London, 1892.

Monteiro (J. J.), *Angola and the River Congo*. 2 vols. London, 1875.

Montesquieu (Charles de Secondat de), *De l'esprit des loix*. 3 vols. Genève, 1753.

Montgomery (J. A.), *The Samaritans*. Philadelphia, 1907.

Montgomery (James), *Journal of Voyages and Travels by the Rev. Daniel Tyerman and George Bennet*. 2 vols. London, 1831.

Monumenta Historica Britannica, or Materials for the History of Britain. Vol. I. Ed. by Henry Petrie assisted by John Sharpe. London, 1848.

Mooney (James), ' The Cheyenne Indians '; in *Memoirs of the American Anthropological Association*, vol. i. Lancaster, 1905–07.

Moorcroft (William) and Trebeck (George), *Travels in the Himalayan Provinces of Hindustan and the Panjab*. Ed. by H. H. Wilson. 2 vols. London, 1841.

Moore (Lewis), *Malabar Law and Custom*. Madras, 1905.

Moore (Theofilus), *Marriage Customs, Modes of Courtship, and Singular Propensities of the various Nations of the Universe*. London, 1814.

Morelet (A.), *Reisen in Central-Amerika*. German trans. Jena, 1872.

Morga (Antonio de), *The Philippine Islands, Moluccas, Siam, Cambodia, Japan, and China, at the close of the Sixteenth Century*. Trans. by H. E. J. Stanley. London, 1868.

Morgan (C. Lloyd), *Animal Behaviour*. London, 1900.

Morgan (H. D.), *The Doctrine and Law of Marriage, Adultery, and Divorce*. 2 vols. Oxford, 1826.

Morgan (J. de), ' Mœurs, coutumes et langages des Négritos de l'intérieur de la presqu'île Malaise ' ; in *Société normande de Géographie, Bulletin de l'année* 1885, vol. vii. Rouen, 1885.
—— ' Négritos de la presqu'île Malaise ' ; in *L'homme*, vol. ii. Paris, 1885.
Morgan (L. H.), *Ancient Society.* London, 1877.
—— *League of the Ho-de'-no-sau-nee, or Iroquois.* Rochester, 1851.
—— *Systems of Consanguinity and Affinity of the Human Family.* (*Smithsonian Contributions to Knowledge*, vol. xvii.) Washington, 1871.
Morgan (T. H.), *Experimental Zoölogy.* New York, 1907.
Morice (*Father* A. G.), ' The Great Déné Race ' ; in *Anthropos*, vols. i.–ii. Salzburg, 1906–07.
—— ' Notes Archæological, Industrial and Sociological on the Western Dénés ' ; in *Transactions of the Canadian Institute*, vol. iv. 1892–93. Toronto, 1895.
Mornand (F.), *La Vie arabe.* Paris, 1856.
Mortimer (Geoffrey), *Chapters on Human Love.* London, 1898.
Mortimer-Ternaux (Louis), *Histoire de la Terreur* 1792–1794. 8 vols. Paris, 1862–1881.
Moseley (H. N.), *Notes by a Naturalist on the " Challenger."* London, 1879.
' On the Inhabitants of the Admiralty Islands, &c.' ; in *Jour. Anthr. Inst.* vol. vi. London, 1877.
Moszkowski (Max), *Auf neuen Wegen durch Sumatra.* Berlin, 1909.
—— ' Die Völkerstämme am Mamberamo in Holländisch-Neuguinea und auf den vorgelagerten Inseln ' ; in *Zeitschr. f. Ethnol.* vol. xliii. Berlin, 1911.
—— ' Über zwei nicht-malayische Stämme von Ost-Sumatra ' ; in *Zeitschr. f. Ethnol.* vol. xl. Berlin, 1908.
Mouhot (H.), *Travels in the Central Parts of Indo-China.* 2 vols. London, 1864.
Mouliéras (A.), *Le Maroc inconnu.* 2 vols. Oran, 1895–99.
—— *Une Tribu Zénète anti-musulmane au Maroc (les Zkara).* Paris, 1905.
Moulton (J. H.), *Early Zoroastrianism.* London, 1913.
Moy (E. von), *Das Eherecht der Christen in der morgenländischen und abendländischen Kirche bis zur Zeit Karls des Grossen.* Regensburg, 1833.
Mozo (Antonio), *Noticia histórico natural de los gloriosos triumphos . . . . por los religiosos del orden de N. P. S. Agustin en las missiones que tienen à su cargo en las Islas Philipinas, y en el grande Imperio de la China.* Madrid, 1763.
Mülinen (E. von), ' Beiträge zur Kenntnis des Karmels ' ; in *Zeitschr. des Deutschen Palästina-Vereins*, vol. xxx. Leipzig, 1907.
Müller (C.). See *Fragmenta Historicorum Græcorum ; Geographi Græci minores ;* and *Oratores Attici.*
Müller (C. O.), *Dissertations on the Eumenides of Æschylus.* Trans. London & Cambridge, 1853.
—— *The History and Antiquities of the Doric Race.* Trans. 2 vols. London, 1830.
Müller (Friedrich), *Allgemeine Ethnographie.* Wien, 1879.
Müller (Friedrich Max), *Chips from a German Workshop.* 4 vols. London, 1867–75.

Müller (Herbert), *Untersuchungen über die Geschichte der poly-andrischen Eheformen in Südindien.* Berlin, 1909.
Müller (*Custos* Hermann), *Am Neste.* Berlin, [1881].
Müller (*Oberlehrer* Hermann), *The Fertilisation of Flowers.* Trans. London, 1883.
Müller (Josef), *Das sexuelle Leben der alten Kulturvölker.* Leipzig, 1902.
—— *Das sexuelle Leben der christlichen Kulturvölker.* Leipzig, 1904.
Müller (Otto), ' Untersuchungen zur Geschichte des attischen Bürger-und Eherechts ' ; in *Jahrbücher für classische Philologie. XXV. Supplementsband.* Leipzig, 1899.
Müller (R.).   See Hirsch (E.).
Müller (W.), ' Über die Wildenstämme der Insel Formosa ' ; in *Zeitschr. f. Ethnol.* vol. xlii. Berlin, 1910.
Müller (W. Max), *Die Liebespoesie der alten Ägypter.* Leipzig, 1899.
Müller-Lyer (F.), *Die Familie.* München, 1912.
Muḥammad, *The Sayings of.* See Abdullah al-Māmūn al-Suhrawardy.
Muḥammad ibn 'Umar, Al-Tūnusī, *Travels of an Arab Merchant in Soudan.* Abridged from the French by Bayle Saint John. London, 1854.
Muir (John), ' On the Lax Observance of Caste Rules, and other Features of Social and Religious Life, in Ancient India ' ; in *The Indian Antiquary,* vol. vi.   Bombay, 1877.
—— *Original Sanskrit Texts.* 5 vols. London, 1868–84.
Mundt (Theodor), *Pariser Kaiser-Skizzen.* 2 vols. Berlin, 1857.
Munshi, ' Iron, &c. ' ; in *Panjab Notes and Queries,* vol. i.   Allahabad, 1883.
Munzinger (W.), *Ostafrikanische Studien.* Schaffhausen, 1864.
—— *Ueber die Sitten und das Recht der Bogos.* Winterthur, 1859.
Murdoch (John), ' Ethnological Results of the Point Barrow Ex-pedition ' ; in *Ann. Rep. Bur. Ethnol.* vol. ix. Washington, 1892.
Murray (Gilbert), *The Rise of the Greek Epic.* Oxford, 1911.
Murray (James A. H.), *A New English Dictionary on Historical Principles.* Ed. by. Oxford, 1884 &c.   *In progress.*
Murray's (John) *Handbook for Travellers in Durham and Northum-berland.* London, 1890.
Murray (Margaret), ' Royal Marriages and Matrilineal Descent ' ; in *Jour. Roy. Anthr. Inst.* vol. xlv. London, 1915.
Musters (G. C.), *At Home with the Patagonians.* London, 1873.
—— ' On the Races of Patagonia ' ; in *Jour. Anthr. Inst.* vol. i. London, 1872.
Mygge (Johannes), *Om Aegteskaber mellem Blodbeslaegtede.* Kjøben-havn, 1879.

Nachrichten über Kaiser Wilhelms-Land und den Bismarck-Archipel. Berlin.
—— *von der Königlichen Gesellschaft der Wissenschaften und der Georg-Augusts-Universität zu Göttingen.*
Nachtigal (G.), *Sahara und Sudan.* 3 vols. Berlin, 1879–89.
Nagam Aiya (V.), *The Travancore State Manual.* 3 vols. Trivan-drum, 1906.
Nakajima (T.), ' Marriage (Japanese and Korean) ' ; in Hastings, *Encyclopædia of Religion and Ethics,* vol. viii. Edinburgh, 1915.

Nalimov (Vasilij), *Zur Frage nach den ursprünglichen Beziehungen der Geschlechter bei den Syrjänen*. (*Suomalais-Ugrilaisen Seuran Aikauskirja—Journal de la Société Finno-ougrienne*, vol. xxv.) Helsingfors, 1908.

Nanjundayya (H. V.), *The Ethnographical Survey of Mysore*. Preliminary issue. Bangalore, 1906 &c.

Nansen (Fridtjof), *Eskimo Life*. Trans. London, 1893.

—— *The First Crossing of Greenland*. Trans. 2 vols. London, 1890.

Napier (James), *Folk Lore : or, Superstitious Beliefs in the West of Scotland within this Century*. Paisley, 1879.

' Nârada,' trans. by J. Jolly ; in *The Sacred Books of the East*, vol. xxxiii. Oxford, 1889.

Narratives of the Rites and Laws of the Yncas. Trans. and ed. by C. R. Markham. London, 1873.

Nassau (R. H.), *Fetichism in West Africa*. London, 1904.

Natesa Sastri (S. M.), *Hindu Feasts Fasts and Ceremonies*. Madras, 1903.

Nation (The) : a Weekly Journal. New York.

Native Races of the British Empire (The). [Ed. by N. W. Thomas.] London, 1906 &c. *In progress*.

Nature : a Weekly Illustrated Journal of Science. London & New York.

Natuurkundig Tijdschrift voor Nederlandsch Indie. Batavia.

Nauhaus (C. T.), ' Familienleben, Heiralhsgebräuche und Erbrecht der Kaffern ' ; in *Verhandl. Berliner Gesellsch. Anthr.* 1882. Berlin.

Naumann (W.), *Untersuchungen über den apokryphen Jeremiasbrief*. (*Beihefte zur Zeitschrift für die alttestamentliche Wissenschaft, XXV.*) Giessen, 1913.

Navarette (M. F.), ' An Account of the Empire of China.' Trans. ; in Churchill, *Collection of Voyages and Travels*, vol. i. London, 1704.

Nayar (K. Kannan), ' The Matrimonial Customs ot the Nayars ' ; in *The Malabar Quarterly Review*, vol. vii. Trivandrum, 1908.

Neander (Joseph), *General History of the Christian Religion and Church*. Trans. 9 vols. Edinburgh, 1847–55.

' Negersitten ' ; in *Das Ausland*, vol. liv. Stuttgart, 1881.

Nelson (E. W.), ' The Eskimo about Bering Strait ' ; in *Ann. Rep. Bur. Ethnol.* vol. xviii. Washington, 1899.

Nelson (J. H.), *The Madura Country*. 5 parts. Madras, 1868.

—— *A View of the Hindū Law as administered by the High Court of Judicature at Madras*. Madras, Calcutta, & Bombay, 1877.

Nesfield (John C.), *Brief View of the Caste System of the North-Western Provinces and Oudh*. Allahabad, 1885.

Nestor, *Chronique dite de Nestor*. French trans. by Louis Leger. Paris, 1884.

Neubauer (A.), ' Notes on the Race-Types of the Jews ' ; in *Jour. Anthr. Inst.* vol. xv. London, 1886.

Neue Jahrbücher für das klassische Altertum Geschichte und deutsche Literatur und für Pädagogik. Ed. by J. Ilberg and B. Gerth. Leipzig.

Neue Zeit (Die). *Revue des geistigen und öffentlichen Lebens. Ergänzungshefte*. Stuttgart.

Neues Archiv der Gesellschaft für ältere deutsche Geschichtskunde. Hannover & Leipzig.

Neuhauss (R.), *Deutsch Neu-Guinea.* 3 vols. Berlin, 1911.
Neumann (C. F.), *Asiatische Studien.* Vol. I. Leipzig, 1837.
—— *Russland und die Tscherkessen.* Stuttgart & Tübingen, 1840.
Neumann (J. B.), ' Het Pane- en Bila-stroomgebied op het eiland
    Sumatra ' ; in *Tijdschrift van het Nederlandsch Aardrijkskundig
    Genootschap,* ser. ii. vol. iii. Amsterdam, 1887.
Nevill (Hugh), ' Vaeddas of Ceylon ' ; in *The Taprobanian,* vols.
    i.–ii. Bombay, 1887–88.
New (Charles), *Life, Wanderings, &c. in Eastern Africa.* London,
    1874.
New Dictionary on Historical Principles (A). See Murray (James
    A. H.).
Newbold (T. J.), *Political and Statistical Account of the British
    Settlements in the Straits of Malacca.* 2 vols. London, 1839.
Newcomb (Simon), *A Statistical Inquiry into the Probability of
    Causes of the Production of Sex in Human Offspring.* (*Car-
    negie Institution of Washington Publication No.* 11.) Wash-
    ington, 1904.
Newland (S.), ' The Parkengees, or Aboriginal Tribes on the Darling
    River ' ; in *Proceed. Roy. Geo. Soc. Australasia : South
    Australian Branch,* vol. ii. Session 1887–88. Adelaide, 1890.
Nicholas (F. C.), ' The Aborigines of the Province of Santa Marta,
    Colombia ' ; in *American Anthropologist,* new ser. vol. iii.
    New York, 1901.
Nichols (J. B.), ' The Numerical Proportions of the Sexes at Birth ' ;
    in *Memoirs of the American Anthropological Association,*
    vol. i. Lancaster, 1905–07.
Nicholson (F. A.), *Madras District Manuals : Coimbatore.* Ed. by
    H. A. Stuart. Madras, 1898.
Nicholson (H. A.), *Sexual Selection in Man.* [Toronto, 1872].
Nicolaus Damascenus, ' Morum mirabilium collectio, e Stobaei
    Florilegio ' ; in *Fragmenta Historicorum Græcorum,* ed. by
    C. Müller, vol. iii. Parisiis, 1849.
Nicolovius (Nils Lovén), *Folklifvet i Skytts Härad i Skåne vid början
    af detta århundrade.* Lund, 1868.
Niebuhr (Carsten), ' Travels in Arabia.' Trans. ; in Pinkerton,
    Collection of Voyages and Travels, vol. x. London, 1811.
Nietzold (J.), *Die Ehe in Ägypten zur ptolemäisch-römischen Zeit
    nach den griechischen Heiratskontrakten und verwandten
    Urkunden.* Leipzig, 1903.
Nigmann (E.), *Die Wahehe.* Berlin, 1908.
Nikander (Gabriel), Manuscript Notes relating to Marriage Rites in
    Swedish-speaking Communities in Finland.
Nilsson (Martin P.), *Griechische Feste von religiöser Bedeutung mit
    Ausschluss der attischen.* Leipzig, 1906.
Nind (Scott), ' Description of the Natives of King George's Sound
    (Swan River Colony) and adjoining Country ' ; in *Jour. Roy.
    Geo. Soc.* vol. i. London, 1832.
*Niti-Nighanduva ; or, the Vocabulary of Law. As it existed in the last
    days of the Kandyan Kingdom.* Trans. by C. J. R. Le
    Mesurier and T. B. Pa'nabokke. Colombo, 1880.
Nixon (Francis R.), *The Cruise of the Beacon.* London, 1857.
Noel (V.), ' Ile de Madagascar. Recherches sur les Sakkalava ' ;
    in *Bull. de la Société de Géographie,* ser. ii. vol. xx. Paris,
    1843.

Nöldeke (Th.), Review of Robertson Smith's *Kinship and Marriage in Early Arabia* ; in *Zeitschr. Deutsch. Morgenländ. Gesellsch.* vol. xl. Leipzig, 1886.

—— Review of Wilken's *Het Matriarchaat bij de oude Arabieren* ; in *Oesterreichische Monatsschrift für den Orient,* vol. x. Wien, 1884.

Noorden (C. von) and Kaminer (S.), *Krankheiten und Ehe.* Leipzig, 1916.

Nordau (Max), *Die conventionellen Lügen der Kulturmenschheit.* Leipzig, 1884.

Nordenskiöld (A. E.), *Den andra Dicksonska expeditionen till Grönland.* Stockholm, 1885.

—— *Vegas färd kring Asien och Europa.* 2 vols. Stockholm, 1880–81.

Nordenskiöld (Erland), *Indianliv i El Gran Chaco (Syd-Amerika).* Stockholm, 1910.

Nordman, (Lennart), ' Bröllop i Houtskär ' ; in *Hembygden,* vol. vi. Helsingfors, 1915.

Nordström (J. J.), *Bidrag till den svenska samhälls-författningens historia.* 2 vols. Helsingfors, 1839–40.

Nore (Alfred de), *Coutumes mythes et traditions des provinces de France.* Paris & Lyon, 1846.

Norlind (Tobias), *Gamla bröllopsseder hos svenska allmogen.* Stockholm, 1919.

Northcote (G. A. S.), ' The Nilotic Kavirondo ' ; in *Jour. Roy. Anthr. Inst.* vol. xxxvii. London, 1907.

Notes and Queries. London.

Nott (J. C.) and Gliddon (G. R.), *Types of Mankind.* Philadelphia, 1854.

Nowack (W.), ' Blessing and Cursing ' ; in *The Jewish Encyclopedia,* vol. iii. New York & London, *s.d.*

—— *Lehrbuch der hebräischen Archäologie.* 2 vols. Freiburg i.B. & Leipzig, 1894.

Nuñez de la Peña (Iuan), *Conqvista y antigvedades de las islas de la Gran Canaria.* Madrid, 1676.

Nya Pressen. Helsingfors.

Nyare bidrag till kännedom om de svenska landsmålen ock svenskt folklif. Stockholm & Uppsala.

Nyland. Samlingar utgifna af Nyländska Afdelningen. Helsingfors.

Oberländer (R.), ' Die Eingeborenen der australischen Kolonie Victoria ' ; in *Globus,* vol. iv. Hildburghausen, 1863.

Occasional Papers of the Natural History Society of Wisconsin. Milwaukee.

O'Curry (Eugene), *On the Manners and Customs of the Ancient Irish.* Ed. by W. K. Sullivan. 3 vols. London & Dublin, 1873.

Odoric of Pordenone (*Friar*), ' The Travels of.' Trans. ; in Yule, *Cathay and the Way thither,* vol. ii. London, 1913.

Oesterreichische Monatsschrift für den Orient. Wien.

Oettingen (A. von), *Die Moralstatistik in ihrer Bedeutung für eine Socialethik.* Erlangen, 1882.

Öfversigt af Finska Vetenskaps-Societetens Förhandlingar. Helsingfors.

Ogée (Jean), *Dictionnaire historique et géographique de la province de Bretagne.* Ed. by A. Marteville and P. Varin. 2 vols. Rennes, 1843–53.

Ogle (William), ' On Marriage-Rates and Marriage-Ages, with special reference to the Growth of Population ' ; in *Jour. Roy. Statistical Soc.* vol. liii. London, 1890.

O'Kearney (Nicholas), *The Battle of Gabhra : Garristown in the County of Dublin, fought* A.D. 283. Ed. by. (*Transactions of the Ossianic Society,* vol. i.) Dublin, 1853.

Olaus Magnus, *Historia de Gentibus Septentrionalibus.* Romae, 1555.

Oldenberg (Hermann), *Buddha : His Life, his Doctrine, his Order.* Trans. by W. Hoey. London, 1882.

—— *Die Religion des Veda.* Berlin, 1894.

Oldfield (A.), ' On the Aborigines of Australia ' ; in *Trans. Ethn. Soc. London,* new ser. vol. iii. London, 1865.

Oldham (C. F.), *The Sun and the Serpent.* London, 1905.

Oldham (T.), ' Communications respecting the Cassia Tribe ' ; in *Jour. Ethn. Soc. London,* vol. iii. London, 1854.

Olivecrona (S. R. D. K.), *Om makars giftorätt i bo.* 4th edition. Stockholm.

O'Malley (L. S. S.), *Census of India,* 1911. *Vol. V. Bengal, Bihar and Orissa and Sikkim,* pt. i. Report. Calcutta, 1913.

Ophuijsen (C. A. van), ' De Loeboes ' ; in *Tijdschrift voor indische taal-, land- en volkenkunde,* vol. xxix. Batavia, 1884.

Oppert (Gustav), ' On the Classification of Languages in conformity with Ethnology ' ; in *Jour. Anthr. Inst.* vol. xiii. London, 1884.

—— *On the Original Inhabitants of Bharatavarsa or India.* Westminster & Leipzig, 1893.

Oppert (J.), Review of P. Haupt's *Die sumerischen Familiengesetze ;* in *Göttingische gelehrte Anzeigen,* 1879. Göttingen.

Oratores Attici. Ed. by C. Müller. 2 vols. Parisiis, 1847–58.

Orientalist (The). Kandy, Bombay.

Original-Mittheilungen aus der ethnologischen Abtheilung der königlichen Museen zu Berlin.

Ortolan (J.), *Histoire de la législation romaine.* Paris, 1876.

Orton (James), *The Andes and the Amazon.* New York, 1876.

Ostermann (*Father* Leopold), ' The Navajo Indians of New Mexico and Arizona ' ; in *Anthropos,* vol. iii. Wien, 1908.

O'Sullivan (Hugh), ' Dinka Laws and Customs ' ; in *Jour. Roy. Anthr. Inst.* vol. xl. London, 1910.

Ovidius Naso (P.), [*Opera*]. Ed. by R. Merkel. 3 vols. Lipsiae, 1908–1910.

Oviedo y Valdés (G. Fernandez de), *Historia general y natural de las Indias.* 4 vols. Madrid, 1851–55.

Padfield (J. E.), *The Hindu at Home.* Madras, 1908.

Palestine Exploration Fund. Quarterly Statements. London.

Palgrave (W. G.), *Narrative of a Year's Journey through Central and Eastern Arabia.* London & Cambridge, 1865.

Pallas (P. S.), *Merkwürdigkeiten der Morduanen, Kasaken, Kalmücken, &c.* Frankfurt & Leipzig, 1773.

—— *Merkwürdigkeiten der obischen Ostjaken, Samojeden, &c.* Frankfurt & Leipzig, 1777.

Pallas (P. S.), *Reise durch verschiedene Provinzen des Russischen Reichs.* 3 vols. Frankfurt & Leipzig, 1776–78.
Pallme (Ignatius), *Travels in Kordofan.* Trans. London, 1844.
Palmer (Edward), ' Notes on some Australian Tribes '; in *Jour. Anthr. Inst.* vol. xiii. London, 1884.
Palmer (Edward H.), *The Desert of the Exodus.* Cambridge, 1871.
Pandit Harikishan Kaul, *Census of India,* 1911. *Vol. XIV. Punjab,* pt. i. Report. Lahore, 1912.
Panikkar (K. M.), ' Some Aspects of Nāyar Life '; in *Jour. Roy. Anthr. Inst.* vol. xlviii. London, 1918.
Panjab Notes and Queries, a Monthly Periodical. Ed. by R. C. Temple. Allahabad.
Paolino da S. Bartolomeo (Fra), *Viaggio alle Indie Orientali.* Roma, 1796.
Papers relating to the Laws of Marriage and Divorce in Self-governing British Colonies. Presented to both Houses of Parliament, October, 1903. London, 1903.
[Papi (L.),] *Lettere sull' Indie Orientali.* 2 vols. Filadelfia, 1802.
' Pâraskara-Grihya-Sûtra,' trans. by H. Oldenberg ; in *The Sacred Books of the East,* vol. xxix. Oxford, 1886.
Pardessus (J. M.), *Loi Salique.* Paris, 1843.
Pardo de Tavera (T. H.), ' Las costumbres de los tagalos de Filipinas, según el padre Plasencia '; in *Revista Contemporánea,* vol. lxxxvi. Madrid, 1892.
—— ' Die Sitten und Bräuche der alten Tagalen. Manuscript des P. Juan de Plasencia. 1589.' Trans. by F. Blumentritt ; in *Zeitschr. f. Ethnol.* vol. xxv. Berlin, 1893.
Parent-Duchâtelet (A. J. B.), *De la prostitution dans la ville de Paris.* 2 vols. Paris, 1857.
Park (Mungo), *Travels in the Interior of Africa.* Edinburgh, 1858.
Parker (E. H.), ' Comparative Chinese Family Law '; in *The China Review,* vol. viii. Hongkong, 1879–80.
Parker (*Mrs.* K. Langloh), *The Euahlayi Tribe.* London, 1905.
Parkinson (J.), ' Note on the Asaba People (Ibos) of the Niger '; in *Jour. Anthr. Inst.* vol. xxxvi. London, 1906.
Parkinson (R.), *Dreissig Jahre in der Südsee.* Stuttgart, 1907.
—— *Im Bismarck-Archipel. Erlebnisse und Beobachtungen auf der Insel Neu-Pommern (Neu-Britannien).* Leipzig, 1887.
—— *Zur Ethnographie der nordwestlichen Salomo Inseln. (Abhandlungen und Berichte des Königl. Zoologischen und Anthropologisch-Ethnographischen Museums zu Dresden,* 1898–99, vol. vii. no. 6.) Berlin, 1899.
Parkman (Francis), *The Jesuits in North America in the Seventeenth Century.* London, 1885.
Parkyns (M.), *Life in Abyssinia.* 2 vols. London, 1853.
Parry (W. E.), *Journal of a Second Voyage for the Discovery of a North-West Passage from the Atlantic to the Pacific.* London, 1824.
Parsons (E. C.), ' The Reluctant Bridegroom '; in *Anthropos,* vols. x.–xi. Wien, 1915–16.
Partridge (Charles), *Cross River Natives.* London, 1905.
—— ' Native Law and Custom in Egbaland '; in *Jour. African Soc.* vol. x. London, 1911.
Passarge (S.), ' Die Buschmänner der Kalahari '; in *Mittheil. Deutsch. Schutzgeb.* vol. xviii. Berlin 1905.

Patkanov (S.), *Die Irtysch-Ostjaken und ihre Volkspoesie.* 2 vols. St. Petersburg, 1897.
Patriota (O). *Jornal litterario, politico, mercantil, &c. do Rio de Janeiro.*
Paul (Hermann), *Grundriss der germanischen Philologie,* ed. by. 3 vols. Strassburg, 1900–07.
Paulitschke (Ph.), *Ethnographie Nordost-Afrikas.* 2 vols. Berlin, 1893–96.
Pausanias, *Descriptio Græciæ.* Ed. by L. Dindorf. Parisiis, 1845.
—— See Frazer (*Sir* James G.).
Pearl (R.) and Salaman (R. N.), ' The Relative Time of Fertilization of the Ovum and the Sex Ratio amongst Jews ' ; in *American Anthropologist,* new ser. vol. xv. Lancaster, 1913.
Pearson (Karl), *The Chances of Death and other Studies in Evolution.* 2 vols. London, 1897.
Peckel (P. G.), ' Die Verwandtschaftsnamen des mittleren Neu-mecklenburg ' ; in *Anthropos,* vol. iii. Wien, 1908.
Peckham (George W. and Elizabeth G.), ' Observations on Sexual Selection in Spiders of the Family Attidæ ' ; in *Occasional Papers of the Natural History Society of Wisconsin,* vol. i. Milwaukee, 1889.
Peiser (F. E.), *Skizze der babylonischen Gesellschaft. (Mitteilungen der Vorderasiatischen Gesellschaft,* 1896, no. 3.) Berlin, 1896.
Pelleprat (*P.* Pierre), *Relation des missions des PP. de la Compagnie de Jesus dans les Isles, et dans la terre ferme de l'Amerique Meridionale.* 2 pts. Paris, 1655.
Pemberton (R. B.), *Report on Bootan.* Calcutta, 1839.
Penha (Geo. d'), ' Superstitions and Customs in Salsette ' ; in *The Indian Antiquary,* vol. xxviii. Bombay, 1899.
Penna di Billi (Francesco Orazio), *Breve notizia del regno del Thibet.* 1730. (Reprinted from *Nouveau Journal Asiatique,* January 1835.) [Paris].
Pennell (T. L.), *Among the Wild Tribes of the Afghan Frontier.* London, 1909.
Penny (Alfred), *Ten Years in Melanesia.* London, 1887.
Percival (Robert), *An Account of the Island of Ceylon.* London, 1803.
Perelaer (M. T. H.), *Ethnographische beschrijving der Dajaks.* Zalt-Bommel, 1870.
Perera (A. A.), *Glimpses of Singhalese Social Life.* Bombay, 1904.
Périer (J. A. N.), ' Essai sur les croisements ethniques ' ; in *Mémoires Soc. d'Anthr. Paris,* vols. i.–ii. Paris, 1860–65.
Perrin du Lac (F. M.), ' Travels through the Two Louisianas, and among the Savage Nations of the Missouri.' Trans. ; in *A Collection of Modern and Contemporary Voyages and Travels,* vol. vi. London, 1807.
Perron (N.), *Femmes arabes avant et depuis l'islamisme.* Paris & Alger, 1858.
Perrot (Nicolas), ' Memoir on the Manners, Customs, and Religion of the Savages of North America ' ; in Emma Helen Blair, *The Indian Tribes of the Upper Mississippi Valley and Region of the Great Lakes,* vol. i. Cleveland, 1911.
Pertz (G. H.), *Monumenta Germaniæ historica.* Hannoverae, 1826 &c.
Peschel (O.), *The Races of Man.* Trans. London, 1876.

Petermann (A.), *Mittheilungen aus Justhus Perthes' geographischer Anstalt.* Gotha.

Petersen (Eugen) and Luschan (Felix von), *Reisen in Lykien Milyas und Kibyratis.* Wien, 1889.

Petherick (John), *Egypt, the Soudan and Central Africa.* Edinburgh & London, 1861.

—— and Petherick (*Mrs.*), *Travels in Central Africa, and Explorations of the Western Nile Tributaries.* 2 vols. London, 1869.

Petrie (Tom), *Reminiscences of Early Queensland (Dating from 1837).* Recorded by his daughter. Brisbane, 1904.

Petroff (Ivan), ' Report on the Population, Industries, and Resources of Alaska ' ; in *Tenth Census of the United States.* Washington, 1884.

Pfannenschmid (*Dr.*), ' Jus primae noctis ' ; in *Das Ausland*, vol. lvi. Stuttgart & München, 1883.

Pfeil (Joachim, *Graf*), *Studien und Beobachtungen aus der Südsee.* Braunschweig, 1899.

Philippine Islands.—Department of the Interior. Ethnological Survey Publications. Manila.

Philippine Journal of Science (The). Manila.

Philippson (Ludwig), *Die Israelitische Religionslehre.* 3 vols. Leipzig, 1861–65.

Phillips (R. C.), ' The Lower Congo ; a Sociological Study ' ; in *Jour. Anthr. Inst.* vol. xvii. London, 1888.

Philo Judaeus, *Opera.* Ed. by Th. Mangey. 2 vols. London, 1742.

Philologische und historische Abhandlungen der Königl. Akademie der Wissenschaften zu Berlin.

Philosophical Transactions of the Royal Society of London.

Piedrahita (L. Fernandez de), *Historia general de las conquistas del nuevo reyno de Granada.* Amberes, [1688].

Piehler (A. B.), ' Die Ajitas (Aëtas) der Philippinen ' ; in *Globus*, vol. xcvi. Braunschweig, 1909.

Pietro della Valle, *The Travels of, in India.* From the translation of 1664, by G. Havers, ed. by Edward Grey. 2 vols. London, 1892.

Pindar, *Carmina.* Ed. by C. I. T. Mommsen. Berolini, 1864.

Pinkerton (John), *A General Collection of Voyages and Travels.* 17 vols. London, 1808–14.

Piprek (Johannes), *Slawische Brautwerbungs- und Hochzeitsgebräuche. (Ergänzungsheft X [zu Band XX] der Zeitschrift für oester-reichische Volkskunde.)* Stuttgart, 1914.

Pischon (C. N.), *Der Einfluss des Islâm auf das häusliche, sociale und politische Leben seiner Bekenner.* Leipzig, 1881.

Pistorius (A. W. P. Verkerk), *Studien over de inlandsche huishouding in de Padangsche Bovenlanden.* Zalt-Bommel, 1871.

Pitcairn (W. D.), *Two Years among the Savages of New Guinea.* London, 1891.

Pitrè (Giuseppe), *Usi e costumi credenze e pregiudizi del popolo siciliano.* 4 vols. (*Biblioteca delle tradizioni popolari siciliane*, vols. xiv.–xvii.) Palermo, 1889.

Pittier de Fábrega (H.), *Die Sprache der Bribri-Indianer in Costa Rica. (Sitzungsberichte der philosophisch-historischen Classe der kaiserl. Akademie der Wissenschaften*, vol. cxxxviii. pt. vi.) Wien, 1898.

Placucci (M.), *Usi e pregiudizj dei contadini della Romagna*. Palermo, 1885.
Plato, *Dialogues*. Trans. by B. Jowett. 5 vols. Oxford, 1892.
—— *Opera*. 3 vols. Parisiis, 1846–73.
Plautus (T. M.), *Comœdiæ*. Ed. by G. Goetz and F. Schoell. 7 vols. Lipsiae, 1893–96.
Playfair (A.), *The Garos*. London, 1909.
Plehn (A.), ' Beobachtungen in Kamerun ' ; in *Zeitschr. f. Ethnol.* vol. xxxvi. Berlin, 1904.
Pleyte (C. M.), ' Ethnographische Beschrijving der Kei-Eilanden ' ; in *Tijdschrift van het Kon. Nederlandsch Aardrijkskundig Genootschap*, ser. ii. vol. x. Leiden, 1893.
—— Review of the first edition of the present work, in *De Indische Gids*, 1891. Amsterdam.
Plinius Secundus (C.), *Naturalis historiæ libri XXXVII*. Ed. by C. Mayhoff. Lipsiae, 1906.
Ploss (H.), *Das Kind im Brauch und Sitte der Völker*. Ed. by B. Renz. 2 vols. Leipzig, 1911–12.
—— *Das Weib in der Natur- und Völkerkunde*. Ed. by Max Bartels. 2 vols. Leipzig, 1887. (Quoted *supra*, i. 96.)
—— The same work. Eighth edition, ed. by Max Bartels. 2 vols. Leipzig, 1905.
—— ' Ueber die das Geschlechtsverhältniss der Kinder bedingenden Ursachen ' ; in *Monatsschrift für Geburtskunde und Frauenkrankheiten*, vol. xii. Berlin, 1858.
Plutarch, *Romane Questions*. Trans. ed. by F. B. Jevons. London, 1892.
—— *Scripta moralia*. 2 vols. Parisiis, 1839–41.
—— *Vitæ*. Ed. by Th. Dœhner. 2 vols. Parisiis, 1846–47.
Pöch (Rudolf), ' Vierter Bericht über meine Reise nach Neuguinea (Niederländisch-Neuguinea) ' ; in *Sitzungsberichte der mathematisch-naturwissenschaftlichen Klasse der kaiserl. Akademie der Wissenschaften*, vol. cxv. pt. i. Wien, 1906.
Pœnitentiale Theodori. See Theodore.
Poeppig (E.), *Reise in Chile, Peru und auf dem Amazonenstrome*. 2 vols. Leipzig, 1835–36.
[Poincy (Louis de),] *Histoire naturelle et morale des Iles Antilles de l'Amerique*. [Ed. by C. de Rochefort.] Rotterdam, 1681.
Polack (J. S.), *Manners and Customs of the New Zealanders*. 2 vols. London, 1840.
Polak (J. E.), *Persien*. 2 vols. Leipzig, 1865.
Political Science Quarterly. A Review . . . edited by the University Faculty of Political Science of Columbia College. New York, Boston, & Chicago.
Pollock (*Sir* Frederick) and Maitland (F. W.), *The History of the English Law before the Time of Edward I*. 2 vols. Cambridge, 1898.
Pollux (Julius), *Onomasticum*. 2 vols. Amstelædami, 1706.
Polo (Marco), *The Book of Ser M. P. the Venetian concerning the Kingdoms and Marvels of the East*. Trans. and ed. by Sir Henry Yule. Third edition, revised by Henri Cordier. 2 vols. London, 1903.
Polybius, *Historia*. Ed. by L. Dindorf and Th. Büttner-Wobst. 5 vols. Lipsiae, 1866–1905.
Poole (F.), *Queen Charlotte Islands*. London, 1872.

Popular Science Monthly (The). New York.
Porter (David), *Journal of a Cruise made to the Pacific Ocean . . . in the Years* 1812, 1813, and 1814. 2 vols. New York, 1822.
Porthan (H. G.), ' Anmärkningar rörande Finska Folkets läge och tillstånd ' ; in *Kongliga Vitterhets, Historie och Antiquitets Academiens Handlingar,* vol. iv. Stockholm, 1795.
Portman (M. V.), *A History of Our Relations with the Andamanese.* 2 vols. Calcutta, 1899.
Post (A. H.), *Afrikanische Jurisprudenz.* 2 vols. Oldenburg & Leipzig, 1887.
—— *Die Anfänge des Staats- und Rechtslebens.* Oldenburg, 1878.
—— *Bausteine für eine allgemeine Rechtswissenschaft auf vergleichend-ethnologischer Basis.* 2 vols. Oldenburg, 1880–81.
—— *Die Geschlechtsgenossenschaft der Urzeit und die Entstehung der Ehe.* Oldenburg, 1875.
—— *Die Grundlagen des Rechts.* Oldenburg, 1884.
—— *Grundriss der ethnologischen Jurisprudenz.* 2 vols. Oldenburg & Leipzig, 1894–95.
—— *Studien zur Entwicklungsgeschichte des Familienrechts.* Oldenburg & Leipzig, 1890.
—— *Der Ursprung des Rechts.* Oldenburg, 1876.
Postans (—), ' Bilúchi Tribes inhabiting Sindh ' ; in *Jour. Ethn. Soc. London,* vol. i. Edinburgh (printed), 1848.
Potter (M. A.), *Sohrab and Rustem.* London, 1902.
Pouchet (George), *The Plurality of the Human Race.* Trans. ed. by H. J. C. Beavan. London, 1864.
Poulton (E. B.), *The Colours of Animals.* London, 1890.
—— *Essays on Evolution* 1889–1907. Oxford, 1908.
Poupon (A.), ' Étude ethnographique des Baya de la circonscription du M'Bimou ' ; in *L'Anthropologie,* vol. xxvi. Paris, 1915.
Powell (J. W.), ' Sociology ' ; in *American Anthropologist,* new ser. vol. i. New York, 1899.
—— ' Wyandot Government ' ; in *Ann. Rep. Bur. Ethnol.* vol. i. Washington, 1881.
Powell (Wilfred), *Wanderings in a Wild Country; or, Three Years amongst the Cannibals of New Britain.* London, 1883.
Powers (Stephan), *Tribes of California. (U.S. Geograph. and Geolog. Survey of the Rocky Mountain Region :—Contributions to North American Ethnology,* vol. iii.) Washington, 1877.
Prado (F. A. do), ' Historia dos Indios Cavalleiros, da Nação Guaycurú ' ; in *O Patriota,* 1814, no. 4. Rio de Janeiro.
Prain (David), ' The Angami Nagas ' ; in *Revue coloniale internationale,* vol. v. Amsterdam, 1887.
Prejevalsky (N.), *From Kulja, across the Tian Shan to Lob-nor.* Trans. London, 1879.
—— *Mongolia, the Tangut Country and the Solitudes of Northern Tibet.* Trans. 2 vols. London, 1876.
Preller (L.), *Römische Mythologie.* Berlin, 1865.
Prescott (W. H.), *History of the Conquest of Mexico.* London, 1878.
—— *History of the Conquest of Peru.* London, 1878.
Preyer (W.), *Die Seele des Kindes.* Leipzig, 1884.
—— *Specielle Physiologie des Embryo.* Leipzig, 1885.
Price (F. G. H.), ' A Description of the Quissama Tribe ' ; in *Jour. Anthr. Inst.* vol. i. London, 1872.
Prichard (H. H.), *Through the Heart of Patagonia.* London, 1902.

Prichard (J. C.), *Researches into the Physical History of Mankind*. 5 vols. London, 1836–47.
Pridham (Charles), *An Historical, Political, and Statistical Account of Ceylon*. 2 vols. London, 1849.
Prinsep (*Mrs. A.*), *The Journal of a Voyage from Calcutta to Van Diemen's Land*. London, 1833.
Pritchard (W. T.), *Polynesian Reminiscences*. London, 1866.
Proceedings of the American Academy of Arts and Sciences. Boston.
—— *of the British Academy*. London.
—— *of the Cambridge Philosophical Society*.
—— *of the Royal Geographical Society and Monthly Record of Geography*. London.
—— *of the Royal Geographical Society of Australasia : South Australian Branch*. Adelaide.
—— *of the Royal Irish Academy*. Dublin.
—— *of the Royal Society of Edinburgh*.
Procopius. Ed. by G. Dindorf. 3 vols. Bonnae, 1833–38.
Project des Corporis Juris Fridericiani. Halle, 1749.
Proust de la Girondière (Paul), *Twenty Years in the Philippines*. Trans. London, [1853].
Provenzal (Dino), *Usanze e feste del popolo italiano*. Bologna, 1912.
Proyart (L. B.), 'History of Loango, Kakongo, and other Kingdoms in Africa.' Trans. ; in Pinkerton; *Collection of Voyages and Travels*, vol. xvi. London, 1814.
Ptah-Hotep, 'The Precepts of.' Trans. by Ph. Virey ; in *Records of the Past*, new ser. vol. iii. London, *s.d.*
Publications de l'École des langues orientales vivantes. Paris.
—— *of the American Economic Association*. New York.
—— *of the Jesup North Pacific Expedition*. Ed. by F. Boas. Leiden & New York, 1900 (1898–1900) &c. *In progress.*
—— *of the Manx Society* (*The*). Douglas.
Puini (Carlo), *Il Tibet* (*geografia, storia, religione, costumi*) *secondo la relazione del viaggio del P. Ippolito Desideri* (1715–1721). (*Memorie della Società Geographica Italiana*, vol. x.) Roma, 1904.
Punnett (R. C.), 'On Nutrition and Sex-determination in Man ' ; in *Proceed. Cambridge Philosophical Soc.* vol. xii. Cambridge, 1904.
—— 'On the Proportion of the Sexes among the Todas ' ; in *Proceed. Cambridge Philosophical Soc.* vol. xii. Cambridge, 1904.
Purcell (B. H.), 'The Aborigines of Australia ' ; in *Transactions of the Royal Geographical Society of Australasia* (*Victoria Branch*), vol. xi. Melbourne, 1894.
—— 'Rites and Customs of Australian Aborigines ' ; in *Verhandl. Berliner Gesellsch. Anthr.* 1893. Berlin.
Purchas (Samuel), *Purchas his Pilgrimes*. 20 vols. Glasgow, 1905–07.
Pyrard (François), *The Voyage of F. P. of Laval to the East Indies, the Maldives, the Moluccas, and Brazil*. Trans. ed. by Albert Gray assisted by H. C. P. Bell. 2 vols. London, 1887–90.

Quarterly Journal of Microscopical Science (*The*). London.
Quatrefages (A. de), *The Human Species*. London, 1879.
Quetelet (A.), *A Treatise on Man*. Trans. Edinburgh, 1842.

Qur'ân (The). Trans. by E. H. Palmer. 2 vols. (*The Sacred Books of the East*, vols. vi. and ix.) Oxford, 1880.

Rääf (L. F.), *Samlingar och Anteckningar till en beskrifning öfver Ydre härad i Östergöthland.* 5 vols. Linköping, Örebro, Norrköping, 1856–75.

' Racenanlage und verschiedene Begabung zum Arbeiten ' ; in *Globus*, vol. xxv. Braunschweig, 1874.

Raffles (*Sir* Th. Stamford), *The History of Java.* 2 vols. London, 1830.

Rajacsich (*Baron*), *Das Leben, die Sitten und Gebräuche, der im Kaiserthume Oesterreich lebenden Südslaven.* Wien, 1873.

Ralegh (W.), *The Discovery of the . . . Empire of Guiana.* Ed. by Sir R. H. Schomburgk. London, 1848.

Ralston (W. R. S.), *The Songs of the Russian People.* London, 1872.

Ramsay (*Sir* W. M.), *The Cities and Bishoprics of Phrygia.* 2 vols. Oxford, 1895–97.

Ramusio (G. B.), *Navigationi et viaggi.* 3 vols. Venetia, 1554–59.
—— The same work. 3 vols. Venetia, 1563–74.

Ranga Rao (T.), ' The Yánádis of the Nellore District ' ; in the Madras Government Museum's *Bulletin*, vol. iv. Madras, 1901.

Ranke (Johannes), *Der Mensch.* 2 vols. Leipzig & Wien, 1894.

Rannie (Douglas), *My Adventures among South Sea Cannibals.* London, 1912.

Rapp (Adolf), ' Die Religion und Sitte der Perser und übrigen Iranier nach den griechischen und römischen Quellen ' ; in *Zeitschr. Deutsch. Morgenländ. Gesellsch.* vol. xx. Leipzig, 1866.

Rasmussen (J. L.), *Historia præcipuorum Arabum regnorum rerumque ab iis gestarum ante islamismum.* Hauniae, 1817.

Rat (J. N.), ' The Carib Language as now spoken in Dominica, West Indies ' ; in *Jour. Anthr. Inst.* vol. xxvii. London, 1898.

Rattray (R. S.), *Some Folk-Lore Stories and Songs in Chinyanja.* London, 1907.

Ratzel (F.), *Völkerkunde.* 3 vols. Leipzig, 1885–88.

Rauber (A.), *Der Überschuss an Knabengeburten und seine biologische Bedeutung.* Leipzig, 1900.

Ravenstein (E. G.), *The Russians on the Amur.* London, 1861.

Rawling (C. G.), *The Land of the New Guinea Pygmies.* London, 1913.

Rawlinson (George), *The Five Great Monarchies of the Ancient Eastern World.* 3 vols. London, 1871.

Ray (Sidney H.), ' The People and Language of Lifu, Loyalty Islands ' ; in *Jour. Roy. Anthr. Inst.* vol. xlvii. London, 1917.

Read (Carveth), ' No Paternity ' ; in *Jour. Roy. Anthr. Inst.* vol. xlviii. London, 1918.

Reade (W. Winwood), *Savage Africa.* London, 1863.

Reclus (Élie), *Primitive Folk.* London, *s.d.*

Reclus (Élisée), *Nouvelle géographie universelle.* 19 vols. Paris, 1876–94.

Records of the Past. London.

Recueil de divers voyages faits en Afrique et en l'Amerique qui n'ont point esté encore publiez. [Ed. by H. Justel.] Paris, 1674.

Reed (W. A.), *Negritos of Zambales*. (*Philippine Islands.—Department of the Interior, Ethnological Survey Publications*, vol. ii. pt. i.) Manila, 1904.

Registrar-General of Births, Deaths, and Marriages in England and Wales, Annual Report of the. London.

Regnard (J. F.), ' A Journey to Lapland.' Trans. ; in Pinkerton, *Collection of Voyages and Travels*, vol. i. London, 1808.

Reich (Eduard), *Geschichte, Natur- und Gesundheitslehre des ehelichen Lebens*. Cassel, 1864.

Rein (J. J.), *Japan : Travels and Researches*. Trans. London, 1884.

—— *Japan nach Reisen und Studien*. Vol. I. Leipzig, 1905.

Rein (Wilhelm), *Das Römische Privatrecht und der Civilprozess bis in das erste Jahrhundert der Kaiserherrschaft*. Leipzig, 1836.

Reinach (Salomon), *Cultes, mythes et religions*. 4 vols. Paris, 1905–12.

—— ' Le gendre et la belle-mère ' ; in *L'Anthropologie*, vol. xxii. Paris, 1911.

—— ' La prohibition de l'inceste et ses origines ' ; in *L'Anthropologie*, vol. x. Paris, 1899.

Reiser (Karl), *Sagen, Gebräuche und Sprichwörter des Allgäus*. 2 vols. Kempten, 1892–94.

Reitzenstein (Ferdinand von), ' Der Kausalzusammenhang zwischen Geschlechtsverkehr und Empfängnis in Glaube und Brauch der Natur- und Kulturvölker ' ; in *Zeitschr. f. Ethnol.* vol. xli. Berlin, 1909.

Rémusat (J. P.), *Nouveaux mélanges asiatiques*. 2 vols. Paris, 1829.

Remy (Jules), *Ka Mooolelo Hawaii*. Paris & Leipzig, 1862.

Rengger (J. R.), *Naturgeschichte der Säugethiere von Paraguay*. Basel, 1830.

Renooz (Céline), *Psychologie comparée de l'homme et de la femme*. Passy-Paris, 1897.

Renouvier (Ch.) and Prat (L.), *La nouvelle monadologie*. Paris, 1899.

Report on the Work of the Horn Scientific Expedition to Central Australia. Ed. by B. Spencer. Part IV. London & Melbourne, 1896.

Reports of the Cambridge Anthropological Expedition to Torres Straits. Ed. by A. C. Haddon. Vol. V. Cambridge, 1904.

—— *of Meetings of the Australasian Association for the Advancement of Science.*

—— *of Meetings of the British Association for the Advancement of Science.*

—— *on the Laws of (on) Marriage and Divorce in the Colonies and in Foreign Countries, presented to the House of Commons*, 1893. 2 parts. London, 1894.

Reuss (L.), *La prostitution au point de vue de l'hygiène et de l'administration en France et à l'étranger*. Paris, 1889.

Reuter (O. M.), *Lebensgewohnheiten und Instinkte der Insekten bis zum Erwachen der sozialen Instinkte*. Berlin, 1913.

Révész (Géza), *Das Trauerjahr der Witwe im Lichte der ethnologisch vergleichenden Rechtswissenschaft.* (Reprinted from *Zeitschr. f. vergl. Rechtswiss.* vol. xv.) Stuttgart, 1902.

Réville (Albert), *La Religion Chinoise*. Paris, 1889.

Revista Contemporánea. Madrid.

Revista trimensal do Instituto Historico Geografico e Ethnographico do Brasil. Rio de Janeiro.
Revue africaine. Constantine.
—— *archéologique.* Paris.
—— *coloniale internationale.* Amsterdam.
—— *d'anthropologie.* Paris.
—— *de l'École d'anthropologie de Paris.*
—— *d'ethnographie.* Paris.
—— *d'ethnographie et de sociologie.* Ed. by A. van Gennep. Paris.
—— *de législation et de jurisprudence.* Paris.
—— *des études ethnographiques et sociologiques.* Ed. by A. van Gennep. Paris.
—— *des traditions populaires.* Paris.
—— *tunisienne.* Tunis.
Rheinisches Museum für Philologie. Frankfurt a. M.
Rhys (*Sir* John), *Celtic Britain.* London, 1904.
—— in the Discussion on M. Winternitz' paper ' On a Comparative Study of Indo-European Customs ' ; in *Transactions of the International Folk-Lore Congress*, 1891. London, 1892.
—— and Brynmor-Jones (*Sir* David), *The Welsh People.* London, 1906.
Ribbe (Carl), *Zwei Jahre unter den Kannibalen der Salomo-Inseln.* Dresden-Blasewitz, 1903.
Ribbe (Charles de), *Les familles et la société en France avant la Révolution.* Paris, 1873.
Richard (—), History of Tonquin ' ; in Pinkerton, *Collection of Voyages and Travels*, vol. ix. London, 1811.
Richards (F. J.), ' Cross Cousin Marriage in South India ' ; in *Man*, vol. xiv. London, 1914.
Richardson (John), *Arctic Searching Expedition.* 2 vols. London, 1851.
Richter (*Oberleutnant*), ' Der Bezirk Bukoba ' ; in *Mittheil. Deutsch. Schutzgeb.* vol. xii. Berlin, 1899.
Richter (G.), *Manual of Coorg.* Mangalore, 1870.
Richter (Ludwig), *Beiträge zur Geschichte des Ehescheidungsrechts in der evangelischen Kirche.* Berlin, 1858.
Riddle (Oscar), ' Sex Control and Known Correlations in Pigeons ' ; in *The American Naturalist*, vol. l. New York, 1916.
Ridgeway (*Sir* William), ' Who were the Romans ? ' ; in *Proceedings of the British Academy*, 1907–08. London.
Ridley (William), *The Aborigines of Australia.* Sydney, 1864.
—— *Kamilaroi, Dippil, and Turrubul.* New South Wales, 1866.
—— ' Report on Australian Languages and Traditions ' ; in *Jour. Anthr. Inst.* vol. ii. London, 1873.
Riedel (J. G. F.), ' Galela und Tobeloresen ' ; in *Zeitschr. f. Ethnol.* vol. xvii. Berlin, 1885.
—— *De sluik- en kroesharige rassen tusschen Selebes en Papua.* 's-Gravenhage, 1886.
Rigveda (Der). German trans. by A. Ludwig. 6 vols. Prag, 1876–88.
Rink (H. J.), *The Eskimo Tribes.* Copenhagen & London, 1887.
—— *Tales and Traditions of the Eskimo.* Edinburgh & London, 1875.
Ripley (W. Z.), ' The European Population of the United States ' ; in *Jour. Roy. Anthr. Inst.* vol. xxxviii. London, 1908.

Ripley (W. Z.), *The Races of Europe*. London, 1900.
Ris (H.), ' De onderafdeeling Klein Mandailing Oeloe en Pahantan en hare bevolking met uitzondering van de Oeloe's ' ; in *Bijdragen tot de taal-, land- en volkenkunde van Nederlandsch-Indië*, vol. xlvi. 's-Gravenhage, 1896.
Risley (*Sir* Herbert), *The People of India*. Ed. by W. Crooke. London, 1915.
—— *Tribes and Castes of Bengal*. *Ethnographic Glossary*. 2 vols. Calcutta, 1891.
—— and Gait (E. A.), *Census of India*, 1901. *Vol. I. India*, pt. i. Report. Calcutta, 1903.
Rivers (W. H. R.), *Address to the Anthropological Section of the British Association for the Advancement of Science*. *Portsmouth*, 1911. (Reprint of ' The Ethnological Analysis of Culture ' ; in *Report of the Eighty-first Meeting of the British Association*.) [London, 1912].
—— *The History of Melanesian Society*. 2 vols. Cambridge, 1914.
—— ' Kin, Kinship ' ; in Hastings, *Encyclopædia of Religion and Ethics*, vol. vii. Edinburgh, 1914.
—— *Kinship and Social Organisation*. London, 1914.
—— ' Marriage (Introductory and Primitive) ' ; in Hastings, *Encyclopædia of Religion and Ethics*, vol. viii. Edinburgh, 1915.
—— ' The Marriage of Cousins in India ' ; in *Jour. Roy. Asiatic Soc.* 1907. London.
—— ' Mother-Right ' ; in Hastings, *Encyclopædia of Religion and Ethics*, vol. viii. Edinburgh, 1915.
—— ' On the Origin of the Classificatory System of Relationships ' ; in *Anthropological Essays presented to E. B. Tylor*. Oxford, 1907.
—— ' Sociology and Psychology ' ; in *The Sociological Review*, vol. ix. London, 1916.
—— ' Survival in Sociology ' ; in *The Sociological Review*, vol. vi. London, 1913.
—— *The Todas*. London, 1906.
—— ' Totemism in Polynesia and Melanesia ' ; in *Jour. Roy. Anthr. Inst.* vol. xxxix. London, 1909.
—— in *Reports of the Cambridge Anthropological Expedition to Torres Straits*, vol. v. Cambridge, 1904.
Rivet (*Dr.*), ' Les Indiens Jibaros ' ; in *L'Anthropologie*, vol. xviii. Paris, 1907.
—— Review of Guevara's *Psicolojia del pueblo Araucano ;* in *L'Anthropologie*, vol. xxi. Paris, 1910.
Robertson (*Sir* G. Scott), *The Káfirs of the Hindu-Kush*. London, 1896.
Robertson (H. A.), *Erromanga, the Martyr Isle*. Ed. by J. Fraser. London, 1902.
Robley (H. G.), *Moko ; or, Maori Tattooing*. London, 1896.
Rochas (V. de), *La Nouvelle Calédonie et ses habitants*. Paris, 1862.
Rochefort (C. de). See Poincy (Louis de).
Rochholz (E. L.), *Schweizersagen aus dem Aargau*. 2 vols. Aarau, 1856.
Rochon (A. M.), ' A Voyage to Madagascar and the East Indies.' Trans. ; in Pinkerton, *Collection of Voyages and Travels*, vol. xvi. London, 1814.

Rockhill (W. W.), *The Land of the Lamas.* London, 1891.
—— 'Tibet. A Geographical, Ethnographical, and Historical Sketch, derived from Chinese Sources'; in *Jour. Roy. Asiatic Soc.* 1891, new ser. vol. xxiii. London, 1891.
Rodd (Rennell), *The Customs and Lore of Modern Greece.* London, 1892.
Rodway (James), *Guiana : British, Dutch, and French.* London, 1912.
Roeder (Fritz), *Die Familie bei den Angelsachsen.* Halle a. S., 1899.
Roemer (Th.), Review of de Chapeaurouge's *Einiges über Inzucht und ihre Leistung auf verschiedenen Zuchtgebieten ;* in *Archiv f. Rassen- und Gesellschafts-Biologie,* vol. vii. München, 1910.
—— Review of Schmehl's *Inzuchtstudien in einer deutschen Rambouillet-Stammschäferei ;* in *Archiv f. Rassen- und Gesellschafts-Biologie,* vol. x. Leipzig & Berlin, 1913.
Rogers (Charles), *Scotland, Social and Domestic.* London, 1869.
Roggewein (Roggeveen ; Jacob), 'An Account of Commodore Roggewein's Expedition . . . for the Discovery of Southern Lands '; in Harris, *Navigantium atque Itinerantium Bibliotheca,* vol. i. London, 1744.
Roguin (Ernest), *Traité de droit civil comparé. Le mariage.* Paris, 1904.
Rohde (Erwin), 'Paralipomena '; in *Rheinisches Museum für Philologie,* new ser. vol. xv. Frankfurt a.M., 1895.
—— *Psyche.* Freiburg i.B. & Leipzig, 1894.
Rohleder (Hermann), *Die Zeugung unter Blutsverwandten (Konsanguinität, Inzucht, Inzest).* Leipzig, 1912.
Rohlfs (Gerhard), ' Henry Noël von Bagermi '; in *Zeitschr. f. Ethnol.* vol. iii. Berlin, 1871.
Romanoff (H. C.), *Sketches of the Rites and Customs of the Greco-Russian Church.* London, Oxford, & Cambridge, 1869.
Romilly (H. H.), ' The Islands of the New Britain Group '; in *Proceed. Roy. Geo. Soc.* new ser. vol. ix. London, 1887.
—— *The Western Pacific and New Guinea.* London, 1887.
Roos (S.), ' Iets over Endeh '; in *Tijdschrift voor indische taal-, land- en volkenkunde,* vol. xxiv. Batavia & 's Hage, 1877.
Roquefeuil (C. de), *Journal d'un voyage autour du monde, pendant les années 1816, 1817, 1818 et 1819.* 2 vols. Paris, 1823.
Rorie (David), ' Stray Notes on the Folk-lore of Aberdeenshire and North-east of Scotland '; in *Folk-Lore,* vol. xxv. London, 1914.
Roscoe (John), *The Baganda.* London, 1911.
—— ' The Bahima '; in *Jour. Roy. Anthr. Inst.* vol. xxxvii. London, 1907.
—— *The Northern Bantu. An Account of some Central African Tribes of the Uganda Protectorate.* Cambridge, 1915.
—— ' Notes on the Bageshu '; in *Jour. Roy. Anthr. Inst.* vol. xxxix. London, 1909.
—— ' Notes on the Manners and Customs of the Baganda '; in *Jour. Anthr. Inst.* vol. xxxi. London, 1901.
Rose (Archibald) and Brown (J. Coggin), ' Lisu (Yawyin) Tribes of the Burma-China Frontier '; in *Memoirs Asiatic Soc. Bengal,* vol. iii. Calcutta, 1910.
Rose (*Sir* H. A.), *A Glossary of the Tribes and Castes of the Punjab and North-West Frontier Province.* Lahore, 1911 &c. *In progress.*

Rose (*Sir* H. A.), ' The Khokhars and the Gakhars in Panjab History ' ; in *Indian Antiquary*, vol. xxxvi. Bombay, 1907.
—— ' Note on Female Tattooing in the Panjâb ' ; in *The Indian Antiquary*, vol. xxxi. Bombay, 1902.
Rose (H. J.), ' On the alleged Evidence for Mother-right in Early Greece ' ; in *Folk-Lore*, vol. xxii. London, 1911.
Rosen (Eric von), *Träskfolket. Svenska Rhodesia-Kongo-expeditionens etnografiska forskningsresultat.* Stockholm, 1916.
Rosén (Helge), *Om dödsrike och dödsbruk i fornnordisk religion.* Lund, 1918.
Rosenau (William), *Jewish Ceremonial Institutions and Customs.* Baltimore, 1903.
Rosenbaum (Julius), *Geschichte der Lustseuche im Alterthume.* Halle, 1845.
Rosenberg (H. von), *Der malayische Archipel.* Leipzig, 1878.
Rosenstadt (B.), ' Zur Frage nach den Ursachen, welche die Zahl der Conceptionen beim Menschen in gewissen Monaten des Jahres regelmässig steigern ' ; in *Mittheilungen aus dem embryologischen Institute der K.K. Universität in Wien*, ser. ii. fasc. 4. Wien, 1890.
Ross (B. R.), ' The Eastern Tinneh ' ; in *Smithsonian Report*, 1866. Washington, 1867.
Ross (J. C.), *A Voyage of Discovery and Research in the Southern and Antarctic Regions, during the Years 1839-43.* 2 vols. London, 1847.
Ross (John), *History of Corea, Ancient and Modern.* Pasley, [1879].
Ross (*Sir* John), *Narrative of a Second Voyage in search of a North-West Passage.* London, 1835.
—— *A Voyage of Discovery for the purpose of exploring Baffin's Bay.* 2 vols. London, 1819.
Rossbach (A.), *Römische Hochzeits- und Ehedenkmäler.* Leipzig, 1871.
—— *Untersuchungen über die römische Ehe.* Stuttgart, 1853.
Rosset (C. W.), ' On the Maldive Islands, more especially treating of Málé Atol ' ; in *Jour. Anthr. Inst.* vol. xvi. London, 1887.
Rossillon (*le Père*), ' Mœurs et Coutumes du peuple *Kui*, Indes Anglaises ' ; in *Anthropos*, vol. vii. Wien, 1912.
Roth (H. Ling), ' The Aborigines of Hispaniola ' ; in *Jour. Anthr. Inst.* vol. xvi. London, 1887.
—— *The Aborigines of Tasmania.* Halifax, 1899.
—— *Great Benin.* Halifax, 1903.
—— *The Natives of Sarawak and British North Borneo.* 2 vols. London, 1896.
Roth (Rudolph), ' On the Morality of the Veda.' Trans. ; in *Journal of the American Oriental Society*, vol. iii. New York, 1853.
Roth (Walter E.), *Ethnological Studies among the North-West-Central Queensland Aborigines.* Brisbane & London, 1897.
—— *North Queensland Ethnography : Bulletin No. 5. Superstition, Magic, and Medicine.* Brisbane, 1903.
—— *North Queensland Ethnography : Bulletin No. 8. Notes on Government, Morals, and Crime.* Brisbane, 1906.
Rousselet (Louis), *India and its Native Princes.* Trans. London, 1876.
Routledge (W. Scoresby and Katherine), *With a Prehistoric People. The Akikúyu of British East Africa.* London, 1910.

Rowlatt (E. A.), ' Report of an Expedition into the Mishmee Hills ' ; in *Jour. Asiatic Soc. Bengal*, vol. xiv. pt. ii. Calcutta, 1845.
Rowley (Henry), *Africa Unveiled*. London, 1876.
Rowney (H. B.), *The Wild Tribes of India*. London, 1882.
Royal Commission on Divorce and Matrimonial Causes. Appendices to the Minutes of Evidence and Report. London, 1912.
Royal Geographical Society. Supplementary Papers. London.
Rubruquis (G. de), ' Travels into Tartary and China.' Trans. ; in Pinkerton, *Collection of Voyages and Travels*, vol. vii. London, 1811.
Rüdin (E.), Review of Feer's *Der Einfluss der Blutsverwandtschaft der Eltern auf die Kinder* ; in *Archiv f. Rassen- und Gesell-schafts-Biologie*, vol. v. München, 1908.
Ruelle (E.), ' Notes anthropologiques, ethnographiques et socio-logiques sur quelques populations noires du 2ᵉ territoire militaire de l'Afrique occidentale française ' ; in *L'Anthro-pologie*, vol. xv. Paris, 1904.
Russell (A. D.) and Abdullah al-Ma'mun Suhrawardy, ' *A Manual of the Law of Marriage* ' from the *Mukhtasar of Sīdī Khalīl*. [London,] *s.d.*
Russell (Frank), ' The Pima Indians ' ; in *Ann. Rep. Bur. American Ethnol*. vol. xxvi. 1904–05. Washington, 1908.
Russell (R. V.), *The Tribes and Castes of the Central Provinces of India*. 4 vols. London, 1916.
Russkaya Starina. St. Petersburg.
Rutland (Joshua), ' On the Survivals of Ancient Customs in Oceania ' ; in *Jour. Polynesian Soc*. vol. xiii. Wellington, 1904.

Saalschütz (J. L.), *Das mosaische Recht*. 2 vols. Berlin, 1853.
Sachau (E.), *Muhammedanisches Recht nach Schafiitischer Lehre*. Stuttgart & Berlin, 1897.
Sachs (Julius), *Text-Book of Botany*. Trans. Oxford, 1882.
Sacred Books of the East (The). Ed. by F. Max Müller. Oxford, 1879 &c.
Sacred Laws of the Âryas as taught in the Schools of Âpastamba, Gautama, Vâsishtha, and Baudhâyana (The). Trans. by G. Bühler. 2 vols. (*The Sacred Books of the East*, vols. ii., xiv.) Oxford, 1897, 1882.
Safford (W. E.), ' Guam and its People ' ; in *American Anthropologist*, new ser. vol. iv. New York, 1902.
Sahagun (F. Bernardino de), *Historia general de las cosas de Nueva España*. 3 vols. México, 1829–30.
Saïd Boulifa, *Textes berbères en dialecte de l'Atlas marocain*. Paris, 1908.
St. Elie (P. A. M.), ' La Femme du désert autrefois et aujourd'hui ' ; in *Anthropos*, vol. iii. Wien, 1908.
St. John (Bayle), *Adventures in the Libyan Desert*. London, 1849.
—— See Muḥammad ibn 'Umar, Al-Tūnusī.
St. John (H. C.), ' The Ainos : Aborigines of Yeso ' ; in *Jour. Anthr. Inst*. vol. ii. London, 1873.
St. John (Spenser), *Life in the Forests of the Far East*. 2 vols. London, 1862.
—— ' Wild Tribes of the North-West Coast of Borneo ' ; in *Trans. Ethn. Soc. London*, new ser. vol. ii. London, 1863.

Sakellarios (Ph.), *Die Sitten und Gebräuche der Hochzeit bei den Neugriechen verglichen mit denen der alten Griechen. (Inaugural-Dissertation.)* Halle a.S., 1880.

Salmon (G.), 'Les Bdadoua'; in *Archives marocaines*, vol. ii. Paris, 1905.

Salvado (R.), *Mémoires historiques sur l'Australie.* French trans. Paris, 1854.

—— *Voyage en Australie.* French trans. Paris, 1861.

Samter (Ernst), *Familienfeste der Griechen und Römer.* Berlin, 1901.

—— *Geburt, Hochzeit und Tod.* Leipzig & Berlin, 1911.

—— 'Hochzeitsbräuche'; in *Neue Jahrbücher für das klassische Altertum*, vol. xix. Leipzig, 1907.

Samuelson (James), *India, Past and Present.* London, 1890.

Sánchez Labrador (P. José), *El Paraguay Católico.* 2 vols. Buenos Aires, 1910.

Sanderson (John), 'Polygamous Marriage among the Kafirs of Natal and Countries around'; in *Jour. Anthr. Inst.* vol. viii. London, 1879.

Sandys (George), *A Relation of a Journey begun An. Dom.* 1610. London, 1637.

Sankara Menon (M.), *Census of India*, 1901. *Vol. XX. Cochin,* pt. i. Report. Ernakulam, 1903.

'Sânkhâyana-Grihya-Sûtra,' trans. by H. Oldenberg; in *The Sacred Books of the East*, vol. xxix. Oxford, 1886.

Sapir (Edward), 'Indian Tribes of the Coast'; in *Canada and its Provinces, vol. XXI. The Pacific Province*, pt. i. Toronto, 1914.

—— 'Notes on the Takelma Indians of Southwestern Oregon'; in *American Anthropologist*, new ser. vol. ix. Lancaster, 1907.

—— *A Sketch of the Social Organization of the Nass River Indians. (Canada Department of Mines. Geological Survey Museum Bulletin No.* 19. *Anthropological Series, No.* 7.) Ottawa, 1915.

Sapper (Carl), 'Mittelamericanische Caraiben'; in *Internationales Archiv für Ethnographie*, vol. x. Leiden, 1897.

Sarasin (Paul and Fritz), *Ergebnisse naturwissenschaftlicher Forschungen auf Ceylon.* 3 vols. Wiesbaden, 1887–93.

—— 'Über die Toála von Süd-Celebes'; in *Globus*, vol. lxxxiii. Braunschweig, 1903.

Sarat Chandra Das, *Journey to Lhasa and Central Tibet.* Ed. by W. W. Rockhill. London, 1904.

—— 'The Marriage Customs of Tibet'; in *Jour. Asiatic Soc. Bengal*, vol. lxii. pt. iii. Calcutta, 1893.

Sarat Chandra Roy, *The Mundas and their Country.* Calcutta, 1912.

—— *The Orāons of Chōtā Nāgpur.* Ranchi, 1915.

Sarbah (J. M.), *Fanti Customary Laws.* London, 1904.

Sartori (Paul), 'Der Schuh im Volksglauben'; in *Zeitschrift des Vereins für Volkskunde*, vol. iv. Berlin, 1894.

—— *Sitte und Brauch.* Vol. I. Leipzig, 1910.

Sarytschew (G.), 'Account of a Voyage of Discovery to the North-East of Siberia, the Frozen Ocean, and the North-East Sea.' Trans.; in *A Collection of Modern and Contemporary Voyages and Travels*, vols. v.–vi. London, 1807.

Sathapata-Brâhmana (The). Trans. by J. Eggeling. 5 vols. *(The Sacred Books of the East*, vols. xii., xxvi., xli., xliii., xliv.) Oxford, 1882–1900.

Sauer (M.), *An Account of a Geographical and Astronomical Expedition to the Northern Parts of Russia performed by Joseph Billings*. London, 1802.

Saunderson (H. S.), ' Notes on Corea and its People ' ; in *Jour. Anthr. Inst.* vol. xxiv. London, 1895.

Sautayra (Édouard) and Cherbonneau (Eugène), *Droit musulman. Du statut personnel et des successions*. 2 vols. Paris, 1873–74.

Sauvé (L. F.), *Le Folk-Lore des Hautes-Vosges*. Paris, 1889.

Savage (T. S.), *A Description of the Characters and Habits of Troglodytes Gorilla*. Boston, 1847.

—— ' Observations on the External Characters and Habits of the *Troglodytes Niger* ' ; in *Boston Journal of Natural History*, vol. iv. Boston, 1844.

Saxo Grammaticus, *Historia Danica*. Ed. by P. E. Müller and J. M. Velschow. 2 vols. Havniae, 1839–58.

Scaramucci (F.) and Giglioli (E. H.), ' Notizie sui Danakil ' ; in *Archivio per l'antropologia e la etnologia*, vol. xiv. Firenze, 1884.

Schaaffhausen (Hermann), ' Darwinism and Anthropology ' ; in *The Anthropological Review*, vol. vi. London, 1868.

—— ' On the Primitive Form of the Human Skull.' Trans. ; in *The Anthropological Review*, vol. vi. London, 1868.

Schadee (M. C.), ' Heirats- und andere Gebräuche bei den Mansela und Nusawele Alfuren in der Untertheilung Wahaai der Insel Seram (Ceram) ' ; in *Internationales Archiv für Ethnographie*, vol. xxii. Leiden, 1913.

Schadenberg (Alex.), ' Die Bewohner von Süd-Mindanao und der Insel Samal ' ; in *Zeitschr. f. Ethnol.* vol. xvii. Berlin, 1885.

—— ' Über die Negritos der Philippinen ' ; in *Zeitschr. f. Ethnol.* vol. xii. Berlin, 1880.

Schaeffner (W.), *Geschichte der Rechtsverfassung Frankreichs*. 4 vols. Frankfurt a. M., 1845–50.

Schell (O.), Bergische Hochzeitsgebräuche ' ; in *Zeitschr. des Vereins für Volkskunde*, vol. x. Berlin, 1900.

—— ' Nachträge zu den " Bergischen Hochzeitsgebräuchen " ' ; in *Zeitschr. des Vereins für Volkskunde*, vol. x. Berlin, 1900.

—— ' Das Salz im Volksglauben ' ; in *Zeitschr. des Vereins für Volkskunde*, vol. xv. Berlin, 1905.

Schellong (O.), ' Ueber Familienleben und Gebräuche der Papuas der Umgebung von Finschhafen ' ; in *Zeitschr. f. Ethnol.* vol. xxi. Berlin, 1889.

—— ' Weitere Mitteilungen über die Papuas (Jabim) der Gegend des Finschhafens in Nordost-Neu-Guinea (Kaiserwilhelmsland) ' ; in *Zeitschr. f. Ethnol.* vol. xxxvii. Berlin, 1905.

Scheurl (A. von), *Das gemeine deutsche Eherecht*. Erlangen, 1882.

—— and Sehling (Emil), ' Eherecht ' ; in Herzog-Hauck, *Realencyklopädie für protestantische Theologie und Kirche*, vol. v. Leipzig, 1898.

Schinz (Hans), *Deutsch-Süd-West-Afrika*. Oldenburg & Leipzig, [1891].

Schlagintweit (Emil), *Indien im Wort und Bild*. 2 vols. Leipzig, 1880–81.

Schlegel (—), ' Om Morgengavens Oprindelse ' ; in *Astræa*, vol. ii.
  Kjøbenhavn, 1799.
Schlyter (C. J.), *Juridiska afhandlingar*. 2 vols. Upsala, 1836–79.
Schmehl (R.). See Roemer (Th.).
Schmid (van), ' Aanteekeningen nopens de zeden, gewoonten en
  gebruiken, benevens de vooroordeelen en bijgeloovigheden
  der bevolking van de eilanden Saparoea, Haroekoe, Noessa
  Laut, en van een geedeelte van de zuid-kust van Ceram ' ;
  in *Tijdschrift voor Neêrlands Indie*, vol. v. pt. ii. Batavia,
  1843.
Schmidt (Emil), *Ceylon*. Berlin, [1897].
Schmidt (Karl), *Jus primae noctis*. Freiburg i.B., 1881.
—— ' Das Streit über das jus primae noctis ' ; in *Zeitschr. f. Ethnol.*
  vol. xvi. Berlin, 1884.
Schmidt (Leopold), *Die Ethik der alten Griechen*. 2 vols. Berlin,
  1882.
Schmidt (Max), ' Die Guató ' ; in *Verhandl. Berliner Gesellsch.
  Anthr.* 1902. Berlin.
—— ' Über das Recht der tropischen Naturvölker Südamerikas ' ;
  in *Zeitschr. f. vergl. Rechtswiss.* vol. xiii. Stuttgart, 1899.
Schmidt (Richard), *Beiträge zur Indischen Erotik. Das Liebesleben
  des Sanskritvolkes*. Berlin, 1911.
—— *Liebe und Ehe im alten und modernen Indien*. Berlin, 1904.
Schmidt (P. W.), *Die Stellung der Pygmäenvölker in der Entwick-
  lungsgeschichte des Menschen*. Stuttgart, 1910.
—— ' Totemismus, viehzüchterischer Nomadismus und Mutter-
  recht ' ; in *Anthropos*, vols. x.–xi. Wien, 1915–16.
—— *Der Ursprung der Gottesidee. I. Historisch-kritischer Teil*.
  Münster i. W., 1912.
—— Review of Buschan's *Illustrierte Völkerkunde*, vol. i. ; in
  Anthropos, vol. v. Wien, 1910.
Schmolck (*Dr.*), ' Mehrfacher Zwergwuchs in verwandten Familien
  eines Hochgebirgstales ' ; in *Virchows Archiv für pathologische
  Anatomie und Physiologie und für klinische Medizin*, vol.
  clxxxvii. Berlin, 1907.
Schnee (Heinrich), *Bilder aus der Südsee. Unter den kannibalischen
  Stämmen des Bismarck-Archipels*. Berlin, 1904.
Schneider (Wilhelm), *Die Naturvölker*. 2 vols. Paderborn &
  Münster, 1885–86.
Schönwerth (Fr.), *Aus der Oberpfalz. Sitten und Sagen*. 3 vols.
  Augsburg, 1857–59.
Schomburgk (Richard), *Reisen in Britisch-Guiana*. 3 vols. Leipzig,
  1847–48.
—— ' Über einige Sitten und Gebräuche der tief im Innern Süd-
  australiens, am Peake-Flusse und dessen Umgebung, hausen-
  den Stämme ' ; in *Verhandl. Berliner Gesellsch. Anthr.* 1879.
  Berlin.
Schomburgk (*Sir* Robert H.), ' On the Natives of Guiana ' ; in *Jour.
  Ethn. Soc. London*, vol. i. Edinburgh (printed), 1848.
Schoolcraft (H. R.), *Historical and Statistical Information respecting
  the History, Condition, and Prospects of the Indian Tribes of
  the United States* (the title-pages of vols. iv.–vi. read : *Archives
  of Aboriginal Knowledge, &c.*). 6 vols. Philadelphia,
  1851–60.
—— *The Indian in his Wigwam*. New York, 1848.

Schotter (*P.* Aloys), ' Notes ethnographiques sur les Tribus de Kouy-
tcheou (Chine) ' ; in *Anthropos*, vol. vi.   Wien, 1911.
Schouten (Wouter), *Ost-Indische Reyse.*   German trans.   Amster-
dam, 1676.
Schrader (Eberhard), *Die Keilinschriften und das Alte Testament.*
Ed. by H. Zimmern and H. Winckler.   Berlin, 1903.
Schrader (O.), ' Family (Teutonic and Balto-Slavic) ' ; in Hastings,
Encyclopædia of Religion and Ethics, vol. v.   Edinburgh,
1912.
—— *Prehistoric Antiquities of the Aryan Peoples.*   Trans. by F. B.
Jevons.   London, 1890.
—— *Reallexikon der indogermanischen Altertumskunde.*   Strassburg,
1901.
Schriften des Naturwissenschaftlichen Vereins für Schleswig-Holstein.
Kiel.
Schroeder (Leopold von), *Die Hochzeitsgebräuche der Esten und
einiger anderer finnisch-ugrischer Völkerschaften in Ver-
gleichung mit denen der indo-germanischen Völker.*   Berlin,
1888.
—— *Indiens Literatur und Cultur in historischer Entwicklung.*
Leipzig, 1887.
—— *Mysterium und Mimus im Rigveda.*   Leipzig, 1908.
Schroeder (Richard), *Lehrbuch der deutschen Rechtsgeschichte.*
Leipzig, 1902.
Schuermann (C. W.), ' The Aboriginal Tribes of Port Lincoln ' ; in
Woods, *Native Tribes of South Australia.*   Adelaide, 1879.
Schütz-Holzhausen (D. von), *Der Amazonas.*   Freiburg i.B., 1883.
Schulchan Aruch oder die vier jüdischen Gesetzbücher.   German
trans. by H. G. F. Löwe.   2 vols.   Wien, 1896.
Schultz (E.), ' The most important Principles of Samoan Family
Law.'   Trans. ; in *Jour. Polynesian Soc.* vol. xx.   New
Plymouth, 1911.
Schultze (Oskar), ' Zur Frage von den geschlechtsbildenden Ur-
sachen ' ; in *Archiv für Mikroskopische Anatomie und Ent-
wicklungsgeschichte*, vol. lxiii.   Bonn, 1903.
Schulze (Louis), ' The Aborigines of the Upper and Middle Finke
River : their Habits and Customs ' ; in *Transactions and
Proceedings and Report of the Royal Society of South Australia*,
vol. xiv. 1890–91.   Adelaide, 1891.
Schumacher (*P. P.*), ' Das Eherecht in Ruanda ' ; in *Anthropos*,
vol. vii.   Wien, 1912.
Schurtz (Heinrich), *Altersklassen und Männerbünde.*   Berlin, 1902.
—— *Grundzüge einer Philosophie der Tracht.*   Stuttgart, 1891.
Schuster (Ernest J.), *The Principles of German Civil Law.*   Oxford,
1907.
Schuster (Fr.), ' Die sozialen Verhältnisse des Banjange-Stammes
(Kamerun) ' ; in *Anthropos*, vol. ix.   Wien, 1914.
Schuyler (E.), *Turkistan.*   2 vols.   London, 1876.
Schwabenspiegel (Der).   Ed. by F. L. A. von Lassberg.   Tübingen,
1840.
Schwalbe (G.), ' Die Hautfarbe des Menschen ' ; in *Mitteil. Anthr.
Gesellsch, Wien*, vol. xxxiv.   Wien, 1904.
—— *Studien zur Vorgeschichte des Menschen.*   Stuttgart, 1906.
—— ' Zur Frage der Abstammung des Menschen ' ; in *Globus*,
vol. lxxxviii, Braunschweig, 1905.

Schwally (F.), *Der heilige Krieg im alten Israel*. Leipzig, 1901.
Schwaner (C. A. L. M.), *Bórneo. Beschrijving van het stroomgebied van den Barito, &c.* 2 vols. Amsterdam, 1853–54.
Schweinfurth (Georg), *Im Herzen von Afrika*. 2 vols. Leipzig, 1874.
—— *The Heart of Africa*. Trans. 2 vols. London, 1873.
Schweizerisches Zivilgesetzbuch vom 10. *Dezember* 1907. Zürich, 1912.
Science, an Illustrated Journal published weekly. New York.
Scott (*Sir* James George), assisted by Hardiman (J. P.), *Gazetteer of Upper Burma and the Shan States*. 5 vols. Rangoon, 1900–01.
—— See Shway Yoe.
Seaver (James E.), *A Narrative of the Life of Mrs. Mary Jemison, Who was taken by the Indians, in the Year* 1755. Howden, 1826.
Sébillot (Paul), *Coutumes populaires de la Haute-Bretagne*. Paris, 1886.
—— *Le Folk-Lore de France*. 4 vols. Paris, 1904–07.
Sebright (*Sir* John S.), *The Art of Improving the Breeds of Domestic Animals*. London, 1809.
Seebohm (F.), *The English Village Community*. London, 1883.
—— *The Tribal System in Wales*. London, 1895.
Seemann (B.), *Narrative of the Voyage of H.M.S. Herald during the Years* 1845–1851. 2 vols. London, 1853.
—— *Viti*. Cambridge, 1862.
Sehling (Emil). See Scheurl (A. von) and Sehling.
Seidlitz (N. von), ' Die Abchasen ' ; in *Globus*, vol. lxvi. Braunschweig, 1894.
Selbie (J. A.), ' Sodomite ' ; in Hastings, *Dictionary of the Bible*, vol. iv. Edinburgh, 1902.
Selenka (Emil and Lenore), *Sonnige Welten. Ostasiatische Reise-Skizzen*. Wiesbaden, 1896.
Seligman (C. G.), ' Dinka ' ; in Hastings, *Encyclopædia of Religion and Ethics*, vol. iv. Edinburgh, 1911.
—— *The Melanesians of British New Guinea*. Cambridge, 1910.
—— *Report on Totemism and Religion of the Dinka of the White Nile*. Khartoum, s.d.
—— and Seligman (Brenda Z.), ' The Kabâbîsh, a Sudan Arab Tribe ' ; in *Harvard African Studies*, vol. ii. Cambridge (Mass.), 1918.
—— and Seligman (Brenda Z.), *The Veddas*. Cambridge, 1911.
Sellami (M. S.), ' La femme musulmane ' ; in *Revue tunisienne*, vol. iii. Tunis, 1896.
Selous (Edmund), *Bird Watching*. London, 1901.
Semper (Karl), *Die Palau-Inseln*. Leipzig, 1873.
Seneca (L. A.), *Opera quæ supersunt*. Ed. by F. Haase. 3 vols. Lipsiae, 1853–62.
Senfft (——), ' Die Insel Nauru ' ; in *Mittheil. Deutsch. Schutzgeb.* vol. ix. Berlin, 1896.
—— ' Die Marshall-Insulaner ' ; in Steinmetz, *Rechtsverhältnisse von eingeborenen Völkern in Afrika und Ozeanien*. Berlin, 1903.
Sepp (Johannes), *Völkerbrauch bei Hochzeit, Geburt und Tod*. München, 1891.

Serbelov (Gerda), ' The Social Position of Men and Women among
the Natives of East Malekula, New Hebrides ' ; in *American
Anthropologist*, new ser. vol. xv. Lancaster, 1913.
Serpa Pinto (Alexandre de), *How I crossed Africa*. Trans. 2 vols.
London, 1881.
Servius Maurus Honoratus, *Commentarii in Virgilium*. Ed. by
H. A. Lion. Gottingae, 1826.
Settegast (H.), *Die Thierzucht*. Breslau, 1868.
Shakespear (J.), *The Lushei Kuki Clans*. London, 1912.
Shakespeare (W.), *Works*. Ed. by A. Dyce. 9 vols. London,
1864–67.
Shand (Alexander), ' The Moriori People of the Chatham Islands ' ;
in *Jour. Polynesian Soc.* vol. vi. Wellington, 1897.
Shand (Alex. F.), *The Foundations of Character*. London, 1914.
Shastri (B. V.), ' Maratha, &c. ' ; in *Panjab Notes and Queries*,
vol. i. Allahabad, 1883.
Shaw (G. A.), ' The Betsileo : Religious and Social Customs ' ; in
Antananarivo Annual and Madagascar Magazine, no. iv.
Antananarivo, 1878.
Shaw (Thomas), ' On the Inhabitants of the Hills near Rájamahall ' ;
in *Asiatick Researches*, vol. iv. Calcutta, 1795.
Sheldon (J. P.), *Dairy Farming*. London, *s.d.*
—— *Live Stock in Health and Disease*. London, *s.d.*
Sherring (Charles A.), ' Notes on the Bhotias of Almora and British
Garhwal ' ; in *Memoirs Asiatic Soc. Bengal*, vol. i. 1905–07.
Calcutta, 1907.
—— *Western Tibet and the British Borderland*. London, 1906.
Sherwill (W. S.), ' Notes upon a Tour through the Rájmahal
Hills ' ; in *Jour. Asiatic Soc. Bengal*. vol. xx. Calcutta,
1852.
Shinji Ishii, ' The Life of the Mountain People in Formosa ' ; in
Folk-Lore, vol. xxviii. London, 1917.
Shklovsky (I. W.), *In Far North-East Siberia*. London, 1916.
Shooter (Joseph), *The Kafirs of Natal and the Zulu Country*. London,
1857.
Shortland (Edward), *Traditions and Superstitions of the New Zea-
landers*. London, 1854.
Shortt (John), ' An Account of the Hill Tribes of the Neilgherries ' ;
in *Trans. Ethn. Soc. London*, new ser. vol. vii. London,
1869.
—— ' A Contribution to the Ethnology of Jeypore ' ; in *Trans.
Ethn. Soc. London*, new ser. vol. vi. London, 1868.
—— *The Hill Ranges of Southern India*. 5 pts. Madras, 1870–76.
Shulḥān 'Ārūkh. See *Schulchan Aruch*.
Shway Yoe (*i.e.*, Sir James George Scott), *The Burman*. London,
1910.
Sibree (James), *The Great African Island. Chapters on Madagascar*.
London, 1880.
Sīdī Ḥalīl, *Muḥtaṣar*. See Russell (A. D.) and Abdullah al-Ma'mun
Suhrawardy.
Siebold (H. von), *Ethnologische Studien über die Aino auf der Insel
Yesso*. Berlin, 1881.
Sieroshevski. See Sumner (W. G.).
Simmel (Georg), ' Die Verwandtenehe ' ; in *Vossische Zeitung*,
June 3rd and 10th, 1894. Berlin.

Simon (Pedro), *Primera parte de las Noticias historiales de las Conquistas de tierra firme en las Indias Occidentales.* Cuenca, 1627.

Simons (F. A. A.), 'An Exploration of the Goajira Peninsula, U.S. of Colombia'; in *Proceed. Roy. Geo. Soc.* new ser. vol. vii. London, 1885.

Simpkins (J. E.), *County Folk-Lore. Vol. VII. Examples of printed Folk-Lore concerning Fife, with some Notes on Clackmannan and Kinross-shires.* London, 1914.

Simrock (Karl), *Handbuch der Deutschen Mythologie mit Einschluss der nordischen.* Bonn, 1887.

Simson (Alfred), *Travels in the Wilds of Ecuador.* London, 1886.

Sinclair (A. T.), 'Tattooing of the North American Indians'; in *American Anthropologist,* new ser. vol. xi. Lancaster, 1909.

Sirr (H. Charles), *Ceylon and the Cingalese.* 2 vols. London, 1850.

Sitzungsberichte der matematisch-naturwissenschaftlichen Klasse der kaiserl. Akademie der Wissenschaften. Wien.

—— *der philosophisch-historischen Classe der kaiserl. Akademie der Wissenschaften.* Wien.

Sjöberg (Wilhelm), 'Brudstugugåendet i Replot'; in *Hembygden,* vol. vii. Helsingfors, 1916.

Sjögren (A. J.), *Livische Grammatik nebst Sprachproben.* Ed. by F. J. Wiedemann. (*Gesammelte Schriften,* vol. ii. pt. i.) St. Petersburg, 1861.

Skeat (W. W.), *Malay Magic.* London, 1900.

—— and Blagden (Charles O.), *Pagan Races of the Malay Peninsula.* 2 vols. London, 1906.

Skottsberg (Carl), 'Observations on the Natives of the Patagonian Channel Region'; in *American Anthropologist,* new ser. vol. xv. Lancaster, 1913.

—— *The Wilds of Patagonia.* London, 1911.

Skrefsrud (L. O.), 'Traces of Fraternal Polyandry amongst the Santāls'; in *Jour. Asiatic Soc. Bengal,* vol. lxxii. pt. iii. Calcutta, 1904.

—— See Hertel (Ludvig).

Skrifter utgivna av Svenska Litteratursällskapet i Finland. Helsingfors.

Sleeman (*Sir* W. H.), *Rambles and Recollections of an Indian Official.* 2 vols. London, 1844.

Smirnov (J. N.), *Les populations finnoises des bassins de la Volga et de la Kama.* Part I. French trans. by P. Bayer. Paris, 1898.

Smith (E. R.), *The Araucanians.* New York, 1855.

Smith (Edward), *Health and Disease as influenced by the Daily, Seasonal, and other Cyclical Changes in the Human System.* London, 1861.

Smith (S. Percy), 'Futuna'; in *Jour. Polynesian Soc.* vol. i. Wellington, 1892.

—— 'Niuē Island, and its People'; in *Jour. Polynesian Soc.* vol. xi. Wellington, 1902.

Smith (Thomas), *Narrative of a Five Years' Residence at Nepaul.* 2 vols. London, 1852.

Smith (W. Robertson), *Kinship and Marriage in Early Arabia.* Cambridge, 1885.

—— Review of the first edition of the present work; in *Nature,* vol. xliv. London, 1891.

Smith (William) and Cheetham (Samuel), *A Dictionary of Christian Antiquities.* 2 vols. London, 1875-80.
—— Wayte (William), and Marindin (G. E.), *A Dictionary of Greek and Roman Antiquities.* 2 vols. London, 1890-91.
Smithsonian Contributions to Knowledge. Washington.
Smithsonian Institution, Annual Reports of the Board of Regents. Washington.
—— *Annual Reports of the Bureau of American Ethnology.* Washington.
—— *Bureau of American Ethnology, Bulletins.* Washington.
Smyth (R. Brough), *The Aborigines of Victoria.* 2 vols. London, 1878.
Snorri Sturluson, *Heimskringla. Nóregs konunga sǫgur I.* Ed. by Finnur Jónsson. København, 1893-1900.
—— *The Heimskringla or the Sagas of the Norse Kings.* Trans. by S. Laing, ed. by R. B. Anderson. 4 vols. London, 1889.
—— *Ynglingasaga.* Ed. by Finnur Jónsson. København, 1912.
Snow (W. Parker), ' Remarks on the Wild Tribes of Tierra del Fuego ' ; in *Trans. Ethn. Soc. London,* new ser. vol. i. London, 1861.
—— *A Two Years' Cruise off Tierra del Fuego.* 2 vols. London, 1857.
Société normande de Géographie, Bulletins. Rouen.
Sociological Review (The). London.
Socrates, ' Historia ecclesiastica ' ; in Migne, *Patrologiæ cursus,* Ser. Graeca, vol. lxvii. Parisiis, 1859.
Sohm (Rudolph), *The Institutes.* Trans. by J. C. Ledlie. Oxford, 1907.
—— *Das Recht der Eheschliessung aus dem deutschen und canonischen Recht geschichtlich entwickelt.* Weimar, 1875.
Solberg (O.), ' Gebräuche der Mittelmesa-Hopi (Moqui) bei Namengebung, Heirat und Tod ' ; in *Zeitschr. f. Ethnol.* vol. xxxvii. Berlin, 1905.
Soleillet (Paul), *L'Afrique occidentale.* Avignon, 1877.
Solinus (C. J.), *Collectanea rerum memorabilium.* Ed. by Th. Mommsen. Berolini, 1895.
Solotaroff (H.), ' On the Origin of the Family ' ; in *American Anthropologist,* vol. xi. Washington, 1898.
' Sommario di tutti li regni, città, & popoli orientali.' Trans. into Italian from Portuguese ; in Ramusio, *Delle navigationi et viaggi,* vol. i. Venetia, 1563.
Sommerville (B. T.), ' Ethnographical Notes on New Hebrides ' ; in *Jour. Anthr. Inst.* vol. xxiii. London, 1894.
Sonnerat (Pierre), *Voyage aux Indes orientales et à la Chine, fait par ordre du Roi, depuis 1774 jusqu'en 1781.* 2 vols. Paris, 1782.
—— *A Voyage to the East Indies and China.* Trans. 3 vols. Calcutta, 1788-89.
Sophocles, *Tragœdiæ et Fragmenta.* Ed. by E. A. J. Ahrens. Parisiis, 1842.
Soppitt (C. A.), *A Short Account of the Kuki-Lushai Tribes on the North-East Frontier.* Shillong, 1887.
Sorge (F.), ' Nissan-Inseln im Bismarck-Archipel ' ; in Steinmetz, *Rechtsverhältnisse von eingeborenen Völkern in Afrika und Ozeanien.* Berlin, 1903.
South American Missionary Magazine (The). London.

Southey (R.), *History of Brazil.* 3 vols. London, 1810–19.
' Soviet Law of Marriage and the Family.' Trans.; in *The Contemporary Review,* vol. cxvii. London, 1920.
Soyaux (Hermann), *Aus West-Afrika.* Leipzig, 1879.
Sozomenus (Hermias), ' Historia ecclesiastica ' ; in Migne, *Patrologiæ cursus,* Ser. Graeca, vol. lxvii. Parisiis, 1859.
Sparkman (Ph. Stedman), ' The Culture of the Luiseño Indians ' ; in *University of California Publications in American Archæology and Ethnology,* vol. viii. Berkeley, 1908.
Sparrman (A.), *A Voyage to the Cape of Good Hope.* Trans. 2 vols. London, 1786.
Speck (Frank G.), ' The Creek Indians of Taskigi Town ' ; in *Memoirs of the American Anthropological Association,* vol. ii. Lancaster, 1907.
—— *Ethnology of the Yuchi Indians.* (*University of Pennsylvania. Anthropological Publications of the University Museum,* vol. i. no. 1.) Philadelphia, 1909.
—— *Family Hunting Territories and Social Life of Various Algonkian Bands of the Ottawa Valley.* (*Canada Department of Mines. Geological Survey. Memoir 70. No. 8, Anthropological Series.*) Ottawa, 1915.
Speiser (Felix), ' Beiträge zur Ethnographie der Orang Mamma auf Sumatra ' ; in *Archiv f. Anthropologie,* new ser. vol. ix. Braunschweig, 1910.
—— *Two Years with the Natives in the Western Pacific.* London, 1913.
Spencer (Herbert), *Descriptive Sociology.* 8 vols. London, 1873–81.
—— *Essays : Scientific, Political, and Speculative.* 2 vols. London, 1883.
—— *The Principles of Psychology.* 2 vols. London, 1890.
—— *The Principles of Sociology.* 3 vols. London, 1882–96.
—— ' A Short Rejoinder ' [to McLennan's article ' The Levirate and Polyandry '] ; in *The Fortnightly Review,* new ser. vol. xxi. London, 1877.
Spencer (*Sir* Walter Baldwin), *Native Tribes of the Northern Territory of Australia.* London, 1914.
—— and Gillen (F. J.), *The Native Tribes of Central Australia.* London, 1899.
—— and Gillen (F. J.), *The Northern Tribes of Central Australia.* London, 1904.
Spiegel (F.), *Erânische Alterthumskunde.* 3 vols. Leipzig, 1871–78.
Spieth (Jakob), *Die Ewe-Stämme. Material zur Kunde des Ewe-Volkes in Deutsch-Togo.* Berlin, 1906.
Spix (J. B. von) and Martius (C. F. Ph. von), *Reise in Brasilien.* 3 vols. München, 1823–31.
—— *Travels in Brazil in the Years 1817–1820.* Trans. 2 vols. London, 1824.
Sprenger (A.), ' Acclimatisationsfähigkeit der Europäer in Asien ' ; in *Verhandl. Berliner Gesellsch. Anthr. Berlin,* 1885. Berlin.
Sproat (G. M.), *Scenes and Studies of Savage Life.* London, 1868.
Squier (E. G.), ' Observations on the Archaeology and Ethnology of Nicaragua ' ; in *Trans. American Ethn. Soc.* vol. iii. pt. i. New York, 1853.
—— *The States of Central America.* London, 1858.
Stack (Edward), *The Mikirs.* Ed. by Sir Charles Lyall. London, 1908.

Stade (Hans), *The Captivity of Hans Stade of Hesse, in A.D.* 1547–1555, *among the Wild Tribes of Eastern Brazil.* Trans. by A. Tootal, and annotated by R. F. Burton. London, 1874.

Stair (John B.), *Old Samoa.* London, 1897.

Stanbridge (W. E.), ' Some Particulars of the General Characteristics, Astronomy, and Mythology of the Tribes in the Central Part of Victoria, Southern Australia '; in *Trans. Ethn. Soc. London,* new ser. vol. i. London, 1861.

Stannus (H. S.), ' Notes on some Tribes of British Central Africa '; in *Jour. Roy. Anthr. Inst.* vol. xl. London, 1910.

Starcke (C. N.), *The Primitive Family in its Origin and Development.* London, 1889.

Starkweather (G. B.), *The Law of Sex.* London, 1883.

' Statistik der Eingeborenen-Bevölkerung der Neu-Lauenburg-Gruppe '; in *Mittheil. Deutsch. Schutzgeb.* vol. xiv. Berlin, 1901.

Steel (E. H.), ' On the Kasia Tribe '; in *Trans. Ethn. Soc. London,* new ser. vol. vii. London, 1869.

Steele (Arthur), *The Law and Custom of Hindoo Castes.* London, 1868.

Steinau (J. H.), *A Pathological and Philosophical Essay on Hereditary Diseases.* London, 1843.

Steinen (Karl von den), *Durch Central-Brasilien.* Leipzig, 1886.

—— *Unter den Naturvölkern Zentral-Brasiliens.* Berlin, 1894.

Steinmetz (S. R.), ' Die neueren Forschungen zur Geschichte der menschlichen Familie '; in *Zeitschr. f. Socialwissenschaft,* vol. ii. Berlin, 1899.

—— *Rechtsverhältnisse von eingeborenen Völkern in Afrika und Ozeanien.* Ed. by. Berlin, 1903.

Steller (G. W.), *Beschreibung von dem Lande Kamtschatka.* Frankfurt & Leipzig, 1774.

Stendhal, *M.* de (*i.e.,* M. H. Beyle), *De l'amour.* Paris, 1853.

—— *On Love.* Trans. with an introduction and notes by P. S. and C. N. Woolf. London, 1915.

Stenin (P. von), ' Das Gewohnheitsrecht der Samojeden '; in *Globus,* vol. lx. Braunschweig, 1891.

Stephan (Emil) and Graebner (Fritz), *Neu-Mecklenburg (Bismarck-Archipel).* Berlin, 1907.

Stephen (A. M.), ' The Navajo '; in *American Anthropologist,* vol. vi. Washington, 1893.

Stephen (H. J.), *New Commentaries on the Laws of England.* Ed. by E. Jenks. 4 vols. London, 1914.

Stephens (Edward), ' The Aborigines of Australia '; in *Jour. and Proceed. Roy. Soc. N. S. Wales,* vol. xxiii. Sydney & London, 1889.

Stern (Bernhard), *Medizin, Aberglaube und Geschlechtsleben in der Türkei.* 2 vols. Berlin, 1903.

Sternberg (L.), ' Die Giljaken '; in *Verhandl. Berliner Gesellsch. Anthr.* 1901. Berlin.

—— Reviewed in *L'Anthropologie,* vol. v. Paris, 1894.

Stevens (H. Vaughan), *Materialien zur Kenntniss der Wilden Stämme auf der Halbinsel Maláka.* 2 pts. Ed. by Albert Grünwedel. (*Königliche Museen zu Berlin. Veröffentlichungen aus dem königl. Museum für Völkerkunde,* vol. ii. fasc. 3–4, and vol. iii. fasc. 3–4.) Berlin, 1892–94.

Stevens (H. Vaughan), 'Mittheilungen aus dem Frauenleben der Ôrang Bĕlendas, der Ôrang Djâkun und der Ôrang Lâut.' Ed. by Max Bartels; in *Zeitschr. f. Ethnol.* vol. xxviii. Berlin, 1896.

—— See Grünwedel (Albert).

Stevenson (Matilda C.), 'The Sia'; in *Ann. Rep. Bur. Ethnol.* vol. xi. Washington, 1894.

Stewart (C. S.), *Journal of a Residence in the Sandwich Islands, during the Years 1823, 1824, and 1825.* London, 1830.

Stewart (R.), 'Notes on Northern Cachar'; in *Jour. Asiatic Soc. Bengal,* vol. xxiv. Calcutta, 1855.

Stewart Lockhart (J. H.), 'Chinese Folk-Lore'; in *Folk-Lore,* vol i. London, 1890.

—— 'The Marriage Ceremonies of the Manchus'; in *Folk-Lore,* vol. i. London, 1890.

Sticotti (P.), 'Zu griechischen Hochzeitsgebräuchen'; in *Festschrift für Otto Benndorf.* Wien, 1898.

Stieda (Ludwig), 'Anatomisch-archäologische Studien. III. Die Infibulation bei Griechen und Römern'; in *Anatomische Hefte,* vol. xix. Wiesbaden, 1902.

Stieda (W.), 'Les mariages consanguins'; in *Annales de démographie internationale,* vol. iii. Paris, 1879.

Stigand (C. H.), 'Notes on the Natives of Nyassaland, N.E. Rhodesia, and Portuguese Zambezia, their Arts, Customs, and Modes of Subsistence'; in *Jour. Roy. Anthr. Inst.* vol. xxxvii. London, 1907.

Stirling (E. C.), 'Anthropology'; in *Report on the Work of the Horn Scientific Expedition to Central Australia,* pt. iv. London & Melbourne, 1896.

Stirling (W. H.), 'A Residence in Tierra del Fuego'; in *The South American Missionary Magazine,* vol. iv. London, 1870.

Stjernstedt (Georg), *Den nya äktenskapslagen.* Stockholm, 1916.

Stoecklein (J.), *Der Neue Welt-Bott.* 4 vols. Augspurg, Grätz, Wien, 1728–55.

Stoll (Otto), *Das Geschlechtsleben in der Völkerpsychologie.* Leipzig, 1908.

Stoll (W. G.), 'Notes on the Yoon-tha-lin Karens'; in *Madras Journal of Literature and Science,* new ser. vol. vi. Madras, 1861.

Stolpe (Hjalmar), 'Påsk-ön'; in *Ymer,* vol. iii. Stockholm, 1882.

Stone (O. C.), 'Description of the Country and Natives of Port Moresby and Neighbourhood, New Guinea'; in *Jour. Roy. Geo. Soc.* vol. xlvi. London, 1876.

—— *A Few Months in New Guinea.* London, 1880.

Storch (——), 'Sitten, Gebräuche und Rechtspflege bei den Bewohnern Usambaras und Pares'; in *Mittheil. Deutsch. Schutzgeb.* vol. viii. Berlin, 1895.

Stow (G. W.), *The Native Races of South Africa.* Ed. by G. McCall Theal. London, 1905.

Strabo, *Geographica.* 3 vols. Ed. by A. Meineke. Lipsiae, 1852–53.

—— The same work. Ed. by C. Müller and F. Dübner. Parisiis, 1853.

—— The same work. Trans. into French by A. Tardieu. 4 vols. Paris, 1873–90.

Strabo, The same work. Trans. into German by C. G. Groskurd. 4 vols. Berlin & Stettin, 1831–34.

Strachey (William), *The Historie of Travaile into Virginia Britannia*. Ed. by R. H. Major. London, 1849.

Strackerjan (L.), *Aberglaube und Sagen aus dem Herzogthum Oldenburg*. 2 vols. Oldenburg, 1867.

Strampff (H. L. von), *Dr. Martin Luther : Ueber die Ehe*. Berlin, 1857.

Strauch (H.), 'Allgemeine Bemerkungen ethnologischen Inhalts über Neu-Guinea, die Anachoreten-Inseln, Neu-Hannover, Neu-Irland, Neu-Britannien und Bougainville'; in *Zeitschr. f. Ethnol.* vol. ix. Berlin, 1877.

Strehlow (Carl), *Die Aranda- und Loritja-Stämme in Zentral-Australien*. Ed. by Moritz von Leonhardi. 4 vols. (*Veröffentlichungen aus dem städtischen Völker-Museum Frankfurt am Main, I.*) Frankfurt a. M., 1907–13.

Stricker (W.), 'Der Fuss der Chinesinnen'; in *Archiv f. Anthropologie*, vol. iv. Braunschweig, 1870.

Strzoda (Walter), 'Die Li auf Hainan und ihre Beziehungen zum asiatischen Kontinent'; in *Zeitschr. f. Ethnol.* vol. xliii. Berlin, 1911.

Stuart (H. A.), *Madras District Manuals : South Canara*, vol. ii. Madras, 1895.

Stuart (T. P. Anderson), 'The "Mika" or "Kulpi" Operation of the Australian Aborigines'; in *Jour. and Proceed. Roy. Soc. N. S. Wales*, 1896, vol. xxx. Sydney, 1897.

Studies in History, Economics and Public Law. Edited by the University Faculty of Political Science of Columbia College. New York.

Stuhlmann (Franz), *Mit Emin Pascha ins Herz von Afrika*. Berlin, 1894.

Stulpnagel (C. R.), 'Polyandry in the Himâlayas'; in *The Indian Antiquary*, vol. vii. Bombay, 1878.

Sturrock (J.), *Madras District Manuals : South Canara*, vol. i. Madras, 1894.

Sturt (Charles), *Narrative of an Expedition into Central Australia* 2 vols. London, 1849.

Subramhanya Aiyar (N.), *Census of India*, 1901. *Vol. XXVI. Travancore*, pt. i. Report. Trivandrum, 1903.

—— *Census of India*, 1911. *Vol. XXIII. Travancore*, pt. i. Report. Trivandrum, 1912.

Suessmilch (J. P.), *Die göttliche Ordnung in den Veränderungen des menschlichen Geschlechts*. 2 vols. Berlin, 1761–62.

Sugenheim (S.), *Geschichte der Aufhebung der Leibeigenschaft und Hörigkeit in Europa*. St. Petersburg, 1861.

Suidas, *Lexicon Græce et Latine*. Ed. by G. Bernhardy. 2 vols. Halis & Brunsvigae, 1853.

Sully (Maximilian de Bethune, *Duc de*), *Memoirs*. Trans. 5 vols. London, 1778.

Sumner (W. G.), 'The Yakuts, abridged from the Russian of Sieroshevski'; in *Jour. Anthr. Inst.* vol. xxxi. London, 1901.

Suomalais-Ugrilaisen Seuran Aikauskirja—Journal de la Société Finno-ougrienne. Helsingfors.

Sutherland (Alex.), *The Origin and Growth of the Moral Instinct*. 2 vols. London, 1898.

Sutherland (P. C.), 'On the Esquimaux'; in *Jour. Ethn. Soc. London*, vol. iv. London, 1856.
Sutton (T. M.), 'The Adjahdurah Tribe of Aborigines on Yorke's Peninsula : some of their Early Customs and Traditions '; in *Proceed. Roy. Geograph. Soc. Australasia : South Australian Branch*, vol. ii. 1887–88. Adelaide, 1890.
Sveriges Rikes Lag, till efterlefnad stadfästad år 1736. Ed. by N. W. Lundequist. Stockholm, 1874.
Swan (J. G.), *The Northwest Coast ; or, Three Years' Residence in Washington Territory*. New York, 1857.
Swanton (J. R.), *The Haida*. (*Publications of the Jesup North Pacific Expedition*, vol. v. pt. i.) Leiden & New York, 1905.
—— 'Social Condition, Beliefs, and Linguistic Relationship of the Tlingit Indians '; in *Ann. Rep. Bur. American Ethnol.* vol. xxvi. 1904–05. Washington, 1908.
—— 'The Social Organization of American Tribes '; in *American Anthropologist*, new ser. vol. vii. Lancaster, 1905.
—— Review of Frazer's *Lectures on the Early History of Kingship ;* in *American Anthropologist*, new ser. vol. viii. Lancaster, 1906.
—— Review of Thomas' *Kinship Organisations and Group Marriage in Australia ;* in *American Anthropologist*, new ser. vol. ix. Lancaster, 1907.
Swettenham (F. A.), 'Comparative Vocabulary of the Dialects of some of the Wild Tribes inhabiting the Malayan Peninsula, Borneo, &c. '; in *Jour. Straits Branch Roy. Asiatic Soc.* no. v. Singapore, 1880.

Ta Tsing Leu Lee. Trans. by Sir G. Th. Staunton. London, 1810.
Tacitus (C. C.), *Libri qui supersunt*. Ed. by C. Halm. 2 vols. Lipsiae, 1850–57.
Taine (H.), *Les origines de la France contemporaine*. 6 vols. Paris, 1876–1894.
Taintor (E. C.), *The Aborigines of Northern Formosa*. A paper read before the North China Branch of the Royal Asiatic Society, 1874. Shanghai, 1874.
Talbot (P. A.), 'The Buduma of Lake Chad '; in *Jour. Roy. Anthr. Inst.* vol. xli. London, 1911.
—— *In the Shadow of the Bush*. London, 1912.
Taplin (George), *The Folklore, Manners, Customs, and Languages of the South Australian Aborigines*. Ed. by. Adelaide, 1879.
—— 'The Narrinyeri '; in Woods, *Native Tribes of South Australia*. Adelaide, 1879.
Taprobanian (The). Bombay.
Tasmanian Journal of Natural Science, &c. Hobart Town.
Tauern (O. D.), 'Ceram '; in *Zeitschr. f. Ethnol.* vol. xlv. Berlin, 1913.
Taunton (E.), *The Law of the Church*. London, 1906.
Taupin (M.-J.). See Delisle (F.).
Tautain (*Dr.*), 'Étude sur la dépopulation de l'archipel des Marquises '; in *L'Anthropologie*, vol. ix. Paris, 1898.
—— 'Étude sur le mariage chez les Polynésiens (Mao'i) des îles Marquises '; in *L'Anthropologie*, vol. vi. Paris, 1895.
—— 'Sur le tatouage aux îles Marquises '; in *L'Anthropologie*, vol. vii. Paris, 1896.

Tauxier (Louis), *Le Noir du Soudan*. Paris, 1912.
Tavernier (J. B.), *Les six voyages de J. B. Tavernier*. 2 vols. Paris, 1676.
Taylor (R.), *Te Ika a Maui ; or, New Zealand and its Inhabitants*. London, 1870.
Tegengren (Jacob), ' Bröllopsbruk i Vörå ' ; in *Hembygden*, vols. viii.–ix. Helsingfors, 1917–18.
—— ' Magi och vidskepelse, hänförande sig till trolovning, bröllop o.s.v. (Från Österbotten) ' ; in *Hembygden*, vol. iii. Helsingfors, 1912.
Teit (J. A.), ' Indian Tribes of the Interior ' ; in *Canada and its Provinces, vol. XXI. The Pacific Province*, pt. i. Toronto, 1914.
—— ' The Lillooet Indians ' ; in *Publications of the Jesup North Pacific Expedition*, vol. ii. Leiden & New York, 1900–08.
—— ' The Shuswap ' ; in *Publications of the Jesup North Pacific Expedition*, vol. ii. Leiden & New York, 1900–08.
—— ' The Thompson Indians of British Columbia ' ; in *Publications of the Jesup North Pacific Expedition*, vol. i. (*Memoirs of the American Museum of Natural History*, vol. ii. Anthropology, vol. i.) New York, 1900.
Tekelija (Sava), ' Autobiografija ' ; in *Letopis Matice Srpske*, vol. cxix. Novi-Sad, 1876.
Tellier (G.), ' Kreis Kita, Französischer Sudan ' ; in *Steinmetz, Rechtsverhältnisse von eingeborenen Völkern in Afrika und Ozeanien*. Berlin, 1903.
Temme (J. D. H.), *Die Volkssagen der Altmark*. Berlin, 1839.
Tench (Watkin), *A Narrative of the Expedition to Botany Bay*. Dublin, 1789.
Tennent (*Sir* James Emerson), *Ceylon*. 2 vols. London, 1860.
Tenth Census of the United States. Ed. by F. A. Walker. 22 vols. Washington, 1883–88.
Tertullian, *Opera omnia*. 3 vols. (Migne, *Patrologiæ cursus*, vols. i.–iii.) Parisiis, 1844.
Teschauer (C.), ' Die Caingang oder Coroados-Indianer im brasilianischen Staate Rio Grande do Sul ' ; in *Anthropos*, vol. ix. Wien, 1914.
Tessmann (Günter), *Die Pangwe. Völkerkundliche Monographie eines westafrikanischen Negerstammes*. 2 vols. Berlin, 1913.
Testaments of the Twelve Patriarchs (*The*). Trans. and ed. by R. H. Charles. London, 1908.
Tetzner (Franz), ' Die Drawehner im hannöverschen Wendlande um das Jahr 1700 ' ; in *Globus*, vol. lxxxi. Braunschweig, 1902.
—— *Die Slawen in Deutschland*. Braunschweig, 1902.
Theal (G. M. McCall), *History of the Boers in South Africa*. London, 1887.
—— *The Yellow and Dark-skinned People of Africa south of the Zambesi*. London, 1910.
Theodore, ' Poenitentiale Theodori ' ; in Haddan and Stubbs, *Councils and Ecclesiastical Documents relating to Great Britain and Ireland*, vol. iii. Oxford, 1871.
Thesleff (A.), ' Zigenarlif i Finland ' ; in *Nya Pressen*, 1897, no. 331 B. Helsingfors.
Thierry (Augustin), *Narratives of the Merovingian Era*. Trans. London, [1845].

Thiers (J. B.), *Traité des superstitions qui regardent les sacremens.*
4 vols. Avignon, 1777.
Thomas (N. W.), *Anthropological Report on the Edo-speaking Peoples
of Nigeria.* 2 vols. London, 1910.
—— *Anthropological Report on Ibo-speaking Peoples of Nigeria.*
6 vols. London, 1913–14.
—— *Anthropological Report on Sierra Leone. Part I. Law and
Custom of the Timne and other Tribes.* London, 1916.
—— *Kinship Organisations and Group Marriage in Australia.*
Cambridge, 1906.
Thomas (W. I.), *Sex and Society.* Chicago & London, 1907.
—— *Source Book for Social Origins.* Chicago & London, 1909.
Thomas Aquinas (*Saint*), *Summa theologica.* 4 vols. (Migne,
Patrologiæ cursus, Ser. Secunda, vols. i.–iv.) Parisiis,
1845–46.
Thompson (T. W.), ' The Ceremonial Customs of the British Gipsies ';
in *Folk-Lore,* vol. xxiv. London, 1913.
Thomson (A. S.), *The Story of New Zealand.* 2 vols. London,
1859.
Thomson (*Sir* Basil Home), *The Fijians. A Study of the Decay of
Custom.* London, 1908.
—— *Savage Island.* London, 1902.
Thomson (J. P.), *British New Guinea.* London, 1892.
Thomson (J. T.), ' Remarks on the Sletar and Sabimba Tribes ';
in *Jour. Indian Archipelago,* vol. i. Singapore, 1847.
Thomson (Joseph), ' Notes on the Basin of the River Rovuma,
East Africa '; in *Proceed. Roy. Geo. Soc.* new ser. vol. iv.
London, 1882.
—— *Through Masai Land.* London, 1887.
Thomson (T. R. H.), ' Observations on the reported Incompetency
of the " Gins " or aboriginal Females of New Holland '; in
Jour. Ethn. Soc. London, vol. iii. London, 1854.
Thorpe (Benjamin), *Northern Mythology.* 3 vols. London, 1851–52.
Thucydides, *Historia belli Peloponnesiaci.* Ed. by F. G. H. C.
Haase. Parisiis, 1840.
Thulié (—), ' Instructions anthropologiques aux voyageurs. Sur
les Bochimans '; in *Bull. Soc. d'Anthr. Paris,* ser. iii. vol. iv.
Paris, 1881.
Thunberg (C. P.), ' An Account of the Cape of Good Hope.' Trans. ;
in Pinkerton, *Collection of Voyages and Travels,* vol. xvi.
London, 1814.
—— *Travels in Europe, Africa, and Asia. Performed between the
Years 1770 and 1779.* 4 vols. London, [1793–]1795.
Thurnwald (Richard), ' Bánaro Society. Social Organization and
Kinship System of a Tribe in the Interior of New Guinea ';
in *Memoirs of the American Anthropological Association,*
vol. iii. Lancaster, 1916.
—— ' Ermittlungen über Eingeborenenrechte der Südsee. A.
Buin auf Bougainville (Deutsche Salomo-Inseln) '; in
Zeitschr. f. vergl. Rechtswiss. vol. xxiii. Stuttgart, 1910.
—— *Forschungen auf den Salomo-Inseln und dem Bismarck-Archipel.*
Berlin, 1912 &c. *In progress.*
Thurston (Edgar) ' Anthropology of the Todas and Kotas of the
Nilgiri Hills '; in the Madras Government Museum's *Bulletin,*
vol. i. Madras, 1896.

Thurston (Edgar), ' The Badágas of the Nilgiris ' ; in the Madras Government Museum's *Bulletin*, vol. ii. Madras, 1897.
—— *Castes and Tribes of Southern India.* 7 vols. Madras, 1909.
—— *Ethnographic Notes in Southern India.* Madras, 1906.
Thwaites (R. G.), *Early Western Travels* 1748–1846. A series of annotated reprints of volumes of travel, ed. by. 32 vols. Cleveland, 1904–07.
Thyagaraja Aiyar (V. R.), *Census of India*, 1911. *Vol. XXI. Mysore*, pt. i. Report. Bangalore, 1912.
Tigerstedt (Robert), *Lehrbuch der Physiologie des Menschen.* 2 vols. Leipzig, 1911.
Tijdschrift van het (Koninklijk) Nederlandsch Aardrijkskundig Genootschap. Amsterdam, Leiden.
—— *voor indische taal-, land- en volkenkunde.* Batavia & 's Hage.
—— *voor Nederlandsch Indië.* Zalt-Bommel.
—— *voor Neêrlands Indie.* Batavia.
Tillier (L.), *L'instinct sexuel chez l'homme et chez les animaux.* Paris, 1889.
—— *Le mariage : sa genèse, son évolution.* Paris, 1898.
Times (The). London.
' Tobit, The Book of ' ; in *The Apocrypha and Pseudepigrapha of the Old Testament in English*, ed. by R. H. Charles, vol. i. Oxford, 1913.
—— See *Liber Tobiæ.*
Tocantins (A. M. G.), ' Estudos sobre a tribu " Mundurucu " ' ; in *Revista trimensal do Instituto Historico Geographico e Ethnographico do Brasil*, vol. xl. pt. ii. Rio de Janeiro, 1877.
Tocqueville (Alexis de), *Democracy in America.* Trans. 2 vols. London, 1889.
Tod (James), *Annals and Antiquities of Rajast'han.* 2 vols. Madras, 1873.
Todd (*Mrs.* M. L.), *Tripoli the Mysterious.* London, 1912.
Tonkes (H.), *Volkskunde von Bali.* Halle a. S., 1888.
Topelius (Zachris), *De modo matrimonia jungendi apud Fennos quondam vigente.* Helsingfors, 1847.
Topinard (Paul), *Anthropology.* Trans. London, 1878.
—— ' Note sur les métis d'Australiens et d'Européens ' ; in *Revue d'anthropologie*, vol. iv. Paris, 1875.
Torday (E.), *Camp and Tramp in African Wilds.* London, 1913.
—— and Joyce (T. A.), *Notes ethnographiques sur les peuples communément appelés Bakuba, ainsi que sur les peuplades apparentées. Les Bushongo.* Bruxelles, 1910.
—— and Joyce (T. A.), ' Notes on the Ethnography of the Ba-Huana ' ; in *Jour. Anthr. Inst.* vol. xxxvi. London, 1906.
—— and Joyce (T. A.), ' Notes on the Ethnography of the Ba-Mbala ' ; in *Jour. Anthr. Inst.* vol. xxxv. London, 1905.
—— and Joyce (T. A.), ' Notes on the Ethnography of the Ba-Yaka ' ; in *Jour. Anthr. Inst.* vol. xxxvi. London, 1906.
Torquemada (Juan de), *Veinte y un libros rituales y Monarchia Indiana.* 3 vols. Madrid, 1723.
Tout (C. Hill), *The Far West the Home of the Salish and Déné.* (*The Native Races of the British Empire. British North America*, vol. i.) London, 1907.

Tout (C. Hill), ' Report on the Ethnology of the South-Eastern Tribes of Vancouver Island, British Columbia ' ; in *Jour. Roy. Anthr. Inst.* vol. xxxvii. London, 1907.
—— ' Report on the Ethnology of the Stlatlumh of British Columbia ' ; in *Jour. Anthr. Inst.* vol. xxxv. London, 1905.
Train (Joseph), *An Historical and Statistical Account of the Isle of Man.* 2 vols. Douglas, 1845.
Transactions (and Proceedings and Report) of the Royal Society of South Australia. Adelaide.
—— *and Proceedings of the New Zealand Institute.* Wellington.
—— *of the American Ethnological Society.* New York.
—— *of the Asiatic Society of Japan.* Yokohama.
—— *of the Canadian Institute.* Toronto.
—— *of the China Branch of the Royal Asiatic Society.* Hongkong.
—— *of the Ethnological Society of London.* New Series. London.
—— *of the International Folk-Lore Congress*, 1891. London, 1892.
—— *of the Ossianic Society.* Dublin.
—— *of the Royal Geographical Society of Australasia (Victoria Branch).* Melbourne.
—— *of the Royal Society of Edinburgh.*
—— *of the Royal Society of Victoria.* Melbourne.
Travels of an Arab Merchant in Soudan. See Muḥammad ibn 'Umar, Al-Tūnusī.
Treffers (F.), ' Het landschap Laiwoei in Z. O. Celebes en zijne bevolking ' ; in *Tijdschrift van het Koninklijk Nederlandsch Aardrijkskundig Genootschap*, ser. ii. vol. xxxi. Leiden, 1914.
Tregear (Edward), ' Easter Island ' ; in *Jour. Polynesian Soc.* vol. i. Wellington, 1892.
—— *The Maori Race.* Wanganui, N.Z., 1904.
Tremearne (A. J. N.), *Hausa Superstitions and Customs.* London, 1913.
—— ' Notes on the Kagoro and other Nigerian Head-Hunters ' ; in *Jour. Roy. Anthr. Inst.* vol. xlii. London, 1912.
Trenk (*Oberleutnant*), ' Die Buschleute der Namib, ihre Rechts- und Familienverhältnisse ' ; in *Mittheil. Deutsch. Schutzgeb.* vol. xxiii. Berlin, 1910.
Trevelyan (E. J.), *Hindu Family Law as administered in British India.* London, 1908.
Trevelyan (Marie), *Folk-Lore and Folk-Stories of Wales.* London, 1909.
Troels-Lund (T. F.), *Dagligt Liv i Norden i det 16 Aarhundrede.* 14 vols. København, 1903–04.
Trumbull (H. C.), *Studies in Oriental Social Life.* Philadelphia, 1894.
—— *The Threshold Covenant.* New York, 1896.
Trusen (J. P.), *Die Sitten, Gebräuche und Krankheiten der alten Hebräer.* Breslau, 1853.
Tschudi (J. J. von), *Reisen durch Südamerika.* 5 vols. Leipzig, 1866–69.
Tuchmann (J.), ' La fascination ' ; in *Mélusine*, vol. vii. Paris, 1894–95.
Tuckey (J. K.), *Narrative of an Expedition to explore the River Zaire.* London, 1818.
Tupper (C. L.), *Punjab Customary Law.* 3 vols. Calcutta, 1881.

Turnbull (John), *A Voyage round the World, in the Years* 1800–1804. London, 1813.
Turner (George), *Nineteen Years in Polynesia.* London, 1861.
—— *Samoa a Hundred Years ago and long before.* London, 1884.
Turner (L. M.), ' Ethnology of the Ungava District, Hudson Bay Territory ' ; in *Ann. Rep. Bur. Ethnol.* vol. xi. Washington, 1894.
Turner (Samuel), *An Account of an Embassy to the Court of the Teshoo Lama, in Tibet.* London, 1800.
Tutuila (—), ' The Line Islanders ' ; in *Jour. Polynesian Soc.* vol. i. Wellington, 1892.
Tyler (Josiah), *Forty Years among the Zulus.* Boston & Chicago, [1891].
Tylor (*Sir* E. B.), *Anthropology.* London, 1881.
—— ' On a Method of investigating the Development of Institutions ; applied to Laws of Marriage and Descent ' ; in *Jour. Anthr. Inst.* vol. xviii. London, 1889.
—— *Primitive Culture.* 2 vols. London, 1903.
—— *Researches into the Early History of Mankind.* London, 1878.
—— Review of the first edition of the present work ; in *The Academy* vol. xl. London, 1891.

Ujfalvy (K. E. von), *Aus dem westlichen Himalaja.* Leipzig, 1884.
—— ' Die Ptolemäer. Ein Beitrag zur historischen Anthropologie ' ; in *Archiv f. Anthropologie,* new ser. vol. ii. Braunschweig, 1904.
—— ' Voyage dans l'Himalaya occidental (le Koulou, le Cachemire et le petit Thibet) ' ; in *Bull. Soc. d'Anthr.* Paris, ser. iii. vol. v. Paris, 1882.
Ullberg (Emil), ' Bröllopsseder i Södra Sibbo ' ; in *Hembygden,* vols. viii.–ix. Helsingfors, 1917–18.
United States Geographical and Geological Survey of the Rocky Mountain Region :—Contributions to North American Ethnology. Washington.
United States Geological and Geographical Survey, Miscellaneous Publications. Washington.
University of California Publications in American Archæology and Ethnology. Berkeley.
University of Pennsylvania. Anthropological Publications of the University Museum, Philadelphia.
Uplands-Lagen. Ed. by C. J. Schlyter. (*Corpus Juris Sueo-Gotorum Antiqui,* vol. iii.) Stockholm, 1834.
Usener (H.), ' Italische Mythen ' ; in *Rheinisches Museum für Philologie,* vol. xxx. Frankfurt a. M., 1875.
Utiešenović (O. M.), *Die Hauskommunionen der Südslaven.* Wien, 1859.

Valdau (G.), ' Om Ba-kwileh-folket ' ; in *Ymer,* vol. v. Stockholm, 1886.
Valerius Maximus, *Factorum dictorumque memorabilium libri novem.* Ed. by C. Kempf. Lipsiae, 1888.
Valikhanof (—) and Others, *The Russians in Central Asia.* Trans. by J. and R. Michell. London, 1865.
Vámbéry (H.), *Die primitive Cultur des turko-tatarischen Volkes.* Leipzig, 1879.

Vámbéry (H.), *Travels in Central Asia.* London, 1864.
—— *Das Türkenvolk.* Leipzig, 1885.
Vancouver (G.), *A Voyage of Discovery to the North Pacific Ocean, and round the World.* 3 vols. London, 1798.
Van-Lennep (H. J.), *Bible Lands.* London, 1875.
'Vâsishtha,' trans. by G. Bühler ; in *The Sacred Books of the East,* vol. xiv. Oxford, 1882.
Västgötalagen, Äldre. Ed. by B. Sjöros. (*Skrifter utgivna av Svenska Litteratursällskapet i Finland,* vol. cxliv.) Helsingfors, 1919.
Velten (C.), *Sitten und Gebräuche der Suaheli.* Göttingen, 1903.
Vendîdâd (The). Trans. by J. Darmesteter. (*The Sacred Books of the East,* vol. iv.) Oxford, 1880.
—— The same work. Oxford, 1895.
'Venedotian Code (The) ' ; in *Ancient Laws and Institutes of Wales.* London, 1841.
Venette (N.), *La génération de l'homme, ou tableau de l'amour conjugal.* 2 vols. Amsterdam, 1778.
Vergette (E. Dudley), *Certain Marriage Customs of some of the Tribes in the Protectorate of Sierra Leone.* Sierra Leone, 1917.
Vergilius Maro (P.), *Opera.* Ed. by A. Forbiger. 3 vols. Lipsiae, 1872–75.
Verhandelingen van het Bataviaasch Genootschap van kunsten en wetenschappen. Batavia.
Verhandlungen der Berliner Gesellschaft für Anthropologie, Ethnologie und Urgeschichte. Berlin.
—— *des Vereins für naturwissenschaftliche Unterhaltung zu Hamburg.*
Verhoeven (P. W.), *Kurtze Beschreibung einer Reyse, so von den Holländern und Seeländern, in die Ost Indien . . . under der Admiralschafft P. W. Verhuffen &c. in Jahren 1607. 1608. und 1609. verrichtet worden.* Franckfurt am Mayn, 1612–13.
Veröffentlichungen aus dem königl. Museum für Völkerkunde. Berlin.
—— *aus dem städtischen Völker-Museum Frankfurt am Main.*
Veth (P. J.), *Java, geographisch, ethnologisch, historisch.* Ed. by J. F. Snelleman and J. F. Niermeyer. 4 vols. Haarlem, 1896–1907.
Vetter (Konrad), ' Bericht des Missionars Herrn Konrad Vetter in Simbang über papuanische Rechtsverhältnisse, wie solche namentlich bei den Jabim beobachtet wurden ' ; in *Nachrichten über Kaiser Wilhelms-Land und den Bismarck-Archipel,* 1897. Berlin.
Veuillot (Louis), *Le droit du seigneur au moyen âge.* Paris, 1854.
Viehe (G.), ' Die Ovaherero ' ; in Steinmetz, *Rechtsverhältnisse von eingeborenen Völkern in Afrika und Ozeanien.* Berlin, 1903.
Vienna Oriental Journal. Vienna, London, &c.
Viera y Clavijo (Joseph de), *Noticias de la historia general de las islas de Canaria.* 4 vols. Madrid, 1772–83.
Vigfusson (Gudbrand) and Powell (F. York), *Corpus Poeticum Boreale.* 2 vols. Oxford, 1883.
Vigne (G. T.), *Travels in Kashmir, Ladak, Iskardo, the Countries adjoining the Mountain-Course of the Indus, and the Himalaya, north of the Panjab.* 2 vols. London, 1842.
Vigström (Eva), ' Folkseder i Östra Göinge härad i Skåne ' ; in *Bidrag till vår odlings häfder* (ed. by A. Hazelius). 2. *Ur de nordiska folkens lif,* vol. i. Stockholm, 1882.

Villot (E.), *Mœurs, coutumes et institutions des indigènes de l'Algérie.* Alger, 1888.

Vincendon-Dumoulin (C. A.) and Desgraz (C.), *Iles Marquises ou Nouka-Hiva.* Paris, 1843.

Vincentius Bellovacensis, *Speculum naturale.* Venetijs, 1494.

Vinnius (A.), *In quatuor libros institutionum imperialium commentarius.* Lugduni, 1747.

Vinson (—), in the Discussion on M. de Ujfalvy's paper ' Voyage dans l'Himalaya occidental ' ; in *Bull. Soc. d'Anthr. Paris,* ser. iii. vol. v. Paris, 1882.

Virchow (Rudolf), ' Acclimatisation ' ; in *Verhandl. Berliner Gesellsch. Anthr.* 1885. Berlin.

—— ' Rassenbildung und Erblichkeit ' ; in *Festschrift für Adolf Bastian zu seinem 70. Geburtstage.* Berlin, 1896.

—— ' Ueber Erblichkeit. I. Die Theorie Darwin's ' ; in *Deutsche Jahrbücher für Politik und Literatur,* vol. vi. Berlin, 1863.

—— *Untersuchungen über die Entwickelung des Schädelgrundes im gesunden und krankhaften Zustande.* Berlin, 1857.

Virchows Archiv für pathologische Anatomie und Physiologie und für klinische Medizin. Berlin.

Virey (J. J.), *De la femme sous ses rapports physiologique, moral et littéraire.* Paris, 1823.

Vishnu, *The Institutes of.* See *Institutes of Vishnu (The).*

Vishvanáth Náráyan Mandlik, *The Vyavahára Mayúkha, in Original, with an English Translation.* With an introduction and appendices containing notes on Hindu Law. 2 vols. Bombay, 1880.

Visscher (J. C.), *Letters from Malabar.* Trans. from the original Dutch by H. Drury. Madras, 1862.

Vogel (E.), ' Reise nach Central-Afrika ' ; in Petermann's *Mittheilungen,* 1857. Gotha.

Vogel (Hans), *Eine Forschungsreise im Bismarck-Archipel.* Hamburg, 1911.

Vogt (Carl), *Lectures on Man.* Trans. ed. by J. Hunt. London, 1864.

Vogt (P. F.), ' Material zur Ethnographie und Sprache der Guayaki-Indianer ' ; in *Zeitschr. f. Ethnol.* vol. xxxiv. Berlin, 1902.

Vogt (Hermann), ' Die Bewohner von Lagos ' ; in *Globus,* vol. xli. Braunschweig, 1882.

Voice for South America (A). London.

Voisin (A.), ' Contribution à l'histoire des mariages entre consanguins ' ; in *Mémoirs Soc. d'Anthr. Paris,* vol. ii. Paris, 1865.

Volkens (Georg), *Der Kilimandscharo.* Berlin, 1897.

Volkov (Théodore), ' Rites et usages nuptiaux en Ukraïne ' ; in *L'Anthropologie,* vols. ii.–iii. Paris, 1891–92.

—— Review of an article by Mendiarov on the Cheremiss of the government of Oufa ; in *L'Anthropologie,* vol. vi. Paris, 1895.

Volz (Wilhelm), ' Zur Kenntniss der Kubus in Südsumatra ' ; in *Archiv f. Anthropologie,* new ser. vol. vii. Braunschweig, 1908.

Vossische Zeitung. Berlin.

Voth (H. R.), ' Oraibi Marriage Customs ' ; in *American Anthropologist,* new ser. vol. ii. New York, 1900.

Wachsmuth (Curt), *Das alte Griechenland im neuen.* Bonn, 1864.
Wachsmuth (Wilhelm), *Hellenische Alterthumskunde.* Halle, 1846.
Waddell (L. A.), *Among the Himalayas.* Westminster, 1899.
—— ' Celibacy (Tibetan) ' ; in Hastings, *Encyclopædia of Religion and Ethics,* vol. iii. Edinburgh, 1910.
—— *Lhasa and its Mysteries.* London, 1905.
Wadström (Aina), ' Frieri- och bröllopsbruk från Dagsmark i Lappfjärd ' ; in *Hembygden,* vol. ii. Helsingfors, 1911.
Wagner (Moritz), ' Die Kulturzüchtung des Menschen gegenüber der Naturzüchtung im Tierreich ' ; in *Kosmos,* vol. i. Stuttgart, 1886.
Wagner (Rudolph), *Handwörterbuch der Physiologie.* Ed. by. 4 vols. Braunschweig, 1842–53.
Waitz (Th.), *Anthropologie der Naturvölker.* 6 vols. (vol. v. pt. ii. and vol. vi. by G. Gerland). Leipzig, 1859–72.
—— *Introduction to Anthropology.* Trans. ed. by J. F. Collingwood. London, 1863.
Wake (C. S.), *The Development of Marriage and Kinship.* London, 1889.
Wakefield (E. S.), ' Marriage Customs of the Southern Gallas ' ; in *Folk-Lore,* vol. xviii. London, 1907.
Walckenaer (C. A.), *Histoire générale des voyages.* 21 vols. Paris, 1826–31
Waldron (George), *A Description of the Isle of Man.* (*Publications of the Manx Society,* vol. xi.) Douglas, 1865.
Walen (A.), ' The Sakalava ' ; in *Antananarivo Annual and Madagascar Magazine,* no. viii. Antananarivo, 1884.
Walker (Alex.), *Beauty.* London, 1846.
Wallace (A. R.), *Contributions to the Theory of Natural Selection.* London, 1871.
—— *Darwinism.* London, 1889.
—— *The Malay Archipelago.* 2 vols. London, 1869.
—— *Travels on the Amazon and Rio Negro.* London, 1853.
—— *Tropical Nature and other Essays.* London, 1878.
Wallace (D. Mackenzie), *Russia.* 2 vols. London, 1877.
Wallaschek (Richard), *Anfänge der Tonkunst.* Leipzig, 1903.
—— *Primitive Music.* London, 1893.
Wallin (G. A.), *Reseanteckningar från Orienten åren* 1843–1849. Ed. by S. G. Elmgren. 4 vols. Helsingfors, 1864–66.
Walter (Ferdinand), *Lehrbuch des Kirchenrechts aller christlichen Confessionen.* Ed. by H. Gerlach. Bonn, 1871.
Walter (P.), ' Die Inseln Nossi-Bé und Mayotte ' ; in Steinmetz, *Rechtsverhältnisse von eingeborenen Völkern in Afrika und Ozeanien.* Berlin, 1903.
Wandrer (C.), ' Die Khoi-Khoin oder Naman ' ; in Steinmetz, *Rechtsverhältnisse von eingeborenen Völkern in Afrika und Ozeanien.* Berlin, 1903.
Wappäus (J. E.), *Allgemeine Bevölkerungsstatistik.* 2 vols. Leipzig, 1859–61.
Ward (B. C.), ' Geographical and Statistical Memoir of a Survey of the Neelgherry Mountains in the Province of Coimbatore made in 1821 ' ; in Grigg, *A Manual of the Nílagiri District in the Madras Presidency.* Madras, 1880.
Ward (F. Kingdon), *The Land of the Blue Poppy. Travels of a Naturalist in Eastern Tibet.* Cambridge, 1913.

Ward (Herbert), *A Voice from the Congo.* London, 1910.
Ward (Lester F.), *Dynamic Sociology or Applied Social Science.*
 2 vols. New York, 1907.
Ward (W.), *A View of the History, Literature, and Religion of the
 Hindoos.* 4 vols. London, 1817–20.
Wargentin (P.), ' Uti hvilka månader flera Människor födas och dö
 i Sverige ' ; in *Kongliga Vetenskaps-academiens Handlingar,*
 vol. xxviii. Stockholm, 1767.
Warnkoenig (L. A.) and Stein (L.), *Französische Staats- und Rechts-
 geschichte.* 3 vols. Basel, 1846–48.
Warren (Willar W.), ' History of the Ojibways, based upon Tra-
 ditions and oral Statements ' ; in *Collections of the Minnesota
 Historical Society,* vol. v. Saint Paul (Minn.), 1885.
Wasserschleben (F. W. H.), *Die Bussordnungen der abendländischen
 Kirche.* Halle, 1851.
Watkins (O. D.), *Holy Matrimony.* London, 1895.
Watson (J. F.) and Kaye (J. W.), *The People of India.* 6 vols.
 London, 1868.
Watt (George), ' The Aboriginal Tribes of Manipur ' ; in *Jour. Anthr.
 Inst.* vol. xvi. London, 1887.
Weber (Albrecht), ' Collectanea über die Kastenverhältnisse in den
 Brâhmana und Sûtra ' ; in *Indische Studien,* vol. x. Leipzig,
 1868.
—— *Indische Studien.* Ed. by. Berlin, Leipzig.
—— ' Vedische Hochzeitssprüche ' ; in *Indische Studien,* vol. v.
 Berlin, 1861.
Weber (E. von), *Vier Jahre in Afrika.* 2 vols. Leipzig, 1878.
Weddell (James), *A Voyage towards the South Pole.* London, 1825.
Weeks (John H.), *Among Congo Cannibals.* London, 1913.
—— *Among the Primitive Bakongo.* London, 1914.
—— ' Anthropological Notes on the Bangala of the Upper Congo
 River ' ; in *Jour. Roy. Anthr. Inst.* vols. xxxix.–xl. London,
 1909–1910.
—— ' Notes on some Customs of the Lower Congo People ' ; in
 Folk-Lore, vol. xix. London, 1908.
Weil (G.), *Biblische Legenden der Muselmänner.* Frankfurt a. M.,
 1845.
Weinhold (Karl), *Altnordisches Leben.* Berlin, 1856.
—— *Die deutschen Frauen in dem Mittelalter.* 2 vols. Wien,
 1882.
Weiss (Max), *Die Völkerstämme im Norden Deutsch-Ostafrikas.*
 Berlin, 1910.
Welcker (H.), ' Die Füsse der Chinesinnen, Zweite Mittheilung ' ;
 in *Archiv f. Anthropologie,* vol. v. Braunschweig, 1871.
Wellhausen (J.), ' Die Ehe bei den Arabern ' ; in *Nachrichten von
 der Königl. Gesellschaft der Wissenschaften und der Georg-
 Augusts-Universität zu Göttingen,* 1893. Göttingen.
—— *Prolegomena to the History of Israel.* Trans. London, 1885.
—— *Reste des arabischen Heidentums.* Berlin, 1897.
Werner (*Miss* Alice), *The Natives of British Central Africa.* London,
 1906.
Wesnitsch (M. R.), ' Die Blutrache bei den Südslaven ' ; in *Zeitschr.
 f. vergl. Rechtswiss.* vol. ix. Stuttgart, 1891.
Wessman (V. E. V.), ' Folktro i Ekenäs ' ; in *Hembygden,* vol. vii.
 Helsingfors, 1916

Wessmann (R.), ' Reife-Unsitten bei den Bawenda in Nord-Trans-
vaal ' ; in *Verhandl. Berliner Gesellsch. Anthr.* 1896. Berlin.
West (E. W.), ' The Meaning of Khvêtûk-das or Khvêtûdâd ' ; in
The Sacred Books of the East, vol. xviii. Oxford, 1882.
West (John), *The History of Tasmania.* 2 vols. Tasmania, 1852.
West (Thomas), *Ten Years in South-Central Polynesia.* London,
1865.
Westermann (Diedrich), *The Shilluk People. Their Language and
Folklore.* Philadelphia, [1912].
Westermarck (Edward), ' *L-'ár*, or the Transference of Conditional
Curses in Morocco ' ; in *Anthropological Essays presented to
E. B. Tylor.* Oxford, 1907.
—— *The Belief in Spirits in Morocco.* (*Acta Academiæ Aboensis.
Humaniora*, vol. i. no. 1.) Åbo, 1920.
—— *Ceremonies and Beliefs connected with Agriculture, certain
Dates of the Solar Year, and the Weather in Morocco.*
(*Öfversigt af Finska Vetenskaps-Societetens Förhandlingar.
Bd. LIV.*, 1911–1912. *Afd. B. N:o* 1.) Helsingfors, 1913.
—— ' The Magic Origin of Moorish Designs ' ; in *Jour. Anthr. Inst.*
vol. xxxiv. London, 1904.
—— *Marriage Ceremonies in Morocco.* London, 1914.
—— ' Midsummer Customs in Morocco ' ; in *Folk-Lore*, vol. xvi.
London, 1905.
—— *The Moorish Conception of Holiness (Baraka).* (*Öfversigt af
Finska Vetenskaps-Societetens Förhandlingar. Bd. LVIII.*,
1915–1916. *Afd. B. N:o* 1.) Helsingfors, 1916.
—— ' The Nature of the Arab Ġinn, illustrated by the present
Beliefs of the People of Morocco ' ; in *Jour. Anthr. Inst.*
vol. xxix. London, 1900.
—— *The Origin and Development of the Moral Ideas.* 2 vols.
London, 1912–17.
—— *The Origin of Human Marriage.* Helsingfors, 1889.
—— ' The Popular Ritual of the Great Feast in Morocco ' ; in
Folk-Lore, vol. xxii. London, 1911.
—— ' Prefatory Note ' to *The Tribe, and Intertribal Relations in
Australia*, by G. C. Wheeler. London, 1910.
Westgarth (William), *Australia Felix ; or, a Historical and Descriptive
Account of the Settlement of Port Phillip, New South Wales.*
Edinburgh, 1848.
Westropp (H. M.) and Wake (C. S.), *Ancient Symbol Worship.* New
York, 1874.
Wetzstein (J. G.), ' Die syrische Dreschtafel ' ; in *Zeitschr. f. Ethnol.*
vol. v. Berlin, 1873.
Weule (Karl), *Native Life in East Africa.* Trans. by Alice Werner.
London, 1909.
—— *Wissenschaftliche Ergebnisse meiner ethnographischen For-
schungsreise in den Südosten Deutsch-Ostafrikas.* (*Mittheil.
Deutsch. Schutzgeb. Ergänzungsheft Nr.* 1.) Berlin, 1908.
Wheeler (G. C.), *The Tribe, and Intertribal Relations in Australia.*
London, 1910.
Wheeler (J. Talboys), *The History of India.* 4 vols. London,
1867–74.
Whiffen (Thomas), *The North-West Amazons.* London, 1915.
White (J. Claude), *Sikhim and Bhutan. Twenty-one Years on the
North East Frontier* 1887–1908. London, 1909.

White (Rachel Evelyn), 'Women in Ptolemaic Egypt'; in *The Journal of Hellenic Studies,* vol. xviii. London, 1898.

Whitehead (G.), 'Notes on the Chins of Burma'; in *The Indian Antiquary,* vol. xxxvi. Bombay, 1907.

'Why is Single Life becoming more General?'; in *The Nation,* vol. vi. New York, 1868.

Wied-Neuwied (Maximilian *Prinz zu*), *Reise nach Brasilien in den Jahren* 1815 *bis* 1817. 2 vols. Frankfurt a.M., 1820–21.

—— *Travels in Brasil.* Trans. London, 1820.

Wiedemann (Alfred), *Herodots zweites Buch mit sachlichen Erläuterungen.* Ed. by. Leipzig, 1890.

Wiese (Carl), 'Beiträge zur Geschichte der Zulu im Norden des Zambesi, namentlich der Angoni'; in *Zeitschr. f. Ethnol.* vol. xxxii. Berlin, 1900.

Wikman (K. R. V.), ' Frieri, förlofning och bröllop i Delsbo. Anteckningar samlade af Einar Spjut och sammanställda af '; in *Fataburen,* 1913. Stockholm.

—— 'Magiska bindebruk'; in *Hembygden,* vol. iii. Helsingfors, 1912.

Wilamowitz-Moellendorff (U. von) and Niese (B.), *Staat und Gesellschaft der Griechen und Römer. (Die Kultur der Gegenwart,* vol. ii. pt. iv. 1.) Berlin, 1910.

Wilda (W. E.), *Das Strafrecht der Germanen.* Halle, 1842.

Wilhelmi (Charles), 'Manners and Customs of the Australian Natives, in particular of the Port Lincoln District '; in *Transactions of the Royal Society of Victoria,* vol. v. Melbourne, 1860.

Wilken (G. A.), 'Bijdrage tot de kennis der Alfoeren van het eiland Boeroe'; in *Verhandelingen van het Bataviaasch Genootschap van kunsten en wetenschappen,* vol. xxxviii. Batavia, 1875.

—— *Huwelijken tusschen bloedverwanten.* (Reprinted from *De Gids,* 1890, no. 6.) Amsterdam.

—— *Das Matriarchat (das Mutterrecht) bei den alten Arabern.* German trans. Leipzig, 1884.

—— ' Over het huwelijks- en erfrecht bij de volken van Zuid-Sumatra'; in *Bijdragen tot de taal-, land- en volkenkunde van Nederlandsch-Indië,* vol. xl. 's Gravenhage, 1891.

—— ' Over de primitieve vormen van het huwelijk en den oorsprong van het gezin '; in *De Indische Gids,* 1880, vol. ii. and 1881, vol. ii. Amsterdam.

—— *Over de verwantschap en het huwelijks- en erfrecht bij de volken van het maleische ras.* (Reprinted from *De Indische Gids,* 1883, May.) Amsterdam.

—— 'Plechtigheden en gebruiken bij verlovingen en huwelijken bij de volken van den Indischen Archipel '; in *Bijdragen tot de taal-, land- en volkenkunde van Nederlandsch-Indië,* ser. v. vols. i. and iv. 's Gravenhage, 1886, 1889.

Wilkes (Charles), *Narrative of the United States Exploring Expedition during the Years* 1838–1842. 5 vols. Philadelphia & London, 1845.

Wilks (Mark), *Historical Sketches of the South of India, in an Attempt to trace the history of Mysoor.* 2 vols. Madras, 1869.

Willcox (W. F.), 'Divorce '; in *Encyclopædia Britannica,* vol. viii. London, 1910.

Willcox (W. F.), *The Divorce Problem. A Study in Statistics.* (*Studies in History, Economics and Public Law.* Edited by the University Faculty of Political Science of Columbia College, vol. i. no. 1.) New York, 1891.
—— ' A Study in Vital Statistics ' ; in *Political Science Quarterly,* vol. viii. New York, Boston, & Chicago, 1893.
Willer (T. J.), *Het eiland Boeroe.* Amsterdam, 1858.
Williams (John), *A Narrative of Missionary Enterprises in the South Sea Islands.* London, 1837.
Williams (Monier). See Monier-Williams (Monier).
Williams (S. Wells), *The Middle Kingdom.* 2 vols. New York, 1883.
Williams (Thomas) and Calvert (James), *Fiji and the Fijians ; and Missionary Labours among the Cannibals.* London, 1870.
Williamson (R. W.), *The Mafulu Mountain People of British New Guinea.* London, 1912.
—— ' Some unrecorded Customs of the Mekeo People of British New Guinea ' ; in *Jour. Roy. Anthr. Inst.* vol. xliii. London, 1913.
—— *The Ways of the South Sea Savage.* London, 1914.
Willigerod (J. E. Ph.), *Geschichte Ehstlands.* Reval, 1830.
Willshire (W. H.), *The Aborigines of Central Australia.* Adelaide, 1891.
Wilson (Andrew), *The Abode of Snow.* Edinburgh & London, 1876.
Wilson (C. T.), *Peasant Life in the Holy Land.* London, 1906.
—— and Felkin (R. W.), *Uganda and the Egyptian Soudan.* 2 vols. London, 1882.
Wilson (J. Leighton), *Western Africa.* London, 1856.
Wilson (S. G.), *Persian Life and Customs.* Edinburgh & London, 1896.
Wilutzky (Paul), *Vorgeschichte des Rechts.* 3 vols. Breslau, 1903.
Winckler (Hugo), *Altorientalische Forschungen.* 3 vols. Leipzig, 1893–1906.
—— ' Polyandrie bei Semiten ' ; in *Verhandl. Berliner Gesellsch. Anthr.* 1898. Berlin.
Winroth (A.), *Offentlig rätt. Familjerätt : Äktenskapshindren.* Lund, 1890.
Winter (C. F.), ' Instellingen, gewoonten en gebruiken der Javanen te Soerakarta ' ; in *Tijdschrift voor Neêrlands Indie,* vol. v. pt. i. Batavia, 1843.
Winterbottom (Thomas), *An Account of the Native Africans in the Neighbourhood of Sierra Leone.* 2 vols. London, 1803.
Winternitz (M.), ' Das altindische Hochzeitsrituell nach dem Āpastambīya-Grihyasūtra und einigen anderen verwandten Werken ' ; in *Denkschriften der kaiserlichen Akademie der Wissenschaften. Philosophisch-historische Classe,* vol. xl. Wien, 1892.
—— ' Notes on the Mahābhārata, with special reference to Dahlmann's " Mahābhārata " ' ; in *Jour. Roy. Asiatic Soc.* 1897. London.
—— ' On a Comparative Study of Indo-European Customs, with special reference to the Marriage Customs ' ; in *Transactions of the International Folk-Lore Congress,* 1891. London, 1892.
Wissmann (H. von), *Unter deutscher Flagge quer durch Afrika.* Berlin, 1889.
—— Wolf (L.), François (C. von), and Mueller (H.), *Im Innern Afrikas.* Leipzig, 1891.

Withnell (J. G.), *The Customs and Traditions of the Aboriginal Natives of North Western Australia.* Roebourne, 1901.
Witkowski (G. J.), *La génération humaine.* Paris, 1881.
Wlislocki (H. von), *Vom wandernden Zigeunervolke.* Hamburg, 1890.
Woeste (F.), ' Aberglaube und Gebräuche in Südwestfalen ' ; in *Jahrbuch des Vereins für niederdeutsche Sprachforschung,* 1877. Bremen, 1878.
Woldt (A.), *Capitain Jacobsen's Reise an der Nordwestküste Amerikas* 1881–1883. Leipzig, 1884.
Wolf (P. Franz), ' Beitrag zur Ethnographie der Fō-Neger in Togo ' ; in *Anthropos,* vol. vii. Wien, 1912.
Wood (Andrew), in the Discussion on Dr. Mitchell's Paper on ' Marriages of Consanguinity, their Influence on Offspring ' ; in *Edinburgh Medical Journal,* vol. vii. pt. ii. Edinburgh, 1862.
Wood (J. G.), *The Illustrated Natural History.* 3 vols. London, 1861–63.
Wood-Martin (W. G.), *Traces of the Elder Faiths of Ireland.* 2 vols. London, 1902.
Woods (J. D.), *The Native Tribes of South Australia ;* with an Introductory Chapter by. Adelaide, 1879.
Woodthorpe (R. G.), ' Some Account of the Shans and Hill Tribes of the States on the Mekong ' ; in *Jour. Anthr. Inst.* vol. xxvi. London, 1897.
Worcester (Dean C.), ' The Non-Christian Tribes of Northern Luzon ' ; in *The Philippine Journal of Science,* vol. i. Manila, 1906.
—— *The Philippine Islands and their People.* New York, 1898.
Wrede (A. von), *Reise in Ḥadhramaut.* Ed. by H. von Maltzan. Braunschweig, 1870.
Wright (Carroll D.), *A Report on Marriage and Divorce in the United States, 1867 to 1886. (Report of the Commissioner of Labor,* 1889.) Washington, 1891.
Wright (Thomas), *Womankind in Western Europe, from the Earliest Times to the Seventeenth Century.* London, 1869.
Wundt (W.), *Elemente der Völkerpsychologie.* Leipzig, 1912.
—— *Elements of Folk Psychology.* Trans. by E. L. Schaub. London & New York, 1916.
—— *Ethik.* 3 vols. Stuttgart, 1912.
Wuttke (A.), *Der deutsche Volksaberglaube der Gegenwart.* Ed. by E. H. Meyer. Berlin, 1900.

Xenophon, *Scripta quæ supersunt.* Parisiis, 1838.

' Yasts (The),' trans. by J. Darmesteter ; in *The Sacred Books of the East,* vol. xxiii. Oxford, 1883.
Yate (William), *An Account of New Zealand.* London, 1835.
Yavorski (——), Reviewed in *L'Anthropologie,* vol. viii. Paris, 1897.
Ymer. Tidskrift utgifven af Svenska Sällskapet för Antropologi och Geografi. Stockholm.
Young (Arthur), ' A Tour in Ireland ' ; in Pinkerton, *Collection of Voyages and Travels,* vol. iii. London, 1809.
Young (Ernest), *The Kingdom of the Yellow Robe.* Westminster, 1900.

Yule (G. Udny), ' On the Changes of the Marriage- and Birth-Rates in England and Wales during the Past Half Century ' ; in *Jour. Roy. Statistical Soc.* vol. lxix. London, 1906.

Yule (*Sir* Henry), *Cathay and the Way thither, being a Collection of Medieval Notices of China*, trans. and ed. by. New edition revised by Henri Cordier. 4 vols. London, 1913–16.

—— ' Notes on the Kasia Hills, and People ' ; in *Jour. Asiatic Soc. Bengal*, vol. xiii. pt. ii. Calcutta, 1844.

Zaborowski (—), ' La circoncision, ses origines et sa répartition en Afrique et à Madagascar ' ; in *L'Anthropologie*, vol. vii. Paris, 1896.

Zachariae (Th.), ' Zum altindischen Hochzeitsritual ' ; in *Vienna Oriental Journal*, vol. xvii. Wien, 1903.

Zache (Hans), ' Sitten und Gebräuche der Suaheli ' ; in *Zeitschr. f. Ethnol.* vol. xxxi. Berlin, 1899.

' Zahnverstümmelung der Hereros ' ; in *Verhandl. Berliner Gesellsch. Anthr.* 1908. Berlin.

Zeen-ud-deen (*Sheikh*), *Tohfut-ul-mujahideen*. Trans. by M. J. Rowlandson. London, 1833.

Zeitschrift der Deutschen Morgenländischen Gesellschaft. Leipzig.

—— *der Gesellschaft für Erdkunde zu Berlin.*

—— *der Savigny-Stiftung für Rechtsgeschichte.* Weimar.

—— *des Deutschen Palaestina-Vereins.* Leipzig.

—— *des Vereins für Volkskunde.* Berlin.

—— *für Ägyptische Sprache und Altertumskunde.* Leipzig.

—— *für die alttestamentliche Wissenschaft.* Giessen.

—— *für Ethnologie.* Berlin.

—— *für induktive Abstammungs- und Vererbungslehre.* Berlin.

—— *für oesterreichische Volkskunde. Ergänzungshefte.* Stuttgart.

—— *für Socialwissenschaft.* Ed. by J. Wolf. Berlin.

—— *für vergleichende Rechtswissenschaft.* Ed. by F. Bernhöft, G. Cohn, and J. Kohler. Stuttgart.

—— *für Völkerpsychologie und Sprachwissenschaft.* Leipzig.

Zeumer (Karl), ' Geschichte der westgothischen Gesetzgebung ' ; in *Neues Archiv der Gesellschaft für ältere deutsche Geschichtskunde*, vol. xxiv. Hannover & Leipzig, 1899.

Zhishman (Jos.), *Das Eherecht der Orientalischen Kirche.* Wien, 1863.

Zimmer (Heinrich), *Altindisches Leben.* Berlin, 1879.

—— ' Das Mutterrecht der Pikten und seine Bedeutung für die arische Alterthumswissenschaft ' ; in *Zeitschr. der Savigny-Stiftung für Rechtsgeschichte*, vol. xv. Weimar, 1894.

Zimmermann (W. F. A.), *Die Inseln des indischen und stillen Meeres.* 3 vols. Berlin, 1863–65.

Żmigrodzki (M. von), *Die Mutter bei den Völkern des arischen Stammes.* München, 1886.

Zöller (Hugo), *Forschungsreisen in der deutschen Colonie Kamerun.* 3 vols. Berlin & Stuttgart, 1885.

—— *Das Togoland und die Sklavenküste.* Berlin & Stuttgart, 1885.

Zollinger (H.), ' The Lampong Districts and their Present Condition ' ; in *Jour. Indian Archipelago*, vol. v. Singapore, 1851.

Zündel (G.), ' Land und Volk der Eweer auf der Sclavenküste in Westafrika ' ; in *Zeitschr. der Gesellschaft für Erdkunde zu Berlin*, vol. xii. Berlin, 1877.

INDEX

A

L L

G

Lawrence, W., on tribal physiognomy among savages, ii. 14 n. 2.

Le Bon, G., on communism in women, i. 225 n. 1, 299 n. 2 ; on jealousy, i. 300 ; on polygyny, iii. 94, 105.

Lebong (Palembang), Malays of, ii. 121 n. 4.

Lei-chou, peninsula of (Southern China), i. 84 *sq.*

Lendu (Central Africa), i. 153, 449 ; ii. 306, 379, 574 n. 1 ; iii. 213 n. 2.

Lengua Indians (Paraguayan Chaco), i. 72, 73, 135 n. 2, 337 ; ii. 195, 287, 593 n. 1 ; iii. 2 n. 2, 53, 108, 196, 287.

Lepchas (Himalayas), ii. 173, 361 n. 5, 389 n. 6, 453 ; iii. 117, 156 n. 7, 162.

Lepers' Island (New Hebrides), i. 437 n. 4, 438 ; ii. 320 n., 382, 449 ; iii. 18.

Let-htas (Burma), i. 143, 144, 500.

Leti (Indian Archipelago), ii. 123 n. 1 ; iii. 14 *sq.*

Letourneau, Ch., on the origin of clothing, i. 537 n. 5 ; on disregard for the woman's wishes among savages, ii. 316 ; on monogamy, iii. 105.

Leuckart, R., on the sexual season of animals, i. 78.

Levirate, the, i. 53 ; iii. 207–220, 261–263 ; a cause of polygyny, iii. 9, 11, 84.

Lewa Kunbis (Baroda), ii. 159 *sq.*

Lewis, C. J., and J. Norman, on the effect of cross-breeding upon the sex of the offspring, iii. 177 n. 2.

Leyté (Philippine Islands), Bisayans of, ii. 366.

Lhasa, ii. 262 ; iii. 112, 113, 159, 159 n. 7.

Li (Hainan), i. 75 n. 5, 84 ; ii. 298, 397 n., 438 n. 1, 527 n. 6 ; iii. 208 n. 1, 290 n. 3.

Liburnes (Illyria), i. 107.

Libyans, i. 108 *sq.*

Licata (Sicily), marriage rite at, ii. 479.

Liebrecht, F., on the *jus primae noctis*, i. 166 n. 1.

Lifu (Loyalty Islands), i. 84, 147, 148, 243, 366, 438 ; ii. 128, 405 ; iii. 148 *sq.*

Lihsaws (Burma-China frontier), ii. 320 n., 321 n. 2.

Lillooet Indians (British Columbia), i. 330, 459 n. 1 ; ii. 290, 291, 388 n. 2.

Limbus (Sikkim and Nepal), ii. 361 *sq.* n. 5, 370 n.

Limestone (Queensland), ii. 439.

Lincolnshire, marriage rites in, ii. 536 n. 10, 588 n. 4 ; unlucky and lucky days for marriage, ii. 570 n. 4, 572.

Line Islanders (Gilbert Group), i. 136, 137, 148, 321 ; ii. 62, 65 ; iii. 95 n. 1.

Lip ornaments, i. 502–505.

Lippert, J., on primitive promiscuity, i. 103, 225 n. 1 ; on paternity, i. 286 n. 2.

Lipplapps (Java), alleged sterility of, ii. 45 ; proportion between the sexes among, iii. 175.

Lisu tribes (Burma-China frontier), i. 76 n. 2, 144, 426 n. 2 ; ii. 266, 294, 295, 383 n. 5 ; iii. 270. *See* Lihsaws.

Lithuania, days for weddings in, ii. 569 n. 1.

Livonians, marriage rites among the, ii. 452, 526.

Loango, i. 40, 156, 200 n. 10, 285, 530, 545 ; ii. 307 n. 5, 404 n. 1, 490 ; iii. 21, 24, 212 n. 4. *See* Bafióte, Bavili.

Lobi (French West Africa), i. 41 ; ii. 594 n. 3 ; iii. 284 n. 3, 297 n. 1.

Lob-Nor, Lake Dwellers of, i. 350.

Lodhis (Central India), ii. 117 n. 7.

Loh (Torres Islands), iii. 243.

Lolos (China), ii. 254 n. 2, 271 n. 1, 274.

Lombroso, C., and Ferrero, G., on the origin of female modesty, i. 539.

London, cousin marriages in, ii. 236.

Loon, G. van, on the *merchet*, i. 178 n. 2.

11 *sq.* ; change of colour of,
ii. 17 ; colour of children
among, ii. 21 n. 1 ; the position
of the first wife, iii. 34 n. 1 ;
conjugal intercourse interrupted during menstruation,
iii. 65 n. 6 ; during pregnancy, iii. 66 n. 1 ; short
duration of female youthfulness, iii. 73 ; absorbing passion
for one, iii. 103.

Negroes, American, i. 335 ; mixture between whites and, ii.
38, 41 *sq.* ; marriages between
white women and, rare or
prohibited, ii. 41 ; proportion
between the sexes among the,
iii. 63.

Negros. *See* Negritos of Negros.

Nenenot (Ungava district of
Labrador), ii. 291, 385 n. 2 ;
iii. 89 n. 4, 279 n. 2.

Nepal, adultery in, i. 314 n. ;
love-matches, ii. 292 ; polygyny, iii. 9 n. 1 ; mock marriage and freedom of women
among the Newars of, iii.
199 *sq.*

Nerike (Sweden), marriage rites
in, ii. 489, 530 n. 2, 584 n. 7 ;
regular day for weddings, ii.
569 n. 6.

Nestorians of Syria, ii. 40, 268 *sq.*

Netchilirmiut (Central Eskimo),
iii. 6 n. 1, 55, 108, 207 n. 5.

Netchillik. *See* Netchilirmiut.

Nevada, marriage age in, i. 387 ;
divorce, iii. 364 *sq.*

New Britain, i. 137 n. 4, 354 n. 1,
364 n. 2, 428, 436, 460 n. 3,
507, 542 n. 8, 561 n. 4, 563
n. 10 ; ii. 49, 50, 98, 126 nn. 1,
2, and 4, 127, 299, 362, 382
n. 9, 594 n. 1 ; iii. 209 n. *See*
Gazelle Peninsula, Sulka.

New Caledonia, i. 147, 183, 190,
309, 312 n. 4, 341, 354 n. 1,
356, 407, 437 n. 4, 537 n. 4,
550, 550 n. 5, 568 ; ii. 74,
84, 125, 127, 128, 128 n. 1,
154, 155, 247, 299, 382 n. 9,
594 n. 1 ; iii. 17 n. 7, 18 *sq.*
n. 11, 56, 57, 90 n., 102 n. 8, 148,
165, 209 n., 214 n. 4, 298 n. 1,
366 n. 4. *See* Belep Islands.

New Granada, i. 197 ; ii. 549.

New Guinea, pre-nuptial chastity
in, i. 127, 146 *sq.* ; classificatory system of relationship,
i. 237 ; masculine jealousy,
i. 309 ; remarriage of widows
prohibited for some time after
the husband's death, i. 324
n. 7 ; frequency of marriage,
i. 340 ; betrothal of children,
i. 354 n. 1 ; marriage age,
i. 355 ; marriage proposals
made by the girls, i. 460 ;
tattooing, i. 515, 522 ; nakedness of the men, i. 542, 543,
543 n. ; pubic covering, i.
550 n. 6 ; head-hunting, ii. 2 ;
conjugal affection, ii. 26 *sq.* ;
exogamy, ii. 124 *sq.* ; female
infanticide, ii. 163 n. 3 ;
marriage by capture, ii. 246 ;
love-matches, ii. 298 *sq.* ;
elopement, ii. 320 n., 321 n. 2 ;
exchange of women as wives,
ii. 355 ; marriage by consideration, ii. 382 ; marriage
rites, ii. 449 ; consummation
of marriage deferred, ii. 547,
552 ; monogamy and poly-
gyny, iii. 16 *sq.* ; proportion
of the sexes, iii. 56 ; levirate,
209 n., 212 n. 2 ; group-
relations, iii. 236 *sq.* ; divorce,
iii. 274, 276 n., 277, 281 *sq.*
n. 4, 282 *sq.*

——, British, i. 312, 421, 424 n. 5,
460 n. 2, 503 n. 4, 522 ; ii.
124 n. 7, 382 ; iii. 17 n. 4.
See Bartle Bay, Bogaboga,
Hood Bay, Kiwai, Koiari,
Koita, Kworafi tribe, Mafulu
mountain people, Mailu, Mas-
sim, Mekeo, Motu, Mowat,
Mukaua, Naiabui, Orangerie
Bay, Roro, Samarai, Toaripi,
Trobriand Islands, Wagawaga,
Wanigela River, Yule Island.

——, Dutch, i. 146 n. 8, 355 ;
iii. 282 *sq. See* Dorey, Geel-
vink Bay, Humboldt Bay,
Kaya-Kaya, Maclay Coast,
Mamberamo, Mimika district,
Nufors, Outanatas.

——, the part which formerly
belonged to Germany, i. 43 n. 2,

Risano (Dalmatia), consummation of marriage deferred at, ii. 557.

Risley, Sir Herbert, on infant-marriage in India, i. 381.

Riukiu (between Formosa and Japan), ii. 554.

Riverina, natives of, i. 65, 203, 204 n. 2 ; ii. 248 n. 5, 301 n. 6, 355 n. 1, 593 n. 2 ; iii. 164 n. 3, 166, 210 n., 283 n. 3.

Rivers, W. H. R., on resemblances of culture-phenomena, i. 4 *sq.* ; on the study of social phenomena, i. 8–11 ; on systems of relationship, i. 237 *sq.* ; on the classificatory system of relationship, i. 237, 238, 240, 241, 252–254, 257–263, 264 n., 266–271, 274, iii. 242 ; on group-marriage or sexual communism, i. 241, 267–271, iii. 241–246 ; definition of "clan" given by, i. 249 n. 6 ; on cross-cousin marriage, i. 260–262, ii. 78 *sq.* ; on mother-right in Africa, i. 283 ; on rules of avoidance, i. 444 ; on consanguineous marriages in royal families, ii. 202 n. 3 ; on the connection between polyandry and female infanticide, iii. 185 n. 4.

Rîwa (Central India), i. 195.

Rochas, V. de, on avoidance between brother and sister, i. 437.

Rockhill, W. W., on polyandry, iii. 187, 188, 188 n. 1.

Rocky Mountains, Indians on the eastern side of the, i. 307, 338, 424 n. 5, 441, iii. 272 ; Indians of the, ii. 39 n. 7.

Rohleder, H., on in-breeding, ii. 221 n. 7, 224 n. 4.

Romagna, marriage rites in, ii. 260 n. 1, 269 n. 2, 451 n. 2, 565 n. 2, 579 ; marriage taboo, ii. 544 n. 2 ; consummation of marriage deferred, ii. 558.

Romang (Indian Archipelago), ii. 123 n. 5.

Rome, ancient, April connected with Venus in, i. 89 ; phallic rites, i. 218 ; regard for guests, i. 228 ; doctrine about adultery, i. 301 n. 6, iii. 50 ; re-marriage of widows, i. 322 *sq.* ; soldiers prohibited from marrying, i. 370, iii. 202 ; views on marriage, i. 385 ; marriage age, i. 385 *sq.* ; Vestal virgins, i. 399 ; tattooing, i. 515 ; pugilists and athletes concealing the glans, i. 536 n. 1 ; endogamy, ii. 41, 52, 63 ; origin of class distinctions, ii. 65 ; marriage with a niece, ii. 99, 149 ; prohibition of marriage between kindred, ii. 149, 207 *sq.* ; between relatives by alliance, ii. 154 ; between relatives by adoption, ii. 155 ; on account of "spiritual relationship," ii. 156 ; households, ii. 207 ; marriage by capture, ii. 251 *sq.* ; resistance made by the bride, ii. 269 ; paternal authority, ii. 332, 333, 338 ; consent to marriage, ii. 333, 338 ; reverence for parents, ii. 347 ; curses of parents and of offended guests, ii. 350 ; *coëmtio* and *arrha sponsalitia*, ii. 411, 421 ; *dos*, ii. 428–430 ; *confarreatio*, ii. 411, 436, 450, 576, iii. 319 *sq.* ; betrothal, ii. 433, 444 ; marriage rites, ii. 436, 437, 440, 447 n. 1, 450, 451, 465, 466, 470, 473, 474, 488, 507, 510, 512, 527, 536, 565 n. 2, 576, 582 ; unlucky periods for marriage, ii. 567, 572 ; polygyny not allowed, iii. 49 ; concubinage, *ib.* ; divorce, iii. 319–323, 331, 332, 353. *See* Maximinus.

Roro (British New Guinea), i. 428, 524 n. 3 ; ii. 257, 320 n., 321 n. 2, 387, 389, 552.

Rose, H. J., on the alleged mother-right in ancient Greece, i. 106 n. 4.

Rosehearty (Aberdeenshire), marriage rite in, ii. 476 *sq.*

Rosén, H., on the ceremonial use of shoes, ii. 540.

Rosenbaum, J., on the defloration of brides, i. 189 n. 5.

P P

Printed in Great Britain by
Richard Clay & Sons, Limited,
BUNGAY, SUFFOLK.